D1601906

# LANDSCAPE ECOLOGY

Richard T. T. Forman
*Harvard University*

Michel Godron
*Université de Montpellier*

JOHN WILEY & SONS
New York • Chichester • Brisbane • Toronto • Singapore

(1) Sand dunes in Death Valley, California (Photo by Ruth and Louis Kirk).
(2) Forest and agriculture by Richmond, Virginia (USDA Soil Conservation
Service). (3) Bull reindeer on western Alaska tundra (D. R. Klein).

*Library of Congress Cataloging in Publication Data:*

Forman, Richard T. T.
  Landscape ecology.

  Includes index.
  1. Ecology.   2. Landscape protection.
3. Human ecology.   I. Godron, Michael.   II. Title.
QH541.F67    1986        712        85-12306
ISBN 0-471-87037-4

Printed in the United States of America

10   9   8   7   6

Printed and bound by Quinn - Woodbine, Inc..

*We dedicate this book to*
Catherine de Maintenant Godron
*and to*
Barbara Lee Forman

# Foreword

As one who has spent his professional and academic career disturbing landscapes, I find it enlightening to see a work that offers a way of understanding the structure, function, and dynamics of those landscapes which are altered by design.

The book recognizes that disturbance, whether caused by humans or induced by natural forces, is a "normal" condition. This perspective differs from the ideological position of much of the literature in ecology, and it moves this book toward a more balanced (yet not anthropocentric) position.

The theoretical assumption underlying this book—that all landscapes, from the wilderness to the central city and from the "natural" to the "developed," share a similar structural model—is an important one. The book outlines a powerful model—a spatial language for analysis—that enables us to view our disturbed and undisturbed landscapes in a new way. It opens the possibility of taking a more comprehensive and synergistic view of a considerable literature in ecology.

This book should be of great interest and value to planners, designers, and managers of our land resources, whose actions must be understood from the perspectives of many natural systems with particular attention to spatial and temporal impacts. The language of landscape ecology offers the possibility of a mediating role between the natural sciences and the changers of landscapes. Without this mediating role—the translating role of a common language of structure, function, and change—we can continue to act only under our current conditions of relative ignorance.

At this point the full implications of landscape ecology for theory and practice cannot be foreseen, but it holds the promise of a more integrated analytic framework. This ground-breaking book impels us in the direction of a more comprehensive understanding of the spatial dynamics of landscapes.

**Carl Steinitz**
*Professor of Landscape Architecture and Planning*
*Graduate School of Design*
*Harvard University*

# Preface

Each of us lives in a landscape. We fulfill most of our needs from the diversity of that landscape. We explore and relax in its mixture of ecosystems. We are awed by its natural forces, and care about its aesthetics. We alter, degrade, and sometimes enhance it. Yet, we also are impressed by the wildness and power of nature in far-off pristine landscapes.

The landscape emerges as a central focus in many disciplines, from forestry to wildlife management, from geography to planning and art. We can and must understand it as a distinct object, using both the breadth of human knowledge and the emerging perspective of modern ecology. This book builds from this premise.

Landscape ecology explores how a heterogeneous combination of ecosystems—such as woods, meadows, marshes, corridors and villages—is structured, functions, and changes. From wilderness to urban landscapes, our focus is on (a) the distribution patterns of landscape elements or ecosystems; (b) the flows of animals, plants, energy, mineral nutrients, and water among these elements; and (c) the ecological changes in the landscape mosaic over time.

Landscape ecology has a unique role to play in our lives. When we focus on the heterogeneity in a landscape, we sense how intertwined its ecological systems are. An action here and now produces an effect there and then. Since the system is interlocking, it is critical to understand the spatial relationships among the landscape elements; the flows of species, energy and materials; and the ecological dynamics of the landscape mosaic. Thus, an understanding of the whole—landscape ecology with its practical tools for scholars, citizens, and decision makers—emerges. The quality of the landscape in which each of us lives depends on how rapidly we grasp the ecology of landscapes.

Why have the two of us written this book? At the outset, the idea of landscape ecology sounded appealing, almost ethereal, yet we both sensed an obvious gap in our understanding of the environment. Urgency and a sense of responsibility for the quality of landscapes motivated us. Our background as ecologists provided a scientific base, but it was incomplete, and we realized that the integration of ecology and human activities was not only necessary but could bring new insights to the study of landscapes. Our sense of discovery and enthusiasm grew with time, as colleagues and students from many disciplines encouraged and helped us. Frankly, it was fun to explore this frontier.

From primordial beginnings, human knowledge has accumulated from generation to generation. Disciplines have formed and have been followed by emerging subdisciplines, each with its frontier of discovery. Breakthroughs have also appeared from the synthesis of disciplines. Landscape ecology seems to have evolved along both routes. Ecologists increasingly recognize it as a challenging emerging subdiscipline within ecology. Yet scholars in many larger and older disciplines perceive landscape ecology as a promising frontier emerging in its own right, synthesizing several areas of knowledge.

The future of the field will be catalyzed by basic ecologists and by geographers, wildlife biologists, foresters, planners and landscape architects, agricultural scientists, and others. Important principles will be drawn from each field and added to a central, growing body of landscape ecology theory.

Landscape management decisions cannot wait until the last datum is in. Similarly, we know that many critical hypotheses need to be posed and many new data are needed before the concepts presented in this book evolve into facts and laws; but we cannot wait. Where lines of evidence appear to converge on a single point, we have attempted to decipher that point and articulate the concept. We understand the limitations and consequent tentativeness of some points, and we expect them to lead to discussion, controversy, hypothesis, observation, experiment, modeling, and fact. We invite the reader to join in this process of discovery.

We have written this book for students. We hope professionals in several fields will also be stimulated and will help solidify the foundations of landscape ecology. No college level prerequisite course should be necessary. A course in biology or another related field would enrich the reader's perceptions and ability to see the implications of the landscape ecology material. We have added an optional chapter, "Ecological Concepts in Brief," for students without previous experience in biology or ecology, but the volume is complete without this chapter. We think the concepts and terminology used in landscape ecology stand on their own and should be readily understandable by students in a wide range of disciplines.

Periodically throughout the text we have inserted scientific names, alternate terms, clarifications, and embellishments in parentheses. These may be included or excluded depending upon student interest and level; the text is complete without the items in parentheses. To help launch landscape ecology on a solid footing, we have relied when possible on observations and experiments and have supplemented these with simple models useful for studying a complex landscape system. We have attempted to use examples from around the world, and we hope that future work and bibliographies in this field will transcend nations and languages, as landscapes do.

A wealth of empirical studies, emergent theory, and applications lies ahead. The lag period between research and the amelioration of environmental and societal problems should be brief in this field. Let the young in spirit look to the future and "think landscape."

**Richard Forman**

**Michel Godron**

# Acknowledgments

The idea for this concept of landscape ecology emerged in 1978 following a year together at the Centre d'Etudes Phytosociologiques et Ecologiques L. Emberger in Montpellier, France. For their broad support we are pleased to acknowledge Rutgers University, the Université de Montpellier, and the Centre Emberger. We also thank the National Science Foundation and the Centre National de la Recherche Scientifique for their financial support, and the Defenders of Wildlife for its aid in selecting photographs.

As this book took shape, we valued especially the criticisms and refinements offered by Mark J. McDonnell, Bruce T. Milne, Ralph E. J. Boerner, Steward T. A. Pickett, Edmund W. Stiles, James R. Karr, Paul G. Risser, David M. Sharpe, a 1984 Rutgers University biogeography class, and a 1983 group of landscape architecture and planning students at Harvard University. Elliott A. Norse, Jane E. Sherwood, and Peter J. Grubb also contributed significantly to the quality of our presentation. Individual chapters have benefitted significantly from the ideas of Warren G. Abrahamson, Allan N. Auclair, James E. Applegate, Thomas F. Breden, Grace S. Brush, Marie B. Connett, Julie S. Denslow, David C. Glenn-Lewin, James R. Gosz, Miron L. Heinselman, Calvin J. Heusser, Henry S. Horn, W. Carter Johnson, James R. Karr, Robert P. McIntosh, Samuel J. McNaughton, Bruce T. Milne, William A. Niering, Michel Phipps, Steward T. A. Pickett, Amos Rapoport, William A. Reiners, Paul G. Risser, David M. Sharpe, Hermon H. Shugart, Donald J. Shure, Edmund W. Stiles, Edmund V. J. Tanner, John C. F. Tedrow, Walter E. Westman, Dennis F. Whigham, F. Ian Woodward, and John A. Wiens.

For R. Forman the intellectual background for this book developed particularly in discussions with Paul G. Pearson, Edmund W. Stiles, Steward T. A. Pickett, the late Robert H. Whittaker, and eighteen years of graduate students and ecology seminar speakers at Rutgers. For M. Godron an ecological perception of the landscape first emerged when mapping with Louis Emberger and Gilbert Long in the late 1950s; since then, it has been richly enhanced through collaborations with Philippe Daget, Jacques Poissonet, Christian Floret, and many other friends and students.

Each of you has contributed in a significant way to help build the foundations of landscape ecology. It is an honor to express our appreciation and respect.

**Richard Forman**

**Michel Godron**

# Contents

**Part I.**
Overview

**1. Landscape and Principles**    *3*

   PERCEPTIONS OF THE LANDSCAPE                                      4

   Breadth of Concepts. The Artist's Landscape. The Concept in the
   Social and Natural Sciences.

   A LANDSCAPE FROM AN ECOLOGICAL PERSPECTIVE                        8

   What Makes a Landscape? A Usable Scientific Concept. Landscape
   Elements and Tesserae. Related Concepts.

   CONCEPT AREAS AND PRINCIPLES OF LANDSCAPE ECOLOGY               17

   Diversity Among Landscapes. Concept Areas. Emerging
   General Principles.

   THE EMERGENCE OF LANDSCAPE ECOLOGY:
   MAJOR LITERATURE                                                 28

   Geography and Ecology. Related Disciplines. International
   Perspectives Today.

   SUMMARY                                                          31

   QUESTIONS                                                        31

**2. Ecological Concepts in Brief**    *33*

   THE PHYSICAL ENVIRONMENT                                         35

   Climate. Soil. Fire.

   AQUATIC ENVIRONMENTS                                             44

   Hydrologic Cycle. Lotic and Lentic Environments.
   Marine Environments.

   POPULATIONS AND THEIR REGULATION                                 49

   Populations and Growth. Competition. Predation.
   Population Regulation.

EVOLUTIONARY ECOLOGY                                                  57

Variation and Selection. Speciation.

ECOLOGICAL COMMUNITIES                                               60

Spatial Structure of a Community. Ecological Niche and Species
Diversity. Succession. Island Biogeography. Biogeography in
Geologic Time.

ENERGY AND MATTER IN ECOSYSTEMS                                      68

Energy. Plant and Animal Production. Food Chains and Webs.
Mineral Nutrient Cycling. Ecosystem Models.

SUMMARY                                                              77

QUESTIONS                                                            78


## Part II.
## Landscape Structure

### Chapter 3. Patches     83

PATCH ORIGINS AND CHANGE                                             83

Basic Concepts. Disturbance Patches. Remnant Patches.
Environmental Resource Patches. Introduced Patches.
Additional Concepts.

PATCH SIZE                                                          98

Effects on Energy and Nutrients. Effects on Species.

PATCH SHAPE                                                        106

Significance in Ecology. Edge Effect. Isodiametric and Elongated
Patches. Rings. Peninsulas.

PATCH NUMBER AND CONFIGURATION                                     117

SUMMARY                                                            119

QUESTIONS                                                          120

### Chapter 4. Corridors     121

CORRIDORS AND THEIR ORIGINS                                        122

CORRIDOR STRUCTURE                                                 125

The Vulture's View. The Hiker's View. Microenvironment
Within a Corridor.

LINE CORRIDORS                                                     131

Hedgerows as Line Corridors. Animal Communities of Hedgerows.
Other Types of Line Corridors.

STRIP CORRIDORS                                                    142

Corridors Lower Than Surroundings. Corridors Higher
Than Surroundings.

STREAM CORRIDORS                                                   146

SUMMARY                                                            153

QUESTIONS                                                          155


## 5. Matrix and Network    157

DISTINGUISHING A MATRIX                                            159

Three Matrix Criteria. How the Matrix Criteria Influence Change: The
Desertification Example.

POROSITY AND BOUNDARY SHAPE                                        168

The Concept and Its Implications. Porosity Patterns in Different
Landscapes. Boundary Shape.

NETWORKS                                                           178

Intersections in the Network. Reticulate Pattern. Mesh Size. Factors
Determining Network Structure.

MATRIX HETEROGENEITY                                               184

SUMMARY                                                            186

QUESTIONS                                                          186

APPENDIX: MEASURES OF PATCH CHARACTERISTICS
IN A MATRIX                                                        188


## 6. Overall Structure    191

MICROHETEROGENEITY AND MACROHETEROGENEITY                         194

Analysis of a Microheterogeneous Landscape. Analysis of a
Macroheterogeneous Landscape.

CONFIGURATION OF PATCHES, CORRIDOR, AND MATRIX                    204

A Few Distinctive Configurations. Determining
Distinctive Configurations.

CONTRAST IN THE LANDSCAPE                                          211

Low-Contrast Structure. High-Contrast Structure.

GRAIN SIZE OF THE LANDSCAPE                                        216

ADDITIONAL STRUCTURAL CONSIDERATIONS                              218

SUMMARY                                                            220

QUESTIONS                                                        220

APPENDIX: A METHOD FOR MEASURING
LANDSCAPE HETEROGENEITY                                          222

## Part III.
## Landscape Dynamics

### 7. Natural Processes in Landscape Development    229

GEOMORPHOLOGY                                                    230

Landforms and Their Effects. River Systems. Bedrock, Climate, and
Stasic Processes. Geomorphic Processes Under Different Climates.

ESTABLISHMENT OF LIFE FORMS                                      241

Plant Establishment. Animal Establishment. Speciation in Landscapes.

Increase in Vegetation Stature.

SOIL DEVELOPMENT                                                 259

Law of Zonality. Toward a Soil Classification Based on Origin and
Development. The Role of Decomposers.

NATURAL DISTURBANCE                                              265

SUMMARY                                                          268

QUESTIONS                                                        269

APPENDIX: GEOLOGICAL TIME                                        270

### 8. The Human Role in Landscape Development    273

MODIFICATION OF NATURAL RHYTHMS                                  274

Disturbance and Rhythms. Daily Rhythms. Seasonal Rhythms.
Rhythms of Several Years or Centuries.

METHODS OR TOOLS USED IN LANDSCAPE MODIFICATION                  281

Natural Resource Extraction and Alteration. Introduction of
Agricultural Methods. Decision Catalysts.

A LANDSCAPE MODIFICATION GRADIENT                                286

Natural Landscapes. Managed Landscapes. Cultivated Landscapes.
Suburban Landscapes. Urban Landscapes. The Megalopolis.

SUMMARY                                                          310

QUESTIONS                                                        311

## 9. *Flows Between Adjacent Landscape Elements*    *313*

MECHANISMS UNDERLYING LINKAGES    315
Vectors. Forces.

AIRFLOW AND LOCOMOTION    320
Wind Patterns. Sound. Gases, Aerosols, and Particulate
Matter. Locomotion.

SOIL FLOWS    335
General Concepts. Erosion and Surface Flow. Subsurface Flow.

INTERACTION BETWEEN LAND AND STREAM    342
The Stream Corridor Role. Corridor Filtration of Mineral Nutrients.

HEDGEROW INTERACTIONS WITH ADJACENT
LANDSCAPE ELEMENTS    347
How Hedgerows Affect Fields. How Fields, Woods, and Homes
Affect Hedgerows.

SUMMARY    354

QUESTIONS    354

## 10. *Animal and Plant Movement Across a Landscape*    *357*

PATTERNS OF MOVEMENT    357
Continuous Movement. Saltatory Movement.

MOVEMENT OF ANIMALS    361
Home Range, Dispersal, and Migration. Barriers and Conduits
Perceived by Different Species. Patterns Based on the
Radiotracking Studies.

MOVEMENT OF PLANTS    381
The Cheatgrass Invasion of the American West. Australian Eucalypt
versus California Pine. Forest Species in Hedgerows.

SOME SPECIES MOVEMENTS IN AGRICULTURE
AND PEST CONTROL    392

SUMMARY    394

QUESTIONS    394

## 11. *Landscape Functioning*    *397*

CORRIDORS AND FLOWS    397
The Functioning of Conduits, Barriers, and Breaks.
Hedgerow Function.

FLOWS AND THE MATRIX                                                404

Matrix Connectivity. Landscape Resistance. Narrows. Porosity and
Interaction Among Patches. Influence Fields. Peninsular
Interdigitation. Spatial Orientation Relative to Flows. Distance.

NETWORKS                                                            415

Nodes and Corridors. Network Connectivity. Loops and Circuitry.
Gravity Model. Spatial Diffusion Processes. Optimization.

SUMMARY                                                            425

QUESTIONS                                                          426

12. *Landscape Change*     *427*

STABILITY                                                          428

Variation Curves. Stability and Instability. An Example of Stability
Followed by Degradation.

METASTABILITY                                                      435

Models. Species Coexistence Patterns.

PATTERNS OF OVERALL LANDSCAPE CHANGE                               440

The Transition Matrix. The Shifting Mosaic.

LANDSCAPE DYNAMICS                                                 446

Active Forces. Levels of Force. Stabilizing Properties.

LINKAGES AMONG LANDSCAPES                                          456

SUMMARY                                                            458

QUESTIONS                                                          458

*Part IV.*
Heterogeneity and Management

13. *Heterogeneity and Typology*     *463*

LANDSCAPE HETEROGENEITY                                            463

Thermodynamic Laws. Mechanisms Causing Heterogeneity.

ANIMAL RESPONSE TO HETEROGENEITY                                   470

GUIDELINES FOR LANDSCAPE TYPOLOGY                                  473

THE INHERENT HIERARCHY IN NATURE                                   477

Five Levels in a Descending Hierarchy. A Parallel Hierarchy. Map
Overlay Approach.

ASCENDING TYPOLOGY                                          484

The Landscape Attributes. Multivariate and Direct Methods for
Typology Construction.

TOWARD A PHYLOGENETIC TYPOLOGY                              490

SUMMARY                                                     491

QUESTIONS                                                   492

**14. Landscape Management**    *495*

WHERE HUMANS GATHER                                         496

PRODUCTION IN LANDSCAPES                                    498

PLANNING AND MANAGEMENT OF MAJOR LANDSCAPE TYPES            499

The Natural Landscape. Landscapes With Forestry. The Agricultural
Landscape. The Built Landscape.

LANDSCAPE QUALITY                                           509

A Direct Method of Estimating Landscape Quality. Survey
Questionnaires. Perception of Landscape Quality by Animals.
Protection of Landscape Quality.

MODELLING AND LANDSCAPE MANAGEMENT                          515

Models from Maps. Model Construction. Tensor Models in
Management. Model Sensitivity, Risks, and Timing.

SOME BROADER PERSPECTIVES                                   526

SUMMARY                                                     528

QUESTIONS                                                   530

*References*    *533*

*Glossary*    *589*

*Index*    *603*

# Part *1*
## Overview

# 1
# Landscape and Principles

*An endless feedback loop:*
*Past functioning has produced today's structure;*
*today's structure produces today's functioning;*
*today's functioning will produce future structure.*

Imagine filling a large glass bowl on your dining table with water from the bottom of a stream or lake near home, and watching it whenever you eat. You find it structurally quite heterogeneous, with hunks of decaying matter, sticks, and plants. You watch it function, with movements of minuscule animals, air bubbles, and the water in the bowl. Finally, over several days you see major changes; as the water turns green with algae, countless slimy animals appear. You become convinced that algae from such a system are not a very delectable way to solve the world food shortage. But you have also witnessed three fundamental characteristics of the object: its structure, its function, and how it changes.

The endless feedback loop above shows how these three characteristics are linked almost inseparably. A landscape, of course, is our object of interest, and we will study (in order) its structure, its function, and its change. First, however, we must determine what a landscape is and delineate a rigorous concept that is scientifically usable. This concept will help catalyze ecological theory at the landscape level of interest, and will lead to the application of such theory within several closely related sister disciplines. Indeed, as many of us in ecology, geography, wildlife biology, forestry, planning and landscape architecture, agricultural science, and so on, work to develop the concepts and principles of landscape ecology, an enjoyable and significant interaction is emerging.

Ponder the following words, and the significance of landscape will unfold. ". . . [L]andscapes mirror and landscapes matter, they tell us much about the values we hold and at the same time affect the quality of the lives we lead. . . ." (Meinig, 1979a).

3

## PERCEPTIONS OF THE LANDSCAPE

### Breadth of Concepts

Dictionaries offer several definitions of the word landscape (Webster's, 1963; The Oxford English Dictionary, 1933), including: (a) a picture representing a view of natural inland scenery (as of prairie, woodland, mountains, etc.); (b) the landforms of a region in the aggregate; (c) a portion of land or expanse of natural scenery as seen by the eye in a single view (Figure 1.1). The dictionary further describes "landscape architecture" as the arranging and modifying of natural scenery over a tract of land for aesthetic effect.

Quizzing a wide range of people produces an astonishing array of landscape concepts. Most can be readily classified as either aesthetic, professional, cultural, physical landform, or photographic-artistic. Spatially, the concepts range broadly from "the North American landscape"

**Figure 1.1**  *Sand dunes and mountains in Death Valley, California. Note that the view of the landforms from a point would differ if the observer was down between the dunes. (Photo by Ruth and Louis Kirk.)*

to that of a terrarium. An insect specialist may even think of the landscape of entangling and toxic hairs on a leaf surface as viewed by the eyes of a microscopic insect attempting to crawl across the leaf. The different ways of seeing a landscape can be described (Meinig, 1979a) as (a) nature, (b) habitat, (c) artifact, (d) system, (e) problem, (f) wealth, (g) ideology, (h) history, (i) place, and (j) aesthetic. People also have feelings about landscapes. For example, what do you feel about the landscape you live in? Beauty? Pride of ownership? Site of a job? Danger? Revulsion? Belonging? Needs protection? The word for landscape in other languages, such as "landschaft" in German or "paysage" in French, has a range of meanings similar to that of English.

In short, landscape perspectives are diverse, perhaps too diverse to usefully synthesize. For the purposes of landscape ecology we must select from the array of meanings.

## The Artist's Landscape

Paintings of landscapes were uncommon in ancient times. Hellenistic styles of painting, which developed in the Mediterranean region around the first century A.D., included paintings of the outdoor landscape. Rather than drawing details of specific landscapes the artists invented idyllic scenes to please the town dweller. Ancient Oriental painters depicted natural forms as background for scenes of human life or military campaigns. In China during the twelfth and thirteenth centuries, dramatic landscape scenes (e.g., by MaYuan and Kao K'o-Kung) were painted out of a sense of reverence, the objective being to aid the practice of meditation. In fifteenth-century Europe natural scenes on tapestries, glass and miniatures became common, and artists began to include the real as well as the beautiful in their paintings (e.g., Van Eyck, Witz). During the sixteenth century (e.g., Altdorfer, El Greco) paintings of nature appeared that were a monument to the skill of the artist, sometimes telling no story but providing direct aesthetic shock. In the seventeenth century, the focus was on paintings depicting the sublime beauty of nature and even the poetry of a scene (e.g., Lorrain, Van Ruisdael). During the age of reason (and of landscape gardeners) in the following century, the composition of landscape paintings was especially stressed, the object being to evoke or reflect a mood (e.g., Gainsborough). The nineteenth and twentieth centuries have seen numerous further developments and breaks with artistic tradition. Landscape painters (e.g., Constable, Turner, Friedrich, Monet, Hokusai, Cezanne, Van Gogh, Rousseau, Wood, Wyeth) portrayed action and change, led a viewer step by step through a landscape, provided depth without a linear perspective, drew from an aerial perspective, and even used a rash of colors and forms to accomplish what the artist wished others to feel.

Several aspects of the artistic notion of landscape are useful toward understanding landscape ecology. Most striking is the diversity or heterogeneity present in the scene painted (Figure 1.2). Two or more distinct objects or visual foci are present, such as a woods and a farmyard, a meadow and a cliff, or a village and a riverside.

A second point of ecological relevance found in most landscape paintings is the spatial scale portrayed by the artist. The field of view depicted is generally similar to what the eye can see from one point. The spans of landscapes in paintings typically range from a few meters to several kilometers.

The subject matter is a third characteristic of ecological interest. Landscape paintings normally include vegetation or animals, but buildings, roads, and rocks are also common (Figure 1.2). Furthermore, people or human influences are usually evident in the picture and sometimes dominate. Landscape painting, like landscape ecology, runs the entire gamut from the urban setting to the scene with no significant human influence evident.

Finally, we note that artists often use the term seascape to refer to

**Figure 1.2** *Landscape painting, "Hunters in the Snow," by Pieter Bruegel the Elder (1565). Note the distance visible, the heterogeneity, and the movement of objects between different portions of the landscape. (Courtesy of Collection H. Roger Viollet.)*

**6** OVERVIEW

scenes predominantly or entirely on water. This book concerns landscape ecology and is limited to that third of our planet characterized by land.

## The Concept in the Social and Natural Sciences

Historians usually use the term landscape to refer to a relatively extensive land area. This would be the terrain where battles took place, food was grown, colonists established settlements, architects built monuments, or through which people moved.

Geography, where the landscape plays a central role and may be considered a fundamental unit, is of particular importance in the attempt to delineate a clear, scientifically useful concept of landscape. The definitions in geography (Mikesell, 1968; Grossman, 1977; Luder, 1981) essentially focus on the dynamic relationship between (a) natural landforms or physiographic regions and (b) human cultural groups.

The astute geographer J. B. Jackson wrote about the landscape (Zube, 1970; Meinig, 1979b) that

. . . the concept continues to elude me. Perhaps one reason for this is that I persist in seeing it not as a scenic or ecological entity but as a political or cultural entity; changing in the course of history. . . . I have come to the point where instead of trying to establish distinctions between landscapes, I try to discover similarities . . . [and am] more concerned with . . . perceiving the universal which presumably lies behind diversity.

He did, however, provide a spatial idea along with his landscape concept in the inaugural issue of the magazine he launched. "*Landscape* is interested in original articles . . . suited to illustration by aerial photographs."

Landscape ecologists have largely come from geographical or biological backgrounds and, not surprisingly, have drawn heavily from these disciplines in understanding a landscape. The pioneer landscape ecologist, C. Troll (1950, 1968, 1971), defined landscape ecology as the study of the physico-biological relationships that govern the different spatial units of a region. He considered the relationships to be both vertical (within a spatial unit) and horizontal (between spatial units). Much of the broad field of ecology, however, particularly over the past few decades, has focused on the "vertical," that is, the relationships among plants, animals, air, water, and soil within a relatively homogeneous spatial unit. In contrast, what makes landscape ecology unique is its focus on the "horizontal," that is, the relationships among spatial units.

Zonneveld (1979) provided the following definition of a landscape: ". . . [A] part of the space on the earth's surface, consisting of a complex of systems, formed by the activity of rock, water, air, plants, animals and man and that by its physiognomy forms a recognizable entity." Note the presence of several systems (a complex), and that the landscape appears (physiognomy) as a distinct entity.

## A LANDSCAPE FROM AN ECOLOGICAL PERSPECTIVE

### What Makes a Landscape?

Fortunately, many elements of the above definitions converge in a nice scientifically rigorous and useful landscape concept. We can discover its essence clearly by exploring a specific landscape.

Let us begin with a typical agricultural landscape such as that shown in Figure 1.3 and go to a randomly chosen point in it. We explore around, say within several hundred meters of the point. We cross a field, a hedge-

**Figure 1.3**  *Agricultural landscape showing cluster of ecosystems repeated throughout. Contour planting of corn (Zea) and grain in center. Dodge County, Wisconsin, United States. (Courtesy of USDA Soil Conservation Service.)*

row, a wood, a highway (with roadside plants and animals), a dirt road, and a farmyard. These six types are quite different from one another and readily distinguished. Ecologists would call each a type of **ecosystem**; the term refers to all of the organisms in a given place in interaction with their nonliving environment. Near our random point we are likely to encounter more than one example of several of the ecosystem types. For example, several fields and hedgerows are likely to be present.

Now let us move to another random point in this landscape, perhaps a few kilometers away, and walk around that new point. Here we are likely to find almost the same **cluster of ecosystem types** as before. Perhaps here no woods are nearby, or we come across a pond. Nevertheless, the second cluster is quite similar to the first. Of course the number of farmyards may be greater, or perhaps fewer dirt roads are present. The relative abundance or frequency of individual ecosystems within a cluster is easily determined by counting, and is an additional measure for comparing random points.

We then repeat the same process at a third point, a fourth point, and so on. At each point we encounter a similar cluster of ecosystem types. At some considerable distance from the center of the landscape, however, we will eventually encounter a quite different cluster of ecosystem types, such as residential area, school yard, railroad, woods, paved road, commercial center, and abandoned field. Now we are in a new landscape, in this case a suburban one. Similarly, we would encounter a quite different cluster of ecosystems if we entered a landscape of ridges and valleys, for example, or a sandy forested plain.

Returning to the first point in the agricultural landscape (Figure 1.3) reveals further interesting patterns. If we stayed at that point for a long time and studied the ecosystems, we would find considerable interaction among them. Animals move from one to another. Plant seeds, pollen, and spores also move. Indeed, many aspects of the physical environment such as heat, wind, sound, water, and mineral nutrients also flow among the clustered ecosystems. If we repeated our visits to many points in the landscape, we would find similar flows or interactions within each cluster of ecosystem types.

Three other characteristics important to a landscape can be discovered by visiting different points in it. First, all points in a landscape are under the influence of the same broad climate. Second, most points in the landscape have a similar **geomorphology.** This concept will be delineated in more detail in Chapter 7; in essence it refers to the underlying rocks or parent materials and to the landforms present, which were formed in geological time.

Third, a similar **set of disturbance regimes** is found throughout a landscape. A **disturbance** (or perturbation) is an event that causes a significant change from the normal pattern in an ecological system such as an ecosystem or landscape. Over days, years, or even centuries, many disturbances mold a landscape. They include natural events such as hurricanes, lightning fires, and pest outbreaks, and human interventions such as plowing, logging, and spraying. Each ecosystem type has a distinctive disturbance regime, that is, the intensities, frequencies, and types of disturbances that occur in it. Therefore, with a similar cluster of ecosystem types around each point, the set of disturbance regimes around points is similar across the landscape.

We have just observed four characteristics that are repeated in similar form across a landscape: (a) the cluster of ecosystem types, (b) the flows or interactions among the ecosystems of a cluster, (c) the geomorphology and climate, and (d) the set of disturbance regimes. A fifth characteristic, the relative abundance of ecosystems within a cluster, may vary more across a landscape.

Of course, we may encounter a rare or unusual feature in the landscape, such as a single lake or rare hill, that differs significantly, in one or more of the four characteristics, from virtually any other area of the landscape. For example, a single village in a remote forested landscape may be the source of most of the people, vehicles, and nonnative species that spread over and significantly modify the entire landscape (Figure 1.4).

**Figure 1.4** *Remote coniferous forest landscape containing a village. The only village within 25 km is on an arm of the lake at right edge of photograph; a ski trail is in the foreground. Rangeley region, Maine, United States. (R. Forman.)*

## A Usable Scientific Concept

The above observations form the heart of the landscape concept. We now can define **landscape** as a heterogeneous land area composed of a cluster of interacting ecosystems that is repeated in similar form throughout. Landscapes vary in size down to a few kilometers in diameter. Aerial photography is often useful in portraying the ecosystems composing a landscape as well as its boundary, which is usually relatively distinct, especially in vegetation structure. Localized areas of a few meters or hundreds of meters across are at a finer scale than a landscape. Nevertheless, most of the principles of landscape ecology apply to ecological mosaics at any level of scale.

**Landscape development** or formation results from three mechanisms operating within a landscape's boundary: specific geomorphological processes taking place over a long time, colonization patterns of organisms, and local disturbances of individual ecosystems over a shorter time.

We now see the landscape as a distinct, measurable unit defined by its recognizable and spatially repetitive cluster of interacting ecosystems, geomorphology, and disturbance regimes. *Landscape ecology* focuses on three characteristics of the landscape:

1. **Structure,** the spatial relationships among the distinctive ecosystems or "elements" present—more specifically, the distribution of energy, materials, and species in relation to the sizes, shapes, numbers, kinds, and configurations of the ecosystems.
2. **Function,** the interactions among the spatial elements, that is, the flows of energy, materials, and species among the component ecosystems.
3. **Change,** the alteration in the structure and function of the ecological mosaic over time.

A landscape, therefore, exhibits the same three fundamental characteristics as a vertebrate or an economic system, for example, and represents a challenging research frontier. Finally, it should be clear that landscape ecology studies both the principles concerning structure, function, and change, and their application, that is, the use of these principles in the formulation and solving of problems.

## Landscape Elements and Tesserae

We now need to see what elements or units make up a landscape. The terms ecotope—that is, the smallest possible land unit that is still a holistic

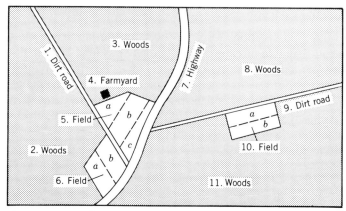

**Figure 1.5** *Landscape elements and tesseras. Five types of landscape element are present—woods, dirt road, highway, farmyard, and field. There are 11 specific landscape elements (numbered). Tesseras (a, b, and c) are visible within the fields.*

unit[1]—and biotope are used by some landscape ecologists as the basic landscape element or unit (Troll, 1966; Neef, 1967; Schmithusen, 1967; Schreiber, 1977; Zonneveld, 1979; Agger and Brandt, 1984). Other terms used include landscape unit, landscape cell, geotope, facies, habitat, and site (Christian and Stewart, 1968; Vinogradov, 1966, 1976; Zonneveld, 1979). Ruzicka et al. (1978) recognize landscape structure at two levels. "Landscape components" are the units within a landscape determined by the physical or natural environment; superimposed on these are "landscape elements" mainly determined by human influences.

Any of these terms, when defined, seems quite satisfactory according to the preference of the investigator. In this volume we will simply refer to the basic, relatively homogeneous, ecological elements or units on land as **landscape elements** (whether they are of natural or human origin). From an ecological perspective these elements may be considered ecosystems, but generally we will simply call them landscape elements. Landscape elements are usually identifiable in aerial photography and often range from around 10 m to 1 km or more in width.

In the agricultural landscape example we recognized *element types*—namely, woods, dirt road (including roadside), highway, farmyard, and field. In Figure 1.5 we can observe these five types of landscape elements. Each element type is represented by one or more actual elements: woods, four elements; field, three elements; dirt road, two elements; highway, one element; and farmyard, one element.

We notice that although there are three field landscape elements, well

---

[1]But see contrasting definitions by Tansley (1935), Sukachev and Dylis (1964), Whittaker et al. (1973), Naveh and Lieberman (1984).

delineated around their boundaries by other element types, within a field two or three portions have been marked off. These portions may be different crops or the same crop planted at different times. Any landscape element, such as a field here, can be recognized as heterogeneous, and we will refer to the most homogeneous portions within it as tesserae. A **tessera**, like the basic piece of stone in an artistic mosaic, is the smallest homogeneous unit visible at the spatial scale of a landscape. Similarly, the farmyard might include a number of tesserae, such as the house, the yard, and the barn.

In studying a landscape, therefore, we have considerable flexibility in how finely we can dissect it. At the broadest scale, we could simply recognize two types of landscape elements in Figure 1.5, forest and field, and view highway, roads, and farmyard as part of the heterogeneity within them. For our example above, we recognized five landscape element types. At the finest scale, we could recognize nine element types: field type *a*, field type *b*, field type *c*, woods, highway, dirt road, house, yard, and barn. In this last case, each landscape element would also be a tessera, since none can be further subdivided.

Hereafter in this book, we will most often use the term landscape element, thereby simplifying the explanation of principles. At times, however, the reader will find it useful to consider the applicability of a principle to the homogeneous tessera rather than to the more flexible concept of the landscape element.

## Related Concepts

Several terms or concepts are related to and should be differentiated from a landscape. A **watershed** or **basin** is the area drained by a river or stream and its tributaries (Horton, 1945; Webster's, 1963; Gregory and Walling, 1973; Likens et al., 1977). Generally many watersheds are included in a landscape, and a landscape boundary may or may not correspond to the boundaries of watersheds.

The area of a **region** is determined by a complex of climatic, physiographic, biological, economic, social, and cultural characteristics (Dickinson, 1970; Isard, 1975). A region therefore almost always contains a number of landscapes (Miller, 1978a); the greater Tokyo region, for example, combines an urban landscape with one or more surrounding suburban landscapes. Similarly, the New England (United States) region includes landscapes in the high mountains, forested hilly landscapes, agricultural landscapes, suburban landscapes, and a number of urban landscapes. Many principles and ideas in this book can also apply to a region and provide a useful foundation for a regional ecology.

The **ecosystem** concept, which includes structure, function, and development, may be applied at any level of spatial scale, from the size of a rabbit dropping, say, to the planet (Tansley, 1935; Evans, 1956; Odum, 1971). For example, in Figure 1.6 the whole desert area may be studied as an ecosystem. Similarly, a single oasis village, or even two adjacent fields within the oasis, may be delineated as an ecosystem. However, in practice ecologists look for a relative homogeneity enabling them to characterize and understand the ecosystem with a reasonable number of measurements (Odum, 1971; Woodwell and Whittaker, 1968; Bormann and Likens, 1981). Thus, typically a single field within the oasis would be studied as an ecosystem (Figure 1.6). Although one may apply the ecosystem concept to a heterogeneous region, landscape, or landscape fragment, in this volume we basically limit its use to relatively homogeneous areas within a landscape (Miller, 1978a).

The terms **biogeocenosis** and **biocenosis** differ little from the ecosystem concept. Biogeocenosis is used particularly in the Soviet Union (Sukachev and Dylis, 1964; Johnson and French, 1981) and in certain areas of

**Figure 1.6** *Desert area with oases near Kerman, Iran. Tiny rectangular fields are visible within the oasis villages. (E. Laporte.)*

Europe. Like the ecosystem, the biogeocenosis includes both the living and nonliving components and, more significantly, specifies the ecological dynamics in a specific area (e.g., of land) that is homogeneous. Thus, the biogeocenosis is exactly synonymous with the ecosystem of a landscape element. Biocenosis, a common term in many areas of Europe, normally includes, like ecosystem, both the living and nonliving components (Moebius, 1877), but in some cases it only refers to the animal and plant community.

Of course, one may call a whole landscape an ecosystem. Examples include the urban landscape ecosystem (Stearns and Montag, 1974; Meier, 1976; Spirn, 1984), the Pine Barrens, New Jersey, landscape ecosystem (Forman, 1979a), or a river delta landscape ecosystem near New Orleans (United States) (Costanza et al., 1983). Such studies are important in landscape ecology (Odum and Odum, 1981) and offer valuable insights into landscape mosaic patterns on a broad scale.

The landscape element discussion has already raised the question of **scale,** the level of spatial resolution perceived or considered. For example, the single, bare buffalo wallow a few meters in diameter (Figure 1.7) is conspicuous and important on a very local scale. But on the landscape

**Figure 1.7**  *Bison (American buffalo) on a "buffalo wallow" in grassland. The bison (Bison bison) rolls in the wallow, accumulating dust that inhibits biting flies.* Niabara National Wildlife Refuge, Nebraska, United States. (See Collins and Uno, 1983; Risser et al., 1981.) (Courtesy of USDA Soil Conservation Service.)

level of scale, we see the grassy landscape elements extending for hundreds of meters while the buffalo wallow is essentially invisible. Scale is important in several aspects of landscape ecology, from factors affecting single organisms to continental plate tectonics and the evolution of floras and faunas (Figure 1.8). Indeed, as the graphs show, spatial scale is closely related to temporal scale for a particular phenomenon. In ecological studies of scale, most approaches focus on a single species (Erickson, 1945; Levins, 1968; Kershaw, 1975) although some consider assemblages of species or ecosystems (Allen and Starr, 1982; Wiens, 1985).

At this point we must raise one question, even though the answer may leave us hanging. As we go progressively from a fine scale to a coarse scale, do spatial patterns of organisms change smoothly and gradually, or abruptly in a stair-step fashion? For example, if we could view nature

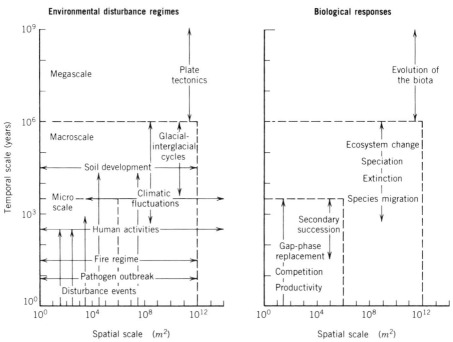

**Figure 1.8** *Relationship between spatial scale and temporal scale for various ecological phenomena. At the microscale, natural and human disturbances affect the establishment and succession of species. At the macroscale, regional climatic changes affect processes such as species migration and displacement of ecosystems. At the megascale, plate tectonics, evolution of major groups, and development of global vegetation patterns are prominent. The five vertical arrows on the lower left represent disturbance events such as wildfire, wind damage, clear cutting, flood, and earthquake. (From Delcourt et al., 1983; reprinted with permission of Pergamon Press, Ltd.)*

through an enormous camera zoom lens through which the focus is gradually and evenly changed, would we see even changes in the clustering of individual organisms (Richardson, 1926; Mandelbrot, 1977; Lovejoy, 1982)? Or would we observe patches within patches, that is, a patch at one distinct level of scale followed by a rapid change to another patch at a next level of scale? We do not have a certain answer but suspect the latter is most likely, as suggested for the distribution of leather flower, a *Clematis* species (Figure 1.9). The objective of the *Clematis* study in the Ozark Mountains (United States) was to determine the levels of scale at which cross-fertilization and the exchange of genes (gene flow) took place (Erickson, 1945). A similar study determined the environmental factors controlling the spread of a moss species in North America at each level of scale (Forman, 1964). The basic question posed here (of the nature of spatial heterogeneity with changing scale) is of interest in landscape ecology, because if there are clear mosaics only at distinct and separate levels of scale, the causes for the heterogeneity at each level are likely also to be distinct (Figures 1.7 and 1.9). Hence the landscape, with its heterogeneity and causative mechanisms, would be a single distinct recognizable level of spatial scale.

We have presented the landscape as being composed of landscape elements that are relatively homogeneous ecosystems. In nature we can find patches separated from one another with abrupt boundaries, with various kinds of transition zones, or with a gradual continuous change in species. The gradual change is most characteristic of certain natural landscapes without significant human influence evident. Other natural landscapes have predominantly abrupt boundaries, due either to abrupt changes in the physical environment through space, or to frequent natural disturbances (Figure 1.7). Human influences in landscapes tend to eliminate gradual changes and to produce abrupt boundaries (Figure 1.3).

## CONCEPT AREAS AND PRINCIPLES OF LANDSCAPE ECOLOGY

### Diversity Among Landscapes

We are now ready to observe some quite different kinds of landscapes to see what they have in common. The acid test of the usefulness of landscape ecology is to see if we can find general patterns that provide predictive ability and are applicable to any landscape.

The four landscapes presented below differ primarily in the degree of contrast, or distinctness, of landscape elements, present in each. They also vary in degree of human influence, natural disturbance regime, and topographic relief. We will visit an agricultural landscape in Wisconsin (midwestern United States) like the one discussed above (Figure 1.3), a

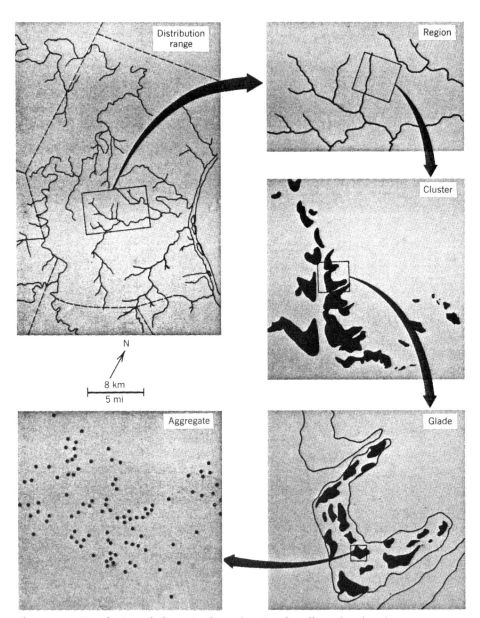

**Figure 1.9** *Distribution of* Clematis *plants showing the effect of scale. Plants were mapped in the Ozark Mountains of Missouri, United States. (After Erickson, 1945; credit Missouri Botanical Garden.)*

coniferous forest landscape in Labrador (Canada), a tropical rainforest landscape in Colombia, and a Mediterranean landscape in southern France.

Initially the best way to look for landscape patterns is to move about slowly a few hundred meters above the vegetation. For this purpose we recommend a glider, a single-seated aircraft without an engine, which has long wings, and glides nicely on a sunny day with hot air rising from the land. Even if you have not piloted one before it is possible to learn. Just grab the stick and move it in the direction you wish to go. There are no gears or accelerator and no brakes. You feel only silence and air as you watch a fantastic landscape spread out below you.

Assuming you are ready to go (and have a pilot's license), we now tow you up with a motorized airplane and cut you loose to glide on your own over a glorious agricultural landscape (Figure 1.3). Your job is to find the patterns. After a few practice turns you look down and over the next few hours record the following in your notebook.

Very distinct patches. Fields, woods, housing areas. Vary widely in size. Also in shape. Linear boundaries along patches very common. Patches often rectangular. Narrow strips or corridors widespread. Paved roads, dirt roads, railroad, powerlines, hedgerows, corridors along streams. Most are narrow, a few wider. Intersections and networks common. Usually fields form the background matrix. Only two isolated lakes present. Intense human influence or disturbance evident throughout landscape. Field plowing, road maintenance, woods cutting, building construction, and lawn mowing. Am hungry, ready to go down.

You spot a smooth, recently mowed pasture and touch down beautifully on your single wheel.

Before analyzing what you saw, let us go north to Labrador and the remote coniferous forest landscape (Figure 1.10). Again you are cut loose in your glider and with cold hands write the following.

No evidence of people anywhere. Yet patches very distinct. Peatlands, recent burned areas, lakes, beaver meadows, insect defoliation area. Patch sizes and shapes vary greatly. No straight borders on patches. Patches odd-shaped like clouds. Narrow corridors present, though not very common. Stream corridors and low curving sandy ridges covered with pine or larch (*Pinus, Larix*). Occasional intersections where stream tributaries come together. Background forested matrix of spruce and fir. A single hill with bare summit visible. Natural disturbances evident. Fire, insect pest outbreaks. Evidence of geomorphic formation by glaciation predominant everywhere. Am freezing, must go down.

You then ruin the glider and almost yourself when you try to land along a shallow lake margin.

Next, you find yourself gliding over the extensive rain forests of South America (Figure 1.11).

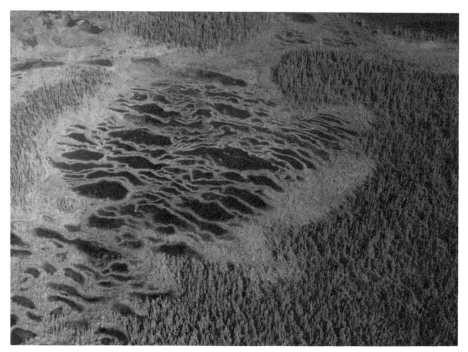

**Figure 1.10** *Coniferous forest with boggy areas. Forest of spruces (Picea) and firs (Abies). Curvy lines in central wet area are string bogs (Foster and King, 1984) with peat moss and shrubs, and are solid to walk on. South-central Labrador. (D. Foster.)*

Not a sign of human activity. Hardly a patch visible here. Heterogeneous, but different landscape elements tend to grade into one another. The rather indistinct patches are dominated by different tree species. Patches vary widely in size and shape. No linear boundaries. Corridors fairly widespread. All are stream or river corridors. Curvy and of different widths. Background matrix is forest. Occasional evidence of natural disturbance such as blowdowns or huge floods. Widespread evidence of geomorphic smoothing of relief by chemical alteration and by deposition. A single large river cuts through landscape. Need a bathroom. Where does one land?

Finally a distinct patch, produced by human activity, comes into view. The jungle has been cut back and replaced by a house, plantings, and a landing strip.

Finally, you try gliding over an area of Mediterranean vegetation in France (Figure 1.12).

Landscape incredibly complex. Low mountains and wide valleys. Some patches very distinct, others indistinct. Villages, farmyards, cultivated fields, woodlots, pastures, orchards, several types of oak forest (*Quercus*), tall shrublands, low

**Figure 1.11** *Montane tropical rain forest in the Andes Mountains southeast of Bogotá, Colombia. The canopy differs, but intergrades, in different portions of the slope. (R. Forman.)*

shrublands, swamps, and more. Abrupt boundaries due to geomorphic breaks, natural disturbance, and human influence. Indistinct boundary gradients due to gradual soil or topographic changes. Patch size and shape varied. Curvilinearity of boundaries varies. Corridors widespread. Roads, hedgerows, powerlines, canals, stream corridors. Stream corridors relatively straight in mountains. Dendritic stream tributary pattern rather symmetrical. Roads curvy in mountains, straight

**Figure 1.12** *Mediterranean landscape with a complexity of natural features and human influences. Flat valleys, low hills with natural oak (Quercus) and shrub vegetation, limestone mountains with rugged slopes, roads, pastures, cultivation, a dammed lake, a village, and isolated homes are present. Near Lodève, Languedoc, France. (Courtesy of Claude O'Sughrue, Montpellier.)*

in valleys. Hard to determine which type of landscape element is matrix. Belts of vegetation tend to parallel elevational levels. Cliffs appear as linear corridors. Human influences appear to go back millennia, hard to separate from geomorphology. Two large towns visible. Lonely up in this single-seater. Am going down to analyze these data with someone sunbathing on a secluded Mediterranean beach.

The differences among these four landscapes are striking and of considerable interest ecologically. The agricultural and coniferous landscapes had small distinct patches, the rain forest landscape indistinct patches, and the Mediterranean landscape contained a mixture of large, small, distinct, and indistinct patches. Geomorphic controls predominate in the rain forest, natural disturbances and geomorphology in the coniferous forest, human influence in the agricultural landscape, and all three in the Mediterranean case. Corridors and linearity are most pronounced in the agricultural landscape and least evident in the rain forest and the coniferous forest. The background matrix is field in the agricultural landscape, forest in the next two, and hard to determine in the Mediterranean case. The diversity of patch types is highest in the Mediterranean, low in the coniferous forest, and hard to determine in the rain forest. Rare or unusual features are present within each landscape.

## Concept Areas

Despite their extreme differences, all these landscapes share a common, fundamental structure. They are composed entirely of patches, corridors, and a background matrix. Both specific concepts and broad principles apply to all these landscapes (Forman and Godron, 1984). This book presents many concepts that help tie the field of landscape ecology together. They focus on specific phenomena and processes and thus provide predictive ability within relatively narrow limits. Some of these concepts may be quite tentative, reflecting the growth phase of the field, and no doubt will be modified over time. If some concepts or principles introduced at this point are difficult to follow, do not worry. They will be developed and explained in the chapters ahead.

Chapters 3, 4, and 5 deal with patches, corridors or strips, and the surrounding matrix, that is, the three basic types of landscape elements that make up a landscape. Origins or causative mechanisms determine to a large extent the species dynamics and stability of a landscape element. Size, shape, and the nature of the edge are particularly important patch characteristics. Corridor characteristics such as width, connectivity, curvilinearity, narrows, breaks, and nodes control the important conduit and barrier functions of a corridor. Stream corridors play additional critical roles in controlling water and nutrient relations in a landscape. Networks are characterized by differences in intersection types, reticulate structure, and mesh size. The landscape matrix, as the most extensive and connected landscape element type, plays the predominant role in landscape dynamics.

The discussion of overall landscape structure in Chapter 6 ties some of this material together and considers the additional factors of scale and heterogeneity. The degree of contrast and the level and type of heterogeneity are key characteristics of landscape structure.

The origin and development of landscapes by both natural processes and human influences are presented in Chapters 7 and 8. Landscapes reflect four pervasive natural processes: geomorphology interacting strongly with climate; plant and animal establishment and speciation; soil development; and disturbance. Processes take place involving the accumulation of potential energy and the increasing uniformity in landscape elements. Humans generally increase landscape heterogeneity by modifying the rhythms of natural disturbance, diversifying the tools of landscape modification, and creating the built-up environment associated with increasing human aggregation, the development of politics, and the input of fossil fuel energy. Human influence also leads to distinctive patterns of change in patches, corridors, and matrix.

In considering the functioning of a landscape in Chapters 9, 10, and 11 we examine the flows of energy, materials, and species. The forces of mass flow and locomotion cause almost all flows and change the density and distribution of the objects moved. Airflow, soil surface flow, and subsurface flow differ markedly in the rate and types of objects transported. Animals and plants moving across a landscape are highly sensitive to certain landscape features, such as large patches and wide corridors, but appear to ignore others. Many animals require two or more landscape elements to live, that is, landscape heterogeneity. Movement is dependent on landscape porosity and the direction of flow relative to the shape of patches. Network complexity as a function of connectivity and circuitry appears to be a useful index of movement through a network.

The patterns of landscape change seen in Chapter 12 show that a landscape may not be in equilibrium or may exist in several kinds of equilibria, depending largely on the amount of potential energy or biomass, the level of resistance to disturbance, and the ability to recover from disturbance. The absorption of useful energy by the landscape combats thermodynamic entropy and builds heterogeneity, in addition to inertia and metastability.

The final two chapters introduce concepts for landscape applications. People require and contribute to landscape heterogeneity, striving for an optimum level that spatially balances high resistance to disturbance, high biotic diversity, low maintenance energy required, and high harvestable yield. The nature of heterogeneity is also important to landscape typology. Guidelines and modeling are presented for landscape quality, planning, and management.

## Emerging General Principles

The information and specific concepts in this volume lead logically to at least seven major statements of principle. The first two focus on landscape structure, the next three on function, and the last two on change.

### Landscape Structure and Function Principle

Each individual ecosystem (or landscape element) at the scale of a landscape can be recognized as either a patch with significant width, a narrow corridor, or the background matrix (Figure 1.13). Ecological objects (in the broad sense) such as animals, plants, biomass, heat energy, water, and mineral nutrients are heterogeneously distributed among these landscape elements, which in turn vary in size, shape, number, type,

**Figure 1.13** *Heterogeneous foothill and high mountain landscapes. The snow, ice, and rock landscape is topped here by Mount Kazbek at an elevation of 5033 meters (16,508 feet). The foothill landscape has alpine vegetation, pastures, cliffs, woods, roads, and a village as distinct landscape elements. Flows between landscapes and landscape elements are widespread. Caucasus Mountains, Georgia, Soviet Union. (W. C. Johnson.)*

and configuration. Determining these spatial distributions is to understand landscape structure. Ecological objects, however, continually move or flow between landscape elements. Determining and predicting these flows or interactions among landscape elements is understanding landscape function. This first principle provides a common language or framework for the multidisciplinary understanding of landscapes.

> *Landscapes are heterogeneous and differ structurally in the distribution of species, energy, and materials among the patches, corridors, and matrix present. Consequently, landscapes differ functionally in the flows of species, energy, and materials among these structural landscape elements.*

### Biotic Diversity Principle

A high degree of heterogeneity in a landscape (whether due to natural disturbance, human activity, or environmental heterogeneity) results on the one hand in few large patches, and therefore relatively few of the species that require the interior environment of large patches. On the other hand, such a landscape contains an extensive amount of edge habitat with edge species, and also favors animals that use more than one ecosystem in close proximity, say for breeding, feeding, and resting. Total species diversity of the landscape is high however, because many ecosystem types are usually present, each with its distinctive biota or pool of species.

> *Landscape heterogeneity decreases the abundance of rare interior species, increases the abundance of edge species and animals requiring two or more landscape elements, and enhances the potential total species coexistence.*

### Species Flow Principle

Species distribution and landscape structure are linked in a feedback loop. Natural or human disturbance that forms landscape elements causes sensitive species to decrease in distribution, while favoring the spread of other species into disturbed areas. At the same time, the reproduction and dispersal of species may eliminate, change, or create whole landscape elements. Heterogeneity, a difference between locations, is a fundamental cause of species movements and other flows.

> *The expansion and contraction of species among landscape elements has both a major effect on, and is controlled by, landscape heterogeneity.*

### Nutrient Redistribution Principle

Mineral nutrients may flow in or out of a landscape, or be redistributed from one ecosystem to another within the landscape by wind, water, or animals (Figure 1.13). In general, disturbance, especially when severe, disrupts the conservation or regulatory mechanisms holding mineral nutrients in an ecosystem. This facilitates their transport to adjacent or other ecosystems.

> *The rate of redistribution of mineral nutrients among landscape elements increases with disturbance intensity in those landscape elements.*

### Energy Flow Principle

With increasing spatial heterogeneity, more energy flows across the boundaries of landscape elements within a landscape. Consider a square painted red on the left and black on the right versus a checkerboard of red and black patches. A heterogeneous checkerboard landscape has a high energy flow rate because of a long total length of boundary (or high perimeter-to-area ratio), as well as a high rate across a single boundary because of the cumulative effect of flows from many nearby small patches. For example, air movement over a heterogeneous landscape with small patches exhibits considerable turbulence, and a large portion of the landscape is edge habitat readily penetrated by wind. Heat energy carried horizontally by the wind (advection) is thus readily moved from one landscape element to another (e.g., the "oasis effect" where advection desiccates a moist area). Furthermore, with smaller patches present there is a greater proportion of edge animals that frequently move between adjacent landscape elements and, through herbivory, transport plant material.

*The flows of heat energy and biomass across boundaries separating the patches, corridors, and matrix of a landscape increase with increasing landscape heterogeneity.*

### Landscape Change Principle

Horizontal structure relates species, energy, and materials to the size, shape, number, type, and configuration of patches, corridors, and matrix. Following disturbance, a homogenizing effect is provided by the process of plant colonization and growth, soil modification, and animal colonization. However, a homogeneous landscape is never attained because the rates of change differ in each landscape element, and because disturbances intervene. Moderate disturbances normally establish more patches or corridors in the landscape (Figure 1.13). Severe disturbance may eliminate many patches and corridors resulting, for example, in a more homogeneous sandy landscape, or alternatively an even vegetative cover may be eliminated to expose a heterogeneous substrate beneath.

*When undisturbed, horizontal landscape structure tends progressively toward homogeneity; moderate disturbance rapidly increases heterogeneity, and severe disturbance may increase or decrease heterogeneity.*

### Landscape Stability Principle

Stability refers to the resistance of a landscape to disturbance and its recovery from disturbance. Each landscape element has its own degree of stability, and so the overall stability of the landscape reflects the proportion of each type of landscape element present. When virtually no biomass is present in a landscape element, such as a highway or bare sand dune, the system may readily change its physical properties (temperature or heat radiation, for example). Without a photosynthetic surface to capture useful sunlight, however, the system is nearly constant biologically. With a low level of biomass present (relative to the same habitats elsewhere in the landscape), the system has little resistance to change but may recover rapidly from disturbance, as in the case of a cultivated field. With considerable biomass present, as in a forest, the system is usually rather resistant to disturbance but recovers slowly from it. Note that biomass (sometimes considered an index of the "information" in a system) is not only a photosynthetic surface but also includes a huge number of organic and inorganic chemicals involved in protection, growth, reproduction, and much more.

> *Stability of the landscape mosaic may increase in three distinct ways, toward (a) physical system stability (characterized by the absence of biomass), (b) rapid recovery from disturbance (low biomass present), or (c) high resistance to disturbance (usually high biomass present).*

We label the seven statements as *emerging general principles* or theory of landscape ecology. They are supported by considerable direct and indirect evidence, rather than being conclusively proven. They deal with major issues of the field, have predictive ability within broad limits, and are applicable to any landscape.

The emerging principles are briefly introduced here to allow the reader to see the breadth of the field. Much of the rationale for them emerges in the following chapters. It is instructive to try to think of examples that may be inconsistent with a statement and to consider whether a given example is an exception or the norm for landscapes in general. It is also instructive to articulate additional general statements (especially applicable to landscapes), either equivalent in breadth to the emerging principles above or more narrowly focused in a hierarchy of generalization. Such is the process of developing human knowledge.

## THE EMERGENCE OF LANDSCAPE ECOLOGY: MAJOR LITERATURE

### Geography and Ecology

Since humans have always lived in landscapes, the roots of landscape ecology could be traced to the writings of scholars in every period of history. In their own way, for example, Herodotus (484–420 B.C.), von Humboldt (1769–1859 A.D.), Darwin (1809–1882), and countless others have contributed to the foundations of landscape ecology. However, the outlines of a distinct discipline or field of study were provided by a series of pioneering geographers and biogeographers, primarily during the 1960s, who interpreted the landscape as being composed of landscape elements (or biotopes or ecotopes). The term "landscape ecology" is credited to the German geographer, C. Troll (1950, 1968).

E. Neef (1963, 1967), J. Schmithusen (1964, 1967; Bobek and Schmithusen, 1967), and G. Haase (1964), all in Germany, provided early insights into the ecological structure of landscapes, with Neef going into particular detail. The Americans C. Sauer (1925, 1963) and J. Jackson (Meinig, 1979b) analyzed landscape structure, particularly as influenced by human culture. G. A. Hills (1960) in Canada, H. Carol (1956) in Switzerland, V. Vinogradov (1966) and V. Sochava (1967) in the Soviet Union, and I. Zonneveld (1979) in the Netherlands provided additional important insights into landscape structure from studies in diverse regions. R. Park (1968) and K. Lynch (1960) particularly elucidated structure and change in the urban landscape. Concepts of landscape function or dynamics received less attention. C. Troll discussed dynamics, but C. Van Leeuwen (1966, 1973) in the Netherlands provided an original perspective by linking temporal variation to spatial heterogeneity in landscapes (the relation theory).

Landscape ecologists quickly recognized the relevance of work in several sister disciplines. From ecology, the development of the ecosystem concept (e.g., Tansley, 1935; Odum, 1959, 1971; Woodwell and Whittaker, 1968; Bormann and Likens, 1967), in the United States and elsewhere, provided an essential holistic view. Sukachev in the Soviet Union particularly developed the similar biogeocenosis concept (Sukachev and Dylis, 1964; Johnson and French, 1981). In England, C. Elton (1958) focused attention on the invasions of animals and plants. R. MacArthur and E. Wilson (1967), in the United States, catalyzed interest in island biogeography and changed its focus to species diversity, rates of species flow, and island characteristics. Traditional animal and plant geography (e.g., Schimper, 1903, 1935; Darlington, 1957; Dansereau, 1957; Eyre, 1977; Ozenda, 1964; Walter, 1964, 1968; Udvardy, 1970) and vegetation methodology (Braun-Blanquet, 1932, 1964; Greig-Smith, 1964; Godron et al., 1968; Kershaw, 1975; Mueller-Dombois and Ellenberg, 1974) are related to landscape ecology and have provided some useful contributions.

A specific series of integrated ecological investigations on hedges or hedgerows in Britain and France (Pollard et al., 1974; Les Bocages, 1976) turn out to be exceptionally instructive for landscape ecology. These studies not only elucidate aspects of landscape structure, function, and change but also consider animals, plants, soil, meteorology, people, land use, and more. Therefore, we will periodically refer to hedgerow studies as examples in this volume.

## Related Disciplines

The field of regional studies (e.g., Rey, 1960; Dickinson, 1970; Cliff and Ord, 1973; Isard, 1975) has provided many useful perspectives on landscapes within regions (Miller, 1978a). Urbanization theory (Christaller, 1938; Rapoport, 1982a) and transportation theory, studying the movement of people, have also proven valuable, especially in understanding corridors and networks (Taaffe and Gauthier, 1973; Lowe and Moryadas, 1975; Haggett et al., 1977). Planning and landscape architecture have provided valuable information on landscape structure, function, and change, as well as underlining the roles of aesthetics and of human perceptions of the landscape (Eckbo, 1975; Kiemstedt, 1975; Zube et al., 1975; Fabos, 1979; Steinitz, 1979; Haber, 1980; Ruzicka and Miklos, 1981, 1984). McHarg's treatise (1969), on designing with nature, focused people's attention on landscape modification within ecological constraints. The land evaluation techniques of Zonneveld (1979) in The Netherlands, Christian and Stewart (1968) in Australia, and Long (1974) in France have given us valuable perspectives on scale and landscape structure. Finally, pioneering individuals in wildlife biology, forestry, and pest management have provided excellent case studies for landscape ecology.

### International Perspectives Today

A broad schematic look at the present status of landscape ecology suggests the following in different regions. In North America, landscape ecology has just been born and seems to have an initial major focus on ecology. But several related disciplines are involved, and the primary focus is on developing basic concepts (Burgess and Sharpe, 1981; Forman and Godron, 1981, 1984; Romme and Knight, 1982; Phipps, 1984; Merriam, 1984; Risser et al., 1984).

In the Soviet Union, under the umbrella of biology and especially of geography, landscape ecology has a strong economic and social planning component. Emphasis is on the complex of land development, increasing productivity, and recognition of environmental impacts (Vinogradov, 1980; Gerasimov et al., 1979; Johnson and French, 1981; Preobrazhensky, 1984).

In Europe and the Middle East, a rich mixture of approaches—including nature conservation, planning, landscape architecture, wildlife biology, land evaluation, geography, environmental science, forestry, landscape history, and concept development—promises important synergisms.[2] Interest in landscape ecology is present in many other countries, as evidenced by participation in international meetings in recent years, and is growing rapidly (Tjallingii and de Veer, 1982; Ruzicka et al., 1982;

[2]See, for example, Van Leeuwen, 1973, 1982; Rackham, 1975, 1976, 1980; Haase, 1975, 1984; Peterken, 1977; Ruzicka and Miklos, 1981, 1984; Ruzicka et al., 1982; Schreiber, 1977; Naveh, 1982a; Naveh and Lieberman, 1984; Godron and Forman, 1983; Vink, 1980; ten Houte de Lange, 1984; Agger and Brandt, 1984; Antrop, 1984; Baudry, 1984; Opdam, 1984; Harms et al., 1984.

Preobrazhensky, 1984; Risser et al., 1984; Brandt and Agger, 1984). Such signs indicate that this new field, as it is weeded and cultivated, will be used to solve many theoretical and practical problems of tomorrow.

## SUMMARY

Common threads from several disciplines help provide a rigorous scientific concept of the landscape. It may be usefully defined as a heterogeneous land area composed of a cluster of interacting ecosystems which is repeated in similar form throughout its kilometers-wide extent. Geomorphic processes, colonization of organisms, and disturbance mold the structure of landscapes. Landscape ecology, therefore, focuses on (a) structure, the spatial patterns of landscape elements and ecological objects (such as animals, biomass, and mineral nutrients); (b) function, the flows of objects between landscape elements; and (c) change, alterations in the mosaic through time.

Views of four contrasting landscapes show a common fundamental structure of patches, corridors, and a matrix; their configurations indicate the wide variety of landscapes on earth. From an array of concept areas, seven general principles of landscape ecology have emerged. These involve structure and function, biotic diversity, species flow, nutrient redistribution, energy flow, landscape change, and landscape stability.

The combination of modern ecological principles with a geographical foundation developed since the 1960s has provided a synergism for the present burst of activity in landscape ecology. Important contributions from related disciplines have helped establish the importance of an ecological understanding, not only of ecosystems, but also of the heterogeneous landscapes in which they coexist.

## QUESTIONS

1. What characteristics are repeated in similar form across a landscape?
2. How would you have defined the word *landscape* before reading this chapter? How does your definition differ from that of the dictionary? Of geography? Of ecology? Why are the concepts so diverse?
3. How would you differentiate a landscape from an ecosystem? A region? A watershed or basin? A landscape element? A tessera?
4. Compare the agricultural, boreal forest, tropical rainforest, and Mediterranean landscapes. Which had the greatest contrast? Diversity of corridor types? Prevalence of linear features? Evidence of recent natural disturbances?
5. In what ways are the structure, function, and change of a landscape similar to those of the human body? Explain any fundamental differences.

6. Describe two of the emerging general principles, explaining how each could be useful in landscape management.
7. If you were a wildlife manager responsible for both protecting rare species and maximizing wildlife for hunting, how would you use the biotic diversity principle?
8. If you were a forester faced with managing a whole forested landscape for both maximum wood production and soil conservation, how would you use the nutrient redistribution principle?
9. If you were a planner or landscape architect designing a suburban landscape, how would you use the energy flow principle?
10. In geography, the scale of a map is always given in the legend as a ratio of map distance to actual distance. What would be the approximate scale of a map of your immediate neighborhood? For a map of the continent? For the landscape in which you live? Briefly describe your landscape.
11. The landscape change principle concerns changing structure, while the landscape stability principle concerns the types of stability. What insight might be gained by integrating the two principles together?
12. What are the major areas of thought contributing to landscape ecology, and how have they meshed to produce the current state of the field?

# 2
# Ecological Concepts in Brief

Nature.
*A vast, tightly interwoven fabric of activity.*
**Paul B. Sears, 1962**
*The Biology of the Living Landscape*

Isaac Newton, the noted physicist and discoverer of gravitation, observed that he could see further than his predecessors because he was able to stand on the shoulders of giants. So, too, we can develop landscape ecology only by standing on earlier foundations. Several foundations underpin landscape ecology. **Ecology,** the scientific study of the relationships between organisms and their environments, is one. If ecology is part of your repertoire, feel free to move directly to Chapter 3. If not, the present chapter, laying out most of the main ideas of the science of ecology, should provide a useful background to landscape ecology.

Early Greek and Roman scholars discussed how plants and animals were related to the environment (Figure 2.1). But today's ecological principles mainly have their roots in the work of seventeenth- and eighteenth-century natural historians, agriculturalists, geographers, and human demographers. During the nineteenth-century, plant geographers, aquatic biologists, and zoologists developed principles that gave birth to the discipline. The early twentieth century saw a quickening and broadening of the ecological sphere to include the work of animal behaviorists, evolutionists, statisticians, animal geographers, and plant community ecologists (phytosociologists). As in any field, scholars of many more disciplines have contributed and continue to contribute significantly.

Two broad perspectives permeate all branches of ecology. The first concerns feedback systems. In a **feedback** loop, or system, one component affects a second component that in turn affects the first component; such loops underlie most ecological processes. Feedback loops may be positive or negative. When one component stimulates a second, but the second inhibits the first, we call it a **negative feedback.** In this case, both components may oscillate within a relatively predictable range through time, thus operating as a regulating or control mechanism to produce a relatively stable equilibrium. Certain predator and prey cycles are familiar examples of a negative feedback system. Other examples are

**Figure 2.1**  *Rattlesnakes* (Crotalus) *crossing gravel road in the short-grass plains. Near Loveington, New Mexico, United States. (Courtesy of USDA Soil Conservation Service.)*

temperature regulation through sweating by mammals, or the amount of harvest extracted from a forest, which affects the next input effort, which in turn determines the future harvest output. In a **positive feedback** system, one component stimulates the second, which in turn stimulates the first. For example, parents reproduce and increase the number of offspring; offspring grow up and increase the number of parents. The result is exponential population growth.

Second, ecologists look for both **proximate** and **ultimate factors** in determining organism-environment interactions. A proximate factor has a direct or relatively direct effect on an organism, whereas an ultimate factor causes or controls the proximate factor. The questions ecologists pose provide the key. They ask *what, how,* and *why,* as in any field of science. What and how questions basically have proximate factor answers, while why questions have ultimate factor answers. Generally, ultimate factors are past evolutionary characteristics of a species, past environmental changes, or fundamental energy relationships embodied in thermodynamics. Thus, in answering the *what, how,* and *why* of the rattlesnake (Figure 2.1) and rodent relationship, we first describe the number and distribution of both species. Next, we look at how the snakes hunt and how the rodents avoid being caught. Finally, we consider the evolutionary processes producing poison in snakes and rodents that hop, plus the historical migrations of the species.

Many of the topics of this chapter will be used again in the perspective of landscape ecology. Landscapes combine to form regions, which combine to form continents, which combine with oceans to form the biosphere. Thus, landscapes play a key interacting role, linking nearby ecosystems together to form basic structural and functional units of the global system (Woodwell, 1983).


## THE PHYSICAL ENVIRONMENT

### Climate

Temperature, moisture, wind, and light are primary environmental controls on terrestrial organisms. We begin with sunlight, or solar energy, which largely controls all of the others, and like energy of any sort may be measured in calories or kilocalories. Much of the middle latitude of the globe annually receives around 140 kcal of solar energy per square centimeter (120–160 kcal/cm$^2$/yr or 30–40 joules/cm$^2$/yr). For comparison, two cloudless midsummer days in temperate or tropical areas typically give 1 kcal/cm$^2$. A single large area from the Sahara to India, plus four scattered smaller areas (Arizona, Chile, Kalahari, and Australia) receive more than 200 kcal in a year. A relatively even decrease in sunlight is present above about 40° north and south latitudes, where the sun hits the earth at quite an oblique angle, thus providing fewer calories per unit area. The solar input is also reduced in the cloudy equatorial rain forest areas of South America, central Africa, and the Pacific Islands.

At an average spot about half of the incoming calories arrive as heat (long wavelength or infrared radiation), and about half in the shorter visible and ultraviolet wavelengths. The visible violet-to-red spectrum is usable in plant photosynthesis, whereas the ultra-violet and other short wave lengths may kill cells. Of the short wavelength energy arriving from space, about 37% is reflected or absorbed by the atmosphere, meaning that about 63% reaches the vegetation and ground (Figure 2.2). Most of the energy absorbed by the ground and plants is reradiated upward at night as long wavelengths, but some does not penetrate through the atmosphere and is reradiated back downward. Both the ground and the air are heated from this process, plus direct incoming heat energy from the sun. Although a considerable amount of energy strikes the ground, typically less than 1% of it is used in plant photosynthesis.

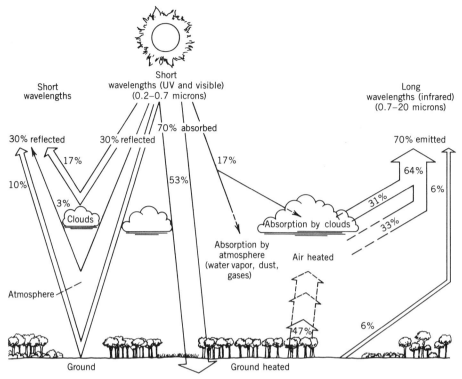

**Figure 2.2**  *Energy flows through the atmosphere, soil, and ecosystem. The incoming short wavelengths constitute nearly half of the total solar energy, the remainder being long wavelengths. The percentages are rough global averages and vary from one landscape or ecosystem to another. For example, within a landscape, reflection of incoming energy (albedo) from bare soil is greater than that from an uneven canopy. This variation in albedo is the basis for the usefulness of aerial infrared photographs.*

The heat from solar radiation combines with the earth's rotation to produce the familiar major climatic zones on earth. Along the equator is a low pressure rainy area. At about 30° north and south latitudes is a high pressure dry area. And again at 50° to 60° a low-pressure wet area is present. The ecological results of these global climatic patterns are evident in the equatorial rain forests, the major deserts and arid areas of the world at about 30° latitude, and the cool, moist forests (e.g., boreal forests) at about 50° to 60° latitude (Figure 2.3).

Between these latitudes are winds with rather predictable directions. Between 30° and the equator are the warm, easterly **trade winds**, between 30° and 40° to 60° the **prevailing westerlies,** and beyond 60° the cold, easterly flowing **polar fronts** (Figure 2.3). The trade wind zone is char-

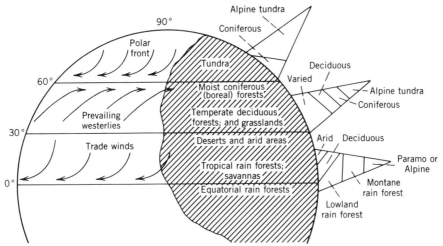

**Figure 2.3** *Winds, latitudinal zonation, and altitudinal zonation. Zones on mountains extend higher on the equatorial side because the incoming solar radiation is greater there. In tropical areas, rainforests or arid areas may occur on any exposure.*

acterized by tropical rain forests and savannas, the prevailing westerly zone by temperate deciduous forest and grassland, and the polar front zone by tundra and drier coniferous forest.

Looking within a continent, we see the directions of these airflows are significant in determining major vegetation distributions. Of course, land near a coast has a climate moderated by the water body, that is, with fewer extremes in temperature. Wind carrying moisture from the sea, for example in the prevailing westerly zone, flows across the United States or southern South America. But when the wind encounters mountains, the air laden with moisture from the sea is forced upward and cools, causing water condensation and precipitation. Therefore, the mountains here, like the Sierra Nevadas or the Andes, have moist forests on their western slopes. But this leaves the air dry as it flows over land downwind of the mountains, producing dry deserts or grasslands such as the Great Basin desert or the Patagonian grassland (steppe). This process, called the **rain shadow** effect, causes marked west to east vegetation differences within continents. A striking example (mainly in the tradewind zone) is northeastern Australia. The easterly warm, moist winds hit and drop rain on the Queensland mountains along the east coast, producing lush tropical rain forests but leaving much of the remainder of the continent arid grassland and desert. Climates near the middle of continents are commonly called continental; that is, they are generally dry but with wide, seasonal temperature variations. These climates support grasslands, shrublands, and deserts.

Within mountainous areas, a further striking climatic pattern is evident with altitudinal zonation. Since climate varies vertically in a similar manner to latitudinal variation, similarities in altitudinal and latitudinal vegetation zones are often, but not always, present (Figure 2.3).

As implied above, the amount of precipitation is a major control on vegetation type. Thus, the dramatic differences between deserts and wet rain forests in equatorial and tropical areas are a result of differences in both total rainfall and how it is distributed throughout the year.

These diverse climatic threads determine vegetation type, and may be tied together in a diagram showing their quantitative relationship (Figure 2.4). Here we see the wide range of vegetation types in tropical regions, showing, for example, how they change as one goes up a mountain (diagonally up the right side of the diagram), or proceeds from wet to dry areas at low elevation (vertically in the center of the diagram). In nontropical, cooler regions (above about 30° latitude), the major vegetation types are generally more strongly influenced by temperature (diagonally up the left side of the diagram). Finally, the vertical axis in the tropical zone indicates that seasonality and total amount of precipitation tend to compensate for one another in that zone.

(These predictions of vegetation types based on climate must be modified to account for two additional major factors, soil and human land use. Human land use, of course, can dramatically change land, such as through suburbanization, cultivation, irrigation, desertification, and the like, in ways that we will explore later in the book. Soil characteristics such as poor drainage, high acidity, low nutrient levels, and shallowness or coarseness also have profound effects on the vegetation.)

Climatic changes over thousands of years (e.g., since the last Ice Age) cause whole floras and faunas to move across the land. Yet in a much shorter time scale, seasonal precipitation changes (in latitudes below about 30°) also result primarily from heat. During seasons when the sun is overhead or nearly so, high incoming heat causes considerable **evapotranspiration** (the evaporation of water molecules from the surfaces of plants, soil, etc.). The water moves vertically in the atmosphere, cools, condenses, and falls as rain. Hence, rainy seasons are generally year-round near the equator where the sun is always nearly overhead. But as one approaches the Tropics of Cancer and Capricorn, at $23\frac{1}{2}°$ north and south latitudes, the pattern gradually shifts to a six-month wet and a six-month dry season. The wet season then corresponds to the period when the sun is overhead in that hemisphere, and most plant growth takes place then.

Diurnal (daily) meteorologic changes are also significant to the activity and behavioral patterns of animals, and, of course, to plant photosynthesis. In open areas, heat from sunlight is absorbed by the ground surface during the day and then reradiated vertically at night (Figure 2.2), leaving

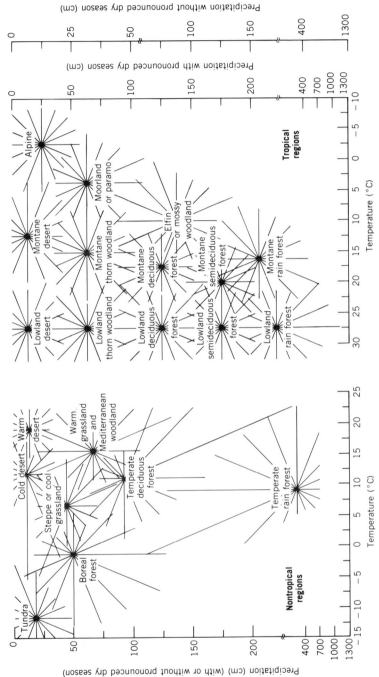

**Figure 2.4** Major vegetation types on earth related to climate. Axes are average annual temperature and precipitation. Based primarily on climatic data of Rumney (1968), with additional insights from Beard (1955), Holdridge (1967), Whittaker (1973), and discussions with R. H. Whittaker.

the soil surface cooler at dawn. While weather fronts several days long move across the land in temperate regions, in warm rain forest areas, weather patterns are generally daily. Basically, the sun comes out in the morning and heats up the vegetation and soil, stimulating evapotranspiration. The water rises and cools, and rain falls regularly in late afternoon. Much animal activity is related to this diurnal rainfall pattern.

We have focused on climate affecting plants and animals, yet the relationship is really a feedback loop, since organisms may affect climate. For example, as the stems in a field of corn (Zea) grow, **microclimatic** (climate of a small area) changes in light, temperature, moisture, and wind beneath the foliage are striking. Similarly, the tiny hummingbird (*Trochilidae*) controls the microclimate of its nest so that its eggs stay at about the same temperature as the human body even when the air surrounding the nest is only slightly above freezing. Cows or bison that huddle together to provide warmth during the cold hours of the day also illustrate a feedback, with animals affecting climate and climate affecting animals.

## Soil

Dirt is dirty, ground is what we walk on, and **soil** is the top layer of the earth's surface where rocks have been broken down into relatively small particles through biological, chemical, and physical processes. That layer is enormously heterogeneous and active. It is composed of mineral particles, organic matter, water, and air. Soil is also composed of numerous small animals, fungi, bacteria and other microorganisms. Many specialists consider the larger organisms present, like mammals, salamanders, and plant roots not to be components of the soil but merely to be located in it.

The basic process of forming soil from the breakdown of rock or other parent material is called **weathering** and may include both physical and chemical processes. The most frequent physical process is the splitting of rocks in regions with frost. Here, water penetrates into rock fissures, expands during freezing, and causes the rock to crack into smaller pieces. Biological and chemical breakdown processes are much more widespread. On exposed rocks, small plants such as lichens, mosses, and some flowering plants commonly become established. The growth of roots in fine cracks helps split rocks. Acids produced either directly by the plants (especially organic acids from lichens), or in the microbial decomposition process at the base of the plant, combine with water to dissolve minerals or cracks between minerals. Acids, such as sulfuric, nitric, and carbonic acids from $SO_2$, $NO_2$, and $CO_2$ in the atmosphere, also dissolve minerals from rock. Probably most soil formation takes place at the lower surface of already established soil, where rock particles are chemically broken down with organic and other acids carried down from the upper microbial decomposition portion of the soil.

Once formed, soil is readily transported to and deposited on other sites by erosion. Water erosion carries soil to lower elevations and drops it as **alluvial deposits.** Wind erosion carries soil as dust or sand to either lower or higher elevations where it is dropped as a (loess) deposit or sand dunes. Organisms colonize this new soil surface, which may cover a former soil or even bare rock.

When we dig a deep hole through the soil we can often see layers or horizons in the cut surface. The so-called **A-horizon** is a zone of leaching, that is, where rock constituents such as mineral nutrients are dissolved and carried downward by water. The **B-horizon** is the zone of accumulation where some of these materials collect. The **C-horizon** is weathered, mineral particles normally derived from the rock beneath. These broad horizons are usefully subdivided and tell us a lot about the vegetation, animals, and history of the site. At the top of the A-horizon is the **litter,** relatively undecomposed, dead organic matter. Beneath the litter is typically well-decomposed, organic matter called **humus.** Under the humus is an $A_1$-layer, where organic matter is visibly mixed with mineral soil. Beneath that is an $A_2$-layer, where the organic matter is no longer visible, and the mineral soil is leached of many of its mineral nutrients. Few soil profiles contain all possible layers; in fact, the presence or absence of layers is used in classifying types of soils.

Climate, vegetation, soil animals, and bedrock chemistry are tightly bound together with feedbacks in determining a wide variety of soil types (Figure 2.5). We can recognize broad soil types associated with each major vegetation type. For example, tundra soil is thin and little stratified because of little biological activity in the soil. In contrast, grassland soil (chernozem) has a deep A-horizon rich in organic matter and nutrients. The tropical rain forest soil (oxisol, latosol, or laterite) is deep, little-stratified, and low in organic matter or nutrients, because they are rapidly removed by heavy rainfall and rapid microbial decomposition activity.

Even at a fine scale, such as near a stream in the temperate zone, soil structural differences are striking and revealing. In high, well-drained soils considerable stratification and weathering are present. In low, water-logged soil, little oxygen penetrates through the A-horizon, leaving organic matter little decomposed, and beneath this are layers of rather impermeable, heavy, oxygenless material. Just as at the broader continental scale, each type of soil has a somewhat different animal community and vegetation, which in turn affect the soil. The feedback loop between soil and organisms is illustrated by the fact that different vegetation planted on identical soil can produce two quite different soil types over time.

Earthworms are familiar in soils of many temperate areas, mites (*Acarina*) and springtails (*Collembola*) in boreal forest soils, and ants and ter-

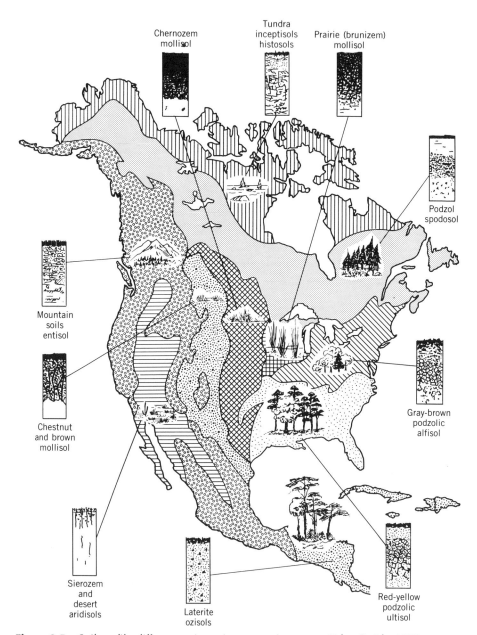

**Figure 2.5** *Soil profile differences in major vegetation types. (After Smith, 1979; courtesy of Harper & Row, Inc., Publishers.)*

mites in many tropical soils. Besides these decomposers the soil ecosystem includes many more kinds of animals, including predators. Fungi, bacteria, protozoa, and algae are also usually present. A few key soil characteristics, including texture, porosity, chemistry, and moisture, largely determine the relative abundance of the different organisms and their activity.

**Soil texture** refers to the relative amounts of different sized soil particles present. Thus, a soil sample with sand particles predominant is considered coarse, soil with abundant silt particles is intermediate, and soil with abundant clay particles is fine. In fact, soil texture based only on particle sizes is a basis for describing any soil (Figure 2.6). For example, a soil containing nearly all clay particles is called a *clay soil*. A mixture of 50% clay and 50% sand is a *sandy clay*. *Clay loam* and *loam soils* have relatively similar proportions of the three particle sizes.

**Soil porosity** refers to the proportion of air space in a soil, which affects the ability of air or water to move through it. Sandy soil is porous, while clay soil normally has low porosity. However, porosity is not simply a

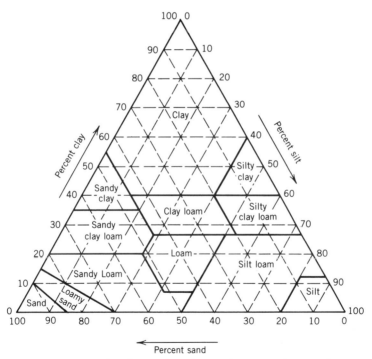

**Figure 2.6** *General soil types based on soil texture. The triangle indicates the relative proportions of three particle sizes, sand, silt, and clay. The names are according to the U.S. Department of Agriculture*

reflection of texture, because many holes of a good earthworm population will increase porosity, and liming a clay soil usually causes the clay particles to aggregate in clusters, leaving larger spaces and hence higher porosity. High porosity is essential for getting oxygen down to animals and for the survival of roots.

Soil chemistry refers to the mineral nutrients and organic acids present. Acidity (or pH) is an overall indication of soil chemistry conditions. Highly acid soils have few mineral nutrients, and somewhat basic soils have more nutrients. When the farmer puts fertilizer on the field, he or she is recognizing that more nitrogen, phosphorus, or potassium will support more plant growth.

Soil moisture is equally significant. Both wet soils, as in a stream bottom, and dry soils, as in the desert (Figure 2.5), have few animals present and support little plant growth. After saturation of a soil by rain or irrigation, some water drains away by gravity, and some water is so tightly bound to particles that it is unavailable to organisms. A third portion of the water, called **capillary water,** is available to plant roots and other organisms.

In short, soil is home to a complex and intriguing natural community as well as being a key substrate for the vegetation in and above it. Soil comes largely from rocks, in the presence of organisms, and can move from place to place. In its profile much is written about the biota, texture, porosity, chemistry, moisture, and history of the site.

## Fire

Some areas undergo frequent fires on which the animals and plants can literally be said to depend. They have adaptations to frequent fire, such as burrowing in the soil, sprouting from roots, opening cones only when hot, or feeding on fruits of other fire-adapted species. At the other extreme are areas where fires are rare and can be considered a severe disturbance. Here, few fire adaptations are present, and it may take a long time for the ecosystem to recover from fire to its pre-burned state, especially if fire is followed by soil erosion.

An important feedback links fire and vegetation. The fire affects the vegetation by combustion, and the vegetation encourages fire by reaching a certain amount of cover, or a certain height, or containing a certain percentage of especially flammable species.

## AQUATIC ENVIRONMENTS

Most ecological concepts apply equally to aquatic (including marine) and land environments. The concepts presented below are essentially unique to aquatic ecosystems.

## Hydrologic Cycle

Water evaporates from the surface of oceans and land to the air, falls on the land in precipitation, runs off in streams and rivers (passing through lakes and ponds), enters estuaries, and finally returns to oceans (Figure 2.7). In this simplified *hydrologic cycle* a particular water molecule could, at least theoretically, return to a previous spot.

Several variations of this basic cycle are important ecologically. Precipitation may arrive as snow, in which case a time lag of hours, months, or longer may intervene before water runs off into a stream. Water moving to a stream may pass over the surface as **surface runoff,** or underground as **subsurface flow** (Figure 2.7). The critical difference is that the former may cause erosion of soil particles, whereas the latter basically carries dissolved nutrients to the stream. Where a layer of sand or porous rock is under the soil, it fills up with water to form an underground *aquifer,* and the subsurface flow may enter the aquifer. Aquifer water flows slowly to rivers at lower elevations.

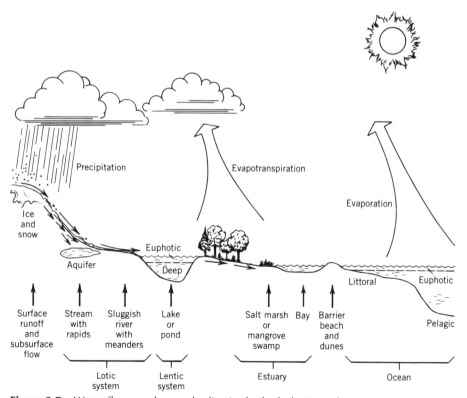

**Figure 2.7**   *Water flows and water bodies in the hydrologic cycle.*

## Lotic and Lentic Environments

Water bodies with fast moving water, such as streams and rivers, are called **lotic** environments. Those with slow moving water, such as lakes, ponds, and bogs, are **lentic** environments (Figure 2.7).

In the lotic environments, we are particularly interested in flow rate, turbidity, and the effects of temperature on the biota of rapids and pools. With a high flow rate over rocks or logs, the surface of a stream is broken, and considerable water turbulence occurs. High levels of oxygen are usually provided from top to bottom, supporting organisms such as trout and salmon that require abundant oxygen. A high flow rate cleans out small particles and leaves the bottom composed of large particles like rocks. The rocks are usually covered by an assemblage of tiny, often slimy species, called **aufwuchs** (or periphyton), which are dominated by algae.

If the flow rate of the stream is lower, smaller particles such as sand and silt can accumulate on the bottom, in which some aquatic plants may be loosely rooted. Aquatic insect larvae are the major consumers in any lotic environment, but in these lower flow rate situations burrowing worms play major roles.

On flatter land, long stretches of rivers may become winding and sluggish (Figure 2.7). Here most of the bottom will be covered with silt, and in addition to rooted aquatic plants, **phytoplankton** (floating aquatic plants composed of essentially all algae) largely replace the aufwuchs. Two other major physical factors change the fauna here. More of the stream or river is directly exposed to the sun, so the water temperature is higher, which means less oxygen is dissolved in the water. Secondly, the river is more muddy or *turbid,* that is, has more suspended particulate matter. These factors tend to eliminate the oxygen-demanding species and favor warmer water, bottom-feeding species such as sunfish and carp (*Lepomis, Cyprinus*). Most of the invertebrates are bottom-burrowing species. The base of the food chain is highly dependent on **detritus,** dead organic matter, from upstream or streamside.

Lakes and ponds (lentic ecosystems), with their much lower flow rates, may have bottoms entirely covered with silt, clay, or organic matter. A **littoral zone** with rooted aquatic plants around the edge surrounds an open water or **euphotic zone** (also called photic or limnetic), where light penetrates and phytoplankton dominate (Figure 2.7). Food chains are based primarily on the phytoplankton, although detritus input may sometimes be considerable. A deep zone below the euphotic zone may contain cold water and oxygen-demanding species that depend on food from the upper zones.

The seasonal aspects of temperate lakes are of particular interest. In deep lakes a prominent vertical stratification commonly appears in summer. An upper layer of warm water is separated from the deeper cold water by a **thermocline,** a narrow horizontal zone in which a sharp temperature change occurs. Ecologically, this means that phytoplankton growth takes place in the warm water, and the cool water organisms accumulate at the thermocline, where their food sources are coming down from above. Fishermen in midsummer know they must have their hooks down at the thermocline to catch anything they could talk about.

In a remarkable process, such a lake turns over each year in fall and spring. As a result of temperature and wind changes, the surface water sinks and forces bottom water up, moving oxygen to deep levels. Of major ecological significance is the fact that nutrients deposited on the lake bottom are also sucked back up to the surface layer, where they become available to phytoplankton for **production,** the accumulation of organic material by organisms.

These physical, seasonal changes also help catalyze a dramatic series of seasonal, biological changes. Most striking in lakes is the sequence of phytoplankton *blooms,* where one species of algae is enormously abundant and productive for a short time, followed by another species, and then another. Major changes, though less pronounced, also occur in the **zooplankton** (floating animals). The herbivorous zooplankton besides responding to the amount of phytoplankton present, also control the phytoplankton abundance (hence how green the lake appears), by the amount of grazing they do. This intriguing feedback between phytoplankton and grazers is still little understood.

## Marine Environments

When fresh water from the land mixes with salt water from the ocean, it produces the brackish water of the estuary (Figure 2.8). This type of aquatic environment plays a special ecological role because it receives nutrients from four sources: fresh water flowing off the land, the ocean tides, the atmosphere, and sediments from its bottom. This nutrient input supports an exceptionally high production. Animal species diversity (the number of species) is relatively high, even though plant species diversity is usually low.

Two distinct areas are commonly present in estuaries: a bay of open water separated from the ocean by a narrow, sandy barrier beach, and a salt marsh (or mangrove woodland in tropical areas) where tides leave exposed mud surfaces (Figures 2.7 and 2.8). The open water portion has abundant phytoplankton and a rich food web leading to a rather high density of fish and birds. The mud flat area of the marsh or mangrove has high production from the rooted plants, but surprisingly little of it is consumed by herbivores. Rather, the production turns into detritus, and two major routes may follow. Animals such as crabs and mudworms may

**Figure 2.8** *Linkage of river, estuary, and ocean. River brings fresh water from the land to the estuary, which also receives salt water from the ocean. The estuary, composed of the salt marsh and bay, is tidal and has the highest salt concentrations in the upper portions of the salt marsh, where evaporation of water is high. Plum Island, Massachusetts, United States. (M. J. McDonnell.)*

feed on the detritus, thus supporting a major food chain. Or the twice daily tides may wash the detritus out to the bay or near-shore portion of the ocean, where another diverse food chain is supported by detritus.

Two-thirds of the globe is covered by oceans, yet much of this vast area has been termed a *biological desert*. This term refers to the fact that only a few rather limited areas in oceans have really high production and species diversity. These areas are scattered, for example, from near the equator to the Arctic Circle on both eastern and western sides of different oceans. They all have one thing in common: high nutrient levels.

To see the reason for this, we must first explore the underwater ecological zones (Figure 2.7). Again we see a littoral zone, and a light-penetrated euphotic zone. We may recognize a **continental shelf (or neritic) zone** and an open ocean **pelagic zone.** Phytoplankton are the major source of food throughout, except in some littoral situations, and food chains are predominantly based on the grazing of phytoplankton. Detritus filtering down from the euphotic zone forms the base of the food webs at deeper layers. Fish are found essentially from top to bottom, but because of the tremendous gradient of pressure present, a species (at adulthood) remains at the particular depth to which it is adapted. (Fish brought up from down deep simply explode because of the pressure change.)

In addition to nutrients, the second factor important in understanding the presence of highly productive spots is ocean currents. Globally, the major currents flow counterclockwise in oceans south of the equator, and in the opposite direction north of the equator. In counterclockwise movement, for example, the current flows northward along the west coast of South America, bringing cold Antarctic water toward the equator. When this cold water begins to flow over the warmer water, it sinks. This process is called *upwelling*, just like the lake overturn in which water from deep down is forced to rise, bringing nutrients to the surface. There phytoplankton bloom, supporting a food chain with high densities of fish and birds. So it happens that one of the major anchovy and tuna fishing areas of the world is off the coast of Peru and Ecuador.

Upwelling also takes place at localized spots above submerged ancient river valleys or canyons, which are visible from a submarine at the lip of the continental shelf. Water from the shelf flows in an underwater current down through a submerged canyon to deeper levels in the pelagic zone (Figure 2.7), forcing up deeper water containing mineral nutrients from the sediments. Right over these submerged canyons we find blooms of phytoplankton, schools of fish, coveys of fishing boats, and flocks of squawking, screaming seabirds.

The littoral zone is pounded by the surf and subject to the tides. Hence, the beach and rocky, intertidal organisms tend to be highly distinctive. Invertebrates and algae with strong attachment mechanisms characterize the rocky zone, while the beach zone residents are primarily burrowing invertebrates. Birds and mammals also are frequent in the littoral zone but move elsewhere during periods of environmental severity.

One other marine habitat is highly distinctive, the **coral reef.** It is found in warm, shallow seas and is therefore mainly tropical. Here algae and corals combine to make a heterogeneous structure on the bottom that is home to a vast array of invertebrates and fish. Productivity is high and species diversity extremely high.

## POPULATIONS AND THEIR REGULATION

### Populations and Growth

A **population** is a group of individuals of the same species located at a particular time and place. (Some definitions add that the individuals regularly exchange genes through reproduction.) The people in a town today and the koala bears in an isolated Australian valley in winter are populations. The individual organism is considered a unit in ecology and is studied in relation to environmental factors (physiological ecology). The population, also a unit in ecology, has additional characteristics. The population is a single species, but its individuals differ genetically. Interbreeding is followed by natural selection, and in some cases the formation of new species.

Populations are commonly measured or estimated in terms of **density,** the number present per unit area of suitable habitat. Density is particularly informative because it provides a rough indication of the resources necessary or consumed, the interactions among individuals of the population, and the amount of physiological stress present. Numbers and density may be relatively poor measures, however, for some populations, such as many plant species, whose size is of more importance than their numbers. In such cases we measure the plant **cover** (the proportion of the substrate covered) or **biomass** (the total weight of the living organisms). Furthermore, individuals are usually not evenly or regularly distributed in their habitat, so we are interested also in their **dispersion**, that is, the pattern of spatial arrangement of individuals. The three major patterns are random, regular, and clustered. It turns out that random dispersion is quite rare, and regular dispersion in most areas is uncommon. Clustered dispersion is the rule. Dispersion patterns provide direct insight into what major factors control a population.

Spatial patterns are easy to determine compared with temporal ones. For temporal patterns, we must consider birth rates (natality), death rates (mortality), and the age structure of the population. The result of integrating these characteristics is the **survivorship curve** (Figure 2.9), which shows the proportion of the individuals at each age group that survives to reach the next age group. For example, the curve of the maple (*Acer*) shows that mortality is high in the early stages of life; relatively few individuals reach the sapling stage. The latter portion of the curve shows that once an individual has reached sapling stage, where mortality is low, it is apt to grow into an old tree. The human curve, conversely, shows low mortality until old age, at which time mortality is high. The curve for white-tailed deer (*Odocoileus virginianus*) shows an initial drop, reflecting mortality of fawns, followed by a number of later steep drops reflecting mortality during the hunting and cold seasons of each year.

When we plot the number of individuals at each age in a population, we produce what is called an **age pyramid.** When divided into three categories—prereproductive, reproductive, and postreproductive individuals—the pyramids provide considerable insight into future growth of a population. For example, a wide pyramid base (a large proportion of prereproductive individuals) indicates that the population should expand

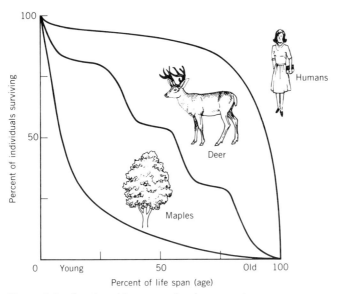

**Figure 2.9** *Survivorship curves for three species.*

as more individuals enter the reproductive age. If the base and middle of the pyramid are similar in width, we conclude that the population should remain relatively constant; and a narrow base points to a population decrease.

These concepts lead to a direct consideration of patterns of population growth. If a population grows with no limitations in available resources, it will resemble an exponential (or J-shaped) curve described by the equation for growth rate

$$\frac{dN}{dt} = rN$$

where $N$ is the population size, $dN/dt$ is the change in population size in a time interval $t$, and $r$ is the **intrinsic rate of increase** of the species. The $r$ is simply equal to the birth rate minus the death rate. Thus, this equation expresses the inherent biotic potential $rN$ of the population unhindered by environmental resistance or limitation. The growth rate is simply a function of the population size times the birth rate minus the death rate.

Perhaps the most important characteristic of the exponential curve is its shape. Throughout the early time intervals growth is gradual and small. But the population always reaches a point where the curve shoots upward sharply. This sudden, large increase often comes unexpectedly and out-strips resources. It is an inherent characteristic of exponential growth.

Since environmental resources do become limiting, a term for **environmental resistance** must be brought into the growth rate equation.

$$\frac{dN}{dt} = rN \left( \frac{K - N}{K} \right)$$

Here $K$ is the **carrying capacity** of the environment, that is, the maximum number of individuals (or biomass) that the particular environment can support. So if the present population size $N$ is tiny compared with the carrying capacity $K$, the population growth rate will be high, almost exponential. In contrast, if $N$ is nearly up to the $K$ level, the population will barely grow.

This equation or mathematical model takes a sigmoid (S-shaped, or logistic) form. The model is based on certain simplifying assumptions that are rarely, if ever, found in nature. Nevertheless, as a generalization it is conceptually useful and stimulates us to further examine both the assumptions and their exceptions, with an eye to modifying the equation to better fit reality.

(Of course, other growth curve shapes are possible. We note particularly the regularly oscillating curve and the curve with oscillations of decreasing amplitude through time. These will be discussed below. Another possibility is a curve with oscillations of increasing amplitude. Such a population goes extinct; when the curve hits the horizontal axis, the population size is zero. Finally, environmental change may alter the carrying capacity $K$, resulting in a change in the growth rate curve.)

## Competition

A population may grow in isolation, but generally it interacts with populations of many other species. When two populations are inhibited by the interaction, we have competition. For example, farmers put up scarecrows to keep the seeds in the fields. They are competing with birds to harvest as much of the limited supply of grain as possible. Competition may lead to evolutionary change; for example, two kangaroo populations competing for limited grass cover change genetically over many generations.

The equation for population growth of a species can be easily modified to account for competition in the case of the presence of a second population. Where $N_1$ is the population size of the first species, $r_1$ is its intrinsic rate of increase, and $K_1$ is its carrying capacity, population growth of the first species can be shown as:

$$\frac{dN_1}{dt} = r_1 N_1 \left( \frac{K_1 - N_1 - \alpha N_2}{K_1} \right)$$

Note that we have simply added a new term expressing the competitive or inhibitory effect of the second population. The population size of the second species is $N_2$, and a constant $\alpha$ is present that is a measure of the inhibitory effect of one individual of the second population on the first population. In essence, adding the competition term to the growth rate equation means that the environmental resistance will have a greater modifying or leveling-off effect on the exponential biotic potential term $r_1 N_1$. Therefore, the added competition will lower the growth rate of the first species $N_1$.

We know this model describing the effects of competition on the population growth of two species is a simplification. It has been useful in developing theory, but success in applying it to plants and many other populations has been limited. Presumably the lack of constancy in carrying capacity level, biotic potential, and disturbance level maintains populations in nonequilibrium and requires new models accounting for environmental heterogeneity.

In the case of competition, where both species are inhibited by the interaction, either local extinction or coexistence results. It would seem that one species is always a somewhat more effective competitor, and that through time the second species will go extinct locally. This idea is embodied in the **competitive exclusion** (or **Gause's**) **principle**—two species that are complete competitors cannot coexist indefinitely. In other words, if two competitors long coexist, they must be using somewhat different resources.

## Predation

As in the case of competition, equations have been developed that include the effect of predation on population growth rate. These equations typically predict oscillating populations of both predators and prey (Figure 2.10a). According to the mathematics developed to mimic the available data, for each population the interval between peaks (oscillation period), the amplitude (height) of peaks, and the slopes of peaks (rates of increase and decrease) should all be constant. The oscillations of the two populations should be out of phase; that is, the predator peaks slightly following the prey peaks.

A negative feedback loop is present: prey stimulate predators, and predators inhibit prey. Within a single oscillation or cycle, the feedback loop can be described in four phases (Figure 2.10a). As prey increase, predators increase. As predators increase, prey decrease. As prey de-

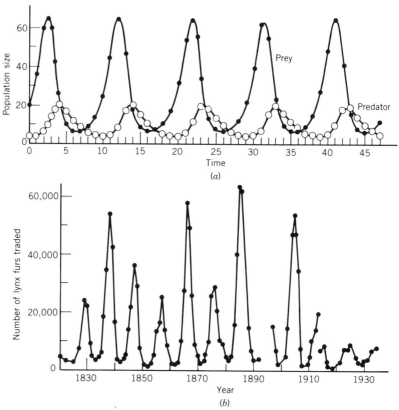

**Figure 2.10** *Predator and prey cycles. Curves in (a) are predicted from equations, while curve (b) represents lynx population data estimated from the fur trade in parts of Canada. (Curve a is from Krebs, 1972; courtesy of Harper and Row, Inc., Publishers. Curve b is from Elton and Nicholson, 1942; permission of Blackwell Scientific Publications Ltd.)*

crease, predators decrease. As predators decrease, prey increase. Then the cycle begins again. In this way, both populations may coexist indefinitely.

This simplified mathematical model has provided a conceptual framework for interpreting oscillating populations in general. Over a century, the lynx populations (*Lynx canadensis*) in Canada oscillated over a regular period of nearly ten years (Figure 2.10b). The amplitude of the oscillations varied widely, however. Populations of the snowshoe hare (*Lepus americanus*), the main lynx prey, also varied during this century with almost precisely the same ten-year oscillation period. The hazard in applying the model was brought out by the discovery that in two areas snowshoe hare cycles were present even though lynxes were absent. Thus, while we know lynxes depend on hares, we really do not understand the cause of the hare cycles. Having recognized the limitation of the model, we can still hypothesize that oscillating populations are controlled by predator-prey loops, and then we can test the hypothesis by examining several possible controlling factors.

Most populations, including prey, are distributed in clusters or patches. Thus, predator movement is highly nonrandom in foraging. Furthermore, we believe the foraging animal optimizes its movements on a kind of cost-benefit basis in what is called the **optimal foraging** process. The predator first forages where large prey clusters are present and where the prey are its preferred food, or at least where foraging provides the highest cost-benefit ratio. Later the predator moves to small clusters and to less preferred items of its diet. In foraging, the predator switches to other dietary items at the point where preferred food items are too costly to capture.

How does the predator accomplish this apparent optimization? In some cases, as it moves the predator is making decisions about the direction to move and the type of food item. In other cases, a considerable amount of learning is involved whereby specific favorable feeding locations are remembered and revisited. A further elaboration of this is the development of a search image whereby a predator learns certain characteristics about a prey type and forms a mental image that aids in locating prey in low-density times and places. Finally, predators that make foraging forays from a common location may enhance their cost-benefit ratio by following the routes of other individuals who have located good feeding locations.

## Population Regulation

Regulation of populations results from extrinsic factors such as food supply, weather, shelter, diseases, and natural enemies, or intrinsic factors like behavior, physiology, and genetic characteristics determining population density. Some factors, such as behavior, are primarily **density dependent** and tend to limit population growth more as its density rises. Other factors, such as weather, are called **density independent** because they often affect the same proportion of the population no matter how dense it is. Most populations are limited by a combination of both types of factors, though density dependence seems of greatest importance for vertebrates, and density independence of greatest importance for insects and plants.

Regulation by competition sometimes produces a more constant equilibrium than the oscillations of predation. Parasitism and disease often function as population regulators very much like predators. A **nonequi-**

**librium coexistence,** in which disturbance or unpredictable (stochastic) events permit continuation of the population, but with irregular fluctuations, is increasingly considered common. There is virtually always a suitable site available for a species because the disturbances are dispersed in time and space. Weather controls population size, but the population normally has little feedback effect on the weather.

As the population size builds, a number of density dependent results considered to be intrinsic to the population may follow. Dispersal of individuals from an area takes place. (Conversely, at low density, dispersal into the area may occur.) Some physiological responses involving hormones somehow triggered by crowding have also been identified in a number of vertebrates. In certain mammals and birds, the rate of egg production (or ovulation) in the female may drop, or the rate of natural abortion of embryos may rise, in either case limiting population growth. In the case of certain salamanders, crowding has induced cannibalism, with a similar limiting effect on population growth.

The on-site behavioral controls of vertebrates are perhaps the most familiar intrinsic regulatory mechanisms. Social dominance hierarchies and territoriality both have the effect of limiting reproduction and the number of individuals in an area. In a **social dominance hierarchy,** as occurs in the case of chickens or baboons, a pecking order is established beginning with the most dominant individual and continuing down to the least dominant individual. In the dominance hierarchy only certain of the individuals are permitted enough food or resources to survive, and only certain of the individuals reproduce. **Territorial behavior,** the establishment (and usually defense) of a certain small area against other individuals in the population, results in a limited number of possible individuals being present in a given area.

An example of how territoriality works to regulate population size is seen in grouse (Figure 2.11). In late summer the old cocks defend their territories, but at the end of the warm season the population is above the carrying capacity. The family groups break up. One group of birds is displaced from the territories, and by January almost all of them are dead. Of the birds remaining in the territories, some are unable to defend their territories and in the autumn form a second group of resident surplus birds that gradually move to marginal habitats, do not breed, and almost all die by spring. The third group successfully defends its territories, survives the winter well, and is the breeding stock for the following spring and summer. In this manner territorial behavior may regulate an equilibrium population level of grouse.

Population regulation is a fascinating, controversial, and highly significant ecological research area, made all the more relevant by its relative applicability to the exponential human population growth on earth.

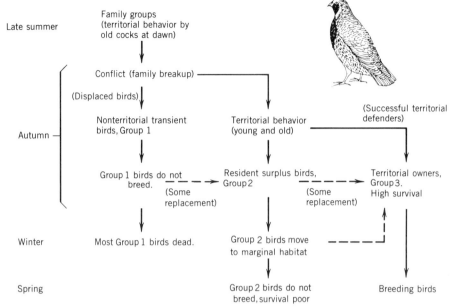

Late summer    Family groups
(territorial behavior by
old cocks at dawn)

Conflict (family breakup)

(Displaced birds)

Autumn

Nonterritorial transient
birds, Group 1

Territorial behavior
(young and old)

(Successful territorial
defenders)

Group 1 birds do not
breed.
(Some
replacement)

Resident surplus birds,
Group 2

(Some
replacement)

Territorial owners,
Group 3.
High survival

Winter    Most Group 1 birds dead.

Group 2 birds move
to marginal habitat

Spring

Group 2 birds do not
breed, survival poor

Breeding birds

**Figure 2.11** *Territoriality and social behavior regulating population size in grouse. (From Smith, 1979; courtesy of Harper and Row, Inc., Publishers.)*

## EVOLUTIONARY ECOLOGY

### Variation and Selection

So far, we have treated all the individuals of a population as if they were genetically identical, which is rarely the case. Variations among individuals is the rule, as is vividly evident at a hog show or on a lively dance floor. Such variations are partly due to physiological adjustment or acclimation, and partly inherited. The genetically determined characteristics transmitted from generation to generation are not identical. In fact, variation among individuals in a population permits gradual change that results in **adaptation.** Without such change, there would be no evolution. Changes in the population through time may even lead up to the formation of new species, called **speciation.**

What are the sources of genetic change? That is, how do the genes in the DNA of cells change? We recognize two major ways, mutation and recombination. **Mutation,** such as that caused by irradiation or certain chemicals, is a change in the sequence of building blocks of a DNA molecule. Most mutations are lethal or damaging, but reproductive cells that survive mutations contain an altered DNA structure. **Recombination** causes variation in offspring by a different process. When male and female parents reproduce, each offspring may receive a different combination of chromosomes from the parents, and so each offspring differs. In this manner no DNA is altered, but the existing DNA of the male and female parents is simply combined in a different way in the offspring. Variation also results from alterations in chromosome structure or number during the cell division process.

Changes in the frequencies of genes in a population from generation to generation are **evolutionary changes.** Four factors tend to make genetic change and evolution ubiquitous.

1. Nonrandom mating among members of the population occurs, so genes of frequently mating individuals increase.
2. Immigration brings new genes and emigration eliminates certain genes from the population.
3. Mutations often occur and introduce or eliminate certain genes.
4. When populations are small, changes in the frequency of genes may take place by chance (genetic drift and founder effect).

Any of these factors causes changes in gene frequencies from generation to generation, and thereby the evolution of the species, through the general process of **natural selection.**

If we go into the field, we may observe at least the essence of natural selection as originally described by Darwin. An overpopulation of off-spring occurs. The population contains variability among the offspring. Competition for resources ensues. Finally, survival of the fittest (best-adapted) offspring results. This natural selection process, going on around us all the time, does not eliminate the variability in a population. But it does lead to organisms better adapted to their environment and it permits adaptation to new or changing environments.

Natural selection as described focuses on individuals within a population. **Kin selection,** in contrast, refers to changes in small groups of individuals, such as family groups, that function as units relative to other units in the population. In kin selection the fitness of small related groups changes. Intriguingly, the fitness of individuals may change in a direction opposite to that of the kin group. Thus, in certain vertebrate species the group appears to be more important than the individual.

## Speciation

If there were random reproduction among all members of a population, genetic change and evolution might not occur. But in real populations, many factors prevent random reproduction. We call them **isolating mechanisms** or barriers. Geographical barriers such as mountains and large bodies of water are obvious. But other barriers may effectively separate patches at a finer scale within a landscape. For example, various reproductive and other isolating mechanisms are just as effective as geographic barriers in preventing random reproduction in a population. An isolation mechanism causes two (or more) groups of individuals to become increasingly different, because individuals interbreed and mix genes within their group, but mating and **gene flow** between groups is inhibited.

When the gene pools of two groups are only slightly different (whether geographically isolated or not), we may refer to them as populations within a species (Figure 2.12). If gene flow between such populations remains limited over time, they will diverge to the point at which we call them races, ecotypes, varieties, or subspecies. Individuals of such populations can potentially interbreed if brought together under appropriate conditions, so there is still only one species. However, if gene flow between these populations remains limited, they will diverge still further genetically, and gene flow will cease altogether. When they are no longer able to interbreed when brought together, we have two species. This process is called **gradual speciation.** A process of **punctuated speciation** has also been proposed, in which a population splits off from a species and becomes a new species rapidly, not by the long, gradual process of reproduction over numerous generations.

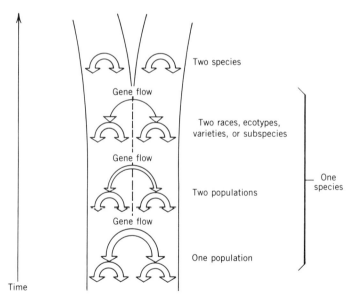

**Figure 2.12** *A gradual speciation process. An isolating mechanism appears and divides the initial population in two parts. The amount of gene flow within or between populations is indicated by the thickness of arrows.*

Many patterns of speciation can be recognized around the globe; we note here two particularly distinctive or frequent ones. A species is often found in a series of populations with progressively different characteristics, extending over a geographic area. This pattern, called a **cline,** may result over time in the extremes being so different they become different species, while intermediate forms are still present between them. In a second case, **adaptive radiation,** a species encounters new environmental conditions and diversifies into a number of species.

## ECOLOGICAL COMMUNITIES

### Spatial Structure of a Community

In studying a population, we examine the individual organisms and how they are clustered by age, sex, and genetic makeup. The ecological **community,** at the next higher organizational level, may be described as the assemblage of species populations at a particular place and time. Usually there are interactions among the species of a community, and in many regions distinctive species clusters are recognizable. Because both species and species clusters differ greatly, a wide range of patterns and measurements is found in community ecology. We study **species composition** (what particular species are present), **species diversity** or richness (how many species are present), **dominance** (which species are most abundant and by how much), **rare species,** and the **growth forms** or **life forms** present (such as trees, shrubs, succulents). We also look for **guilds,** groups of species which use a type of resource in a similar way.

The vertical structure of an above ground plant community is a product of the size and the branching and leaf characteristics of plants, and the internal distribution of leaves is largely dependent on light penetration. More or less distinct vegetation layers may be present, as in a forest with canopy, subcanopy, understory, shrub layer, and herb layer, each receiving progressively less light. The animal species also sort out vertically, with certain animals mainly in the canopy, others mainly in the understory, and so on. Vertical stratification in animal and microbial communities in the soil is also marked. Oxygen level is a primary determinant of this vertical pattern, though the amounts of organic matter, mineral nutrients, water, and heat also strongly correlate with depth. In aquatic communities, vertical stratification is pronounced and largely due to temperature, oxygen, and light gradients.

The horizontal distributions of species exhibit complex patterns. At one extreme, the boundary between two types of vegetation, such as field and forest, may be relatively abrupt. In this case the overlap zone or **ecotone** is narrow and composed mainly of species from both sides intermixed. Sometimes the overlap zone is wide, and in it a mosaic of patches of each vegetation type intermingle (Rapoport, 1982b). At the other extreme, no ecotone is easily distinguishable, and we find a gradual change in species composition over distance, called a **continuum.**

These different separations of vegetation types have sparked considerable controversy and have given rise to two theories about the essential nature of a community. If a continuum is present everywhere, interactions among species vary continuously over space. Thus the integrated nature of a community is minimal; that is, a species apparently does not require the presence of other specific species. From this perspective, called the **individualistic theory,** the community is simply the assemblage of species that happen to coexist at some point in time and at some point along the continuum. The types of communities are as numerous as the points along the continuum, and no community type is much more frequent than any other. Alternatively, the so-called **community unit theory** recognizes the existence of primary community types separated by ecotones. This theory assumes some interdependence among the species of a community.

In a continuum, when we plot the abundance of species against some controlling environmental factor such as food supply or soil moisture, a series of broadly overlapping bell-shaped curves (each representing a species) may appear (Figure 2.13a). When we plot the same species abundances against distance on land, we sometimes find the same result (Figure 2.13b). Usually, though, we find flatter curves with several species dropping out at about the same place and less overlap at that place, basically an ecotone between communities (Figure 2.13c). Why? Apparently the continuum is present where the major controlling environmental factor varies evenly (linearly) with distance, as when temperature changes evenly from the bottom to the top of a mountain. Usually, however, environmental factors are unevenly or patchily distributed over space. The result is a sharper ecotone, where the amount of a factor changes abruptly in a short space (Figure 2.13c), such as that along the edge of certain swamps or between a forest and adjacent cultivation.

When individual trees or small groups of trees within a community die, a gap is produced where high light conditions prevail down to the ground. Larger patches in the community may be produced by disturbances such as fire or pest defoliation. Furthermore, the physical environment itself may be patchy, having rock outcrops or wet spots. In all cases the **patchiness** of the community forms a mosaic.

Continuua observed over lengthy spans are primarily limited to natural landscapes, in areas with little disturbance or environmental patchiness. Natural landscapes with frequent environmental patchiness or natural disturbance primarily have ecotones, and this pattern is even more pronounced in landscapes modified by human influences.

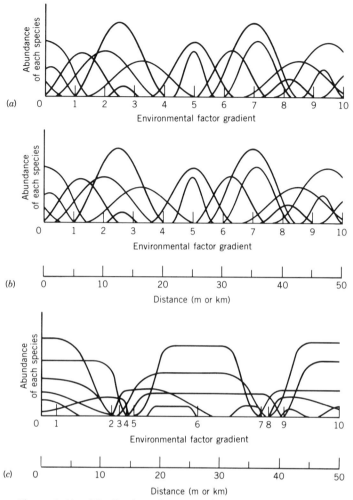

**Figure 2.13** *Distribution of species along environmental and distance gradients. Each bell-shaped or flat-topped curve represents a species. The gradients of environmental factors such as temperature, phosphorus level, or food supply range from low to high. (a) Response of each species to an environmental factor determined by laboratory experiments. (b) Species distributions where the controlling environmental factor is directly correlated with distance, and (c) where the controlling environmental factor is patchily distributed. Pattern c is common in landscapes.*

Plant and animal communities are often mapped, and to do this they are named and classified, as much as possible to show their relationships to one another. The primary criteria used in classifications are appearance (physiognomy), species composition, dominant species, and habitat. The major divisions in the various classification systems differ in their use of these criteria, but at finer divisions, species composition is almost always used as the classification criterion.

## Ecological Niche and Species Diversity

Many ecologists agree that the **ecological niche** is the functional role of a species in a community, including the environmental variables affecting the species. The totality of environmental variables and functional roles to which a species is adapted is called a **fundamental niche.** However, a species normally does not occupy that totality but only a portion of it, called a **realized niche.** The difference between the fundamental and realized niches is often ascribed to competition, though other factors may be important.

**Niche width,** a measure of the variety of different resources exploited by an organism, provides further insight into the roles of a species in a community. A broad niche indicates that the species is a **generalist,** sacrificing efficiency in the use of a narrow range of resources in order to use a wide range of resources. A narrow niche indicates a **specialist** species, one that exploits efficiently a narrow range of resources on which it depends. One way many species coexist in a community is by specialization, since it reduces competition.

Ecologists use species diversity as one important measure of the structural heterogeneity of a community. There are many ways a community can be diverse in species. They may vary in number (richness) of species, degree of dominance by one or a few species, relative abundance of all species (evenness), number of rare species, number of nonnative species, vertical stratification of species, horizontal patchiness, number of growth or life forms, and so forth. Species diversity measurements are used to help interpret mechanisms operating in the community.

Various indices have been constructed that combine two or more of these measures into a single number. For example, the *Shannon-Wiener* (or information) *index* combines number and relative abundance of species (Peet, 1974). A synthetic index is convenient in reducing two or more variables to a single number, but because the variables are not separated the mechanisms behind them are less likely to be identified. Number of species is the single clearest measure of species diversity, although measuring additional separate variables adds interpretive power.

Measurements of bird species diversity, plant species diversity, and the like, turn out to be very coarse measurements. Thus, as a finer community characteristic, guild diversity is measured, for example, birds that feed on seeds, catch flying insects, or eat flesh. In this way a more penetrating view of the several mechanisms operating in the community emerges than if species diversity of birds as a whole, for example, is measured.

## Succession

When disturbance causes the formation of a bare area, plants and animals colonize this bare area (Figure 2.14). Then, over time, species replace one another until the community consists primarily of species which can successfully reproduce where they are, that is, a **climax community**. This directional species replacement process is called **succession.**

We mentioned the case of small clusters of trees blowing down or dying in a forest, producing scattered gaps. If we study such gaps over time, we may see an initial colonization by herbaceous plants, followed by takeover by small woody plants, followed by takeover by trees, fol-

**Figure 2.14** *Succession on slides (landslips) in the boreal forest. The disturbance patch resulted from vegetation and soil (and perhaps snow and ice) sliding down the slope, probably when the soil was saturated with water. Note that the older slide to the right has revegetated with birches (Betula) and aspens (Populus). The remainder of the forest is spruce (Picea) and fir (Abies). Parc de la Gaspésie, Québec, Canada. (R. Forman.)*

lowed by a blowing down, and the cycle starts again. This process is called **cyclic succession** since it progresses through a series of stages and returns to a former stage. In this example, the tree stage lasts much longer than the other stages, but in the cyclic successions of bogs, tundra, grassland, and shrubland the stages are more equal in length.

In the above case the primary energy source is plant photosynthesis. In **heterotrophic succession** the primary energy source is nonphotosynthetic organic matter such as elephant droppings, a fallen log, or organic waste dumped in a stream. The organic matter is consumed by decomposers, and a series of stages then occurs that involves a food web based on those decomposers. In all these examples of succession, colonization, species composition changes, and local extinction rates are high in the early phases and decline over time.

In an abandoned tobacco field in the southeastern United States, the main successional stages progress from herbaceous annuals to herbaceous perennials, to grass, to shrubs, to successional trees such as pine (*Pinus*), to climax trees such as oak and hickory (*Quercus, Carya*). However, one specific point within the field may go through this sequence but skip the shrub stage by having a pine seedling directly colonize the grass there. In similar fashion, other points in the field could skip the grass stage or even two stages. In other words, in **point succession** each adjacent point may undergo a different sequence, while the field as a whole goes through all the stages listed as a kind of average of all the points in the field.

Disturbance is an important mechanism of succession, as are external modifications of the environment such as weather or dust deposition. Each community includes its own proportion of species that replace one another in various ways, and each differs in the relative importance of disturbance and external factors during succession.

The climax community is a mosaic containing patches with species of earlier successional stages (Figure 2.14). The mosaic may simply include small patches relating to natural deaths of organisms, by herbivore grazing, hunting by people, or tree falls, for example. It may also include large patches caused by disturbances such as fire and pest outbreaks.

When fires or pest outbreaks, for example, are frequent and widespread, species adapt to them, and it becomes questionable what the climax is. In New Jersey (United States) Pine Barrens fires have been frequent and widespread, so the area is always dominated by pine. But in a few isolated spots near old human settlements wildfire has been eliminated or minimized for a century or more, and an old oak forest is present. Which is the climax, pine or oak forest? Oak is the theoretical climax if fire could be artificially eliminated. Pine, though, is the actual climax, since it maintains itself with fire as a part of its ecosystem. Indeed, here wildfire prevention is a significant disturbance because it effectively leads to elimination of the pine forest.

## Island Biogeography

Charles Darwin wrote a book on island biogeography, and island communities have always intrigued ecologists. For understanding the species diversity (number of species) on an island, a model was recently developed that interrelates the colonization and extinction rates of species (Figure 2.15). The hypothesis is that with more species present on an island, hence increased competition, the rate of colonization of new arrivals would be lower. Also, the rate of extinction of species would be higher. The point at which the idealized colonization and extinction curves cross is thus the predicted number of species on an island.

It was additionally proposed that islands near a species source, such as a mainland, would have more diversity than isolated islands, because the rate of arriving species and colonists would be higher on nearby islands (Figure 2.15). Similarly, more species are predicted on large islands than small islands because the extinction rate is lower on large islands. Confirmation of the island biogeographic model has proven elusive despite much interest. Several studies have supported aspects of it and certain predictions from it, but other studies have demonstrated quite different patterns. The model has been applied to patches on land with

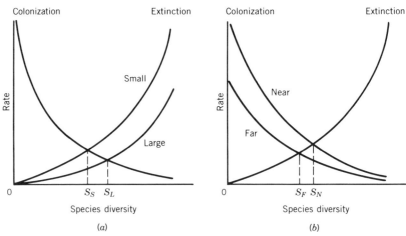

**Figure 2.15** *Hypothesized effects of colonization and extinction on species diversity of islands with different characteristics. (a) Island size: $S_S$ and $S_L$ are the number of species on small and large islands, respectively. (b) Island isolation: $S_F$ and $S_N$ are the number of species on islands far from and near a species source, respectively. After MacArthur and Wilson (1967).*

limited success. The problems in testing the model are the limited knowledge of extinction rates, the difficulty of eliminating other major variables, and the difficulty of doing appropriate experiments.

The model has stimulated empirical studies on archipelagoes and the plotting of species-area curves (Figure 2.16). These curves agree with the prediction that larger islands will have more species, but the mechanism is quite different, namely, there is more habitat diversity on larger islands. The curves seem to better support the idea that islands near species sources have more species. By plotting an archipelago curve based on samples of a few islands one may predict the species diversity on other islands with some accuracy.

An equation relating species diversity $S$ to island area $A$

$$S = cA^z$$

has generated interest because $z$, the slope of the line relating species and area (Figure 2.16), appears to be relatively similar in different archipelagoes and for different types of organisms. ($c$ is a constant measuring the number of species in a unit area of island). The variation in $z$ may simply be a mathematical property or may be indicative of different ecological patterns on archipelagoes.

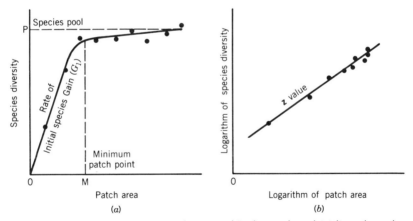

**Figure 2.16**  *Species–area curve for an archipelago, plotted (a) linearly and (b) logarithmically. The linear plot shows only a slight gain in species between the minimum patch point M and the asymptote diversity level or species pool P. A steep $G_i$ slope (initial species gain) characterizes relative homogeneity in the distribution of species over the archipelago, whereas a lower slope is produced by relative heterogeneity or an abundance of rare species.*

## Biogeography in Geologic Time

The animal and plant communities of today are the latest word in a long history of evolutionary developments and species migrations. Violent geological events took place in the middle of the Tertiary period, about 20 million years ago (see Chapter 7, Appendix). Huge mountain chains were thrown up: the Rocky Mountains, the Andes, the Himalayas, and the Alps. Extensive dry regions formed downwind of these mountains as rain shadows, often near the centers of continents. Pockets of arid evergreens and grasses spread rapidly, forming deserts, grasslands, and Mediterranean type vegetation. Temperate forests at high latitudes and tropical forests at low latitudes were separated from one another.

During the Tertiary, most of the plant species that are dominant on earth today evolved. Birds, mammals, and insects also became widespread around the globe, replacing the dinosaurs and other reptiles which had previously predominated (Figure 2.17). By the end of the Tertiary, many of today's families and genera (subdivisions of families) of these animals had evolved, though most of the species were different.

Between two million years ago and about 8000 B.C. came the Pleistocene period, during which at least four massive glaciations occurred, separated by warmer periods when much of the ice melted. Faunas and floras were constantly moving or migrating across the land, at times being compressed into one or many isolated pockets and at times spreading to cover large expanses. During this process many of our present terrestrial animal species evolved (Figure 2.17).

The past ten or so millennia since the Pleistocene compose the present period, the Holocene, a time marked by two major factors affecting animal and plant communities. First, climate has changed, primarily with a general warming trend over the whole period, but also with a hot phase that began about 7500 years ago and later cooled. Second, human activity has become widespread. Deforestation and agriculture, in particular, which began some 8000 years ago, accelerated in the past four millennia. Very recently the effect of an industrial society has changed the earth's flora and fauna at a pace even more rapid than that of glaciation, climatic change, or agriculture.

## ENERGY AND MATTER IN ECOSYSTEMS

### Energy

Energy flows in a predictable way through an ecosystem. Solar energy is converted by photosynthesis to chemical energy in plants. A portion of the energy then returns directly to the atmosphere by the respiration of plants. Another portion of the energy goes to herbivores (see Figure 2.17),

**Figure 2.17** *Mayan stone turtle, a herbivorous reptile. Carved 1100 years ago at Copan, Honduras, this animal probably represents the huge sea turtle that breeds today on nearby beaches and feeds largely on phytoplankton. This turtle is a descendent from the age of reptiles that was followed by the diversification of birds, mammals, and insects of the later Mesozoic and Tertiary periods. (R. Forman.)*

to carnivores, to higher carnivores, and to the atmosphere in a **grazing food chain.** A third portion of the energy always goes to dead organic matter, to detritus feeders, and to the atmosphere, or from detritus feeders to carnivores, to higher carnivores, and to the atmosphere in a **detritus food chain.** In all these cases the energy returns to the atmosphere as heat, unusable for further photosynthesis. Therefore we say energy flows one way through an ecosystem.

Each of the steps in these chains is called a **trophic level.** If we gather all the organisms in a trophic level together and weigh them, we have a measure of the biomass of each trophic level. When we compare the biomass of each trophic level, distinctive **biomass pyramid** forms emerge (Figure 2.18). On land, four or five trophic levels are common, and in aquatic ecosystems five or six.

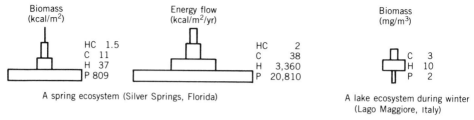

Biomass (kcal/m²)

| HC | 1.5 |
| C | 11 |
| H | 37 |
| P | 809 |

A spring ecosystem (Silver Springs, Florida)

Energy flow (kcal/m²/yr)

| HC | 2 |
| C | 38 |
| H | 3,360 |
| P | 20,810 |

Biomass (mg/m³)

| C | 3 |
| H | 10 |
| P | 2 |

A lake ecosystem during winter (Lago Maggiore, Italy)

**Figure 2.18** *Biomass and energy flow pyramids. Each layer in a pyramid is a trophic level, and its width is approximately proportional to the amount of biomass or energy flow present. P = producers; H = herbivores; C = carnivores, HC = higher carnivores. (Silver Springs data from "Trophic structure and productivity of Silver Springs, Florida," by H. T. Odum, Ecol. Monogr., 1957, 27, 55–112. Copyright 1966 by Ecological Society of America. Reprinted by permission. Lago Maggiore data from Ravera, 1969; courtesy of Verhandlungen der Internationalen Vereinigung fur theoretische und angewante Limnologie.)*

In terrestrial ecosystems, total biomass always decreases as we progress through the trophic levels. In aquatic ecosystems a reverse hourglass or inverted biomass pyramid is sometimes present, with less producer than herbivore biomass (Figure 2.18). This is possible because the herbivores are longer-lived than the producers and heavily graze down the producers. In this case, the producer turnover is high; that is, phytoplankton mature and die in a day or so, whereas terrestrial woody plants require years to complete their life cycle.

When we diagram the amount of energy flowing through each trophic level, rather than simply how much biomass is present at each level, we have an **energy flow pyramid.** In it, each succeeding level is always less than the preceding level (Figure 2.18). Why is this so? A simple law, the **second law of thermodynamics,** governs energy flow through any system, including an ecosystem. In transforming energy from one level or form to another (say, from herbivore to carnivore), some energy is always given off or lost as heat. Therefore, an energy flow pyramid must progressively decrease at each level.

### Plant and Animal Production

The photosynthetic process by itself produces a certain quantity of organic matter called **gross production.** However, we never see gross production because the plant must expend energy in respiration to function as a living organism. The amount produced after plant respiration is termed **net production** (Figure 2.19). Again, we rarely see it because parts of plants die and because herbivores are almost always consuming some of that energy. So-called **standing crop** (or biomass or phytomass) remains. We may harvest this standing crop but we almost never eat the whole

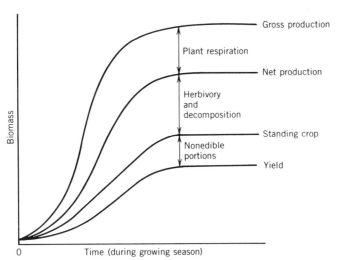

**Figure 2.19** *Biomass (or energy) losses in primary production. The relative amounts of loss differ in each ecosystem. The present foci of agriculture and forestry are on increasing gross production and decreasing herbivory.*

plant. We discard the nonedible portions, leaving **yield** as the biomass or energy which may be consumed by humans.

Four processes, therefore, decrease gross production to end up with yield: plant respiration, herbivory, decomposition, and discarding of nonedible portions (Figure 2.19). One major focus of agriculture is on reducing energy loss to herbivory through the use of pesticides. The other major focus of agriculture, as well as forestry, is the attempt to increase gross production through breeding, fertilization, and planting or cultivation techniques.

When net production is compared on a worldwide basis, interesting patterns emerge (Figure 2.20). The highest production regions include most of the hot tropical areas, and the lowest production is in the cold tundra and in the arid desert regions (generally in the 30° north and south latitudes). These are the inherent patterns for natural vegetation. Agricultural production for yield, however, is quite different. The bread baskets or rice paddies of the world are in the central United States, western and central Europe, eastern China, and some parts of southern Asia and South America. These are intermediate zones of about 200 to 400 gC/m²/yr production, in terms of natural vegetation (Figure 2.20). This paradox results from the fact that the high natural production zones generally have high rainfall, and thus more nutrient poor soils that are less suitable for extensive agricultural production.

The biomass accumulated per unit of time by green plants is called **plant** (or **primary**) **production.** When net plant production is ingested by

ECOLOGICAL CONCEPTS IN BRIEF   **71**

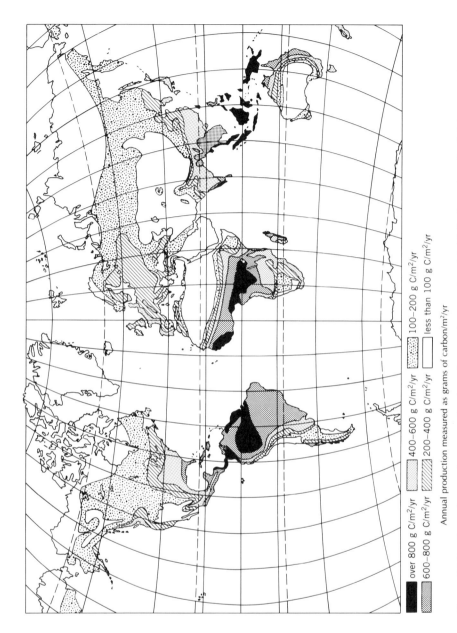

over 800 g C/m²/yr

600–800 g C/m²/yr

400–600 g C/m²/yr

200–400 g C/m²/yr

100–200 g C/m²/yr

less than 100 g C/m²/yr

Annual production measured as grams of carbon/m²/yr

**Figure 2.20** *Annual net primary production of natural vegetation. Multiply the values by 2.5 for an estimate of grams of dry matter/m²/yr. (Courtesy of H. Leith, 1975, and Springer-Verlag.)*

herbivores, the energy taken in goes to several sources. Some of the biomass is nondigestible and passes right through the digestive tube and out as feces. The remainder passes from the digestive tube into the body tissue and is called **assimilation.** Some of the assimilated energy is then given off as heat in respiration, with less given off by insects than warm-blooded mammals and birds. Another smaller loss of energy is metabolic waste such as urine. The remaining (stored) energy (or "net production") is called **consumer** or **secondary production.** It is available for two basic consumer processes, growth and reproduction.

Exactly the same process takes place when carnivores ingest herbivores, or higher carnivores ingest carnivores. Overall, high secondary production is correlated with high growth rates or high birth rates and usually with high net plant production.

## Food Chains and Webs

Energy from gross plant production basically goes in three directions: to the atmosphere in respiration, to herbivores in ingestion, and to decomposers in nonliving plant biomass, for example, when leaves drop off or roots die. In a grazing food chain, if we trace the energy ingested by herbivores (grazers), exactly the same three energy flows are present, respiration (by the herbivores), ingestion (by carnivores), and decomposition (of nonliving herbivore tissue) (Figure 2.21). Similarly, at each higher trophic level the same three energy flows follow. The food chain ends when there is no ingestion of a trophic level.

In a grazing food chain, the decomposers break the nonliving organic matter down until none is left. In this process all of the energy from the organic matter is given off to the atmosphere by respiration of the decomposers. In a detritus food chain, fungi and bacteria are usually consumed by tiny animals, such animals are ingested by carnivores, and so on to higher carnivores (Figure 2.21). All the original energy is returned to the atmosphere as heat in respiration from the trophic levels of this detritus food chain, and through decomposition of these consumers in turn.

The efficiency of the ecological process that takes place, say, between one trophic level and the next, has been of considerable interest. In the transfer of energy between trophic levels in a grazing food chain, some 80% to 100% of the energy goes to respiration and decomposers. This leaves relatively little energy to be incorporated into the biomass of the next trophic level. Efficiencies vary within this range and provide insight about energy flow in the ecosystem.

Food chains, however, are only part of the food web that characterizes each ecosystem. The food web integrates species diversity, with energy flow through trophic levels. In this case we focus on feeding links among

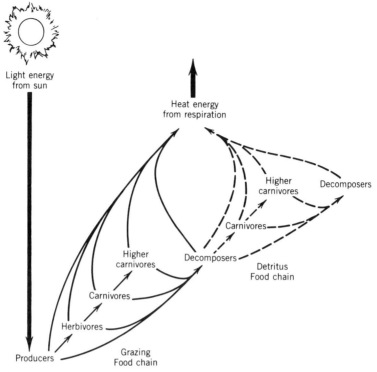

**Figure 2.21** *Energy flow through grazing and detritus food chains. Most energy fixed by producers flows through decomposers, particularly in terrestrial systems.*

species of different trophic levels rather than on competition among species at the same trophic level. In working out a food web, we learn several key aspects of it that relate ultimately to the stability of the ecosystem. For example, how specialized or generalized is a species—that is, how many feeding links does it have to the next lower trophic level? Where are the major energy flows through the web? Are there relatively distinct sub-webs within the food web? How likely is it that an ecosystem will lose a (top) trophic level? How could one manage to channel more energy into a certain species for harvest? In short, energy flow analysis through food webs is of major theoretical and applied interest.

## Mineral Nutrient Cycling

The **law of conservation of matter** states that matter can neither be created nor destroyed. Matter or materials such as mineral nutrients simply cycle, combining with different materials at each time and place they pass through. Unlike energy, which flows one way through an ecosystem, mineral nutrients may cycle within an ecosystem or flow from one ecosystem to another. We saw the water or hydrologic cycle earlier. Here we consider briefly the carbon and phosphorus cycles.

Carbon in atmospheric $CO_2$ is incorporated by photosynthesis into organic compounds that are passed from producer to herbivore, to carnivore, to higher carnivore, or at each step to decomposer. Respiration of all these organisms releases not only heat but also $CO_2$ into the atmosphere. The carbon atom originally in the atmospheric $CO_2$, after cycling through the organisms, is exactly the same carbon atom released in respiration to the atmosphere. We call this an *atmosphere-organism cycle*.

Phosphorus, in contrast, is in the soil in the form of phosphate. There it is absorbed by plant roots, fed through the food chain mainly attached to organic compounds, and released by decomposers back into the soil (Figure 2.22). Thus, phosphorus moves in a *soil-organism* cycle without a significant atmospheric phase. Calcium, potassium, and magnesium also move in soil-organism cycles. In contrast, nitrogen moves in an atmosphere-organism-soil cycle that depends on several types of bacteria for its completion.

These nutrient examples illustrate cycling within a single ecosystem. But each has at least one *sink*, that is, a place where huge amounts of the mineral nutrient have accumulated outside the ecosystem. For carbon, the oceans are a sink (containing carbon in the form of $CO_2$, bicarbonate ion, and carbonic acid). Phosphorus has two sinks, rocks and deep sea sediments (Figure 2.22). The atmosphere is the nitrogen sink. The sinks appear to participate in a stabilizing feedback by both absorbing and liberating mineral nutrients, perhaps according to the levels available in ecosystems.

The food web patterns discussed for energy also apply to mineral nutrients. In fact, ecologists have used radioactive elements such as carbon and phosphorus, and even pesticides, to work out the food webs of ecosystems. A striking pattern that emerges from these studies is the presence of **ecological** (biological) **magnification** and **dilution** in food webs. Basically, as a particular material moves through the trophic levels of a food chain, the feeding and tissues of the organisms either concentrate the material, leading to a food chain magnification, or discriminate against the material, leading to dilution or decreased concentration at higher trophic levels. Following ecological magnification, high concentrations of materials such as the pesticide DDT have proven toxic to organisms at high trophic levels and have therefore shortened the food web of the ecosystem.

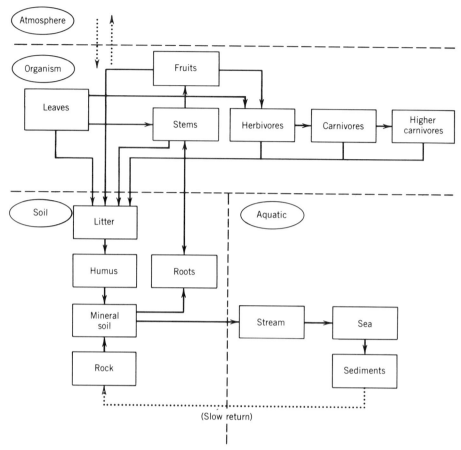

**Figure 2.22** *The phosphorus cycle. Some phosphorus reaches the atmosphere, particularly in dust in arid and agricultural areas; hence it may also be an atmospheric input to the ecosystem.*

## Ecosystem Models

The development of models to describe the functioning of an ecosystem has been highly informative and has stimulated interactions among diverse sciences. One of the most commonly used models is a series of compartments or boxes connected by arrows (Figure 22.2), often followed by mathematical equations describing ecosystem changes. The compartments represent the amount of biomass, energy, or mineral nutrients in various components of the ecosystem such as leaves, stems, fruit, herbivores, or humus. The arrows represent flows of energy or material from one compartment to the next. The compartments are standing crops measured, say, in grams per square meter, and the arrows are rates of flow measured, for example, in grams per square meter per year.

In using such models we are frequently interested in ecosystem stability and in what would happen if a particular disturbance occurred. To find out, we may plug in hypothetical values for compartment sizes or flow rates, or if possible use actual values from available studies of disturbance effects on the ecosystem. The model then predicts which compartments or flow rates might be changed significantly by the disturbance.

Models, of course, are to be used cautiously, as they are by nature simplifications involving necessary assumptions. Four interrelated cautions are required. First, certain assumptions may be unrealistic, such as assuming the importance of pollinators is proportional to their biomass, or assuming no spatial heterogeneity is present. Second, since measuring all the characteristics of an ecosystem is a huge time, energy, and money consuming operation, usually certain characteristics are simply estimated by subtraction, that is, for example, measuring two characteristics and subtracting (or adding) them to estimate a third characteristic. Most models have many such subtracted estimations that provide ample opportunity for compounded errors. Third, stochastic or random inputs that are non-systematic through time, such as many weather related phenomena, are exceedingly common in the ecosystem but are rarely mimicked adequately in the model. Fourth, the mechanisms causing ecological changes may be missed altogether, since mimicking of the data by the model may be due to inherent mathematical, not ecological, properties or may be due to quite spurious mechanisms. In short, models are essential for analyzing complex systems, such as ecosystems or landscapes, but it is equally essential to use caution in interpreting such models.

## SUMMARY

The science of ecology, focusing on organisms interacting with their environment, builds on the study of energy flow, material cycles, and evolution. Solar radiation is the primary factor controlling spatial and temporal climatic patterns. Soils, which contain a rich biological community, are typically formed by the weathering of bedrock and the incorporation of organic matter. The movements of water, gases, materials, and organisms through soil depend largely on soil structure, particularly its horizons, texture, and porosity. The hydrologic cycle intimately links the land to aquatic ecosystems. In the latter, water flow rate significantly controls the biological community. Nutrient levels are also primary controllers in lakes and seas, where different types of species and production occur in conspicuous vertical and horizontal zones.

A population of individuals is structured in several ways, and these affect its growth rate, which is commonly described quantitatively as the inherent rate of increase modified by the environmental resistance present. The regulation of populations often results from feedback systems that involve predator-prey cycles, competition, animal behavior, and spatial patterns or temporal rhythms in the environment. Evolutionary changes, including speciation, depend on natural selection and on differential gene flows caused by isolating mechanisms.

The structure of animal and plant communities is characterized by vertical layering, horizontal patchiness or gradients, and species diversity that reflects differences in the ecological niches of species. Succession may lead the community to a mosaic-like climax, or may be cyclic. The spatial patterns and species compositions of today's communities result particularly from the climatic change, species migrations, and evolution that occurred during the Tertiary, the Pleistocene and the Holocene periods.

Ecosystems are characterized by one way energy flow, and by the one way or cyclic movements of mineral nutrients. Plant production is at the base of both the grazing and the detritus food chains, which contain progressively less energy at higher trophic levels. We construct models to simplify the complexity of ecosystems, including food webs and mineral nutrient cycles, and especially to understand ecosystem stability.

## QUESTIONS

1. How does heat energy determine the distribution of major vegetation types around the globe?
2. Diagram and label the typical layers in a soil. How was each layer formed? What currently moves through each layer?
3. Compare the importance of mineral nutrients and water flow rate in the major types of water bodies.
4. What are the key characteristics to know in predicting the growth rate of a population?
5. How is the population growth equation modified to account for competition? The carrying capacity sometimes varies through time. How could you modify the basic equation to account for that?
6. How are populations regulated so as not to explode or crash continually and not to become extinct?
7. How is selection important in speciation? Geography is commonly important in speciation; explain a case where it is not.
8. In what ways is the ecological niche concept important in understanding the structure of an animal community? How is it important in island biogeography theory?
9. Describe the climax in each of the following cases: cyclic, heterotrophic, and point succession. How could this information aid in landscape planning?

10. How are net plant production, trophic levels, and the second law of thermodynamics important in the management of wildlife?

11. Herbivore populations such as caterpillars, locusts, or rodents often explode to become a pest faced in agriculture or forestry. Show in one or more diagrams what the effects of such an explosion would be on a particular mineral nutrient cycle of your choice. How do such diagrams differ from a model?

12. A hierarchy of levels has been proposed as follows: molecules, cells, organisms, populations, communities, and ecosystems. To understand the main principles at one level, some suggest that understanding the main patterns and principles at the next lower level is required, some suggest that understanding the main patterns and principles at all lower levels is required, and some suggest that understanding lower levels never suffices. Using specific examples, assess this statement.

# Part *II*
# Landscape Structure

# 3
# Patches

Many objects are patchy, including quilts, mosaics, soil, and clouds in the sky. However, in this book we restrict the concept to the distribution of organisms. We may define **patch** as a nonlinear surface area differing in appearance from its surroundings (Figure 3.1). Patches vary widely in size, shape, type, heterogeneity, and boundary characteristics. In addition, patches are often embedded in a **matrix,** a surrounding area that has a different species structure or composition (see Chapter 5). Normally, patches in a landscape are plant and animal communities, that is, assemblages of species. However, some patches could be lifeless, or at least contain primarily microorganisms, and are then much more prominently characterized by the presence, for example, of rock, soil, pavement, or buildings.

## PATCH ORIGINS AND CHANGE

### Basic Concepts

The morning after the big fire we couldn't wait to explore the blackened landscape. An awesome sight it was! Most intriguing to us were the many types of patches scattered across the landscape. Two separate fires had ignited. A single small patch was blackened nearby, and an extensive fire had swept the area beyond. We explored the latter and discovered several patches of remaining vegetation that the flames had skipped. Returning through an unburned area, we crossed a little swamp, a patch with quite different vegetation and animals because of its water-soaked soil. Later we reached a clearing and gazed at a patch of grain waving gently in the breeze.

At least four types of patches were observed during this exploration, each with a fundamentally different origin. The small burned area was

**Figure 3.1** *Remnant patches skipped by a wildfire. Patches are dominated by spruce* (Picea) *and fir* (Abies). *Regrowth in the burned area is dominated by cherry* (Prunus pensylvanica), *birch* (Betula papyrifera), *and aspen* (Populus tremuloides). *Parc de la Gaspesie, Quebec, Canada. (R. Forman.)*

created by a local disturbance, fire. The vegetation patches skipped by the extensive fire also resulted from a disturbance, but in this case, the disturbance left the patches (Figure 3.1). The little swamp resulted from wet soil, and the clearing resulted from cutting the vegetation and planting the crop. The key **causative mechanisms,** or **origins,** for these patches involved disturbance, environmental heterogeneity, and human planting.

If one observed these patches for years to come, the differences in their **species dynamics** would become still more evident. That is, the particular sequence and rate of species disappearances and arrivals in a patch would vary, and so would the changes in population size of the species present. For example, the species dynamics might be relatively slight in the nearly permanent swamp, whereas they would probably be rapid and striking in the small burned patch as a succession of organisms occurred there.

If succession in the burned patch proceeded long enough, the area of the patch would probably become indistinguishable from the surrounding vegetation. The patch would disappear. In contrast, the swamp patch would remain distinct because the saturated soil is relatively permanent.

These examples illustrate **patch turnover,** the rate at which patches appear and disappear, which also varies widely and is an important characteristic in understanding the landscape.

Patches may be categorized according to their origins or causative mechanisms. In considering each type of patch recognized below, we briefly examine its causative mechanism, its species dynamics, and its turnover. In this way, we gain insight into the history, the stability, and the future of patches. (We also must remember that all phenomena may not be understandable as simple cause and effect. Indeed, many scientists recognize a considerable amount of apparent randomness [stochasticism] in nature.) We will then progressively explore the fascinating ramifications of patch size, shape, number and configuration in the landscape.

## Disturbance Patches

Disturbance of a small area in a matrix produces a **disturbance patch.** A wide variety of disturbances causes these. Mud slides (Figure 2.14), avalanches, windstorms, ice storms, herbivore outbreaks, mammal trampling, and many other natural changes give rise to patches (Flaccus, 1959; Webb, 1958; Wright, 1974; Sprugel, 1976; Siccama et al., 1976; Mattson and Addy, 1975; Platt, 1975; Garwood et al., 1979; Runkle, 1981). Patches caused by fire are common in dry regions and occasional in wet regions (Nye and Greenland, 1960; Kozlowski and Ahlgren, 1974; Heinselman, 1973; Forman and Boerner, 1981; Trabaud, 1984). The frequency, and the extent, of each causal agent are often unpredictable, since in most cases they reflect environmental factors both outside and inside the patch area (Pickett and Thompson, 1978).

Human activities also cause disturbance patches. Logging in forests (Figure 3.2), burning in grassland, and strip mining for surface coal or minerals are examples of widespread disturbance patches on earth.

What happens when an area is disturbed? This is one of the most important questions in ecology today. At this point, we will select a few of the major patterns that are nearly universal, regardless of the type of disturbance and the ecosystem disturbed (Dyksterhuis, 1949; Woodwell and Whittaker, 1968). Here we examine the *post-disturbance species dynamics.* Initially, population sizes of many species change rapidly, usually dropping sharply as a result of death or damage of individuals caused directly by the disturbance (Figure 3.2). Usually certain species become locally extinct, that is, they disappear from the patch area. Some species normally survive the disturbance (depending upon its intensity) and remain in lowered population sizes, or even in dormant forms such as seeds, spores, eggs, or cysts.

The second response, which usually follows quickly, is another drastic change in population size of many of the surviving species. Numbers

**Figure 3.2** *Cable logging (or skyline) system forming disturbance patches in coniferous forest. Note forested strips between patches, network of bare trails from logging operations, partial elimination of stream corridor, and beginning regrowth of vegetation on opposite slope. Gifford Pinchot National Forest, Washington, United States. Mount St. Helens volcano is visible shortly before its 1980 eruption. (Bob and Ira Spring.)*

increase, often more than compensating for the initial loss of individuals. The third response in rapid order is immigration, the arrival of species previously absent in the patch area. For example, animals, seeds, and spores colonize the newly opened space.

From this point on, succession or recovery from disturbance involves all three of the above processes: major population size changes, extinctions, and immigrations. Some species also remain relatively stable. Although all three processes continue, the proportion of species involved in these changes gradually declines. This means that the rate of extinction, immigration, and major population size change decreases, but does not drop to zero. More and more of the species present persist and with smaller population size changes, but the processes of change continue, even in the most stable communities (Levin and Paine, 1974; Connell, 1978; Levin, 1976; Pickett and Thompson, 1978; Pickett, 1980, 1982; Sousa, 1980).

This sequence of responses and recovery from disturbance results in relative community stability in the patch area. At this point, the patch has disappeared because it has converged in similarity with the matrix and is now indistinguishable. The species composition, the relative abundances of species, and the rates of change are no longer significantly different between the former patch and matrix areas.

Disturbance patches are generally the patch types that most rapidly disappear. That is, they have the highest patch turnover rates, or the lowest average age or persistence time. However, patches are also formed by **chronic** (or **repeated**) **disturbance** that persists for a long time. Certain air pollution occurs every day at a local spot, or an unplanted pasture is grazed repeatedly. In such cases the successional process is continually or repeatedly set back or restarted, and a kind of stability within the patch may result. This type of disturbance patch has a long persistence time.

The first two rows in Figure 3.3 compare the immigration and extinction rates over time in patches produced by single versus chronic disturbance. In the former case, a single disturbance causes a large increase in the rate of immigration and extinction in the patch. This rate gradually decreases and ultimately the patch disappears. In contrast, in the latter case, the initial disturbance causes a large increase in extinction, but immigration only increases somewhat, because the second, third, and subsequent disturbances prevent the establishment of the normal sequence of species in succession. The diagram indicates that the patch then enters a stable phase with low immigration and extinction rates. If the chronic disturbance is terminated, we see another large increase in the immigration and extinction rates as succession begins again, and this time ultimately leads to disappearance of the patch.

In both cases, after the initial disturbance a slight increase in immigration in the matrix is hypothesized, but no increase in extinction (Figure

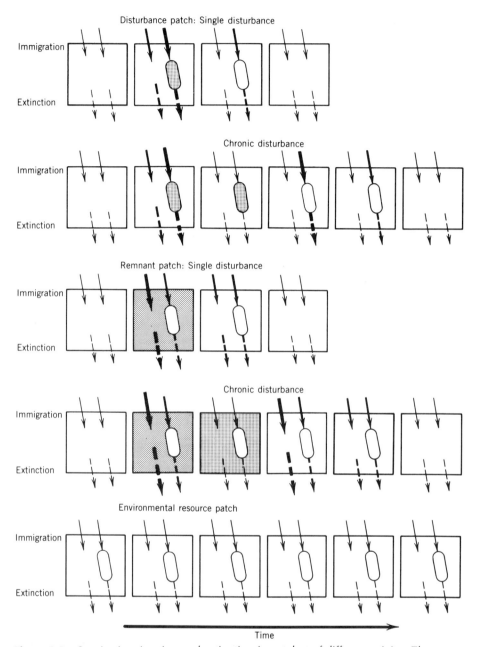

**Figure 3.3** *Species immigration and extinction in patches of different origins. The square is an area of matrix containing an oblong patch. Shading indicates an area being disturbed. The solid arrow is immigration and the dashed arrow is extinction. The thickness of an arrow is proportional to the estimated rate of immigration or extinction.*

3.3), because immigrating species enter the patch and then spread into the matrix, simply enriching the matrix with species. An alternative hypothesis is that these immigrant species may cause extinctions in the matrix, such as cowbirds entering large blow-downs in eastern North American forests and driving out the less common tropical migrant bird species (Robbins, 1980). In the chronic disturbance patch, a second immigration increase into the matrix is probably present, as immigrants spread from the patch during the final successional phase.

Chronic disturbance patches are mainly caused by human disturbances. Chronic natural disturbance over a long time, such as regular flooding, large mammal trampling, or wildfire, normally results in patch species that have adapted to the disturbance regime. Therefore, the patch area, with a distinctive environment or resources, remains different from the surrounding matrix and is in equilibrium with it.

## Remnant Patches

A remnant patch is caused by widespread disturbance surrounding a small area, the inverse of the mechanism for the disturbance patch. In this case, a remnant of the previous plant and animal community is embedded in a matrix which has been disturbed (Figure 3.4).

The patches of vegetation skipped by the extensive fire of the blackened landscape are remnant patches (Figure 3.1), as are vegetation remnants missed by a plague of locusts (*Schistocerca migratoria*), spruce budworms (*Choristoneura fumiferana*), or gypsy moths (*Porthetria dispar*). Remnant animal patches also occur, such as a nesting warbler community on a warmer slope that survived a rare freeze which eliminated the birds of the surrounding area, or a pocket of herbivores that escaped the invasion of an aggressive predator species.

Several parallels between remnant patches and disturbance patches are evident. Both originate with disturbance, either natural or human. In both cases large changes in population size, immigration, and extinction occur at the beginning and are followed by succession. Both disappear as the matrix and patch converge in similarity (Figure 3.3). Both have a high turnover rate.

However, this last characteristic raises a new issue. Studies of islands formed by flooding the surroundings suggest that an elevated species extinction rate is found right after the island is formed. This elevated extinction rate is hypothesized to be rapid at first, and gradually to decline to near zero as the island reaches a stable equilibrium number of species. The time following disturbance, during which the extinction rate is elevated, is referred to as a **relaxation period.** The species lost are often those with low population sizes or with large territory requirements, such as certain birds and mammals. Hence, in addition to those species earlier

**Figure 3.4** *Remnant and chronic disturbance patches in an agricultural area of eastern Britain. Most features shown are of medieval origin. The large wood on the left, the small woods in the upper portion, and most hedges were indicated on a 1613 map almost as they are today. The woods in the lower portion date mainly from the late seventeenth and early eighteenth centuries. Recent changes include some hedge removal and plantations in the large wood. Area shown is about 1.6 × 1.6 km (one square mile). Long Medford, Suffolk, England. (From Rackham, 1976; courtesy of Cambridge University Collection: copyright reserved.)*

eliminated from the flooded area, additional species on the island are lost during the relaxation period (Diamond, 1972; Terborgh, 1974; Willis, 1974; Miller and Harris, 1977; Miller, 1978b; Soule et al., 1979; Karr, 1982).

However, especially in the case of remnant patches in the landscape, a relaxation period appears to be just one portion of a longer modulation or **adjustment period** that is characterized by an elevated rate of species dynamics. Following disturbance of a landscape matrix, some species will immigrate to the remnant and a portion of these will become established (Lovejoy et al., 1983; Lovejoy et al., 1984). This initial patch enrichment will then be followed by the more gradual species extinctions of the relaxation period. However, the matrix is also undergoing rapid species changes as succession proceeds. The relaxation process, therefore, is followed not by a stable number of species but rather by periods when immigration exceeds extinction (e.g., species that disappeared reinvade from the matrix), alternating with periods when extinction exceeds immigration (the initial colonizers now disappear). This adjustment period for species in the patch may extend throughout the life of the patch, that is, until the patch converges with the matrix.

This sequence of events provides a message of caution for us. A remnant patch such as a woods may superficially resemble the original predisturbance forest. Yet, since the species lost in the relaxation process are also commonly eliminated from the matrix by the disturbance, recolonization of the species depends on distant sources and is often slow. Therefore, even after the matrix and patch have converged, the resulting extensive ecosystem may be a species-poor mimic of the original ecosystem.

Remnant patches may also result from chronic disturbance (Figures 3.4 and 3.5). Woodlots surrounded by agriculture or suburban development are familiar, though usually impoverished examples (Curtis, 1956; Peterken, 1974; Rackham, 1976; Wegner and Merriam, 1979; Robbins, 1980; Sharpe et al., 1981). In this case, chronic human disturbance of the matrix has left the remnant isolated for long periods (Figure 3.5). Species extinctions are caused by diverse factors, but random chance alone may be used to explain the loss of many rare species (e.g., those with low population sizes). The longer the remnant patch with species of low population size exists, the more chance there is that a species will become locally extinct. Hence, we expect chronic remnant patches to have longer relaxation periods, and more species lost, than short-lived remnant patches. When the long-lived remnant patch and its matrix ultimately converge, the resulting landscape may be expected to be rather different from that existing before disturbance.

In some landscapes, **regenerated patches** occur, resembling remnant patches but with a different origin. In this case, a spot within a large area of chronic disturbance becomes free of disturbance, permitting succession to take place (D. Sharpe, F. Stearns, and R. Burgess, personal communication). Examples are new "natural" woodlots in an agricultural landscape (Raup, 1966; Sharpe et al., 1981), and ecosystems newly protected in an area of frequent fire caused by humans. Although the regenerated patch may have the appearance of a remnant patch in a sea of disturbance, its pattern of species dynamics through succession resembles that of a disturbance patch.

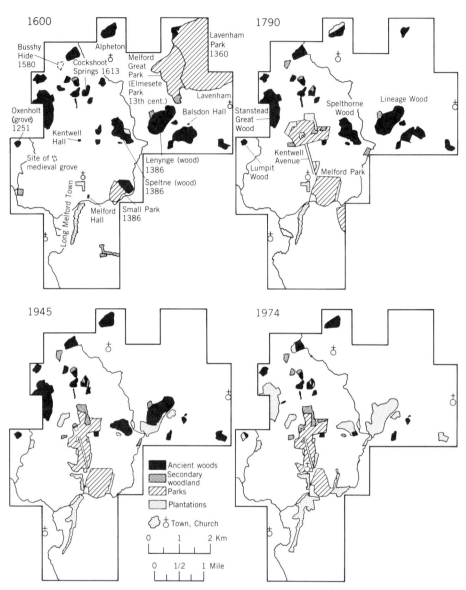

**Figure 3.5** *Four-hundred-year history of an English agricultural landscape. Ancient wooded area is considered to have escaped cultivation, whereas secondary woods regenerated after cultivation. Ancient woods have progressively decreased, while the total areas of woods and of cultivation have remained relatively unchanged over the four centuries. Figure 3.4 is of area in upper left. (From Rackham, 1976; Trees and Woodlands in the British Landscape courtesy of J. M. Dent and Sons, Ltd.)*

Before we proceed, we must note that some statements above have been phrased cautiously. Landscape ecology is a new and growing field, and in some areas very few studies have been done. The perceptive reader will see many opportunities for specific investigations of major potential import. As its quantitative base grows, landscape ecology will increasingly take its place as a predictive science alongside older fields of knowledge.

## Environmental Resource Patches

The previous types of patches owe their existence to disturbance. On the other hand, we have all seen patches that seemed rather stable and unrelated to disturbance. A peatland (or bog) left by glacial activity, a heath area on an exposed mountain ridge, wet depressions in limestone country (Figure 3.6), a concentration of amphibians and reptiles around a desert oasis, or a special group of pollinating insect species in a moist alpine valley are all **environmental resource patches.** What do they have

**Figure 3.6** *Wet depressions as environmental resource patches in limestone grassland. These "prairie potholes" are on the Nature Conservancy–Ordway Prairie Reserve, South Dakota, United States. (Jim Brandenburg.)*

in common? In each case, the organisms of the patch differ from those of the surrounding matrix because the environmental conditions or resources of the patch are different. In other words, the origin of each patch is due to the heterogeneous or patchy distribution in space of environmental resources, such as water and soil for the plants, or water and flowers for the animal communities.

In many cases the **ecotone,** or overlap zone, separating a patch from the matrix is relatively sharply defined, as is commonly the case in disturbance-caused patches (Figures 3.1, 3.2 and 3.4). But since environmental resources often are not distributed with sharp boundaries separating them, the ecotone may be extremely wide and form a gradually changing gradient (Ramensky, 1924; Gleason, 1926; Curtis, 1959; McIntosh, 1967; Whittaker, 1967; Daubenmire, 1968; Rapoport, 1982b). The significance of this difference will be discussed in Chapter 11. As a preliminary hypothesis, we may look for greater movement of species between patch and matrix if the boundary is less abrupt.

The above examples of environmental resource patches have several other characteristics in common. Since the distribution of resources is relatively permanent, the patches are relatively permanent and patch turnover is extremely low (Figure 3.3). In these stable patches the dynamic processes of population fluctuation, immigration, and extinction are present, but at a low level. No relaxation or adjustment period is present, because the species changes are simply those normal for a patch community in equilibrium with a surrounding matrix community.

## Introduced Patches

When humans introduce organisms to an area, an *introduced patch* results. It resembles a disturbance patch in the sense that disturbance of a small area initiates the patch. In all cases the introduced species, whether they are plants, animals, or people, exert a dominating and continuing effect on the patch. Such patches, therefore, are among the most widespread on earth (Marschner, 1959; Lebeau, 1969).

**Planted Patches.**   People introducing plants, as for example in wheat fields, rice paddies, pine or eucalypt plantations, golf courses, and arboreta, form *planted patches* in a matrix.

In planted patches, the species dynamics and patch turnover depend largely upon the maintenance activities of people. For example, if no maintenance takes place, the patch will be invaded by species from the matrix, and succession and ultimate disappearance of the patch will follow, just as in a disturbance patch. The only difference is that the introduced species, such as in tree plantations, may remain dominant for a long time and therefore retard the successional process.

But foresters and farmers want production from their plantings, so planting is normally followed by a range of maintenance activities aimed at preventing succession. Weeds are dug, cut, or killed with chemicals. Herbivores are shot, trapped, scared, or sprayed. The introduced plants are thinned or trimmed. Even the soil is turned over, fertilized, watered, or drained. Such maintenance activities result in persistence of the planted patches for long periods.

In shifting (or swidden or slash-and-burn) cultivation in the moist tropics of Asia, Africa, and Latin America, the farmer often cuts a clearing in the forest, plants crops for two or three years, abandons the site to succession, and repeats the process at another site. Such planted patches are relatively short-lived and have a rapid turnover (Nye and Greenland, 1960). Most other planted patches in the world, though, remain for decades or even centuries (Figure 3.5), with chronic human maintenance activities preventing takeover by succession. In short, the species dynamics of planted patches include a brief initial period of sharp change associated with disturbance and planting, a (usually) long period of relative stability during maintenance activity, and a second period of major change during abandonment and succession. The sequence terminates when the patch disappears by converging with the matrix.

An identical overall process takes place when animals are introduced into a concentrated area. A herd of sheep, goats, or cattle introduced into a matrix is effectively a patch within the matrix animal community. A feeding station, say, for mammals in the African savanna, or for birds in a temperate region, which attracts vertebrate species to a small area is in essence an introduced patch. The persistence of such patches depends almost totally on the duration of human maintenance activity.

**Homes or Habitations.**   People are major components of most landscapes on earth today. We have seen their role in planting patches and in disturbing the matrix with many activities that produce both disturbance and remnant patches. One of the most conspicuous, and nearly universal, components of these landscapes is the human *habitation* or *home* (Figure 3.4). It includes the house, associated yard, courtyard, farm buildings, and immediate surroundings (Hoskins, 1955; Rapoport, 1969, 1982a; Eckbo, 1975; Meinig, 1979a; Tuan, 1974; Watts, 1975; Lowenthal, 1976).

The origin of habitations is, of course, disturbance, involving the partial or nearly total elimination of the natural ecosystem at that spot. Next comes building construction and, usually, the introduction of new species. Often the habitation remains stable as a patch for years, decades, or even centuries, before disappearing.

The ecological structure within habitations is based on the types of organisms that have replaced the natural ecosystem. People are foremost. Not only are they large consumers, but also they provide the predominant disturbance regime that maintains the habitation. Most of the plant species present are those introduced by people for consumption or to adorn gardens, yards, and public places. Some may be native species, but humans exhibit a propensity for surrounding themselves with a diverse and exotic species assemblage (Schmid, 1975; Spirn, 1984). Animals, too, are introduced, and in most cases we prefer domestic animals and livestock such as cats, cows, and canaries, rather than native species such as bobcats, buffalo, and bats. The habitation ecosystem is further enriched with plant and animal pests that are inadvertently introduced. Rats, mice, fleas, termites, cockroaches, crabgrass, ragweed, dysentery amoebas, and hoof-and-mouth organisms illustrate the wide range of possibilities. These species, however, must compete with the "rain" of native species constantly immigrating to the patch from the surrounding matrix. Seeds may bring weeds, and animals may bring trouble: for example, caterpillars defoliate ornamentals, rabbits consume gardens, and mongoose catch chickens.

In short, the habitation ecosystem includes four types of species: people, introduced plants and animals, inadvertently introduced pests, and immigrating native species. Since it is highly artificial, its success depends in part upon the degree and constancy of human maintenance. Human activity varies over time, and the typical instability of the habitation ecosystem mirrors this.

The distance between habitations largely differentiates urban, suburban, town, village, and various rural areas (Hoskins, 1955; McHarg, 1969; Lebeau, 1969; Zube, 1970; Rapoport, 1982a). Urban and suburban areas may be extensive enough to be termed landscapes in their own right. In contrast, a small city, town, village, or isolated cluster of houses forms a multi-dwelling habitation patch within a rural landscape. Single-dwelling habitation patches are also usually common in such a landscape.

Urban and suburban landscapes, with numerous contiguous dwellings, are dominated by people and nonnative species (Schmid, 1975). In rural areas with isolated homes, the habitation contains people and nonnative species, but the role of native species from the surrounding matrix is far greater. Here the entire area of the habitation is close to the matrix, and so interaction between them is maximized.

In summary, the habitation and the planted patch might both be considered analogous to a zoo built in the wilderness. The zoo contains an assortment of relatively incompatible species of diverse origins that are coexisting thanks to enormous human input and effort. Whenever the human effort lags, rapid and large changes are evident in the zoo's population. When the zookeeper's budget eventually dries up, the wilderness swallows the zoo. So, too, is the existence and fate of the human habitation.

## Additional Concepts

The types of patches analyzed in the preceding pages are the principal structural components of landscapes. However, we must also recognize that patches of organisms may be considered in several other contexts.

It is common to see transient aggregations of species in nature (Figure 3.7), such as a localized bloom of annuals in the desert, a shrubby area in field-to-forest succession, a tree-fall gap community in a forest, or mammals feeding at dawn around a mudhole in the savanna. **Ephemeral patches** such as these are caused by social interactions, or by normal, short-lived fluctuations in environmental factors. That is, the levels of biotic or abiotic environmental change are frequent, and of such low intensity, that species have adapted to them. (Unusual or severe environmental changes are considered disturbances, which in turn cause

**Figure 3.7** *Caribou herd as a transient or ephemeral patch in arctic tundra. Such migratory accumulations have recently become increasingly infrequent largely because of human activities. Interior Alaska (Charlie Ott; courtesy of Photo Researchers.)*

disturbance and remnant patches.) The ephemeral patch with a rapid turnover, such as a clump of berry bushes in a woods or a small flock of birds in a field, appears to be more prominent at finer levels of scale than the landscape, and thus is not analyzed further in this book.

When a landscape is mapped, particular types of communities (e.g., vegetation, mammals, insects) are usually mapped separately. The maps may then be superimposed to provide an overview of the horizontal distribution of ecosystems. In some cases the boundaries on several maps coincide, that is, the patches are "congruous." In many cases, however, the boundaries of different community patches do not coincide spatially. The degree of *congruity* probably varies widely among landscapes and may be an important index of landscape structure (Forman, 1979b; Opdam et al., 1983; Opdam, 1984).

In analyzing a landscape, we must observe the *vegetation types* or *animal communities* present in patches, in addition to patch characteristics such as origin and size. Vegetation types or animal communities are named by their predominant species or structure, such as pine woods, wet meadow, thorn woodland, salmon-trout community, and banana plantation. The distribution of particular communities among the patches present plays an important role in the flows of objects across a landscape, and in landscape change.

In this chapter we have analyzed four categories of landscape patches, with origins based on disturbance, environmental resource distribution, and human introduction. The patches differ sharply in their *persistence,* or stability (Figure 3.8). Environmental resource patches are long-lived. The other patch types are short-lived if a single disturbance is the causative mechanism. More commonly, though, the disturbance is chronic, resulting in a temporary stable phase and a somewhat longer-lived patch. Thus the persistence, or turnover, of patches varies widely; seen together in a landscape, they appear like the night lights of a town blinking on and off.

## PATCH SIZE

The most easily recognized aspect of patches is their size, or area (Figure 3.9). Ask a forester, a farmer, a bird watcher, and a landscape architect to describe patches, and striking differences between large and small patches will be described. These will include not only species, but also energy and materials.

Two questions are constantly faced by local leaders, planners, environmentalists, decision-makers, citizen groups, and any person concerned with land use. What is the minimum patch size needed to accomplish a particular objective? And what is the optimum patch size?

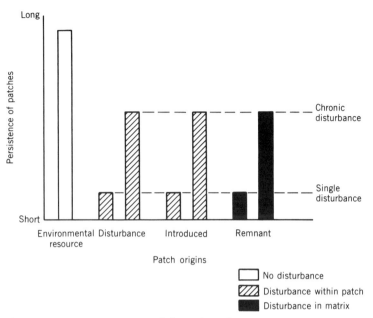

**Figure 3.8** *Persistence, or stability, of patches.*

For example, there are minimum and optimum patch sizes for efficiently growing corn, keeping livestock, or harvesting wood (Smith, 1962; Stoddard, 1968; Brown, 1971b; Row, 1978; Cubbage, 1983). The answers to these questions are crucial to the understanding and management of landscapes.

Note that the primary characteristics considered below are ecological: energy, mineral nutrients, and species. Other important characteristics also relate to the patch size question, such as the ability to operate planting and harvesting machinery, the distance to habitations and markets, or topographic variation. In the following discussion one should keep in mind the roles these other factors may play.

### Effects on Energy and Nutrients

In general terms, the amount of energy storage or flow in a plot of a given size is the same whether the plot is within a small patch or a large patch (Figure 3.9). The same is true for nutrient storage or flow. Therefore, the total amount of energy or nutrients in a patch is simply proportional to the area of a patch. Large patches contain more energy and mineral nutrients than smaller patches.

One important modification in this argument needs to be made. When we walk from the edge portion of a large patch into its interior, the

**Figure 3.9** *Tiny wooded patch with edge conditions throughout. Eleven woody plant species are present, dominated by maple (Acer). Glacial boulders from clearing the field, and the single individuals of white birch (Betula papyrifera), white pine (Pinus strobus), and red cedar (Juniperus virginiana) are visible. Note characteristic persistent branches along lower tree trunks. Near Woodstock, New York. (R. Forman.)*

differences are striking. For example, let us examine energy and nutrient patterns for remnant patches. (Disturbance and other types of patches exhibit different or even opposite patterns.) The edge portion of a remnant patch, such as a woodlot surrounded by fields or an area missed by a fire (Figures 3.4 and 3.1), generally has denser vegetation than the patch interior (Figure 3.10). The biomass per unit area is greater on the edge. In fact measurements would probably show that the biological production of the edge exceeds that of the interior. This appears to be due to the higher light availability at the edge and to reduced plant competition on the open side. We hasten to add that, although edge production is higher, the predominant plants, such as trees, are often shorter and commonly have bent or misshapen stems with branches along the stems, probably because of light conditions on the open side of the edge (Figure 3.10).

**Figure 3.10** *Patch edge showing mantel of dense shrubs and small trees. The canopy trees along the edge lean outward toward the field and have a "misshapen" appearance, with large lower horizontal branches on the outward side. Other canopy trees in woods have mainly straight trunks with branches only at top. Canopy trees are black oak (Quercus velutina), white oak (Q. alba), red oak (Q. borealis), and tulip poplar (Liriodendron tulipifera), with some large sassafras (Sassafras albidum) along the edge. Small trees are predominantly flowering dogwood (white blossoms), cherries and ash (Cornus florida, Prunus serotina, P. avium, Fraxinus americana). Shrubs are mainly blackberry (Rubus spp.), poison ivy (Toxicodendron radicans), and honeysuckle (Lonicera japonica). The herbaceous saum is hardly visible in spring. Near Princeton, New Jersey, United States. (R. Forman.)*

Therefore, yield, in the form of harvestable wood products, for example, is sometimes lower near the edge than in the interior of a large patch. Certain harvestable plant species, however, may be more abundant in the edge or may produce more flowers and fruits there, and thus attract different pollinators, herbivores, or berry pickers.

Vertebrate biomass and productivity are also typically higher in the edge than in the interior of a remnant patch. Indeed, this has been a central concept in wildlife management (Leopold, 1933; Lay, 1938; McAtee, 1945; Giles, 1978). Many wildlife, such as rabbits (*Sylvilagus*), quail (*Colinus*), and pheasant (*Phasianus*), have higher densities in the edges of patches. Animal activity, herbivory, and predation are often high along edges (Bider, 1968; Gates and Gysel, 1978). Nevertheless, large patches appear to have more species of vertebrates than small patches and perhaps longer food chains, since the species most sensitive to patch size usually are animals at higher feeding (trophic) levels (Johnston, 1947; Forman et al., 1976; Robbins, 1980; Karr and Freemark, 1985). Therefore, a landscape with both many large patches, and a considerable length of edge around small patches and along corridors, will combine a wealth of sensitive interior species with edge species and wildlife.

If the vegetation is denser in the edge of remnant patches, the nutrient storage in that vegetation is probably greater than that in the same area of forest interior. On the other hand, the total nutrients in the soil may be either greater or less in the edge than the interior. (In temperate and boreal regions soil nutrients typically far exceed nutrients in plant biomass.) Factors that can be expected to produce greater soil nutrients per unit area of edge include: accumulations of leaves and other plant materials, greater total plant production, and greater impaction of airborne nutrients on edge plant surfaces. Factors that may produce fewer soil nutrients include the loss of leaves by wind and decreased organic matter in the soil resulting from more rapid decomposition at the edge.

These differences between the energy and nutrients in the interior and in the edge are central to the basic question of the effect of patch size. Small patches have a higher proportion of edge area than large patches (Figure 3.9). We are reasonably certain that small remnant patches normally differ from large patches in the amount of energy and nutrients per unit area, and (as just described) we know the general factors causing increases or decreases. However, apparently no studies have compared patches of different size on the basis of their energy and nutrient characteristics; there appears to be fertile ground for investigation (Dierschke, 1974; Cubbage, 1983).

## Effects on Species

**Islands.**   The effect of patch size on the numbers, types, and flows of species has generated considerable study, insight, and controversy. The basic question is illustrated by the following episode. A class was shipwrecked. Each member is cast ashore on a different island of a tropical archipelago. The smallest island, of course, had only a palm tree and a little lizard. Some islands were flat, others were mountainous. Some were pristine and others contained abandoned fields and dwellings. As inquisitive observers, each member of the class carefully recorded all species seen while searching for food. The class eventually was rescued.

When the number of species for each island was plotted on a graph, what could the class tell the news media about that archipelago?

Large islands have more species than small islands, they would report. However, the relationship between species diversity and island size is not linear but curvilinear; that is, there is a rapid initial increase through the smaller island sizes and a slight, but continued, increase through the larger sizes. Mountainous islands have more species than flat islands of the same size. Islands with evidence of considerable human disturbance activity often (but not always) have fewer species than those without such activity.

The relationship plotted between increasing area and the number of species is called a **species-area curve** (see, e.g., Figure 2.16). Ecologists commonly record the species present in a series of plots within a community and then draw a species-area curve on graph paper as a rough first step to determine the minimum area for an adequate sample of the community (Arrhenius, 1921; Vestal, 1949; Cain and Castro, 1959; Preston, 1962; Greig-Smith, 1964; Connor and McCoy, 1979). In contrast, in the archipelago example, each size along the horizontal axis includes a complete island ecosystem including its border or edge. The species-area curve based on complete islands provides different information from a curve based on samples within an island or community. When the species number on a sample of islands in an archipelago is measured, the number of species on any other island can then be estimated or predicted.

Islands have attracted an enormous amount of study of their natural history and types of species, from the time of the perceptive nineteenth-century naturalists Darwin (1842) and Wallace (1880), to the present (e.g., Carlquist, 1974). A different approach to understanding islands and archipelagos has emerged in recent years, called **island biogeographic theory** (MacArthur and Wilson, 1967; Hamilton et al., 1964; Simberloff and Wilson, 1970; Gilbert, 1980). In this approach the number of species (species diversity or richness) on an island is related directly to three factors in order: the island's area, its isolation, and its age (MacArthur and Wilson, 1967). Many studies on an array of types of organisms have confirmed the major importance of island area. The isolation effect is intuitively satisfying and is supported by several studies. The island age effect is least well documented but also seems to be a logical hypothesis.

Notice the difference between what the class found and what island biogeographic theory indicates. Both sources suggest island area has a major effect on species diversity. The class observed an effect of environmental heterogeneity (mountains) and disturbance (fields and dwellings), while island biogeographic theory indicates the importance of isolation and age of the island. Surely all five factors play a role. The basic island area effect in island biogeographic theory has been considered to be mainly due to habitat diversity; in most cases, larger islands simply have more habitats that, therefore, support more species. However, there is also an area effect in the sense that even when habitat diversity does not differ, somewhat more species are typically found on large than on small islands (or patches) (Forman et al., 1976; Simberloff, 1976). Finally, one of the major factors determining species diversity on an island is the history and present regime of disturbance (Carlquist, 1974; Pickett and Thompson, 1978).

To summarize, species diversity (number of species) $S$ is a function $f$ of certain island characteristics, listed here in their probable order of overall importance.

$$S = f \,(+ \text{ habitat diversity}, \; - \text{ disturbance},$$
$$+ \text{ area}, \; - \text{ isolation}, \; + \text{ age})$$

where $+$ means positively related to species diversity, and $-$ means negatively related. (Disturbance is usually negatively but sometimes positively related.) Species diversity commonly refers to all species, though often it is useful to restrict the concept to native species.

**Terrestrial Landscapes.** Patches in the landscape differ significantly from islands surrounded by water (Forman, 1979b; Gilbert, 1980). For example, landscape patches may have high average turnover rates, whereas islands are essentially permanent. Similarly, the sharpness of the patch boundary varies greatly in the landscape (Whittaker, 1973), and gradual gradients may be more conducive to the movement of species between patch and matrix (van Leeuwen, 1965, 1966). Unlike water, the landscape matrix often has extremely high heterogeneity. This implies a large number of potential colonizing species in the matrix, as well as marked species differences in the matrix on different sides of the patch. The landscape matrix may be used as a rest stop for many species moving between patches, particularly in the limited area of a landscape compared with the extensiveness of oceanic archipelagos. Thus, in a landscape the importance of isolation, a central characteristic of island biogeographic theory, is reduced. These factors mean that we should not expect the previous equation for islands to suffice for understanding landscape patches. Rather, species diversity of patches in a landscape mosaic should be related to the characteristics and processes of the mosaic.

Within a landscape, the rate of species immigration appears to be high. That is, individuals or propagules of most species reach most patches within the time period required to complete their life cycle. Therefore, when species become extinct in patches, rapid recolonization is facilitated, and the effect of isolation is minimized (see also Chapter 5). While this high species immigration rate applies to the community as a whole (as measured by species diversity), some species have limited dispersability within the landscape. Isolation in the landscape may be critical for these individual species, many of which are typically uncommon. Conservation activities thus must consider not only the basic animal or plant community but also these specific populations (Terborgh, 1974, 1976; Diamond, 1975; Diamond and May, 1976; Simberloff, 1976; Pickett and Thompson, 1978; Council on Environmental Quality, 1980; Soule and Wilcox, 1980; Wilcox, 1980; Shaffer, 1981; Higgs, 1981).

The species diversity pattern for landscape patches appears to be related to patch characteristics in the following order (compare with the pattern for islands above).

$$S = f (+ \text{ habitat diversity}, - (+) \text{ disturbance}, + \text{ area}, + \text{ age},$$
$$+ \text{ matrix heterogeneity}, - \text{ isolation}, - \text{ boundary discreteness})$$

Species diversity has been shown to correlate strongly with landscape patch size (Peterken, 1974, 1977; Moore and Hooper, 1975; Galli et al., 1976; Whitcomb, 1977; Gottfried, 1979; Robbins, 1980; Ambuel and Temple, 1983; Lynch and Whigham, 1984), but area has rarely been considered separately from habitat diversity (Buckley, 1982). When patch area alone is evaluated, we find it to be an important determinant of species diversity. Furthermore, each species group, such as trees, mushrooms, butterflies, seed-eating birds, and insectivorous birds, responds differently to patch area (Elfstrom, 1974; Forman et al., 1976; Forman and Godron, 1981).

How to design nature reserves that maintain (a) high native species diversity, (b) rare and endangered species, and (c) stable ecosystems is a question of considerable interest in the field of conservation. The area of a nature reserve is the primary factor considered, whereas isolation, age, shape, disturbance regime, and other factors are generally given secondary importance. If the species diversity of patches and the distribution of rare species are already known, conservation of course must focus on them rather than on the abstract patch variables (Terborgh and Winter, 1983; Game and Peterken, 1984). However, the complex of landscape features, rather than a single patch, may be the critical characteristic in protecting certain birds (Morris and Lemon, 1983; Arnold, 1983) and in accomplishing the other nature reserve objectives (Westhoff, 1970; Ratcliffe, 1977; Bakker, 1979). In view of the suggested interactions among ecosystems in a landscape (Chapter 1; see also Chapters 9, 10, and 11), a cluster of ecosystems—rather than a particular landscape element—may be an appropriate unit for many nature reserves.

## PATCH SHAPE

### Significance in Ecology

The shape of patches is just as striking as patch size (Figures 3.1 and 3.4). Curiously, however, we know relatively little about the effects of shape on the ecosystem. These effects must be considerable though, since standing in the middle of a large round patch gives a very different sensation from standing in the middle of a long strip of equal area. Again our attention is drawn to the importance of the edge. But first let us mention some other ways shape has been studied or is important.

The shape of lakes has been of particular interest because shoreline processes are major factors affecting the productivity and organisms present in the body of the lake (Hutchinson, 1957; Lind, 1979; Cole, 1983). The degree of development of a lake shoreline $D$ is considered to be the ratio of shoreline length $L$ to the circumference of a circle which has the same area $A$ as the lake.

$$D = \frac{L}{2\sqrt{\pi A}}$$

The smallest possible shoreline development level would be 1.0 for a circular lake. Some volcanic, meteoritic, and glacial lakes have low development values ($D$). Examples in the United States are Montezuma Well in Arizona ($D = 1.04$) and Crater Lake in Oregon ($D = 1.10$) (excluding an island); and in southern Africa, Avenue Pan ($D = 1.02$). Many elongated glacial lakes, such as Lake Baikal in the Soviet Union and Cayuga Lake in New York, have $D$ values of about 3 to 4, and very high values are often observed for dammed reservoirs which partially flood many stream tributaries. Over time, shoreline development values may decrease because of erosion of promontories and filling in of bays, or increase because of the depositing of deltas and sand spits.

In biogeography, investigators often draw dot maps or shade in areas on a map to indicate where a species lives. The shapes of distributions of species vary widely, from circular to long and narrow, from having smooth borders to having convoluted borders. Biogeographers analyze these shapes to gain insight into the dynamics of the species, in other words, whether the species distribution is stable, expanding, contracting, or migrating (Darlington, 1957; Udvardy, 1970; Daubenmire, 1978; Rapoport, 1982b). Even the migration route may often be inferred from the shape.

Shape has also been important in sampling theory. If you wish to sample some aspect of an ecosystem, what is the *optimum shape of plots* to be sampled? Squares and circles have been widely used for convenience (Raunkiaer, 1934). However, less variable results can be obtained by using strip or rectangular plots. This procedure is valid for low cropland, herbaceous vegetation, shrub-grassland, and forest (Ilvessalo, 1920; Clapham, 1932; Kalambar, 1932; Hasel, 1938; Pechanec and Stewart, 1940; Bormann, 1953). It is particularly valid if the long axis of the plot is perpendicular to the topographic contours or any obvious vegetational differences. None of these sampling conclusions would be valid if the species were randomly distributed, but the conclusions are almost always true because species tend to be distributed in clusters (Greig-Smith, 1964). Although less variation is found between rectangular plots than between square plots, more variation is found within rectangular plots, hence in this case sampling effort per plot is greater (Godron, 1966; Mueller-Dombois and Ellenberg, 1974). A final aspect of the shape of plot samples relates to human bias. In comparing equal sized plots whose length-to-width ratios varied from 1 : 1 (square) to 200 : 1 (strip), a forest ecologist found the lowest variability in results with the 200 : 1 shape, but recommended use of a rectangular shape with a 4 : 1 length-to-width ratio (Bormann, 1953). The strip plot has a much longer total border than the rectangular plot, and along a border an investigator must make a decision whether an organism is inside or outside the plot. So many decisions must be made over a long border that inadvertent bias by the investigator may creep in. Thus, a rectangular plot with about a 4 : 1 length-to-width ratio is commonly used in ecological sampling.

Patch shape is undoubtedly important in the dispersal and foraging of organisms. For example, insects or vertebrates moving through a woods, or birds flying over it, are more apt to find a long narrow clearing that is oriented perpendicular to their direction of movement, whereas they may miss a round clearing. Conversely, the long narrow clearing parallel to their movement may also be missed. Hence, both patch shape and orientation are critical in the dispersal of animals and plants across a landscape. These and related questions have spawned an exciting field of study focusing on animal foraging strategies (Schoener, 1971; Krebs et al., 1974; Covich, 1976; Emlen, 1981).

The importance of shape has also been studied for geographic districts, drainage basins, coral reefs, and cloud areas (Richardson, 1926; Gibbs, 1961; Blair and Biss, 1967; Austin, 1981; Horton, 1945; Chorley et al., 1957; Stoddart, 1965; Gregory and Walling, 1973; Lovejoy, 1982). The shape of forest stands and openings is particularly important for wildlife, because habitat conditions and shape are often closely interrelated (Patton, 1975; Covich, 1976; Marcot and Meretsky, 1983). Finally, the shape of animal home ranges varies from circular to nearly linear, but is usually elongated and described empirically or mathematically as polygonal or elliptical (Knowlton, 1960; Mitchell, 1961; Stumpf and Mohr, 1962;

Jennrich and Turner, 1969; Metzgar, 1972; Koeppl et al., 1975; Smith, 1983).

## Edge Effect

The primary significance of shape in determining the nature of patches in a landscape appears to be related to the edge effect. As previously noted, the microenvironment in the center of a tiny patch of woods differs strikingly from that in the center of an extensive woods. Wind from the surrounding matrix whistles through the tiny woods but only penetrates a limited distance past the boundary of the extensive forest. This outer band, which has an environment significantly different from the interior of the patch, is known as the **edge** of the patch. A different species composition and abundance is found in the edge, the so-called **edge effect** (Figure 3.10). For example, differences between the edge and interior of deciduous forests in North America and Europe have been documented for a host of meteorological factors, vegetational character-istics (Gysel, 1951; Hagar, 1960; Trimble and Tryon, 1966; Wales, 1967, 1972; Jakucs, 1972; Dierschke, 1974; Chasko and Gates, 1982; Wil-manns and Brun-Hool, 1982; De Walle, 1983), and animal communities (Leopold, 1933; Lay, 1938; Kendeigh, 1944; Johnston, 1947; Johnston and Odum, 1956; Schuerholz, 1974; Patton, 1975; Thomas et al., 1976; Galli et al., 1976; Taylor, 1977; Gates and Gysel, 1978; Thompson and Willson, 1978; Ferris, 1979; Thomas, 1979; Gates and Mosher, 1981; Kroodsma, 1982; Morgan and Gates, 1982). Soil and fire characteristics probably also differ, as (for example) in the savannas of Australia or Brazil.

Several factors affect the width of the edge. The angle of the sun plays a major role. Edges facing the equator are typically wider than those facing the poles (Wales, 1972; Ranney et al., 1981; Carpenter, 1935), and edges in temperate areas are usually wider than those in tropical areas. Wind, usually causing desiccation or nutrient input, also exerts a major influence; the prevailing wind direction during the active or growth period causes a wider edge than on other sides. Wider edges can be expected where the patch and matrix differ more in vertical structure. To a lesser extent this is also the case for differences in species composition. Edges may be more pronounced when a patch is older or has better soil (Yi, 1976).

The structure of a forest edge adjacent to cultivation or a pasture can be understood by visualizing a cross section through the edge (Figure 3.11). A herbaceous layer like the hem of a skirt, called a *saum* or *perennial herb border,* is on the outside. Then comes a woody layer of shrubs and small trees called a *mantel* or *woody mantle* (named for an overcoat that surrounds and protects the forest interior from outside weather), that in turn borders or is under the canopy trees (Figure 3.10) (Tuxen,

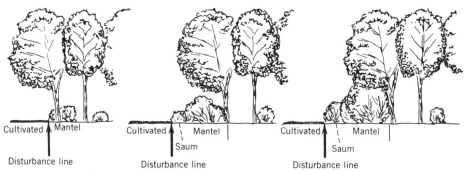

**Figure 3.11** *Different edge structures relating the saum and mantel to disturbance line location. The saum is dominated by perennial herbs, and the mantel by shrubs and small trees. After Tuxen (1967), Wilmanns and Brun-hool (1982), Ranney et al. (1981) and data of R. Forman.*

1967; Muller, 1962; Kopecky, 1969; Dierschke, 1974; Mueller-Dombois and Ellenberg, 1974; Braakhekke and Braakhekke-Ilsink, 1976; Ellenberg, 1978; Wilmanns and Brun-Hool, 1982). The juxtaposition of the outer edges of saum, mantel, and canopy varies according to how close disturbance, such as plowing, in the open area comes to the trunks of canopy trees (Figure 3.11). If disturbance is close to the tree trunks and canopy branches overlap the field, usually the mantel is poorly developed and the saum is sparse. However, if the disturbance line lies outside the tree canopy branches, a well-developed saum is usually present with a dense and wide mantel extending back to the tree trunk area (Gysel, 1951; Trimble and Tryon, 1966; Wales, 1972; Ranney et al., 1981). The vertebrate and invertebrate communities also differ considerably according to edge structure (Leopold, 1933; Carpenter, 1935; Hagar, 1960; Julander and Jeffery, 1964; Patton, 1975; Thomas et al., 1976; Ghiselin, 1977; Thompson and Willson, 1978; Thomas, 1979; Lyon and Jensen, 1980; Gates and Mosher, 1981; Chasko and Gates, 1982; Hanley, 1983; Opdam et al., 1983).

Within a landscape element, **edge species** are those only or primarily near the perimeter, and **interior species** are those located only or primarily away from the perimeter. Patch edges appear to vary in width from a few meters to a few tens of meters in patches at the landscape level. Different groups of organisms respond differently to the environmentally determined edge width. For example, avian and tree communities in woodlots appear to be different from the interior communities only in the outer portion of a forest edge. In contrast, butterflies and ground dwelling organisms such as herbs and mosses appear to vary over essentially the entire span of the edge.

## Isodiametric and Elongated Patches

A large isodiametric patch such as a circle or square consists mostly of interior, with a band of edge in the outer portion of the patch. A rectangular patch of the same area has proportionally less patch interior and more patch edge. Finally, a narrow patch of the same area may be all edge (Figure 3.12). Since community and population characteristics of animals and plants differ between the interior and the edge, the importance of patch shape in a landscape may be estimated by comparing these characteristics with the **interior-to-edge ratio** of patches.

In comparing a truly isodiametric form, the circular patch, with the square patch—nearly isodiametric but with four corners—the interior-to-edge ratio is noticeably higher for the circle than for the square. Furthermore, it would take a wider band of edge to completely eliminate the interior of a round patch than that of a square patch. Since interior and edge species differ, ecological differences can be expected in these two shapes. In elongated patches the interior-to-edge ratio is much lower, and relatively narrow edge widths may eliminate the patch interior altogether. The interior-to-edge ratio appears to be a useful indication of certain ecological conditions in a patch but, of course, is not a cause of those conditions. The cause is the penetration of the edge by wind and other factors from the surrounding matrix.

Few investigators have studied patch shape, or width, as an ecological variable (Patton, 1975; Game, 1980). Whitmore (1975) noted that plant species composition and community structure varied according to the shape of open gaps in Malaysian tropical rain forest. Stiles (1979) found sharp differences in wasp nesting density in the New Jersey (United States)

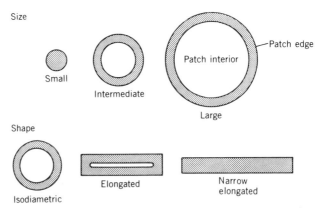

**Figure 3.12** *Interior and edge areas as affected by patch size and shape. (From Forman, 1981; courtesy of Pudoc– Centre for Agricultural Publishing and Documentation.)*

Pine Barrens according to the width of the habitat. In rockslides in Idaho (United States), small mammal density best correlated with the length of the rockslide perimeter (Bunnell and Johnson, 1974). Unpublished data (Forman and Clay) on mushroom diversity in old New Jersey two-hectare oak woods indicate a halving of species diversity and a threshold response in proceeding from isodiametric to narrow elongated patches. These examples are consistent with the idea that patch width or shape is a major ecological variable in the landscape.

Some of the possible areas where patch shape may be significant are summarized in Figure 3.13. It is evident that a high interior-to-edge ratio facilitates certain ecological processes, whereas a low ratio enhances other important processes. We will return to this concept when considering landscape dynamics; at this point, however, we note that the functional effect of shape depends strongly on the orientation of the long axis of the patch within a landscape.

## Rings

In northern tundra and boreal regions, many animal and plant groups or species have circumpolar distributions; that is, they completely encircle

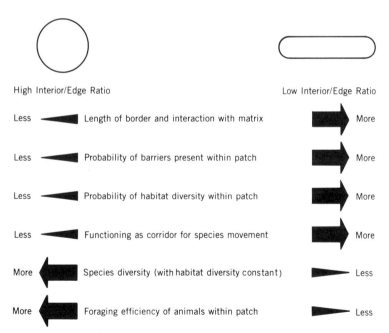

**Figre 3.13**  *The interior-to-edge effect on several ecological characteristics. The pattern for foraging efficiency is a hypothesis.*

the polar ice cap (Figure 3.7). Similarly, species may encircle a large mountain range, or amphibians may surround a pond. At a landscape scale, we recognize belts of vegetation, commonly within a particular altitudinal range. These extend around a mountain or depression and encircle a "hole" of different vegetation at a different altitude (Hedberg, 1955; MacArthur and Wilson, 1967). Such an encircling belt might be called a *ring* or "doughnut," a form with well-known mathematical characteristics (Hocking and Young, 1961; Kasriel, 1971; Kuratowski, 1972).

A common gaming strategy is to encircle your opponent. However, if your opponent then encircles your ring, you have a long perimeter or battlefront to protect. Similarly, an ecosystem in the shape of a ring has a long total border with considerable edge (Figure 3.14). No studies apparently have been done on this, but the resulting low interior-to-edge ratio suggests that rings resemble elongated patches more than isodi-

**Figure 3.14** *A ring patch surrounding a field. The forested ring has a low interior-to-edge ratio. The woods affects the field by shading and reducing wind, as suggested by the persistent snow cover. Northern New York State. (R. Forman.)*

ametric patches. Hence, a relative scarcity of interior species would be expected in rings. In fact, cutting a clearing within a forest patch produces a ring with the resulting increase in edge and expected decrease in interior species (Figure 3.14).

## Peninsulas

Another exceedingly common shape in landscapes is a narrow extension or lobe of a patch called a **peninsula** (or peninsuloid). Even the corner of a square or rectangular patch appears to function as a peninsula. We may also envision peninsulas as truncated corridors. In this sense, they function as routes for the movement of species across a landscape and indeed may be important funnels or concentrators of animal species movement. A high density of animal tracks at the tip of a peninsula is often evidence of this **funnel effect.** Conversely, the peninsula also functions as a barrier between patches on its opposite sides.

Despite the near ubiquity of the peninsula at the landscape scale, no studies on the subject are known to us, so for ecological clues we must initially look at peninsulas at the scale of continents. Biogeographically, such peninsulas as Florida and Baja California have been of interest because species diversity is often lower on the peninsula than on the **mainland,** that is, the wide patch area from which the peninsula extends. Not only is diversity lower on the peninsula, at least for several animal groups, but commonly there is a gradual decrease in species from the base to the tip of the peninsula (Figure 3.15).

The reason for this decreasing species diversity pattern is unknown. Several hypotheses or models have been posed to account for the pattern (Milne and Forman, unpublished).

1. *Equilibrium (colonization-extinction)* hypothesis. On the basis of patterns of mammal species on major North American peninsulas, Simpson (1964) infers that the geometry of the peninsula makes the mainland the primary **species source,** and that species can thus be considered to colonize the peninsula in one direction only. A population is less likely to colonize, and more likely to become extinct, at a point far from the species source. The decreasing diversity gradient from base to tip along a peninsula, therefore, results from the dynamic balance between extinction and recolonization. Only the best colonizers reach the tip frequently enough to counteract local extinctions.
2. *Ongoing colonization* hypothesis. The diversity pattern is produced when a new peninsula is formed, or when species are eliminated from a peninsula (e.g., during the ice age, or by recent disturbance). Species progressively spread into relatively vacant areas along the peninsula, and extinction has not yet equilibrated with the colonization process.

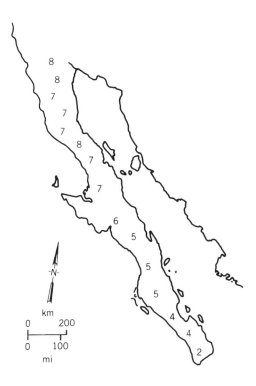

**Figure 3.15** *Vertebrate species diversity from base to tip of a peninsula. Rodent diversity is given on the map. Baja California, Mexico. (From Taylor and Regal, (1978, and personal communication), (Hall and Kelson, 1959), Seib (1980), Lawlor (1983); courtesy of R. J. Taylor and the University of Chicago Press; © 1978 by the University of Chicago.)*

| Vertebrate group | Species present at northern end | Species present at southern end | Percent change |
|---|---|---|---|
| Rodents (heteromyid) | 8 | 2 | −75% |
| All mammals | 49 | 45 | −8% |
| Mammals excluding bats | 33 | 26 | −21% |
| Bats | 16 | 19 | +19% |
| Birds (breeding) | 107 | 95 | −11% |
| All lizards | 18 | 18 | 0 |
| Southern desert lizards | 4 | 8 | +100% |
| Northern desert lizards | 12 | 8 | −33% |
| All snakes | 16 | 20 | +25% |
| Southern desert snakes | 1 | 8 | +700% |
| Northern desert snakes | 15 | 11 | −27% |

3. *Interior-to-edge* hypothesis. An interior environment along the center of a peninsula is sandwiched between edge environments on each side, and the result is a kind of lateral environmental heterogeneity.

Peninsulas also frequently become progressively narrower toward their ends. Therefore, although the frequency of edge species remains the same along a peninsula, interior species decrease from base to tip. The tip of a peninsula is all edge habitat.

4. *Environmental heterogeneity* hypothesis. The diversity of habitats, and thus the diversity of species, decreases from base to tip along the peninsula.
5. *Environmental gradient* hypothesis. A gradient in environmental conditions—say from cool to warm, or moist to dry—extends gradually along the peninsula, and fewer species tolerate the conditions of this gradient near the peninsula tip.
6. *Sequence of barriers* hypothesis. Barriers to species dispersal are scattered along the peninsula, and the species diversity pattern reflects the differing abilities of the species spreading from the mainland to cross these barriers.
7. A combination of two or more of the above hypotheses. Note that hypotheses 4 and 5 would also explain a gradient of species diversity anywhere [such as within the mainland (Emlen, 1978)], whereas the other hypotheses depend on the distinctive shape of peninsulas.

Which hypothesis does the available evidence support? The equilibrium colonization-extinction idea was tested by a computer simulation model of rodent species distributions on the Baja California peninsula (Figure 3.15) (Taylor and Regal, 1978; Gilpin, 1981). The investigators found that this hypothesis could explain the rodent pattern observed, but that the model would accurately describe the pattern only if somewhat unrealistic assumptions were made. In other words, the colonization-extinction mechanism is possible for the rodent pattern but its probability remains in doubt. Some support for the environmental gradient hypothesis was provided by a study of a group of lizards on Baja California and a similar mainland Mexican desert area (Seib, 1980).

None of the other hypotheses, apparently, has been tested. Farmers have long known that the climate of peninsulas is strongly modified by the surrounding matrix of water. In cold regions, fruits can often only be grown on peninsulas, because there the water ameliorates the climate and decreases the probability of frost. To some degree, the climate is modified according to the width of the peninsula and how far inland the climate can change, in other words, the width of the edge effect. This supports the interior-to-edge hypothesis. In the rodent study of Baja California (Figure 3.15), the authors considered progressive changes in climate, and hence vegetation, along the peninsula (that is, the environmental gradient hypothesis) to be the most reasonable alternative to their colonization-extinction model. Some cases of constant or increasing species diversity from base to tip along a peninsula are also known (Figure

**Figure 3.16** *Interdigitating peninsulas in a landscape. In upper-right portion, wooded peninsulas project into the field area, and field peninsulas project into the wooded area. Contour plowing and strip cropping (alternating crops) are widespread in this landscape of rolling hills. Note also the abundance of corridors, though some have breaks. Near Millersburg, Ohio, United States. (Courtesy of USDA Soil Conservation Service.)*

3.15; Savage, 1960; Seib, 1980; Busack and Hedges, 1984), which warrant further study.

We know of no published data on finer scale peninsulas within a landscape (Figure 3.16). However, our preliminary observations in New Jersey oak woods suggest that the pattern of gradually decreasing species diversity from base to tip also occurs at the landscape scale, at least for birds and vascular plants. We suggest that the decreasing species diversity from base to tip of a peninsula is caused mainly by the loss of interior species as the peninsula narrows or the edge widens, that is, as the interior-to-edge ratio decreases. The tip seems to differ markedly from the middle and base of the peninsula in terms of the species present. Nevertheless, it seems likely that the interior-to-edge mechanism combines or interacts with at least one other mechanism, the colonization-extinction process, to produce the commonly observed pattern of decreasing species diversity along a peninsula.

Figure 3.16 shows the striking case of **peninsular interdigitation** where peninsulas of one landscape element type interfinger with those of a second type. In this example, cultivated peninsulas interdigitate with forested peninsulas. This pattern is widespread and results from the basic process of erosion. Vegetation of low stream gully areas interdigitates with vegetation of drier ridge areas between the stream gullies. We hypothesize that the interdigitation zone is an area of high total species diversity, since two vegetation types are in close proximity. However, it would also appear to be a zone of low diversity of interior species, since interior species would be concentrated in the mainlands.

Another peninsular pattern appears to be common at the continental level. At the tips of many mountain ranges, population differentiation or speciation is often present. At the southern tip of the Appalachian Mountains, the Frazier fir (*Abies fraseri*) has speciated from balsam fir (*A. balsamea*), which is widespread in the remainder of the peninsula and in the "mainland" of Canada (Braun, 1950). Several similar cases of mammals, birds, and trees are familiar at the southern end of the Rocky Mountains (Kendeigh, 1974; Rydberg, 1954). In these cases the differentiation may be related to isolation during the ice age, but probably results at least in part from the relative isolation at the tip of a peninsula (see also Emlen (1978) for bird density differences along the Florida peninsula). The differentiation process that produces distinctive populations within a species (Chapter 2) could also take place at the tips of (patch) peninsulas within a landscape. However, because patch turnover is so high the organisms at the tip are not isolated long enough to produce new species. Despite this fact, the idea of *population differentiation at peninsula tips* needs to be evaluated at various levels of scale, including the landscape.

## PATCH NUMBER AND CONFIGURATION

So far, we have focused on the characteristics of individual patches. However, patches generally do not exist singly but are numerous in a landscape.

A lively discussion has arisen on the critical question of how many nature reserves are needed to maximize the species diversity in a landscape. Does one large patch of a particular vegetation type contain a larger or smaller number of native species than the same total area subdivided into smaller patches (Wilson and Willis, 1975; Simberloff and Abele, 1976; Diamond and May, 1976; Terborgh, 1976; Higgs and Usher, 1980)? Although few data are available, it appears that a single large patch contains more species than several smaller patches, if a nearby portion of a landscape is considered. More species are found in several patches if the patches are widely scattered (Forman et al., 1976; Cole, 1981; Forman, 1981). These differences occur because all the patches contain similar edge species, but the large patches usually contain sensitive interior species also. In addition, widely scattered patches are located in somewhat different regional faunas and floras (species pools). Within a nearby portion of a landscape, Forman et al. (1976) concluded, more than three large patches are needed to maximize landscape species diversity. Based on several characteristics, Game and Peterken (1984) concluded that at least nine woods are needed.

The importance of patch numbers will be considered further in Chapter 5. However, it bears mention here that patch density is critical in wildlife management and forestry (Julander and Jeffery, 1964; Resler, 1972; Telfer, 1974; Thomas et al., 1976; Hansson, 1977; Giles, 1978; Vance, 1976; Martin, 1980; Lyon and Jensen, 1980).

In understanding a landscape, we must determine the number of patches in each of at least four categories. (1) How many patches of each community type are present? (2) Of each patch origin or causative mechanism (remnant, disturbance, etc.? (3) Of each patch size? (4) And of each patch shape?

Determining the numbers of patches in each of these four categories is not difficult in some landscapes. A subsample of each category can then be selected for measurement of the species, energy, or nutrient component of interest. By simple multiplication, the status of the component in the patches of a landscape is thus estimated, together with a measure of variability.

However, this estimation is inadequate for a full understanding because the spatial configuration or juxtaposition among the patches has been ignored (Kozova, 1982). For example, let us consider a landscape with ten patches clustered at one end, versus a second landscape with ten patches scattered evenly throughout. In this case the patches are habitations. In the first landscape a person may easily meander over to neighbors' homes after supper to discuss the weather, borrow a toilet plunger, or start a romance. Even underground, the sewage of the neighboring houses quietly coalesces in the ground water. In contrast, the second landscape has the same number of habitations; but since they are scattered, little of such interaction takes place. The flows of energy, nutrients, and species among patches in the two landscapes differ dramatically because of their patch configurations.

Are there particular spatial configurations that are repeated in different landscapes? Standard statistical techniques are available to evaluate spatial patterns (Godron, 1966; Kershaw, 1975; Chessel, 1978; Daget, 1979). These tests help determine whether patches are random, regular, or aggregated, or whether positive or negative associations among patches of different categories are present. Finding these patterns provides insight not only into the cause of the patches but also into the potential for patch interaction. For example, familiar nonrandom patterns of patches are seen in limestone (karst or sink) topography, dendritic (branching) stream systems, along roads, railroads, and property lines, or encircling towns.

Interactions among patches are discussed in Chapters 6 and 10. However, let us mention here certain interactive aspects of patch configuration. A patch may be the source of a disturbance such as a fire or pest explosion. If the patch is isolated in a landscape, the disturbance may go no farther. On the other hand, if the patch is near others like it, the disturbance may readily spread. Or a different patch type—such as a marsh or bog—interspersed with the first patches, may be an effective barrier. Whether a particular patch is a source of, or a barrier to, a disturbance, the configuration of patches in space will be crucial to the spread of the disturbance.

If the disturbance in turn destroys the patch, we are led to the interesting conclusion that a *negative feedback system* with stimulatory and inhibitory loops is operating. The more patches there are, the more the disturbance spreads. The more the disturbance spreads, the fewer patches there are. The fewer patches there are, the less the disturbance spreads. The less the disturbance spreads, the more patches develop. The more patches there are, the more the disturbance spreads—and on and on it goes. The system has a stimulatory loop and an inhibitory loop. The result is stability, as both patch density and disturbance level oscillate within a limited range. Understanding stability at the landscape level is an important challenge (Chapter 12), and the search for possible operating feedback systems may prove extremely rewarding in our further consideration of landscape structural characteristics.

## SUMMARY

Patches are prominent and ubiquitous structural features of landscapes. Disturbance, heterogeneity of environmental resources, and introduction by people cause these patches of organisms, and the end result is highly diverse patterns of species dynamics, stability, and turnover among patches. Five patch types are recognized based on their differing origins: disturbance patches, remnant patches, environmental resource patches, planted patches, and habitations. Environmental resource patches are relatively permanent, but the other types vary widely in persistence depending upon whether the causative disturbance is single or chronic.

Patch size is a major variable that affects biomass, production, and nutrient storage per unit area, as well as species composition and diversity. However, species diversity of a landscape patch appears to be mainly determined by habitat diversity and the disturbance regime. Patch shape is also of major importance in the landscape, particularly as a result of the edge effect. The interior-to-edge ratio appears useful in interpreting species differences in isodiametric and elongated patches. The latter include the peninsula, a common shape of patch that has been little studied. Once we understand the effects of patch origin, size, and shape, we must examine the lesser-known but equally critical significance of patch number and configuration.

## QUESTIONS

1. What are the most common patch shapes in your own landscape? How do shapes of patches vary in different landscapes?
2. What might cause the gradient of decreasing species diversity from base to tip in a peninsula?
3. How do patches in a landscape differ from islands in an oceanic archipelago? In a patch you know, roughly what proportion of the species appear to be isolated from surrounding patches?
4. What human activities are focused on patch edges? How do they affect the energy, nutrients, or species of those edges?
5. How do you define disturbance? Can it be defined independently of stability?
6. Which of the patch types described lasts the shortest time? Which is not caused by disturbance? Which is caused only by human disturbance? Which has the highest turnover rate? Which is not found at other levels of scale? Which has the highest species diversity?
7. Patches are prominent in the visual landscape. What combinations of patch sizes and shapes, irrespective of species, are most pleasing to the eye?
8. Is it possible for a patch caused by one mechanism to change into a patch caused by a different mechanism? Explain.
9. What is the optimum size and shape of a housing development based on ecological criteria? How about a field for crops? A logging operation? A grazing area? Why?
10. What feedback systems involving patches might be hypothesized to be operating in a landscape?
11. In what other areas of human knowledge do we study the origin, size, shape, number, and configuration of items? Are the patterns for these characteristics universal, or are there special patterns in each area of human knowledge?

# 4
# *Corridors*

*A barely discernible track, marked in the earth by the four-footed
dwellers of the forest. I have walked along the track many times, yet
. . . I never know whether I shall meet several wild neighbors or none.
They all use the trail.*

**Helen Hoover, 1963**
*The Long-Shadowed Forest*

The use of corridors for transportation, protection, resources, and aesthetics permeates nearly every landscape in one way or another. The
most obvious use of corridors is for transportation. Railroads, highways,
and canals have the direct economic benefit of efficiently moving people
and goods across a landscape. Hiking trails provide a recreation function.
Livestock paths are an efficient mechanism for moving animals. Energy
is transported along power line and gas pipeline corridors. Indeed, the
construction, maintenance, and use of corridors involves not only the
energy expended by human muscles but increasingly the energy extracted
from fossil fuels.

With the onset of deforestation for agriculture a few millennia ago,
humankind faced a whole new set of problems, basically problems of
protection. Corridors have been used for defense in warfare (Seignobos,
1978). Fields have been cleared of rocks, and stone walls have been
constructed. Windbreaks are required to reduce crop desiccation and
soil loss by wind. Fences or thorny shrubs are needed to keep livestock
either in or out of a field. Vegetation strips are used to inhibit soil nutrient
loss and erosion by water. Barriers are erected to identify property boundaries, protect property, and provide privacy. Road, ditch, and canal banks
are protected with lines of vegetation. In addition, stream corridors protect
against excess water, sediment, and mineral nutrient flows.

Corridors provide more than protection, though; they also provide
resources. For example, wildlife is especially abundant in some corridors
and is a source of meat (Vance, 1976). Similarly, corridors are critical
resources in the conservation of various nongame species.

Plant products of many sorts come from hedgerows. Firewood is usually the most important product of wooded corridors, and is often critical
in times of war or fuel shortages. In landscapes where woodlots are scarce,

such corridors may be the only local source of firewood (Ferguson, 1916; The Shelterbelt Project, 1934; Steavenson et al., 1943). Firewood from hedgerows has been shown to cover the needs of a French parish where almost every house is heated with wood (Chevallier, 1980). Firewood is a major world fuel, especially in developing nations, and wooded corridors should be an important resource as its scarcity increases.

Wood from corridors is also used for fenceposts, furniture, and building (Pollard et al., 1974; The Shelterbelt Project, 1934; Steavenson et al., 1943; Harmon, 1948). With abundant light and with limited tree competition, productivity is high. Coppicing, the cutting of trunks and basal shoots to promote resprouting, is possible for many species and provides fuel wood of relatively constant diameter. Pollarding, the clipping of tree branches of species such as ash (*Fraxinus*) and elm (*Ulmus*), provides food for livestock (Rackham, 1976; Pollard et al., 1974). Pollarded species may thus be especially abundant in corridors near villages (Baudry and Burel, unpublished data)—an example of species distributions more related to socioeconomic than ecological factors.

Windbreaks planted with species for fruit production, such as apple (*Malus*) or hazel (*Corylus*), provide a double economic value. Berries are often abundant in wooded strips, and the delectable fruits of bird-dispersed shrubs such as blackberries (*Rubus*), raspberries, and elderberries (*Sambucus*) are harvested for human consumption.

For many people, corridors play a critical role in the aesthetics of the landscape. The Flemish paintings that depict the rural landscape, the tree-lined trails walked by hikers, and the rows of fenceposts that sprout leaves and flowers in the moist tropics are all manifestations of the beauty provided by corridors.

Perhaps the clearest way to pinpoint the roles and values of corridors is to try to visualize a suitable agricultural landscape without them. Such a prospect is not fantasy; hedgerow removal has been and is an active process in America, Britain, and France (Harmon, 1948; Pollard et al., 1974; Les Bocages, 1976; Vance, 1976).

## CORRIDORS AND THEIR ORIGINS

A hunter and a wild animal play out a life-and-death drama in which corridors often determine the winner. An animal moves quietly along a hedgerow between two fields and the hunter follows close behind. The animal turns along a dense stream corridor; so does the persistent hunter. In desperation, the scared animal glides through a woods to a powerline cut, and down its corridor. In exasperation, the puffing hunter spurts after it, but can't close in. Some time later, both hunter and hunted are heading for home—along different roads.

The hunter and the hunted both know the landscape is crisscrossed with corridors. In simplest terms, **corridors** are narrow strips of land which differ from the matrix on either side. Corridors may be isolated strips, but are usually attached to a patch of somewhat similar vegetation. Thus, a hedgerow may be completely surrounded by open area but more commonly is attached to a woods, at least at one end. Similarly, powerline corridors connect open areas, and roads connect built up areas.

Nearly all landscapes are both divided and at the same time tied together by corridors (see Figure 4.1). These dual and somewhat opposing properties characterize the major roles of corridors in a landscape (Forman, 1983; Forman and Godron, 1984). Such roles are well known in the fields of transportation and communications, because paths, railroads, and powerlines tie different areas together, and in agriculture and water resource studies, because hedgerows and stream corridors form barriers between areas. Although corridors are of central importance in a range of disciplines, from economics to study of the visual landscape, our focus is on their ecological roles.

In the hunt described above, the corridors were used as routes or conduits for movement. Corridors perform several other critical functions (analyzed in Chapters 10 and 11)—they act as species filters (Figure 4.1),

**Figure 4.1** *Antelope crossing a superhighway corridor with roadside and median vegetation. Vehicles and people move along the corridor, while pronghorn antelope (Antilocarpa americana) and blowing soil particles cross it. The corridor area is also a source of heat, salt, and vehicular outputs that influence adjacent areas. Shortgrass plains, western USA. (Photographer unknown; Courtesy of Defenders of Wildlife.)*

as habitats for certain species, and as sources of environmental and biological effects on their surroundings.

In this chapter we focus on their structural characteristics. Corridors may differ in origin, width, degree of connectivity, amount of curvilinearity, whether a stream is present, and whether they are interconnected to form a network. Linear features characterize all landscapes, but stand out especially in landscapes with major human influence. The structural characteristics of corridors appear to have a strong effect on the ecology of a landscape.

Corridors originate in the same ways as patches (Chapter 3). *Disturbance corridors* result from disturbance in a strip, for example, linear logging operations, railroads, and powerline cuts (Niering and Goodwin, 1974; Anderson et al., 1977). *Remnant corridors* result from disturbance in the surrounding matrix. Thus, a strip of trees left from cutting a forest, or a strip of native prairie alongside a railroad that runs through cultivated land, are both remnants of former extensive vegetation (Pollard et al., 1974). *Environmental resource corridors* result from the heterogeneous, linear distribution of environmental resources through space. Stream corridors or animal paths along narrow ridges are examples (Schlosser and Karr, 1981b). *Planted corridors* such as shelterbelts, expressways through suburban areas, or many low thorny hedgerows, result from human planting (Van Eimern et al., 1964; The Shelterbelt Project, 1934; Pollard et al., 1974). Finally, *regenerated corridors* result from regrowth of a strip in a disturbed area. Many hedgerows grown up along fences, and some urban green belts, are regenerated corridors.

The species dynamics—that is, the direction and rate of change of species over time—within a corridor vary widely according to its origin. In fact, the persistence or stability of the corridor itself follows directly from the mechanism causing it. For example, an environmental resource corridor like a stream corridor is relatively permanent, whereas a disturbance corridor like a linear logging operation may be short-lived, as forest trees regrow.

Just as in the case of patches, the other overriding factor controlling corridor stability and species dynamics is management of the corridor. Vegetation along powerlines, railroads, and roadsides (Figure 4.1) may be repeatedly sprayed with herbicides or, alternatively, managed with natural succession for a stable aesthetic diversity of native wildflowers or shrubs (Niering and Goodwin, 1974). Tops of hedgerow shrubs may be clipped and interwoven with the bases to form an impassable barrier (Pollard et al., 1974). In such cases the human effort in management is directed at the corridor. Human activities in the adjacent landscape elements are often also of primary importance in maintaining a corridor. The plowing, cutting, or grazing of fields may prevent an area from turning into a forest that would effectively obliterate a hedgerow. Most corridors, therefore, except for environmental resource corridors, owe their continued existence to chronic and major human inputs of energy, particularly fossil fuel. These inputs may be either in the corridor area itself or in the area adjacent to it.

## CORRIDOR STRUCTURE

### The Vulture's View

The vulture or eagle gliding over a landscape in search of food sees the forms of corridors from above (Figure 4.2). The degree of corridor **curvilinearity** (or linearity) is conspicuous. Stream corridors in mountainous terrain are often relatively straight, while in flat terrain they wind exten-

**Figure 4.2** *Stream corridors winding through a banana plantation. Note breaks and nodes in the highly connected and curvilinear corridors (gallery forest), that link mountains above with lowland tropical forest below. Southwestern Costa Rica (R. Forman.)*

sively. Despite several negative ecological impacts, winding streams are often straightened for purposes of boat transportation, drainage, or flood control. Railroad, powerline, and hedgerow corridors tend to be especially straight. The primary ecological importance of the degree of corridor curvilinearity has to do with movement along the corridor. The straighter the corridor, the shorter the distance and, generally, the faster the movement between two points in the landscape. It takes longer for water in a stream, animals in a wooded strip, or hikers on a path to cross a landscape via a winding corridor.

The vulture may also see irregularities in the width of the corridor (Figure 4.2). **Breaks** in the corridor are long or short discontinuities (Figure 4.3). They appear to be of considerable significance for movement both along and across corridors (Schreiber and Graves, 1977). **Narrows,** where the corridor has the form of an isthmus, must have similar though less pronounced effects. Patches of similar vegetation attached to the corridor appear in the form of **nodes** (or **mini-nodes,** if widenings of the corridor

**Figure 4.3** *Wide forested corridor and narrow hedgerow corridors connecting forested nodes. The node in center foreground is connected to five corridors; a distinct break is evident in the foreground corridor. Northern New York State. (R. Forman.)*

**126** LANDSCAPE STRUCTURE

are too small to be recognized as separate landscape elements). Such nodes are significant in their own right relative to the patch principles described in the previous chapter. Additionally, these patches are significant in the movement of objects, since they are attached to the corridor conduits (Figure 4.3) (Merriam, 1984).

The distribution of breaks and nodes along corridors is decidedly non-random. Several distinct patterns may be recognized. Nodes are particularly common at the intersections of corridors. An interchange area of vegetation at the intersection of two major highways is a node; a tiny cluster of trees at the intersection of hedgerows is a mini-node. In the typical *dendritic* pattern of stream corridors, that is, tree-like branching, we often see nodes surrounding the joining of two tributaries. Nodes are also frequently found at the concave sides of sharp stream bends in flat terrain. These nodes are often wooded on flood plains. The basic dendritic pattern of erosion imprinted on landscapes apparently dictates many of the locations of corridor nodes and breaks. A series of nodes attached to a long corridor, such as a stream corridor, has the appearance of a *string of lights* or beads. This pattern may be useful in planning and management because it provides many connected species sources that facilitate re-colonization when species disappear from patches in the landscape.

Breaks, too, result to a large extent from direct human activities. For example, breaks in hedgerows are frequently found within 30 meters (m) of the end of a plowed field, for the simple reason that farmers commonly move their farm machinery to the adjoining field at such a point (Figure 4.3). Breaks in the continuity of vegetation and fauna along country roads are characteristic, because the roads often pass through villages where roadside vegetation is absent or different (Getz et al., 1978). Breaks are also common where one type of corridor crosses another type of corridor.

**Connectivity** is a measure of how connected or spatially continuous a corridor is, which may be quantified simply by the number of breaks per unit length of corridor. Since the presence or absence of breaks in a corridor is considered the most important factor in determining the effectiveness of both the conduit and barrier functions, connectivity is the primary measure of corridor structure (Merriam, 1984; Baudry, 1984; Forman and Godron, 1984).

## The Hiker's View

The hiker, like the hunter and the hunted, spends a large proportion of travel time inside corridors. In this sense, the hiker gets a biased view of the landscape, since the foreground, at least, is almost always corridor vegetation and fauna (Figure 4.4). This is reminiscent of some early travelers exploring the tropics. As they proceeded up narrow rivers by boat, fascinating exotic vegetation and animals were described for the world

**Figure 4.4** *Footpath corridor through temperate rainforest. Corridor soil is compacted beneath an unbroken canopy of cedar (*Thuja plicata*) and douglas-fir (*Pseudotsuga menziesii*). Olympic Peninsula, Washington, United States. (Bob and Ira Spring.)*

to read about. These exciting stories primarily depicted streamside vegetation, highly specialized species in corridors that snaked through the extensive surrounding forest or savanna.

Although the types of corridors on earth vary widely, a number of structural characteristics common to many types may be recognized. Most have a sharp change in species composition from center to edges. Most have a very different central zone bounded by two side strips that may be similar, depending on the nature of the surrounding landscape elements (Figures 4.4 and 4.5). The beaten down path for hikers, the ruts of a wagon or logging road, the pavement of a highway, the track area of a railroad, and the water of a stream corridor, canal, or irrigation ditch

**Figure 4.5** *Trough effect of road corridor. Road corridor includes the road surface and roadside (verge) areas. The distinct but sparse roadside vegetation is absent in this surrounding jack pine* (Pinus banksiana) *forest. Western New Brunswick, Canada.* (R. Forman.)

are all used to transport people, goods, or resources. But all also function as a partial internal barrier between the two sides of a corridor.

The principles relating to corridors in this chapter appear to apply just as well to corridors of vegetation of greater height than the adjacent landscape elements, such as hedgerows, as to those that are lower, like a trail through shrubland. The degree of difference in stature between a corridor and its surroundings does have an important effect on how wide the edge effect is in a corridor. For example, a wooded stream corridor in a grassland may have a wide edge controlled by wind from the grassland. On the other hand, a strip of prairie vegetation surrounded by hay fields, or a flood plain woods winding through an upland forest, receives little wind from the matrix, and may have narrow edges or may gradually intergrade with the matrix.

If you hike along a logging road, a paved road, or a power-line cut through woods, you are apt to feel hotter on sunny days, and cooler on cold windy days, than if you did not walk in the corridor (Figure 4.5). The main factor in this case is the canopy opening, which permits more solar radiation and wind to enter. It is like walking in a giant *trough.* The environment in the trough is both more extreme and more variable than in the adjacent woods. However, when hiking along a narrow path through a woods one may be walking down strips of low plants that are absent or uncommon in the surrounding woods, and that result from the disturbance of litter and from soil compaction (by hikers' feet) (Figure 4.4). The microclimate of the path differs little from that of the woods, since the forest canopy over the path is basically unchanged.

The inverse of the trough is a wooded corridor through open country. The following example of a class returning from a field trip in agricultural land near a prairie-forest boundary in the United States illustrates how different organisms respond to such a corridor. When the bus entered a long double row of trees bordering an avenue, where arching branches touched high above the road, one student observed, "This dark tunnel we've entered gives me claustrophobia." Her neighbor countered, "Finally we're out of that dusty barren land; now we can enjoy the lush intimate woods." The first student grew up in prairie country, the second in a forested landscape. Species, like these students, have different environmental preferences. The microenvironments within a tree-lined avenue and within a hedgerow differ sharply from their surroundings; hence so do the species found there.

## Microenvironment Within a Corridor

In this section we will discuss the hedgerow, but the general principles can be extended to many other types of microenvironments within corridors. Solar radiation, wind, and precipitation are normally the three major inputs to a hedgerow. A hedgerow has lower *albedo* (i.e., radiation reflection) than a field, and so absorbs more heat energy. During the day the sunny side of a hedgerow often has higher soil temperatures than the shady side by 5° to 10°C (Figure 4.3). Air temperature only differs by about 0.5° to 2°C. A shaded ground layer environment that has relative humidity higher than in adjacent fields is generally present (Wales, 1972; Dierschke, 1974; Guyot and Seguin, 1976; Damagnez, 1976).

At the top of the hedgerow, wind velocity exceeds that in the adjacent field, whereas at the bottom center of the hedgerow it is considerably lower than in the field. Even on the upwind side of the hedgerow, wind velocity is lower near the ground. The entire downwind side has reduced wind velocity. However, for dense, relatively nonpermeable hedgerows, considerable turbulence will take place in strong winds (Pollard et al., 1974; Caborn, 1976).

Evaporation from the soil in a hedgerow is less than from that in a field, but plant transpiration must be higher, perhaps much higher, because of wind exposure (Ballard, 1979; Geiger, 1965). Snow persists longer in portions of temperate hedgerows because of accumulation by wind and subsequent shading. Thus, more soil moisture is expected in spring. Water percolation through the soil is considered greater if the hedgerow is on a slope and impedes surface runoff (Merot and Ruellan, 1980; Buson, 1979). In contrast, on flatter land, percolation is probably lower than in the field because of hedgerow evapotranspiration (Blavoux et al., 1976; Ballard, 1979). Soil in hedgerows typically has more organic matter than do field soils. The presence of stones in hedgerows provides suitable habitats for special species such as lichens and mice (Bates, 1937; Sinclair et al., 1967; Roze, 1981). Less soil is blown away from hedgerows than from fields. More soil may be deposited by wind (aeolian deposits), gradually producing a low ridge along the hedgerow (Harmon, 1948; Damagnez, 1976).

In short, microenvironmental conditions vary widely from top to bottom, and from one side to the other of a hedgerow. The top of a hedgerow is perhaps subjected to greater environmental extremes than the adjoining field, but the inside bottom of a hedgerow is a significantly more mesic microhabitat.

Since a corridor extends for some distance in a landscape, it is apt to differ also at one end from the other. Commonly, a **gradient** is present; that is, gradual changes in species composition and relative abundance occur along the corridor, as has been suggested for peninsulas (Chapter 3). The gradient may correspond to a gradual environmental change, or a colonization-extinction pattern, or may be a product of disturbance.

## LINE CORRIDORS

There are three basic types of corridor structure. They are independent of origin, human use, and type of landscape. Much of the richness and functioning of corridors arises from these structures.

**Line corridors,** such as most paths, roads, hedgerows, property boundaries, drainage ditches, and irrigation channels, are narrow bands essentially dominated throughout by edge species. **Strip corridors** are wider bands, with a central interior environment that contains an abundance of interior organisms (Figure 4.6). **Stream corridors** border water courses and vary in width according to the size of the stream. They control water and mineral nutrient runoff, thus reducing flooding, siltation, and soil fertility loss (Figure 4.7). Some overlap among the three basic types exists. For example, edge species may move in all three, or a wide stream corridor may also function as a strip corridor for movement of patch interior species. Networks, formed by intersecting or interconnecting corridors, are discussed in Chapter 5.

At least seven types of line corridors have been studied ecologically: roads (including roadsides or verges), railroads, dikes, ditches, power-

## Line corridors

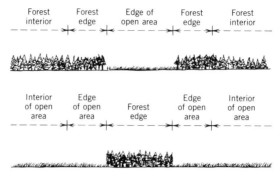

## Strip corridors

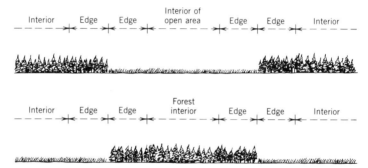

**Figure 4.6** *Comparison of line and strip corridors. From Forman (1983).* *(Courtesy of* Ekologia CSSR.)

lines (transmission lines), hedgerows, and herbaceous or shrubby strips for wildlife management. Apparently no species is completely restricted to line corridors. The line corridor environment and species are highly affected by conditions in the adjacent matrix, such as wind, human activities, and species and soil present.

### Hedgerows as Line Corridors

One of the most prominent features in a moist temperate landscape is the hedgerow, a line corridor bordering a pasture or cultivated field. Agriculture and hedgerows apparently developed together and today coexist over about 10% of our planet's land surface.

Early studies recognized hedgerows as part of agriculture or wildlife management (Section d'Agriculture de l'Institut de France, 1822; Dic-

**132** LANDSCAPE STRUCTURE

**Figure 4.7** *Line, strip and stream corridors. The narrow road (including roadside) is a line corridor. Both the open strips and the intervening woods are strip corridors. In the foreground and in the distance are stream corridors, running from left to right, that help control erosion and flooding. Open wildlife management areas are planted with panic grass (*Panicum*) primarily to attract higher populations of white-tailed deer (*Odocoileus virginianus*) and wild turkey (*Meleagris gallopavo*). Small bare spots indicate rodent burrows. Near Pearsall, Texas. (Courtesy of USDA Soil Conservation Service.)*

kerman, 1869; Powell, 1900; Ferguson, 1916; Alexander, 1932; Richards, 1928; Bates, 1937; Petrides, 1942; Hewes and Jung, 1981). The most significant contributions to hedgerow ecology emanate from multidisciplinary studies of many scholars in England (Pollard et al., 1974) and France (Les Bocages, 1976). In both countries, certain government programs had accelerated the removal of hedgerows, and new land-use problems had emerged. Windbreaks in grassland or overexploited landscapes have been studied for their function in protecting soil and plants (Van Eimern et al., 1964; Harmon, 1948; The Shelterbelt Project, 1934). The role of hedgerows in maintaining populations of game is often emphasized in wildlife management (McAtee, 1945; Yoakum et al., 1980; Yahner, 1983a, 1983b). Intriguing patterns of spatial structure and changing human-land interactions over time are described by geographers and historians (Lebeau, 1969; Rackham, 1976).

We will now focus on the origin, structure, and dynamics of hedgerows, including their characteristic flora and fauna. Throughout our analysis we will see that a theme of overriding importance is the degree of human interest in the origin and management of the hedgerow. A second important theme is the great difference in hedgerow structure; while some functions or patterns apply universally, other functions vary with structure.

**Hedgerow Origin and Structure.**   Hedgerows may be either planted, regenerated (spontaneous), or remnant (Forman and Godron, 1981). Planted hedgerows (Figure 4.3) usually are dominated by a single species such as hawthorn (*Crataegus*) or cypress (*Cupressus*) in Europe, and Osage orange (*Maclura*), pine (*Pinus*), or willow (*Salix*) in parts of the United States. The shrubs or trees are generally planted in a single row, though in **shelterbelts** they are planted in a number of rows. On slopes, a ditch (up to a meter in depth) and often a bank (up to 2 m high), with or without stones, may be constructed in addition to the plantings. Planted hedgerows tend to have dominants of equal age, relative homogeneity in vertical and horizontal structure, and rather low species diversity (Figure 4.3) (Pollard et al., 1974; Les Bocages, 1976).

In regenerated hedgerows, trees and/or shrubs grow along a fence, stone wall, or ditch, from seeds dispersed by animals and the wind (Figure 4.8). A fence attracts many birds that drop seeds and also limits cultivation and livestock grazing, thus permitting development of the hedgerow biota. In regenerated hedgerows spatial diversity and species diversity—particularly of bird-dispersed plant species—tend to be high.

Forest remnant hedgerows (Hooper, 1976) result from the process of forest clearing; for example, a row of trees and shrubs are commonly left along a property line. Such hedgerows generally have old individuals of various species, considerable spatial heterogeneity, high species diversity, and many forest species.

Hedgerow vegetation is exceptionally varied, primarily because of differences in hedgerow origin and management (Delelis-Dusollier, 1973; Roze, 1981). Several additional factors underlie differences in hedgerows, including:

**Figure 4.8** *Hedgerow regenerated along an old fence between fields. Near Millstone, New Jersey, United States. See Table 4.1 for common plant species of hedgerows in this landscape. (R. Forman.)*

1. *Whether shrubs, trees, or both shrubs and trees predominate.*
2. *Whether one or several species predominate(s).*
3. *Species composition.*
4. *Abundance of thorns.*
5. *Height and width.*
6. *Human-made structures such as ditches, banks, stone walls, woods, or wire fences.*

**Vegetation of Hedgerows.** About 500 to 600 vascular plant species are known to grow in hedgerows in England, although only half as many occur frequently enough to be thought of as hedgerow plants (Pollard et al., 1974). In the available studies (done in England, France, and New Jersey) no plant species is known to be limited to hedgerows. All species are found in other nearby habitats. Some plants are predominantly open field species, a few are forest interior species, and many are forest edge species. In general, hedgerows are similar to forest edges in vegetation. For example, Pollard et al. (1974) describe hedgerows as "woodland edges without the woods." In areas with an abundance of both woods and fields, hedgerow species are more common in either the woods or the fields. In a landscape with few woods, though, hedgerows are especially important, because some species may occur primarily in hedgerows, as in the case of endangered species in ditches (Ruthsatz, 1983). The predominant species of hedgerow trees and shrubs in temperate zone landscapes differ, although the genera are rather similar. For example, ash (*Fraxinus*), cherry (*Prunus*), oak (*Quercus*), elm (*Ulmus*), maple (*Acer*), blackberry (*Rubus*), and rose (*Rosa*) are common hedgerow plants in both Europe and North America (Table 4.1).

The origins of hedgerows differ among landscapes. In New Jersey, almost all the hedgerows are regenerated (between fields) (Figure 4.8). The Great Plains hedgerows in North America are almost all planted; the grassland climate does not support extensive forests. European hedgerows are largely planted but include some regenerated and remnant hedgerows. Hedgerow origin plays an important role in determining the types of species present (Table 4.1). Almost all the woody plant species in the New Jersey regenerated hedgerows are bird-dispersed. The Great Plains species are largely wind-dispersed, although they mostly arrived by planting. English hedgerows have mainly wind-dispersed tree species, but bird-dispersed shrub species. Note that all the hedgerow areas include at least some thorny species that deter the movement of livestock. The North American hedgerows have several nonnative species in abundance. The reasons for some of these patterns remain to be studied.

Several other important variables in the landscape help determine what species predominate in hedgerows. For example, on the Isle of Purbeck in England, mixed hedgerows predominated on sandy soils, blackthorn (*Prunus spinosa*) hedgerows on one type of clay soil and elm (*Ulmus*) hedgerows on another, and hawthorn (*Crataegus*) hedgerows on chalk soils (Hooper, 1976). Ash (*Fraxinus*), elm (*Ulmus*), and field maple (*Acer campestre*) were about twice as frequent in unmanaged hedgerows as in those that were regularly trimmed. Bramble (*Rubus fruticosus*), rose (*Rosa* spp.), honeysuckle (*Lonicera periclymenum*), and ivy (*Hedera helix*) were about twice as frequent in the managed hedgerows. In central England, hedgerows between fields were observed to be largely planted and managed while those by brooks were largely regenerated. Those by gardens and houses were planted and managed and contained many nonnative species (Willmot, 1980). Hedgerows by roads had more woody species than those between fields. In central Africa, particular species were planted in hedgerows that were maintained for defense (Seignobos, 1978).

Microenvironmental conditions, and hence plant species composition and abundance, varies in different parts of a hedgerow. For example, measurements of a hedgerow in Ille et Vilaine in France revealed differences in the species of woody plants, herbs, and mosses growing on the sunny versus the shady sides of an east-west oriented hedgerow (J. Baudry, personal communication). The number of woody species did not differ significantly, but the sunny side had more than twice as many herbaceous species as the shady side. Mosses were restricted to the shady side. Of the thirty-six species present, fewer than one quarter grew on both sides of the hedgerows. As expected, most of the species limited to the sunny side were open field species and most of those limited to the shady side were woodland species. Forest interior species (such as herbs) could be expected to grow near the center of a hedgerow in the most shaded area.

## Animal Communities of Hedgerows

A large proportion of the fauna in an agricultural landscape is observed at some time in hedgerows. For example, Hooper (1970) estimates about four out of five woodland wildlife species in England now breed in hedgerows. Similarly, about two out of three lowland terrestrial birds, and the same proportion of lowland mammals, use hedgerows. The hedgerows provide access to foods in adjacent fields, as well as providing cover from predators. However, striking seasonal changes occur in the structure of the bird, mammal, reptile, amphibian, and insect communities of hedgerows (Sinclair et al., 1967; Pollard and Relton, 1970; Wegner and Merriam, 1979; Martin, 1980; Yoakum et al., 1980).

In view of the high proportion of bird-dispersed plants in most hedgerows, a positive feedback system involving plants and birds is evident. The plants produce fruits that attract large numbers of birds. The birds disperse the seeds and they in turn produce more of the plants (Debussche et al., 1982; McDonnell and Stiles, 1983; McDonnell, 1984). Avian diversity is relatively high in hedgerows for both feeding and nesting species (McAtee, 1945; Harmon, 1948; Pollard et al., 1974; Yoakum et al., 1980).

While birds are conspicuous in hedgerows, mammals appear to be scarce because most are nocturnal or secretive. In the New Jersey hedgerows, white-footed mice (*Peromyscus*), woodchucks (*Marmota*), and deer (*Odocoileus*) are among the most common species in summer. Hedgerows also provide cover for woodland rodents such as bank voles (*Clethrionomys*) and eastern chipmunks (*Tamias*) (Pollard and Relton, 1970; Eldridge, 1971; Wegner and Merriam, 1979; Yahner, 1983b). Other mammals using hedgerow cover include rabbits (*Oryctolagus*), squirrels (*Sciurus*) (Harmon, 1948), red-back voles (*Clethrionomys*) (Sinclair et al.,

TABLE 4.1  **Hedgerow vegetation in Europe and North America.**[a]

| A. 110 Hedgerows Near Millstone, New Jersey (USA) | | B. Shelterbelts and Hedgerows in the Great Plains (USA) | |
|---|---|---|---|
| Black cherry (*Prunus serotina*) | B, E | Osage orange (*Maclura pomifera*) | M, T |
| Sassafras (*Sassafras albidum*) | B, E | Cottonwood (*Populus deltoides*) | W |
| White ash (*Fraxinus americana*) | W, E | Green ash (*Fraxinus pennsylvanica*) | W |
| Choke cherry (*Prunus avium*) | B, N, E | Red cedar (*Juniperus virginiana*) | B |
| Pin oak (*Quercus palustris*) | B, M, E, F | Chinese elm (*Ulmus parvifolia*) | W, N |
| Red cedar (*Juniperus virginiana*) | B, O | Russian olive (*Elaeagnus angustifolius*) | N, T |
| | | Ponderosa pine (*Pinus ponderosa*) | W |
| Black haw (*Viburnum prunifolium*) | B, E, F | Box elder (*Acer negundo*) | W |
| Honeysuckle (*Lonicera japonica*) | B, N, E | Willow (*Salix*) | |
| Multiflora rose (*Rosa multiflora*) | B, N, T, O | Caragana (*Caragana arborescens*) | N |
| Blackberry, raspberry (*Rubus* spp.) | B, T, O, E | | |
| Poison ivy (*Toxicodendron radicans*) | B, E, F | | |
| Wild grape (*Vitis*) | B, E, F | | |

## C. 125 Hedgerows in a Small Area of Brittany, France

| | |
|---|---|
| Chene pedoncule (Quercus pendunculata) | B, M, E, F |
| Châtaignier (Castanea sativa) | M, E, F |
| Merisier (Prunus avium) | B, E |
| Aubépine (Crataegus monogyna) | B, T, E, F |
| Noisetier (Corylus avellana) | M, E, F |
| Eglantier (Rosa spp.) | B, T, E |
| Prunellier (Prunus spinosa) | B, T, E, O |
| Ajonc (Ulex europaeus) | W, O |
| Genêt (Sarothamnus scoparius) | W, O |
| Saule (Salix atrocinerea) | W, O, F |
| Houx (Ilex aquifolium) | B, F |
| Alisier (Sorbus terminalis) | B, F, E |
| Néflier (Mespilus germanica) | F, E |

## D. 121 Wiltshire, England Hedgerows

| | |
|---|---|
| Ash (Fraxinus excelsior) | W |
| Hazel (Corylus avellana) | W |
| Field maple (Acer campestre) | W |
| Oak (Quercus spp.) | M, B |
| Elm (Ulmus) | W |
| Ivy (Hedera helix) | B |
| Hawthorn (Crataegus monogyna) | B, T |
| Brambles (Rubus spp.) | B, T |
| Wild roses (Rosa spp.) | B, T |
| Blackthorn (Prunus spinosa) | B, T |
| Elder (Sambucus nigra) | B |
| Privet (Ligustrum vulgare) | B |

NOTE: Species are listed in the approximate order of abundance, with trees first and shrubs and vines second in each category. A. The New Jersey data (Figure 4.8) are from unpublished studies of J. Baudry and R. Forman. B. The Great Plains data are a synthesis of species widespread between Minnesota, North Dakota, Colorado, Oklahoma, and Missouri, based on The Shelterbelt Project (1934), Steavenson et al. (1943), McAtee (1945), and Harmon (1948). C. The Brittany data are unpublished data of J. Baudry. D. The Wiltshire data are from Grose (1957) as cited in Pollard et al. (1974) with oak and elm added, based on a broad survey over much of England.

[a]Abbreviations are as follows:

| | | |
|---|---|---|
| B, bird-dispersed | N, nonnative species | E, forest edge species |
| W, wind-dispersed | T, thorny species | F, forest interior species |
| M, mammal-dispersed | | O, old-field species |

1967), hedgehogs (*Erinaceus*), moles (*Talpidae*), common and pygmy shrews (*Sorex*), water shrews (*Microsorex*), harvest mice, and house mice (*Mus*) (Pollard et al., 1974).

Many hedgerow animal studies suggest that species diversity is higher there than in fields, apparently because of the microhabitat heterogeneity within the hedgerow (Lefeuvre et al., 1976). For example, the following birds use different portions of English hedgerows for different functions (Pollard et al., 1974):

|  | Nesting | Feeding |
| --- | --- | --- |
| Upper branches | Carrion crow, rook | Blue tit, chaffinch |
| Trunks and holes | Barn owl, jackdaw, starling | Treecreeper |
| Shrubs | Turtle dove, magpie | Fieldfare, redwing, robin |
| Herbs, low brambles | — | Goldfinch, Greenfinch |
| Ground | Skylark | Hedge sparrow, song thrush, wren |

There is a high species diversity of invertebrates in hedgerows as well as vertebrates. Thus, summer insect diversity was higher in an English hedgerow than in an adjoining bean field and pasture (Lewis, 1969b). The most abundant groups in the hedgerows (with number of individuals) were as follows:

716 Parasitoids on other insects—*Hymenoptera* (especially *Chalcidoidea, Proctotrupoidea, Ichneumonoidea*)
641 Flies—*Diptera* (especially *Empididae, Muscidae*)
245 Plant lice and aphids—*Homoptera* (especially *Psyllidae, Aphididae*)
205 Plant bugs—*Hemiptera* (especially *Miridae*)
204 Beetles—*Coleoptera* (especially *Nitidulidae*)
168 Thrips—*Thysanoptera*
  50 Other insects
2229 Total

Hymenopterans, especially insect "parasites," and dipterans (the flies) were most abundant, but overall there is a lack of dominance (high evenness) among the insect groups. Although insect diversity of the hedgerow exceeded that of the bean field and pasture, the density of insects was highest in the pasture. Also, a large number of insects was collected in the air downwind of the hedgerow.

Hedgerow animal diversity has also been correlated with various attributes of the flora. For example, in France, the number of species of plant bugs (*Miridae*) was directly correlated with the number of hedgerow plant species (Ehanno, 1976). Vegetation structure, as measured by the number of layers in a hedgerow, has also been related to faunal diversity. Hence in Europe, about 20 species of breeding birds are common in hedgerows with well developed shrub and tree layers. With either layer absent, however, only about seven to eight bird species are expected (Constant et al., 1976). In two New Jersey hedgerows, 84 and 168 meters in length, with tree and shrub layers present, we observed 15 individuals in each hedgerow during the breeding season, representing six and eight bird species, respectively. On the other hand, in a nearby hedgerow 384 meters in length, where cattle had essentially eliminated the shrub layer, only five individuals of four species were found. Thus vertical hedgerow structure, particularly the shrub layer, is a key determinant of the animal community present.

Animal abundance in hedgerows has also been correlated with plant species composition. In 1 kilometer lengths of hedgerow in Brittany, France, Constant et al. (1976) found an average of (a) 49 birds of 20 species in an oak-dominated hedgerow and (b) 20 birds of 10 species in a coniferous hedgerow. The oak-dominated hedgerow had at least twice the density and diversity of birds as the coniferous hedgerow. In England, oak and hawthorn hedgerows appear to support the most diverse insect fauna (Pollard et al., 1974). In contrast, hedgerow origin rather than vegetation was found to be the best correlate with development of snail faunas (Cameron et al., 1980).

Finally, hedgerows are of critical importance in a landscape with few woods, because forest animals, as in the case of forest plants discussed above, may be essentially limited to hedgerows. This pattern has been observed for reptiles in western France and for birds in several countries (Chapman, 1939; Snow, 1965; Tomek, 1973; Wiens, 1973; Wiens and Dyer, 1975; Saint-Girons and Duguy, 1976; Martin, 1980; Bongiorno, 1982; Yahner, 1983a).

## Other Types of Line Corridors

Several other types of line corridors that crisscross landscapes have been studied:

1. Roads, including roadsides or verges (Clements, 1920; Bates, 1937; Buckner, 1957; Hodson, 1966; Joselyn et al., 1968; Lagerwerff and Specht, 1970; Smith, 1971; Oetting and Cassel,1971; Hofstra and Hall, 1971; Taylor, 1971; Baker, 1971; Yapp, 1973; Oxley et al.,

1974; Puglisi et al., 1974; Getz et al., 1978; Collins et al., 1978; Rost and Bailey, 1979; Irwin and Peek, 1983).
2. Railroads (Thellung, 1905; Matthies, 1925; Messenger, 1968; Niemi, 1969; Suominen, 1969; Stapleton and Kiviat, 1979; Muehlenbach, 1979; Lienenbecker and Raabe, 1981).
3. Dikes (Nip-Van der Voort et al., 1979).
4. Ditches (McAtee, 1945; Marsh and Luey, 1982; Ruthsatz, 1983).
5. Power lines (transmission lines) (Niering and Goodwin, 1974; Johnson et al., 1979; Anderson, 1979; Kroodsma, 1982; Chasko and Gates, 1982).
6. Herbaceous and shrubby strips for wildlife management (Davison, 1941; Vance, 1976; Chapman and Feldhamer, 1982; Morgan and Gates, 1982).

These are all composed largely of edge species. In addition, most have a central portion relatively barren of terrestrial plants and animals, because of chronic disturbance. The disturbance, of course, results from the frequent use of the corridors by people for the transport of goods. Furthermore, the persistence of these corridors requires considerable human maintenance effort. Narrow stream or riparian corridors may also have a line corridor structure (Figure 4.2) (Sands, 1980; Schlosser and Karr, 1981a).

## STRIP CORRIDORS

The strip corridor with an edge effect on each side is wide enough to contain an interior environment (Figure 4.9). This fundamental ecological difference between line and strip corridors, based solely on width, has important functional ramifications (Forman and Godron, 1981; Forman, 1983). Strip corridors are generally less frequent than line corridors in a landscape. Superhighways (Bellis and Graves, 1971; Oxley et al., 1974; Ferris, 1979), wide strips of woods (Morgan and Gates, 1982), and wide power-lines (Figure 4.9) (Anderson et al., 1977; Hessing et al., 1981) are common examples. They exhibit the same characteristics as line corridors, except that down their center is an interior environment.

### Corridors Lower than Surroundings

The difference between strip and line corridors is illustrated by power lines that cross a forested area of Tennessee (in the United States), and which vary from 12 to over 90 m in width (Table 4.2). The bird community in the forest was quite dissimilar to that in all of the corridors (only 28 to 42% similarity). The avian communities in the narrow corridors 12

**Figure 4.9** *Power-line strip corridor. It connects cleared patches and also shows signs of erosion resulting from disturbance and the limited vegetation cover maintained. The forested area is composed of both coniferous (pine) and deciduous patches of various sizes and shapes, largely reflecting logging history and soil moisture patterns. Near Holly Springs, Mississippi, United States. (Courtesy of USDA Soil Conservation Service.)*

and 30.5 m in width were rather similar to one another (77% similarity). They were less similar, however, to the birds in the wide corridors (61 and 91.5 m in width) (62–74%). This was because the narrow power lines functioned as line corridors containing mainly edge species, while the wide power-lines functioned as strip corridors also containing open country birds.

TABLE 4.2. **Similarity of bird communities in forest and in four power-line corridors varying in width.**[a]

| Corridor width | Forest | Corridor Width | | | |
| | | 12 m | 30.5 m | 61 m | 91.5 m |
|---|---|---|---|---|---|
| 12 m | 42% | — | 77% | 72% | 62% |
| 30.5 m | 42% | | — | 74% | 64% |
| 61 m | 28% | | | — | 83% |
| 91.5 m | 32% | | | | — |

*Source:* Anderson et al., 1977. (Courtesy of the American Midland Naturalist.)

[a]To read the table, choose a corridor in the left column, and compare it with the forest or any corridor of the other columns. For example, the 12 m wide corridor and the forest have bird communities that are only 42% similar. A similarity of 100% would indicate two bird communities with identical species and abundances of each species.

Another common type of strip corridor is the strip cut or thinning in forest logging operations. In this case, strips of trees are clear cut to increase penetration of light and growth of the trees remaining in the intervening forested strips (Bucht and Elfving, 1977; McCreary and Perry, 1983). Growth of trees in the edges of the forested strips increases, but the interior trees are often not significantly affected.

### Corridors Higher than Surroundings

We expect species diversity patterns for edge and interior species to differ as a function of corridor width (Figure 4.10). Thus an extremely narrow corridor, such as a line of shrubs, would have few edge and almost no forest interior species. A somewhat wider wooded corridor would contain most of the edge species in the area, but still not have a microenvironment sufficiently favorable to support many interior species. A very wide corridor would contain a favorable microenvironment and would support many interior species.

Wide hedgerows, for example, might contain several forest interior species, but the community would probably be a highly depauperate representative of a forest interior community. In fact, in Figure 4.10, the horizontal axis would probably have to be extended a considerable distance before the interior species curve levels off. At this point—where the plant or animal community near the center of the landscape element is similar to the interior community of a large forest—we call the woods a patch rather than a corridor.

In a study of 30 hedgerows varying from 3 to 20 m in width, no significant effect of width on number of edge species of herbs was found (Figure 4.11). In contrast, the diversity of forest interior herb species

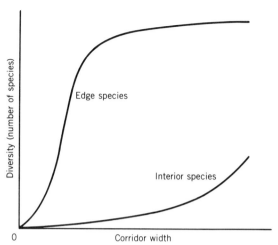

**Figure 4.10** *Hypothesized effect of narrow corridor width on edge and interior species. From J. Baudry and R. Forman (unpublished.)*

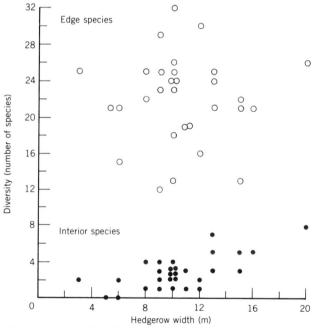

**Figure 4.11** *Width effect on edge and interior species in hedgerows. Each point represents the number of herbaceous species in a 100-m length of hedgerow. Thirty hedgerows were sampled near Hutcheson Memorial Forest, Millstone, New Jersey, United States, by J. Baudry and R. Forman.*

increased significantly with corridor width. Although the linear correlation between hedgerow width and forest herb diversity is significant, a closer look at the pattern reveals an apparent threshold at a width of about 12 m. From 3 to 12 m, the correlation between width and diversity is not significantly different from zero. The hedgerows greater than 12 m in width, however, average more than twice as many forest herbs as the narrower ones.

In summary, a corridor **width effect** is apparent. Higher forest herb diversity and abundance occurs in wider hedgerows, especially those wider than the apparent threshold of 12 m. Edge species diversity does not correlate with width. One study that evaluated the effect of hedgerow width on plants in narrow English shrub hedges found no hedgerow width effect up to 7 m (Helliwell, 1975). This result is consistent with the New Jersey study indicating that the width effect only occurs at widths greater than 12 m.

We conclude, therefore, that for herb species in the New Jersey study, hedgerows less than about 12 m wide are line corridors and those wider than 12 m are strip corridors. Note that the designation of the two corridor types is dependent on the organisms being considered, in this case, herbs. In landscape management, the natural community as a whole is the appropriate consideration for differentiating the two corridor types by width.

## STREAM CORRIDORS

A stream corridor is the band of vegetation along a stream that differs from the surrounding matrix (Figures 4.2 and 4.12). This corridor may cover the edges of the stream channel, the flood plain, the banks above the flood plain, and part of the upland above the banks (Wistendahl, 1958; Rowe, 1963; Wilson, 1967; Heller, 1969; Johnson, 1970; Van Hylckama, 1970; Hynes, 1975; Hasler, 1975; Marsh and Luey, 1982; Karr and Schlosser, 1978; Schlosser and Karr, 1981a, 1981b). The variation in the width of stream corridors from stream to stream, and along a single stream system, should have major functional implications.

Stream corridors (riparian vegetation) are well-known for their roles in controlling water and mineral nutrient flows. Water runoff and consequent flooding are both minimized when effective stream corridors extend to the uplands on both sides of a stream. Bank erosion and mineral nutrient runoff are also inhibited. Consequently, the amount of sedimentation (including siltation) and suspended particulate matter in the stream is minimized. Stream water quality is usually high in a wide stream corridor (Figure 4.13).

Less well-known is the role of stream corridors as routes for movement

**Figure 4.12** *Deciduous stream corridor through scrub oak woodland. Scouring by floods on the narrow limestone flood plain dominated by ash (Fraxinus), poplar (Populus), and willow (Salix), is evident. The surrounding matrix is Mediterranean "garrigue" vegetation dominated by green and white oak (Quercus ilex, Q. pubescens). View is from top of the Pont du Gard Roman aqueduct built about 44 B.C. by a proconsul of Augustus Caesar near Nîmes in southern France. (R. Forman.)*

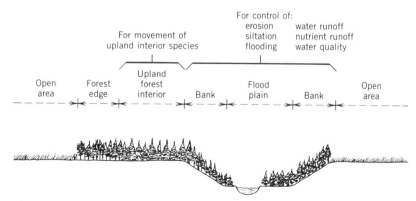

**Figure 4.13** *Structure and functions of a stream corridor. From Forman (1983). (Courtesy of Ekologia CSSR.)*

of terrestrial plants and animals across the landscape. Some species move readily along the wet soil of the flood plain. However, many species cannot tolerate flood plain conditions such as high soil moisture or periodic flooding. These species require an upland environment such as that found above the stream bank. Certain of these upland species are forest interior species that are absent or infrequent in edge conditions.

The functional characteristics of a stream corridor, involving the flows of water, mineral nutrients, and species, provide a guiding principle for the perennial planning question, *How wide should a stream corridor be?* The stream corridor should be wide enough to effectively perform the functions of both controlling water and nutrient flows from upland to stream, and facilitating the movement of upland forest interior animals and plants along the stream system. To accomplish all these objectives, the stream corridor should cover the flood plain, both banks, and an area of upland—at least on one side—that is wider than an edge effect (Figure 4.13).

Two additional points emerge when a stream system is viewed from above. First, as a stream winds through a landscape, the corridor typically becomes wider on one side and then wider on the other side. Since some species are inhibited by flood plain conditions, they would not be expected to move efficiently along most stream corridors, because they would have to repeatedly cross the flood plain barrier to get from one upland side to the other. For such species, therefore, a continuous band of upland forest interior on one side of the stream would be most effective as a corridor.

Second, the stream corridor form just described results from the basic process of erosion. Tiny streamlets coalesce to form tributaries that progressively coalesce to form streams and rivers. The result is a dendritic system. A wide range of variations on this basic dendritic form (Figure 4.14) provides considerable insight into the structure of landscapes. For example, meandering streams characterize flat terrain, and nonintegrated drainage patterns are often found in certain sandy or limestone areas with underground water movement.

The smallest streams that flow year round or nearly so are called *first-order streams.* Two first-order streams coalesce to form a *second-order stream,* two second-order streams combine to form a *third-order stream,* and so on (Figure 4.15) (Horton, 1945; Strahler, 1957; Hynes, 1975; Vannote et al., 1980; Barila et al., 1981; MacDonald, 1983; Decamps, 1984). Usually species change as the **stream order** increases, though some species in a system may be found from first to highest-order streams. Environmental changes such as flow rate and oxygen level are pronounced going downstream, especially in agricultural and urbanized areas. For example, in Indiana (United States), tiny first-order (feeder) streams may be clear and well shaded by vegetation, thus supporting

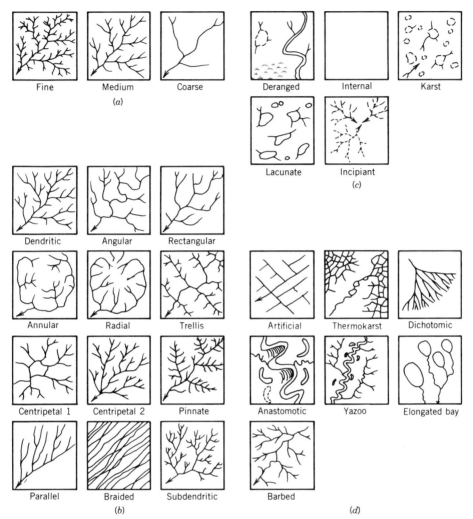

Fine    Medium    Coarse
(a)

Deranged    Internal    Karst

Lacunate    Incipiant
(c)

Dendritic    Angular    Rectangular

Annular    Radial    Trellis    Artificial    Thermokarst    Dichotomic

Centripetal 1    Centripetal 2    Pinnate    Anastomotic    Yazoo    Elongated bay

Parallel    Braided    Subdendritic    Barbed
(b)    (d)

**Figure 4.14** *Natural drainage densities and patterns. (a) Drainage densities. (b) Integrated drainage patterns. (c) Nonintegrated drainage patterns. (d) Other drainage patterns. The densities of tributaries generally indicate differences in resistance of rock to weathering, soil permeability, or erosion. Patterns are characteristic of different geological and climatic areas. From Way (1973). (Courtesy of Van Nostrand Reinhold.)*

certain fish species (Karr and Schlosser, 1978). Somewhat higher-order streams are muddy because of erosion from cultivated fields and support different fish species.' The highest-order streams contain yet another fish community, resulting from the combined inputs of sediment and pesticides from agriculture, urban wastes, and sluggish flow with little shading (Figure 4.15). In such a stream system, individuals in certain first-order

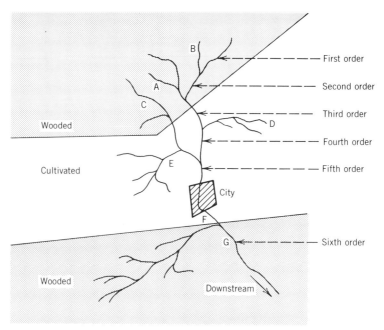

First order
Second order
Third order
Fourth order
Fifth order
Sixth order

B
A
C
D
E
F
G

Wooded
Cultivated
City
Wooded
Downstream

**Figure 4.15** *Stream orders. Typically fish may move from point A to point B, but not to points C or D because of agricultural runoff (and often higher temperature and lower oxygen) in the cultivated area. Similarly, fish may move from point D to point E, but not to points F or G because of urban water pollution.*

streams are effectively isolated from those in other first-order streams, because the species cannot tolerate the muddy connecting higher-order streams (Luey and Adelman, 1980; Barila et al., 1981; Marsh and Luey, 1982). Fish isolated in different low-order streams in the Amazon basin have evolved and become quite different from one another over time.

The cross section of a stream valley also varies considerably. Streams actively cutting the bedrock beneath them, as on mountain slopes, are somewhat V-shaped in cross section, whereas streams meandering across

**Figure 4.16** *Flood levels and flood frequencies in a stream valley. In (a), the levels of alluvial deposits are related to flooding in a climate with somewhat regular precipitation patterns from year to year. In climates with markedly irregular annual precipitation patterns—such as in many dry climates—the lower levels are more apt to result from the last flood, which may be a 1-year, 10-year, or longer flood. Diagrams (b), (c), and (d) illustrate the effects of building flood control banks.*

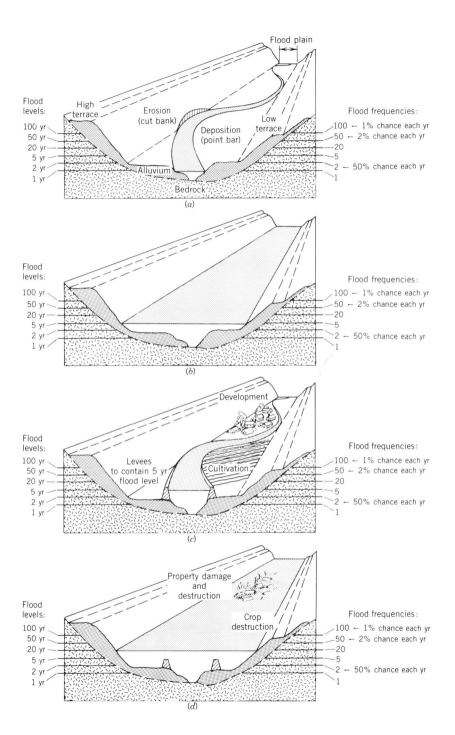

Flood plain

Flood levels:

100 yr
50 yr
20 yr
5 yr
2 yr
1 yr

High terrace

Erosion (cut bank)

Deposition (point bar)

Low terrace

Alluvium

Bedrock

(a)

Flood frequencies:

100 ← 1% chance each yr
50 ← 2% chance each yr
20
5
2 ← 50% chance each yr
1

Flood levels:

100 yr
50 yr
20 yr
5 yr
2 yr
1 yr

(b)

Flood frequencies:

100 ← 1% chance each yr
50 ← 2% chance each yr
20
5
2 ← 50% chance each yr
1

Development

Flood levels:

100 yr
50 yr
20 yr
5 yr
2 yr
1 yr

Levees to contain 5 yr flood level

Cultivation

(c)

Flood frequencies:

100 ← 1% chance each yr
50 ← 2% chance each yr
20
5
2 ← 50% chance each yr
1

Property damage and destruction

Crop destruction

Flood levels:

100 yr
50 yr
20 yr
5 yr
2 yr
1 yr

(d)

Flood frequencies:

100 ← 1% chance each yr
50 ← 2% chance each yr
20
5
2 ← 50% chance each yr
1

a nearly flat plain normally have a wide flood plain between two stream banks. An intermediate case, diagrammed in Figure 4.16, shows a typical flat alluvial deposit covering the flood plain. Note also the presence of higher terraces on the stream banks, the result of former geomorphic processes such as forming flood plains in the valley. The diagram also shows **flood levels** or stages and **flood frequencies.** For example, the 100-year flood level or stage is considered to have only a 1% frequency or chance of being attained in any given year. In Figure 4.16, the flood plain is approximately the width of the two-year flood stage. In climates with irregular rainfall, the flood plain may correspond with a level attained only once in ten or even 30 years. The lower diagrams (Figure 4.16) illustrate a common result of the building of flood control structures to channel stream water. The channel height may prevent a five-year flood, for example, thus encouraging development on the flood plain. Eventually, however, the less frequent flood arrives and causes extensive damage and perhaps loss of life in the misplaced development (Figure 4.17).

Ongoing processes such as flooding, droughts, ice scouring, and sedimentation help determine the heterogeneity within a stream corridor. A sharp environmental gradient from stream to upland is also present. Some stream corridor vegetation and animals, adapted to both high levels and high variability in soil moisture and flooding, are distinctive and widespread along the stream system. The substrate is almost always rich in nutrients deposited by former floods (Figure 4.17). Hence, flood plain plants tend to be highly productive, and many sprout rapidly following flood damage. [Corridor species on and above the stream bank, of course, are different and reflect upland conditions (Geier and Best, 1980)].

Clearly, the corridor vegetation also has a direct major impact on the stream. Cool water is maintained by shading (often necessary for trout), litter is deposited in the stream and provides the base of much of the stream food web, logs dropped into the stream form pools, and abundant nutrients enter in widespread caterpillar droppings. Over high-order streams, the vegetation canopy is open (Figure 4.12). Various butterflies, birds, and other species commonly use, and in some cases depend on, this open strip within the stream corridor.

One stream corridor animal, the beaver (*Castor*), plays an unusually significant role when present. (Except in certain arid areas, this species was undoubtedly once present in every temperate and boreal stream of the northern hemisphere.) By forming dams and shallow ponds along a stream, which are periodically washed away, and feeding on the woody plants of the flood plain, the beaver maintains the flood plain in a state of vegetation flux (Figure 4.18). The habitat diversity and species diversity are probably higher in streams where some beaver are present. When much of the woody cover in the flood plain is cut, surface runoff can be

**Figure 4.17** *Bridge washed out by low-frequency flood. Mineral nutrients and sediments from surrounding agricultural land are carried downstream, and many are deposited on the flood plains with stream corridor vegetation. (Courtesy of USDA Soil Conservation Service.)*

expected to increase and evapotranspiration of water decrease. Higher water flow in the stream results, despite the ponds and dams. Of course, the presence of beaver ponds and the cutting of surrounding woody vegetation also forms breaks in the connectivity of a stream corridor.

## SUMMARY

Corridors originate by the same mechanisms as patches. As seen from the air, a key characteristic of corridors is connectivity, or presence of breaks. Nodes containing interior species are commonly attached to a corridor to form a string-of-lights structure. Corridors have sharp microclimatic and soil gradients from one side to the other. The center is typically a unique habitat partly determined by the transportation or movement taking place along the corridor.

**Figure 4.18** *Beaver pond with dam and lodge along a stream. The thin film of ice on the pond. The dam provides a constant water level so that the beaver living in the rounded lodge, made largely of sticks, stay dry and warm only slightly above the water level. (Len Rue, Jr.) Inset. The beaver carries aspen (Populus tremuloides) branches underwater for dam or lodge construction. Larger diameter branches often are cut in short sections and buried in the bottom of the pond for winter food. Most of the stream corridor woody vegetation here has been cut by the beaver. (Irene Vandermolen.) Western North America.*

Line corridors are narrow and composed basically of edge species. Strip corridors are wider and contain an abundance of interior species along their center line. From the microenvironment, the plants, and the animals of hedgerows, we can discover much about the heterogeneity and patterns of line corridors. The width effect exerts a key control over the nature of a corridor. These characteristics apply whether it is lower or higher than its surroundings.

Stream corridors regulate the movement of water and materials from the surrounding land to the stream and also affect transport in the stream itself. Erosion, nutrient runoff, water runoff, flooding, sedimentation, and water quality are all modified by stream corridor width. In addition, terrestrial species moving along stream corridors may require a well-drained strip above the stream bank. Corridors are very important in human society, providing transportation routes, several kinds of protection, and harvestable resources.

## QUESTIONS

1. List the types of corridors in your landscape and give an approximate percentage of relative frequency for each. Which persist in their present form because of natural or human disturbance in the corridor? Disturbance in the matrix? No disturbance?
2. What inherent geographic or geologic features produce high linearity in a landscape? What human influences produce high curvilinearity in a landscape?
3. Diagram and label the microenvironmental variation in cross sections of one corridor that is higher than its surroundings, and one that is lower than its surroundings.
4. How do the European and North American hedgerows discussed differ?
5. Could a visitor new to a landscape differentiate among a line corridor, a strip corridor, and an elongated patch? How?
6. Which is better for wildlife, a line corridor, a strip corridor, or the edge of a patch? Why?
7. Is a stream corridor more critical in controlling water movement or mineral nutrient movement? Explain in detail how the stream corridor operates in the more critical case identified.
8. Diagram and label a stream corridor that contains as many basic characteristics inhibiting movement of animals and plants along it as possible.
9. In what ways is a stream corridor important in forestry?
10. How would you design a corridor to maximize the movement of organisms both along and across it?
11. What other fields of knowledge focus on lines or strips? What spatial or structural patterns are similar to those for landscape corridors? Are there any additional corridor patterns not discussed in this chapter?

# 5
# Matrix and Network

How many red spots make a white cow red?
How many clearings make a forest, prairie?
A score? More? A coalescing core?
A threshold reached?

A farmer thrives in a dry but fertile agricultural plain. *Clear blue sky.* An occasional field in the plain is too heavily cultivated. *An occasional muddy stream.* A few pastures are overgrazed. *Sunsets redder.* The farmer notices several eroded fields. *Some streams now dry out at times.* Bare fields become common in the plain. *A brief dust storm one afternoon.* Barren area now equals the cover of greenery. *Clearwater fish largely gone.* Green areas, no longer connected, are still overused. *Roads often blocked by windblown soil.* Farmer's remaining vegetated patches are shrinking. *Well went dry.* Scattered green spots are used heavily. *Huge sandstorm.* Desertified.

At the outset of this desertification process, the farmer lived in a background or matrix of green agricultural land. At the end, the matrix was barren land (Figure 5.1). This chapter takes on the challenge of understanding the nature of the landscape matrix (Kuchler, 1969). In the preceding chapters we assumed that patches are distinct fragments embedded in a matrix. When walking through a landscape, however, we often encounter areas where distinguishing the boundaries between patch and matrix is quite a challenge. The simplest strategy is to study air photographs or maps and to draw boundaries between landscape elements, even though boundaries remain unclear in places.

At one extreme, some landscapes have an extensive homogeneous matrix containing scattered distinct patches analogous to scattered knots on a wood panelled wall. At the other extreme, an entire landscape may be composed of small patches that differ from one another like the pieces of a puzzle. Most landscapes fall between these extremes and contain highly diverse proportions and spatial configurations of patches, corridors, and matrix. Would it be possible to describe the entire area of a landscape as either patch or corridor? The extensive, relatively homogeneous landscape element that encloses scattered distinct patches of a different type illustrates the fact that the matrix (i.e., the extensive land-

**Figure 5.1** *Farm during the 1930s "dust bowl" in the American Midwest. Soil deposited by wind has covered both the farmyard and the fields in the background. Gregory County, South Dakota. (Courtesy of USDA Soil Conservation Service.)*

**Figure 5.2** *Landscape of Woodstock, New York. Pastures and homes are scattered in a forest matrix of oaks (Quercus) and other deciduous trees. Woodstock is known for the three-day rainy festival of rock music and harmony of life that converted an alfalfa field some kilometers away into a quagmire. (R. Forman.)*

scape element) has special properties and is conceptually different from a patch. Therefore, before analyzing landscape structure as a whole (in Chapter 6), we must examine in precise terms the characteristics of the matrix.

A landscape is composed of several types of landscape elements. Of these, the **matrix** is the most extensive and most connected landscape element type, and therefore plays the dominant role in the functioning of the landscape (i.e., the flows of energy, materials, and species). However, when observing a landscape it is sometimes difficult to estimate the role each landscape element plays. So we are obliged to proceed step by step, beginning with the most conspicuous matrix characteristics. The first consideration in differentiating patches from matrix concerns their relative proportion and configuration, which vary widely from landscape to landscape. The matrix is very much larger in total area. It generally has concave boundaries enclosing other landscape elements. It is interconnected with narrows where enclosed patches are close together. And it exerts an overriding influence on the dynamics of the landscape as a whole.

## DISTINGUISHING A MATRIX

### Three Matrix Criteria

The following definitions of the idea of a matrix are used in quite diverse areas of human knowledge.

1. *the homogeneous mass in which small differentiated elements appear (for example, in soil science, the matrix of fine material in which stones are embedded);*
2. *the binding material that surrounds and cements independent elements;*
3. *the mold in which a metal sculpture is produced, or, in vertebrates, the organ in which an embryo develops.*

Since these ideas appear to be useful in understanding a landscape, we will develop each into a formal criterion and attempt to determine the relative importance of each.

To illustrate the reasoning to be followed, we will examine two landscapes. The first is a sparsely populated landscape near Woodstock, New York (120 km north of New York City), where one sees cows grazing peacefully, woodcutters in the paper producing forest, charming villages, and isolated homes (Figure 5.2). The second is a cultivated, level calcareous plain near Agde, Languedoc (on the French Mediterranean), where one sees grape-growers watching the wine flow, stone houses clustered in medieval villages, and sun-seekers relaxing in the European sunbelt (Figure 5.3). In each case, we placed a line equivalent to 8.2 km on a map of the landscape. Each line was divided into 128 segments, each 64 m long. The landscape elements—woods, vineyards, dirt roads, power-lines, and so forth—observed under each segment were recorded. The resulting table, showing the presence or absence of the types of landscape elements in each of the 128 segments, serves as a basis for elucidating several concepts presented below (Table 5.1).

**Relative Area.**    When one type of element in a landscape is considerably more extensive than the others, it seems logical to say that this element type is the matrix. And so the species that are dominant in the matrix are also predominant in the landscape. For example, scientists who study pollen deposits in lake or bog sediments of cool temperate landscapes (Heusser, 1974; Davis, 1976; Richard, 1977; Webb, 1981; Huntley and Birks, 1983), find pollen predominantly from plants of the landscape matrix.

**Figure 5.3**   *Mediterranean landscape near Agde, France. Vineyards and pastures are bounded by strips of pines (Pinus), oaks (Quercus), and other plants. (M. Godron.)*

TABLE 5.1   *Frequency of landscape elements in Woodstock and Agde.*[a]

|  | Woodstock 2 | | Agde 4 | |
|---|---|---|---|---|
|  | Absolute Frequency | Relative Frequency | Absolute Frequency | Relative Frequency |
| Forests and woods | 91 | 71% | 0 | 0 |
| Fields | 55 | 42% | 9 | 7% |
| Roads and highways | 16 | 12% | 5 | 4% |
| Homes | 8 | 6% | 0 | 0 |
| Streams and rivers | 7 | 5% | 8 | 6% |
| Quarries | 3 | 2% | 0 | 0 |
| Standing water | 2 | 2% | 1 | 1% |
| Dirt roads | 3 | 2% | 36 | 28% |
| Power-lines | 1 | 1% | 0 | 0 |
| Vineyards | 0 | 0 | 119 | 93% |
| Bare soil | 0 | 0 | 2 | 2% |
| Hedgerows | 0 | 0 | 10 | 8% |
| Orchards | 0 | 0 | 3 | 2% |
| Railroads | 0 | 0 | 1 | 1% |

[a]*Absolute frequency* is the number of segments in which a particular landscape element type was observed; *relative frequency* is the percentage of segments which contained the type of landscape element. The sum of relative frequencies exceeds 100% because several element types often coexist in a segment. Woodstock 2 (New York) was the second of several parallel lines sampled, and Agde 4 is the fourth sample line near Agde (southern France).

The most extensive element type also often controls flows in the landscape. For example, heat from a desert matrix permeates and desiccates oases, and sandstorms from a desert matrix sweep through villages and croplands. In fact, the *oasis effect* refers to desiccation of an area due to advection, and *advection* is the horizontal movement of heat energy between two areas.

In Chapter 3, we emphasized the importance of the area of a patch in affecting the animals and plants within the patch. This importance is due largely to the extensiveness and isolation of the patch interior. In the case of the matrix as well, area is an important index of its role in the landscape. And so we adopt relative area as the first criterion for defining a matrix: generally, *the area of the matrix exceeds the total area of any other landscape element type present.*

This criterion of relative area leads us to suggest that the matrix around Woodstock is deciduous forest and the matrix near Agde is vineyard (Table 5.1). If a type of landscape element covers more than 50% of a landscape (Curtis, 1956; Sharpe et al., 1981), it is very likely to be the matrix. If the most extensive landscape element type covers less than

50% of a landscape, additional characteristics will be important in determining the matrix type.

The patterns of relative frequency of landscape elements in Table 5.1 provide additional insight into the relative importance of the matrix in the two landscapes. We see that forest near Woodstock has a relative frequency of 71% versus 93% for vineyard in the Agde landscape. Near Agde, dirt roads are the second most frequent landscape element; near Woodstock, fields are in second place. The difference between the relative frequency of the two leading elements was 29% near Woodstock and 65% near Agde, where the matrix is clearly more predominant. This difference suggests another useful characteristic of the matrix. Landscapes differ in how evenly distributed through space the various landscape elements are. This spatial evenness or unevenness is easily determined by various methods (e.g., Daget and Godron, 1982) that suggest that the area of the matrix is usually not a sufficient sole criterion in recognizing a matrix. Therefore, although relative area is a key criterion in determining a matrix, we must remember also the uneven distribution of the matrix across the landscape.

**Connectivity.** The case of a hedgerow or ("bocage") landscape is one where relative area as the only criterion for a matrix may be misleading. Hedgerows generally cover less than a tenth of the total area (Pollard et al., 1974; Les Bocages, 1976), yet intuitively one suspects that the network of hedgerows may be the matrix (Figure 5.4). This impression is due to the shape of the network: it encloses the fields. In this sense, the hedgerows constitute a single continuous piece of terrain that, for example, can be painted on a map without lifting the paintbrush. It is, in the language of our second concept above, "the binding that surrounds and cements the independent elements." In contrast, each field in the landscape must be colored separately with a brush.

To describe this property of the matrix in a precise manner, it is convenient to use the mathematical concept of **connectivity** (Hocking and Young, 1961; Kasriel, 1971; Lelong-Ferrand and Arnaudies, 1980). That is, a space is completely connected if it is not divided into two open wholes (i.e., is not crossed by a boundary whose ends join the perimeter of the space). A high level of connectivity in a landscape element type (Figure 5.4) has several consequences.

1. *The element may function as a physical barrier separating the other elements. Hence, a wind-break or fire-break may be an effective physical, chemical, and biological barrier (e.g., for insects or seeds) between two landscape elements.*
2. *When the connectivity takes the form of an intersecting of thin, elon-*

**Figure 5.4** *Hedgerow network surrounding pastures and cultivation. A farm pond is visible in the upper left and cows are enclosed in a pasture near the lower woods. This glaciated landscape is in northern New York state. (R. Forman.)*

gated strips, the element may function as a series of corridors facilitating both migration and gene exchange among species. The spatial and mathematical basis for analyzing movement along interlocking corridors is familiar in transportation theory and in the geography of movement (e.g., Whyte, 1968; Taaffe and Gauthier, 1973; Wolkowitsch, 1973; Lowe and Moryadas, 1975; Haggett et al., 1977).

3. The element may encircle other landscape elements to create isolated biological "islands." Thus, livestock in separated fields may eye each other without mixing genes, and populations of mice, butterflies, and clover may become genetically different when separated within a landscape (Antonovics and Bradshaw, 1970; Bradshaw, 1972; Ehrlich et al., 1974; Harper, 1977; White, 1979).

Because of these significant effects, when one landscape element is completely (perfectly) connected and encircles all the others, it has to be considered the matrix. However, the matrix is usually not completely connected but is broken into several fragments. Therefore, it is prudent to begin the analysis of a landscape by simply identifying each element present before deciding which type of element is the matrix and which element types are patches and corridors. Thus, in a cultivated plain sprinkled with woodlots and homes, the matrix is the cultivated area. It may be a single element, such as the extensive wheat cultivation in Canada and the Soviet Union. In parts of Brazil, and India, on the other hand, the cultivated area has a heterogeneous mixture of rice, manioc, and banana fields, and one may consider these to be separate landscape element types. Alternatively, depending upon the objective of the analysis, one may consider cultivation to be the landscape element type and each field within it to be a homogeneous tessera. In mountainous forested terrain such as the Rocky Mountains, spruce-fir forest (*Picea-Abies*), pine forest (*Pinus*), and aspen forest (*Populus*) may be categorized as separate landscape element types. On the other hand, forest may be considered a single landscape element type with spruce-fir, pine, and aspen stands as individual tesserae.

The second criterion, therefore, in identifying a matrix is *degree of connectivity. The matrix is more connected than any other landscape element type present.*

The matrix of the line observed in the Agde landscape has high connectivity; that is, we would have to lift the paint brush only four times (because of a river, orchard, and fields) along the 8-km line. The forests along the line near Woodstock are less connected; we would have to raise the brush ten times because of fields, roads, houses, and a power line corridor.

**Control Over Dynamics.** The hedgerow landscape example suggests a third and more sensitive criterion for determining a matrix. In a hedgerow network, the hedgerows may be highly dynamic, especially when they are made up of pioneer successional species—such as cherry (*Prunus*) and hawthorn (*Crataegus*) in moist temperate areas—mixed with late succession species like oak (*Quercus*) (Pollard et al., 1974; Les Bocages, 1976; Wegner and Merriam, 1979). Winged seeds from the hedgerows are blown and deposited in nearby fields. Birds and mammals feed on the hedgerow fruits and drop seeds widely across the landscape (Ridley, 1930; McQuilkin, 1940; Beckwith, 1954; Smith, 1975; Stiles, 1980; McDonnell and Stiles, 1983). Consequently, the hedgerows act as species sources (Figure 5.4) and are ready to initiate the dynamics leading the entire area toward a possible former steady state or other condition. Thus, the matrix exerts a major control over landscape dynamics by giving rise to the future landscape.

The preceding reasoning appears to be widely but not universally applicable. In the case of a heavily cultivated plain where a mere handful of old woodlots remains, we can only estimate the role they would play if cultivation ceased. Most of the abandoned fields would be rapidly invaded by wind-disseminated species (anemochores) and not by the heavy-fruited species (barochores) that commonly predominate in old woods (Molinier and Muller, 1938; Van der Pijl, 1969). This result is in part due to the fact that bird and mammal communities that must disperse the forest seeds are depauperate. In North America and some other temperate regions, the forest climax will usually reconstitute itself rather rapidly following disturbance (Clements, 1916; Oosting, 1942; Bard, 1952), but elsewhere this is not always the case. In the Mediterranean region, for example in Egypt, Israel, and Syria, the human imprint is so intense and ancient that the former natural ecosystems can no longer be reconstituted. In dry tropical regions, several vegetational formations that developed in a moister climatic period are now maintained in an unstable equilibrium and are in risk of disappearing forever. In New Zealand, Chile, and elsewhere, several landscape areas are now dominated by nonnative species imported from other temperate areas of the world. In these examples, the tree and shrub species that presently grow in the landscape, though quite different from the original climax species, play a significant role in the dynamics of the new environment.

According to the third criterion, therefore, *the matrix exerts a greater degree of control over landscape dynamics than any other landscape element type present.*

**Combining the Three Criteria.** The first criterion, relative area, is the easiest to estimate. The third, control over dynamics, is the most difficult to evaluate, and the second, connectivity, is intermediate. In many landscapes, control over dynamics appears to have much more weight (i.e., greater ecological significance) than relative area, and somewhat more weight than connectivity, in determining a matrix.

Therefore, to determine which type of element is the matrix in an unfamiliar landscape, we suggest that one first calculate the relative area and connectivity levels for all landscape element types. If one type of landscape element covers far more area than any other element, we designate it as the matrix. If the areas of the most frequent element types are relatively similar, the type with the highest connectivity may be considered the matrix. However, if designation of the matrix is still uncertain after calculating the area and connectivity criteria, we must make field measurements or obtain published information on species composition and life history characteristics. This information will enable us to estimate which landscape element type present exerts the greatest degree of control over landscape dynamics.

### How the Matrix Criteria Influence Change: The Desertification Example

**Desertification** is the process of severe reduction of biological productivity and soil quality, leading to desertlike conditions. An impoverishment of dependent human livelihood systems is usually associated with desertification (Mabbutt, 1976). Indicators of the process include a significant increase in soil erosion by water or wind, a reduction of surface water, a drop in the water table, and salt buildup in water or soil.

Based on climate, about a third of the global land surface is desert or semidesert. Based on data of soil and vegetation conditions, the figure is about 43% (United Nations, 1977). The difference (9.1 million km$^2$ or more than the area of Brazil) represents desertification caused by humans (Figure 5.5). Huge areas of the United States, Africa, the Middle East, Australia, and Central and South America are currently undergoing this process (Dregne, 1977; United Nations, 1977; Meckelein, 1980; Spooner and Mann, 1982).

We began this matrix chapter with an oversimplified example of desertification. At the beginning and end of the example, the matrix type was obvious (green agricultural land, then barren land). How to define the matrix type in the intermediate phases is less clear. At the midpoint, when the green and barren lands covered equal areas, the degree of connectivity (and perhaps control over dynamics) of each of the two types would determine the matrix. As long as the degraded areas are isolated patches easily reconquered by grasses, the matrix is green. But it is brown if degraded patches, once started, tend to expand with convex boundaries and to interconnect leaving isolated green patches. At some point along the desertification gradient, the barren land exerts a controlling influence on landscape dynamics, as heat, dust, and stream sediments permeate the surrounding agricultural land. It would be interesting to know at what point control over landscape dynamics becomes the predominant determiner of the matrix, overriding in importance the other two changing characteristics, area and connectivity.

The most widespread cause of desertification is overgrazing. When native plant cover decreases, native animals decrease, new or noxious plants first spread and then decrease, bare soil increases, water and wind erosion increases (Figure 5.5), and finally eroded sediments build up elsewhere on land and in streams (Stewart et al., 1940; Dyksterhuis, 1949, 1957; Weaver and Albertson, 1956; Jacobsen and Adams, 1958; Sears, 1962; Charley and Cowling, 1968; Brown, 1971b; Noy-Meir, 1973; Floret, 1981).

**Figure 5.5** *Soil loss by erosion in Senegal, central Africa. Overgrazing of limited vegetation cover in this semiarid climate becomes particularly evident and serious during the periodic droughts. The exposed roots indicate the loss of nearly a meter of soil, and an unstable substrate is left. (Courtesy of A. Cornet.)*

Many other human influences cause or contribute to desertification as well. Dramatic localized manifestations of desertification are sand dunes that overrun villages or fields. A much more common pattern is the linking up of separated patches which have been subject to overuse by livestock or water removal (Mabbutt, 1976; United Nations, 1977; Spooner and Mann, 1982). The overused patches may remain static during wet or normal rainfall years but are subject to rapid degradation in droughts. Thus, the spreading process—of bare patches interconnecting—is accelerated during droughts. Once barren land is interconnected, enclosed green patches are likely to succumb to the process, because of both heavy human or animal pressure on the remaining green spots (Pellek, 1983) and pervasive flows of heat and sediments from the surrounding bare areas. In short, the changes in the land depend greatly on the three characteristics of a matrix: relative area of landscape element types, level of connectivity present, and degree of control over landscape dynamics.


## POROSITY AND BOUNDARY SHAPE

### The Concept and its Implications

**Porosity** is the measure of the density of patches in a landscape. To evaluate the level of matrix porosity, we simply count the number of patches present, that is, the number of closed boundaries which are included within a unit area of matrix (Figure 5.6). *Closed boundaries*, such as circles and polygons, are those that do not touch the perimeter of the space or landscape studied, whereas *open boundaries* have both ends intersecting the perimeter.

In the simplest case, the landscape studied is traversed by a single boundary that intersects the perimeter at its two ends (Figure 5.6a). Here the porosity is zero. If a single closed boundary is present, the encircling element is normally the matrix, and the patch is enclosed within it (Figure 5.6b). The encircling element may not always be the matrix, and the species composition of the two elements plays a role in this determination. Other things being equal, though, there is a greater probability that the surrounding element imposes its control, for example, over the successional dynamics of the inside element than vice versa.

The greater the number of patches with closed boundaries present, the more porous the matrix. Diagrams b-e of Figure 5.6 depict matrix porosities of 1, 2, 3, and 11. These examples show that porosity is a concept independent of connectivity. The connectivity of the matrix remains unchanged in the four cases, whereas the porosity varies from one to eleven. (Now we see more clearly why it is necessary to use precise criteria to characterize the matrix.) The distinction becomes more difficult

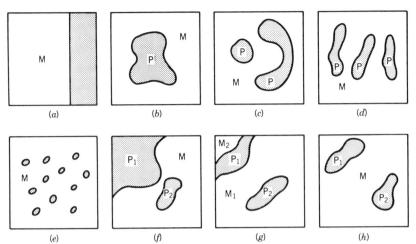

**Figure 5.6** *Porosity and connectivity of the matrix. M = matrix, P = patch. (a) The simplest case where porosity = 0. (b) Porosity = 1. (c) Porosity = 2. (d) Porosity = 3. (e) Porosity = 11. (f) Porosity = 2, and matrix connectivity is complete, but it is unclear whether type M or type P should be the matrix. (g) Porosity = 2, but connectivity is not complete. (h) Porosity = 2, and connectivity is complete.*

when the area under study is both traversed by open boundaries and perforated by closed boundaries (Figure 5.6f). In this case, it is imperative to estimate connectivity and porosity separately. Diagrams g and h illustrate how the level of connectivity may vary without a change in porosity. In both cases the porosity level is equal to two, but connectivity is directly visible only in h. (It would be nice to know whether those portions of the matrix of Figure 5.6g which appear unconnected are actually connected outside the observed map. The only remedy to this puzzle seems to be to increase the area examined, but such an approach is merely tantalizing, because the solution may not appear until one has observed the entire surface of the earth.)

Note that porosity is a measure of the number of patches, regardless of patch size. In view of the important differences between small and large patches, it may often be useful when considering a landscape to distinguish a number of patch size classes and calculate porosity for each.

The porosity of a matrix appears to be important in several contexts. For example, within a coniferous forest matrix, small mouse-like animals called voles (*Microtus*) are common in wet grassy patches (Hansson, 1977). During certain seasons, the voles move into the forest matrix and consume seedlings that would regenerate the forest. When the porosity of grassy patches is low, the voles have little effect on the forest. However, when porosity is high, vole damage is considerable.

Porosity should also provide an overall clue to the degree of species isolation present and to the potential genetic variability present within populations of animals and plants in a landscape (Mayr, 1974; Brown, 1971a; Blondel, 1979). Generally, porosity should be an index of the amount of edge effect present, a factor that has many implications for wildlife management (Leopold, 1933; Giles, 1978; Schemnitz, 1980) and influences numerous energy, material, and species flows. Conversely, low porosity should often indicate the presence of considerable remote area in a landscape, a condition that is critical for certain animals requiring a habitat distant from boundaries (F. E. Smith, personal communication). Landscape porosity is also quite relevant to animal foraging, because the density of suitable patches is critical to obtaining sufficient food for survival and to supporting young at a den or nest (central place foraging) (Schuster, 1950; Durango, 1951; Horn, 1968; Schoener, 1971; Wiens, 1973; Brown and Lieberman, 1973; Haggett et al., 1977; Krebs et al., 1974; Orians and Pearson, 1978). The porosity of clear cuts in forested landscapes is also critical in wildlife management (Julander and Jeffery, 1964; Resler, 1972; Telfer, 1974; Thomas et al., 1976; Thomas, 1979; Lyon and Jensen, 1980; Hanley, 1983).

Studies comparing species in woodlots in a landscape are particularly common, but little information directly bearing on porosity is yet available because only a few of the woodlots present in a landscape are studied (Curtis, 1956; Peet and Loucks, 1977; Burgess and Sharpe, 1981). For many species, low porosity would seem to inhibit the interchange among patch species, and so isolation would become important in determining species diversity and composition in patches (Auclair and Cottam, 1971; Gottfried, 1979; Ranney and Johnson, 1977; MacClintock et al., 1977; DeAngelis et al., 1980; Butcher et al., 1981; Lynch and Whigham, 1984; Merriam, 1984; see also Appendix to this chapter). However, many studies of woodlot species in a landscape find no significant isolation effect (Helliwell, 1976; Forman et al., 1976; Weaver and Kellman, 1981), suggesting that porosity level of the landscape matrix is not significantly inhibiting the woods species studied.

In the human sphere, porosity is a factor in the economics of harvesting wood, since the size and proximity of forest patches strongly affects whether intensive harvesting methods are used (Row, 1978; Cubbage, 1983). Porosity is also a familiar subject in human geography, as it studies the patterns of distribution of homes and villages in a matrix.

## Porosity Patterns in Different Landscapes

One study that compares different landscapes in Ohio (USA) is particularly informative because it includes all patches present in several quite distinct landscapes, and it provides simple analytic tools for understanding spatial patterns (Bowen and Burgess, 1981). Aerial photographs and maps of fifteen landscapes were studied, using a plot equivalent to 10 km on a side [10,000 hectares (ha)] in each. We will concentrate on six of these landscape parcels (Figure 5.7). What characteristics in these landscapes vary? Certainly patch sizes, patch shapes, the distance between patches, and the total forested cover differ.

To understand these patterns, measurements of the perimeter and area of each forest patch and of the distance separating patches were made for each landscape parcel. Statistical techniques (factor analysis and discriminant analysis) were used to analyze different landscape patterns and to relate them to site conditions such as topography, soils, glacial history, and vegetation type. Landscape patterns were compared against a theoretical model assuming circular patches of varying density and total cover. Additional landscape patterns such as connectivity, dispersion (aggregated, regular, or random), and associations of particular pairs of

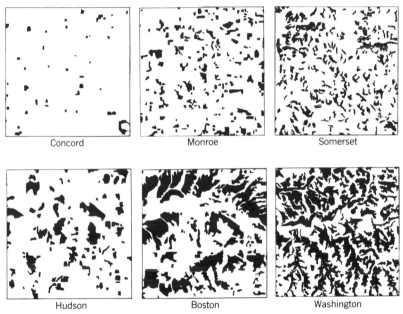

**Figure 5.7** *Forest patches in six Ohio (United States) landscapes. Each landscape parcel is approximately 10 km on a side and is named for a nearby town. The shaded areas represent land remaining or reverting to forest in the 1930s. Forest cover in landscapes increases from left to right. Patch density (number per 10,000 hectares) increases from left to right in the top three landscapes, and remains constant in the bottom three landscapes. (From Bowen and Burgess, 1981; also see Sharpe et al, 1981; courtesy of R. Burgess and Pudoc-Centre for Agricultural Publishing and Documentation.)*

TABLE 5.2 **Characteristics of the pattern of forest patches in six Ohio (U.S.A.) landscapes** *(see* **Figure 5.7**).

| Name of Landscape | Total Forest Cover (%) | Patch Density (number per 10,000 hectares) | Average Distance Between Patches (m) | Median Patch Area (hectares) | Median Patch Shape[a] |
|---|---|---|---|---|---|
| Concord | 2.7 | 46 | 3520 | 4.1 | 1.15 |
| Monroe | 11.8 | 180 | 1000 | 3.6 | 1.24 |
| Somerset | 22.7 | 244 | 728 | 5.6 | 1.39 |
| Hudson | 14.5 | 102 | 1419 | 6.4 | 1.29 |
| Boston | 33.8 | 83 | 625 | 8.0 | 1.36 |
| Washington | 43.6 | 132 | 403 | 11.2 | 1.60 |

[a]Patch shape $(P/2\sqrt{\pi A})$ is the perimeter $P$ of a patch divided by the perimeter of a circle of equal area $A$.
*Source:* Bowen and Burgess, 1981.

patch sizes or shapes, are perhaps discernible (Figure 5.7), but not considered in this analysis (see Appendix to this chapter for simple mathematical indices for several characteristics related to matrix porosity).

The quantitative data show that the total forest cover ranged from less than 3% to over 40%, a fourteen-fold range (Table 5.2). Patch density showed a five-fold range (from 46 to 244), but the landscapes with the highest and lowest densities were not the same as those with the highest and lowest percent cover. The average distance between patches also varied over a nine-fold range, from 403 to 3520, but again the extremes were in different landscapes. Patch area and patch shape also varied, though over somewhat narrower ranges. The fact that different landscapes represent the extremes for different characteristics suggests that a number of major factors, rather than a single factor, are controlling the differences in matrix patterns. A statistical analysis of these and related data showed that two primary variables accounted for an impressive 90% of the variability among landscape patterns. We will call the variables total percent forest cover and density of patches.

When the landscapes are compared on the basis of these primary variables, two major trends emerge. For one group of landscapes (including Concord, Monroe, and Somerset), patch density increases as total percent cover increases (Figure 5.8a). For the other group of landscapes (including Hudson, Boston, and Washington), patch density remains nearly constant as total percent cover increases.

When these patterns are compared with site conditions, we see that the patterns for both groups correlate with their topography (Figure 5.8b).

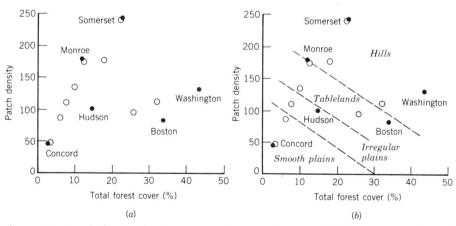

**Figure 5.8** *Patch density, forest cover, and topography of six Ohio landscapes. (a) Patch density and forest cover of landscapes are compared. Open circles represent nine additional landscapes studied. (b) Topographic patterns superimposed on graph (a). See Figure 5.7 and Table 5.2. (From Bowen and Burgess, 1981; courtesy of R. Burgess.)*

Smooth plains (e.g., Concord) have few woodlots and low total forest cover. Hilly areas have higher cover but may have either many patches (Somerset) or few patches (Washington). Hilly landscapes have the highest density of woodlots (Somerset), the largest patches, the most dissected patch shapes (Washington). They also have the greatest differences between average and median values (i.e., the most skewed values) for both patch size and patch shape (Washington, Boston). Conversely, in these characteristics smooth plains were most homogeneous.

In the Ohio region, the overriding cause of open areas is removal of forest by people for agriculture. The landscape is believed to have been essentially completely forested 300 years ago. Steepness of slope is a primary indicator of the value of land for agriculture, so much of the pattern in the landscapes of Figure 5.8b relates to slope. In each of the two groups of landscapes recognized in Figure 5.8a, the hilly areas are quite different geomorphically. Of course, superimposed on this basic geomorphic or topographic control is a whole range of secondary factors that modify the pattern—for example, remoteness from markets, wetland drainage, surface strip mining, parks, protected natural areas, and farmers maintaining woodlots for firewood and wildlife.

This comparison of landscapes again pinpoints the importance of both the relative area of a landscape element and the overall porosity of the matrix. In addition, several related characteristics of importance emerge, including patch areas, patch shapes, and distances between patches. A similar type of analysis can readily be used to understand patterns of landscape change over time (Raup, 1966; Curtis, 1956; Auclair, 1976; Debussche et al., 1977; Gallusser, 1978; Sharpe et al., 1981; Ruzicka et al., 1982). However, apparently no study yet exists that integrates these spatial patterns with those of species, energy, or materials.

## Boundary Shape

In most of the examples just presented, the boundaries were drawn to look relatively smooth. Obviously, however, the shape of a boundary may be convoluted in various ways (Rapoport, 1982b). A simple case is presented in Figure 5.9a. One may hesitate a long time before deciding whether the matrix of this landscape is the element on the left or the element on the right. We propose to solve this dilemma as brusquely as Alexander when he slashed the Gordian knot with his sword.

Let us imagine what would happen if one element gained area at the expense of the other. To simplify [and borrow an idea developed by Matheron (1965) for mining strategy], we assume that a constant width is gained along the entire length of the boundary, and we temporarily ignore species composition and life history differences. If the element on the left spreads (Figure 5.9b), the forward points become effective bridge-

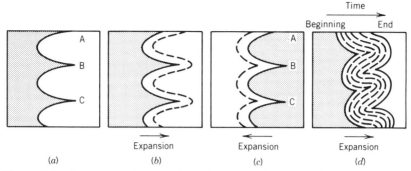

**Figure 5.9** *Concave and convex boundaries. (a) Element on left with concave boundaries, element on right with convex boundaries. (b) Dashed line indicates the new frontier as element on left spreads. (c) Dashed line indicates the new frontier as element on right spreads. (d) Over time, the concave margin of the spreading element on left becomes convex.*

heads to conquer terrain. The conquered area will clearly be larger than in the case of the element on the right spreading (Figure 5.9c), because in the latter case the conquest efforts are duplicated in the frontier portions near points A, B, and C. This is a case where the third matrix criterion, control over dynamics, brings its weight to bear. The element on the left, with concave boundaries, gains territory more efficiently and therefore is the matrix. We can observe an analogy with animal foraging (Schoener, 1971; Root, 1973; Emlen, 1981; Charnov, 1976; Covich, 1976; Krebs et al., 1974; Orians and Pearson, 1978; Kareiva, 1982), where predators at points A, B, and C would search for nearby food more efficiently in the element on the right, than in the one on the left. Inasmuch as the boundary between landscape elements may function as an important filter or semipermeable membrane, boundary shape is significant in interactions between matrix and patch (J. Wiens, C. Crawford, and J. Gosz, personal communication).

   This type of reasoning differentiates **spreading elements** (or tesserae), i.e., those which are most likely expanding at their periphery from convex boundaries, from **relict elements** (or tesserae), i.e., those that are in the process of diminishing and have concave boundaries (Figure 5.10a and b). Note that spreading elements may change rapidly from having a concave boundary with acute bridgeheads to having a convex boundary (Figure 5.9d). A clear example of a spreading element is the woody fire-adapted species that resprouts after fire from an extensive network of roots and underground stems. For example, a patch of the Kermes (or prickly) oak (*Quercus coccifera*) of Mediterranean shrubland or maquis often looks like a huge cauliflower in aerial photographs taken a few years after

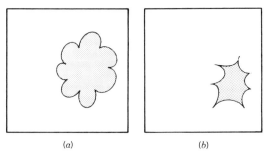

**Figure 5.10** *Spreading and relict landscape elements. (a) Convex boundaries of spreading element. (b) Concave boundaries of relict element*

a fire. As soon as the Kermes oak patches are connected, they must be considered the matrix.

The spreading and relict element rule just proposed has a number of apparent exceptions. For example, on hillsides ravaged by overgrazing and fire, perennial vegetation and associated invertebrate and vertebrate communities recolonize slopes by first invading the valley bottoms. A helicopter view of the colonizing element would show many protruding fingers of vegetation with concave boundaries between them (Figure 5.11).

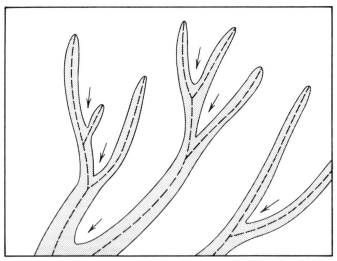

**Figure 5.11** *A spreading element in an environmentally heterogeneous area. The shaded element invades along valley bottoms (upward to the right), resulting in the concave or acute margins (indicated with arrows).*

The explanation for this apparent exception is that since the environment is strongly heterogeneous, initially the boundary shape simply reflects the sharp environmental differences. Progressively the area between the fingers tends to fill in and make a smoother boundary.

It appears that when the geomorphic substrate is homogeneous, the ultimate natural progression of boundaries leads from convexity to a wavy line that in time tends to become smooth, as in the cases of Figure 5.9b or c. Of course, the convoluted margins of environmental resource patches or those subject to chronic disturbance would change at extremely slow rates, if at all.

A so-called **form and function principle** (Thompson, 1961; Margalef, 1963; Portmann, 1969) also applies to landscapes (Harris and Kangas, 1979) and is particularly appropriate in the context of boundary shapes. The interaction between two objects is proportional to their common boundary surface. The rounded or compact form with minimal appendages, that is, with a minimal perimeter-to-area ratio, is characteristic of systems where it is important to conserve resources like energy, materials, or organisms. This form is important in animal ecology (Allen's law) or for a military force. In contrast, a convoluted boundary with a high perimeter-to-area ratio is characteristic of systems with considerable interchanges of energy, materials, or organisms with the surroundings— e.g., lungs or tree foliage (Van Leeuwen, 1966, 1973). A third shape, the dendritic, is mainly associated with transport—e.g., nerves or a railroad yard (MacDonald, 1983). These fundamental principles relate the shapes of boundaries and landscape elements to their function, namely the flows in and out of the surrounding matrix.

The structural characteristics of the matrix presented above are oversimplified in some respects but provide a framework for analyzing the dynamics of the matrix. The mathematically-inclined reader will have already recognized some familiar patterns and will find landscape structure fertile ground for analysis and elucidation. Set theory (e.g., Wilder, 1965; Cantor, 1969; Fairchild and Tulcea, 1970), fractals and topology (e.g., Kuratowski, 1972; Hocking and Young, 1961; Kasriel, 1971; Fairchild and Tulcea, 1971; Mandelbrot, 1981; Porteous, 1981; Burrough, 1981), and spatial statistics (Cliff et al., 1975; Burgess et al., 1981; Ripley, 1981; Kincaid and Bryant, 1983) routinely deal with similar spatial phenomena. Indeed, theories of topological spaces, topological mapping, homology, connectedness, filters, and nets seem directly applicable to landscape structure. Applications of these theories to spatial patterns such as networks, nodes, connectivity, and flows have been made in geography and transportation (King, 1969; Chorley and Haggett, 1970; Taaffe and Gauthier, 1973; Lowe and Moryadas, 1975; Isard, 1975; Bartlett, 1975; Haggett et al., 1977; Hastings et al., 1982). Their applicability to landscape ecology will be introduced in later chapters.

# NETWORKS

In Chapter 4 we observed that corridors often interconnect to form networks that enclose landscape elements. In this chapter, we converge on the subject of networks from another perspective. Now our concern is the matrix that encloses patches. When the enclosed landscape elements are large, or the landscape is highly porous, the matrix appears as interconnected strands and may be a corridor network. Many linear landscape features, such as roads or ditches, interconnect to form networks. We will focus on hedgerows because they are best known ecologically. In Chapter 11 we will explore the fascinating ways networks may function in the flows across a landscape.

## Intersections in the Network

As described previously, individual hedgerows differ markedly in internal structure. For purposes of simplicity, we will here ignore this structural richness and consider the hedgerow network to be composed of equivalent lines. Almost all such networks also include scattered or frequent woodlots. Thus, one important structural characteristic of the network is the type of connection that occurs where lines intersect or end (Hopkins and Odum, 1953). These types may have the shape of a cross, a *T*, an *L*, an end, or a connection with woods (Figure 5.12) (Forman and Baudry, 1984; Baudry, 1984).

Another network property is the presence, and length, of breaks in lines. In some hedgerow landscapes, the cross-shaped connection is rather uncommon, and experience in New Jersey (United States) and in Europe suggests that the *T* and cross-shaped connections commonly have short breaks near the intersection that are caused by the movement of farm machinery between fields.

Some intersections may serve as mini-nodes, spots that are wider than the corridors but too small to be recognized as separate landscape elements (Figure 5.12). Constant et al. (1976) reported more bird species in intersections than in the surrounding corridors.

If intersections in the network serve as mini-nodes for interior species, we would expect quite different patterns of distribution for interior and edge species (Wales, 1972) as a function of their distance from the intersection. The number of interior species should decrease rapidly with distance, since the spatial effect of a connecting hedgerow would presumably be quite limited (Figure 5.13). No effect of distance would be expected for edge species, except perhaps almost at the intersection point.

The hypothesized mechanism underlying this *intersection effect*, i.e., ecological conditions altered by an interconnection of corridors, is microclimatic modification. Although no microclimatic study of hedgerow

**Figure 5.12**  *A network of planted shelterbelts showing connection types. T connections are prevalent, but L, cross, and ends are also present. Isolated shelterbelts and a stream corridor with breaks are visible in the distance. This landscape near Vernon, Texas and Alta, Oklahoma was imprinted by a square mile (1.6 km) grid of roads in the nineteenth century. (Courtesy of USDA Soil Conservation Service)*

intersections is available, we can extrapolate from general microenvironmental studies of hedgerows. We expect a small area—of less than ten meters to a few tens of meters—that surrounds an intersection to have a lowered wind speed, more shade, higher atmospheric and soil moisture, higher soil organic matter, and less temperature variation (Pollard et al., 1974; Guyot and Verbrugghe, 1976; Barloy, 1980; Barloy et al., 1976). In essence, intersections are mini-nodes with a mesic microenvironment.

In a landscape of corn and bean fields in New Jersey, herb species diversity showed a significant negative correlation with distance from intersections (Figure 5.14) (Baudry and Forman, unpublished data). Diversity was markedly higher within 30 m of an intersection, and no significant effect of distance on herb diversity was present beyond that distance.

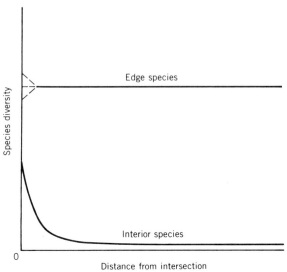

**Figure 5.13** *Hypothesized species distribution pattern for a network intersection of line corridors. The number of edge species in the intersection area itself may increase or decrease slightly as indicated by the dotted lines. (From J. Baudry and R. Forman, unpublished).*

Underlying the diversity pattern of Figure 5.14 was a significant negative correlation between the presence of 12 species and distance from an intersection. These species represented nearly 40% of the common hedgerow herbs. Although many forest interior species were present in the hedgerows, only two herb species—jewelweed (*Impatiens capensis*), and avens (*Geum canadense*)—and one woody species—choke cherry seedlings (*Prunus avium*)—were frequent enough to show a statistically significant intersection effect. The distribution patterns for these three species near intersections were then plotted to estimate how far an intersection effect extends. Jewelweed decreased significantly in abundance only in the first 14 m, avens decreased over the whole 30 m, and choke cherry decreased significantly from 20 to 30 m. In view of the drop in herb species diversity after 30 m (Figure 5.14), it appears that the intersection effect in this New Jersey network extends out to about 30 m.

## Reticulate Pattern

Linear features that interconnect and contain loops constitute a *reticulate pattern*. While a hedgerow network forms barriers around species in fields, it also provides loops and alternative pathways to species moving

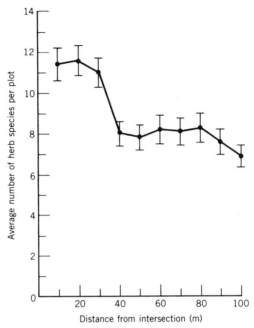

**Figure 5.14** *Intersection effect for herb species diversity in a hedgerow network. Near Hutcheson Memorial Forest and Millstone, New Jersey (United States). Each point is the average of 30 plots (30 hedgerows were sampled, with a plot being 10 m in length along the hedgerow, times the hedgerow width). Vertical lines (representing 95% LSI confidence limits) that do not overlap indicate that those diversity points are significantly different. Note that the above curve is equivalent to the sum of the curves in Figure 5.13. See Davison and Forman (1982) and Buell and Forman (1983) for information on the species present. (From J. Baudry and R. Forman, unpublished).*

along it (Figure 5.12) (Forman and Godron, 1981; Forman, 1983; Baudry and Burel, 1985; Merriam, 1984). We would expect such a reticulate structure to reduce the extent to which breaks, disturbances, and predators within the corridors inhibit the movement of species.

Unfortunately, this hypothesis has not been tested. The relative importance of hedgerows, narrow or wide, in determining the movement of plants and animals between woods in a landscape is still unclear, though it is probably great in some situations (Pollard and Relton, 1970; Helliwell, 1975; Bull et al., 1976; Wegner and Merriam, 1979; Merriam, 1984). Some evidence indicates that hedgerows attached to a woods have higher species diversity near the woods than at greater distance, possibly implying movement from woods to hedgerow (Helliwell, 1975; Willmot, 1980; Yahner, 1983b).

The hedgerow network is a grid with mostly rectangular elements. Other reticulate patterns exist, such as the polygonal or hexagonal tundra soils (see Figure 13.4) (Lachenbruch, 1962; Billings and Peterson, 1980; Tedrow, 1977), and the irregular animal paths of East African savannas. Possible flows along a network are discussed later in terms of transportation theory, mathematical network analysis, and ecological flows (Chapter 11).

### Mesh Size

The characteristics of enclosed landscape elements, such as their size, shape, environmental conditions, species richness, and human activities, exert a major effect on the network itself. The average distance between network lines, or the average area of landscape elements enclosed by the lines, are measurements of **mesh size.**

Mesh size is considered particularly important in relation to the **grain size of a species** (Levins, 1968), that is, the distance or area to which the species is sensitive in carrying out its functions, such as foraging, defending a nesting territory, or absorbing sunlight and water. For example, in a landscape in Brittany, France, a predatory ground beetle [*Poecilus capreus* (Carabidae)]—a relatively fine grained species—disappeared where the average mesh size of fields was greater than 4 ha (Figure 5.15) (Deveaux, 1976). In contrast, coarser grained species such as owls (*Strigidae*) were common up to a mesh size of 7 ha (Leduc, 1979).

Fine mesh            Intermediate mesh            Coarse mesh

**Figure 5.15** *Grain size related to mesh size of networks. When the mesh size becomes too great, the food or other resources of these network species becomes too scarce. In contrast, species characteristic of the spaces within the network would disappear as the mesh size becomes smaller.*

For comparison, the fields in the foreground of Figure 5.12 average 32 ha.

In the northwestern United States, elk (*Cervus elaphus*) avoid the vicinity of roads, and so suitable elk habitat decreases rapidly as the density of roads increases. So-called *road density* is the total length of roads in a unit area of terrain, and is an indirect measure of network mesh size. For example, barely a quarter of the forest terrain is suitable for elk when the road density has reached 2 km/km² (6 miles per square mile) (Thomas et al., 1979; Lyon, 1979, 1983; Yapp, 1973).

Mesh size is also important in logging operations (Peters, 1978; Bryer, 1983), and in agricultural economics. Farmers observe that it takes more time to cultivate several small fields than one large field of equal total area. In fact, an economist concluded that 4 ha appeared to be the minimum economic threshold for field size in Brittany (Le Clezio, 1976). (This figure is based only on the immediate cost of mechanized agriculture. Such a threshold size would doubtless be different if critical ecological factors were considered.)

## Factors Determining Network Structure

Usually, historical or cultural factors underlie the spatial relationship between a hedgerow network and landscape physiography. Landscape networks developed and changed markedly through time in response to numerous economic, social, and ecological factors (The Shelterbelt Project, 1934; Hoskins, 1955; Pollard et al., 1974; Rackham, 1976). For example, a parcel of land is divided among the children of a family, and hedgerows are planted to delineate the new smaller fields. These divisions result in a fine mesh network (Figure 5.16). In other areas, fields are communally owned and cultivated by the whole community. In this situation hedgerows may be planted only around a set of fields, resulting in a coarse mesh network. Later a fine mesh may be superimposed on the coarse mesh network as individual landowners obtain parcels. In many parts of the world, however, mesh size is increasing as more machines are used in agriculture (Figures 5.4 and 5.16).

Other networks, such as roads and power-lines, may have spatial relationships with hedgerows. For example, roads are usually the primary orienting lines in landscapes with major human imprint, and hedgerows start from, and parallel, roads (Figure 5.12) (Lebeau, 1969). Roadside vegetation, like that of hedgerows, has its own linear distinctiveness (Bates, 1937), and Willmot (1980) showed that hedgerows along roads in England are more diverse than those away from roads.

Since farmers generally use different soil types for different purposes, a hedgerow may mark the boundary between two soil types. Soil drainage characteristics also play an important role in both the orientation and the

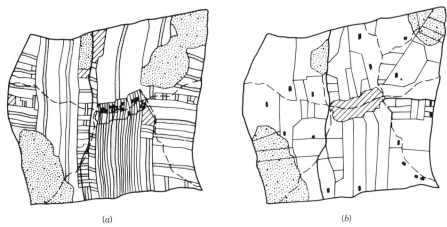

(a)                                                    (b)

**Figure 5.16**  *Transformation of a landscape by agrarian reform. (a) Surrounding a village is a fine mesh landscape produced by centuries of subdividing the land. After land redistribution (b) the village was abandoned, the homes were dispersed over the surface, and the fields were grouped into large parcels. Dotted areas are forested, including wooded strip corridors in (a); the former village site became agricultural fields. Village of Seesken, near Trentburg, eastern Prussia (Soviet Union). See Burel (1984) for a similar pattern in France. (From Lebeau, 1969; courtesy of Editeur Masson, © Masson, 1969).*

type of hedgerow. In poorly drained soils, hedgerows generally run up and down the slope and improve drainage. In better drained soils, where low moisture may limit productivity, hedgerows commonly run in contours or terraces and may include a ditch and bank to impede drainage. These examples emphasize how the spatial structure of hedgerow networks is determined by physiographic, communication, and sociological factors.

Network structure is not determined only by human influences. On mountains the basic geological process of erosion largely determines the spatial configuration of the intersecting patterns of stream corridors. Steeply descending streams with rapids tend to be relatively straight and to have narrow valleys with steep sides. In wide valleys, rivers and tributaries with little slope tend to meander.

## MATRIX HETEROGENEITY

One central problem of matrix structure remains to be considered. How homogeneous or heterogeneous is it? In effect, the matrix is always somewhat heterogeneous. This heterogeneity may weaken the distinction between matrix and patches, because every part of the matrix that differs slightly from the rest of the matrix could be considered a patch.

In the most general sense, an object is *homogeneous* if it is identical to itself in all its parts. Obviously, no real object exists that is absolutely homogeneous, since everything is composed of several types of atoms, and the atoms themselves are constituted of electrons, protons, and neutrons, which in turn are composed of quarks, and so on. The degree of homogeneity is never absolute; it always depends on the size of the smallest elements that are distinguished. Thus, the first step in characterizing the homogeneity of an object is to decide on the degree of fineness, or degree of resolution, we wish to observe.

A bronze bar is considered homogeneous if the proportions of copper and tin are approximately constant throughout. A flock of flamingos or a herd of caribou is homogeneous if the density of individuals of each age and sex are constant throughout. A population of maples (*Acer*) in a forest is considered homogeneous if the proportions of various genetic or morphological forms do not change significantly through space. A plant community is homogeneous if the covers of the component species remain constant in a group of plots (Raunkiaer, 1918; Emberger, 1954; Curtis and McIntosh, 1951; Greig-Smith, 1964; Daubenmire, 1968; Moravec, 1975; Mueller-Dombois and Ellenberg, 1974). Finally, a landscape may be considered homogeneous if the clusters of adjacent landscape elements do not differ significantly throughout the landscape. These examples emphasize that it is possible to describe homogeneity statistically, that is, an object may be considered homogeneous if its heterogeneity is below some arbitrary level. How then do we measure the level of heterogeneity?

For precision in considering methodology, we will begin with another analogy. The degree of fineness attained by an optical instrument (i.e., its power of resolution) depends directly on the wavelength of the radiant energy used by the instrument. Hence, an ordinary microscope using the visible wavelengths will permit one to observe only the surface of a stone, whereas X-rays (much shorter wavelengths) are used to gain an idea of the internal structure of crystals.

In studying the Woodstock and Agde landscapes (Figures 5.2 and 5.3), we used a line divided into segments of equal length (or a linear set of plots) to determine the frequency of the various landscape elements (Table 5.1). The line functions as a fisherman's net, with the mesh of the net equivalent to the length of the segments (or the size of the plots). Such a line with small segments, say, 10–200 cm long, has proven useful in studying plant species assemblages, where individual organisms can be distinguished (Godron, 1966, 1968, 1982). However, in studying a landscape, we want a level of resolution (i.e., a segment length) that is sensitive to the size of tesserae and that will help determine the limits between them. Thus, for most landscapes, the line segments generally should range from ten to several tens of meters in length. To have confidence in the major frequencies determined, more than a hundred segments should be measured along a line. This type of line is particularly useful in analyzing overall landscape structure and will be used to understand heterogeneity in the upcoming chapter.

## SUMMARY

The matrix, a major landscape element category (along with the patch and the corridor), exhibits at least six important structural characteristics. There are three criteria for determining the matrix: (a) it has a greater relative area than any patch type within it, (b) it is the most connected portion of the landscape, and (c) it plays a predominant role in the dynamics of the landscape. The landscape element type that clearly predominates in total area is the matrix. If no type is predominant, the degree of connectivity, together with relative area, determines the matrix. If no landscape element type is clearly predominant, the relative role in overall landscape dynamics determines the matrix.

The matrix may vary from slight to high porosity, irrespective of its degree of connectivity. The external boundaries of matrix elements are more often convex than concave, and boundary shape is a useful indication of the expansion or contraction of landscape elements. The role of a network in the landscape is reflected in the types of intersections present, the reticulate pattern of corridors, and the mesh size of the enclosed landscape elements. The structure of most networks is determined largely by human influences, though a stream network determined by erosion is a widespread exception.

To examine matrix heterogeneity, we must determine the level of resolution desired and select a method of measuring that has that degree of fineness. Observing the landscape elements present on segments of a long line is a simple method for evaluating matrix heterogeneity.

## QUESTIONS

1. How could one directly observe dynamic characteristics to determine which landscape element is the matrix?
2. What is the matrix in your landscape? In qualitative terms, how would you rate that type of element against the other leading element types in the landscape for each of the three matrix criteria?
3. The hedgerow network was evaluated as a possible matrix in an agricultural landscape. How would the evaluation differ for a road (with roadsides) network in a suburban landscape? Or ditches (with embankments) in an irrigated desert landscape?

4. Assume you are a regional landscape designer. Diagram a series of landscapes which combine each of the two following characteristics:
   (a) high connectivity and minimal matrix area
   (b) minimal patch edge and low connectivity
   (c) high porosity and minimal matrix area
   (d) relict tesserae and low connectivity
   (e) abundant patch edge and an extensive remote area of matrix
5. How would various kinds of disturbance affect the level of porosity in a matrix? The level of connectivity?
6. How can one resolve the apparent paradox that a matrix can exert a dynamic control over an embedded patch, whereas a patch with convex boundaries can spread at the expense of the matrix?
7. Why is scale so critical in determining heterogeneity?
8. In some landscapes the matrix is covered with people's homes. Draw a map of such a landscape having a matrix with a high degree of connectivity. Do the same for one with high porosity; a low relative area; high heterogeneity.
9. Can you think of any other structural characteristics of a matrix? How important might they be in terms of dynamics?

# Appendix: Measures of Patch Characteristics in a Matrix

The following measures proposed by different authors should be used with appropriate caution, since their dependability and generality in describing ecological patterns are as yet unclear. (See also Chapter 11.)

## Shape of a Patch

$$D_i = \frac{P}{2\sqrt{A\pi}}$$

where $D_i$ is an index of the shape of patch $i$; $P$ is the perimeter of the patch; and $A$ is the area of the patch (see Chapter 3; Patton, 1975; Game, 1980; and Bowen and Burgess, 1981. Several other measures of shape are summarized by Haggett et al., 1977).

## Isolation of a Patch

$$r_i = \frac{1}{n} \sum_{j=1}^{j=n} d_{ij}$$

where $r_i$ is an index of the isolation of patch $i$; $n$ is the number of neighboring patches considered; $\sum$ is the sum of; and $d_{ij}$ is the distance between patch $i$ and any neighboring patch $j$ (see King, 1969; Bowen and Burgess, 1981).

## Accessibility of a Patch

$$a_i = \sum_{j=1}^{j=n} d_{ij}$$

where $a_i$ is an index of the accessibility of patch $i$; $d_{ij}$ is the distance along a linkage (e.g., a forest corridor or hedgerow) between patch $i$ and any of the $n$ neighboring patches $j$ (see Lowe and Moryadas, 1975; Bowen and Burgess, 1981).

## Interaction Among Patches

$$I_i = \sum_{j=1}^{j=n} \frac{A_j}{d_j^2}$$

where $I_i$ is the degree of interaction of patch $i$ with $n$ neighboring patches; $A_j$ is the area of any neighboring patch $j$; and $d_j$ is the distance between the edges of patch $i$ and any patch $j$ (see Whitcomb et al., 1981; MacClintock et al., 1977).

## Isolation of Patches

$$D = \sum (\sigma_x^2 + \sigma_y^2)$$

where $D$ is an index of the isolation of all patches present. Patches are located on a grid with $x$ and $y$ coordinates. The average location and the variance for all patches are calculated for the $y$ coordinate. $\sigma_x^2$ and $\sigma_y^2$ are the variances on the $x$ and $y$ coordinates, respectively. This equation is based on the "standard distance index" (see Lowe and Moryadas, 1975; Bowen and Burgess, 1981).

## Dispersion of Patches

$$R_c = 2\, d_c \left( \frac{\lambda}{\pi} \right)$$

where $R_c$ is an index of dispersion; $d_c$ is the average distance from a patch (its center or centroid) to its nearest neighboring patch; and $\lambda$ is the average density of patches. Here $R_c = 1$ with randomly distributed patches; $R_c < 1$ for aggregated patches; and $R_c > 1$ (up to a maximum of 2.149) for regularly distributed patches. This equation is a measure of aggregation (see Clark and Evans, 1954, 1979; Pielou, 1977).

# 6
# *Overall Structure*

*The world is a beautiful book,*
*but of little use to him who cannot read it.*
**Pamela Goldoni**

In a valley at the bottom of a high mountain, a group of climbers walks easily by cultivated patches, woodlots, gardens, homes, streams, and roads. Each of these landscape elements is generally 10 to 100 meters across, and the entire landscape can be represented in the area of a few square kilometers (Figure 6.1a).

Halfway up the mountain, the valley landscape is still visible, but the individual landscape elements previously noticed are tiny. The climbers can clearly view mountainside landscapes composed of rocky cliffs, avalanche tracks, and various forest patches (Figure 6.1b). Each of the landscape elements visible is perhaps a hundred to a few thousand meters across, and it may require a hundred square kilometers to describe the whole landscape adequately.

Many hours later, the climbers feel the euphoria as they reach the summit. The panorama embraces numerous landscapes, including a system of valleys, warm sunny mountainsides, cool forested slopes, and rugged or rounded summits of mountain ranges (Figure 6.2). Each visible landscape measures several kilometers across, and the whole panorama easily covers ten thousand square kilometers. These landscapes are still composed of individual landscape elements that are often difficult to distinguish from this vantage point. With a pair of binoculars, though, the tiny garden where the climbers received their send-off can still be seen from the top of the peak.

This example emphasizes the importance of **scale,** that is, spatial proportion, or the ratio of length on a map to true length. Scale has been studied by many authors (e.g., Kershaw, 1960; Greig-Smith, 1964; Godron et al., 1968; King, 1969; Herz, 1973; Long, 1974; Bartlett, 1975; Isard, 1975; Miller, 1978a; Mandelbrot, 1981; Delcourt et al., 1983). Scholars in various disciplines use small and large scale in opposite senses. Therefore, in this book, we use the terms **fine scale**—referring to a small area, where the ratio of map length to true length is large, as for example in Figure 6.1a—and **broad** or **coarse scale**—referring to a large

(b)

(a)

**Figure 6.2** *Broad scale view from atop Aiguille de Midi, Chamonix, France (R. Forman).*

area where the ratio is small, as in Figure 6.2. The mountain-climbing expedition also illustrates the importance of degree of **resolution,** that is, the ability to distinguish small objects. As the climbers progressed, their view was increasingly broad in scale, while their degree of resolution diminished.

The landscape concept is flexible (see Chapter 1), and for certain purposes, such as mapping, it may be useful to consider the entire panorama seen from the summit (Figure 6.2) as one landscape, not many. In such a case, the valleys, mountainsides, and summits or ranges would be the landscape elements repeated over an extensive mountainous landscape.

The elements that constitute a landscape can be assembled in a hi-

**Figure 6.1** *Fine scale and medium scale views in the Alps (Chamonix, France). a. Fine scale view of individual homes, vegetation patches, and so forth (the mountain is Mont Blanc, 4807 m high, the highest mountain in Europe). b. Medium scale view of avalanche tracks, built areas, and so forth with ski area in upper right (the mountain is Le Brevent). (R. Forman).*

erarchy. For example, the garden is an element when seen at the beginning of the trip but it is drowned in the element called "valley" when seen from the summit. In this sense, the structure of the landscape as a whole is a **true synthesis,** in that the elements are transformed into new forms when combined. It is like building large molecules (with unique characteristics) out of simpler components in the chemistry laboratory. This synthesis produces new objects, the properties of which are usually not predictable before the synthesis. Knowing that a molecule of water is composed of two atoms of hydrogen and one of oxygen does not tell us much about such functional characteristics of water as freezing at 0°C or being able to refresh a parched throat (even when mixed with a few molecules of coffee or alcohol).

In short, the landscape as a whole has properties that its parts do not possess. Therefore, we cannot describe a landscape only as the sum of cultivated fields, homes, roads, streams, and pastures. As in a synthesis, the **configuration** of elements—their locations and their juxtaposition—is a characteristic that must also be described. For example, the elements may be clustered together in a corner of an extensive open area, distributed evenly throughout, or even aligned linearly as are dwellings along a cliff face or a line of springs in an arid zone. Therefore, we must observe how the landscape elements are assembled and make use of the concepts of microheterogeneity and macroheterogeneity.

## MICROHETEROGENEITY AND MACROHETEROGENEITY

In certain dry tropical areas—for example, in parts of Australia or Africa—trees can grow nearly anywhere, and aerial photographs show that they are essentially scattered throughout the landscape. The limited amount of available water in the soil, however, prevents young trees from thriving when the roots of an older tree already occupy a spot. Consequently, a relatively bare circular area appears around each mature tree (Rossetti, 1962). Mammal herbivory and the release of toxic organic chemicals (allelochemics) are also controlling factors in some areas (Muller and del Moral, 1966; Muller, 1970; Rood, 1970; Bartholomew, 1970).

On aerial photographs, each tree or shrub patch surrounded by its bare ring appears as a quite distinct patch in a herbaceous matrix (Figure 6.3). The matrix in this case can be described as quite homogeneous, clearly predominant, highly connected, and very porous. But one further characteristic is striking in the aerial photographs: the patch configuration. The woody patches are quite regularly spaced across the matrix, because a seedling can only mature if it is sufficiently far from existing mature plants (Figure 6.3). This configuration is a typical example of **microheterogeneity.** That is, the assemblage of landscape element types around

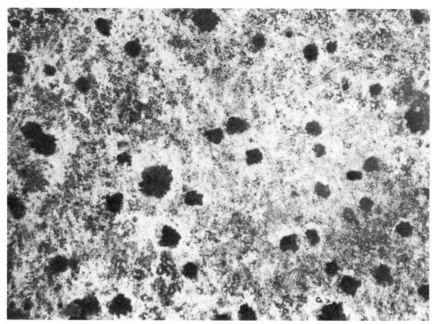

**Figure 6.3** *Microheterogeneous distribution of woody plants in dry savanna. Large dark spots are individual trees or shrub patches, most of which are surrounded by a light colored ring nearly bare of vegetation. This vegetation experiences severe drought and is widespread in the Mauritania region (in the Sahel) south of the Sahara. (From the* Bulletin de la Carte Phytogeographique, *B-VII-2, 1962, Paris, C.N.R.S.; courtesy of the Ministère de la Recherche et de l'Industrie.)*

a point is similar wherever the point is located in an area. Another example of microheterogeneity in dry savanna (steppe) regions are the woody patches that are grouped in numerous parallel bands, producing a distinctive "tiger scrub" vegetation.

In contrast, on a mountain slope in the Sierra Nevadas or Himalayas or Alps (Figures 6.1 and 6.2), for example, the landscape elements near the top are completely different from those near the valley bottom. This configuration is an example of **macroheterogeneity;** that is, the assemblage of landscape element types differs markedly in the extreme portions of the area observed. Here the environmental gradient is rather constant through space, a condition that generally produces a relatively gradual continuous change (continuum) in the vegetation and fauna. In this case, there is more similarity in the clusters of landscape elements around nearby points than around points widely separated along the gradient.

These two examples suggest that overall landscape structure embraces an intriguing richness of pattern. No landscape is completely microheterogeneous or completely macroheterogeneous. To determine the level of these contrasting characteristics in a landscape, it is convenient to employ a linear sample for measuring heterogeneity, as was done in Chapter 5 to distinguish matrix from patches. Lines are laid out across a landscape, aerial photograph, or map, and segments of equal length are marked off along the lines. In each segment the presence or absence of each type of landscape element is then recorded. This simple method (see Appendix of this chapter) is efficient for sampling and for later statistical analysis of the observations (Kershaw, 1958; Godron, 1966; Zarnovican, 1972; Poissonet et al., 1973). We will now use it to study more precisely two quite different landscapes.

## Analysis of a Microheterogeneous Landscape

Vineyards were tended more than twenty centuries ago on the Languedoc plains in southern France. The Romans transported wine in their wide-bellied galleys (whose wreckage was strewn along Mediterranean shores) and engaged in time-honored arguments over the quality of the wine. Nowadays, the traveler who crosses the hills and coastlines of Languedoc has the impression of navigating in a sea of vineyards and crops that seems about to engulf the fortified villages perched on little buttes. To find out if this landscape is really as homogeneous as it appears, we placed five parallel lines on a map (1/25,000 scale) of the landscape near the old port of Agde. The lines were approximately 8 km long and were divided into 128 segments that were each 64 m long. The presence of each landscape element type was recorded for each segment.

Below is an example of the results for the second line near Agde (Figure 6.4), where fields of cultivated crops are particularly common.

| Landscape Element Types | Relative Frequency |
|---|---|
| Cultivated crops | 57% |
| Vineyards | 43% |
| Dirt roads | 23% |
| Paved roads | 19% |
| Streams and rivers | 18% |
| Homes | 10% |
| Orchards | 7% |
| Hedgerows | 5% |
| Marshes | 2% |
| Town | 1% |

**Figure 6.4** *The Agde landscape of Languedoc, southern France. The approximately 8 km Line Number 2 is marked on the map.*
© *IGN-Paris 19-Aut. no. 700932. Carte Au 1/50,000 (No. 2645)/(No. 2641).*

Cultivated crops are present in 57% of the segments, vineyards in 43%, dirt roads in 23%, and town in only 1%. The three landscape element types with the highest frequency (cultivation, vineyards, and dirt roads) are distributed throughout the length of the line rather than being only at one end or in the middle of the line (Figure 6.5a).

A closer look at the distribution of elements reveals that the dirt roads are fairly evenly or regularly distributed along the line. On the other hand, the cultivated fields tend to be clustered together, as do the vineyards (Figure 6.5a). In this sense, where you encounter one cultivated field, another field is usually next to it, and the same pattern is evident for vineyards.

The less frequent landscape elements exhibit less clear distribution patterns along the line. The marshes are only present on the extreme right end (Figure 6.5a). Homes, paved roads, and hedgerows are especially frequent in the middle. We can analyze the observations quantitatively and document these results objectively instead of subjectively as we have just done. Our goal is to determine the **distinctive configurations** present, that is, the significant nonrandom spatial patterns. If we quantitatively evaluate and compare the distributions of all the landscape elements along the line (see the Appendix to this chapter), the most remarkable or distinctive configuration of heterogeneity present turns out to be the clustered distribution of the cultivated fields and of the vineyards.

At the beginning of this chapter, we emphasized the importance of scale in interpreting landscape elements and pattern. Heterogeneity also depends on scale, as becomes evident when we go to the summit of a small mountain near Agde and view the landscape analyzed above. Now that the view is broader, the resolution power of the eye is inadequate to distinguish many of the details just discussed. This transformation is dealt with in the analysis of the line of segments by grouping the segments in twos. When this is done, we have half as many new segments, each 128 m long, and the new image of the line is reduced (Figure 6.5b).

If a bit of volcanic activity nudged the mountain higher (and you dared to stay atop the volcanic cone with all the explosions, gases, ash, heat, lava, and moving ground), as the cone grew higher your view would progressively broaden, while your Agde 2 line would seem to diminish, as from Figure 6.5b to 6.5c to 6.5d and 6.5e. What happens to the heterogeneity of the landscape during this process? In Figure 6.5c, the cultivated fields appear to be present throughout, and in 6.5d, the vineyards are also found continuously along the line. Originally the clustering of these two landscape elements was the most distinctive heterogeneity pattern in the landscape (Figure 6.5a), but now the landscape has become homogeneous for them. This happened simply by changing the scale of observation. An increase in homogeneity when the scale of observation is broadened is, therefore, another characteristic of a microheterogeneous

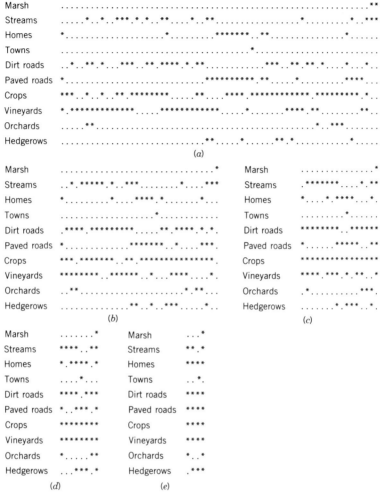

**Figure 6.5** *Effect of progressively grouping sampled segments along a line. The Agde 2 line (Figure 6.4) was sampled with 128 segments each 64 m long. Data for segments were then grouped by twos, so (a) appears as 64 segments each representing 128 m length. Dots indicate the absence of a type of landscape element, and asterisks indicate presences. At each step from (a) to (e), segments are grouped by twos, such that a dot or asterisk represents the absence or presence of a landscape element in two segments of the previous level.*

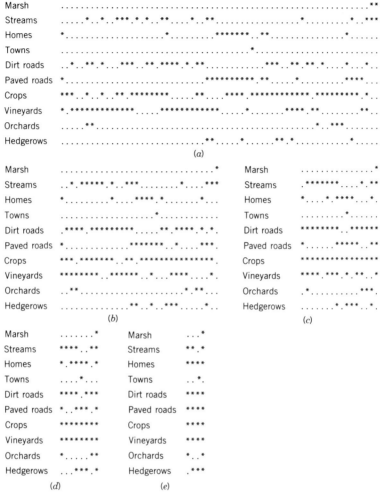

landscape (and is described mathematically in the Appendix to this chapter). In this case, heterogeneity of the landscape is greatest when viewed close up, as if looking through a microscope at the myriad microorganisms in pond water.

In fact, no landscape is perfectly microheterogeneous, because certain landscape element types are inevitably more frequent toward one end of the line or the other. Thus, in the Agde line (Figures 6.4 and 6.5a) cultivated fields and vineyards are clearly microheterogeneous, but the marshes, which are at one end of the line only, are not. In this manner, we can characterize the overall structure of a landscape in terms of its degree of microheterogeneity, but we can also describe each type of landscape element in terms of microheterogeneity.

The precise calculation of the amount of heterogeneity present at each level of scale (see Appendix to this chapter) shows that the contrasts between landscape elements appear most strongly at the level of Figure 6.5b. **Contrast,** the degree of difference and the abruptness of transition between adjacent areas, is another distinctive and useful characteristic of overall landscape structure (Kuchler, 1973). We will consider it further later in this chapter. Like microheterogeneity, contrast may vary continuously in degree from high to low. When the amount of heterogeneity present is calculated mathematically for each level of scale in the Agde landscape (Figure 6.5a-e), the highest level of contrast between landscape elements appears at level 6.5b in the landscape. Thus, like microheterogeneity, contrast differs at different levels of scale. But contrast is a relatively independent characteristic and may peak at almost any level of scale.

### Analysis of a Macroheterogeneous Landscape

In the central Atlas Mountains of Morocco is a plateau scattered with volcanos and covered by pastures and magnificent forests of stately Atlas cedars (*Cedrus atlantica*). (This species, an evergreen with bluish foliage and excellent wood that was used long ago to build the nearby city of Fez, presently graces the lawns of estates around the world.) The boundaries of the cedar forest on the plateau are often sharp, and the landscape is very heterogeneous. To analyze this typical case of macroheterogeneity, landscape structure was studied by measuring vegetation along the length of 51-km lines that were extended across the plateau and down into the adjacent semi-arid and arid valleys (Lecompte, 1973). The 64 consecutive segments, each 800 m in length, along one line, will be examined here for the presence or absence of the predominant woody plants.

The line begins in the high elevation cedar forests, passes through mid-elevation pastures, and finally descends into the drier Moulouya valley.

The data show that cedar, oak, barberry, and chickweed are present only in the highest portion of the line (to the left of Figure 6.6). The next two species, mainly in the highest portion, are followed by four species that appear to be distributed more or less along the entire line. The last six species are increasingly limited to the lower elevations (to the right of Figure 6.6).

Each of the first four species has a typical macroheterogeneous distribution. That is, when we observe the line from afar without analyzing the details, the first four species appear to be clearly concentrated toward one end of the line (Figure 6.6). The last six species, which are absent from the highest portion of the line, are macroheterogeneous also. Since other lines parallel to this line show the same pattern, we conclude that this landscape is predominantly macroheterogeneous.

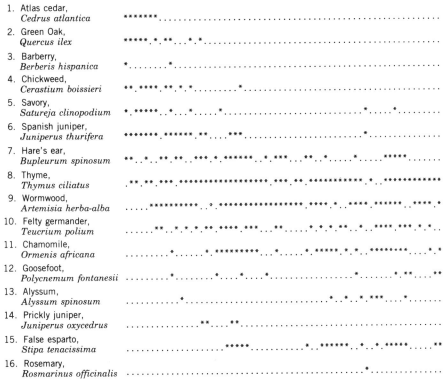

**Figure 6.6** *Woody plants along a 51 km line from high to low elevation in the Atlas Mountains, Morocco. Presence of a predominant species is indicated by an asterisk, absence by a dot. Each of the 64 segments is approximately 800 m long. Note that the mountains are covered with cooking herbs. (From Lecompte, 1973).*

We can also measure precisely the degree of heterogeneity of each species. Using the example of the Atlas cedar, we may visualize a shuttle—resembling a weaver's shuttle—that is progressively passed along the line. The shuttle is long enough to cover exactly two of the 64 segments at any time. When the shuttle is placed in its first position, it covers the first two segments of the data for cedar. Since cedar is present in both segments (Figure 6.6), the distribution of cedar in this position of the shuttle appears homogeneous. More precisely, we say the amount of heterogeneity is zero for cedar in the first two segments. When the shuttle is moved one notch to the right, it covers segments 2 and 3, both of which contain cedar, and so again no heterogeneity is present. The shuttle is moved in this fashion progressively down the line, recording zero heterogeneity until it covers segments 7 and 8 (Figure 6.6). Here, one presence and one absence of the species are observed.

This observation is equivalent to one unit of **information** about the degree of heterogeneity of this species on the line (Godron, 1966; for other uses of information theory, see Margalef, 1957; Pielou, 1966; Medvedkov, 1967; Morowitz, 1970; Tribus and McIrvine, 1971; Webber, 1972; Phipps, 1981b). Information is knowledge gained from observing an event. [It is measured (in information theory) by the logarithm—base 2—of the inverse of the probability of an event; see the Appendix to this chapter.] In communications theory, a unit of information is called a *binon* (according to the International Telegraph and Telephone Committee), or a *bit* (when used with computers).

As the movement of the shuttle continues down the line, it thereafter records two absences of cedar at each notch (Figure 6.6); there are, therefore, no additional binons or bits relative to heterogeneity.

In summary, for the 63 possible shuttle positions, we obtain only one unit of information. Therefore, the average information level for the samples along this line is

$$1/63 \text{ or } 0.016 \text{ binons or bits}$$

It is possible to "stand back" from the line and effectively change the scale, so that finer details drop out and broader patterns become clearer. This change can be made here by grouping the segments along the line by twos. Doing so is essentially equivalent to recording the presence and absence of species along 1600 m segments, instead of the original 800-m segments. The line for cedar would then appear as follows.

Atlas cedar (*Cedrus atlantica*) ****...........................

In this case, the shuttle covers two segments equivalent to a total length of 3,200 m. The first three notches for the shuttle cover only species presences and thus contain no units of information on heterogeneity. When the shuttle is in the fourth position, it covers one presence and one absence, thus providing information equal to one binon. The 27 following shuttle positions contain no information on heterogeneity because they are situated along the line only where the species is absent. The average information on heterogeneity obtained along this line is

1/31 or 0.032 binons or bits

By the same reasoning, grouping the original segments in fours to produce 6400 m segments gives a line for cedar

Atlas cedar (*Cedrus atlantica*) **.............

The second shuttle position contains one binon, while the fourteen other positions provide no information units. The average information level is

1/15 or 0.066 binons or bits

If we continue to group the segments in this fashion, the average information level will continue to increase. In summary, as the scale becomes progressively broader, the average information has the following values.

$0.016 \rightarrow 0.032 \rightarrow 0.066 \rightarrow 0.143 \rightarrow 0.333 \rightarrow 1.000$ binon or bit

This regular increase in information level is the typical indication of a macroheterogeneous distribution, of cedar along a line in this case. Heterogeneity is greater when we observe the pattern from afar than when we observe the details.

In a microheterogeneous pattern such as that observed near Agde, the result would be the opposite. If the "shuttle analysis" is applied in that case (Figure 6.5), both information and heterogeneity decrease as we broaden our view ($0.43 \rightarrow 0.39 \rightarrow 0.29 \rightarrow 0.13 \rightarrow 0.00$ binons or bits).

When the same reasoning and measurements are made for the other species along the line in the Atlas Mountain landscape of Morocco, it appears that most of the species have a macroheterogeneous distribution (Figure 6.6). In this case, regional climatic gradients—from cool moist high elevations to hot dry low elevations—are the primary cause of the macroheterogeneity of the vegetation. Controlling biotic factors, such as the influence of humans and sheep, reinforce the pattern imposed by climatic factors.

Marine or river shorelines with bands of vegetation and animal communities are also, at a finer scale, typically macroheterogeneous. For example, the extensive marshlands along the St. Lawrence River in Quebec have been similarly analyzed—calculating the amount of information provided by the distributions of species—and found to be macroheterogeneous (Gauthier, 1979).

The Agde landscape is microheterogeneous, and the Moroccan mountain landscape is macroheterogeneous. Few if any landscapes, though, are completely one or the other, that is, composed only of micro- or macroheterogeneously distributed landscape elements. Rather, landscapes are normally composed of a mixture of both landscape element distributions. Hence, absolute micro- and macroheterogeneity are opposite ends of a spectrum, and landscapes can be directly compared on the basis of where they fall along it.

## CONFIGURATION OF PATCHES, CORRIDORS, AND MATRIX

The above analysis of heterogeneity provided an overview of landscape structure that is based on the distribution patterns of landscape elements (or of predominant species). We now turn to the question of how patches, corridors, and the matrix are spatially distributed across a landscape.

The possibilities seem limitless: patches lined up like the beads on a rosary, clusters of tiny patches, small patches next to large patches, two types of patches always separated as if repelling one another, and so forth. Certainly these different structural possibilities play critical roles in how a landscape functions (Van Leeuwen, 1966; King, 1977; Ruzicka et al., 1982). For example, landscape structure—as indicated by the numbers, types, and configuration of landscape elements—in a 2.5 km² area surrounding a site has a major effect on the bird community at that site (Arnold, 1983).

To identify such spatial configurations, many methods may be used, such as mathematical morphology (Matheron, 1965), autocorrelation (Moran, 1953), spatial statistics (Cliff et al., 1975; Burgess et al., 1981; Ripley, 1981; Kincaid and Bryant, 1983), and spectral analysis or fractals (Mandelbrot, 1981; Burrough, 1981; Hastings et al., 1982). To illustrate landscape concepts, we will use information theory from communications which offers a broad perspective and is easily used. Indeed, a recent landscape book (Gonzalez-Bernaldez, 1981) began with the following lines: "We must recognize that the subject of the landscape embraces many and varied dimensions. Therefore, it seems necessary to me to select a unifying focus, and I have chosen the perspective of information."

## A Few Distinctive Configurations

Virtually all configurations of landscape elements are nonrandom. How can we detect all the myriad possible spatial patterns? There is no need, nor is it possible, to be complete. Here are five important patterns with a few illustrations of each.

1. *Regular* or even distributions are those where the distance between the landscape elements of a particular type is relatively uniform. For example, school fields in suburbia usually are regularly distributed, because each school draws children from its surrounding neighborhood. Homes or farm ponds in some agricultural areas are commonly distributed regularly, because each is surrounded by its farmland. Other examples are wetlands in certain limestone sinkhole or karst landscapes, wet sedge areas in polygon shaped soil patches in the tundra (see Figure 13.4), and clearings cut in certain forests (Figure 6.7).

**Figure 6.7** *Regular distribution of clearcut patches in coniferous forest on slopes of Mt. Baker in Washington State (United States). Note the variation in patch sizes, shapes, distances between patches, slopes, and connecting logging road corridors. (B. Eustus; courtesy of Defenders of Wildlife.)*

2. *Aggregated* distributions are seen, for example, in many tropical agricultural areas where a series of fields is clustered in the general vicinity of a village or the end of a road. In hilly terrain, rice paddies are often in clusters, and villages also are clustered in major valleys.
3. *Linear* patterns are illustrated by homes scattered along a road or cultivated fields along streams in arid or mountainous terrain. Glacial processes often leave linear bands of sand along which patches of pine woods may be found.
4. Examples of *parallel* patterns are parallel stream corridors in rapidly eroding terrain and nutrient-poor woodlands along hilltops in ridge and valley landscapes (Figure 6.8). Some glaciated landscapes have distinctive parallel wetlands resulting from gouging of the land by the glacier.
5. Distinctive associations, or *spatial linkage*, may exist between different types of landscape elements. For example, rice paddies and cranberry bogs are always associated with streams or canals. Roads and golf courses often exhibit a positive spatial linkage with towns and villages. In arid areas, fanlike sediment deposits inevitably are at the end of

**Figure 6.8** *Parallel landscape elements in ridge and valley topography. Washington County, Tennessee (United States.) Ridge tops tend to be more acid and less fertile here and are covered with forest corridors. Narrows and breaks are visible in both the forested and open strip corridors. (Courtesy of USDA Soil Conservation Service).*

**206** LANDSCAPE STRUCTURE

stream corridors at the base of mountains. These are cases of positive spatial linkage; that is, one landscape element is present and a high probability exists that the other element will also be nearby. Spatial linkage may also be negative (or "in opposition"). Such was the case for cultivated crops and vineyards on the Agde line (Figure 6.5); if cultivated crops were present in a segment, vineyards were probably absent, and vice versa.

Before we examine how to recognize distinctive configurations in the landscape, it should be noted that overall patchiness of a landscape can also be determined. Porosity refers to the density of patches of a particular type (Chapter 5); **patchiness** is a measure of the density of patches of all types (Greig-Smith, 1952; Evans and Dahl, 1955; Kershaw, 1957; Thompson, 1958; Pielou, 1965, 1967, 1969; Roach, 1968; Hill, 1973; Levin and Paine, 1974; Slatkin, 1974; Bartlett, 1975; Roughgarden, 1978; Diggle, 1981). For example, suburbia with its relatively small patches is patchier than a grassland landscape no matter how many types of landscape elements are present in either case.

In a mosaic composed of several patch types, it is common for three or more types of landscape elements to intersect at a point. Such points may be recognized as *coverts* or *convergency points* and are believed to be of particular importance to wildlife, because at them is found the convergence or proximity of diverse resources (Harris and Kangas, 1979). In addition to a concentration of interactions among the landscape elements, convergency points often are at the peninsula tips (Chapter 3) of two of the landscape elements, and therefore are key points for movement of animals and other objects across a landscape (the funnel effect). Since interactions among three (or more) landscape elements are probably particularly important, we also recognize *convergency lines*. This term refers to line corridors where three types of landscape elements are in close proximity. A windbreak between grassland and cultivation and a logging road between a coniferous plantation and a deciduous forest are convergency lines. Where are the convergency points and lines in Figure 6.8?

## Determining Distinctive Configurations

**The Line Approach.** Four main aspects of landscape structure can be characterized and directly compared along a line, using information levels expressed in binons or bits.

1. The *beginning position* of each landscape element type.
2. The *end position*.

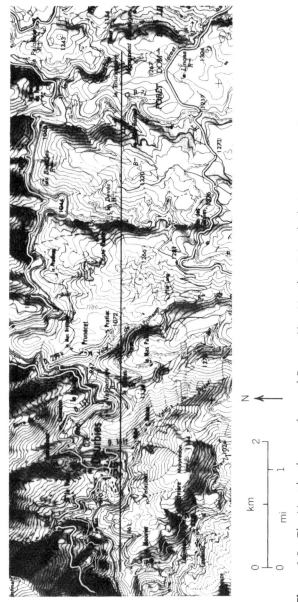

**Figure 6.9** *The Nant landscape of central France. Line Number 7 (marked), is approximately 8 km long.* © IGN-Paris 19-Aut. no. 700932. Carte Au 1/50,000 (No. 2645)/(No. 2641).

3. The *aggregation* or (in contrast) the *regularity* in distribution of occurrences of the elements.
4. The *spatial linkage* between different types of elements.

We will focus on the results of the analyses, using the example of a line, Nant 7, that is one of several 8 km lines used to analyze a hilly wooded and pasture landscape in central France for a management plan (Figure 6.9). Calculation methods are given in the Appendix to this chapter.

The Nant 7 line contains seven types of landscape elements: streams, homes, dirt roads, paved roads, woods, shrublands, and pastures (Figure 6.10a). The matrix is composed of woods, and it is immediately apparent that woods and shrublands have a negative spatial linkage (Figure 6.10a). We also immediately note that paved roads and homes appear to be concentrated along the left side of the line. To go beyond these somewhat subjective impressions, we can calculate the information levels for the above four aspects of landscape structure relative to the overall structure of the line (see Appendix to this chapter). The results, shown on the next page in decreasing order, pinpoint the distinctive configurations in this portion of the landscape (Figure 6.10b).

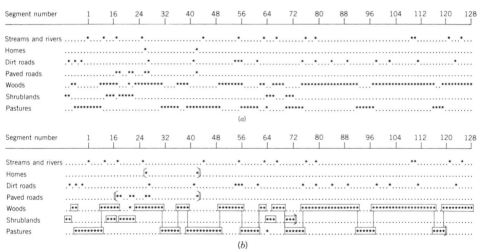

**Figure 6.10** *Overall landscape structure along the Nant 7 line. (a) Presence (\*) or absence (·) of landscape elements is indicated in 128 segments along the line. (b) Significant structural patterns are marked based on data analyses. Rectangles indicate statistically significant aggregations. The beginning for homes (marked [) is also significant (6 binons). Beginnings and ends of species distributions that are highly significant (≥ 7 binons) are indicated by [[ and ]], respectively. (See Appendix to Chapter 6 for statistical methods.)*

1. Pastures are highly aggregated in groups (55 binons or bits).
2. Pastures and woods exhibit a negative spatial linkage (are in opposition) (47 binons).
3. Woods are highly aggregated (41 binons).
4. Shrublands are clearly aggregated (22 binons) and are on the left portion of the line (17 binons, based on information provided by their end position).
5. Paved roads are clearly on the left (16 binons, also based on information on end position).
6. The other information levels are significantly lower (8 binons for the "end" of pastures, 8 for the "end" of homes, 7 for the "beginning" of paved roads, and 6 binons for the "beginning" of homes).

These results lead to a logical ecological and socioeconomic interpretation. The paved roads and homes situated on the left side of the line are the heart of an area of human activity—deforestation, pasturing, and cultivation. More distant from the homes is some land abandonment with consequent invasion of pastures and shrublands, a general process throughout the entire Nant region. The forested matrix is present along the whole line but is especially concentrated on the right side, where a national forest is in fact located.

Other insights into the configuration or patch structure of a landscape may be gained with this approach. For example, we may identify in a precise manner those elements whose "center of gravity" is significantly distant from the center of the line, those with unusual clusterings of presences or absences, and places along the line where mapping boundaries would optimally be located (e.g., to divide the line into landscape sections more homogeneous than the line as a whole) (Godron, 1966, 1971, 1972; Godron and Bacou, 1975).

Determining a landscape configuration opens up two additional dimensions. First, a specific configuration was produced by a specific force or forces, and when we have determined that configuration we are in a better position to attempt to determine those forces. Second, a specific landscape configuration implies a specific landscape functioning or flow of animals, plants, energy, water, or mineral nutrients.

**The Grid Approach.**   We can directly analyze the horizontal distribution of landscape elements or predominant species in two dimensions by using a grid. The method consists of placing a grid of squares over the territory of interest and recording in each square what landscape elements are present or absent there. Then "windows" of increasing size are moved over the interior of the grid just as we previously moved a shuttle along the length of a line. Many descriptions and tests may be performed with this type of data using information analysis and other techniques. One of the more direct methods of analysis is to compare the number of presences of each element observed in each window, with the number expected as a function of window size (see Appendix to this chapter). In fact, the grid approach is used commonly in the interpretation of aerial photography. Here spatial analyses can be performed using information stored in a computer about each square (pixel) of the grid.

## CONTRAST IN THE LANDSCAPE

The examples just presented show that patches, corridors, and the matrix can be combined in many ways and that these are often related to human activities. One of the primary results of activities such as agriculture, forest management, and suburbanization is increased contrast in landscapes. Contrast (as in a photograph) is strong if adjacent landscape elements are very different from each other and transitions between them are narrow or absent.

### Low-Contrast Structure

How would you visualize a landscape with the lowest possible contrast? It would be composed of a single type of landscape element, like the surface of a new purple table in your room, which would be the matrix; no patch or corridor would be present. These conditions rule out all landscapes containing roads, homes, or villages. Also eliminated are most cold or arid landscapes with little vegetation and with high contrast produced by geomorphic processes. Hence, the lowest-contrast landscapes must be natural and must even be free of such natural patches as distinct wet depressions or stream corridors. The primary example appears to be a landscape covered by a uniform blanket of vegetation on deep homogeneous soils. This pattern can be produced in a moist temperate or tropical region, but temperate zones are today so heavily modified by people that the pattern is only found in a few tropical areas.

The most typical illustration of a low contrast landscape is a tropical rain forest, where, away from major water courses, we may choose an aerial photograph almost at random (Figure 6.11). Scrutiny of the photograph may or may not reveal traces of minimal topographic relief. The canopy of the vegetation is usually pockmarked with both deep holes and tall emergent trees, suggesting a many-layered forest that appears to extend over nearly the entire landscape. What, then, is the nature of heterogeneity in the tropical rain forest? Where are the landscape elements?

Ecologists and foresters have known for a long time that it is extremely difficult to find distinct plant associations in these moist tropical forests.

**Figure 6.11**  *Tropical rain forest canopy (montane rain forest, Merida, Venezuela). Note the convoluted canopy surface, and our inability to detect the location of a stream gulley beneath. These canopy trees are festooned with airplants (epiphytes)—especially orchids, ferns, and bromeliads. A small clearing with banana plantings is visible in the upper right. (R. Forman.)*

Most species are rare and few species frequent (Emberger, 1954; Pires et al., 1953; Richards, 1964; Ashton, 1976). The apparent homogeneity of vegetation presents several advantages for animals, particularly herbivores such as fruit-eating vertebrates, which often maintain a highly diversified diet in the forest matrix. Average temperature varies very little from month to month, and numerous plant species do not have a regular annual fruiting cycle (McClure, 1966). Fruit-eating vertebrates in the evergreen forest thus are offered a diverse menu almost anywhere and almost throughout the year.

Furthermore, birds, mammals, and insects play key roles in the dissemination of a variety of seeds throughout the forest. This dispersal process affects spatial landscape homogeneity in two ways. Animals, such as primates living in bands, often choose places with high concentrations of fruit that appear to be suitable "dining rooms" (Figure 6.12) (Perrier de la Bathie, 1921; McClure, 1966; Janzen, 1970). These fruit concentrations are a potential source of future forest heterogeneity, on the one

**Figure 6.12** *Lemurs in tropical rain forest in Madagascar. These monkey relatives (Avahi laniger laniger) feed in certain fruit-producing trees and then distribute the seeds widely through the forest. (Photographer unknown; courtesy of Defenders of Wildlife.)*

hand, because the seeds are dropped mostly near the dining room. On the other hand, such a heterogeneity-producing process may be compensated by the homogenizing process of seed transport over considerable distances, since in the low-contrast rain forest landscape few barriers may exist to inhibit the movement of animals dispersing seeds.

Tropical forests are not as homogeneous, however, as aerial photographs would lead one to believe. When walking through the forest, differences in flora from place to place are evident. In fact, careful measurement of the dispersion of tropical rain forest trees indicates that almost all the common species are aggregated, that is, found in clusters or groves within the continuous forest (Knight, 1975; Ashton, 1976; Hubbell, 1979;

Forman and Hahn, 1981). (Little is yet known about whether the rare species that compose much of the forest are distributed randomly, regularly, or in an aggregated pattern in the rain forest.) This preponderance of aggregated common species suggests that differences in the physical environment may be important (Grubb, 1977) even though they are difficult to detect. In the Ticoporo rain forest reserve in Venezuela, foresters have carefully mapped the distribution of trees of 14 species within a grid measuring 1 km on each side (Carrero, 1983). The reserve is situated on alluvial deposits that produce differences in drainage conditions; eight subtly different types of environmental conditions were distinguished. None of the tree species was randomly distributed over these environmental conditions [based on an analysis of "corrected frequencies" (Daget and Godron, 1982)]. In other words, each tree species was "preferentially" found on one or a few of the environmental conditions. In fact, the two most frequent species were found mainly in the same types of alluvial conditions.

The overall picture, for the tropical rain forest, is of a relatively homogeneous, low-contrast landscape with some heterogeneity present. Although ecological processes in the rain forest are complex, we have at least seen both the homogenizing mechanism of animals dispersing seeds widely, and the heterogeneity-producing mechanisms of environmental variation and aggregated short-distance seed dispersal. A few high-contrast landscape elements such as rivers, large blow-downs, and cultivated plots (Figure 6.11) may be present in the landscape. The predominant pattern, however, is of landscape elements recognizable by groves or aggregations of the more frequent tree species (and associated animals and plants). Such a landscape has low contrast because adjacent landscape elements are relatively similar to one another and because the transitions between landscape elements are broad rather than abrupt.

Landscapes with low-contrast structure are occasionally present under other, quite different climatic conditions, for example in certain unpopulated arid areas. There heterogeneity is basically due to geomorphology, particularly in geological formations where the bedrock is fragmented in small pieces (such as shales, gypsums, and many schists). Erosion has produced countless minuscule watersheds, all resembling one another (Figure 6.13). The major impression when looking at such a landscape as a whole is of an infinite repetition of the same motif—it is monotonous. In the so-called badlands landscape in Figure 6.13, the mode of water and wind erosion is so pervasive that no matter what rock type is present the molded relief always seems to look the same. Apparently it would be possible to consider each slope of each little basin of each bedrock type a patch. But the characteristics common to all the tiny slopes, such as extreme temperature variation, low moisture, and low food supply, are of such overriding ecological importance that we must

**Figure 6.13** *Repetitive structure of badlands. The countless tiny eroded gullies give an impression of relative homogeneity or low contrast. Badlands National Monument, South Dakota (United States). (R. Forman.)*

consider the whole area to be a single matrix. The matrix of course is heterogeneous, and each tiny slope is a tessera that differs from its neighboring tessera only in subtle ecological characteristics.

The vegetation is scattered and repeated in similar form over this geomorphic mold. As in the rain forest example, each plant species exhibits a preference for certain slopes and rock types but grows widely over the environmental conditions present, producing the image of gradual vegetation changes. The matrix is microheterogeneous with low contrast. For most vertebrate species, especially birds, mammals, and reptiles, the home ranges extend widely over the matrix. Again, the landscape as a whole has little contrast from an ecological perspective because it is a single milieu for most animals.

## High-Contrast Structure

**Natural Landscapes.**   Purely natural mechanisms can result in high-contrast structures, particularly where soil conditions control the distribution of dominant plant or animal species. For example, the distinct boundaries between peatlands and boreal forest in Siberia and Scandinavia are natural and produce intense ecological contrasts within a landscape (see Figure 1.10).

Another naturally produced landscape structure with high contrast is the forest-savanna fringe area in semi-arid tropical zones. We see this fringe in Australia, Pakistan, South Africa, along the Sahel in Africa, and in Brazil. Here two principal environments are present—woods and grassland (or shrubland)—differing basically in their amounts of water availability. Forests only survive along rivers at the bottom of alluvial valleys (and in depressions where water accumulates). Where the soil is not capable of holding a reserve of water sufficient for the long dry season, the water balance changes radically, and forest is replaced by savanna. Generally, the soils of these two types of elements are very different, and between forest and savanna there are sharp boundaries only a few meters wide.

**Landscapes Influenced by Humans.**   People may create a high-contrast structure within a large homogeneous matrix. Examples are the farms centered around the deep wells that provide irrigation water in Libya, and the isolated clearings for construction projects in the extensive boreal forest in Canada. These cases appear to be unusual. Generally, high-contrast structures caused by human activity are inserted into landscapes that already have high contrast as a result of natural causes.

In the case of a landscape in Alaska, an aerial photograph reveals a dark matrix corresponding to a coniferous forest (Figure 6.14). Within this matrix, open patches (some along curved topographic contours) appear along with a major highway corridor leading to a small town. Large clearings have been opened by farmers. Within the openings, farmers have also introduced a microheterogeneity, resulting from the planting of differing crops and the maintenance of some hedgerows and tiny patches of woods. This microheterogeneity is reinforced by the presence of scattered farm buildings.

Microheterogeneity introduced by human activity within a natural macroheterogeneity is extremely common and perhaps covers most rural landscapes in the northern hemisphere. In these regions, however, it is difficult to find high-contrast structures resulting solely from human influence because extensive human influences are normally superimposed on, and spatially congruous with, the already existing extensive natural patches of a high contrast landscape.

## GRAIN SIZE OF THE LANDSCAPE

Landscapes are fine grained or coarse grained according to the size of the landscape elements present. We began this chapter on overall landscape structure with a consideration of scale, and it should be noted that grain is closely related to the level of scale considered (Pielou, 1974). Some methods of measuring grain are suggested by Godron (1982). Perhaps the simplest way to determine the **grain size of a landscape** is to

**Figure 6.14** *A high contrast landscape in Alaska. Agriculture and forestry in the Watanuska Valley. (Courtesy of USDA Soil Conservation Service.)*

measure the average diameter or area of the landscape elements present and also estimate the variation in sizes.

Note that grain size for a landscape is different from grain size for an organism (Levins, 1968). The latter concept refers to the area to which an organism is sensitive or uses. For example, an army ant has a much larger grain size than a navy bean.

For specific examples of landscape grain size (van Leeuwen, 1965), let us consider the different landscapes we have explored in this chapter. In each case, grain size is determined relative to the scale of the entire landscape.

1. The dry savanna landscape in the Sahel region south of the Sahara (Figure 6.3) is fine grained, because each tree or shrub with its bare ring is a patch.
2. The Agde landscape of southern France (Figure 6.4) is medium grained with patch size averaging about 1 hectare.
3. The Atlas Mountains landscape of Morocco (Figure 6.6) is coarse grained, with patch sizes a few kilometers in diameter.

4. The marshland along the St. Lawrence River in Quebec is fine grained, because the more or less parallel shoreline strips of vegetation are typically only a few meters or tens of meters wide.
5. The examples of regular and parallel configurations (Figures 6.7 and 6.8), as well as the rolling wooded and pasture landscape of Nant in central France (Figure 6.9) are medium grained, with landscape elements perhaps averaging a few hectares in area.
6. Finally, the tropical rain forest (Figure 6.11) and the Venezuelan Ticoporo rain forest are considered rather coarse grained with landscape elements extending for kilometers, though grain size in the tropical rain forest is difficult to measure.

## ADDITIONAL STRUCTURAL CONSIDERATIONS

Several additional characteristics of overall landscape structure are important and deserve mention. **Unusual landscape features** may be present, that is, types of landscape elements only found once or a few times across an entire landscape. A single small city, three rock outcrops, or a single major river in a landscape are examples. Generally such unusual landscape features are activity centers or "hot spots" where flows of species, energy, or materials are concentrated. A new Amazon highway slicing through diverse primeval forest (Figure 6.15) becomes an unusual landscape feature that concentrates and funnels flows in the landscape. Therefore, these unusual features are normally among the first characteristics we must identify in a landscape study.

The importance of scale in understanding landscape structure has been emphasized. It should also be observed that the controlling factors that produce landscape elements may operate at different levels of scale. For example, the patchiness evident in New England mountains results from finer scale factors—such as avalanches, tree blow-downs, and beaver (*Castor*) activity—being superimposed on broader scale factors such as slope exposure, elevation, and timber harvest patterns (Reiners and Lang, 1979). In the New Jersey Pine Barrens, a striking patchiness results from small fire patches that occurred during the past four decades of effective fire suppression being superimposed on the large fire patches of the previous four decades (Forman and Boerner, 1981).

In exploring the landscape examples presented in this chapter, we have attempted to gain insight into the nature of heterogeneity, a basic property of landscapes. The question of where to place sample lines or grids for measuring a landscape has not been discussed because it is a basic sampling question with theoretical solutions given in classic works (e.g., Greig-Smith, 1964; Desabie, 1966; Kendall and Stuart, 1967; King, 1969; Kershaw, 1975; Mueller-Dombois and Ellenberg, 1974; Isard, 1975;

**Figure 6.15** *New Amazon highway as an unusual landscape feature. Many rain forest animal and plant species can be expected to disappear here as human activities are funneled into the landscape along this corridor. (B. J. Zehnder; courtesy of Defenders of Wildlife.)*

Bartlett, 1975). As a rule of thumb, we look for the major environmental gradient present in the landscape and orient the sampling lines to cross that gradient at right angles. Each line will thus cover a wide range of landscape element patterns, and the mathematical efficiency of sampling will be optimal. If the analysis shows two portions of the area sampled to be extremely different, calculations can be performed to help evaluate whether they are portions of one or two different landscapes (e.g., Cottam and Curtis, 1956; McIntosh, 1967; or "optimal limit" analysis as presented in the Appendix to this chapter).

A wealth of standard ecological techniques is available to help us understand how animals and plants are spatially related to the environment, and to compare ecosystems where the spatial juxtapositions of the ecosystems are not considered (e.g., Greig-Smith, 1964; Godron, 1968; Mueller-Dombois and Ellenberg, 1974; Kershaw, 1975; Phipps, 1981b;

Daget and Godron, 1982). This chapter focuses on spatial (or topological) structure, which is determined by the location, orientation, and distance apart of ecosystems. Clearly, such study of the spatial structure of landscapes can be combined with the study of the distribution of organisms using standard ecological techniques.

## SUMMARY

Landscape elements are combined in a true synthesis to form a landscape with unique characteristics. Scale is very important in understanding overall structure. In a microheterogeneous landscape, the assemblage of landscape element types is similar throughout the area observed. In a macroheterogeneous landscape, the assemblage of element types differs markedly at extreme ends of the area observed. Several distinctive configurations of elements, that is, significant nonrandom patterns, are common. Five main types of configuration are the regular, the aggregated, the linear, the parallel, and the case of spatial linkage between different types.

Landscapes differ markedly in level of contrast (i.e., the degree of difference and the abruptness of transition between adjacent areas). A tropical rain forest typically has low contrast, and savanna-forest boundary areas, as well as virtually all landscapes with a heavy human imprint, have high contrast. Another conspicuous structural characteristic of a landscape that varies is its grain size, which is indicated by the sizes of landscape elements present. Unusual landscape features, namely those elements which are rare in the landscape, are often major centers of activity or flows in the landscape.

In short, overall landscape structure involves a series of characteristics that are superimposed and to some degree interrelated, the most important of which are patch configuration, microheterogeneity and macroheterogeneity, contrast, human influence, and grain size.

## QUESTIONS

1. If a landscape is a true synthesis, what characteristics does it have that are undetectable by focusing only on individual landscape elements?
2. Give and describe one example of microheterogeneity and one of macroheterogeneity in a landscape familiar to you. How could you have a macroheterogeneous species in a microheterogeneous landscape?
3. In a microheterogeneous landscape, how does the amount of heterogeneity vary as you change the level of scale? How does the amount of contrast change?

4. In the "shuttle" analysis of a landscape, what is "information" a measure of? What is a "distinctive configuration"?
5. What are some widespread distinctive configurations in landscapes? Give examples of these in a single landscape.
6. Why is it that rocky deserts are typically high contrast landscapes, while badlands often have low contrast?
7. How is grain size of an organism related to grain size of a landscape?
8. Why is scale so important in studying a landscape?
9. On the Nant 7 line, the highest information level was for the aggregation of pastures. On the Agde line of Chapter 5, the strongest patterns were for the aggregation of vineyards and the aggregation of cultivated fields. What reasons could there be for these distinctive configurations?
10. What mechanisms in the tropical rain forest produce spatial homogeneity? Spatial heterogeneity?
11. How could studying distinctive configurations and overall heterogeneity in a landscape be useful in regional planning and landscape architecture? In forestry? In range management? In crop science? In wildlife management?

# Appendix: A Method for Measuring Landscape Heterogeneity

A problem that arises when looking at the overall structure of a landscape is how to measure its heterogeneity. Here we present a broad and flexible method. We begin by simply looking for the presence of a given type of landscape element at two points, A and B, in a landscape. If this type of element (for example, a marsh) is present only at point A, or only at B, then heterogeneity is present. In this case there is uncertainty, when searching, whether the element is at A or at B. In the mathematical theory of communication (Shannon and Weaver, 1949), this uncertainty is called "entropy" (somewhat analogous to entropy—unavailable energy or disorganization—in a thermodynamic system). When we make our observation that the marsh is present at A and absent at B (or the reverse), this uncertainty (or entropy) vanishes. In this way, we acquire *information* (which is also called *neg-entropy*, because it is an index or measure of the lack of entropy).

If we had equal probabilities of finding the marsh at A or at B, these probabilities are $\frac{1}{2}$ and $\frac{1}{2}$, and the information is, by definition, equal to

$$\tfrac{1}{2} \log 2 \, + \, \tfrac{1}{2} \log 2 \, = \, \log 2$$

If we choose 2 as the base of the logarithm, this basic unit of information is equal to $\log_2 2 = 1$. This basic unit has been called a *binon* when used in communications, or a *bit* when used in computers. Logarithms with the base 2 will be used from now on.

The above measure of heterogeneity may be applied to a line subdivided into segments of equal length. If we check for the presence of a type of element in a line composed of S segments and find that the element is present in F of the segments, F is its *absolute frequency*. The information H obtained from recording the segments containing presences, assuming no *a priori* knowledge, is (Godron, 1966)

$$H = \log \frac{S!}{F! \, (S - F)!}$$

For example, looking at the Nant 7 line (Figure 6.10), pastures are present in 49 of the 128 segments studied. The absolute frequency for pastures is 49 and their relative frequency is 49/128 or 38%. The amount of information, corresponding to knowing the exact position of each of the segments where pastures occur, is

$$H = \log \frac{S!}{F! \, (S - F)!} = 119 \text{ binons or bits}$$

An additional use of this first formula is to find the "optimal" location where limits may be placed in mapping, separating groups of landscape elements in a landscape crossed by a line of segments (Godron, 1972; Godron and Bacou, 1975).

The same type of reasoning is used (Godron, 1971) to compute the information $I_d$ gained when we observe that a type of element first appears in the $D$th segment (i.e., observing that the "beginning" of this type of element is in segment $D$ along the line):

$$I_d = H - \log \frac{(S - D)!}{(F - 1)! \, (S - D - F + 1)!}$$

In the same way, the information gained ($I_f$) when we observe that the "end" of the type of element is in segment $E$ along the line, is:

$$I_f = H - \log \frac{(E - 1)!}{(F - 1)! \, (E - F)!}$$

In the Nant 7 line, paved roads end in the 42nd segment. The information provided by this observation is equal to 11.4 binons. This quantity is greater than 9.9 binons or bits (which corresponds to the statistical threshold of 0.001) in the case of a 128-segment line, and means that the absence of paved roads in the last 86 segments is highly significant.

The degree of clustering of the landscape elements of a given type is measured (Godron, 1966) by, for example, counting the number of groups of pastures present. This number—the number of places along the line where two or more adjacent segments contain pastures—is called $G$, and the information ($I_g$) provided about clustering is

$$I_g = \log \frac{(F-1)! \, (E-D+F)! \, (F-2)! \, (E-D-F+1)!}{(G-1)! \, (F-G)! \, (G-2)! \, (E-D+F-G+2)! \, (E-D-1)!}$$

For the pastures of the Nant 7 line, $G = 7$ binons and $I_g = 55$ binons. This means that the clustering of pastures is very strong along the line.

(It is also possible to measure the information gained when observing how many times two different types of elements are present or "associated" in a segment. We do this by using contingency tables with their mutual presences. Landscape heterogeneity programs computing $H$, $I_d$, $I_f$, $I_g$, and the association between elements are generally available from CEPE-CNRS, Route de Mende, B.P. 5051, Montpellier 34033, France.)

When recording $A$, the number of presences of a type of element in a "shuttle" (see Chapter 6) containing $L$ segments, the information $I_s$ provided by the heterogeneity inside the shuttle is:

$$I_s = \log \frac{L!}{A! \, (L - A)!}$$

(If the numerical values of an ecological parameter are recorded in each segment of the line, the mutual information between these values and the presences of a type of element along the line is obtained by computations detailed by Daget and Godron, 1982.)

If the local contrast between two adjacent segments has to be measured, we count the number of types of elements that are present only in the first segment, and the number of types that are present only in the second segment. The sum of these two numbers (a "Hamming distance") is the measure of local contrast between two consecutive segments along a line.

When two lines of segments are observed in the same region, we may ask whether they are in the same landscape or in two different landscapes? A preliminary answer is obtained by comparing frequencies, as shown in the following example of the Nant 3 and Nant 4 lines.

|  | Nant 3 | Nant 4 |
|---|---|---|
| Streams and rivers | 18 | 12 |
| Homes | 1 | 0 |
| Dirt roads | 24 | 24 |
| Paved roads | 1 | 2 |
| Woods | 90 | 87 |
| Pastures | 49 | 41 |
| Croplands | 0 | 4 |

A Chi-square statistical test cannot be used to test the differences between these two sets of frequencies, because some are too small. Therefore, we compare the individual frequencies directly. For example, the contingency table for the presence or absence of streams and rivers in the 128 segments along each line is as follows:

|                             | Nant 3 | Nant 4 | Total |
|-----------------------------|--------|--------|-------|
| Streams and rivers present  | 18     | 12     | 30    |
| Streams and rivers absent   | 110    | 116    | 226   |
| Total                       | 128    | 128    | 256   |

The probability $P$ of obtaining the results, when only 30 (that is, 18 + 12) of the 256 segments have streams or rivers, is

$$P = \frac{30! \; 226! \; 128! \; 128!}{256! \; 18! \; 12! \; 110! \; 116!} = 0.079$$

The sum of this probability $P$ and the probabilities of more extreme differences in streams and rivers between the two lines is 17%, well above the 5% statistical threshold. This means that these two lines do not differ significantly in the frequencies of streams and rivers present. We may therefore conclude that, based on streams and rivers only, the two lines are in the same landscape.

The same calculation is made for each type of element. It then appears that the clearest difference between the two lines results from the croplands, for which the probability is only 6%. Thus, one can say that these two lines are in the same landscape, but that the croplands present in Nant 4 represent a significant difference between the two lines.

# Part III
# Landscape Dynamics

# 7
# Natural Processes in Landscape Development

*From the boiling rocks has come all of earth's past.*
*From their dust will come all of its future.*
**Helen Hoover**
*The Long Shadowed Forest, 1965*

The first job of a new forester, who has to manage a landscape, in the Rocky Mountains or the Alps, say, is to explore the belts of vegetation present from the bottom to the top of the mountains (Figure 7.1). At the foot of the mountains, he or she will observe that the deciduous or coniferous woods are situated on brownish, often deep soils that can support high production if well watered. Agriculture is frequently introduced into the forest here. At intermediate elevations, the forester will find more striking contrasts, as valleys with scattered lakes and wetlands alternate with slopes streaked with rock slides and coniferous forests. Up at the alpine fringe are clumps of conifers twisted by the wind and blasted by ice crystals. The forester also senses the instability of trickles that transform themselves into dangerous muddy torrents after rain or melting of snow. Such torrents roaring down slopes can disrupt human activities and towns far down in the valley bottoms.

Disentangling the complex of natural processes underlying the origin and development of landscapes—our goal in this chapter—may not be simple but is important for understanding and management. We first ask, "What are the most permanent, primordial characteristics and processes that control the development of landscapes?" An early (600 B.C.) answer was given by the Greek geographer Thales de Milet who identified five major zones on earth: arctic, summer tropics, equator, winter tropics, and antarctic. In so doing, he perhaps articulated the first general ecological concept. He concluded that these zones of life resulted from the apparent movement of the sun, that in turn influenced all living organisms by means of temperature and water availability. Much later, Humboldt (1807) described the vegetational belts in mountains and linked them to climate (thus initiating the field of biogeography).

We now know that climate is a relatively long-term characteristic of

**Figure 7.1** *Vegetation zonation in the southern Rocky Mountains (Sangre de Cristo Mountains, Taos, New Mexico). Bison graze on grassland at bottom. Gentle fan-like slopes are covered with pinyon (Pinus edulis) and juniper (Juniperus spp.). Rocky slopes are covered by ponderosa pine (P. ponderosa) below, and douglas-fir (Pseudotsuga menzeisii) and white fir (Abies concolor) above. The highest forest is spruce (Picea engelmanii) and fir (Abies lasiocarpa), and alpine vegetation is on top. A stream corridor of deciduous poplar trees (Populus) angles down through the pinyon-juniper zone. (R. Forman.)*

a landscape (see Chapters 2 and 13). **Geomorphology,** which considers the forms of the land surface and the processes producing them, is also normally a long-term landscape characteristic (Ruhe, 1975). The two are strongly linked. Therefore, we will begin by exploring how climate combines with geomorphic (geomorphological) characteristics to fashion the land surface and its soils.

## GEOMORPHOLOGY

### Landforms and Their Effects

Four major processes produce the natural geomorphic features of the earth's surface—its **landforms.** *Plate tectonics* refers to the movement of the huge, often continent-size rock shields that compose the earth's surface. Where these plates encounter one another, pressures in them cause the formation of volcanos, rugged mountain ranges, and other landforms. *Erosion,* a second major process, resulting from wind or water (Davis, 1899; Penck, 1910; Hack, 1960; Leopold et al., 1964; Keller, 1972), tends to flatten mountains and ridges. Thirdly, *deposition* of materials fills in low places. A consequence of erosion and the associated deposition process is a smoothing of the landscape, resulting in more rounded landforms and flatter terrain. In fact, in many parts of the world, landscapes marked by steep slopes and sharp jagged ridges are young in geologic time whereas landscapes with smooth rounded or flat contours are old. However, a fourth major process, *glaciation,* also tends to smooth or transform the landscape features.

Our perception of landscapes is strongly affected by landforms. Suppose we are standing in the bottom of a valley in a young mountain chain with high vertical slopes and, therefore, a limited field of vision. In this case the landscape appears *closed* (Observer A in Figure 7.2). But if we look at the same landscape from a summit or from atop a slope (Observer B), our eye now has an extensive view, and the landscape appears *open.* The **depth effect** is also great for Observer B, that is, we see a series of surfaces at different horizontal distances.

In plains country, on the other hand, our view of the landscape is controlled basically by the presence of screens of vegetation capable of

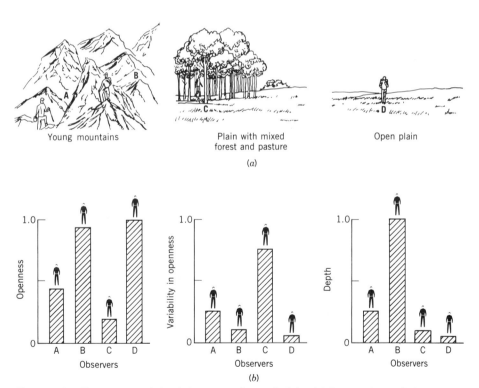

**Figure 7.2** *Openness and depth in mountains and plain.* (a) *Perspectives of observers in locations* A, B, C, *and* D. (b) *Analyses of the perspectives.*

blocking our vision. The **openness** may be small on a completely forested plain (Figure 7.2, Observer C in the forested portion only), but almost infinite in open rangeland or in old salt lake beds essentially devoid of vegetation (Observer D). In these cases, the distance viewed will not change much as we move around on the plain. In other words, on a particular plain with homogeneous natural vegetation, the openness of the landscape may be limited, intermediate, or great, but the variability in openness will normally be low. If, however, the plain has heterogeneous vegetation of mixed forest and pasture (Figure 7.2, Observer C in the whole landscape), variability in the extent of view will be greater.

These subjective observations arise from and describe objective characteristics of the landscape. In a young mountain chain, the elevations, slopes, exposures, bedrocks, and geomorphic processes are more varied than in the plain. This difference in variability of both depth and other parameters is a primary factor in understanding the types of landscapes on earth (see Chapter 13).

The characteristics of openness and depth effect are also useful in understanding the **ruggedness** of a landscape, that is, the sum of the slopes, valleys, peaks, exposures, and elevations present. In some landscapes the distribution of vertebrates is highly sensitive to ruggedness (Strahler, 1952; Schumm, 1956; Leslie and Douglas, 1979; Kramer, 1972; Beasom et al., 1983).

## River Systems

A drop of water flowing from the source of a river to the sea descends in elevation, usually at a progressively decreasing rate. River systems may be directly compared on the basis of their **equilibrium profiles,** that is, a graph of river elevation at a point versus percent of the total distance from source to sea. For example, for the Amazon river system east of the Andes, the equilibrium profile shows an initial steep drop followed by a long nearly horizontal phase. River systems west of the Andes generally have equilibrium profiles that are only slightly curved, because of their relatively short steep drop to the Pacific. For hydrologists, these curves indicate the relative flow rate (or charge capacity) of a river and, indirectly, the size of sediments deposited in the river bed.

For landscape ecologists, the equilibrium profile provides two useful indices that summarize two groups of landscape characteristics. The first is the average slope that the water traverses along a river; that is, an angle that permits direct comparison of this river system, or landscape, to other river systems on earth. Second is the variability in average slopes for the many rivers within a landscape. On a plain, the slopes measured for several rivers are practically the same, so the variability in slopes is low. In a mountainous landscape, wild torrents can join a peacefully meandering river, and thus the variability in average slopes is high. These two characteristics provide a simple index of overall geomorphic structure of landscapes and may be readily used in landscape classification.

The equilibrium profile is influenced by the nature of the bedrock, and several other related characteristics of a river network may be useful (Hynes, 1975; Vannote et al., 1980; Decamps, 1984). Examples are the degree of dissection of the network, the variability in directions of water flow, the presence of major valleys without major rivers (due to "river capture"), and the presence of meanders and meander scars. Such geomorphic characteristics of a landscape are of particular interest in understanding the roles of stream corridors (Chapter 11).

## Bedrock, Climate, and Stasic Processes

Rock type is an important characteristic of a landscape, especially in young mountains, but its importance may vary greatly as a result of climate. A familiar example is limestone, which crumbles and dissolves markedly in cold freezing-and-thawing climates, may produce a mound and hollow topography (karst topography) in humid climates, and may remain in the form of resistant ridges in hot arid climates. In desert climates, the type of bedrock (or parent material) directly determines the type of landscape (Figure 7.3). A more general relationship between bedrock and climate is embodied in the "stasy" system of Erhart (1967), which recognizes two overall alternative sets of processes molding landscapes.

Erhart observed that the history of the earth is that of "crisis periods" (climatic change or mountain building) separated by "calm periods." During crisis periods the predominant phenomenon is mechanical erosion, which flattens mountains and accumulates heavier deposits at their feet. In this process, landscapes are dissected with steep slopes, waterways are torrential or wandering, and stream networks are in continual anarchy (Figure 7.3). These characteristics together describe **rhexistasy** (a terrible word but a useful concept), which applies to the period of erosion following the lifting up of mountain chains, such as the Sierra Nevadas, the Himalayas, and the Andes.

In contrast, during calm periods vegetation protects the slopes, and they are gently rounded. Streams have clear water and rivers flow calmly. The calmness, however, does not mean that nothing is happening. Processes are active, and the landscape is changing. Humic acids from massive leaf litter deposits dissolve chemical elements (especially cations) from rocks and even attack the silica of sand and silt. Rivers arrive at the sea laden with such chemical nutrients. In lagoons and deltas, geochemical transformations take place, particularly under the influence of the marine flora and fauna. Eventually, these processes build up thick layers,

**Figure 7.3** *Desert landscape with channels of sediment deposition and a salt flat below sea level. The salt remains from the evaporation of water molecules from periodic lakes caused by floods. Death Valley, California. (Photo by Ruth and Louis Kirk.)*

composed of skeletons, shells, shellfish, and other elements accumulated by organisms. This total process, called **biostasy**, reigned during much of Mesozoic (Secondary) time in geological history (see Appendix to this chapter).

Such alternating phases, of course, do not explain details but do provide a broad perspective on the geomorphic processes taking place before our very eyes in different parts of continents today. The landscapes of the Andes, or of the Himalayas, are being sculptured by the conspicuous processes of rhexistasy, while the landscapes of the shallow Amazon basin and other tropical rain forest regions undergo the subtle but active biostasic processes in the midst of incessant murmuring of all-encompassing life (Figure 7.4). Rhexistasic landscapes are apparently easier to understand than those dominated by vegetation, the "green leprosy that masks the landforms," as a geomorphologist looking for clues in the landscape once remarked. When the biological mantle covers the ground, the biostasic landscape may be difficult to "read" because its structure is rich in gradations and nuances.

## Geomorphic Processes under Different Climates

**Equatorial Geomorphology.** Certain climatic factors are important in the genesis of landforms (the principal characteristics of equatorial climates were summarized in Chapter 2). Temperature is never low, hence chemical reactions are never slow (based on the Van't Hoff law—when temperature increases 10° C, the average speed of reactions increases by a factor of two). Although it may rain practically throughout the year, usually two wetter phases that coincide with the passage of the sun overhead (the equinoxes, March 21 and September 21) alternate with two drier phases near the winter and summer solstices.

Under these temperatures and moisture conditions, at the bottom of the soil—often ten meters or more down, near the equator—the alteration of bedrock is intense. The rock layers at the surface are covered by vegetation, as by a woolly blanket, smoothing out the relief in the landscape. The landforms often have a profile resembling half an orange. These are the most biostasic landscapes.

Forest vegetation intercepts much of the rainfall (perhaps up to about 60%), but the concentrated flow running down along tree trunks often produces local streamlets on the ground. Alternating flattened knolls and humid depressions (including ponds in some moist areas) are occasionally present. Bare "sugarloafs" that look like the ubiquitous travel poster of Rio de Janeiro or the paintings of the southern mountains of China, may remain conspicuous in the landscape.

In the plains of equatorial climates, the rivers winding through the land often contain too little sand and gravel to effectively cut the hard underlying rocks. Thus, rapids or waterfalls may occur, such as those which flow over occasional geological faults in the Amazon and Congo basins.

Often the only really pronounced contrast in the equatorial landscape is between masses of vegetation and rivers (Figure 7.4). On the vegetation-covered flood plains, drainage patterns determine the primary variations in the landscape. Native residents of the forest usually do not produce major contrasts in the forest, even when they practice shifting (swidden) agriculture (Figures 6.11 and 7.4). The "healing" of vegetation is generally so rapid after burning that the landscape continues to be almost entirely composed of a forest matrix whose patches of cultivation remain small, dispersed, and temporary. The density of the native human population in the equatorial climate remains low. For example, less than one person per ten square kilometers is the average distribution of Brazilian

**Figure 7.4** *Lowland rain forest that receives 10 m (33 ft) of rain per year. Near Buenaventura, Colombia. Temporary cultivated plots are visible in lower left. Plant diversity is high, but vertebrate diversity is said to be lower than in most rain forests due to the unusually high volume of rainfall. (R. Forman.)*

tribes in the Amazon forest. This factor, of course, is altered drastically when outsiders cut large areas of forest for agriculture or wood, as along new highways in the Amazon basin (Figure 6.15).

**Geomorphology in Tropical Climates.**   When traveling from the equator toward the tropics (of Cancer or Capricorn), it is hard to say at what point aridity becomes the principal characteristic determining landscape structure. We note, however, that the transition between equatorial and tropical climates often coincides with the presence of permanent openings that are occupied by savannas or periodic cultivation. For example, in the portion of the Chaco region of northern Argentina called "impenetrable," the forest does not burn, largely because there is practically no herbaceous cover in the understory. As soon as humans intervene, using modern techniques of harvesting trees or sending livestock in to browse, herbaceous plants develop and fires appear. Shrubs and small trees burn, further favoring herbaceous cover, and a cycle begins that could rightly be called infernal. If the cycle of burning during the dry season and grass growing in the wet season is repeated, the forest disappears and is replaced by a low savanna that may burn every year.

The farther from the equator one goes, the more angular or pointed the landforms become. In the so-called sudanian fringe in Africa, the tropical forest would be able to reinvade the savanna, were it not for the regular fires lit by residents. Distinct forest patches, often well isolated from one another, are surrounded by a grassy savanna matrix.

Still farther from the equator, two factors combine to produce still more angular landforms. The first is the increase in aridity that causes the vegetation to be more and more open, thus protecting the soil less and less against water erosion. The second is rain, which is increasingly concentrated in a short wet season and has a considerable erosive power. The fraction of the rain that runs off over the soil surface, thus eroding the soil, may reach 30%, or even 50%, of the total water that falls in hard rains. In this area, erosion here annually may carry off 10 to 20 tons of soil per hectare (about a kilogram in a 2 × 2 m area each year), and may reach 100 tons of soil loss per hectare on steeper slopes (Wishmeier and Smith, 1965). With the same tropical climate, on the same soils, a forest provides effective soil protection and may limit water runoff to about 1%, and annual erosion to less than 0.1 ton per hectare.

Intense erosion, especially just after the onset of the rainy season, often does not carry mineral debris very far. It tends to produce large sloping banks with extensive views, resembling the terraces (glacis) built around forts when muskets were the predominant factor in battles. When a resistant rock landform remains protruding above the surrounding land, it generally has steep slopes that join the surroundings with sharp angles.

These geomorphic changes correspond with climatic changes, that is, as we move toward the poles we go from (a) an equatorial regime with two brief equally long dry phases, to (b) semitropical regimes with one long and one short dry season, to (c) typical tropical regimes with only a single severe dry season. As we proceed still farther from the equator, the vegetation becomes sparse. Large surfaces of bare ground are present, where particles are readily blown by the wind—characteristic of the desert zone.

**Desert Geomorphologies.** The most varied areas on earth are deserts. They have a coarse and conspicuous patchiness, largely because there is not enough vegetation to help make them uniform (Figure 7.3). All deserts are low in moisture, but we must distinguish several types of desert landscapes. There are sandy deserts, rocky deserts, cold deserts, flat deserts, mountain deserts, and more. Absolute deserts, where it "never" rains, are extremely rare. Strong traces of former climates are often preserved in deserts, such as grooved rocks ground by ancient glaciers and the petrified tree trunks in the Sahara or the southwestern United States. Stone engravings at Tassili in the central Sahara show that giraffes, antelopes, and elephants lived there, and that ox keepers drove their herds, just as residents drive cattle today, along the southern edge of the Sahara in Senegal, Mali, and Niger (Lhote, 1973, 1978).

One of the unique characteristics of many desert landscapes is the presence of salt lakes or flats, often dazzling in brightness and perfectly level (Figure 7.3). In other places, wind erosion hollows out sandy rocks and produces bizarre forms that are lived in or that kindle the imagination. Finally, one of the most striking contrasts in desert landscapes is the presence of oases, often grouped in a line of patches that may be linked by corridors (see Figure 1.6).

In several cases, rivers—such as the Euphrates, the Niger, and the Hoang-Ho—arrive at deserts and are swallowed up in interior deltas. This produces distinctive landscapes with interconnecting channels separated by winding levees.

**Geomorphology in the Mediterranean Climate.** The Mediterranean type climate, such as that of southern California, southwestern Australia, and southern Africa (Figure 7.5), is the only major climate on earth where the warmest season is the driest. Precipitation falls largely during the cool season. Movie stars living in Hollywood, California know the side effects of the Mediterranean climate well. In winter, their homes are swept down hills in mud slides, and in summer their homes burn up in brush fires.

Because of the rather intense summer drought, Mediterranean type vegetation does not form a complete cover, and water erosion leaves strong marks on the landscapes. On the other hand, humus is rapidly broken down to minerals, and chemical alteration of rock is weak. Overall, soil development is slow, and the soils are often shallow.

Another important characteristic is basically geological. The major silica-containing rock shields or plates of the world are tropical (as in India, Africa, and Brazil) or cold temperate (as in North America and Siberia). In contrast, the mountain chains produced in the Tertiary period (see Appendix to this chapter) lifted up a considerable amount of limestone originating from earlier warm seas. Such mountains are common in areas with a Mediterranean climate. These mountain chains have sharp

**Figure 7.5** *Cape of Good Hope landscape with Mediterranean type climate. Table Mountain, with characteristic gorges and rocky crests, overlooks Cape Town near the southern tip of Africa. (Courtesy of the South African Tourist Corporation and Satour.)*

angles, rocky crests, and gorges or canyon-like valleys with steep slopes (Figure 7.5).

**Geomorphology of Temperate Zones.**   Here, summer is the rainy season. An oceanic climate is often prevalent near coasts, while the middle portions of a continent usually have a continental climate with pronounced annual temperature variation.

The temperate climate normally produces biostasy, which minimizes dramatic changes in the short term and leaves landforms from former erosion periods. Therefore, when working in temperate climates of large areas of the United States, Europe, and China, for example, we must act as "geodetectives." We must decipher the residual traces in a landscape left by former climates. Deposits of various sorts may be present, including **moraines** (i.e., rocks and debris carried and dropped by glaciers), soil flows due to repeated freezing and thawing, sand dunes, and accumulations of windblown soil (loess) that may produce fertile plains. Even soils formed under a former tropical climate may be present.

In some temperate areas, **ridge and valley topography** (Appalachian relief) may be present as a series of more or less parallel ridges composed of hard resistant rock alternating with valleys of softer rock (see Figure 6.8). In moist areas, such landscapes tend to have fertile valleys and acid, nutrient-poor ridges.

**Cold Regions.**   Proceeding toward the poles, we encounter the cold polar air masses and the season favorable to most animal and plant growth is brief. These polar air masses are quite familiar to inhabitants of the temperate zone too, because they bring the bitter cold days of winter.

When water penetrates into the fine cracks of a rock and freezes, the rock splits into countless tiny angular stones (gelifracts). By this process the landforms often become smooth, as if wrapped in a thick mantle of debris (Figure 7.6). Soils subject to alternating freezing and thawing lose their structure (or develop little structure) and become bloated and almost fluid. Downhill sheet flow of the soil mass occurs on slopes and results in smoothed-over knolls. On flatter plains in cold regions, alternating freezing and thawing produces polygon networks (see Figure 13.4) (Tedrow, 1977; Bliss et al., 1981). All these phenomena are called *periglacial* (Cailleux and Taylor, 1954).

In high mountain chains, glaciers hollow out wide valleys and leave an irregular profile like stair steps. Moraines carpet valley bottoms and add additional relief. As they retreat, large continental glacial masses leave rounded hills and mountains interspersed with elongated lakes (see Figure 1.4). Most of the lakes, such as those in parts of Scotland and

**Figure 7.6** *Snowmelt stream and rocky debris in alpine zone. Water volume and downstream flood threat vary enormously according to air temperature. The angular stones and rocks result from cycles of alternating freezing and thawing. The Alps south of Briacon, France. (M. Godron.)*

along the coast of Maine, are oriented in the direction of flow of the former glacial mass.

Plains left by glaciers may be marked with drumlins, which are rock and sediment deposits often 1 or 2 kilometers long and 20 to 30 meters high. These provide a distinctive landscape appearance, for example, in areas from New England to the Great Lakes in North America.

In conclusion, landforms show in concrete form the traces of past as well as present climate. Furthermore, they determine to a large measure the range of possibilities for vegetation, animals, and people that colonize, adapt to, and further mold the landscape.

## ESTABLISHMENT OF LIFE FORMS

Some four billion years ago, landscapes were only masses of rock convulsed by volcanic eruptions and the lifting up of mountain chains. The land was cut by torrents of water and by winds that deposited sediments in distant locations. Seas formed and expanded, sheltering prebiological activity. The landscapes where life appeared are generally depicted as a series of coastal lagoons or clays containing what might be described as a lukewarm broth of inorganic and organic molecules. Three billion years then passed before plants and animals spread from the seas and conquered the land surface, ultimately to produce the landscapes that we admire today.

### Plant Establishment

Let us step momentarily into science fiction and take a "time capsule" spaceship back to these early landscapes. What do we see? Landforms and geomorphic processes are predominant and striking. Perhaps on moist surfaces a low plant carpet is relatively complete. It is similar to our moist canal or road banks covered with mosses, lichens, or algae (Figure 7.7). There, erosion is noticeably decreased and soil is developing. Rhexistasy is still king on the landscape, but prince biostasy has been born.

Moving our spaceship forward to the *Silurian* period—450 to 400 million years ago (see Appendix to this chapter)—we notice that a major split has taken place in the evolution of plants. **Vascular plants,** those with conducting tissue or tubes for internal movement of material up and down the plant, appear on land. Cautiously getting out to explore, we note that the plants (psilophytes) look something like the bristles of a broom or a cluster of rushes, and if you squint, you might think you were in a marsh or grassland. These plants are taller than the algae- and moss-like plants, and they protect the soil more effectively from the impact of

**Figure 7.7** *Moss and lichen cover inhibiting erosion on a moist road bank in the Catskill Mountains in New York. Polytrichum or hair-cap moss (with leaves) is interspersed with two species of whitish Cladonia lichen. (R. Forman.)*

raindrops and from erosion by wind and floods. Humus develops and remains in the upper layers of soils, and biostasic processes are growing in importance.

From this point in time on, diverse panoramas flash by our spaceship as vegetation changes on land become increasingly rapid. Landscapes of the Paleozoic era (see Appendix to this chapter) are relatively easy for us to imagine, thanks to the rich fossil record they left, especially in today's coal fields. The vascular plants of the Silurian age, now considered primitive relatives of ferns, presumably covered wet habitats for the most part. Not until the *Devonian* period (400 to 350 million years ago) do plants begin to possess many of the structures familiar to us now. Although there are still large deserts, vegetation is getting taller, and during the *Carbon-iferous* period (some 300 million years ago), large forests spread out. Extensive warm lowland forests become visible. Periodically, fallen plants from these forests are covered by soil deposits, later to be squeezed, fossilized, and turned into the coal and oil layers that today run our industrial civilization.

The *Mesozoic* (Secondary) era, of about 200 to 80 million years ago, next comes into view with its forests of *gymnosperms* (i.e., conifers and relatives) predominant. For the first time, animals grazing in the landscapes can be seen from our spacecraft. It is the age of dinosaurs (we decide not to land). An event of enormous import unravels at this time before our eyes. The preceding Paleozoic era, which experienced a series of catastrophic environmental changes, ends with massive species extinctions. There is a single huge continent, *Pangaea*. During the Mesozoic era, new smaller continents form by a "drifting" apart process, or plate tectonics, that results in the seven continents of today. This causes a major isolation of faunas and floras. Finally, near the end of the Mesozoic, flowers appear on earth, a welcome relief from the monotonous greenery.

To grasp the ecological significance of the appearance of *flowering plants* (angiosperms), the last major plant group to evolve, we must realize that they (co)evolved with animal pollinators (Figure 7.8). Most of the pollinators were presumably insects, although some may have been birds and mammals, such as hummingbirds or bats. Such animals, as they consume the nectar and much of the pollen in flowers, also play the crucial role of efficiently transporting pollen from one plant to another. The flamboyance of our walls covered with roses or bougainvillea, and the bright flower colors that paint the grasslands in sequence during spring, have only one "goal": to attract the buzzing pollinators. The increase in types of flowering plants was explosive during the subsequent *Tertiary* (100 to 2 million years ago) and Quaternary (2 million years ago to the present) periods. For example, flowering plants became 30% of North American flora and 35% of the flora of Portugal as early as the middle Tertiary.

In the northern hemisphere, two broad bands of vegetation (geofloras) circled the globe during the early Tertiary period. The **arcto-tertiary flora** of cold-tolerant deciduous and coniferous trees dominated the high latitudes north of the equator, and the *tropical tertiary flora* of cold-intolerant, broad-leaved evergreen trees dominated the lower latitudes (Figure 7.9). During warmer portions of the Tertiary, a mild subtropical climate reigned over large areas of the globe so that, for example, palms extended to Alaska and sequoias (*Sequoia*), elms (*Ulmus*), and beech trees (*Fagus*) extended to Greenland and northern Scandinavia. In the drier and warmer southwestern portions of continents a new type of flora appeared that

**Figure 7.8**   *Tiger swallowtail butterfly* (Pterourus glaucus) *pollinating a field thistle* (Cirsium discolor). *Many flowering plants and insects evolved together in relatively recent geological time. Hutcheson Memorial Forest near Millstone, New Jersey (United States). (Courtesy of Patti Murray.)*

was composed of grasses and leathery-leaved evergreen woody plants, called in North America the *madro-tertiary flora* (Figure 7.9).

The increasingly separate continents meant increasing isolation and the formation of different floras on different continents. Another major event, the lifting up of the highest present mountain chains—such as the Rocky Mountains, the Andes, the Alps, the Himalayas, and the Australian mountains—took place in the middle Tertiary. As a result there was a further drying of the centers of those continents (rain shadow effect),

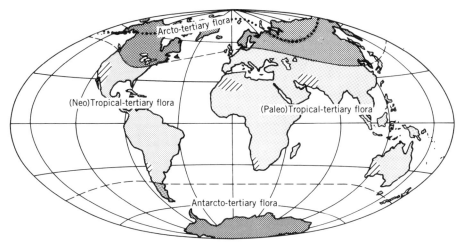

**Figure 7.9** *Distribution of floras in the early Tertiary period. Diagonal lines show areas where semiarid floras were beginning to appear. Above the dotted line, the arcto-tertiary flora had a greater abundance of coniferous species. From Axelrod (1960), based on Chaney (1940), Krystofovich (1957), and other sources. (Copyright 1960 by the University of Chicago.)*

which further fragmented the once-continuous arcto-tertiary flora (Figure 7.9). Not only were continental floras separate, but now floras on the eastern and western sides of continents were isolated and became different. Dry areas spread, and the madro-tertiary-like floras were succeeded by many deserts, grasslands, and Mediterranean-type vegetations (Axelrod, 1960).

By the end of the Tertiary, the spaceship voyageurs feel very much at home because they see most of the genera and many of the species we now know, as well as belts of vegetation similar to those of today. In middle Europe, for example, they see a coniferous forest with pine (*Pinus*), fir (*Abies*), sequoia (*Sequoia*), and rhododendron (*Rhododendron*) at higher elevations, a deciduous forest of oak (*Quercus*), sycamore (*Platanus*), pear (*Pyrus*), and elm (*Ulmus*) on lower slopes, a savanna with scattered palms (*Palmae*) and acacias (*Acacia*) on the plains, and a (gallery) forest of camphor (*Camphor*) and sumac (*Rhus*) trees along rivers (Termier and Termier, 1968).

But then everything changed quickly. The view of the land from space during the past two million years (i.e., the **Quaternary** period) is dramatic, since the action is a series of massive glaciations and species migrations (see Appendix to this chapter). The effect of a number of glacial convulsions on the vegetation of the northern hemisphere is relatively well-known, mainly thanks to studies of successive deposition layers in bogs that contain pollen deposited through time. Two overall patterns emerge. First of all, two types of phases have alternated several times. During cool (and often dry) periods, tundra and boreal forest species extended over most high latitude landscapes. During mild, humid periods, a deciduous forest reigned with many species intermixed in both the canopy and understory. Secondly, during either phase, the predominant vegetation was apparently almost identical to that present several tens of thousands of years earlier. The relatively constant species balance of a phase, under conditions of massive migrations over the land, suggests that the vegetation of temperate regions is endowed with considerable elasticity or adaptability. In tropical regions, the variations in the landscapes during the Quaternary are less well known, although it is certain that major rainy periods have alternated with drier periods in some places (Haffer, 1969; Maley, 1980; Tricart, 1965).

The post-glacial period (**Holocene**) began with ice melt about 14,000 to 10,000 B.C. in today's temperate regions and somewhat later in today's boreal regions (Figure 7.10). By about 7000 B.C., the general zones of vegetation across the northern hemisphere approximated those of today. Marked human influences on the landscape began to appear shortly thereafter with the spread of agricultural plantings. But then the climate changed yet again. A warm moist period of a few millennia occurred and was followed by a more severe warm dry period (Figure 7.10). During these warm periods, low latitude species moved over the land toward the poles, and then retreated when the cooler climate returned. The spread of agriculture accelerated in the past few millennia, modifying and creating whole new landscapes. Urban landscapes appeared, and the rate of landscape change, together with human population numbers, has continued its acceleration to the present.

To sum up, we may say that:

1. Major plant groups developed during the Paleozoic and Mesozoic.
2. Today's genera largely appeared early in the Tertiary.
3. Many of today's plant species had originated by the end of the Tertiary.
4. Migration of these species was the key pattern during the glacial period.
5. Today's vegetation developed in its present location and form largely late in, or subsequent to, the last glacial advance, which ended some 12,000 years ago.

## Animal Establishment

The principal characteristic of animals in this context is that they are **heterotrophs;** that is, they consume chemical energy stored in large molecules rather than building their own chemical energy directly from solar

| Time | Climate (and Stages) | Vegetation | |
|---|---|---|---|
| | | (Eastern North America) | (Northern Europe) |
| 1,000 A.D. | Cooler, moister | Oak, chestnut, beech, | Beech, oak |
| 0 | (sub-Atlantic) | hemlock | |
| 1,000 B.C. | | | |
| 2,000 B.C. | Warm, dry | Oak, hickory, elm, | Oak, beech |
| 3,000 B.C. | (sub-boreal) | prairie peninsula | |
| 4,000 B.C. | | | |
| 5,000 B.C. | Warm, moist | | Oak, elm, linden |
| 6,000 B.C. | (Atlantic) | Oak, beech, hemlock | |
| 7,000 B.C. | Warmer, drier | Pine, oak | Pine, hazel |
| 8,000 B.C. | (boreal) | | Birch, pine |
| 9,000 B.C. | Cool, moist | Spruce, fir | Park-tundra |
| 10,000 B.C. | (pre-boreal) | | Pine, birch |
| 11,000 B.C. | Cold | Tundra | Tundra |
| 12,000 B.C. | (sub-arctic) | Deglaciation | Park-tundra |
| 13,000 B.C. | | | Tundra |
| 14,000 B.C. | | | |

(Hypsithermal spans the warm period from approximately 2,000 B.C. to 7,000 B.C.)

**Figure 7.10** *Climate and vegetation changes during the Holocene. The hypsithermal was a warm phase near the middle of this post-glacial period. In many regions the Paleolithic (Old Stone Age) ended about the middle of the Holocene, and was followed successively by the Copper, Bronze, and Iron Ages. (From S. C. Kendeigh, Ecology: With Special Reference to Animals and Man, copyright 1974, page 310. Adapted by permission of Prentice-Hall, Inc.)*

energy. We know that animals developed and diversified in the sea before the Paleozoic (Primary) era, because fossils from the beginning of that era contain the major invertebrate groups of today (Figure 7.11). During the Paleozoic, some invertebrates such as centipedes, spiders, and wingless insects colonized the land, but it was not until the late Paleozoic that amphibians (i.e., vertebrates) colonized the land near water. A little later, reptiles evolved. They had more freely movable heads useful in catching prey and moving around in the heterogeneous terrestrial landscapes. Reptiles, including the huge dinosaurs and the flying pterodactyls, diversified enormously in the landscapes of the Mesozoic (Secondary) era (Figure 7.11). Near the end of the Mesozoic, birds and tiny mammals evolved. They had a greater ability to regulate their internal body temperature which enhanced their ability to remain active on land during cold periods.

By the beginning of the Tertiary, these warmblooded mammals and birds had massively replaced the reptiles (Figure 7.11). The earliest fossils of monkeys date from this epoch, and the ancestors of horses, pigs,

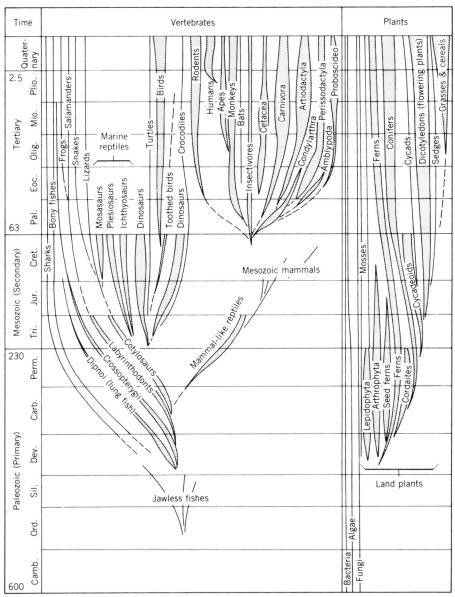

**Figure 7.11** *Relative abundance of major vertebrate and plant groups over geologic time. (See Figure 7.23 for full names and ages of time periods.) Note that many animal and plant groups have become extinct. Among the current groups are Insectivores, including moles and shrews; Cetacea, including whales and dolphins; Carnivora, including cats, foxes, and hyenas; Artiodactyla, or "single-toed ungulates," including horses and rhinos; Perissodactyla, or "two-toed ungulates" including cattle, deer, and giraffes; and Proboscidea, including elephants. (From Dunbar and Waage; copyright 1969, reprinted with permission of John Wiley & Sons, Inc.).*

ruminants, rhinoceroses, and elephants are discernible. Finally in the middle Tertiary—when penguins appeared in the Antarctic—colonization of the continents by today's major animal groups was essentially complete, though catastrophic environmental changes since then have periodically caused extensive species extinctions and colonizations on particular continents.

The establishment of animals in specific landscapes has three important aspects. First, it is much more rapid than that of plants, especially in the case of migrating animals. The minuscule hummingbird descends from Canada to Mexico at the end of the summer and returns in the opposite direction in spring. Migrating birds follow the seasonal cycle and live in an "eternal spring." Ornithologists often say that birds have wings to fly, but that the wings are used to stay in place, that is, in the same type of environment. When certain environmental conditions disappear or move, the animal species typically also disappears or moves. In other words, the presence or absence of an animal in a landscape is closely linked with the recent history and environmental fluctuations in the landscape.

The second observation reinforces this perspective of tight links between animals and changing environments. Natural selection is strong for animals. (Charles Darwin, who was an excellent botanist, chose the majority of his examples of selection from among the animals [Darwin, 1958].) Through natural selection, many animal populations in a new environment tend to lose variability rather rapidly. Thus the average rate of genetic variability (or heterozygosity), compiled from many sources, is only 7% for vertebrates and 13% for invertebrates, but 17% for plants (Godron, 1984).

The third point is that the establishment of animals results in an important feedback loop in a landscape system. We recognize that the constraints that work together to create a landscape are linked in a manner that, without being absolute, is far from random (Figure 7.12).

1. Climate leaves its mark directly on vegetation, on erosion, on the type of sediment deposition, and on landforms.
2. Vegetation depends directly on climate but also plays a leading role in the development and protection of soil.
3. Soil reacts in turn on vegetation through the feedback loop described below.
4. Climate, vegetation, and soil provide the environmental conditions for the establishment of animals. Yet, in a feedback loop, animals modify vegetation (through herbivory, pollination, and seed dispersal) as well as soil.

This last feedback loop, which regulates the equilibrium between animals and plants, has been strongly affected by direct human intervention.

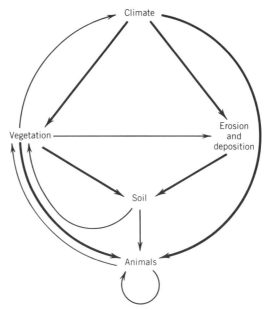

**Figure 7.12** *Major feedback linkages in landscape development. Large arrows indicate predominant controls or effects. Each loop where one factor affects a second, and the second affects the first, is a feedback loop. Note the predominant control by climate, and the nature of the linkages among animals, vegetation, and soil.*

Mammoths, mastodons, giant beaver, giant sloths, and many other abundant large herbivores disappeared rapidly about 15,000 years ago. Several current hypotheses compete in the controversy over these mass extinctions. The estimations and extinction model of Martin (1971), Budyko (1980), and others are impressive. They suggest that the populations of these great herbivores were destroyed, at least in part, by hunters during the Paleolithic (see Appendix to this chapter). Most recently, species extinctions caused by humans have accelerated again in the industrial age.

These three characteristics of animal establishment lead to the conclusion that animals are very sensitive indicators of landscape quality. Once established, some animals also contribute to the heterogeneity of the landscape (as we will see further in Chapter 12). In other words, animals take advantage of the heterogeneity present to colonize and adapt while they also increase that heterogeneity.

## Speciation in Landscapes

Where did all the animal and plant species that are established in today's landscape come from? We have seen massive geomorphic changes and recent climatic changes and we know that landscapes appear and disappear. Through these changes, species adapt, migrate, become extinct, or form new species in the process of **speciation.**

A nice example of speciation is how we got the five closely related, pretty, brightly colored warbler species that fly around in treetops searching for insects over about a third of North America. At the beginning of the Quaternary glacial period (Pleistocene), a single species—similar to our black-throated green warbler (*Dendroica virens*) of today—apparently lived in the deciduous forests of what is now the southeastern United States (Figure 7.13) (Mengel, 1964). During the first of four major glaciations, the species distribution was compressed toward the Florida peninsula. During the following warm interglacial period, the species expanded its range northward all the way to what is now Alaska (Figure 7.13). Then the second glaciation came, and the species distribution was split between the Southeast and the Southwest. Birds in each region of course could only interbreed among themselves. Over tens of thousands of years, the populations in the two regions became increasingly different until finally they were two distinct species. When the next warm interglacial period arrived, both species spread northward. The third glaciation then split the distribution of the new bird species, and so a third species evolved. A similar process followed during the last interglacial and glacial periods, and the fourth and fifth species evolved. Thus, five bird species evolved from one in only two million years (Figure 7.13). This evolutionary sequence, while incompletely known, is also evident for other groups of small birds (Mengel, 1970). By comparison, humans are known to have been on earth for almost four million years.

But do big animal species arise in the same way? Let us consider the moose (*Alces americana*), one of the largest animals in the western hemisphere. The moose thrives in cold regions, feeding on aquatic vegetation in summer and young woody stems in winter. Just before the last of the four glaciations, a single moose species presumably lived from what is now Alaska across Canada to Newfoundland (Peterson, 1955). When the ice moved south, the moose was limited to four isolated populations, located respectively in what are now the Middle Atlantic states, in an area south of Lake Superior, in the American Rocky Mountains, and in Alaska (Figure 7.14). As long as the ice was there, generation followed generation of moose, but reproduction was only within a population. When the ice finally melted some 10,000 years ago and the species spread across its former range, four subspecies were present and still are today (Figure 7.14). As subspecies, they are morphologically distinct and largely

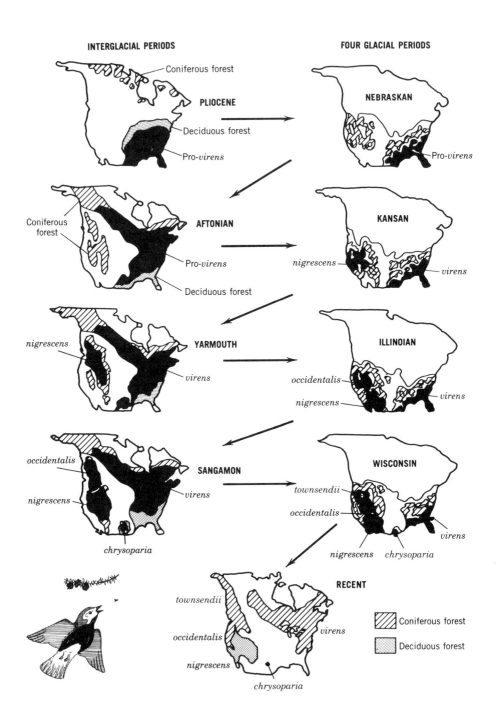

INTERGLACIAL PERIODS

PLIOCENE
- Coniferous forest
- Deciduous forest
- Pro-*virens*

AFTONIAN
- Coniferous forest
- Pro-*virens*
- Deciduous forest

YARMOUTH
- *nigrescens*
- *virens*

SANGAMON
- *occidentalis*
- *nigrescens*
- *virens*
- *chrysoparia*

FOUR GLACIAL PERIODS

NEBRASKAN
- Pro-*virens*

KANSAN
- *nigrescens*
- *virens*

ILLINOIAN
- *occidentalis*
- *nigrescens*
- *virens*

WISCONSIN
- *townsendii*
- *occidentalis*
- *nigrescens*
- *chrysoparia*
- *virens*

RECENT
- *townsendii*
- *occidentalis*
- *nigrescens*
- *virens*
- *chrysoparia*

Coniferous forest
Deciduous forest

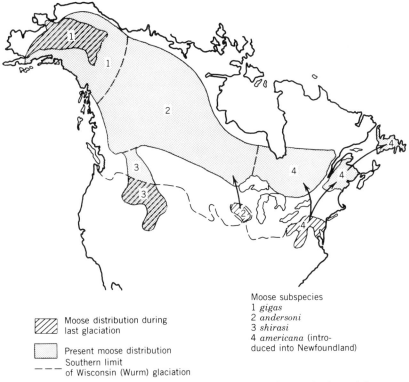

Moose distribution during last glaciation

Present moose distribution

Southern limit of Wisconsin (Wurm) glaciation

Moose subspecies
1 *gigas*
2 *andersoni*
3 *shirasi*
4 *americana* (intro-duced into Newfoundland)

**Figure 7.14**   *Evolution of four subspecies of moose during the last of the major Pleistocene glaciations (from S. C. Kendeigh, Ecology: with Special Reference to Animals and Man, 1974. Permission of Prentice Hall, Inc.) (After Peterson, 1955, copyright and permission of the University of Toronto Press.)*

**Figure 7.13**   *Evolution of five warbler species during the Pleistocene glaciations. The ancestral species is called Dendroica pro-virens. Today's five closely related species and their habitats are as follows.*

1. D. virens *(black-throated green warbler shown in inset) in boreal forest;*
2. D. nigrescens *(black-throated gray warbler) in woodland;*
3. D. occidentalis *(hermit warbler) in Sierran montane forest;*
4. D. townsendii *(Townsend's warbler) in coastal forest;*
5. D. chrysoparia *(golden-cheeked warbler) in mixed deciduous and cedar forest on Edwards Plateau, Texas.*

*Adapted from:* Pleistocene and Recent Environments of the Central Great Plains, *edited by Wakefield Dort, Jr., and J. Knox Jones. © 1970 by the University Press of Kansas. After Mengel, 1964. (Sketch of black-throated green warbler courtesy of Charles F. Leck.)*

separated in different portions of the total range, but if given the chance they can still interbreed. In this way, four subspecies of a huge herbivore evolved in only 150,000 years. While this was going on in North America, in Europe two human subspecies—*Homo sapiens neanderthalii* and *Homo sapiens sapiens*—were competing, and the former disappeared.

Let us now turn to speciation within a single landscape. Two contrasting examples will illustrate the range of possible processes. The old uncut rain forests of Madagascar off the coast of Africa are extremely rich in species, and many species live intermixed side by side in nearly homogeneous forests (Figure 7.15). There, the fineness of the variations in species distributions reminds one of an impressionist painting with its multitude of rainbow colored specks, and shapes drowned in glittering sparkles. Why is the forest like this? Undoubtedly, it is because this huge island has remained isolated for tens of millions of years in a relatively even tropical climate, and almost all the plant and animal species have developed and differentiated in the apparent absence of environmental catastrophes. The spatial homogeneity of the landscape combined with a remarkable stability over time has favored intense speciation.

On the other hand, strong contrasts and large environmental variations over time have also led to high levels of speciation in other landscapes. A striking example are snowfield areas in depressions on the side of a mountain (Figure 7.6). The snow melts slowly and progressively uncovers the herbaceous carpet beneath. Plants situated on the periphery of the snowfield are exposed to light and heat at the beginning of the summer. They grow, reproduce, and set seed well before their neighbors, still smothered in snow, have begun growing, flowering, and producing pollen. Pollen exchange between the interior plants of the snowfield and the peripheral plants, therefore, does not take place. Plants from different portions of the snowfield do not cross-fertilize and mix genes with each other. Thus, the process of speciation is enhanced, in this case, as a result of pronounced environmental contrasts within the landscape.

Climate and geomorphology thus form the framework within which speciation proceeds. They are the scenery in the theatre, and animals and plants are the actors in the play. Present vegetation and animal communities are only the last word in this long ongoing drama. The history of species is strongly controlled by the "struggle and survival of the fittest." However, natural selection is not as absolute as Darwin suggested when he wrote in the *Origin of Species*, "We may feel sure that any variation in the least degree injurious would be rigidly destroyed." We now know that such minor variations are not automatically eliminated by natural selection and that most species are strongly and persistently genetically variable (Mayr, 1974). The history of species continues to be written every day before our eyes in all landscapes—from those with subtle environmental variations like Madagascar to those with

**Figure 7.15** *Diverse and distinctive tropical forest in Madagascar. Areas such as this Alluaudia forest contain large numbers of species found nowhere else in the world (endemic species), the result of long isolation on this large island off eastern Africa. (Photographer unknown; (courtesy of Defenders of Wildlife.)*

marked contrasts like mountain snowfields (Ehrlich et al., 1974; Harper, 1977). In fact, speciation may be accelerating around us as the landscapes marked by a heavy human imprint change rapidly.


## Increase in Vegetation Stature

Has the invasion of continents by the green tide of vegetation that started in the Silurian period stopped? Is the patchy lichen cover on rocks of alpine mountain summits the ultimate response of natural biochemical engineering, or is it a prelude to more vegetation in a few million years? A general trend helps organize our response to this question. Vegetation tends spontaneously and naturally to acquire greater stature, restarting its ascent again after each disturbance.

This observation seems reasonable considering the fact that virtually all classifications of vegetation give the preeminent position to tall woody vegetation (e.g., Brockmann-Jerosch, 1912; Holdridge, 1947; Danser-eau, 1957; Whittaker, 1975). Whittaker's classification scheme (1975) more precisely indicates that vegetation tends to become woody at the point where average annual precipitation reaches 5 cm and temperature reaches $-6°C$.

This commonly accepted view of vegetation development is reinforced by observing the vertical profile of biomass in natural vegetation (Cannell, 1982; Satoo and Madgwick, 1982; Trabaud, 1984). In an old tropical rain forest in Malaysia (Kira, 1978) or an old Canadian boreal forest (taiga), the molecules of organic matter are distributed—from the level of the soil to the level of the terminal buds of the dominant trees—according to a logarithmic curve (Figure 7.16). Analogously, we note that the density of inorganic molecules of the terrestrial atmosphere is also distributed according to a logarithmic curve (at the scale of kilometers) from the soil into the stratosphere. This distribution results from the molecules being subject to the combination of two antagonistic forces, brownian move-ment (the random motion of molecules due to their inherent energy, the net effect of which is to cause molecules to move upward), and gravi-tation, which draws molecules toward the earth (Godron, 1975).

Does the logarithmic curve of inorganic molecules in the atmosphere tell us something about the logarithmic curve of organic molecules in the boreal forest? We think so. The analogy suggests that two opposing forces, operating at the scale of tens of meters, may be determining the vertical distribution of biomass. The first force is the vertical thrust by plant growth toward light, a depositing of photosynthesis-derived organic molecules at the growing tip (Figure 7.17). The second force is a resistance that keeps the molecules near the ground, a combination of gravity with the need for water to be transported to the cells from the ground.

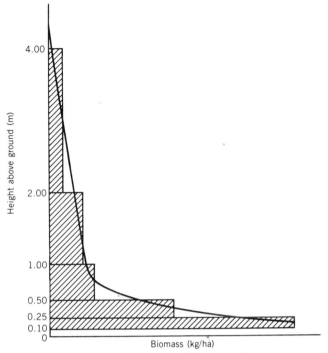

**Figure 7.16** *Vertical distribution of biomass in a mature boreal forest near Poste de la Baleine, Quebec. The total biomass sampled in the six vertical intervals indicated from top to bottom was 0.3, 9.2, 11.7, 7.8, 10.8, and 12.7 kg/ha, respectively. (From Godron, 1975. Courtesy of* Biologia Contemporanea.*)*

The increase in height of vegetation has considerable ecological importance besides the obvious plant characteristics. Increasing vegetation stature is a primary driving force in the establishment of bird species (MacArthur and MacArthur, 1961; Blondel, 1979), the modification of the hydrologic cycle (Perrier, 1975) and light conditions, and the establishment of soil horizons.

Height of vegetation increases in a sigmoid or S-shaped fashion over time, because of the competition for light that leads plants to orient their leaves to optimize its use. When several species are competing, their leaves are placed as high as possible in "making a run for the light," thus causing the general increase in vegetation height (Figure 7.17) (Horn, 1971). Examples are the succession from lichens and mosses on bare rock to herbaceous plants, shrubs, and trees, and from herbaceous plants to taller weedy plants on abandoned fields.

**Figure 7.17** *Tropical rain forest tree and canopy structure (East Kalimantan, Borneo). (Courtesy of Timothy C. Jessup.)*

We hypothesize that many other vegetation types have curves for the vertical distribution of total biomass that resemble the curve for the boreal forest. However, alternative patterns of vegetation stature exist, suggesting that additional mechanisms may be operating. For example:

1. The flat Pampas grasslands of Argentina stretch to the horizon, and the eye may see only endless grass waving in the wind. An occasional ranch projects above the plain, shaded by a cluster of eucalyptus or melia trees. The patch of planted trees near the habitation shows that the environment can readily support trees, yet the Pampas vegetation remains low and herbaceous. Why? A prime hypothesis is that grazing (including trampling) by sheep and cows eliminates woody vegetation.

In the rare places where livestock cannot go, trees begin to grow (Ellenberg, 1962).
2. Near the center of the forested Pine Barrens of New Jersey (United States) are two large patches (2400 ha each) of dwarf pines (*Pinus rigida*) and oaks (*Quercus marilandica, Q. ilicifolia*) that reach to about head height. Yet in the surrounding forest, the same tree species and other oaks and pines grow several times higher. Why is the vegetation so low in these patches of "pine-oak plains"? Several hypotheses have been posed and tested. The most likely cause is the combination of coarse soil conditions, location in the center of an extensive fire area, and long-term adaptation of the plants to an exceptionally high fire frequency (Good et al., 1979; Forman, 1979b; Givnish, 1981).

## SOIL DEVELOPMENT

### Law of Zonality

At the end of the last century Dokuchaev, a Russian scientist studying soils, worked to modernize agriculture in his country. He read as much as he could and was astonished that the books available provided only very general guidelines. Many of the books he read came from European countries, which have a temperate climate, and soils intensely marked by long cultivation and the resulting impoverishment of humus. For several centuries, or even millennia, the recipe for restoring soil fertility could be summed up in two procedures. One was to burn the woody vegetation to furnish mineral elements for the soil. The other was to plow, harrow, and keep turning the soil over in order to compensate for the loss of the natural soil structure and mineral nutrients.

In Russia, however, from the Black Sea to the White Sea, Dokuchaev (1898) recognized a series of soil types linked to distinct climatic zones, from the hot, dry climates of the Ukraine in the Southwest to the arctic climate of the Kola peninsula in the Northeast. During his travels he noticed that the soil types differed markedly following a progression parallel to the series of climates and vegetation belts. The extensive *chernozem* soils favorable for grain cultivation had little in common with the *podzol* soils where coniferous forest accumulated a thick bed of black organic matter over a gray ash-colored mineral layer beneath. He observed the following schematic sequence.

| Climate | Natural Vegetation | Soils |
|---|---|---|
| Semi-arid | Grassland | Chernozems |
| Continental | Deciduous forest | Brown soils |
| Cold continental | Boreal forest (taiga) | Podzols |
| Very cold | Tundra | Arctic soils |

For ecologists, the most important aspect of this soil perspective is that it reemphasizes the primary role that climate plays in directing ecological systems (Figure 7.12). Climate is the primary determinant of vegetation, which in turn shades and provides organic matter to the soil. Hence, if given enough time, vegetation and soil may be surprisingly independent of the underlying rock type.

We can see this result in comparing a sandy soil and a clay soil as they are progressively colonized by vegetation in a temperate continental climate (Figure 7.18). In the beginning, the sand is very porous, low in tiny particles in suspension, and low in available mineral elements. The clay, while it contains a strong ability to retain water and has a high percent of tiny particles in suspension, is "asphyxiated" during the wet season. As vegetation develops and enriches the upper horizons with humus, the properties of the two soils begin to converge (Figure 7.18). The humus increases the capacity of the sandy soil to retain water. In clay soil, the added humus aerates the surface horizons of the soil. The vegetation of each site then spontaneously begins to resemble that of the other as the soils become more and more similar. In addition, the microclimate under the vegetation canopy increasingly exerts a controlling influence on living conditions for the animals, plants, and microbes of the understory and soil.

As the reader may have realized, these processes are linked in a feedback system. The vegetation changed the soil, which in turn changed the vegetation. This feedback loop starts out positive or self-accelerating, as in many biological systems. That is, changes in the soil favor or accelerate the development of vegetation, and the resulting vegetational changes favor or accelerate soil development. When vegetation approaches its maximum height and cover, the rate of both vegetation and soil change diminishes, and a negative feedback system becomes increasingly predominant. Thus the ecological system, including both soil and vegetation, approaches an equilibrium.

The convergence just outlined is sufficiently universal to have been called by some a law, the **law of zonality.** That is, in each climatic zone, soils developed from different underlying rocks, together with their assemblages of plants and animals, tend to converge toward an increasingly uniform ecological system.

Considering the law of zonality, we might legitimately ask why heterogeneous landscapes exist within a climatic zone. One major reason is disturbance. Natural disturbances and human influences are so pervasive and diverse that the convergence process is continually being set back in different ways. Another major reason is that the rates of convergence differ sharply for different bedrocks and geomorphic structures. Some ecosystems change rapidly while others appear almost stable and permanent. Finally, climate and geomorphology themselves may change

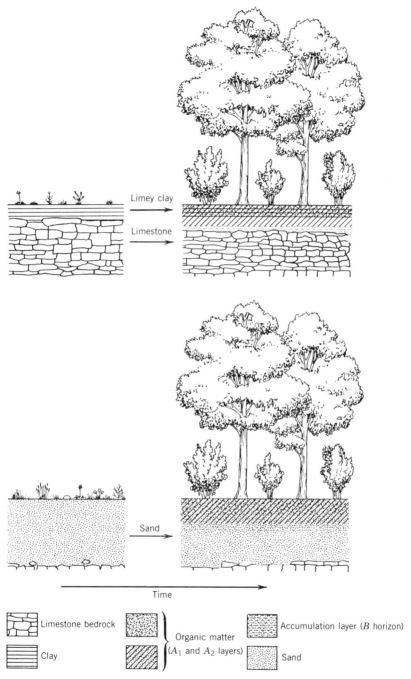

Limey clay

Limestone

Sand

Time

Limestone bedrock

Clay

Organic matter
($A_1$ and $A_2$ layers)

Accumulation layer ($B$ horizon)

Sand

**Figure 7.18** *Convergence of soil and vegetation originating on different substrates. Upper diagram of clay soil derived from limestone, and lower diagram of sandy soil derived from a sand deposit. Both are in a temperate climate (from Godron, 1984; courtesy of Editeur Masson. © Masson 1984, Abrégé d'ecologie de la Végétation Terrestre.)*

more rapidly than do some ecosystems (Botkin and Sobel, 1975; Billings and Peterson, 1980; Walker, 1981). Therefore, at any point in time, numerous ecosystems representing different stages in the long-term convergence process (law of zonality) coexist in a landscape. We must discriminate between these stages when studying a landscape. In effect, our interest in the law of zonality concerns not its end product but rather the process, which is a driving force or general tendency in landscapes.

## Toward a Soil Classification Based on Origin and Development

The fact of differing rates of soil development among different landscape elements relates directly to the problem of classification. The first classifications of soil, dating to Roman antiquity, are purely descriptive or morphologic, in the sense that they describe soils independently of one another and are based only on the properties visible to the naked eye. This approach was used systematically up through the eighteenth century in various disciplines, as for example in the botanical classifications of Tournefort and Linnaeus. The development of plant structure over time was not evident to these botanists, and they depended on appearances. Thereafter, scientists became increasingly certain that plants or animals with similar structures, at least for certain characteristics, developed from a common ancestor. Furthermore, it became evident that the similarity of forms results from a common inheritance that may be represented by a **phylogenetic** tree, that is, a pattern of ancestry which relates current similarities to past relationships. Classification, therefore, is like a photograph or cross section of the major groups in a phylogenetic tree at a particular point in time (Figure 7.19). The genius of the early animal and plant classifiers became apparent when it turned out that their morphologic intuitions were very close to the picture provided by the myriad fossils later discovered by geologists during the nineteenth century.

For soils, two similar approaches to classification—the first based on appearance, and the second based more on origin—also unfolded. Today this schism has not been totally resolved, presumably because the law of zonality is much less rigid in separating soil types than is the usual reproductive barrier separating two species of animals or plants. Thus, soils appear to vary over a more gradual continuum (Jenny, 1980; FitzPatrick, 1983) than do species produced by biological evolution.

Use of the continuum concept in consort with consideration of dynamic processes (including the law of zonality) may provide a solid basis for soil type descriptions, so that soils can ultimately become a pillar in the classification of landscapes.

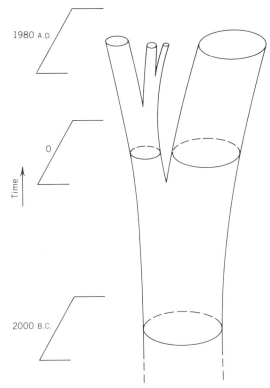

**Figure 7.19** *A "growing phylogenetic tree" showing objects to be classified. A cross section at a point in time indicates the objects for classification, such as different soils or landscapes, and the vertical axis shows their phylogenetic relationships.*

## The Role of Decomposers

A soil, of course, is not simply a collection of mineral particles. It also includes the equally important components of water, air, and organisms, particularly those small animals and microorganisms that decompose organic matter. Because of this critical decomposition process, decomposers play central roles in both the production and the mineral cycling of ecosystems and landscapes.

Typically, some of the organic matter produced in one landscape element is decomposed in an adjacent landscape element. For example, wind readily blows leaves and insects across the boundary separating ecosystems (Lewis, 1969a, 1969b; Orndorff and Lang, 1981). Perhaps more predictably, wild herbivores and livestock graze in one ecosystem but deposit much of their feces in another ecosystem where they rest or raise young (Woodmansee, 1978, 1979).

**Net ecosystem production,** the gain or loss of organic matter in an ecosystem during a certain time period, equals net plant production less the (cellular) respiration of herbivores, carnivores, and decomposers (Woodwell and Whittaker, 1968). It turns out that in terrestrial ecosystems the amount of respiration, or organic matter breakdown, accomplished by herbivores and carnivores is tiny compared with that accomplished by decomposers. Thus, the production of the whole ecosystem largely boils down to whether the net production of organic matter by plants is greater or less than the amount of organic matter broken down by decomposers.

In a mature stable natural ecosystem such as the Amazon rain forest, net ecosystem production is essentially zero. In other words, the forest as a whole is neither increasing nor decreasing in biomass. The amount of $CO_2$ taken up by the rain forest exactly equals the amount given off. In such a stable system, whether net plant production is high or low, the net production of the whole ecosystem is nil.

If, however, the stable system is disturbed by fire, cutting, or the like, decreasing biomass, the system responds by gradually increasing biomass, that is, **aggrading,** until the stable level is reestablished. During this period of increasing biomass, net plant production exceeds decomposition. Foresters take advantage of this phenomenon to grow wood, and farmers do the same in growing crops or forage. In a system undergoing plant succession, biomass is also usually increasing. During this process more $CO_2$ is taken up by the system than is given off. Conversely, more $O_2$ is given off than absorbed.

On the other hand, if a system is **degrading,** it means net plant production is inhibited, say by air pollution, drought, overgrazing, or even irradiation (Figure 7.20) (Dyksterhuis, 1949; Gordon and Gorham, 1963; Whittaker and Woodwell, 1973). In this case, decomposition exceeds plant production and biomass decreases over time (retrogression). In general, then, the balance between decomposer activity and plant production determines whether there is any change in biomass, or $CO_2$ and $O_2$ flows.

A landscape, of course, includes many ecosystems. While some may be degrading (Figure 7.20), most landscapes contain a majority of aggrading ecosystems resulting not only from human influences such as agriculture and forestry but also from previous natural disturbances like fire and herbivore pest outbreaks. In such cases, there is a net uptake of $CO_2$ and a net release of $O_2$. Whether the net amounts of $CO_2$ and $O_2$ are significant relative to the burning of fossil fuels and gas exchanges between the ocean and atmosphere is one of the major critical, and controversial, global issues facing humankind (MacCracken and Moses, 1982; Woodwell, 1983).

**Figure 7.20** *Degrading oak-pine forest resulting from irradiation. Radioactive cesium (a gamma source) has emitted irradiation from the top of the central pole for 12 years (Woodwell, 1967; Whittaker and Woodwell, 1969). In the central sandy area, virtually all species have been killed. The next zone out to about the large pine trunk on left is dominated by* Cladonia *lichens; the next zone by* Carex *(grass-like) sedges; the next zone by blueberry and huckleberry shrubs (*Vaccinium, Gaylusaccia); *the next zone by oak trees (*Quercus alba, Q. coccinea) *(not pictured here); and the final surrounding area by oak and pine (*Pinus rigida). *Brookhaven National Laboratory, Long Island, New York. (R. Forman.)*

## NATURAL DISTURBANCE

*Homo sapiens* has so modified landscapes on the globe that it is not easy to find a landscape that remains absolutely natural or virgin. Human influences have been widespread and are often subtle. Hence, we will refer to **natural landscapes,** in a general sense, as those where human effects, if present, are not ecologically significant to the landscape as a whole. An old road may persist in the tundra or a small hunted area may surround a cluster of huts in a rain forest, but in each case the effect on the landscape as a whole is not ecologically significant.

We have discussed and given examples of natural disturbance in each chapter. We mention it briefly here to pinpoint a few major underlying characteristics and as a reminder that it takes its place alongside geomorphology, plant and animal establishment, and soil development as a major natural process of landscape development.

Fire has been considered the most important natural disturbance because of the extent of area it affects and its high frequency (Figure 7.21). Where fire is frequent, however, the vegetation and fauna adapt to it—indeed, we sometimes speak of "pyrophytic" vegetation. Under such circumstances, fire is a normal component of the landscape and cannot be considered a disturbance. In contrast, fire is a disturbance in all those ecosystems and landscapes where it has been infrequent, and as a result few fire adaptations of animals and plants have developed.

Similarly, flooding and volcanic activity may be so frequent that animals and plants of specific ecosystems—such as flood plains and the slopes of volcanos—may adapt to the environmental changes and even require them for survival. In such cases, the flooding or volcanic activity cannot be considered a natural disturbance but rather part of the normal

**Figure 7.21** *A 600-hectare fire in dry pine forest. Plant and animal species here have various adaptations to fire, which is relatively frequent. Galena Creek Area, Washoe County, Nevada (United States). (Courtesy of USDA Soil Conservation Service)*

range of variation of the system. Typically, however, a whole landscape is not flooded or covered by volcanic material frequently enough for the organisms present to adapt to the environmental changes. The extensive floods and volcanic activities are infrequent, unpredictable, and often so violent that they cause massive disruptions. In short, such environmental changes are not disturbances in the specific ecosystems that they hit repeatedly, but are disturbances in the landscape as a whole, where they are rare.

A final major natural disturbance characteristic relates to hurricanes, tornados (Figure 7.22), and outbreaks of herbivore pest defoliators. Natural disturbances help create the heterogeneity of the landscape. The tornado that uproots large trees and eliminates a farm or village, or the defoliation that opens up a patch in a grassland or forest, significantly alters the patch structure of a landscape (Figures 7.21 and 7.22). The balance between stable and aggrading ecosystems changes, as do the flows of objects across the landscape.

We conclude this first chapter on landscape development by introducing *catastrophe theory*, a concept with a mathematical foundation

**Figure 7.22** *Tornado effect on a village. Elms (Ulmus) remain along Main Street, and grassland is in distance. Boone County, Nebraska (United States). (Courtesy of USDA Soil Conservation Service)*

(Thom, 1969, 1977) that helps us understand the development process of any system, including a landscape [Waddington, 1975 (the "epigenetic landscape"); Jones, 1975; Zeeman, 1976; Woodcock and Davis, 1978; Cancela da Fonseca, 1980]. Consider a straight line beginning at the origin of a graph and rising to the right side. If you could pour water on the line from the upper right end, the water would flow down to the origin of the graph. Now make the line S-shaped, so that to the right of the midpoint the curve is slightly concave upward and to the left it is slightly convex upward. Water would still flow from the upper end across the midpoint to the origin, with only a minor decrease in rate. Now make the line strongly S-shaped, so that the dip on the right side is slightly lower than the midpoint, and the mound on the left is slightly higher. Water now would flow down to the dip but not quite reach the midpoint or, of course, the origin. In this case the midpoint, called the **catastrophe point**, is a threshold where the system can be significantly diverted or altered. (Thom, 1969, found that mathematically only eight shapes or surfaces functioned as catastrophe points: the fold, the crease, the navel, etc.)

Catastrophe theory thus indicates that a gradually changing system (with its characteristics) converges on, and crosses, particular points, and that only a slight change in the immediate vicinity of a point will divert the system in a quite different direction. Major alterations in landscape development take place in this way. For example, a meandering river changes direction as the result of a slightly larger than usual flood, a few individuals of an aggressive nonnative species accidentally colonize a landscape, and—as we will see in the next chapter on the human role in landscape development—someone first hammers some iron into the form of a hoe that can cut up grassland sod for planting crops.

## SUMMARY

Landscapes today result from five broad natural processes: geomorphology, climate, the establishment of plants and animals, soil development, and natural disturbance. Geomorphic processes are heavily dependent on climate, and thus landforms are quite different in each major climatic zone. The complexity of landforms in landscapes can be integrated by evaluating the degree of openness, the depth effect, and the ruggedness present. The plants and animals in landscapes today reflect how they evolved in consort with climatic changes and species migrations, especially during the Mesozoic, Tertiary, and Pleistocene periods. Speciation continues today in both biostasic and rhexistasic landscapes. Vegetation stature increases in a sigmoid fashion, an important recovery process following disturbance.

Soils develop and tend to converge in a climatic zone according to the law of zonality. This developmental process underlies a phylogenetic soil classification. Natural disturbance not only is strongly affected by heterogeneity in a landscape, but also creates heterogeneity. The species most affected by strong environmental changes are those that have been exposed to them infrequently. Degrading landscapes are those with a negative net ecosystem production—that is, respiration, primarily by decomposers, exceeds plant production—while aggrading landscapes have a net gain in carbon. Natural landscapes (those without significant overall human effect) continue to be changed and molded by all these processes together.

## QUESTIONS

1. What are the general differences between plains landscapes and mountain landscapes?
2. Which is more important in controlling geomorphic phenomena, temperature or precipitation? Explain.
3. Are the natural processes that affect a landscape independent of one another? Is there any logical order for studying them? Explain.
4. Briefly trace the history of terrestrial plants and animals over geological time, indicating any times when one group strongly affected speciation in the other group.
5. What major events took place during the Holocene, and in what major climatic zones were they most pronounced?
6. What is the purpose of the colored flowers that adorn our landscapes? If a plant species produced different colored flowers, what would that suggest relative to the topic of this chapter?
7. Summarize the roles of climate, bedrock, vegetation, and animals in landscape development.
8. What factors limit the growth in height of vegetation? Is it possible to predict the maximum height that can be attained by vegetation in a landscape?
9. Why doesn't the tendency toward zonality produce homogeneous landscapes?
10. How would a forester turn a degrading landscape into an aggrading one, and what measurements would be required to confirm his or her success?

# Appendix: Geological Time

| Era | Period | Biological Events | Years Ago |
|---|---|---|---|
| | Permian | Extinction of many kinds of marine animals, including trilobites. Glaciation at low latitudes | 280 ± 10 million |
| Paleozoic (Primary) | Carboniferous | Sharks and amphibians abundant. First reptiles. Large and numerous scale trees and seed ferns. First conifers Great coal forests | 345 ± 10 million |
| | Devonian | First amphibians. Fishes abundant | 405 ± 10 million |
| | Silurian | First terrestrial plants and animals | 425 ± 10 million |
| | Ordovician | Invertebrates dominant. First fishes. | 500 ± 10 million |
| | Cambrian | First abundant record of marine life. Trilobites (arthropods) dominant, followed by extinction of about two-thirds of trilobite families | 600 ± 50 million |
| | Precambrian | Rare fossils of primitive aquatic plants and some simple animals. Evidence of glaciation. Oldest dated algae and bacteria ± 3.3 billion years | > 600 million |

| Era | Period | Biological Events | Years Ago |
|---|---|---|---|
| Cenozoic | Quaternary | Modern humans | 11 thousand |
| | | Early humans. Northern glaciation | 5 to 3 million |
| | Tertiary — Pliocene | Large carnivores | 13 ± 1 million |
| | Miocene | First abundant grazing mammals | 25 ± 1 million |
| | Oligocene | Climax of arcto-tertiary flora | 36 ± 2 million |
| | Eocene | Many modern types of mammals | 58 ± 2 million |
| | Paleocene | First placental mammals | 63 ± 2 million |
| Mesozoic (Secondary) | Cretaceous | Climax of dinosaurs followed by extinction. First flowering plants | 135 ± 5 million |
| | Jurassic | Dinosaurs abundant. First birds, first mammals. | 180 ± 5 million |
| | Triassic | First dinosaurs. Abundant cycads and conifers | 230 ± 10 million |

**Figure 7.23** *Geological time table (from Wilson et al., 1973, and other sources).*

# 8
## The Human Role in Landscape Development

*All art, all education,*
*can be merely a supplement to nature.*
**Aristotle, 384–322 B.C.**

The accompanying photograph of the jewel of Mont Saint Michel, on the northern coast of France, can be viewed from at least two points of view (Figure 8.1). A geologist would see it as an erosional outlier, a remnant of a former plateau that later served to support some buildings. A landscape architect would see it as a fortified abbey, built about 1450, taking advantage of a readily defended site. In a landscape with people, the human role and the role of nature may be alternatively emphasized but cannot be disentangled. How would North American landscapes look today if Chinese instead of Europeans had colonized them? To understand why a landscape looks as it does, we cannot limit ourselves to the natural or physical environment. We must also understand human influences and culture (see, for example, Thomas, 1955; Hoskins, 1955; McHarg, 1969; Detwyler, 1971; Meinig, 1979a).

In the preceding chapters the human role has generally been kept on the sidelines, but now the time has come to spotlight it. Most so-called natural ecosystems, and numerous species within them, have long been influenced by humans. With the exponential growth in human population, ecosystems without this influence are increasingly scarce. Rather than attempting to avoid human influences in ecology, or calling their study applied ecology, we must develop ecological principles based on the characteristics of most of the earth's ecosystems and species. Such principles will be far more powerful and useful. Nevertheless, rigor and caution are essential, because humans become simultaneously the observers and the objects of study.

To begin on solid ground, we will refer to the landscape change principle (Chapter 1), and see how it is linked to rhythms of the environment.

**Figure 8.1** *Mont Saint Michel, an island on the northern coast of France as seen when rapidly rising tides cover the adjoining mud flats. (J. Feuillie/© C.N.M.H.S./S.P.A.D.E.M.; courtesy of Caisse Nationale des Monuments Historiques et des Sites, Paris.)*

## MODIFICATION OF NATURAL RHYTHMS

### Disturbance and Rhythms

When undisturbed, the horizontal structure of a landscape tends to progress toward homogeneity. Moderate disturbance rapidly increases heterogeneity. Severe disturbance may increase or decrease heterogeneity.

A landscape can therefore be said to be in a *dynamic balance* at a point in time; that is, it is subject to two opposing types of forces, development and disturbance. In such a balance, the most fundamental landscape characteristics—vertical structure, horizontal structure, and grain size—shift rapidly when one group of forces becomes predominant over the other.

The preceding chapter presented examples of natural disturbances and suggested that the most important ecological characteristic of a disturbance is its time lag or periodicity. When an environmental factor such as temperature, fire, or food supply oscillates with a rhythm as regular as the pendulum of an antique clock, the *genetic memory* of organisms permits them to take note of the fluctuations. The species progressively adapt until, at some point, this factor can no longer be considered a disturbance.

For animals, the daily rhythm produces a series of waking and sleeping periods. Humans are so habituated to these that they suffer noticeably from disorientation of their biological clock when they cross several time zones in an airplane. The contrast between day and night also permits plants to alternate daytime photosynthesis and evapotranspiration with nighttime cell expansion. Similarly, the annual seasonal cycle in the temperate zone acts like the baton of an orchestra conductor. Its signals launch the explosion of annual plants in spring, gradually build the sustained songs of summer, and lead the decrescendo of fluttering leaves in fall to a final pianissimo of dormancy in winter.

Regular periodicity is striking in climates with a severe dry season, where natural fires appear almost certain when biomass reaches a certain level. The plant species have had time to adapt to the frequent fires with varied mechanisms for resisting death or for rapidly regrowing, while most of the animals either have the ability to burrow in the substrate or flee from the fire.

In effect, periodic variations in the environment can be absorbed by organisms, thanks to their genetic memory. It effectively notes regular fluctuations and permits an adaptation through reproductive cycles. In contrast, unpredictable and infrequent variations are disturbances, in the sense that they significantly alter the ecological system and result in a long recovery period.

These broad principles are recalled here, introducing a chapter on the influence of people, because human actions are sudden and unexpected in the scale of geological time. If the 3.5 billion years since life's beginning were a 365-day year, the first human tribes appeared at about 4:00 P.M. on the 31st of December, and agriculture only appeared at the last minute. The period of human influence has been so brief that, in effect, other species have still not had time enough to adapt to it (Figure 8.2). Confronted with the massive activities of humans, and not having sufficient time to "resist" by adaptation, many species risk disappearing altogether. *Extinction* has been the fate of 120 bird species since 1600 A.D., including the flightless birds of New Zealand and Madagascar and the once-predominant passenger pigeon (*Ectopistes migratorius*) of North America (Owen, 1971; Martin, 1971). Alternatively, species may evolve by benefiting from human construction. For example, the common pigeon or rock dove (*Columba livia*) colonizes the cornices of Venetian palaces and the parks of all American cities, and gulls (*Larus*) live on the mounds of concentrated urban waste (Isenmann, 1976, 1977). We thus begin this

**Figure 8.2** *Waste material from strip mining operations in La Salle County, Illinois (United States). Few species colonize or adapt to this exposed rock material or to the adjacent lake (left) that receives runoff. For scale of this patch, see the huge shovel in lower left and the village in background. (Courtesy of USDA Soil Conservation Service.)*

chapter by considering how human actions directed at altering the rhythm of natural processes lead to direct and widespread effects on landscapes.

## Daily Rhythms

To extend the daily temperature cycle, we construct greenhouses. Their effect on the landscape is considerable in parts of Holland or Israel, where long tunnels of plastic combined with geometric glasshouses extend for kilometers.

The other easily changed daily rhythm is the alternation of light and dark periods. Elongating days with artificial lights increases the production of eggs and chickens. Elongating nights accelerates the fattening of hogs. This type of modification is generally too localized to modify an entire landscape but it helps produce the large farmyards so distinctive and so repetitive on the extensive plains of the American Midwest. These human struggles against a strong regular daily rhythm require a heavy investment in a nearly permanent agricultural infrastructure that leaves a marked imprint on the landscape.

## Seasonal Rhythms

The most spectacular revolution in human history arose from the idea of modifying natural seasonal rhythms. The change from the hunter-gatherer (Figure 8.3) to the cultivator-herder way of life near the end of the *Paleolithic* or Old Stone Age has resulted in the transformation of more than three quarters of the global land surface. (The Paleolithic is the human cultural and technological phase characterized by the use of stone tools,

**Figure 8.3** *Excavation of a Paleolithic site beneath an overhanging cliff. The Altiplano near Bogotá, Colombia. Plaster "vessels" are made to hold archaeological remains, including numerous deer (Odocoileus), guinea pig (Cavia), and human (Homo) bones in place for study. Stone and wooden implements indicate human use for at least 11,000 years, with agriculture in the last 2,500 years, (Van der Hammen and Correal Urrego, 1978). (R. Forman.)*

before the widespread use of metal, and occurred during the Pleistocene ice age and about the first half of the Holocene. The Neolithic or New Stone Age in some regions, approximately the Holocene portion of the period, is characterized by the grinding or polishing of stones [see Figure 7.10]. The stockpiling of provisions to survive the difficult season was an even more basic revolution than the practice of seed planting for legumes and grain. The establishment of permanent settlements, the domestication of ruminants, and cultivation are three convergent means to escape the constraints of seasonal rhythms.

The principal object of plowing and working the soil is to modify the sequence of life cycle changes of perennial plant species (seed germination, flowering, pollination, fruit production, and onset of dormancy). In natural landscapes, a different set of species may be active and productive at each season. In the cultivated landscape, this sequence is replaced by a much more compact cycle. A single species produces at a single moment of the year, whether we plant annuals such as wheat, maize, or beans, or perennials such as sugarcane, grapes, or orchard trees. As a result, the landscape is transformed into a checkerboard on which each type of cultivation represents a square. This checkerboard of mixed plantings could be constructed at the scale of a field parcel, a farm, or an entire landscape (Hoskins, 1955; Auclair, 1976; Pimentel et al., 1975; Meinig, 1979a). Ultimately, the landscape could appear as a monoculture, in which all the squares of the checkerboard are planted with the same crop.

The history of agriculture verifies this basic pattern of modifying seasonal rhythms. The **Age of Copper** and the **Age of Bronze** (the first human cultural and technological phases with a widespread use of metal, about 3000–1200 B.C. in the Middle East, and about 1800–600 B.C. in China), before the advent of iron farm instruments, were characterized more by temporary burned patches for crops than by permanent agricultural clearing. Not until the **Iron Age** (characterized by widespread use of iron, beginning about 1200 B.C. in the Middle East and 600 B.C. in China), could the roots of herbaceous grasses readily be cut by rigid cutting tools. Early writers tell how the Gauls often had to straighten out the blades of their bronze swords by hand and that possessing iron swords that retained their rigidity in spite of clashes and blows was a sign of wealth and power. A bronze spade that twists is of limited agricultural use in digging up and turning over the dense tangle of roots of a mature grassland. It was not until the iron hoe became widespread that the regular cultivation of grasslands or fallow fields became possible.

In America, the introduction of steel tools by European settlers so modified the cultivation process that certain species benefited immediately. A small weed called plantain (*Plantago lanceolata*), which generally cannot survive the normal competition in an old prairie, so dependably colonized the land worked by the pioneers that the native Indians called it "the footstep of the white man." Today the same native European species is perhaps the leading weed in American lawns along with another European species, the dandelion (*Taraxacum officinale*).

In the case of livestock grazing, the transformation of the landscape by modification of the seasonal sequence is less evident, but all ranchers and farmers know that the rhythm of pasturing is the key to good management. In general, overgrazing is basically the result of a poor seasonal or weekly distribution of livestock rather than an average excess of the total number of animals.

Irrigation is generally used, in climates with a very distinct seasonal rhythm, to compensate for the water deficit in the dry season. The endless, monotonous appearance of the landscape in irrigated plains bears witness to the magnitude of investments needed to reduce the constraints of seasonal climatic cycles. The "geometrization" of irrigated landscapes has even left a trace in our scientific vocabulary; "geometry," originally meaning "a measure of the land," was invented in the Middle East before Pythagoras to better distribute irrigation water across a floodable plain (Jacobsen and Adams, 1958). Perhaps the earliest dated example are the canals more than 100 km long that Hammurabi (1728 to 1685 B.C.) used, such as the Khan canal downstream from Babylonia. These canals were large enough to transport troops from place to place by boat.

In each irrigated landscape the form of the canal network, whether fern-like—with principal canals and smaller parallel branches—or hand-like—with canals radiating from a single point—provides a nearly permanent imprint on landscape structure.

## Rhythms of Several Years or Centuries

In environments where fire is a natural factor that controls assemblages of animals and plants, fires appear at relatively regular intervals—when the amount of combustible material builds up to the level where fire spreads easily (Hanes, 1971; Kozlowski and Ahlgren, 1974; Little, 1979; Forman, 1979a; Minnich, 1983). When humans intervene, they generally accelerate the cadence or frequency of fires (Figure 8.4). The clearest example is the tropical savanna in parts of Africa and South America, where millions of hectares are deliberately burned each year. In fact, most specialists now believe that natural savannas are exceptions and that most savannas have been created and maintained by this human influence (Beard, 1953; Budowski, 1956; Richards, 1964).

In some areas, foresters use *control burns* to help manage the forest for wood products. These are intentional, controlled fires undertaken only at certain seasons and at certain well-chosen stages of succession (Kozlowski and Ahlgren, 1974; Little, 1979).

**Figure 8.4** *Fire use was the first widespread human influence on the environment. Forestry precedes fire and shifting agriculture quickly follows it in many tropical rain forest areas today. Large trees are felled, trunks removed for wood, most remaining biomass burned to release mineral nutrients to the soil, crops planted often for only about two years, followed by a fallow period of many years to replenish the impoverished soil fertility, and then cultivation again (East Kalimantan, Borneo). (Courtesy of Cynthia Mackie.)*

Management of European forests provides a significant example of the modification of century-long rhythms. For example, the forest of Blois in the Loire Valley of France was oriented in the seventeenth century toward production of wood for the royal navy. It is still managed with a complete rotation of 240 years, giving the oaks fine-grained wood for producing deluxe furniture.

This type of forest management produces a checkerboard of parcels usually of four identifiable types (Jacquot, 1931). They may be called, by increasing age, (a) seedling brush, (b) sapling thicket, (c) pole stand, and (d) forest grove. Forests resulting from this process are very different from natural forests because woodcutters harvest some wood from the forest about every ten years. The total amount removed is considerable, averaging more than three tons of organic matter per hectare per year. Even more importantly, the first management operation, which thins out seedlings at the seedling brush stage, eliminates those species judged of little value. The result is that the species diversity of the stand remains reduced for centuries. At each harvest the poorest growing trees are selected for removal, so the final forest grove is composed of beautiful, tall, productive trees that in turn give rise to the following forest generation.

Another influence of civilization at the century scale is the increase in the level of atmospheric $CO_2$ (MacCracken and Moses, 1982; Woodwell, 1983; Houghton et al., 1983). This increase affects the entire biosphere and is linked to landscapes because it depends on the annual production and decomposition rhythms of ecosystems. Deforestation of landscapes in the past two decades appears to be a particularly important factor in the overall $CO_2$ increase (Woodwell, 1983).

## METHODS OR TOOLS USED IN LANDSCAPE MODIFICATION

We could spell out other widespread and long-term effects of human actions on landscapes, such as desertification, deforestation, and erosion. It is more interesting now, however, to explore how the methods or tools used by people affect the landscape. Use of tools, of course, is one of the prime characteristics separating the human species from other species on the globe.

### Natural Resource Extraction and Alteration

Doubtless the first influence of prehistoric people was their predation on edible animals and plants (Figure 8.3). This predation did not modify the landscape much more than that of chimpanzees. Modification became somewhat more serious near the end of the Paleolithic (Old Stone Age) with the invention of the bow. During this period, livestock and planted crops allowed some further increases in regular harvest production as well as in human population growth. However, domestication at its beginning probably had little genetic effect on the wild strains used. The earth supported only a few million people (estimates of 2 to 10 million) then, an average density of less than one person for every 20 square kilometers. The total predation effect was still minimal at this time.

It was mainly by using fire that humans came to exert a major influence (Figure 8.4) (Budowski, 1956; Nicholson, 1970; Barrett and Arno, 1982). Traces of human use of fire have been found in deposits more than 200,000 years old, such as those near Aix-en-Provence in southeastern France. Evidence of fire some 35,000 to 80,000 years ago is frequent at nearby Hortus, though of course archaeological traces unfortunately can provide little evidence of fire use across a landscape. Throughout history, sailors who navigated along shores inhabited by "indigenous savages" have described clouds of smoke that decorated the coastlines, both in such temperate regions as North America and such dry tropical regions as southern Africa. Naveh and Dan (1973) suggest that fire has been used in the Middle East since the middle Paleolithic for hunting and making clearings.

Some scholars affirm that native Indians in the northeastern United States set regular fires (Bromley, 1935; Day, 1953). But a careful review of the historical evidence (Russell, 1983) now indicates that before European settlement native Indians did not burn the land either systematically or in a widespread manner. Natural fires, augmented by occasional fires escaping from, and mainly localized near, inhabited areas appear to have been the most likely pattern.

The extraction of minerals also transforms landscapes. Quarries, sand and gravel extraction, open pit mines, and especially surface strip mining for coal and other mineral resources (Figure 8.2) far exceed the abilities of the existing natural ecosystems to adjust and of their species to adapt. These pits and mining activities result in long-term marks on the landscape.

### Introduction of Agricultural Methods

Agriculture is not simply the harvest of usable production. It also involves the favoring of certain native species and the introduction of new species into selected ecosystems of a landscape (Figure 8.5). Since the middle Holocene, humans have intentionally introduced species or strains of plants and animals for domestication on a significant scale. Such species normally cannot compete with wild native species and require human effort to persist (Budowski, 1956; Bell, 1973; Marks, 1983).

**Figure 8.5** *Livestock as an introduced species bred and tended by humans. Cattle are valuable protein sources in many dry climates; but overgrazing, leading to rapid desertification during inevitable droughts, is a hazard. Senegal, central Africa. (Courtesy of A. Cornet.)*

The mechanical energy necessary for cultivation has produced a major effect on the landscape, especially the utilization of draft animals such as oxen and horses. This *innovation* (a new technique or idea that causes a significant effect) has still not reached its peak; most Asian and African farmers, for example, continue today to use a hoe to break up soil and eliminate weeds (Figure 8.6). Harnessed animals increase by about five times the input of energy per cultivated hectare. The use of a tractor may increase energy input a hundred times and thus leaves an indelible mark on the landscape. In addition to making it possible to plow extensive parcels of land, mechanization goes hand in hand with the abandonment of the **fallowing** system, that is, the periodical setting aside of parcels for natural regrowth and refertilization of the soil. (The complex of species introductions and mechanical cultivating methods produces a human-driven process of landscape development that will be analyzed later in this chapter.)

**Figure 8.6** *A highly connected rain forest matrix contrasted with a river corridor and agricultural patches. Temporary huts are built for the two years or so of cultivation in a clearing that is typically a hectare or two in size (see Figure 8.4). East Kalimantan, Borneo. (Courtesy of Herwasono Soedjito.)*

Throughout the historical period, the techniques used to harvest the annual increment of livestock and crop productivity have become ever more powerful. Nevertheless, the rise in human population and the increasing use of fossil fuel are the two main factors in the increase in the amount extracted each year.

At the present time, the major world harvests are wood and grain (see Table 8.1) (Beaujeu-Garnier, 1977). Note that wood harvest by weight is equal to that of all grains combined. Cattle, sheep, and pigs, all basically

TABLE 8.1 *Global harvests.*

| Plant biomass | | Animals | |
|---|---|---|---|
| Wood | $2 \times 10^9$ | Cattle | $1.2 \times 10^9$ |
| Wheat | $5 \times 10^8$ | Sheep and goats | $1.1 \times 10^9$ |
| Rice | $4 \times 10^8$ | Pigs | $7 \times 10^8$ |
| Corn (Maize) | $4 \times 10^8$ | Fish | $7 \times 10^7$ |
| Other grains | $4 \times 10^8$ | | |
| Sugar beets | $3 \times 10^8$ | | |
| Potatoes | $3 \times 10^8$ | | |

NOTE: Plant and fish biomass is given in metric tons per year, and other animals in roughly estimated number of head.
*Source:* Beaujeu-Garnier, 1977. Editions C.D.U. and S.E.D.E.S.

herbivores, provide the major animal harvest for human consumption, a tiny fraction of the weight of plant material harvested.

The inputs of fertilizers and pesticides are also effectively inputs of energy. Their influence on landscapes is often as conspicuous as that of mechanization, because they lead to increasing homogeneity of cultivated parcels with few patches of weeds or parasites evident. With these techniques, the long-term trade-off between higher crop productivity and soil erosion—and impoverishment of the native biota—becomes increasingly clear.

The use of fertilizers and pesticides in mechanized agriculture has reached enormous proportions. For example, in the United States both fertilizers and pesticides are major components of the average farmer's annual budget. Of the pesticides used, about 51% are herbicides, 35% are insecticides, and 14% are fungicides. They are applied over about 34%, 12%, and 2%, respectively, of the nonpasture cropland (Pimentel et al., 1978).

Despite the use of pesticides in many agricultural fields, pest explosions continue in landscapes. In some cases, the pests are native species undergoing cyclic population increases (e.g., continued plagues of locusts) or benefiting from changes wrought by the introduction of agricultural methods. But often the pests are nonnative species which are introduced or arrive spontaneously and, in the absence of the constraints of their native habitat, simply increase to local epidemic proportions.

## Decision Catalysts

The tools used for constructing buildings and cities, as well as transportation and communication routes, are powerful and diverse. We will concentrate later in this chapter on their effects in modifying landscapes. However, before proceeding, we must pinpoint a major factor in landscape ecology that has received only brief mention until now, that is, how political, economic, and social decisions affect the landscape. Nearly all characteristics of landscape structure, functioning, and change operate at levels of—and are confined by—political, economic, and social forces. In many cases, these are concrete decisions, such as to open up a portion of the Amazon rain forest with a trans-Amazonian highway (see Figure 6.15), or to convert a rural landscape to a suburban landscape by introducing a large sewer line, or to consider using a major nuclear explosive. In such cases, specific human decisions act as *triggers* or *decision catalysts* that may be transmitted to another landscape (or landscape element) by communication, and cause change virtually overnight (see Figure 5.16).

## A LANDSCAPE MODIFICATION GRADIENT

We have attempted to detect some of the patterns of the human role in landscape development by focusing on tools and methods. Human influences on landscapes are numerous, however, and it is neither possible nor useful to consider each of these in isolation. A more promising approach is to consider the combined effects of all human influences on a landscape. To do this, we can observe a gradient of landscape modification, extending from a natural landscape without significant human impact to an urban landscape (Godron and Forman, 1983). The natural landscape is in equilibrium with its (zonal) soil, while the city is the highest level of human-caused modification (or "artificialization") considered. We will follow this gradient as if going by limousine from the heart of an extensive natural reserve to the center of a large city. During this trip we will also make historical observations, since each landscape is a product of its historical development.

In a highly diversified region, five primary landscape types will be visited on our journey.

1. **Natural landscape**—without significant human impact (Chapter 7).
2. **Managed landscape**—for example, pastureland or forest, where native species are managed and harvested.
3. **Cultivated landscape**—with villages and patches of natural or managed ecosystems scattered within the predominant cultivation.
4. **Suburban landscape**—a town and country area with a heterogeneous patchy mixture of residential areas, commercial centers, cropland, managed vegetation, and natural areas.
5. **Urban landscape**—with remnant managed park areas scattered in a densely built up matrix several kilometers across.

We will concentrate on the horizontal structure of the landscapes, noting also productivity, mineral nutrient cycling, and species diversity (i.e., species number) while zipping by.

## Natural Landscapes

In our first location we see a highly connected matrix (Figure 8.6) surrounding a relatively low density of natural patches and corridors. The grain of the landscape is usually rather coarse, and in many cases boundaries between landscape elements are indistinct. Most patches are environmental resource patches resulting from spatial variations in physical factors, but disturbance-caused patches are also present (Figure 8.7). The few corridors present are almost always stream corridors (Figure 8.8). In

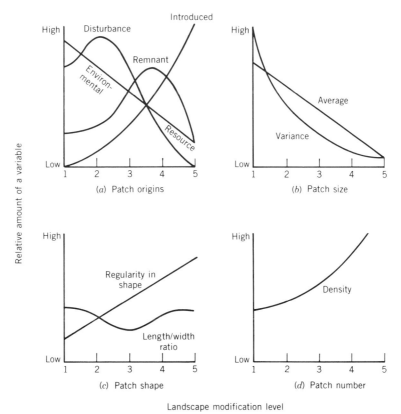

**Figure 8.7** *Patch characteristics changing along a landscape modification gradient. The landscape modification levels are (1) natural, (2) managed, (3) cultivated, (4) suburban, and (5) urban. (Modified from Godron and Forman, 1983). (Courtesy of Springer-Verlag, Inc.)*

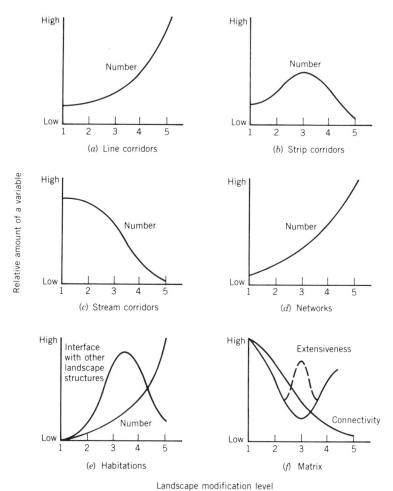

**Figure 8.8** *Corridors and other features changing along a landscape modification gradient. Landscape modification levels are: (1) natural, (2) managed, (3) cultivated, (4) suburban, and (5) urban. The matrix of a cultivated landscape is extensive where a single crop predominates, but low where a few crops predominate in similar proportions. (Modified from Godron and Forman, 1983). (Courtesy of Springer-Verlag, Inc.)*

flat areas, boundaries between landscape elements are commonly parallel to topographic contours, while on slopes their limits are often linked to the depth of soil or water table, resulting in an interdigitating pattern of the vegetation. In either case, boundaries are highly curved and rarely straight. Average patch size is large, but more striking is the high variability in patch size.

Biomass, or potential energy accumulated by the vegetation, is almost always at its maximum. The rate of photosynthesis is high, but because so much energy is required to support the large biomass, and because decomposers are actively breaking down biomass, the net production available for sustained human harvest is minimal (without significantly changing the landscape). Nutrient runoff to streams is present but generally small (Vitousek, 1983). Species diversity is generally high and (in some natural landscapes) extremely rich.

The colonization of natural landscapes may involve nomadic grazing of livestock or the establishment of scattered clearings for cultivation (Figure 8.6). In either case, corridor and patch density increases and matrix connectivity decreases. The major consequence of these new landscape elements is that they serve as nuclei for the spreading of people and tools into the natural matrix of the landscape. Livestock, domestic animals, introduced plants, and people can move readily into the immediate surrounding area that had previously been remote. The other side of the coin, of course, is that those native animals that require remoteness or large tracts of undisturbed land decrease or are eliminated.

## Managed Landscapes

Major changes appear as we drive into pastureland, rangeland, or forests harvested for wood products (Figure 8.9). The matrix remains extensive, though it is now dominated by one or a few species that are managed for production. Humans affect the matrix primarily by harvesting products and by decreasing or increasing fire frequency.

**Hamlets**—little clusters of homes—are present. Line corridors associated with communication and harvest appear in abundance, cutting the connectivity of the matrix sharply (Figure 8.8) (Chisholm, 1962). Patchiness continues to increase, and there are more disturbance patches, while average patch size and variability decrease (Figure 8.7).

Average net production for the whole landscape is positive, with patchy harvests, reflecting the locations of settlements. Harvest patterns also vary temporally, taking place annually in the case of sheep, for example, or at several-decade intervals in the case of wood products.

Mineral nutrient cycles may be extensively disturbed as a result of widespread management and harvest activities along with the cumulative localized effects of clearings, hamlets, and roads. After logging, for example, mineral nutrient losses from an ecosystem typically increase sharply, and then soon drop as vegetative regrowth accelerates. However, if regrowth is inhibited for a period by disturbance, large mineral nutrient losses, especially of nitrate, can be expected (Figure 8.10) (Likens et al., 1967; Gorham et al., 1979; Vitousek et al., 1979; Vitousek, 1983). The loss of the positively charged soil ions (cations) so essential to plant growth

**Figure 8.9** *Geometrization introduced into a managed rangeland landscape near Crystal, Idaho (United States). The straight lines of this stripcropped field, with alternating cultivated strips of spring wheat and summer wheat (Triticum), contrast with the curves and topographic diversity of the grazed rangeland. (Courtesy of USDA Soil Conservation Service.)*

is believed to be related to the loss of negatively charged ions (anions) such as nitrate ($NO_3$) (Figure 8.10). On slopes or highly permeable soils such disturbance may lead to long-term soil impoverishment.

Species diversity in managed landscapes may increase or decrease. Perhaps often the number of native species that disappear is greater than the number of nonnative species that are introduced in patches across the landscape. Even more striking is the relative homogenization of the matrix. While some native species, especially among the vertebrates,

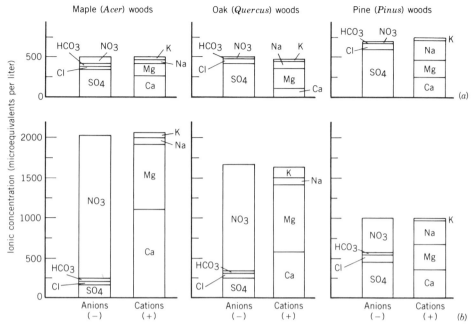

**Figure 8.10** *Dissolved ions leaching out of undisturbed (a) versus disturbed (b) forest ecosystems. Disturbance in these three forests of southern Indiana (United states) is a root trenching technique with prevention of vegetation regrowth. In undisturbed areas, nutrient output from pine woods is slightly higher than that from the deciduous maple and oak woods. After disturbance, mineral nutrient loss is much greater from the deciduous woods. Also a major shift in the proportion of specific nutrients lost, particularly a relative drop in sulfate and increase in nitrate, is evident (from Vitousek, 1983). (Courtesy of Springer-Verlag, Inc.)*

become rare, the few harvest species appear in repetitive monotony across the managed landscape.

Animal species with large home ranges, and often those at high trophic or feeding levels are usually the first to disappear. Mountain lions (*Felis concolor*) and wolves (*Canis lupus*) were probably removed at an early date in the seventeenth century from the colonized landscapes of eastern North America. In a similar manner, bears (*Ursidae*) had been eliminated from Western Europe, and large primates disappeared from the Banco Forest Reserve in southern Ivory Coast.

## Cultivated Landscapes

**The Development of Cultivation.** The cultivation of patches, a major step in human alteration of natural and managed landscapes, was discussed above as an example of the modification of seasonal rhythms. A further development, the transformation of a natural or managed landscape contaning a cultivated patch into an entire cultivated landscape, is so important that we will now explore a specific example.

In flat temperate areas of Europe, agriculture developed and deciduous forest was removed. By late in the Iron Age a so-called **open-field** landscape (Figure 8.11) had formed along with a social system that directly controlled land use practices (Orwin and Orwin, 1967; Hoskins, 1955; Pollard et al., 1974; Rackham, 1975, 1980; Sivery, 1977). Extensive plains were often totally cultivated and typically underwent a system of three-field rotation. While one field was in winter wheat, one would be in summer grain, and one in fallow—that is, abandoned to natural vegetation, soil refertilization, and often a few livestock. The land around a

luy qui veult vaurier aler aures

**Figure 8.11** *A wild boar hunt in a Middle Ages landscape in France. The pasture on the right, with tree branches cut perhaps for firewood, contrasts with the dense forest. Fourteenth-century manuscript, the* Livre de la Chasse *by Gaston Phoebus, Comte de Foix. (Courtesy of Giraudon and the Musée Conde in Chantilly.)*

**292** LANDSCAPE DYNAMICS

village was divided into three relatively large homogeneous sections that were rotated nearly every year, say, clockwise. A new section could be in fallow to prevent soil depletion, while in the other (unfenced) sections all the farmers had to work together to produce the same crop, and then cattle and sheep were permitted to graze those sections.

Initially, the property and its exploitation were often communal, even after deforestation. The division of revenues was determined by the number of workers in each family and their beasts of burden. Later, parcels were generally distributed to the individuals who cultivated them, but collective rotation was still observed, so that livestock could roam widely over the communal fallow section of land.

Seen from above, the plain was characterized by a series of pie-shaped fields radiating from each hamlet or village. Each field in a section was harvested at the same time by all the cultivators. This open-field system developed about 1250 to 1400 A.D. at the end of the great deforestation period in northern France (Sivery, 1977). When the population became moderately dense (about 10 to 20 homes per square kilometer), as for example in the area of Thiérache near Belgium, several villages sometimes formed the center of the radiating fields. This rotating open-field system was less strict where forest land or wet valleys, usually on poor soils, remained unplowed and prevented formation of the symmetrical pie-shaped sections.

The next phase took place when a network of hedgerows was constructed to form **enclosures** for pastures or cultivation. The establishment of enclosed fields that began to develop around the end of the fourteenth century was linked to an increase in livestock. In some places, the enclosure process spread outward with various regroupings of parcels. The grazing of livestock was widespread and even high elevation parcels were carved out of the forest for enclosures.

At the beginning of the sixteenth century, the spread of the field enclosures was accompanied, progressively, by the cultivation of crops such as peas, beans, clover, mustard, and carrots. The rural agricultural system functioned in this manner in all middle European countries up to the nineteenth century. Extensive hedgerow removal then occurred in many of the open plain areas. Although traces of the former enclosure landscapes remain, today's plains have much larger fields and fewer hedgerows, as a consequence of the mechanization of farming.

Agricultural systems can be quite stable in human hands. Certain Chinese plains have remained productive and in similar form for 5,000 years (Needham, 1954), as have plains in Europe and the Ukraine. Agricultural systems on plains, however, remain particularly subject to the hazards of geopolitics. There are numerous examples of "bread baskets" or "granaries" that have been ravaged or altered to become deserts. Two typical cases are Numidia (North Africa), which was flourishing at the end of the Roman period (Gautier, 1952; G'sell, 1913; Murphey, 1951), and the area of present-day Israel, where several million people once lived, before the population dropped to a few hundred thousand in the nineteenth century.

**The Development of Villages.**   A **village** is a cluster of homes in a rural area, somewhat larger than a hamlet, that includes at least one common building or a market place. The location of a village usually has to do with the presence of particular necessities such as access to well water, in regions where the water table is deep, or defense against ravaging during insecure periods (Figure 8.12).

By the late Paleolithic, about 6000 B.C., a village was already installed at the "Iron Gates" site by the Danube River in Yugoslavia. In the Middle East, many traces of villages have been discovered that date to the second half of the fifth millennium B.C. (e.g., Tell Massuna in Mesopotamia, Saktchegozou in Syria, and Sialk in northwestern Iran). Egyptian sites apparently were still hamlets in the fourth millennium B.C.

Villages, of course, do not represent a landscape by themselves but rather represent a new type of landscape element. A village may be linear in shape (Figure 8.12), as is Marschufendorf today in Germany, for example, and the many settlements called "rangs" that line country roads in Quebec. However, most villages are somewhat circular as a result of a physical or social constraint, such as a fortified site or the hub of an open-field agricultural area. Villages may also be a loose cluster of hamlets, often connected by a hedgerow network.

Whatever shape they have, villages cause an increase in the number of patches present in a landscape, leading in turn to a significant increase in corridors and networks. The connectivity of the matrix is therefore low.

This type of rural landscape with a village structure can be very stable and persist over several centuries or even millennia, as has been the case in Numidia and Switzerland, for example. Still, ecological catastrophes such as floods, salinization of irrigated land (Jacobsen and Adams, 1958), and loss of fertility, as well as economic or military setbacks, can cause a long-term loss of the village structure from a landscape.

Finally, it is recognized that a large number of widespread or "cosmopolitan" species "follow" human aggregations around the world. These include such common animals as the Norway rat (*Rattus norvegicus*), the house mouse (*Mus musculus*), and the housefly (*Musca domestica*), and such plants as chickweed (*Stellaria media*), nettle (*Urtica dioica*), shepherd's purse (*Capsella bursa-pastoris*), lamb's quarters (*Chenopodium album*), knotweed (*Polygonum aviculare*), plantain (*Plantago major*), and dandelion (*Taraxacum officinale*). Several of such species are particularly abundant in villages and may be called *village species*. That is, they

**Figure 8.12** *Linear village developed in a gorge for a religious community dating to the tenth century A.D. St. Guilhem le Desert, Languedoc, southern France. A significant part of the cloister from the ancient church is in the Cloisters Museum in New York City. (Courtesy of M. Fournier.)*

survive well neither in pastures and fields nor in cities. Village species provide ecological repeatability to the village landscape elements scattered across a rural landscape.

A modification or extension of the village role in the landscape can be seen today in some landscapes in socialist and other countries where **collectives** have been built in the rural landscape. These are communally run aggregations of people, buildings, and land that are commonly larger than a farm and smaller than a village. The collectives are often roughly the same size and usually are highly specialized around a single industry or type of agricultural crop. The density of collectives though, is typically higher than the density of former villages. The result is an intense and relatively evenly distributed human influence across the landscape; large distinct patches often surround each collective.

**Characteristics of Cultivated Landscapes.**  Agricultural development of a landscape usually progresses through three stages.

1. *Traditional agriculture:* a somewhat heterogeneous fine-grained matrix with scattered, irregularly-shaped field patches—that have just been cultivated—next to grazed fallow patches.
2. *Combined traditional and modern agriculture:* similar except with wide, persistent, homogeneous patches on the best soils.
3. *Modern agriculture with remnants of traditional agriculture:* a matrix of large persistent homogeneous parcels with scattered patches of traditional agriculture and remnant natural patches.

The most general characteristic of the cultivated landscape is that **geometrization**—the formation of linear and polygonal features—has been imposed on it, and straight lines are visible throughout (Hoskins, 1955; Meynier, 1970; Auclair, 1976; Meinig, 1979a). On flat plains, we see roads, field margins, furrows, and irrigation ditches extending in straight lines to the horizon. When there is more topographic relief, the sharp geometric patterns are combined with curves of hills and natural drainage patterns (Figure 8.9).

Stream corridors are often destroyed, and fewer remain (Figure 8.13), while line corridors that connect villages or are used in cultivation and harvest are widespread (Figure 8.8). Corridor networks are usually conspicuous and predominant, and so matrix connectivity is low. If a single crop is prevalent, the matrix covers a large portion of the landscape area. More often a few major crops are intermingled and widespread. In this case the matrix area is minimal, and it may be difficult (as in trying to decide how many red spots a white cow must have to become a red cow) to determine which type is the matrix.

Compared with managed landscapes, in cultivated landscapes patch density increases, while variability in patch size decreases (Figure 8.7). A marked shift in the causes of the patches emerges. Fewer disturbance patches and more introduced cultivated patches are evident, and more remnant patches appear as the natural and managed vegetation is cut into increasingly fine residual parcels.

Net production is maximal, as is yield. This production is widespread over the cultivated landscape, and intervals between harvests are highly

**Figure 8.13** *Intensive cultivation that nearly eliminates a stream corridor. The result is high levels of nutrient loss, stream bank erosion, flooding, stream sedimentation, water temperature, and fish disappearance. A windbreak against soil blowing is also lost in those corn (Zea) fields near Humboldt, Illinois (United States). (Courtesy of USDA Soil Conservation Service.)*

regular. Mineral nutrient inputs in the form of fertilizer are typically high, permitting the very high net production. Outputs of nutrients and eroded particulate matter are also high (Figure 8.13). The muddy streams and rivers with thick sediment loads on their bottoms and actively spreading deltas at their mouths attest to these outputs. Nutrients are also transported by wind in bulk quantities, in the form of dust storms or windblown, frozen soil particles, to other portions of these landscapes or to adjoining landscapes.

Species diversity drops considerably in the cultivated landscape, as a few crop species rule, and others in fields are removed mechanically or by pesticides. Scattered remnant natural ecosystems are species-poor as a result of repeated disturbances of many kinds and because of their isolation, which inhibits recolonization of species following local extinctions.

## Suburban Landscapes

Suburbs are the most heterogeneous and least ecologically understood landscapes. Since they develop around and are linked to cities, we must begin by considering urbanization.

**A Historical Overview of Cities.**   The oldest town site known today is Jericho, founded in the late Paleolithic around 6000 B.C., in the Middle East. The houses were circular and had walls of mud or bricks that were sometimes painted. The city was encircled by rock walls and round towers, from which a ford of the Jordan River could be watched. Burial masks in plaster or clay and rather simple ceramic vessels provide evidence of the life of the inhabitants. Çatal Huyuk of the same period (in Turkey) covered 13 hectares and has also left remarkable remains.

Urban landscapes have always been highly varied, undoubtedly because cities assume several major functions. The first city-states of the Sumerian civilization were also holy cities. The oldest known sanctuary (about 3700 B.C.?) was found at Eridou near the gulf between Iran and Saudi Arabia.

The landscapes of Mesopotamia (now primarily Iraq) were dominated by rounded pyramids with exterior staircases (ziggurats). Those of the Sumerian civilization had four-sided pyramids with five levels. At Our (Ur), which dates to the third millennium B.C. (during the Bronze Age), trees and shrubs formed an island of protective shade—or a sacred wood—on the highest level of the pyramid. Much later (eighth century B.C.) at the same site (then called Assour), Sennacherib, one of the earliest known landscape architects or botanists, planted a large park. He brought together local species, as well as those from territories to the north, the east, and the Mediterranean shores, to form a sort of botanical garden.

The combination of architecture and plants reached its zenith in the suspended gardens of Babylon (Figure 8.14) (Duval, 1980). These gardens, 120 m on a side, had the form of an amphitheater and were bounded by exterior colonnades 25 m high. Trees 4 m in circumference and 60 m high were reported to grow there. The gardens were almost certainly constructed by Nebuchadnezzar II (604 to 561 B.C.) and were to have been dedicated to Amouhid, daughter of King Midas, who languished for the green forests of her childhood. Three wells were found in the center of the suspended gardens during excavations. The water was originally brought up to the summit by an endless chain of buckets.

Egypt is no longer considered the sole progenitor of urban civilizations but it played a key role in the development of the city form. Around the beginning of the third millennium B.C., the peoples of Upper Egypt near the Nile and Lower Egypt accepted a common sovereign, Menes, who initiated an architecture of a gradiose scale. The terraced 60 m pyramid

Seven wonders
of the
Ancient world

1. Egyptian pyramids at Giza

2. Hanging gardens of Babylon

3. Statue of Zeus at Olympia

4. Colossus of Rhodes

5. Temple of Artemis at Ephesus

6. Mausoleum at Halicarnassus

7. Lighthouse at Alexandria

**Figure 8.14** *The seven wonders of the ancient world. All were associated with cities, and most were sacred monuments.*[1]

[1]Reprinted with permission of the *Encyclopedia Americana*, copyright 1982, Grolier, Inc.

(a)

(b)

(c)

**Figure 8.15** *Sacred, government, and financial monuments. (a) Temples and carved alter stones, or stelae, (below) in the former Mayan city of Tikal in the Guatemalan rain forest. (R. Forman.) (b) The Kremlin (in Moscow), the central government building of the Soviet Union. (Courtesy of W. C. Johnson.) (c) The Sears Tower in Chicago, the tallest building in the world. (R. Forman.)*

of Djeser dates from just before 2600 B.C. The great pyramids (Figure 8.14) and the Sphynx (built during the fourth dynasty, 2600–2480 B.C.) attained a maximum height of 146 m—as high as the much later Cathedral of St. Peter in Rome.

These brief examples of landscape development in Mesopotamia and Egypt illustrate the process of **sequent occupance.** This term refers to the landscape changes produced when a sequence of different cultures occupies the same area. The sequence is commonly a series of stages where predominantly natural conditions, often characterized by low productivity, alternate over time with landscapes that bear a heavy human imprint.

Similar trends doubtless took place in other parts of the world (e.g., the early Chinese town Liang Chengzhen, dating to about 3500 B.C.). Astronomy (or geomancy) may also have played a role in the design of some cities. From this history, we see that cities quickly produced monuments of large size which had a unique social significance. That is, the city constituted a novel and special landscape feature. The Greek name for town—polis—expresses the idea that there *politics,* the process of governing, came into being (Plato, 428-348 B.C. *The Republic*). The politically powerful almost inevitably made their role sacred and erected monumental buildings that reflected a new holy or religious mentality.

The large cathedrals of Europe, the Mayan temples (Figure 8.15*a*), the forbidden city of Peking, and the sacred steps of Benares along the River Ganges in India all are *sacred monuments.* In modern times, political power is manifested directly in the buildings that symbolize government—*government monuments* such as the Kremlin (Figure 8.15*b*), Versailles, the Hofburg Imperial Palace, and the Capitol in Washington. Construction now is focused more on "temples to a new god, money"— that is, *financial monuments,* including skyscrapers like the World Trade Center in New York, the Sears Tower in Chicago (Figure 8.15*c*), and commercial buildings in Tokyo and Sao Paulo.

**Characteristics of Suburbia.**  With a historical perspective in mind, we now return to our limousine and move from the cultivated to the suburban landscape (Figure 8.16). Line corridors and networks continue to increase, while stream corridors decrease (Figure 8.8). Matrix area and connectivity are minimal. Patchiness is nearly at its maximum in the suburban landscape (Figure 8.7). The richness of types of landscape elements is very great, and almost all the patches are either introduced or remnants.

Average net productivity for the landscape is always patchy and often low. In the face of increasing human population pressure, cultivated fields and managed remnant patches may soon be gobbled up for other land uses (Figure 8.16). The suburban landscape has a special kind of dynamics since it continues to creep outward from cities, maintaining a consistent form. Mineral nutrient cycling in suburban landscapes is essentially unstudied and difficult to characterize because of the extreme heterogeneity of the landscape.

Species diversity is high, perhaps usually greater than that of the natural landscape. Despite the depauperate nature of the remnant patches, many species characteristic of natural and cultivated landscapes are present overall. The plants and animals from nurseries, florists, and pet stores that are associated with human aggregations are also a large source of species richness. Only some of these species can successfully colonize the more natural portions of the suburban landscape, but those that do

**Figure 8.16** *New housing developments and woodland corridors in a suburban landscape. Undeveloped areas in suburbia are usually under enormous competing land-use pressures, including shopping, industrial, housing, waste disposal, and nature reserve interests. Montgomery County, Maryland (United States). (Courtesy of USDA Soil Conservation Service.)*

often become significant pests. In the built-up portions of the landscape a large biota of nonnative species is present, including pests, parasites, and weeds.

## Urban Landscapes

Cities are a type of organization totally different from the late Paleolithic encampments and hamlets. The development of hamlet into city has analogies with the formation of the first organisms from accumulations of organic substances floating in the warm tidal broth of ancient lagoons. In both cases, a relatively unorganized homogeneous ensemble transforms itself into an organized structure that cycles objects, information, and energy within itself (Wilson et al., 1973; Havlick, 1974; Dorney and McLellan, 1984).

**Specialization.** A **city** has a large human population and functions by having a series of specialized objects flow through a network. Indeed a primary difference between a city and a group of huts is that in a city people have specialized or diversified roles. Let us consider some examples. In villages of Eskimos in the Arctic, Indians of the Matto Grasso in Brazil, and Aborigines of central Australia, each family produces its own needs such as food, clothing, house, tools, ornaments, traps, arms, and the like. In contrast, where bronze or iron making has developed, it is a specialized activity reserved for persons with special wisdom, technical knowledge, and (often) magical power. The blacksmith's products are exchanged for food, and such a person can only live in a group sufficiently large to provide a market for the metal products. Other specialized artisan activities operate in the same fashion, and a town is born when all these exchanges produce a relatively stable system. The city-states of Mesopotamia developed in this manner in the late Paleolithic, as early as the fifth millennium B.C.

**Writing.** The above vision of the birth of cities is reinforced by a remarkable concurrent event. Writing was born when cities appeared. The origins of these two revolutionary developments were not unrelated. Traces of the first of many writings have been found at Ourouk in Sumeria along the Euphrates River. These texts of commercial dealings and inventories are preceded only by trading chips or stones from the late Paleolithic (Lafforgue, 1969; Kramer, 1957). (A linkage between inscriptions on trading chips and commercial lists has left traces in our scientific civilization: small monetary stones called calculi were used as counters by the Romans.)

Several other important innovations originated at about the same time as cities. The potter's wheel and the beginning of copper metallurgy (heralding the Age of Copper, and then Bronze) in this region also date from the fourth millennium B.C. Scholarly classes arose along with the erection of sanctuaries and the origin of holy cities in this epoch. In this manner Mexico City was organized around the temples of the Sun and the Moon, and remained so as late as 1525 when the Spanish soldiers arrived.

**Urban Structure and Function.** The city might remind us of the biological cell, which has specialized structures and a transmissible memory written in its nucleus. But the city is really more analogous to a many-celled heterotrophic organism. That is, it is akin to a system that cannot use the sun to obtain energy but must get it from the surrounding environment. Organisms with constraints most analogous to those of a city are perhaps sponges, which must get their food energy from other organisms in the water. Sponges have a tough but universal problem: they must circulate the food brought in, using the energy available from that food. Similarly, the city has a network of circulatory structures wherein the exchanges, or "metabolism," occur (Figure 8.17). The circulation routes or streets, which were paved even in Babylon (Duval, 1980), carry nourishments such as water, electricity, coal, and wood to the cells, in this case homes. The circulation routes also serve as channels for wastes, where sewers carry liquids, and waste disposal vehicles carry solids.

The urban structures that result from this functioning seem to some designers analogous to biological structures. The architect Saarinen (1965) suggests that the physical order of urban communities compares fundamentally to the organic order of organisms. He uses a cross section of mammalian tissue as a model to discuss the optimization of circulation

**Figure 8.17** *Circulatory network underpinning the urban block or patch structure. Each block is unique and depends on the inputs from, and outputs to, the particular circulatory configuration surrounding it. The city is St. Louis, Missouri (United States) seen from the Arch. (R. Forman.)*

in a city (Figure 8.17). In a similar comparison, Doxiadis (1968) hypothesizes that all human settlements are composed of four indispensable elements—nature, man, society, buildings—and of networks.

Urban landscapes are largely composed of two general types of landscape elements, streets and city blocks, with a scattering of parks and other uncommon landscape features (Stearns and Montag, 1974; Dorney and McLellan, 1984). *Districts,* distinctive groupings of these landscape elements, are usually evident and not uniformly distributed, as illustrated in the following three models of urban spatial structure (De Blij, 1977; Miller, 1981). In the *concentric zone* model, the sequence of districts surrounding a central business district is similar in all directions (Figure 8.18a). In the wedge-shaped *sector* model, a particular type of district, often extends from the central business district to the city limit, so different sides of the city have different districts (Figure 8.18b). In the *multiple nuclei* model, an asymmetric patchwork of districts surrounds the central business district (Figure 8.18c). Such differing spatial patterns result partially from the underlying geomorphic configuration. However, they are primarily the result of cultural characteristics and of the political system. Hence, the present pattern reflects any previous imprint or plan ranging from, for example, the routes chosen by cows (some claim) before Boston arose, to the highly planned city of Brasilia.

**Ecology of the Modern City.**   Relatively few animal and plant species thrive and reproduce in the modern city (Bornkamm et al., 1982; Spirn, 1984). The biological system is totally polarized around the needs of the human species. While unplanned assemblages of species always exist in the city, artificial communities of plants and animals are constructed as a depauperate symbol or reminder of nature. These depauperate species assemblages are important symbols of nature to people, partially fulfilling their *biophilia* need, that is, their affinity and need for plants and animals (Wilson, 1984). A compelling example is the effect of a view of nature from a hospital room in speeding up a patient's recovery rate (Ulrich, 1984).

The accumulation of household wastes in dumps is one of the consequences of urbanization that directly affects landscapes, especially the suburban landscape. In an industrial country (France) with 55 million inhabitants, about one cubic meter of household waste products per person on the average is added each year to the dumps. This production of volume is equivalent to the building of a dual highway 600 km long each year (Langlois, 1973). In the suburbs or shantytowns of the great cities of the developing nations waste accumulation, often forming distinct landscape elements (Figure 8.19), is becoming striking in the landscape.

Today 16 cities of the world have more than five million inhabitants.

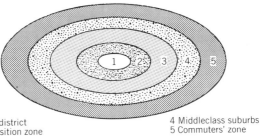

1 Central business district
2 Deteriorating transition zone
3 Workers' homes

4 Middleclass suburbs
5 Commuters' zone

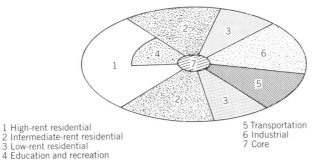

1 High-rent residential
2 Intermediate-rent residential
3 Low-rent residential
4 Education and recreation

5 Transportation
6 Industrial
7 Core

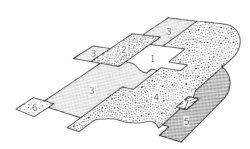

1 Central business district
2 Wholesale, light manufacturing
3 Low-rent residential
4 Medium-class residential
5 High-class residential
6 Heavy manufacturing
7 Outlying business district

**Figure 8.18** *Three patterns of urban spatial structure. (a) The concentric zone model. (b) The sector model. (c) The multiple nuclei model. Additional models exist for different cities of the world. From Living in the Environment by George T. Miller, ©1979 by Wadsworth, Inc., Belmont, California. Reprint by permission of the publisher. After De Blij, 1977.*

**Figure 8.19** *A waste disposal landscape element. Old vehicles rust and decompose slowly in this dry climate. Blaine County, Idaho (United States). (Courtesy of USDA Soil Conservation Service.)*

By the year 2000, UNESCO estimates that three billion people will have squeezed in around urban zones. Most of these inhabitants will be in 60 cities of more than five million people, 47 of which will be in the developing nations. Thus, urban landscapes are rapidly increasing in number, and unique circulation and structural patterns are emerging for each.

We now conclude our journey by limousine with brief observations. An extensive corridor network of streets perforates the urban landscape, producing a tremendous density of tiny equal-sized introduced patches (Figure 8.17). All other patch and corridor types are at a minimum (Figures 8.7 and 8.8). Those that remain, such as the occasional stream corridor, urban woodlot, golf course, or cemetery are conspicuous and of exceptional importance to the biota.

Average net productivity for the landscape is negative, as the entire ecosystem is fundamentally based on massive imports of plant and animal food. Inputs include sunlight, water, fuel, food, manufactured goods, and atmospheric deposits usually containing high pollutant levels. Outputs include sewage, solid wastes, water, heat, and various pollutants. Species diversity of most animal and plant groups is low, although in spots it may be relatively high where nonnative species are abundant (Stearns and Montag, 1974; Schmid, 1975; Balser et al., 1981; Spirn, 1984).

In a sense, the city is two ecological systems, spatially superimposed but with generally minor linkages. The primary productivity of the city grass, trees, and other plants supports a rather simplified trophic structure that involves a few herbivores or carnivores such as squirrels and birds. The other system, centered around humans, involves food and water inputs, waste and sewage outputs, carnivores such as fleas and bedbugs, and decomposers such as bacteria and gulls (*Larus*). A small subsystem centered on pets like monkeys, cats, and canaries is tied into the human ecological system.

## The Megalopolis

Where does the process of increasing human concentration lead? The magnitude of inputs and outputs and of services within a city cannot increase indefinitely without creating problems. Severe drought spells, disruptions in the availability of oil, coal, and electricity, air pollution build-ups, military attacks, and strikes of truckers, railroaders, waste disposal workers, and sewage treatment personnel disrupt the urban ecological system effectively, rapidly, and critically. The political system responds to disruption in varying degrees of rapidity and effectiveness. Basically, the larger the magnitudes of inputs and outputs relative to production or storage within a system, the less stable the system.

An alternative to indefinite urbanization, where a city continues to spread in all directions, is **megalopolization,** the process of forming a number of cities surrounded by suburbia. This process is evident in the Boston-New York-Philadelphia-Baltimore-Washington area, the Rotterdam-Amsterdam-The Hague area, and the Tokyo-Osaka area. The end product of this process is an enormous suburban landscape, on an order of magnitude larger than before, within which cities are scattered. The smaller city centers are simply a distinctive type of landscape element within suburbia. The large cities, as nuclei giving rise to megalopolization, are urban landscapes in their own right and are surrounded by the gigantic suburban landscape.

The two types of landscapes within the megalopolis are tightly bound together. Flows of commuters, information, and pollutants between the landscapes are extensive, for example. Thus, the megalopolis—the tying together of two unlike landscapes that serve different major functions— appears to be a distinctive point along the gradient of concentrating and specializing human processes that began with scattered homes and hamlets.

The megalopolis is anything but the pinnacle of stability. With its enormous inputs and outputs, the megalopolis is more dependent than ever on other landscapes. Massive amounts of fossil fuel sustain the megalopolis. In its unique political system many governmental bodies, most of which are in competition, make decisions. Hence, responses to or recovery from disruption are slower, patchier, and less effective. One worries about the risk of a degeneration that resembles a cancerous ganglion. The ultimate point in the aggregation process has been termed an "ecumenopolis" or "planetopolis," or world city (Rodoman, 1970; Havlick, 1974). These ideas seem to be academic exercises in planning without the constraints of universal ecological principles.

## SUMMARY

Human influences (except where extremely heavy) increase landscape heterogeneity in three primary ways. First, rhythms of natural disturbances, ranging from one day to a few centuries long, are modified through agricultural and forestry practices. Second, the methods of landscape modification—for example, extracting renewable resources, developing agriculture, and constructing buildings and communication routes—have increased in number and effectiveness. Such methods range from early hunting and use of fire to modern machinery and chemical inputs.

Third, the aggregation process, from hamlets to cities, is related to the centralization of necessities, the diversification or specialization of human roles, the construction of sacred and other monuments, and the development of politics. In the cultivated landscape, two prominent features are geometrization and the abundance of villages that develop where special resources exist. Villages contain characteristic species and serve as nuclei for effects on the landscape. The megalopolis is composed of two linked landscapes, the urban and the suburban, with huge inputs, outputs, and internal cycling. It is subject to many disturbances and has a relatively ineffective political system to respond to the disturbances.

When each of the structural characteristics of landscapes is separately examined along a human modification gradient from natural to urban, patterns emerge. Introduced patches increase, whereas disturbance and environmental resource patches decrease. Patch density and regularity in shape increase, whereas patch size and variability decrease. Line corridors and networks increase, and stream corridors decrease. The changes in the landscapes are therefore a product of both human influences and natural processes.

# QUESTIONS

1. How is it that a particular environmental change is a disturbance in one landscape but not in another? To back up your answer, cite and explain examples of two quite different types of natural environmental changes.
2. When were the various human cultural and technological phases? How did humans affect landscapes during each phase?
3. Does altering the periodicity of natural rhythms produce minor or major effects on a landscape? Why? Is it possible for a particular type of human influence to alter natural rhythms of different lengths? Explain.
4. Describe, in the order of their introduction, the major types of agricultural methods that have changed landscapes over time.
5. How do patch origins change along a landscape modification gradient? How about average patch sizes and shapes?
6. How do corridor types change along a landscape modification gradient? How would a geographer describe the patterns of geometrization along the gradient?
7. How does net production change along a landscape modification gradient? How do mineral nutrient outputs change?
8. What characteristics differentiate a hamlet, a village, a city, and a megalopolis?
9. What changes in species diversity and composition take place in proceeding from a natural to a managed landscape? In what order? What major recommendations can you make for biological conservation in this process?
10. What are the ecological advantages and disadvantages for a landscape in the open-field system? Why was it usually replaced by an enclosure landscape?
11. What were the major steps in the historical development of cities? Cite examples.
12. Explain how urban structure and flows would be important to an urban forester; to an urban wildlife manager.

# 9
# *Flows Between Adjacent Landscape Elements*

*Who has seen the wind?*
*Neither you nor I.*
*But when the trees bow down their heads,*
*The wind is passing by.*
### Christina Rosetti, 1872
*Sing-Song*

Once there was a hunter who spent his days tracking the wide prairies of North Dakota with his gun and dog and sometimes with a small boy who would beg to trot along.

"Smart little . . . gophers," the hunter observed, "I mean the way they have things figured out. Whenever you come upon a gopher village you can be sure it will be near a patch of grain where they can get their food, and close by a creek or slough for water. They'll not build their towns near willow clumps or alders for there's where the owls or hawks will be roosting. And you'll not be finding them near a pile of rocks or stony ledges where their enemies the snakes will be hiding ready to snatch them. When these wise little fellows build their towns, they search out the southeast slope or knoll that will catch the full sweep of the sun each day to keep their dens warm and cozy. The winter blizzards that pound out of the north and west and leave the windward slopes of the rises frozen solid will only drift loose powder snow on top of their homes."

"When gophers plan their homes and towns," the boy philosophized, "they seem to do it better than men do."

"Yes," mused the hunter, "and so do most of the animals I know. Sometimes I wonder why." (Simonds, 1983).

Why are the gophers (Figure 9.1) so successful in choosing their village location? They evaluated characteristics of the immediate site such as the southeastern slope for the sun's heat or the presence of grass sod and porous soil. The surroundings, however, were more important. Grain must be nearby for food, and a creek for water. Distance from the flying predators in willow or alder clumps and from the snakes in rocky areas is critical. And there must be protection from winter winds.

This basic importance of evaluating the surroundings first and the immediate site second was implicitly understood by the hunter and the

**Figure 9.1** *A prairie dog (Cynomys) by its burrow entrance. A colony of these animals (also sometimes called "gophers") digs a burrow system resembling an urban subway network but in three dimensions. Washington, D.C. Zoo. (Courtesy of USDA Soil Conservation Service.)*

boy. It is well understood by industry, in selecting a site for a factory or office building, and it is emerging as a critical issue in landscape planning and management. It may also be central to site selection by animals (Arnold, 1983) and to our understanding of natural communities. This idea is a major applied take-home message from the concepts in this chapter.

Before proceeding, we should mention two general ideas relevant to flows between landscape elements. We may hypothesize that the edge portion of a landscape element functions as does a semipermeable membrane, filtering the flows in and out of the element (J. Wiens, C. Crawford, J. Gosz, C. Schonewald-Cox and J. Bayless, personal communications). Although the edge effect refers to the structural characteristics of the edge, particularly the organisms (Chapter 3), this *boundary function* or effect refers to how the edge affects flows. These may be flows across the edge, such as drifting snow or sand being intercepted by the dense vegetation of a woods border, or flows along the edge, such as herbivores and predators using the edge as a conduit. Such a boundary function is likely to be quite significant and needs study.

Second, where adjacent landscape elements differ in their degree of maturity, the younger stage may function as a *source* that gives off things (say, nutrients), and the older stage may function as a *sink* that absorbs things (Margalef, 1963; Van Leeuwen, 1966, 1982). In contrast, in the case of many other objects (e.g., some seeds and animals), the mature stage may be the source, whereas the younger stage is the sink.

For convenience, we recognize airborne, overland, and soil flows. These are three major categories of flows that must be evaluated in all landscape planning and management considerations.

## MECHANISMS UNDERLYING LINKAGES

### Vectors

Energy, nutrients, and most species move from one landscape element to another in a landscape (Miller, 1978a; Van Leeuwen, 1982). None is static. These movements or flows depend on five major **vectors,** or transport mechanisms: wind, water, flying animals, ground animals, and people. Examples of each are discussed below. Several other mechanisms—such as seeds spreading by the explosion of fruits, soil creeping down slopes, and alternating freezing and thawing cycles that move material down slopes—may be important in local areas for transporting objects between landscape elements.

*Wind* carries a range of items, including heat energy, water, dust, aerosols, pollutants, snow, sound, seeds, spores, and many small insects and spiders. *Water,* on the ground surface or underground, carries mineral nutrients, seeds, insects, sewage, fertilizers, and toxic substances. *Flying animals* such as birds, bats, and bees carry various seeds, spores, and insects in their feathers or feet, and also carry seeds in the gut. Similarly, *ground animals*—including many mammals and reptiles—carry species either externally as when small fruits catch in fur, or internally as when seeds pass through the gut and are dropped in feces. Finally, *people* carry a wide range of species—not only attached to their pants or in the gut but also in containers or vehicles of many sorts.

### Forces

To understand where energy, nutrients, and species move, that is, how far and in what direction, we must consider the forces behind the vectors. We do not need to start with Einstein's $e = mc^2$ but rather with a recognition that to move anything requires energy. This energy is stored as potential usable energy and is given off as heat in the moving process, as when we eat a huge meal and "run off" the energy, or when a log burns to ashes. At the landscape level, three forces drive the vectors that underlie movements. Two of the forces, **diffusion** and **mass flow,** depend on temperature differences, and in these cases the energy contained within the things transported is not affected. In the case of the third force, **locomotion,** the animal or person of course expends energy to move but may also carry objects passively from place to place. These three forces will be presented in order of decreasing generality or universality.

**Diffusion,** in the narrow scientific sense, is the movement of dissolved or suspended materials from a region of high concentration to one of lower concentration. The materials move in random directions by means of their own individual agitation. For example, if a perfume bottle spills on one side of a classroom, heads will gradually begin to turn as the luscious scent slowly moves across the room—floral molecules are diffusing from a concentrated area to an area where they are sparse. Diffusion takes place almost everywhere in the universe, though rates vary enormously. Diffusion, since it is absent in a homogeneous system, appears hand in hand with heterogeneity and is particularly appropriate to consider in the context of the heterogeneous landscape.

**Mass flow** (or transport or transfer) is the movement of matter along an energy gradient. Wind, an example of mass flow, is caused by pressure differences in the atmosphere, and air molecules move from high to low pressure areas. If a gust of wind blows the perfume molecules across the room they have moved by mass flow, and everyone's interest will have been stimulated at the same time. Mass flow is also widespread, though it depends on the presence of gradients of (potential and kinetic) energy that of course are patchily distributed through space.

**Locomotion** is the movement of an object from one place to another by its expenditure of energy (Figure 9.2). Animals and people are obvious examples, but we use the term in the broad sense to include vehicles driven by fossil fuel such as cars, boats, and aircraft. Hence, locomotion depends on the presence of mobile animals, which are widespread, but not everywhere, on our planet.

**Diffusion.** This term technically refers only to the movement of molecules, but we commonly broaden the concept and develop a variety of diffusion models that assume random movement of objects in a landscape (Chapter 11). The problem, however, is that random movements appear to be the exception rather than the rule. Random spatial patterns are equally difficult to find in the ecological world. What ecological distributions have you seen that are random? One might expect that the distribution of seeds or tiny weed seedlings in a recently bare field is random.

**Figure 9.2** *Mule deer (*Odocoileus hemionus*) crossing a clearing and fence in western United States. Locomotion involves expenditure of energy by the objects moving, and results in a change in the degree of aggregation of the objects. (Photographer unknown; courtesy of Defenders of Wildlife.)*

Even here, though, the seeds are likely to have been dropped near certain perches or flight paths of birds or channeled by particular nonrandom wind patterns (Buell et al., 1971; Yarranton and Morrison, 1974). A short time after germination, the seedlings compete with one another, and some are eliminated, a process that also produces a nonrandom pattern.

Many proposed random patterns in nature, furthermore, really seem so because of our ignorance or lack of perception. We study something and find no pattern, no predictability, and so we erroneously conclude the phenomenon is random. In the case of the seedlings, for example, perhaps we did not recognize that the birds have certain highly preferred perches and flight paths. Had we designed our study specifically to test for avian flight paths, we would probably have found predictable concentrations of bird-dispersed seeds related to these flight paths.

Diffusion, a low energy process compared with mass flow and locomotion, may be important for movement of objects at an extremely fine level of scale. It does not appear to be an important force for transporting objects between landscape elements or across a landscape. In predicting spatial movements on the landscape, mass flow and locomotion are the major forces.

**Mass Flow.**  The flow of water on and under the ground is strongly affected by gravity. In heavy rains or snow melt, or with relatively impervious soil, a considerable amount of water flows gradually downward over the soil surface as **surface runoff.** Except in arid regions, water that percolates into the soil commonly flows laterally and downward to a nearby stream or other water body in the form of **subsurface flow.** This mass flow of water may carry many things with it. Dissolved substances such as mineral nutrients are always present, as are small organisms and propagules. **Erosion** commonly occurs along with surface runoff, that is, soil particles are removed from the soil and carried with the water (Figure 9.3).

The other important mass flow in landscape ecology is air movement or **wind,** which is caused by differences in atmospheric pressure that often have resulted from differential heating of the earth's surface by solar energy. As a transporting agent, wind may be divided into two categories. Lightweight objects such as spores, aerosols, and water molecules undergo long-distance dispersal at high altitudes. Surface winds blowing through terrestrial ecosystems pick up both lightweight and somewhat heavier items such as winged seeds, moths, and leaves and deposit them in a nearby landscape element. This process is called short-distance dispersal. Wind also carries heat energy, as anyone knows who, on a windy summer afternoon, has stood downwind of a large asphalt parking area or tried unsuccessfully to cool off in a cluster of desert shrubs.

**Locomotion.**  Flying animals illustrate well the difference between mass flow and locomotion. In still air, mosquitos, nighthawks, and bats locomote with their wings to find tasty food. The energy required for flying comes from the animal itself and is derived from organic compounds. However, if a strong wind is blowing, few of these creatures fly—they are at least partially carried by mass flow. A striking example is the excitement early in the morning following a hurricane, when hordes of bird watchers stream out of their houses looking for rare birds blown far out of their range by mass flow.

Locomotion is the force behind the transport of most items by flying

**Figure 9.3** *Movement of people by motorcycles and movement of soil particles by erosion in southwestern United States. The prominent paths are made by squadrons of motorcyclists who climb and descend, using fossil fuel energy. Both wind and water erosion are prevalent in this dry pinyon-juniper area (Pinus edulis, Juniperus supp.), and both are accelerated by the use of off-road vehicles. (Dick Smith; courtesy of Defenders of Wildlife.)*

animals, ground animals, and people (including vehicles) (Figures 9.2 and 9.3). The most important ecological characteristic of movement by locomotion is the highly aggregated nature of most deposits in the recipient landscape element. That is, piles of phosphorus and nitrogen accumulate in bird roosts. Fruit-eating mammals leave droppings full of seeds. Neolithic people gathered seeds of wheat and other wild plants for small agricultural plots. A lady plants an array of beautiful wildflowers in her garden in town. In all these cases, items that were dispersed across one landscape element have been moved to a small concentrated area within another landscape element. Other dispersal patterns result from locomotion. For example, rain forest monkeys feed on a single fig tree (*Ficus*) and disperse the seeds widely. Even in such cases, however, the patterns of collection and of deposition are nonrandom, basically because animals rarely move randomly. On the whole, diffusion produces the least aggregated patterns, mass flow is intermediate, and locomotion produces the most clustered patterns in landscapes.

A word should be added here about directionality. In almost all flows, some items are moving in one direction and others in the opposite direction. The direction of flow is that in which the greatest number of items move during an interval. The amount of flow is the net movement, (for example, across a boundary)—that is, the difference between the number of items moving in opposite directions. Hence, a flow of turtles or spiny succulents from one landscape element to another implies that there is a net movement in that direction but also that some individuals may be moving in the opposite direction.

## AIRFLOW AND LOCOMOTION

### Wind Patterns

Sailors are captains of the wind, and poets bring the wind alive. Landscape ecologists, recognizing the wind as a major vector, see wind patterns etched on the landscape.

Wind whistling along unimpeded has a **laminar airflow**; that is, layers or streams of air are flowing in a parallel fashion, one on top of another (Geiger, 1965; Moen, 1973, 1974; Yoshino, 1975; Grace, 1977; Rosenberg et al., 1983). The layer closest to a surface is the *boundary layer air.* **Turbulent airflow,** in contrast, has an irregular motion, usually with up and down currents (Figure 9.4).

If an object is introduced into free-flowing laminar airflow, either of the airflow types may result, depending upon the shape of the object relative to the direction of airflow. The boundary layer of air flowing past a **streamlined** object closely follows the surface of the object. Also evident are a speedup in the flow of boundary layer air, a minimum of turbulence at the downwind end of the object, and continued laminar airflow after the object is passed. In contrast, the accelerated boundary layer air flowing over a **bluff object**—that is, one with a broad somewhat flattened front—cannot follow the surface of the object and therefore separates. The pressure between the boundary air layer and the adjacent air layers increases, resulting in the separation of the airflow for some distance downwind and (usually) the appearance of turbulent air immediately downwind (Figure 9.4).

The importance of these airflow and object types in the landscape is considerable. A hill that has gradual slopes with laminar air flowing over them acts as a streamlined object, and laminar flow continues up and over the hill (Figure 9.5). A hill with either a steep downwind slope or a steep upwind slope, however, causes turbulent air on the downwind

**Figure 9.4** *Snow banks resulting from turbulent airflow behind a windbreak of pine. The dense windbreak acts as a bluff object. Erie County, New York. (Courtesy of USDA Soil Conservation Service.)*

slope. Note that the turbulent air—hence less predictable weather conditions—extends a longer distance downwind if the upwind slope is steep (Figure 9.5). At any rate, in all three cases the acceleration of the air in the boundary layer means an increased wind speed on the ridge top. This speed when measured is often about 20% higher than on the plain.

If such wind patterns apply to hills, we might ask whether similar patterns apply to windbreaks and patches of vegetation, and at even finer levels of scale. In the laboratory, tiny models of trees were constructed, and windbreaks composed of several rows of trees were simulated. The windbreaks were placed in (and at right angles to) a long, large cylinder. By varying the heights of trees within a windbreak, the investigator was able to compare the effectiveness of windbreaks of three shapes. For these, the top surface of the windbreak encountered by wind was:

1. A gradual slope (that is, the shortest trees were on the upwind side and the tallest trees on the downwind side).
2. An abrupt face (the tallest trees were upwind, grading down to the shortest trees downwind).
3. A rounded face (the tallest trees were near the center).

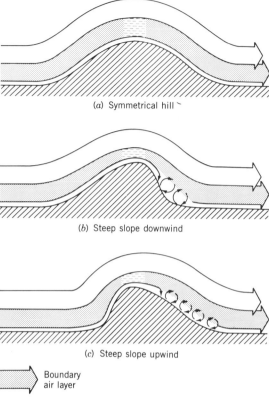

(a) Symmetrical hill

(b) Steep slope downwind

(c) Steep slope upwind

Boundary
air layer

**Figure 9.5** *Airflow over hills with different slopes. Hill (a) functions as a streamlined object, whereas hills (b) and (c) function as bluff objects, causing different patterns of turbulence. Dashes in the boundary air layer indicate maximum wind speed.*

A fan was turned on and airflow patterns were measured in this wind tunnel. Wind velocity was reduced by 50 to 75% at the same distance downwind of all three windbreak shapes. A small reduction in wind speed, however, extended further downwind of the rounded surface than the others (a distance of 30 times the windbreak height, versus 25 times). The highest wind velocity (110% of that away from windbreaks) was recorded downwind of both the gradual slope and the abrupt face. However, this wind speed was only well above the "ground" surface, as would be expected from the hilltop wind pattern (Figure 9.5). The rounded windbreak with the tallest trees near the center best maintained laminar airflow, or produced the least turbulence, and was considered to function best as a windbreak (Robinette, 1972, after N. P. Woodruff and A. W. Zingg).

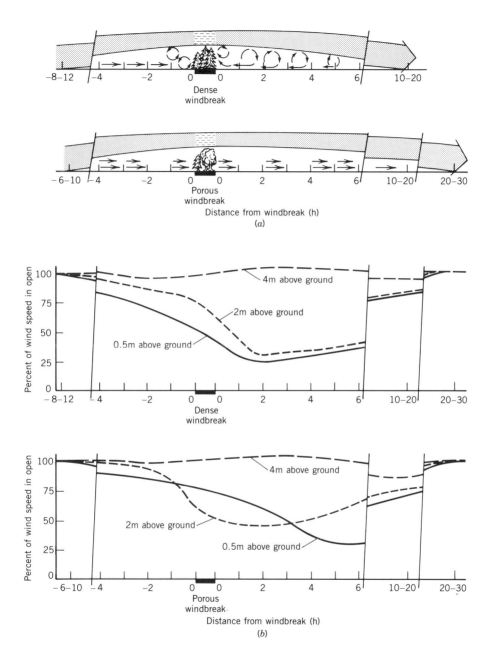

**Figure 9.6** *Wind patterns near dense versus porous windbreaks. (a) Boundary layer air (shaded) and turbulence. (b) Wind speed at three heights above the ground. Distance is the number on the horizontal axis times the height h of the windbreak. The highest wind speed in the boundary layer air is indicated with dashes. (After Caborn, 1957, Van Eimern et al., 1964, Robinette, 1972; Rosenberg et al., 1983, and other sources.)*

The penetrability of barriers also affects air movement downwind. A solid or *dense barrier* produces severe turbulence and weather conditions downwind (Figure 9.6a). A diffuse *porous barrier* that permits wind penetration prevents most turbulence. The effectiveness of a windbreak as a barrier to strong winds is greater, and extends for a greater distance, with the porous barrier than with the dense barrier. Although the windbreak effect of the dense barrier extends only a relatively short distance, the actual rate of wind speed is most reduced in this case. As a rough estimate, a porous windbreak causes a major wind reduction to a distance of perhaps five times the height of the windbreak, and some reduction downwind to about thirty times the windbreak height.

Wind reduction by a windbreak is typically effective only in the 2 m or so next to the ground (Figure 9.6 b). At 0.5 m above the ground, where many grassland and crop plants grow and animals feed, maximum wind reduction occurs some three times as far downwind of a porous windbreak as a dense windbreak (6 h versus 2 h). Nevertheless, the windspeed in both cases is the same, only about a quarter of that in the open.

A woods generally acts as a dense barrier, because (if leaves are on the trees) relatively little wind penetrates. Thus, turbulence is normally present just downwind of a woods. The degree of wind penetration of woods varies, of course, with seasonal changes in wind velocity and foliage density. In the case of an isolated tree without lower branches, in a savanna, say, the boundary layer air moves under the foliage at a higher rate of speed than it does in the open, and the heating and drying effects on animals under the tree or on lower tree branches may be increased.

Snow and soil are carried by wind, and the pattern of snow-drifts relative to windbreaks is instructive (Figure 9.4). Snow accumulates downwind of porous and dense windbreaks to about the same distance (Figure 9.7). Maximum accumulation is immediately adjacent to the porous barrier, whereas behind the dense barrier, peak accumulation is shifted downwind because of the turbulence adjacent to the barrier. The maximum snow depth is considerably greater behind the porous windbreak than the dense windbreak.

These snow patterns are interesting because wind carries many other things passively, and we may expect their accumulations to show similar deposition curves. For example, insects carried by the wind are deposited in peak numbers slightly downwind of a windbreak (Lewis, 1969a, 1969b; Brunel and Cancela da Fonseca, 1979). The peak is shifted if a second hedgerow is nearby that alters airflow patterns (Figure 9.8). Furthermore, insects dispersed over long distances and those originating in the upwind hedgerow show different deposition patterns.

Windbreaks often have gaps or breaks, such as in single rows of trees where a tree has died (Figure 9.8). On the basis of the principles of airflow

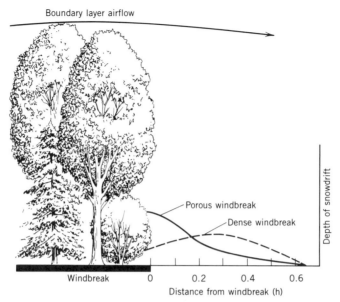

**Figure 9.7** *Snowdrift patterns downwind of windbreaks of different penetrability. Here* h *is the height of the windbreak (see Figure 9.6). (After Caborn, 1957, Van Eimern et al., 1964, Robinette, 1972, and other sources.)*

discussed, we would expect wind to whistle through such breaks. Indeed, measurements around gaps show an increase in wind speed just upwind of a break (the Venturi effect), but a decrease in wind speed just downwind of it. Downwind, some air moves laterally into the area protected by the windbreak.

The fixation of sand dunes and the reclamation of some arid areas for agriculture have been accomplished by the planting or constructing of windbreaks. The so-called dust bowl of the midwestern United States (see Figures 5.1 and 9.8) was overcome in the 1930s in part by this approach (Sears, 1962; The Shelterbelt Project, 1934; Hewes and Jung, 1981). The effects of wind on the evapotranspiration, water balance, and heat balance of an adjacent landscape element are also considerable (Miller, 1956; Rouse, 1984a, 1984b). Similarly, the input of ash from a nearby fire, or heat from the subsequent blackened area, is often significant (Grier, 1975; McColl and Grigal, 1975; Clayton, 1976).

A landscape typically has not just one but several or many structures that alter airflow (Figure 9.8). A glimpse of the airflow patterns around two separate structures reveals the richness of possible wind patterns on a landscape and emphasizes the nonrandom nature of wind deposits. As an illustration, we will consider two structures, a hedge and a building,

**Figure 9.8** *Windbreaks close enough to significantly alter surface meteorological conditions over the whole intervening area. The shadows indicate a break (foreground) where high wind velocities would be present. Willow (Salix) trees are planted here to protect fields growing bluegrass (Poa pratensis) sod on black organic soil. Lapeer County, Michigan (United States). (Courtesy of USDA Soil Conservation Service.)*

and will vary both the height of the hedge and its distance from the building (Robinette, 1972).

In general, low shrubs permit more air to flow through the building than do higher shrubs (Figure 9.9). If the low shrubs are separated from the building at some distance, the airflow through the building is less than if the shrubs are adjacent to the building, because turbulence develops between the shrubs and the building. However, in the case of the high shrubs adjacent to or near the building, very little air passes through the building, and (surprisingly), it flows in the opposite direction (Figure 9.9). In effect, the high shrubs near the building (and not those distant

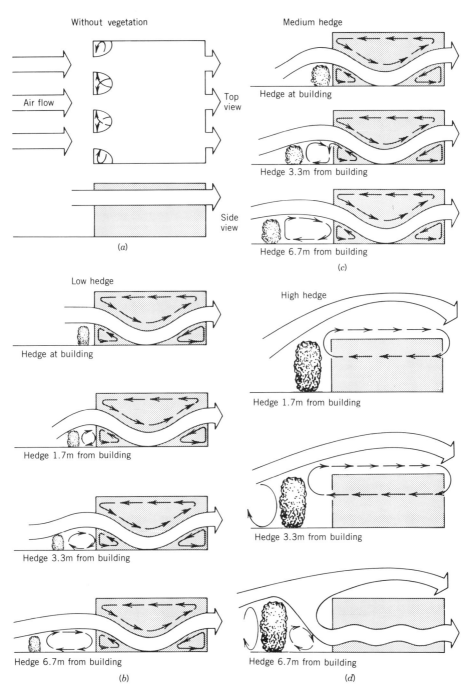

Without vegetation

Air flow

Top view

Side view

(a)

Medium hedge

Hedge at building

Hedge 3.3m from building

Hedge 6.7m from building

(c)

Low hedge

Hedge at building

Hedge 1.7m from building

Hedge 3.3m from building

Hedge 6.7m from building

(b)

High hedge

Hedge 1.7m from building

Hedge 3.3m from building

Hedge 6.7m from building

(d)

**Figure 9.9** *Airflow past two structures (hedge and building) when height and distance apart vary. Top and side views of a building (a) show airflow through windows. Side views of airflow (b, c, and d), with hedges that vary in height and in distance from the building. (After Robinette, 1972, based on studies of R. F. White.)*

from it) force the boundary layer air over the building. Therefore, the downward turbulent air at the opposite end of the building is greater than the air pressure upwind (e.g., see Figure 9.6). Hence, air is forced back into the building in the reverse direction. In summary, both laminar air speed and the presence of turbulence can be either augmented or re-duced—and direction can be altered radically—when two or more projecting structures are present in the landscape.

As wind surfers, hang gliders, and vultures well know, a projecting curved object such as a cliff or point of land, acting as a streamlined object, can noticeably change the wind direction. A similar effect is commonly felt near shelterbelts or valleys oriented diagonally to the direction of the wind. The wind bends and speeds up, following these shelterbelts or valleys.

One special case of air movement is particularly evident at the scale of a landscape. At night, especially in cloudless dry air, the heat absorbed from the sun during the day by the soil and rock is radiated back to the air. The air thus heated rises. Cool air from higher elevations then rushes in to replace the departing warm air. This process of air movement down slopes at night is called **cold air drainage** (Geiger, 1965; Weller and Schreiber, 1965; Schreiber, 1968; Bergen, 1969; Patterson and Haze, 1979; Miller et al., 1983). It is not accidental that in arid land those who camp in dry canyons and river valleys are mainly visitors and tourists, while the natives or cowboys prefer the warmer slopes to the cold valley bottoms.

The implications of these airflow principles and patterns for planners, designers, and land managers are enormous. Evergreen and deciduous trees affect wind differently. Seasonal wind patterns differ markedly. In some areas, exceptional winds, such as those that accompany destructive storms and hurricanes, are the problem. In other areas, the normal daily wind is so strong it makes growing crops, heating your house, and pro-tecting butterfly populations difficult. Too little wind may be present and the heat may be suffocating and the flies unbearable. The homeowner and the planner alike have a multitude of opportunities to channel the wind to their liking. They can speed it up, slow it down, and change and even reverse its direction. Of course, altering wind at one spot usually changes it somewhere else, and the ecological changes at both places must be considered.

**Sound**

The movement of sound and the dissipation of its energy to heat take place in many ways and are of considerable importance in the landscape. Animals broadcasting for mates, and residents adjacent to a jet airport, know well the significance of sound movement.

When the string section in an orchestra is in good form, we hear low throbbing sounds from the base fiddles and melodic high-pitched tones from the violins. The chirps of small insect-feeding edge birds are heard in both woods and field, and the Swiss mountain horns, longer than two men, are heard for tens of kilometers. What is the reason for such tremendous differences in loudness and in the transmission of sound across space?

**Sound** is a form of energy that moves through space in a linear trajectory with undulations or waves around the trajectory. Different sounds have different wavelengths, or *frequencies,* measured in cycles per second (cps) or hertz (hz). For example, most of us hear in the range of about 20 to 20,000 cps. In general, higher frequencies—like that of the violin—sound louder than lower frequencies—like that of the base fiddle. Sound is also described in terms of *intensity* or pressure, which is measured in decibels on a logarithmic scale, by which a doubling of loudness to the human ear represents ten times the amount of sound energy. Loudness, therefore, is determined by both the frequency and the intensity of sound. (See Figure 9.10 for several examples of loudness in the landscape.)

Unlike wind, which moves primarily in a single direction, sound energy radiates in linear trajectories in all directions from its source (Figure 9.11). Eventually sound energy, like other forms of energy on earth, is converted into heat energy.

Sound energy moves through air and is dissipated more rapidly if the air is laden with materials such as moisture. Thus, weather is a major factor affecting sound transmission. Sound bounces readily off hard surfaces and is absorbed and dissipated more rapidly by soft and diffuse surfaces. Wind carries sound energy in its trajectory just as it carries heat energy.

In view of these patterns, vegetation clearly plays a role in the movement and diminishing of sound in the landscape. Vegetation is particularly effective in reducing high frequency sounds, a help in the abatement of **noise**—unwanted sound (Beranek, 1971; U.S. Environmental Protection Agency, 1972). (Except for extreme or sustained cases, low frequency sounds are generally not annoying.) Hedges and narrow plantings are relatively ineffective in reducing noise. For example, such plantings separating a highway corridor from an adjacent residential neighborhood are mainly of visual significance. Wider bands of vegetation, however, may quite effectively reflect and absorb sound energy.

Landscape architects use plantings of many sorts to deal with noise. For example, evergreens tend to reflect more noise, while deciduous plants absorb more. A mixture of several species is considered especially effective at reducing middle frequency noise.

Rock music is an inspiration to some people and a racket to others. While reducing noise is often a goal, there are also cases in which in-

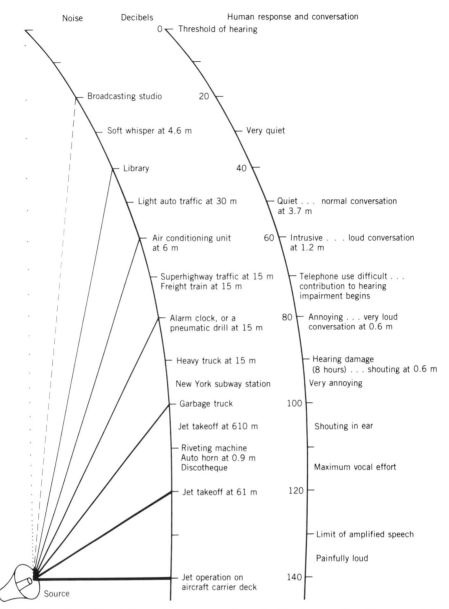

**Figure 9.10** *Sound levels for various sources. Sounds of both natural and human origin span the range. Most sounds over about 60 decibels are commonly considered to be noise. (Based on U.S. Environmental Protection Agency, 1972, and other sources.)*

**Figure 9.11** *Seven wolves howling in a pack ritual. Each wolf (Canis lupus) may choose his or her own note, head angle, and body stance. New York City. (Photo by Scott Barry.)*

creased transmission of sound is important. The migratory bird returning from a long flight, for example, sets up a territory and sings loudly for a mate. A wolf pack joins together for evening choruses (Figure 9.11). Many sounds travel distances at the scale of adjoining landscape elements (Hopkins and Odum, 1953; Fletcher and Busnel, 1978; Grue et al., 1983). Hence, sound transmission is determined to a large extent by the structure of those elements and the relative hardness of the border separating them.

## Gases, Aerosols, and Particulate Matter

If you have not stood immediately downwind of a paper mill, you have an unforgettable experience ahead. You want to run away as fast as you can, but the sulfur oxides in the air smell like rotten eggs up close, and you feel as though you would suffocate if you took a deep breath.

Air from one landscape element that blows into another may contain a wide range of materials foreign to the second landscape element. Dust and smoke blowing from open or arid areas are visible, conspicuous examples. Invisible gases and particles are also prevalent. These include the common industrial pollutants carbon monoxide, sulfur dioxide, and nitrogen oxide, as well as naturally produced organic compounds liberated from evergreens. **Allelochemics,** the organic substances secreted by one organism that affect another organism, are important here. Some substances, such as those from certain aromatic shrubs inhibit other organisms (allelopathy). Other substances are stimulatory—the minuscule amounts of sex attractants (pheromones) liberated by insects, for example.

The gaseous components in the air entering the second landscape element may produce various effects. Hordes of insects may be stimulated to buzz toward the first ecosystem, for example, or toxic pollutants may wipe out certain species. Some gases, such as sulfur dioxide and hydrogen fluoride, have reportedly been absorbed by the vegetation, which may act as a filter to clean the air of the pollutants. Naturally, the effectiveness of such a filtering system varies greatly, depending particularly on the amount of gas entering, the wind speed, and the height, type, and amount of vegetation.

Particulate matter and aerosols also are carried passively in the airstream around both streamlined and bluff objects. Inevitably some of the particles, hitting the leaves and stems of plants, adhere to the vegetation (White and Turner, 1970; Schlesinger and Reiners, 1974; Art et al., 1974; McColl, 1978; Mayer and Ulrich, 1978; Gorham et al., 1979; Brabec et al., 1981; Wiman, 1981; Lindberg et al., 1982; Kovar et al., 1982; Lovett et al., 1982; Graustein and Armstrong, 1983; Gosz et al., 1983). This process, called **impaction,** also functions as a filtering of the air. If you walk in an ecosystem downwind of a large rock quarry area or a dusty road (Tamm and Troedsson, 1955), the vegetation is commonly coated with dust. Residential and natural tracts downwind of most urban areas are peppered with a range of chemicals, in particulate and aerosol form (suspended droplets in a gas), that impact on the vegetation and other structures. The pollen from such plants as ragweed (*Ambrosia*) that afflict hay-fever sufferers is filtered by impaction.

As in the case of gaseous flows, the effectiveness of vegetation as a filter of particulates and aerosols varies widely. Edge vegetation on the windward side of an ecosystem simply by its position receives the greatest amount of impaction, and in some cases is noticeably damaged by the accumulated materials. Unlike the gaseous material filtered, which is generally absorbed into the tissue of organisms, particulate matter and aerosols normally adhere to the outside of leaves and stems. The materials may clog up pores in the organisms or become tightly bound to the surface. Most of the material, however, remains only until the next rain, when it is washed from the plant surfaces and incorporated into the soil. Vertebrate and invertebrate populations, of course, may also be heavily affected by these material inputs and processes.

Finally, as with a drain in the kitchen sink or the old-fashioned sticky flypaper, a filter is effective only until it is saturated or blocked up. When the flypaper is covered with masses of sticky flies, it no longer works. When the vegetation can no longer absorb gases or particulates, it filters no more. A good rain will readily rejuvenate impaction. (Of course, a considerable amount of particulate matter may be deposited on the ground where vegetation decreases wind velocity, rather than by impaction.)

Some arthropods, such as spiders and moths, produce long lightweight threads or nets. The wind catches these lightweight structures with the animals attached and may passively carry them long distances. When the arthropods encounter new vegetation they simply set up homes and live in it. In this fashion, the gypsy moth (*Lymantria dispar*) introduced from Europe has spread widely through the eastern hardwood forests of North America, even though the female moths are flightless. When the caterpillar is tiny it climbs to the top of a tree and hangs down on a long thread. A gust of wind sends thousands of these tiny caterpillars aloft and gives them a free ride to the next woods, where filtration takes place. A sumptuous meal follows that soon leaves many of the trees defoliated. Presumably the impaction and filtration effect rarely involves saturation in the case of animals in the wind.

## Locomotion

Flying animals basically move from one landscape element to another for reasons of food or cover. They are trying either to eat or not to be eaten and, in some species, to find a mate. These are airborne flows but the movement involves locomotion by wings, and energy is expended by these organisms.

Birds, bats, bees, and butterflies are familiar examples. For the most part, the flying species are predators, fruit- or seed-eaters, carrion-feeders, and nectar-feeders and pollinators. The extinct flying dinosaurs—the pterodactyls—were fierce flesh-eating predators. Many furry bats prey on tiny insects today. Giant bats and many colorful birds of the tropical rain forest feed on large juicy fruits, while most temperate birds feed on insects or seeds. Moths and bats at night and butterflies, bees, and birds by day feed on nectar in flowers and by doing so transfer pollen from plant to plant. In fact, without animal pollination, we would have no beans, berries, large juicy fruits, or countless other plants to eat.

The roost or nesting territory of a species may be in one ecosystem, while its feeding territory includes the adjacent ecosystem. A species may feed in one ecosystem but take cover in another. Some species forage in several landscape elements of the same type, such as woods, and must cross the intervening fields to do so. In short, flying animals move between adjacent landscape elements largely in food-related activities.

Flows along the ground are most familiar because we see or participate in many of them. Vehicles consuming fossil fuel commonly cross from one landscape element to another (Figure 9.3) carrying not only people, but also an extensive range of goods. Such vehicles may also transport numerous animals and plants, often inadvertently. When people using their own energy walk or bicycle across landscape element boundaries, they also transport any number of things. The effects of such human movements may even change the landscape element itself to a different size or type.

Ground animals—including most mammals and reptiles plus some amphibians, birds, and arthropods—readily move between landscape elements. Familiar examples are livestock from fields, dogs and cats from residential areas (Liberg, 1980), field mice and house mice from their respective habitats, and weeds from disturbed or natural areas. Less familiar are the nocturnal creatures (Figure 9.12), especially mammals and,

**Figure 9.12** *A desert streambed used by many locomoting animals, mainly at night, in central Arizona (United States). Coyote (Canis latrans) footprints are particularly visible here, suggesting that the streambed corridor is a conduit for them, and a barrier or filter for the movement of their prey, such as certain rodents. Note the well-developed stream corridor vegetation in an arid landscape dominated by scattered shrubs. Water can often be found by digging some tens of centimeters down in the sandy sediments here. (R. Forman.)*

in warmer climates, reptiles. In addition, many plant and arthropod species may be transported to nearby areas in the fur, scales, or feathers of these animals.

## SOIL FLOWS

### General Concepts

Less visible, but highly significant, are the flows on and below the soil surface. A small portion of such flows may be by means of wind—for example, when leaf litter blows along the soil surface (Phillipson et al., 1975; Orndorff and Lang, 1981)—or by animal locomotion, as in the case of burrowing mammals. However, almost all ground flows depend on water as the transporting vector (Figure 9.13). Because water basically flows down slopes, the recipient landscape elements are generally at low elevation. Stream corridors, and the streams in them, are the primary recipients. Swamps, marshes, lakes, and estuaries also receive these ground flows.

The range and magnitude of such flows are staggering. Fertilizers (especially phosphorus and nitrogen), pesticides, nitrogen wastes from livestock, silt, and clay are carried in enormous quantities from fields. Sewage flows from housing areas along with smaller but significant amounts of wastes such as petroleum products, pesticides, and chlorine from swimming pools. The outputs from industrial areas to the ground are diverse and in some cases huge. Such outputs include organic wastes from food processing or organic chemical manufacturing, inorganic wastes such as acids and salts, and toxic substances such as PCBs, arsenic, and dioxin.

Despite the range of materials flowing, the principles underlying these flows are quite easily understood. Curiosity about what is going on right under our feet is basically all that is needed. Water moves as a mass flow with gravity (usually) the predominant force, and materials are passively carried with it. As is not the case with other vectors (wind, animals, and people), the direction of this water flow is fixed—down, down, down—and thus is predictable. On sloping land the direction is obvious to the eye. On flat land, water still goes diagonally down and typically flows underground in the direction of a nearby stream valley. While direction is constant, the rate of flow may vary considerably. A few basic factors govern most of the variability, and an understanding of them makes possible reasonably good predictions of flow rates between landscape elements.

Three primary factors determine flow rates.

1. The amount and timing of water input, primarily precipitation, is critical. The more precipitation enters the ground from above, the

**Figure 9.13** *A clear cool stream transporting relatively low levels of either dissolved or particulate matter. Net River, Carlton County, Minnesota (United States). The low turbidity suggests a rather continuous stream corridor upstream that does not have eroding banks or agricultural, industrial, or sewage inputs. The low water temperature suggests springs and continuous shade. These conditions help make this an excellent trout (Salmo) stream. (Courtesy of USDA Soil Conservation Service.)*

more pressure is exerted on the water below, so that it is pushed downhill faster. Water input in precipitation, of course, varies with the weather, and we all know by reading or listening to the news media how predictable weather is.

2. The structure of the soil is critical, particularly its **porosity**—the measure of the spaces water can flow through.

3. The filtration effect of the soil on the material being carried by the

water is also important. This filtration may involve physical adhesion or chemical attachment of the material to the soil particles.

Let us see what the materials that are being carried in soil flow look like. Basically, they are in the form of either particulate matter or dissolved substances. **Particulates** are materials that are not dissolved in water, although they may be suspended in it. Particulate matter includes both organic matter—such as bacteria, spores, and pieces of decayed leaves— and inorganic matter such as clay and silt. **Dissolved** (or soluble) **substances** are materials that chemically break apart in water and pass into solution. They may also be organic, including humic acid and urea, or inorganic, such as nitrates, sulfates, and calcium. Dissolved substances chemically bond with or attach to other materials both organic and inorganic, including clay particles in the soil and materials flowing through it. This ability to bond chemically is of importance in the general soil filtration process.

A striking pattern emerges when we compare the flows of particulate matter to those of dissolved substances, using measurements taken in streams (Figure 9.13). In the case of particulate matter, we find that very little of it moves under a light rain. Increasing amounts flow during heavier rains, and the relationship is not linear, but exponential (Figure 9.14). Rather than a doubling of rain producing a doubling of particle flow, it may produce four times as much. The familiar exponential or J-shaped curve phenomenon is present—beyond a certain rainstorm level, the curve bends steeply upward. Thus, a single very heavy rain may cause tremendous particulate flow (Figure 9.14) and even landslides (debris avalanches) (Sharpe, 1938; Flaccus, 1959; Miller, 1977; Lee, 1980; Eschener and Patric, 1982).

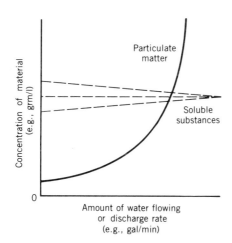

**Figure 9.14** *Stream output of particulate and dissolved materials related to the amount of water flow. The curve for soluble substances may increase or decrease slightly depending on the substance and the environmental conditions. (After Likens et al., 1977.)*

A careful study of particulate flow in a forested mountain stream in New Hampshire (United States) found that the majority of flow for an entire year took place on one April day (Bormann and Likens, 1967). The ecologists estimate that most of that output took place within two hours. This example, and the J-shaped curve of Figure 9.14, well illustrate the pattern of *catastrophic ecology* (see Chapter 7). A single infrequent event may outweigh in significance the sum of all the day-by-day events.

The flow pattern of dissolved substances differs markedly from that of particulate matter (Figure 9.14). The relationship between concentration and water flow rate is believed to be linear or nearly so. In some cases there is little difference in the concentration of dissolved substances whether water is trickling by or pouring by, that is, the curves are nearly horizontal. In these cases the total amount of dissolved material transported is directly proportional to the amount of water that passes. In most cases, however, as the flow rate increases the concentration of dissolved substances decreases.

The concentration of dissolved substances, also differs from the beginning to some time after the termination of a single rainstorm. Early in a rain, little water is flowing and it is rich in dissolved substances. Sometime after the rain stops, again little water is flowing but it is purer; that is, it has fewer dissolved substances. This pattern occurs because the initial rainwater encounters considerable material that has accumulated since the previous rain. Some of this material is picked up by the rainwater and carried through the soil. As the rain continues the accumulated material is gradually washed away, and so the later flow has less dissolved material. The process is analogous to washing vegetables or a baby. Most of the dirt is removed at first, and continued washing carries off fewer and fewer dissolved substances and particulates.

## Erosion and Surface Flow

Another very important characteristic distinguishes the flow of particulates from dissolved substances. Whereas almost all particulate matter flow takes place on the soil surface, almost all dissolved substances flow through the ground. Water **erosion** is the process of removing particulate matter from the soil surface in flowing water. The upper layers of soil are usually rich in particulate organic matter such as litter and humus, and erosion often initially removes such matter. When erosion continues, mineral soil is washed away and increasing amounts of inorganic matter are eliminated (Hack, 1960; Leopold et al., 1964; Keller, 1972; Likens et al., 1977; Young, 1978; Swanson et al., 1982). Extreme erosion results in the removal of all soil and the exposure of the bedrock beneath (Figure 9.15). Naturally, some dissolved substances are carried with the particulate matter in surface water runoff. Mineral nutrient loss in surface runoff

**Figure 9.15** *Exposed bedrock after plant death and erosion of all soil due to chronic air pollution. Palmerton, Pennsylvania (United States). Sixty years of zinc oxide from a nearby smelter killed almost all plants in many square kilometers of oak forest. When the dead roots finally break apart (little microbial decomposition takes place, as a further effect of the pollutant), the soil is rapidly washed away. The tree bases suggest that about 30 cm of soil covered this area. Only five species, all found in distinct patches, remain common: sassafras (Sassafras albidum, tree), black gum (Nyssa sylvatica, tree), catbriar (Smilax rotundifolia, vine), sandwort (Arenaria patula, herb), and a moss (Pottia). The last two are rare species in the region. (See Nash, 1975, Strojan, 1978.) (R. Forman.)*

may be considerable in localized places and at infrequent periods, but generally mineral nutrients in subsurface flow far exceed those in surface runoff.

Erosion also causes the movement in the soil of seeds and other propagules, which may be an important source of new plants in an area. Arthropods, broken pieces of plants, and many other organisms that survive the transport process also invade new areas in this manner.

However, the primary result of the erosion process, other than the baring of an area, is the deposit of sediments down slopes. Generally, these sediments are clay and silt that may cover and indeed nutritionally enrich the recipient landscape element. In areas with inadequate landscape management, too many of these sediments are carried right through the stream corridor and deposited in the stream or even directly into other water bodies. Sediment buildup then occurs in the stream basin and fills up lakes and ponds behind dams.

Almost all erosion is preventable, except in arid areas. Most erosion can be traced to (a) agricultural fields, especially those that are cultivated or strongly herbicided, (b) heavily trampled or overgrazed areas, and (c) logging, road building, and other disturbances on steep slopes. The following basic factors that underlie erosion are evident in these situations and have been documented by soil scientists, ecologists, foresters, agriculturalists, and others in studies of severely disturbed areas (Wischmeier and Smith, 1965; Bormann and Likens, 1967; Ruhe, 1975; Jenny, 1980; McCashion and Rice, 1983).

1. Removal of the above-ground vegetation prevents a large surface from intercepting precipitation, so that more water directly strikes the ground and promotes some erosion. (Interception of precipitation by vegetation in temperate forest areas is often measured or calculated to be 5–20% of incoming precipitation.)
2. Removal of the litter and humus leaves the mineral soil exposed to precipitation, further promoting erosion. The physical force of raindrops striking mineral soil combined with the lack of piles of organic matter to block the formation of tiny surface gullies appears to be the problem.
3. An acceleration of erosion follows upon the death of roots. A major force binding soil particles together—the fine roots too small to be seen without a lens—has disappeared. The rate of erosion increases sharply from this point on and continues until only bedrock is present, as is often seen near heavy metal smelters (Figure 9.15).

The primary erosion factors are described by the "universal" *soil loss equation* (Wischmeier and Smith, 1965; Ruhe, 1975; Jenny, 1980)

$$A = f (R, K, L, S, C)$$

where $A$, the amount of soil eroded, is a function of rainfall intensity ($R$), a soil erodability factor ($K$), length of the slope ($L$), the angle of the slope ($S$), and the vegetation cover ($C$).

The erosion process can generally be stopped and even reversed by the introduction of plants. Returning land to its pre-erosion vegetation and fauna is a long process. Accomplishing this on land that has gone past the root death stage may be impossible.

## Subsurface Flow

We observed that dissolved substances move primarily in subsurface flow. Generally, water that penetrates the ground, and is not absorbed by roots, **percolates** (moves down in a vertical or near vertical direction) through the soil particles. We are interested here in the structure of the soil through which percolation takes place, because soil structure affects both the percolation rate of water and the ability of soil to filter materials in the water.

Unlike dirt, which is a nuisance to be cleaned off, soil has a fascinating structure with many kinds of objects moving about. Viewing this structure is an insight into a frontier as awe-inspiring as snorkeling on a coral reef or wandering around space in a capsule. The structure of soil is analogous to that of a town or a naval flotilla; each depends primarily on the size of its components and how they are aggregated. The distribution of sizes of mineral particles is called **soil texture** and is basically defined in terms of the relative proportions of clay, silt, and sand particles (small, medium and large particles—see Chapter 2).

As in the case of the naval flotilla, not only the size of objects but also their pattern of aggregation is critical in determining their penetrability. The smallest particles—clay (and humus)—contain an immensely significant characteristic, **cation exchange capacity** (CEC). It is the ability of many positively charged nutrients (or cations) such as calcium and magnesium to attach chemically to clay particles and later be released from them. Cation exchange capacity is one major component of **soil fertility.** Soils that have high CEC values are potentially richer than soils with low CEC values (and usually less acid). (The other major component of soil fertility is the amount of positively charged nutrients present. Sand and silt contain neither appreciable CEC nor these nutrients, so the amount of clay or humus is primarily critical in this measure of soil fertility.)

Several factors that together we will call *binding factors* affect the aggregation of soil particles—primarily, the amount of organic matter, acidity, and roots present. With varying amounts of these factors present, the clay or silt particles, for example, may stick together to form larger aggregate particles (peds). Because larger particles have larger spaces between them, the soil porosity is greater.

The net result of the above soil characteristics is that water flows faster through soils with higher porosity. Porosity depends on soil texture (relative amounts of clay, silt, and sand), plus the binding factors (organic matter, acidity, and roots) that in turn are related to cation exchange capacity (clay or humus particles chemically holding nutrients). The other result of all these characteristics is that dissolved substances and particulates carried passively by water are effectively filtered by the soil, that is, some pass readily through while others are retained in the soil.

Except in arid regions, most water that percolates down through soil generally enters the **ground water** (of which the water table is the upper surface). It is a continuous stream of water where spaces between soil particles are saturated, so that substances that enter it may be carried for considerable horizontal distances underground (Pye et al., 1983; Geophysics Research Forum, 1984). In some areas, where sand or porous rock underlie the soil, water may fill the pores to form an **aquifer,** which is like an underground lake. Aquifers are particularly important as sources of pure drinking water for towns or cities. However, when substances enter an aquifer, they readily spread by diffusion or water flow. Pollutants from septic systems, waste landfills, and cattle feedlots (Figure 9.16) are especially apt to seep into ground water or aquifers.

## INTERACTION BETWEEN LAND AND STREAM

Scientists who study streams are sometimes called landscape urologists, because they take a sample of the water in a bottle, analyze its contents, and can then tell what problems appear to be present in the landscape.

The tight linkage between stream quality and the status of the land has long been an area of ecological study in the landscape. We observe a cultivated field extending to the edge of a stream bank (see Figure 8.13), a logging operation on a steep slope (see Figure 3.2), or wastes from a town entering a river. In such cases major changes in stream quality, usually obvious to the eye, are always obvious to the scientist who analyzes the stream water.

### The Stream Corridor Role

Stream corridor (riparian) vegetation commonly separates the surrounding land from a stream (see Figure 9.17) (Wistendahl, 1958; Johnson, 1970; Hasler, 1975; Hynes, 1975; Vannote et al., 1980; Schlosser and Karr, 1981b; Decamps, 1984). The corridor vegetation itself clearly affects the stream in major ways, including shading, litter input, seed input, droppings from herbivorous caterpillars, and fallen wood that creates dams and pools. This vegetation also retards the input of particulate and dissolved substances by preventing erosion of the stream bank, a major factor in controlling stream water quality. But here we are primarily interested in the movement of objects from the land to the stream corridor and in whether *corridor filtration* is important; that is, whether the corridor

**Figure 9.16** *A feedlot with up to 30,000 cattle and a mammoth waste disposal problem, near Hereford, Texas. Nitrogen seeps into the ground water of the area making well water unsafe for drinking. The number of cattle in the American Midwest is similar to the number 200 years ago of native bison, which have now disappeared in most of the area. The cattle, however, are largely maintained in local concentrations. (Courtesy of USDA Soil Conservation Service).*

acts as an effective filter to prevent moving objects from entering the stream.

Mammals move singly and in herds from the land to the stream. Predators in the stream corridor may devour some of the animals entering, but otherwise the stream corridor generally has little filtering effect on mammals. However, as mammals enter they may produce considerable effects on the stream corridor—by, for example, dropping wastes and

**Figure 9.17** *Stream corridor bisecting cultivation in a rain forest climate (central Costa Rica). Large quantities of water and eroded sediment pass from the upland directly through this narrow corridor into the stream. However, a narrow stream corridor may still reduce critical stream bank erosion. Some wild animals or livestock that enter the corridor cause stream bank erosion, some are inhibited by the corridor conditions, and others pass right through the corridor. (R. Forman.)*

seeds, damaging streambanks, feeding on the vegetation, and stirring up the stream water. Birds also commonly enter the corridor for feeding or cover and often introduce seeds. In some areas, wind transport of soil and snow from land to stream is also of considerable significance (Chapter 11).

When vegetation is removed from surrounding land (Figure 9.17), more water flows to a corridor, for two reasons.

1. Plant surface area decreases, so less water is transpired to the atmosphere.
2. The blocking effect of the vegetation on runoff (flow impedance) decreases, so that less water is held on the land to be transpired (Penman, 1948; Likens et al., 1970, 1978; Budyko, 1974; Swank and Douglass,

1974; Baumgartner and Reichel, 1975; Gorham et al., 1979; Lee, 1980; Reiners, 1983).

For example, in a New Hampshire (USA) deciduous forest, after a particular clearcutting process the amount of water in the stream increased 28% in the first year and 39% in the second year (Likens et al., 1970). If a stream corridor had been left along the stream it would have probably had little effect on these results. In other words, in this moist climate, the corridor would have had a minimal filtering effect on the movement of water.

In a drier climate, however, where every drop of water counts, evapotranspiration by exposed stream corridors and by vegetation along irrigation ditches may be quite significant. In effect, the stream corridor acts as a filter, intercepting water flowing from the land toward the stream and pumping it out vertically (Dunford and Fletcher, 1947; Rowe, 1963; Heller, 1969; Campbell, 1970; Van Hylckama, 1970; Brooks and Thorud, 1971; Davenport et al., 1976).

## Corridor Filtration of Mineral Nutrients

The flow of particles and dissolved substances exhibits patterns quite different from the flow of water. On steep slopes, **gravitational transport** (mass wasting) may be considerable, including processes such as soil creep, mud flows, landslides, avalanches, and movement by freeze-thaw cycles (solifluction) (Rapp, 1960; O'Loughlin and Pearce, 1976; Garwood et al., 1979; Swanson et al., 1982; Reiners, 1983). Where the slope is steep, these materials transported by gravity generally move directly to the stream bed, with little resistance from the corridor. On gradual slopes, materials also move directly by gravity, but far more moves passively in water and wind transport.[1]

The rate of movement is highly dependent on the nature of the vegetation. In the New Hampshire study above, most mineral nutrients in the stream water increased several times following the clearcutting process (Likens et al., 1970). The level of nitrate increased 57 times, not changing the appearance of this clear mountain stream but making it unfit for humans to drink. Vegetation in a stream corridor absorbs some of the dissolved mineral nutrients that enter from the surrounding land. Vegetation also inhibits stream bank erosion, particularly of small clay

[1]See, for example, Nye and Greenland, 1960; Ruhe and Walker, 1968; Likens et al., 1969, 1977; Jordan and Kline, 1972; Likens and Bormann, 1974; Golley et al., 1975; Ritchie and McHenry, 1977; Wischmeier and Smith, 1978; Aber et al., 1978; Dietrich and Dunne, 1978; Young, 1978; Wolman and Gerson, 1978; Franklin, 1979; Gorham et al., 1979; Vitousek et al., 1979; Asmussen et al., 1979; Brown et al., 1981; Pimentel and Edwards, 1982; De Jong et al., 1983; Yates and Sheridan, 1983; and Ritchie et al., 1983.

particles that are rich in plant nutrients (Likens and Bormann, 1974; O'Loughlin and Pearce, 1976). In fact, cutting of stream corridor vegetation causes major changes in stream quality and organisms (Johnson, 1970).

While stream scientists agree that the possible filter effect of corridor vegetation on mineral nutrient movement is a critical question, they do not yet agree on how important such filtration might be. Mineral nutrients entering a stream corridor from the upland may take three major routes (ignoring wind transport in dry periods).

1. The nutrients may pass directly through the corridor and enter the stream.
2. The nutrients may accumulate in the soil of the corridor, gradually filling in the valley bottom. (During floods, they may be flushed down to riverbeds, lake bottoms, or deltas.)
3. The nutrients may be absorbed and incorporated into biomass by corridor vegetation as it grows.

The amount of mineral nutrients moving by the first two routes is poorly known. Clearly, the physical blocking by corridor vegetation of eroded particulate matter takes place (Figure 9.17). The accumulation of dissolved nutrients in the organic matter of corridor soils may also be important in some locations.

The third route, involving the role of accumulating plant biomass as a filter, is better known. In an agricultural watershed in the southeastern United States, significant proportions of some mineral nutrients that entered the corridor as subsurface flow were retained by the corridor (Lowrance et al., 1984). Similar or greater amounts were incorporated into the new tissue of the young corridor trees, which were harvested for timber and firewood. These findings lead to the idea that periodic corridor harvests might keep the nutrient filtering process working effectively, since old mature forests generally accumulate little or no biomass (Omernik et al., 1981; Gorham et al., 1979). Other factors, however, may render this proposed filtration effect of limited effectiveness, for example, surface nutrient runoff, deposits of particulate matter by erosion, and heavy flows during periodic storm periods (Brinson et al., 1980). Even these factors, though, could be counterbalanced by wide stream corridors (Karr and Schlosser, 1978; Bingham et al., 1980; Schlosser and Karr, 1981a, 1981b). In fact, in a Minnesota (United States) forest area where the stream corridor included peaty wetlands, about half of the nutrients entering were retained in the corridor and did not reach the stream (Verry and Timmons, 1982). Thus, we conclude that a wide stream corridor is likely to be an important filter of mineral nutrients flowing from the upland toward a stream.

# HEDGEROW INTERACTIONS WITH ADJACENT LANDSCAPE ELEMENTS

At this point, we can examine many of the preceding concepts in action. Because they are so widespread and relatively well known, we have again chosen hedgerow corridors here to explore the richness of interactions between two landscape elements (Pollard et al., 1974; Les Bocages, 1976; Forman and Baudry, 1984). Basically, hedgerows are surrounded by (a) fields, including cultivation and pastures; (b) natural vegetation, such as woodlots, wetlands, shrublands, and stream corridors; and (c) homes, including farmyards and villages.

## How Hedgerows Affect Fields

**Microclimate.** In many places the major objective in maintaining hedgerows is to modify the microclimate of the field, particularly the effect of wind, in order to increase the productivity of the field. This process is embodied in the terms shelterbelt or windbreak (Van Eimern et al., 1964; The Shelterbelt Project, 1934).

Downwind of a hedgerow, essentially all microclimatic variables are modified (Figure 9.18). Shade modifies the environment in a narrow band along the hedgerow. However, wind is the driving force controlling all other microclimatic variables. Compared to an open area without hedgerows, some environmental factors downwind of a hedgerow are elevated, including day temperature, soil, and atmospheric moisture. Others, such as wind speed, evaporation and night temperatures, are generally reduced.

Two environmental factors are modified for a long distance downwind. Evaporation is reduced downwind for a distance about 16 times the hedgerow height (16 h). The wind speed reduction extends to 28 times the hedgerow height (28 h) (Figure 9.18). Thus, wind speed would be significantly reduced for about 56 m downwind of a typical 2-m-high hawthorn hedge (*Crataegus*). A typical 20-m-high tree hedgerow would be expected to reduce wind for some 560 m, the length of about 200 horses in single file.

In many agricultural landscapes hedgerows are interconnected to form a network, and the distance between parallel hedgerows is usually far less than 560 m. In such cases, a second hedgerow modifies the normal wind attenuation pattern seen in Figure 9.18. Wind forced up over the first hedgerow drops rather sharply in a turbulent flow at a distance of about 6 to 8 h before being forced over the second hedgerow (Figure 9.19). Hence, wind speed near the ground is reduced for a considerable distance downwind of a hedgerow but is higher in the 6- to 8-h zone downwind. Then it is reduced again on the upwind side of the second

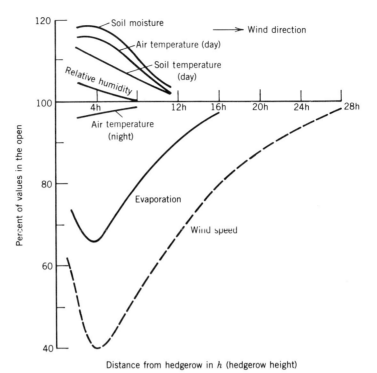

**Figure 9.18** *Hedgerow effects on the microenvironment of a field downwind (from Marshall, 1967; courtesy of* Field Crop Abstracts, Commonwealth Agricultural Bureau.*)*

hedgerow. Potential soil desiccation by wind in the 6- to 8-h distance is therefore high (Figure 9.19).

Except for in the narrow shaded area, heat energy input from sunlight is high near hedgerows. Overall, temperature is high in the wind-protected unshaded areas near the hedgerow and low in the windy, dry 6- to 8-h zone downwind. The spatial pattern of precipitation input parallels that of wind speed (Merot and Ruellan, 1980).

**Water, Erosion, and Mineral Nutrients.** On gentle slopes where precipitation soaks into the soil, the lateral movement of water is a subsurface process. The subsurface water may be absorbed by the deep and/or dense roots of hedgerow plants. Tall hedgerow plants are exposed to high levels of sun and wind, which accelerate water loss by evapotranspiration (Ballard, 1979; Geiger, 1965; Yoshino, 1975; Rosenberg et al., 1983). The presence of a ditch and bank in the hedgerow, which catches surface runoff after a heavy rain or snow melt, therefore also leads to higher evapotranspiration. By catching soil water and pumping it vertically,

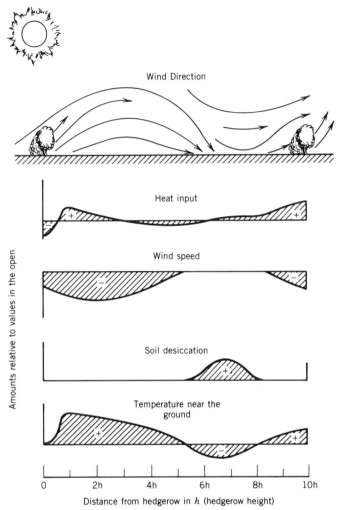

**Figure 9.19** *Expected field microclimatic patterns between two hedgerows (from Forman and Baudry, 1984, based on Guyot and Verbrugghe, 1976). (Courtesy of Springer-Verlag.)*

hedgerows help produce drier soil, less stream flooding, and (perhaps) locally moister air.

In hilly terrain, hedgerows seem to play important roles in inhibiting soil erosion, protecting soil nutrients in the field, and improving nearby stream characteristics such as sedimentation, flooding, and water quality. Soil erosion on slopes is reduced when hedgerows extend along the contours. Indeed, the deposition of soil particles—including organic matter—on the uphill side of a hedgerow, producing a terrace-like effect on the slope, may be pronounced. For example, different soil levels on opposite sides of an old stone wall usually indicate former cultivation on the uphill side (because soil particles that eroded from the field have accumulated by the stone wall). The distance between hedgerows is an important factor in inhibiting soil erosion, and Pihan (1976) estimates that halving the distance between hedgerows results in a 40% reduction in erosion. Similar patterns for mineral nutrient runoff may be expected. In an analogous situation, vegetation along stream corridors has been shown to reduce the amount of the particles suspended in stream water, resulting in less algae growth and better water quality (Schlosser and Karr, 1981b).

**Animals and Plants.** Hedgerows affect the organisms in adjacent fields indirectly—by modifying the microclimate, which in turn determines the species found in the field—and directly, when hedgerow organisms move into the field. Brunel and Cancela da Fonseca (1979), studying a group of flies (*Diptera: Brachyceres*), described what may be a common distribution pattern of passively transported organisms between hedgerows. Fly density was low immediately adjacent to both sides of a hedgerow. Peak fly density was found farther downwind of one hedgerow, and a smaller peak was found upwind of a second hedgerow. These peaks in fly density were separated by a low density area, somewhat downwind of mid-field. A similar pattern was found for the diversity of flies. In contrast, with no second hedgerow downwind, fly density and diversity were high only in the first meter downwind of the hedgerow. The presence of a second hedgerow changes the wind flow patterns and therefore the input of flies. Lewis (1969a, 1969b) found arthropod population peaks 2 to 4 h upwind that extended to 10 h downwind. This pattern, which was found to be predominantly for insects drifting from distant sources, passively mimicked the airflow pattern created by the hedgerow. Lewis (1969b) also showed that insects that apparently originated in the hedgerow, were found in abundance for only a short distance downwind.

Windblown pollen and seeds probably have patterns similar to those of insects. Consequently, patterns of old field succession should differ considerably with increasing distance from hedgerows (Harmon, 1948; McDonnell and Stiles, 1983; McDonnell, 1984). Furthermore, the hedgerow plants that shade the field immediately adjacent send out roots and suckers that extract water and nutrients (Bates, 1937; Harmon, 1948; Steavenson et al., 1943).

Many types of animals move from hedgerows into fields, including mice, birds, and insects (Pollard and Relton, 1970; Pollard et al., 1974; Saint-Girons, 1976; Darley-Hill and Johnson, 1981). Some animals cause economic damage by feeding on crops (van den Bosch and Telford, 1964; Southwood and Way, 1970; Rabb et al., 1976), for example, hedgerow rabbits have a banquet on tender planted shoots of grain. Such movements from hedgerow to field are highly seasonal—for example, some birds studied in Ontario mainly moved into fields in May and June (Wegner and Merriam, 1979).

It has been hypothesized that hedgerows maintain predators that by feeding in fields, reduce agricultural crop loss because they dampen pest population fluctuations. This idea is intuitively appealing, and has great potential economic significance, but as yet the evidence for it is meagre (Pollard, 1968, 1971; Pollard et al., 1974; Lundholm and Stackerud, 1980). Predatory ground beetles (*Coleoptera: Carabidae*) reportedly over-winter in hedgerows and then move out to feed on insects among the crops during the growing season. A study of hoverfly predators (*Diptera: Syrphidae*) on cabbage aphids found that predator species from hedge-rows and woods moved only short distances in the fields, whereas open country predatory species—that apparently did not require hedgerows—fed throughout the fields. The role of birds as pest predators warrants study, both during the breeding period when most are relatively dispersed and feeding on insects, and later when the post-breeding flocks often have insect and seed diets.

**Crop Production.** The hedgerow performs many functions for the farmer and society. If we consider only short-term crop production on a farm, we may ask whether the presence of hedgerows has a net negative or positive effect. There is no unequivocal answer (Les Bocages, 1976). On the negative side, hedgerows decrease the crop area, produce shade, shelter pests, and compete with crop plants for soil moisture and nutrients. Balanced against this is the pattern of microclimate over the field dis-cussed above. Especially productive zones in the field may be expected about 3 to 6 h downwind of a hedgerow, and 2 to 6 h upwind of a second hedgerow. Some measurements of corn production suggest there is no significant difference between a 4-hectare field bordered by hedge-rows and 4 hectares of open country (Barloy, 1980). Similar studies using different field sizes are needed.

Basically, the decision of the farmer (and of society) whether to have hedgerows by fields hinges largely on the multiple functions of hedgerows (Forman and Baudry, 1984). These include providing wildlife, inhibiting potentially damaging wind velocities, harboring pests, harboring potential predators on pests, blocking farm machinery, providing shade for live-stock, marking property boundaries, providing firewood, blocking drifting snow, inhibiting erosion and nutrient runoff, biological conservation, aesthetics, and more.

## How Fields, Woods, and Homes Affect Hedgerows

**Fields.** The driving forces of wind and water cause many flows from fields to hedgerows. Snow and soil particles accumulate in the hedgerow (Figure 9.4), and dust and aerosols impact on its vegetation. Fire spreads across open areas into hedgerows and shelterbelts (Harmon, 1948). Herbicides and insecticides from the field blow into the hedgerow, doubtless killing many insects and some plants and vertebrates (Pollard et al., 1974). Fertilizers from fields readily enter hedgerows and favor some species, such as "nitrogen-loving" plants (nitrophiles), at the expense of other species (Ellenberg, 1939, 1978; Pigott and Taylor, 1964; Tuxen, 1967; Kopecky, 1969; Braakhekke and Braakhekke-Ilsink, 1976; Ruthsatz and Haber, 1981). Even many field animals use hedgerows as temporary shelters (Lefeuvre et al., 1976). In short, the nature of hedgerows as narrow lines of vegetation and animal communities, is heavily controlled by inputs from adjacent fields.

**Woods.** Does a hedgerow attached to a woods differ from an unattached one? Indirect evidence indicates that wrens, butterflies, snails, and shrubs colonize a hedgerow from an attached woods (Williamson, 1969; Pollard et al., 1974; Cameron et al., 1980; Helliwell, 1975). Wegner and Merriam (1979) counted the number of birds moving between woods and hedgerow, woods and field, and hedgerow and field in Ontario, and found that three-quarters of the movements were between woods and hedgerow (Table 9.1). Measurements for small mammals in the same landscape showed the same pattern. A seasonal variation in the pattern was also evident. In early summer some birds moved into the fields via the hedgerows, and in early autumn some small mammals moved directly into the fields from the woods (Table 9.1). Along stone wall hedgerows attached to woods in southern New England, forest mammals were observed to move out into hedgerows, but field species did not move into the woods along the stone walls (Sinclair et al., 1967).

In six hedgerows attached to a woods in New Jersey, R. Forman, L. Goodrich, and B. Milne (unpublished data) found three bird species essentially limited to the first 100 m of hedgerow adjacent to the forest, whereas one bird species was in hedgerow portions almost always more than 50 m from the forest. Most of the possible explanations of this pattern involve the forest affecting the portion of attached hedgerow closest to it. Conversely, a flow from hedgerow to woods was demonstrated in England by experimentally removing a great tit (*Parus major*) from its territory in a woods, and observing its replacement by another bird of the same species from the adjoining hedgerow (Krebs, 1971). This action was interpreted as a movement from a suboptimal to an optimal habitat

TABLE 9.1 *Movements of birds and small mammals among woods,*
*hedgerows, and fields in Ontario.*

| Month | Movement Between: | | |
| | Woods and Hedgerow | Woods and Field | Hedgerow and Field |
|---|---|---|---|
| A. Birds | | | |
|     May | 121 (58%) | 16 (8%) | 71 (34%) |
|     June | 100 (52%) | 18 (9%) | 73 (38%) |
|     July | 64 (80%) | 2 (3%) | 14 (18%) |
|     August | 130 (88%) | 6 (4%) | 11 (8%) |
|     September | 291 (89%) | 24 (7%) | 12 (4%) |
|     October | 66 (79%) | 3 (4%) | 15 (18%) |
|     Total | 772 (74%) | 69 (7%) | 196 (19%) |
| B. Small mammals | | | |
|     May-June | 18 (90%) | 1 (5%) | 1 (5%) |
|     July-August | 36 (100%) | 0 (0%) | 0 (0%) |
|     September-October | 28 (62%) | 14 (31%) | 3 (7%) |
|     Total | 82 (81%) | 15 (15%) | 4 (4%) |

NOTE: Numbers of animals observed are given together with percentages for each time period. Small mammal data are for chipmunk (*Tamias*) and white-footed mouse (*Peromyscus*) combined.
*Source:* Wegner and Merriam, 1979. Blackwell Scientific Publications Ltd.

for the species. In summary, it appears that considerable interaction between woods and attached hedgerows exists, especially in the movement of birds and mammals, though most of the evidence is indirect.

**Homes.** A hodgepodge of unrelated ecological observations indicates that hedgerows near rural homes or habitations are important to, and used by, the people there. Hedgerows are often maintained for privacy, for protection from wind and snow, and to cut fuel costs. Such hedgerows commonly have high plant diversity and dominant species different from those of other hedgerows in the landscape (Willmot, 1980). The bird community may also be distinct—for example, there may be an abundance of robins (*Turdus migratorius*), which forage in farmyards and tolerate farming disturbances (Yahner, 1982). Hedgerows near homes may be maintained for the hunting of many types of wildlife including foxes. Such hedgerows are also enriched by nonnative species from the home, including house mice, cats, and certain plantings (Middleton and Merriam, 1983; Willmot, 1980).

# SUMMARY

The forces of mass flow and locomotion drive the movements of objects between landscape elements. Five vectors transport the objects—wind, water, flying animals, terrestrial animals, and people. Moving in streamlined or turbulent airflows, wind is accelerated, diminished, or changed in direction depending on the configuration of structures in the landscape. Vegetation structure is particularly important in the movement of sound energy and in the filtration or impaction of materials carried by wind.

Flow rates through soil are controlled by precipitation, soil porosity, and the filtration effect of the soil. Particulate matter is eroded and carried by water in surface runoff, particularly during high water input periods. The deposition of sediments goes hand in hand with this process. Dissolved materials move primarily in subsurface flows. Several binding factors aggregate soil particles to make soil porosity and fertility different from what would be expected on the basis of soil particle sizes (texture) alone.

The land-stream interaction is controlled in part by the filtering effect of the stream corridor, which is especially important in the movement of particulate matter, though significant amounts of some mineral nutrients can be absorbed by the corridor vegetation as it grows.

Hedgerows modify the microclimate of fields downwind, especially the wind speed and evaporation, and the patterns are altered noticeably when there is a second hedgerow downwind. Hedgerows also affect the movements of water, particulate matter, wind-blown insects, and many winged and terrestrial animals—as well as crop production—in adjacent fields. Conversely, fields, woods, and homes affect hedgerows. These flows of animals, plants, heat energy, biomass, water, and mineral nutrients between adjacent ecosystems are a major part of landscape functioning.

# QUESTIONS

1. What are the characteristics of a good windbreak in the landscape? Diagram a view from above of the area around a break or gap in a windbreak showing relative wind speeds.
2. How do the major forces underlying movement of objects between landscape elements differ in terms of energy?
3. In the landscape where you live, what are the primary flows between adjacent landscape elements? Indicate the direction of the flows, which flows are general, and which are essentially specific to certain pairs of landscape elements.
4. Evaluate the following statement: The planner can create situations that speed up the wind, slow it down, and change or even reverse its direction. How

does changing wind patterns in one place affect the patterns in surrounding areas?

5. How does locomotion as a transport mechanism typically affect the aggregation of objects? In what ways might this effect be important to a forester?
6. How do the movements of dust and sound differ?
7. Why is subsurface flow between ecosystems so important? What flows? What are the effects?
8. What is erosion? What primary factors determine its rate?
9. In what circumstances is a stream corridor an effective filter of objects moving from the surrounding land to a stream, and in what cases is it relatively ineffective?
10. Which is more important in wildlife management, the effect of hedgerows on adjacent landscape elements, or vice versa? In agriculture? Explain.
11. Does the size or shape of ecosystems affect flows between adjacent ecosystems? How?

# 10
# Animal and Plant Movement Across a Landscape

*Another kind of explosion*
*Was that of the potato fungus from Europe*
*That partly emptied Ireland*
*Through famine a hundred years ago.*
**Charles Elton, 1958**
*The Ecology of Invasions*
*by Animals and Plants*

Suppose you are driving an ambulance across town from an accident site to a hospital. With a straight road connecting the two locations you get your accident victims to the hospital in good time. If you must cross the grid of city streets in a diagonal direction, much precious time will elapse before your arrival. Worse still, if you must go around a large cemetery or a railroad yard the time required will be agonizing for everyone involved.

The speed with which you get your accident victims to the hospital depends largely on the structure of the landscape. The locations of corridors, barriers, and large patches are critical. A second major factor is the direction of movement relative to landscape structure. Your ambulance only makes good time when there is a corridor going your direction. The effect of landscape structure on the movement of animals and plants, the subject of this chapter, is analogous to the above example.

A tight linkage between structure and function is well known for many objects, such as cells, the human body, or a financial system. In this and the following chapter, we will be attuned to how tight is such a linkage between structure and flows in a landscape.

## PATTERNS OF MOVEMENT

An object moving between two points exhibits **continuous movement** if its speed never drops to zero. It may have a constant speed or may significantly accelerate or decelerate its rate of movement. However, commonly an object displays **saltatory movement,** stopping one or several times during its movement between two points.

357

## Continuous Movement

When we focus on the spatial aspects of a landscape, we find that these two movement patterns describe major types of flows of species, energy, and materials. Particles, gases, and heat energy move continuously across a landscape in a steady wind. Many species exhibit uniform movement along corridors or through the landscape matrix. Movement at a relatively constant speed is prevalent in areas of low heterogeneity (Figure 10.1). Landscape elements—a grassland, a forest, or a path, for example—that are favorable to a species will permit continuous movement if they are homogeneous, because no barriers or inhospitable areas exist to slow down the organisms.

Similarly, accelerating or decelerating movement would be expected where one portion of the route is relatively homogeneous and another part heterogeneous. An animal starting in a heterogeneous area where some landscape elements are inhospitable or nearly so moves slowly, on the average (although it might move rapidly across dangerous spots like roads). As it enters a more homogeneous tract of hospitable land, it can move across the tract faster, on the average (unless the tract is the destination, where the animal slows down perhaps to feed). Conversely, an animal beginning in favorable homogeneous habitat often slows down as it encounters heterogeneous land with unfavorable patches.

The influences behind these movement patterns may be described or measured more precisely. At a first level of resolution, we can measure the degree of landscape heterogeneity as described in Chapter 6. In addition to this heterogeneity measure, it is useful to estimate the degree

**Figure 10.1** *Caribou bulls* (Rangifer) *in continuous movement over relatively homogeneous tundra. (Len Rue, Jr.)*

of contrast present among the landscape elements. How different are the various types through which the animal passes? The landscape elements could be categorized on a scale—say from one to ten—based, for example, on how similar each type is to the matrix.

Another approach to understanding influences behind movement patterns is to consider the roles of boundaries between landscape elements. Boundaries are the places where the animal must cross from one element to another. Caution and a pause are generally the watchwords. In Chapters 4 and 5 we presented the concept of connectivity, or the degree to which a particular type of landscape element is separate or continuous in the landscape. Here, we use a somewhat similar concept, **boundary crossing frequency.** Basically, it is a measure of the number of boundaries per unit of length that an object crosses in moving over a landscape. The animal that encounters more spatial homogeneity has a lower boundary crossing frequency and may move rapidly across an area (Figure 10.1). Boundary crossing frequency can be combined with the measure of the degree of landscape element contrast to provide a fairly precise estimate of the relative speed of the animal across the landscape.

Easily measured boundary crossing frequency is likely to be of use in planning and management, because it may be calculated for any number of possible alternative routes between two points. In this way, for example, we may directly compare a straight line with a route that uses corridors and with a route that avoids them. Boundary crossing frequency appears to be of particular interest in understanding the movement of patch interior species, including secretive species that cross few boundaries and require areas remote from edges.

## Saltatory Movement

An object may move for a while, stop, and move again. As it moves across a landscape between two points, certain places along the route serve as stopping points for the object. Movement of this type is called *saltatory movement* or, in the case of species, "jump dispersal" (Pielou, 1979).

Consider a heavy rain falling on a recently plowed field on a hillside. Water running over the soil surface picks up silt particles (erosion), carries them downhill some distance, and deposits them shortly after the rain stops. The silt particles remain where they are until the next heavy rain. Again they are eroded and deposited farther downhill. This moving and stopping process continues on the hillside until the silt particles are dumped into the stream below. In this example of saltatory movement, the particles have little interaction with objects along the path while moving but may have significant interactions at the stopping points. The flows may provide mineral nutrients to plants at those points, for example, or may smother soil animals or seedlings. Thus, the primary importance of saltatory movement lies in the often major interactions between the dispersing object and objects at the stopping spots. In continuous movement such interactions are minimal, or are at least dispersed along the route and not concentrated at points.

The above example also emphasizes how landscape structure affects flows. If a single extensive plowed field with straight vertical furrows covers the hillside right down to the stream, the first heavy rain may carry particles long distances, even all the way to the stream. If, on the other hand, the farmer has done contour plowing, the rate of surface water runoff and erosion is slowed, and the silt does not move as far downhill. If in addition the farmer has relatively flat terraces on the hillside, or has hedgerows parallel to the contours of the hillside, the silt particles move even shorter distances with each rain. Three changes result from this added heterogeneity in landscape structure.

1. A change from continuous movement to saltatory movement of the particles.
2. With the increase in the number of stops along the route, an increase in the amount of interaction between the particles and the environment along the route.
3. A decrease in the rate of movement from hill to stream—in part due to more boundary crossings—from hours perhaps to years or even centuries.

Similarly, an animal moving continuously across a landscape generally has minimal impact on the landscape, while in saltatory animal movement a considerable amount of interaction often takes place at the stops. The animal may heavily browse the spot, trample it, fertilize it, nest in it, or be eaten by a predator on it.

These possible interactions suggest two important types of stops made by dispersing species. When individual animals arrive at a spot, remain for a brief period, and move on, the spot may be called a **rest stop** (Figure 10.2). In contrast, a spot that is colonized by a species—where the species arrives and successfully grows and reproduces—is called a **stepping stone** (Kimura and Weiss, 1964; MacArthur and Wilson, 1967). (In some cases an individual may remain a long time at a rest stop without reproducing, as when a single mammal makes a home, or a seed grows into a mature plant without producing flowers or cones.) What is significant about these two kinds of stops is that when a species uses a particular spot as a stepping stone, the species expands its distribution of successfully reproducing individuals. This provides a new source for further dispersing of individuals. Rest stops, in contrast, are only temporary locations for species (Figure 10.2). The spread of many plant species from South America

**Figure 10.2** *Leopard (*Panthera pardus*) using a cluster of savanna trees as a rest stop. Central Africa. (Courtesy of W. C. Johnson.)*

north across the Caribbean Sea has been made possible by the presence of a linear series of island stepping stones. A similar spread of mainland plant species to Hawaii or the Galapagos Islands has not taken place across the Pacific Ocean, where few stepping stones are present.

## MOVEMENT OF ANIMALS

### Home Range, Dispersal, and Migration

Animals in a landscape move in three ways—within a home range, in dispersal, and in migration (Swingland and Greenwood, 1983). The **home range** of an animal is the area around its home (e.g., nest, den, or burrow) that is used for feeding and other daily activities. Commonly, a pair of animals and their offspring share a home range, though in some species a larger group shares it. **Territory**, a similar concept, is used by many authors to refer to the area defended against intrusions by other individuals of the same species. When animals have defended territories, their home range is normally the larger area, as they commonly feed outside the defended limits.

**Animal dispersal** refers to the one-way movement of an individual from the home range where it was born to a new home range. The new home range is usually far from the origin, normally at a distance many times the diameter of the home range. Subadult animals leaving parents and setting up their own home ranges are the individuals most commonly involved in dispersal, though some adults also disperse in this manner. Dispersal may also extend the overall distribution range of a species. For example, the meadow vole (*Microtus pennsylvanicus*) extended its range rapidly into central Illinois (United States) when a superhighway was constructed (Getz et al., 1978). Apparently, the continuous grassy sides along the superhighway served as a conduit, where villages previously serving as breaks in the grassy corridors of smaller roads had prevented dispersal.

**Migration** is the cyclic movement of animals between separated areas that are used during different seasons. (Analogously, the diurnal vertical movement of zooplankton in bodies of water is often called migration.) Migrating species have adapted to climatic and other conditions associated with the changing seasons and thus tend to avoid unfavorable environmental conditions and to utilize favorable ones. Classic examples are the migration of vast numbers of birds between colder and warmer regions, and the hordes of caribou that migrate between the tundra and the edge of the boreal forest (see Figure 3.7) (Banfield, 1954; Clarke, 1940; Murie, 1951; Moreau, 1972; Griffin, 1973). The flows of some bats and butterflies from north to south and vice versa are equally impressive cases of what is called **latitudinal migration** (Figure 10.3) (Urquhart, 1960; Villa and Cockrum, 1962; Williams and Williams, 1970; Baker, 1978). Such migration commonly crosses several or many landscapes.

**Vertical migration,** the movement of animal species between higher and lower elevations in mountains, is also common and also involves the avoidance of unfavorable and selection of favorable conditions. In the Swiss Alps, for example, the European ibex (*Capra ibex* L.) feeds on alpine vegetation in summer and winters in low elevation meadows (ten Houte de Lange, 1978). Many bird species in the Rocky Mountains breed at high elevations and winter at low elevations (Snyder, 1950). Elk (*Cervus canadensis*), mule deer (*Odocoileus hemionus*) and other hoofed herbivores winter in large herds in low-elevation open areas. In early summer the herd breaks up. Small groups of animals follow snow melt up through several forest zones to the high-elevation open meadows. In autumn (Figure 10.4) they descend again to their winter forage area (Craighead et al., 1972; Murie, 1951). Similarly, in some mountainous landscapes domestic sheep are herded through valley systems from low elevation range in winter to high elevation range in summer.

Some winter-summer animal movements may be considered transitional between migration and home range movement. The home ranges of certain species are constricted during winter when travel is inhibited by snow. Conversely, some species have larger winter home ranges ne-

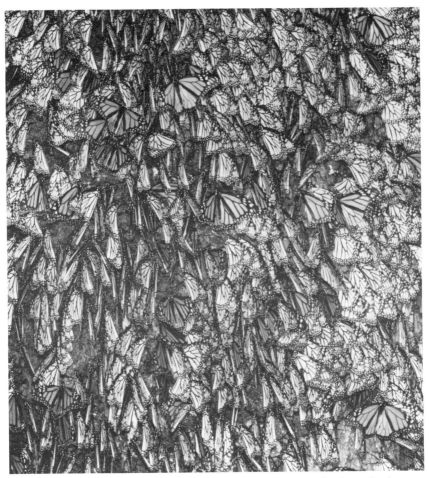

**Figure 10.3** *Monarch butterflies at their overwintering site after latitudinal migration. Masses of these butterflies* (Danaus plexippus: Lepidoptera) *may cover trees at this time, and indeed only tiny patches of tree trunk remain visible in the photograph. (George D. Lepp/BIO-TEC Images.)*

cessitated by the sparse distribution of food. In both cases, the den or nest is within both winter and summer home ranges. Other species simply move to different habitats within a landscape in winter and summer, in a process analogous to vertical migration. In Maine, for example, deer (*Odocoileus virginiana*) accumulate in cedar (*Thuja*) swamps during the winter because these swamps offer food availability, predator protection, and weather protection. Pheasants in Texas moved from wet depressions (playas) in winter, to cool-season crops in spring, and then to a mixture

**Figure 10.4** *A herbivore that undergoes vertical migration. This bull elk (*Cervus canadensis*) is bugling during the rutting season in autumn. Western United States (Len Rue, Jr.)*

of row crops, small grains, and wet depressions in summer and autumn (Whiteside and Guthery, 1983).

## Barriers and Conduits Perceived by Different Species

The movements of several mammal and bird species will now be examined in some detail to see what patterns emerge relative to landscape structure (Forman and Godron, 1984). We will focus on four species, chosen because they represent diverse types of animals and because information on them is available. Briefer accounts will be presented for six additional species. None of these studies had as its major objective determining how landscape structure affects animal movement. Therefore, we have extracted the following information from data presented and from comments made by the authors. Virtually none of the patterns pinpointed here has been demonstrated in the usual scientific sense of statistical significance. They were either observed a few times or suggested by the information published. The richness of suggested patterns linking landscape structure and function is intriguing, though.

The measurement techniques used included trapping, following tracks, field observations, and radiotelemetry. This last technique involves trapping an animal and attaching to it a tiny radiotransmitter (e.g., on a neck collar). The investigators, out of sight and hearing, follow the movement of the animal using portable radio receivers attuned to the transmitter signal. The investigators may be on the ground, in vehicles, or in aircraft, depending on how far and over what terrain the animal moves.

**Skunk (*Mephitis mephitis*).** The striped skunk (Figure 10.5), an omnivore widespread in North America, is famous for squirting out an intense putrid smell when alarmed. The animal lives in subterranean dens that it digs or that have previously been dug by other mammals. The information reported here comes primarily from studies in Illinois (west of the Chicago region) where cultivation predominates and there are scattered hayfields, farmyards, woodlots, hedgerows, and towns (Verts, 1967). Before European settlement the area was mainly prairie. The skunk dens are most common along hedgerows, where accumulated snow remains until late in spring.

Few skunks were recorded more than 1000 meters from their den, suggesting that the approximate home range of the species is less than a square kilometer. The maximum recorded distance traversed by an animal was 3600 m. The distance traversed varies considerably with the seasons. After breeding season in the spring, the male skunks traverse longer distances, feeding primarily on small mammals and other animals in the hedgerows because little food exists in the newly cultivated fields. During summer, the skunks stay closer to their dens where food is presumably more abundant. Again, in the autumn before the deep snows, they move primarily along hedgerows (Figure 10.6). Note in the figure that the skunk studied really only left the proximity of the hedgerows twice, both times in small corn (Zea) fields, and that the hay and oat (Avena) fields were essentially avoided.

The skunks' concentrated use of hedgerows between cultivated fields suggests that these animals may have been less common in the prairie before widespread agriculture was introduced in the 1850s. It also leads to the hypothesis that they would be more common in forested areas. To test this, the investigator cut out a square piece of paper equivalent to

**Figure 10.5** *A striped skunk* (Mephitis mephitis) *ready to spray its potent warning fluid. North America. (Leonard Lee Rue III.)*

16 hectares, and on a topographic map of northwestern Illinois, marked the distribution of large woods present into which the 16 hectare square would fit. The distribution of skunks (encountered in traps over a three-year period) was then compared with the distribution of large woods (that contain a forest interior environment). The hypothesis was rejected, as skunks were found to be most common in open landscape areas with few large woods.

However, the animals are found in all portions of the landscape and are not restricted to open areas. The investigator then examined the landscape at a finer spatial scale by comparing the locations of a particular skunk with specific fields and woods. Although at a broad scale the investigator had found skunks most common in open landscape areas, at this fine scale skunks were often found to live next to or even within woods. This fact illustrates how the effects of landscape structure on species—in this case, the affinity of skunks and woods—differ according to the scale being considered.

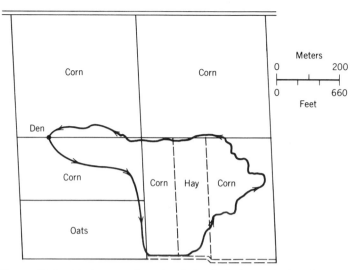

**Figure 10.6** *Movement of a striped skunk during a single winter night, as determined from tracks in snow. Solid lines are hedgerows; single dashed lines indicate borders of crops within a field; double solid lines indicate a road; and double dashed lines indicate a narrow dirt road. (From B. J. Verts,* The Biology of the Striped Skunk, *copyright 1967 by the Board of Trustees of the University of Illinois.)*

Trapping in the three kinds of fields present tended to confirm the results (see Figure 10.6). Skunks were found mainly in corn fields and were less common in hay and oat fields. The investigator hypothesizes that the corn field, with a high canopy and fairly open ground layer, provides good protection from both aerial and ground predators. In addition, plenty of large arthropod food items are present.

Finally, three types of areas, all related to landscape structure, seem to be poor habitats for skunks in Illinois. These are extensive forest, extensive corn field, and areas such as flood plains, where a high water table would cause inundation of dens. All three are examples of high landscape homogeneity. A heterogeneous landscape structure, combining at least two ecosystem types, appears necessary for this species of mammal.

**Red Fox (*Canis vulpes*).** The red fox, a widespread carnivore in North America (Figure 10.7), may have increased in abundance following the hunting of two other canines, the wolf (*Canis lupus*) and coyote (*C. latrans*). Like the skunks, the foxes live in subterranean dens and are nocturnal, but they feed almost entirely on small and medium-sized vertebrates. Storm et al. (1976) studied foxes for several years in an agri-

**Figure 10.7**  *The red fox* (Canis vulpes) *stalking small mammal prey. North America. (Leonard Lee Rue III.)*

cultural landscape in Minnesota, Iowa, and Illinois. It was similar to that of the skunk study but larger, with somewhat more woods, lakes, rivers, and small cities.

In this study, dens were found in all upland habitats except one, that is, near people. Only 8 of the 516 dens located were within 275 m of an occupied building. Dens were found in woods, corn fields, other grain fields, hay fields, pastures, hedgerows, and gravel pits. It appears that **remoteness,** in this case distance from buildings, is the prime limiting factor on the distribution of fox dens.

Home ranges did not overlap. If adjacent, they were usually separated by some distinct barrier such as a highway. The average area of a home range was about 4 × 2.4 km, several times larger than the skunks' home range, indicating that foxes have a larger grain size (Levins, 1968) than skunks. Home ranges were almost always elongated rather than round or square, a pattern that appears widespread for mammals.

In the fall and winter, subadult foxes and some adult foxes leave the home range (Figure 10.7) for reasons that are still unclear, move to a distant area that we cannot predict, and do all this using cues that we know little about. What we do know, based on ear-tagged foxes collected by hunters or from road kills, is how far they disperse. They disperse in all compass directions. The males average a straight-line distance of 31 km (maximum 211 + km), and the females average 11 km (maximum 108 km). The trip takes several days, and of course the distance actually traveled considerably exceeds the straight-line distance.

Radiotelemetry was used to track fox dispersal. At first glance, the fox routes look like drunken squiggles or random diffusion (Figure 10.8), but intriguing patterns are present. Let us follow a few specific dispersing foxes, imagining that we are up in a tiny plane or in a pickup truck with a huge pivoting antenna in back. It is of course nighttime. Snow is on the ground, and even in autumn, Minnesota nights can be bitterly cold.

The routes of two females led toward small cities, and in both cases the city caused a significant change in the direction of movement. Female no. 181 headed southeast toward the small city of Wyoming, Minnesota, and began moving erratically before reaching the city (Figure 10.8). She encountered a high fence along the superhighway just west of the city and circumvented it and the city by moving 1.6 km northeastward, before heading east and crossing the superhighway corridor. The other female, no. 189, traveling southeast toward the northern edge of Hugo, Minnesota, came within 150 m or so of the same superhighway (Figure 10.8). She then reversed her travel for about one-half a kilometer, rested for 10 minutes, proceeded south to the southern edge of Hugo, and crossed the superhighway. Both females continued to travel southeast (their original heading) after bypassing a city and a major highway corridor. Two other foxes, a subadult male and an adult male, also changed direction when each approached a town or small city. Built-up areas such as these towns or small cities apparently were barriers to movement across the landscape.

Lakes also altered the pattern of travel. Subadult male no. 161 was influenced by at least four lakes between Highways 152 and 55 (Figure 10.8). Subadult female no. 181 followed the southwestern boundary of a lake east of Wyoming, Minnesota and subadult male no. 183 traveled westward for nearly 1 kilometer along the northern shore of a lake. Apparently no fox swam across a lake. And so lakes also acted as barriers to be circumvented.

Creeks and rivers did not appear to be major deterrents to dispersal. Changes in movements did occur when the foxes encountered some rivers; their travel slowed and became more erratic until finally they swam the rivers. The widest rivers crossed included the 55-m wide Rum River, which was swum by foxes nos. 161 and 194 (Figure 10.8). Subadult male no. 161 also crossed the mighty Mississippi River, apparently using two islands in crossing. The longest swim was 82 m. In only one case did a river stop the movement of a fox. Male no. 191 arrived at the Rum River (55 m wide), spent several hours along the west bank, and then turned back in a southwesterly direction. It appears that streams, unlike cities and lakes, are not barriers, although rivers decrease the rate of movement of foxes across the landscape and the widest rivers do act as barriers.

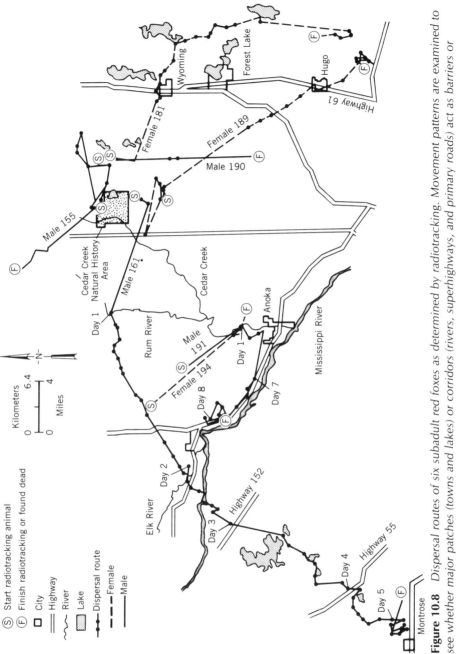

**Figure 10.8** Dispersal routes of six subadult red foxes as determined by radiotracking. Movement patterns are examined to see whether major patches (towns and lakes) or corridors (rivers, superhighways, and primary roads) act as barriers or conduits. Dots along routes indicate radio contacts (from Storm et al., 1976). (© of The Wildlife Society.)

The effect of these distinctive physical features or landscape elements on the rate of movement was specifically examined by comparing the rates where barriers were present to those where they were absent (Figure 10.9). Four of the six foxes studied moved at about the same average rate whether in the presence or absence of such landscape elements (Figure 10.9). The other two moved on the average more slowly through land containing barriers. In addition, the foxes appeared to move more slowly when they approached a potential barrier than when they left it.

These foxes moved in a clearly saltatory, not continuous, manner along their route. They were moving, on the average, approximately 85% of the time during the night and were stopped about 15% of the time. The stops were generally 20 to 60 minutes in duration and were used for rest or a variety of activities. Stops were more frequent when approaching cities and major rivers. For an unexplained reason a few animals stopped for one or a few days at a spot before moving on.

One of the most distinctive and surprising findings of the study is that the foxes avoid corridors. None of the foxes followed along the primary landscape corridors such as rivers, major roads, or superhighways (nor did they move parallel to the corridor in the adjacent matrix area). The animals may well have used small dirt roads or paths, but no information is available on this. The avoidance of larger roads is made further apparent by the locations of the daytime beds of these nocturnal creatures. Beds were always recorded more than 92 m away from roads.

Except for the rivers, lakes, and cities, fox movement through the landscape appeared to be generally independent of its structure (at least, as we perceive landscape structure). This inference is based on other data

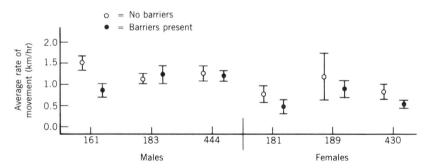

**Figure 10.9** *Rates of fox movement in areas with and without potential major barriers. Three males and three females (each individual is numbered) were studied in areas with and without towns, lakes, rivers, superhighways, and primary roads. The vertical lines indicate statistical standard errors. For an individual animal, if vertical lines overlap, there is no significant difference in rate of movement when barriers are present or absent (from Storm et al., 1976). (© of The Wildlife Society.)*

that show a rate of movement approximately equal in wooded and open areas. In addition, foxes moved at approximately the same rates across both Minnesota—where there are considerably more woods, lakes, wooded stream corridors, and hedgerows—and Iowa, where there is more open area.

Only five times were foxes recorded within 92 m of a farmyard at night, and no fox was detected crossing one. Thus, it appears that not only are large human population centers such as cities a barrier, but the numerous farmyards scattered somewhat regularly across agricultural landscapes are also small barriers that must be detoured.

Apparently, major corridors do not function as conduits but do function as filters, often decreasing the rate of flow or, in extreme cases, blocking passage.

The rather extensive data of ear-tagged foxes collected by hunters or as road kills suggest an additional insight into the effect of a barrier. The Mississippi River where it separates Illinois from Iowa is quite wide, about 0.5 to 0.8 km across. Usually the river remains unfrozen in the autumn until after the fox dispersal period is completed, and foxes remain close to their winter dens after this period. There are no reports of ear-tagged foxes crossing the big river in this area. Thus, the river serves as a barrier to gene flow between fox populations on opposite sides of the river. Iowa foxes breed among themselves, and Illinois foxes breed among themselves, but the mixing of Iowa and Illinois fox genes is at best a rare event.

Interestingly, this barrier apparently has resulted in differences between Iowa and Illinois foxes. In a variety of characteristics of the cranium, the Illinois individuals tended to be slightly larger. Such a study does not conclusively demonstrate, but does suggest, that this barrier within the landscape has led to populations on opposite sides of the river being genetically more different than populations on one side of the river (Storm et al., 1976).

**Desert Bighorn Sheep (*Ovis canadensis*).** Shy, hoofed herbivores with impressively thick horns (Figure 10.10), desert bighorn sheep move around in groups of about four or five in the Nevada (United States) desert, where they were radiotracked (Leslie and Douglas, 1979). Their home ranges are about 3 to 6 km across, and aggregations of 50 to 60 animals occur only around the scattered permanent water sources.

Almost all animals remain within 3 km of a permanent water source, except after a heavy rain. Then they move farther away, using temporary water sources and feeding on the rejuvenated forage, especially along desert stream beds.

In addition to the spots with permanent water, two landscape features appear critical to the movements of the species. The stream beds serve

**Figure 10.10** *Desert bighorn sheep (Ovis canadensis) ewe and ram on cliff in typical rugged terrain in the western United States. (Len Rue, Jr.)*

as conduits both for foraging and for escape from predators. Secondly, the presence of steep rugged terrain apparently provides necessary shady spots during the heat of the desert day. In the entire study, animals were never observed more than 1.3 km away from a refuge of steep rugged land.

One permanent water source only 0.5 km from rugged terrain was little used, however, because some of the area between the water and the steep ridge was kept open for a network of power-lines. The absence of cover meant that only one entrance and escape route to the water existed, an inadequate landscape structure for the bighorn sheep. In another area, the sheep crossed a highway and entered a tract of housing, suggesting that the importance of water to the animals exceeded their need for remoteness.

In summary, desert bighorn sheep are highly sensitive to landscape structure. They require a number of landscape elements in proximity, and use stream bed corridors for movement.

**River Otter (*Lutra canadensis*).** These cute playful mammals (Figure 10.11) are known for their apparent enjoyment of sliding down river banks and landing in the water with a splash. They were studied in a forested high mountain area of Idaho (United States) that is permeated with logging roads (Melquist and Hornocker, 1983). The otters feed primarily on fish and have basically linear home ranges (that may be branched) associated with rivers and streams in valleys. Home ranges are commonly 30 to 80 km long.

**Figure 10.11** *River otter (Lutra canadensis) ready for a dive. North America. (Leonard Lee Rue III.)*

The river otter appeared to use landscape features in its movement. Within the home range, the animals only crossed short distances overland, such as across peninsulas formed by stream meanders. They did traverse meadows as wide as several hundred meters across, although in going overland, they usually followed ditches and low order streams as much as possible.

Two individuals involved in dispersal were radiotracked. A male otter

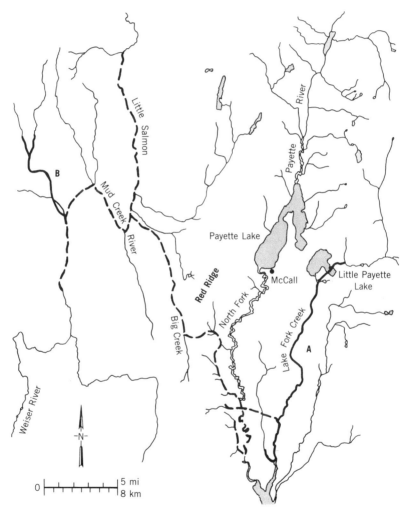

**Figure 10.12** *River otter dispersal in mountainous terrain. A is the birth home range; B is the new home range; the dashed line is the dispersal route of a male, based on 162 daily transmitter locations in Idaho (United States) (from Melquist and Hornocker, 1983.) (© The Wildlife Society.)*

travelled 104 km away from the home range in 30 days, a straight-line distance of only 32 km (Figure 10.12). He generally followed major stream drainage patterns but did not go up to the headwaters of a stream and cross a ridge to the headwaters of a stream on the other side. The headwater areas at high elevations often have deep snow and little food and are inhospitable to the species except in midsummer. Instead, the otter climbed over two major ridges (3 and 5 km wide, respectively), and two smaller ridges, in each case by going directly from one major stream to another. A female that traveled 192 km ended up with a new home range adjacent to her original home range. She also did not cross major ridges and did not go to the stream headwaters. Often she stopped in an area for a few days before continuing. A third radiotracked otter did not disperse but simply extended its home range along valleys, without crossing a ridge or penetrating to headwaters.

The home range of an otter changed markedly over the seasons, and the use of different landscape features within a home range changed sharply from winter to summer. In short, landscape structure exerts a major influence on the movements of river otters.

**Six Other Species in Brief.**  The Canada goose (*Branta canadensis*), a large waterfowl (Figure 10.13a), apparently requires a number of landscape features in proximity for overwintering (Raveling, 1969a, 1969b). These birds roost at night on open water in lakes, feed in surrounding fields in the morning and late afternoon, and rest on mudflats or shorelines in midday. Protected coves are also required by them on windy days.

The yellow-bellied marmot (*Marmota flaviventris*) is a medium-sized mammal species (Figure 10.13b). It has relatively straight narrow home ranges associated with the straight valleys and steep mountain slopes at high elevations in the Colorado Rocky Mountains (Shirer and Downhower, 1969). Some evidence is available that a river is a barrier to movement, and the riverside apparently is not used as a conduit.

The woodchuck or groundhog (*Marmota monax*), (Figure 10.13c), a low elevation relative of the marmot and similar to it in size, digs clusters of burrow systems. This species apparently does not move between two clusters when they are separated by a shallow gulley area. In contrast, considerable movement takes place between clusters without an intervening shallow gulley area.

The white-tailed deer (*Odocoileus virginianus*), a large mammal species (Figure 10.13d), has a home range about 1 to 3 km across in a mixed farmland and forested area of Minnesota (United States) (Rongstad and Tester, 1969). In this area the deer generally have separate summer and winter ranges, some 15 to 25 km apart. The summer ranges are widely dispersed over the landscape, but the winter ranges of animals are concentrated in white cedar swamps (*Thuja occidentalis*) that are dense,

**Figure 10.13**  *Five additional species studied for movement patterns. (a) Canada goose (Branta canadensis) on eggs and nest by pond (North America). (Leonard Lee Rue III.) (b) Hoary marmot (Marmota caligata) with view from the alpine zone in Mt. Rainier National Park, Washington (United States). (Bob and Ira Spring.) (c) Woodchuck or groundhog (Marmota monax) surveying its farm, (eastern United States). (Leonard Lee Rue III.) (d) White-tailed deer (Odocoileus virginianus) with fawn 12 minutes old (eastern United States). (Leonard Lee Rue III.) (e) Ruffed grouse (Bonasa umbellus) ready to fly (eastern North America). (Leonard Lee Rue III.)*

(d)

(c)

(e)

**Figure 10.13** (*continued*)

evergreen, extensive, and relatively homogeneous. Observations on movement between summer and winter grounds indicate that animals crossed paved roads, and moved short distances along snow plowed roads. Some crossed major streams on the ice, yet others did not cross. The deer did not use either roads or streams or the edges of adjacent vegetation as significant conduits. They stopped periodically but still pursued a relatively direct route with little meandering.

Two female white-tailed deer radiotracked during a Minnesota winter spent most of their time in a white cedar swamp (Tester and Heezen, 1965; Heezen and Tester, 1967). Each day they moved out either once or twice to upland forest and open fields. Hence, even in deep snow the animals used the cluster of three primary ecosystem types present nearly every day.

Wolf packs (*Canis lupus*) (see Figure 9.11) were radiotracked in a large flat coniferous forest area with bogs in northwestern Minnesota (Fritts and Mech, 1981). The packs generally were made up of four to six animals and had a home range or territory about 10 to 40 km across. The authors note, "Within all territories there are areas in which the wolves were seldom or never found. Generally they corresponded to the treeless marshes or to homogeneous conifer cover." Later, they report that ". . . near the center of Vacuum Pack (a specific named wolf pack) was a 50 km$^2$ marsh in which the pack was never found" (Fritz and Mech, 1981). Thus, certain large homogeneous patches are inhospitable for the wolf, and must have considerable influence on movement patterns.

Marshes and conifer swamps function as natural buffer zones between many adjacent wolf packs. Wolf activity was generally greatest around wolf dens and rendezvous sites, but in winter was greatest just outside deer wintering areas such as cedar swamps. Pack territory boundaries were not fixed, despite the natural landscape features of marshes and swamps. Boundaries varied with changes in pack size and the appearance or disappearance of adjacent packs. Boundaries of wolf territories with high perimeter-to-area ratios were less stable than those of more rounded territories.

During dispersal, wolves readily crossed farmland and sometimes remained in forest near it. Roads through the landscape were heavily scent-marked with urine during the snowy winter and intensively used as travel routes in both winter and summer. Dispersal routes were perhaps primarily influenced by the distribution of pack territories. Boundaries of territories and strips between territories turned out to be major dispersal routes. Such areas were generally suboptimal habitats such as marshes, swamps, or places near farmland. Frozen drainage ditches were often used for travel in winter, and the banks above them in summer.

Deer and moose were the primary food of the wolves. Significantly, more deer kills per unit area were found in the interior of a wolf territory than in the edge portions of territories. Predation on farm livestock such as calves, sheep, turkeys, cows, and geese occurred but apparently rarely. Although wolves would cross fields containing livestock and indeed have dens within a few kilometers of the fields, large wild herbivores were hunted in lieu of livestock.

The ruffed grouse (*Bonasa umbellus*), a game bird (Figure 10.13e), had a home range in Minnesota about 500 to 800 m across, that tended to be small in winter and larger in spring (Marshall and Kupa, 1963). One male bird that was radiotracked always roosted at night in patches of spruce-fir (*Picea-Abies*) and commonly fed during the day in aspen forest (*Populus*). The birds readily crossed roads and lowland-upland boundaries. Neither landscape feature was a conduit, as the bird seemed to totally avoid moving along them. The birds readily crossed lowlands 50 to 100 m in width, apparently moving at a faster average rate than when in the uplands.

## Patterns Based on the Radiotracking Studies

We can now summarize the patterns for the 10 species just discussed and draw conclusions from the results. *Inhospitable patches* in the landscape, such as marshes, swamps, towns, or lakes were generally circumvented by a species (e.g., skunk, fox, wolf). **Hospitableness** refers to the suitability or avoidance of an area by a species. Thus, large homogeneous areas are inhospitable in many cases, although this may be more because of the remoteness of ecosystems (e.g., fox) than because of homogeneity *per se.*

More than one landscape element in proximity (e.g., the cluster-of-ecosystem concept—see Chapter 1) is required by many species (e.g., skunk, bighorn sheep, goose, white-tailed deer, wolf). Evidence of animal flows among several nearby patch types is present in many studies using a variety of methods (Bider, 1968; Wellington et al., 1975; Stinner et al., 1977; Orians and Pearson, 1978; Thompson et al., 1979; Howe, 1979; Karr, 1982; Karr and Freemark, 1983; Middleton and Merriam, 1983; Fahrig et al., 1983; see also the natural resource management example in Chapter 14). This pattern of multi-ecosystem use suggests that convergency points and lines (Chapter 6) (Harris, 1981) are of particular importance in landscapes.

As corridors, two-lane paved roads are not barriers to relatively large animals (e.g., fox, grouse). With few exceptions, these larger roads and the edges (verges) adjacent them do not serve as conduits, while smaller roads perhaps do. Hedgerows serve as conduits (e.g., skunk). Streams are generally not barriers (e.g., fox, deer), but large rivers are (e.g., fox), and rivers that are crossed decrease the rate of movement (e.g., fox). Stream and river corridors generally do not function as significant conduits (e.g., marmot, fox), although for certain species they may do so (bighorn sheep in dry stream beds; wolf on frozen streams; and river otter when feeding). The barrier effect may lead to population differentiation, that is, genetic differences on opposite sides of the barrier (e.g., fox).

Home ranges are usually elongated and sometimes linear (e.g., wolf, otter) (Knowlton, 1960; Mitchell, 1961; Stumpf and Mohr, 1962; Jennrich and Turner, 1969; Metzgar, 1972; Koeppl et al., 1975; Smith, 1983). Barriers between home ranges such as gullies, streams, marshes, swamps, and fields are common (e.g., woodchuck, wolf, fox), but some home range boundaries fluctuate according to population rather than landscape characteristics (e.g., wolf). Seasonal changes generally cause changes in home range boundaries and may result in twice-yearly seasonal migrations between summer and winter grounds (e.g., otter, deer). Saltatory movement is prevalent, with pauses of minutes, hours, or days (e.g., deer, fox). Alternate routes or loops may be required by some species (e.g., bighorn sheep). Dispersal routes are sometimes funneled into *strips between home ranges* (e.g., wolf).

Unusual features (or "hot spots") in a landscape play particularly important roles in landscape functioning (e.g., permanent water spots for bighorn sheep; lakes for geese; large cedar swamps for wintering deer). Since the grain sizes of animal species differ, landscape features affect each species differently.

Until more species are known relative to use of landscape features, in landscape planning and management it is best to enumerate all the species of interest and determine their expected responses individually. At present, generalizations about movements of communities of animals should be considered hypotheses (Bider, 1968). Nevertheless, there are some patterns of primary interest here, which should be considered when evaluating the relationship of any species to the landscape. Landscape structure clearly has a major effect on the habits and movements of animals.

## MOVEMENT OF PLANTS

Without the limitations of wings or feet, plants have evolved a wide range of ways of moving from place to place. A mature plant, of course, does not move about but produces reproductive *propagules* (or diaspores) such as seeds, fruits, or spores, which disperse to other sites. Hence, the species moves, or "migrates," through reproduction. **Plant dispersal** refers to the process of propagule movement, and a species is only considered to have spread if it successfully colonizes or becomes established at a new site.

Plants get "free rides" by taking advantage of both mass flow and locomotion forces. In fact, we recognize a series of propagule types that differ by their distinctive adaptations for each of the dispersal mechanisms (Ridley, 1930; Dansereau, 1957; Van der Pijl, 1969). Maple (*Acer*), pine (*Pinus*), and dandelion (*Taraxacum*) have wind-blown propagules or *anemochores*. Many riverside or coastal plants produce *hydrochores* that are dispersed by water. Animal-dispersed berries and other fleshy fruits are *zoochores*. Heavy fruits such as walnuts (*Juglans*), and many tropical forest species, are *barochores* that disperse by gravity, although animals may also play a role. A few plants even disperse seeds from fruits that explode. Recently, a botanist (Gleason and Cronquist, 1964) collecting tropical plants returned to camp and was met by an excited field assistant. "Chief—you know that big pod? I just look at him and he say 'POW'!"

The result of this richness in dispersal abilities is that the distances crossed by plants vary widely. **Long-distance dispersal** generally means going to a different landscape altogether. Coconuts float across oceans, seeds are carried thousands of kilometers on the feet and feathers of ducks, and winds loft lightweight propagules and insects over mountain ranges. **Short-distance dispersal,** in contrast, is usually measured in meters to hundreds of meters within a landscape. This travel often involves heavier seeds, terrestrial animals, or nonmigrating birds.

Three general types of plant movement appear to occur no matter what the dispersal mechanism or distance travelled. First, *species distribution boundaries fluctuate* with short-term, usually cyclic environmental changes. Thus, year-to-year precipitation differences in a grassland, or temperature differences in a temperate forest, often produce relatively small or local expansions and contractions in a species range. Second, long-term environmental change makes *species go extinct, adapt, or move.* For example, many tree species have moved across temperate regions in response to climatic changes since the last glaciation (Heusser, 1974; Davis, 1976; Webb, 1981; Delcourt et al., 1983; Huntley and Birks, 1983).

The third plant movement pattern is seen when a *species arrives in a new area and spreads widely* (Elton, 1958). Such species have a galaxy of names—alien, invader, nonnative, introduced, adventive, and exotic. Usually such a species spreads rapidly, as did the blight-fungus (*Endothia parasitica*), which wiped out the extensive chestnut forests (*Castanea dentata*) of North America in about five years. Some invading species have a large economic impact, as when the prickly-pear cactus (*Opuntia*) decimated the prime grazing areas of Australia. Sometimes the species are purposefully introduced by people, as was the North American salt marsh cord-grass (*Spartina alterniflora*) that was planted in English marshes and then hybridized with the native species to produce a new aggressive species (*S. townsendii*). Often the species are introduced inadvertently, as was the purple loosestrife (*Lythrum salicaria*), which may have arrived in a shipment of pulpwood from Eurasia and is now spreading across wet areas of the northeastern United States. Since such nonnative species are so prevalent and important, we will look at one in more detail to see what landscape structural characteristics have played a role in its success (or tragedy, from the perspective of the native flora). Curiously, there is little documentation of how landscape structure affects invading species.

## The Cheatgrass Invasion of the American West

A huge 400,000-km² area that separates the Rocky Mountains from the Sierra Nevada/Cascade Mountains to their west was covered before 1850 with natural vegetation in cool grassland and shrubland (or steppe) landscapes (Mack, 1981). From British Columbia south to Nevada and Utah, wheatgrass (*Agropyron spicatum*) and fescue (*Festuca idahoensis*) grasses predominated in moister portions, and sagebrush (*Artemisia tridentata*), rabbitbrush (*Chrysothamnus* spp.), and antelopebrush (*Purshia tridentata*) shrubs in drier portions. The grasses were low perennial carpetlike plants. Herds of hoofed herbivores were sparse or absent in these landscapes.

From the 1850s to the 1870s, gold and silver were discovered in this intermountain region. What draws people faster? Prospective miners flocked in, and cattle were driven into the region for food, followed by sheep and feral horses, which established trails. The livestock quickly grazed away patches of the fragile grass cover. By the 1880s cattle trail networks were extensive and conspicuous in the landscapes. Then railroads and homesteading arrived. The soil was plowed, wheat (*Triticum*) was planted, and within a decade wheat fields were extensive (Figure 10.14).

Meanwhile, nonnative species arrived and spread. One was cheatgrass (*Bromus tectorum*), an annual from Asia and Europe, where it grows on disturbed sites and sand dunes. Cheatgrass was first found in the 1880s in a wheat-growing area and is presumed to have arrived as a contaminant

**Figure 10.14** *Cultivated wheat fields (*Triticum*) with native wheatgrass (*Agropyron spicatum*) windbreaks. Before the nineteenth-century gold rush, wheatgrass was a widespread dominant species. Barriers of it are now maintained to control wind erosion of the soil and to trap snow to increase stored soil water. The snow here is from an early autumn storm. The average wheatgrass windbreak is about 1.2 m high, and the snow accumulates across the intervals between windbreaks at a fairly uniform depth of about 60 cm. Roosevelt County, Montana (United States). (Courtesy of USDA Soil Conservation Service.)*

in a grain shipment. It arrived again in a government seed shipment that was planted at an experimental research farm in the 1890s (Figure 10.15a). Around 1900, the cheatgrass distribution was composed of small local populations mainly in eastern Washington state (Figure 10.15a,b). Most populations were along railroads and cattle trails. In the two new patch types introduced (rangeland and grain cultivation) which were spreading in the landscape, the species was only scattered.

From 1905 to 1914, the cheatgrass extended its range, and became locally abundant from eastern Washington to the Great Salt Lake area of Utah (Figure 10.15c). At least three factors favored this major spread. First, the seeds moved along railroad or cattle trail corridors mixed in grain shipments, in discarded cattle bedding straw, in dung (where seeds remain viable), in packing straw, and attached to the fur of the animals. Second, wheat threshing machines left piles of chaff in the fields. The cattle fed on them in autumn and then spread the cheatgrass seeds in their movements. Third, further farm mechanization converted much of the summer wheat cultivation to winter wheat, which required autumn plowing and favored the autumn-germinating cheatgrass. In fact, cheat-

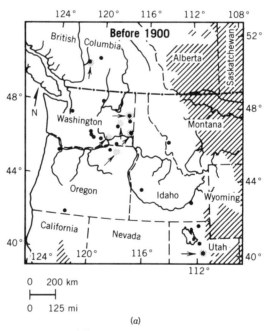

(a)

**Figure 10.15** *Cheatgrass invasion of the Intermountain West region of the United States from 1890 to 1980. Seven locations indicated with arrows are known for this nonnative species before 1900.* Bromus tectorum *(from Mack, 1981). (Courtesy of R. Mack and Elsevier Science Publishers B.V.)*

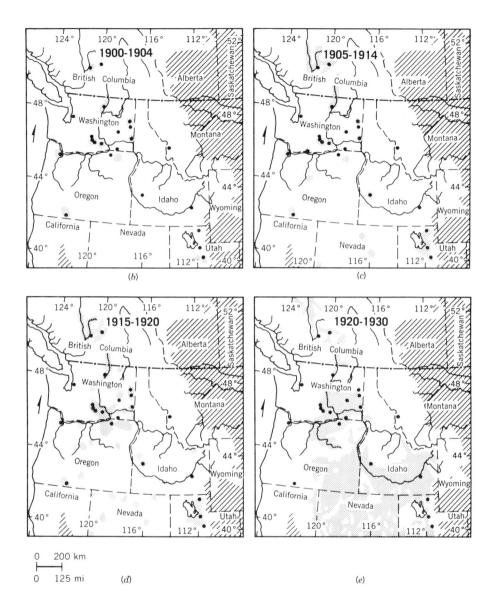

0 200 km
0 125 mi      (d)

(e)

grass seeds persist in the soil, and the species often grows up after winter wheat is harvested in midsummer. This phenomenon led some farmers to conclude that their wheat had degenerated into a weed and thus had "cheated" the farmer.

From 1915 to 1930, cheatgrass became a predominant weed from British Columbia to Nevada (Figure 10.15d,e). It now was abundant in both cultivated fields and other disturbed sites. Finally, from 1930 to

1980 the species expanded to its present range "like a group of coalescing leopard spots" (Mack, 1981). The original dominant, wheatgrass (*Agropyron*) (Figure 10.14), largely disappeared over much of the region.

This spread of a nonnative species, with slow initial growth followed by rapid expansion, exemplified the characteristic exponential or J-shaped growth pattern. The wildlife biologist Leopold (1941) described it this way: "One simply woke up one fine spring to find the range dominated by a new weed."

What can we learn from this grass? The species initially got a toehold in a foreign environment on disturbed sites. It spread considerable distances along corridors. It spread locally into newly-formed patches in the landscape, where it then became a landscape dominant. It was "preadapted" to colonize disturbed sites; that is, before it arrived it contained the necessary genetic adaptations to grow in such places. The species outcompeted and replaced the fescue (*Festuca*) species, which apparently were the native disturbed site colonizers (a process called functional displacement). The native species could not adapt fast enough in the face of a double onslaught, new disturbances, and a superior competitor. Finally, cheatgrass had escaped from its own natural controls in Asia and Europe. No competitor, herbivore, or parasite was present in its new environment to control the invader.

### Australian Eucalypt versus California Pine

Monterrey pine (*Pinus radiata*) is planted on over a million hectares around the world, yet grows natively in only three tiny spots totalling 4,000 ha perched on the California coast (Burdon and Chilvers, 1977). In most of the plantation areas (Figure 10.16), including Australia, pine grows faster and straighter than in its native habitat. There is a certain irony in this, because Australia is the cradle for over 200 eucalypt (*Eucalyptus*) species, and these species are planted even more widely around the world. In California, where eucalypt trees have been widely planted, it is said that the introduced trees grow better there than in their native Australia. Soil and climate in both native and introduced areas are extremely diverse and are generally not considered major causes for the above pattern in either species. The irony remains a puzzle to be pieced together in the future, but biological factors such as native parasites, herbivores, and competitors are probably a keystone.

To find out how the pine can invade a natural forest ecosystem, a study was done of a eucalypt forest next to a Monterrey pine plantation in the Brindabella Mountains of southeastern Australia (Burdon and Chilvers, 1977). Over a 20-year period, pine seedlings and saplings became abundantly established in the native eucalypt forest, but very few eucalypt seedlings, apparently, could invade the pine plantation. The pine seed-

**Figure 10.16** *Monterrey pine (Pinus radiata) growing as a nonnative forest plantation near Rotoroua, North Island, New Zealand. In this forest (left, and in the distance) it grows some five times faster than in its native California. (Photograph courtesy of the New Zealand Tourist Office.)*

lings were most common near the pine stand and steadily decreased to a low density at 160-m distance, with almost none found beyond 500 m. Pine seedlings and saplings tended to grow in little clusters rather than in even or random distribution through the forest, unlike most of the eucalypt trees. Finally, some evidence was found that the invading pines were inhibiting the eucalypt seedlings in the eucalypt forest.

Clearly the study does not solve the overall puzzle, but it does provide a few insights, and challenges us to think more about the questions of invasions of plants and animals (Elton, 1958). Unlike cheatgrass, which invaded via disturbed sites, Monterrey pine is successfully invading a native, relatively homogeneous ecosystem. It spreads in little clusters that outcompete the native species. Once established, the pine also resists invasion by the native species. The investigators note that infrequent individual pines, perhaps carried by birds or vehicles, are scattered broadly through the mountain range. It would be nice to know the routes taken by the seeds that produced such trees, and whether the species will reproduce locally and eventually form "coalescing leopard spots." The study examined invasion of a relatively homogeneous patch. We need to know how such patterns apply to a strongly heterogeneous surface, and at the scale of a landscape.

## Forest Species in Hedgerows

In unusual cases, vegetation patches themselves may move over part of a landscape under the influence of wind (Watt, 1947; Marr, 1977). Much more common, however, is the movement of plant species from patch to patch by means of the dispersal of seeds (Ranney and Johnson, 1977; DeAngelis et al., 1980). A key question—what route do such seeds take—has important landscape management implications. Are corridors critical to this movement (Nip-Van der Voort et al., 1979; Wegner and Merriam, 1979) or not (Pollard et al., 1974)?

A distinctive structural characteristic of most agricultural landscapes is a network of hedgerows among scattered woodlots. To determine whether this network is important in the movement of plant species between woodlots, Baudry and Forman (unpublished data) studied the distribution of forest interior herb species in New Jersey (United States) hedgerows. The focus was on intersections of hedgerows, where a cluster of trees forming a mini-node provides a microenvironment in which certain forest interior species might grow.

Intersections, however, are formed by hedgerows of various widths, and (as described in Chapter 4) forest herbs are highly sensitive to forest width. Therefore, we might hypothesize an interaction between the effects of width and intersections, such that only certain intersections would be effective as mini-nodes containing forest herbs.

Such a pattern was found for the two most abundant forest herbs in the hedgerows, jewelweed (*Impatiens*) and avens (*Geum*). In the narrowest hedgerows (< 8 m wide), the species were absent or nearly so even at intersections. In medium-width (8 to 12 m) hedgerows, a significant *intersection effect*—ecological conditions altered by the presence of an intersection—was present for both species; that is, they were significantly more abundant near intersections. In wide (> 12 m) hedgerows, the intersection effect was only present for jewelweed. Avens grew in all wide hedgerows, so no intersection effect was present here. Thus, the hypothesis was supported, because an interaction between the width effect and the intersection effect was determined for both species.

Three basic patterns of species distribution in hedgerows near intersections appear possible. If species are moving continuously along hedgerows, we would expect patterns such as those in Figure 10.17a. These patterns suggest that species enter the sample area from the hedgerow on the left. On the other hand, if species move longer distances by skipping past some length of hedgerow—saltatory movement—we would

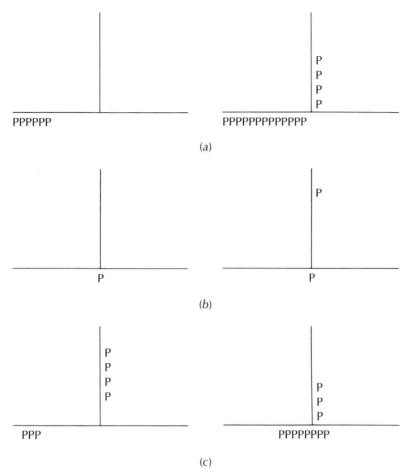

**Figure 10.17** *Hypothesized movement patterns of forest plant species from woods to woods through a hedgerow network (a) Continuous movement, (b) saltatory movement with no local spread, and (c) saltatory movement with local spread. Lines represent hedgerow intersections in T form; P is the location of a plant along a hedgerow (From J. Baudry and R. Forman, unpublished.)*

expect the patterns of Figures 10.17b and 10.17c. Figure 10.17b represents a species that successfully arrived and survived at a point in the network. Figure 10.17c represents a species that arrived, survived, and then spread locally around a point in the network. (An alternative hypothesis, that all the species distributions are remnants of former widespread distributions in the hedgerow network, is considered highly unlikely in this location).

Trying to understand the process of plant species movement across the New Jersey landscape, the investigators looked for evidence of continuous colonization along hedgerows, saltatory movement, and saltatory movement with subsequent local spread. First, for each of ten T-shaped hedgerow intersections, they mapped the distributions of all ten forest herbs frequently encountered within 100 m of an intersection point. For each species on each intersection, they then classified the distribution pattern as one of the three alternatives in Figure 10.17.

No forest herb species near any intersection showed evidence of crossing the landscape by continuous movement along hedgerows (Table 10.1) (i.e., none showed the pattern in Figure 10.17a). Instead, the patterns suggested that forest herb species spread by a saltatory process. The majority of the species manifested saltatory movement without subsequent local spread (Figure 10.17b). However, over a third of the saltatory patterns had clusters of individuals, suggesting that the species may have subsequently spread locally within the intersection (Figure 10.17c).

These distribution patterns of forest herbs in a New Jersey hedgerow network, plus additional evidence collected on woody plant seedlings, indicate primarily saltatory rather than continuous movement of the plants across a landscape, and subsequent local spread of some species in specific suitable spots. In the New Jersey landscape, these spots are wide hedgerows and intersections of intermediate and wide hedgerows.

Other studies have presented evidence relating to continuous colonization of hedgerows. Uniform movement of several animal species along hedgerows, presumably in numbers significantly higher than in adjacent fields, is reported (McAtee, 1945; Wegner and Merriam, 1979; Bull et al., 1976), though not all studies support this conclusion (Pollard et al., 1974; Sinclair et al., 1967). The limited evidence available for plants suggests that few if any forest species move along hedgerows (Pollard et al., 1974; Helliwell, 1975). The difference between this conclusion for plants and the results found in the New Jersey study probably has to do with width effect. The earlier studies were done primarily in managed shrub hedgerows, commonly about 1.5 to 2 m wide. The present results indicate few forest herbs grow in hedgerows narrower than 8 m, and therefore narrow hedgerows would normally be unsuitable routes for such plants moving across a landscape.

The distribution patterns encountered in New Jersey appear to be related to the mechanisms of microclimatic modification and dispersal. Hedgerow intersections and wide hedgerows contain a significantly more mesic microclimate than do narrow hedgerows or surrounding fields (Pollard et al., 1974; Guyot and Verbrugghe, 1976) and thus support certain forest interior species that arrive. Dispersal of many of these species is by the birds and mammals that commonly move along hedgerows (Wegner and Merriam, 1979; McDonnell and Stiles, 1983). Thus seeds are moved, for example, hundreds of meters from a woods (Schuster,

TABLE 10.1 **Apparent hedgerow colonization patterns for forest herbs.**

| Species | Continuous Movement Along Hedgerow | Saltatory Movement with No Local Spread | Saltatory Movement with Local Spread | Pattern Intermediate or Unclear | Species Absent |
|---|---|---|---|---|---|
| Avens (Geum canadense) | 0 | 3 | 7 | 0 | 0 |
| Jewelweed (Impatiens capensis) | 0 | 5 | 3 | 1 | 1 |
| Bedstraw (Galium aparine) | 0 | 5 | 2 | 0 | 3 |
| Buttercup (Ranunculus abortivus) | 0 | 2 | 2 | 1 | 5 |
| Jack-in-the-pulpit (Arisaema triphyllum) | 0 | 4 | 0 | 0 | 6 |
| False Solomon's seal (Smilacina racemosa) | 0 | 3 | 0 | 1 | 6 |
| Enchanter's nightshade (Circaea quadrisculata) | 0 | 1 | 1 | 1 | 7 |
| Solomon's seal (Polygonatum biflorum) | 0 | 1 | 0 | 1 | 8 |
| Black snakeroot (Sanicula gregaria) | 0 | 0 | 1 | 1 | 8 |
| Spring beauty (Claytonia virginica) | 0 | 0 | 0 | 1 | 9 |
| Total | 0 | 24 | 16 | 7 | 53 |

NOTE: Species distributions near each of ten T-intersections were mapped and compared with the three alternative colonization patterns of Figure 10.17. The table gives the number of intersections that fit each colonization pattern. (Unpublished data of Baudry and Forman.)

1950; Chettleburgh, 1952; Ranney and Johnson, 1977; Darley-Hill and Johnson, 1981), and if they are dropped in one of these two special microclimatic sites, will give rise to the pattern of forest herb diversity encountered.

In conclusion, we are impressed with the importance of studying not only hedgerows but hedgerow networks (Forman and Baudry, 1984). The interaction between hedgerows to produce a mini-node intersection, and the important spatial relationship between a hedgerow and woods in facilitating movement across a landscape, emphasize that a landscape is more than the sum of its parts. Understanding the spatial structure is fundamental to understanding landscape functioning, and to date we have astonishingly few structural studies or concepts to guide us in studying function in landscape ecology.

## SOME SPECIES MOVEMENTS IN AGRICULTURE AND PEST CONTROL

The movements of animals in grazing systems offer an opportunity to examine the transport of nutrients across a landscape pattern (Woodmansee, 1979; Risser et al., 1984). Nutrients in rangelands are transported among patches by four principal agents: large animals, water, wind, and people (via supplemental feeding). Large animals, including wild herbivores and livestock, are important transport mechanisms because in grazing they typically remove material from patches containing relatively large amounts of high quality forage (Figure 10.18). Usually these grazing areas (patches) are separated spatially from the areas where the animals water, rest, bed down, and ruminate. Overall, material is removed from the grazed areas and accumulates in the resting areas via defecation and urination.

Most behaviors of livestock in rangelands are determined primarily by soil type and fertility, plant communities, and topography (Figure 10.18) (watering is often partially determined by people). Patterns of livestock are quite similar, for example, to those of wild herbivores of the Serengeti Game Reserve in East Africa (Talbot and Talbot, 1963; Sinclair and Norton-Griffiths, 1979; McNaughton, 1979). The herbivores select certain patches in the landscape mosaic for grazing, and this pattern changes according to the degree of food limitation present (Low et al., 1981; Dudzinski et al., 1982; Coppock et al., 1983; Duncan, 1983). After grazing, the mineral nutrients in the grazed patches are significantly altered, as are the nutrients in the patches where the animals leave their deposits (Lee and Inman, 1975; Woodmansee, 1978; Parton et al., 1980; Risser and Parton, 1982).

Many insect species require resources in two or more landscape elements to complete their complex life cycles. For example, a number of

**Figure 10.18** *Large animals both affected by and affecting landscape heterogeneity. Topographic, vegetational, and soil heterogeneity determines most of the movement patterns of large animals such as horses. In turn, the animals graze, trample, and transfer nutrients in a highly nonrandom manner within the heterogeneity. Montana, near Yellowstone National Park (United States). R. Forman; courtesy of D. and E. Patten.*

herbivorous species feeding within crop fields must move to wooded areas for overwintering. Many predaceous insects—such as the vespid wasp (*Hymenoptera*)—colonize hedgerows but forage in cultivated fields. Thus, the mix of crops and environmental changes over the season have major influences on the flow of insect herbivores. Similar patterns also occur in unmanaged landscapes. Numerous recent studies illustrate the value of a landscape approach in describing, modelling, and explaining spatial and temporal patterns of insects (Van der Plank, 1960; Den Boer, 1970, 1981; Gilg, 1973; Stenseth, 1981; Risser et al., 1981, 1984). Examples include the western tent caterpillar in the Sanich Peninsula of British Columbia (Wellington et al., 1975; Thompson et al., 1979); the spruce budworm in Canada (Royama, 1984); and, in the United States, the cereal leaf beetle in Michigan and the corn earworm (*Lepidoptera: Heliothis zea*) in North Carolina (Stinner et al., 1977).

Plant breeders and pest control scientists are finding it increasingly desirable to use a landscape approach in choosing a strategy for developing and using different types of resistance in a species. For example, an antibiotic property may be genetically bred into a crop variety that is the primary food of an insect herbivore pest. If this crop variety is planted uniformly over the area where a population of the pest species lives, the insect population rapidly develops tolerance to the antibiotic properties of the crop. However, if the crop variety represents only a small fraction of the food of the pest population, tolerance evolves more slowly. Therefore, crop resistance to the insect pest remains longer where the crop is only planted in scattered patches.

## SUMMARY

Saltatory movement with periodic stops is far more common among plants and animals than is continuous movement. Of considerable importance are the concentrated interactions between moving objects and their stopping places, which may be either rest stops or stepping stones. Most animal movements occur either within a home range, in dispersal from the home range, or in latitudinal or altitudinal seasonal migration.

Radiotracking studies suggest that large inhospitable patches are avoided by animals, and that many need more than one landscape element in proximity. In general, roads are neither barriers nor conduits for dispersing animals. Rivers, including river sides, are apparently little used as conduits and are filters when wide. Some species require remoteness. Unusual landscape features are especially important as attractants.

Plant dispersal—long distance and short distance—depends on the movement of propagules. The spread of aggressive nonnative species is likely to be facilitated by disturbance corridors and patches. Three examples—the movement of interior herb species between woodlots; the transport of nutrients in livestock grazing systems; and pest control systems of insects—involve landscape structure as the key controlling factor. Animals and plants cross landscapes by skipping along routes that are highly nonrandom and that are strongly determined by natural disturbance and human influence.

## QUESTIONS

1. Diagram a portion of a typical heterogeneous rural landscape with patches and corridors. Then draw a curvilinear route across the diagram, through the midpoint, that minimizes boundary crossing frequency. Similarly, draw a route through the midpoint that maximizes continuous movement. Draw

another that maximizes rest stops. Finally, draw a straight route that maximizes continuous movement.

2. Why is it that some animal movement patterns are considered transitional between dispersal and migration?

3. What patterns of landscape functioning relative to structure were suggested by the skunk (*Mephitis*) study? The desert bighorn sheep (*Ovis*) study?

4. What is remoteness and how is it important in nature conservation? What evidence for it was detected in this chapter?

5. What evidence was presented that roads and highways are important in wildlife management? What other evidence can you cite?

6. What evidence was presented that streams and rivers are important in wildlife management or in biological conservation? What other evidence can you cite?

7. How are the types of propagules important in determining the type of dispersal used by a plant species?

8. In the cheatgrass (*Bromus tectorum*) invasion, what was the relative importance of native corridors, native patches, introduced corridors, and introduced patches?

9. What evidence is there for an intersection effect? How could intersections affect dispersing animals?

10. If you were designing a portion of a landscape, explain how you would incorporate the concepts of remoteness, inhospitable patches, and animal use of more than one ecosystem.

11. What are the primary barriers to animal and plant movement across landscapes? For each barrier type, indicate the types of species blocked and suggest an optimum solution for overcoming the barrier.

# 11

# Landscape Functioning

*Two roads diverged in a wood, and I—*
*I took the one less traveled by,*
*And that has made all the difference.*
**Robert Frost, 1916**
*The Road Not Taken*

Earlier chapters of this book explored a wide range of landscapes and identified spatial patterns common to them all. In Chapters 9 and 10 we examined flows between adjacent landscape elements and the movement of animals and plants across landscapes. Now we will attempt to tie these approaches together.

The question underlying this exploration is this: How does a landscape function? How do energy, water, and mineral nutrients, in addition to animals and plants, move across landscapes composed of various combinations of structural features? The primary structural characteristics of landscapes considered in this chapter are: corridors, hedgerows, the matrix, and networks.

## CORRIDORS AND FLOWS

### The Functioning of Conduits, Barriers, and Breaks

Chapter 4 presented the basic types of corridor structures. Strip corridors contain an interior environment and interior species, whereas narrow line corridors are composed of edge species (Figure 11.1). Stream corridors are most effective in controlling water and mineral nutrient flows from upland to stream when they cover both flood plain and banks, and when they are wide enough above a bank to enhance the movement of upland interior species along the corridor. Networks contain alternative pathways for species movement, have differing types of intersections, enclose landscape elements, and exhibit varying mesh sizes. Large patches or nodes attached to corridors serve as important species sources for corridors.

We now can pinpoint the four main functions of corridors. They serve as:

**Figure 11.1** *A road corridor through pastureland illustrates the four major functions of corridors. The road with its roadside (verge) acts as a special habitat, conduit, filter, and source of effects on the surroundings. Montana, near Yellowstone National Park (United States). (R. Forman; courtesy of D. and E. Patten.)*

1. A habitat for certain types of species.
2. A conduit for movement along corridors.
3. A barrier or filter separating areas.
4. A source of environmental and biotic effects on the surrounding matrix.

All these functions involve flows of animals and plants; the last two functions also include flows of energy and mineral nutrients. The road corridor, including the roadside banks and ditches, illustrates these four functions (Figure 11.1). First, with its early summer strips of beautiful yellow mustards (*Cruciferae*) and late summer feathery grass, it is a special habitat for species uncommon in the matrix (Joselyn et al., 1968; Oetting and Cassel, 1971; Getz et al., 1978). Second, along with allowing considerable movement of people, the corridor acts as a conduit that channels certain species, such as coyotes (*Canis latrans*) foraging at night, across the fields (Buckner, 1957; Baker, 1971; Getz et al., 1978). Third, the road and ditches are a filter that reduces the movement of small animals between opposite sides of the road (Hodson, 1966; Bellis and Graves, 1971; Oxley et al., 1974). Finally, the road is a source of dust that blows into the adjacent matrix area (Figure 11.1) (Tamm and Troedsson, 1955; Lagerwerff and Specht, 1970; Smith, 1971; Hofstra and Hall, 1971).

The importance of large patches in the landscape for many uncommon interior species has been well documented and discussed (Galli et al., 1976; Simberloff, 1976; Pickett and Thompson, 1978; Robbins, 1980; Burgess and Sharpe, 1981). Thus, the large forest patches or nodes along a stream system are important in their own right, especially if they include considerable upland area. If the patches are connected by a stream corridor that facilitates movement of species, they have an additional significance. Thus, a stream corridor system of adequate width, connected to upland nodes in a "string of lights" configuration, is one of the most important functional structures in a landscape.

Commonly patches are located around the intersection of tributaries. A patch that surrounds the intersection of two streams controls water and nutrient flows from the upland into both streams. It also acts as a species source for species moving along the tributary as well as up and down the mainstream corridors. Furthermore, a predator in such an intersection patch may function as a "gatekeeper," controlling flows of prey both to the upstream tributaries and downstream. Such a mechanism helps to isolate populations in different tributary corridors.

Several functions of corridors have been mentioned earlier in the context of specific corridor structures. These will now be brought together in relation to the four general functions of corridors. **Function** here refers to the flows of energy, mineral nutrients, and species (Forman, 1979b).

**Conduits.** Plants and animals are the primary flows along corridors (other than movements directly related to stream flow or human transport). Surprisingly little documentation exists about this major corridor function. The movement of small mammals along the open edges of large highways (Buckner, 1957; Baker, 1971; Getz et al., 1978), and of plants along roads on dikes (Nip-Van der Voort et al., 1979) have been described, but as yet for roadside corridors no generalization can be made about the rates of movement and types of species (Figure 11.1). Indirect evidence from many studies of hedgerow ecology suggests that whereas only a few plants and small mammals move along hedgerows efficiently (Sinclair et al., 1967; Helliwell, 1975; Merriam, 1984), some birds and many medium-sized and large mammals use them regularly for movement across a landscape (McAtee, 1945; Bull et al., 1976; MacClintock et al., 1977; Wegner and Merriam, 1979). The need for strip corridors for movement of interior species has not been clearly documented, but is a concept consistent with a large literature on edge and interior species, environmental conditions, cover and habitat preferences, and foraging strategies.

When corridors are present, disturbances such as fire or certain pest outbreaks that move along corridors can be expected to spread more readily (Stenseth, 1977; Comins et al., 1980). On the other hand, corridors can also function as bottlenecks, where land managers could effectively control the spread of disturbances.

**Barrier or Filter Effects.** Perhaps the best-known barrier effect is the inhibition of water runoff and erosion by vegetation corridors that are parallel to the contours of sloping terrain. Less visible but also important is the interception of mineral nutrient runoff and of subsurface water movement, which is absorbed by roots of corridor plants and moved vertically in evapotranspiration (Ballard, 1979). Wind, heat energy, wind-blown soil, aerosols, and passively-transported organisms (Pollard et al., 1974; The Shelterbelt Project, 1934; Lewis, 1969b; Les Bocages, 1976) are also partially inhibited in their movement across a corridor. It also appears highly probable that animals and plants on the ground have different abilities to cross corridors (Bider, 1968; Van der Zande et al., 1980). For example, certain forest interior birds and small mammals may not cross narrow road cuts through a forest (Oxley et al., 1974; Wilson and Willis, 1975; Karr, 1982) or small fields (Lynch and Whigham, 1984). Many mammals are killed in crossing, and some avoid road corridors altogether (Hodson, 1966; Bellis and Graves, 1971; Taylor, 1971; Storm et al., 1976; Rost and Bailey, 1979; Irwin and Peek, 1983). In all of the cases mentioned, the effectiveness of the barrier would appear to be closely related to corridor width (Oxley et al., 1974). Note that corridors are semipermeable barriers or filters in a landscape, permitting some objects to pass through readily and inhibiting others.

**Breaks.** Scattered evidence suggests that breaks generally inhibit the movements of species along a corridor, and that the length of the break is a primary determinant of which species will be affected (Schreiber and Graves, 1977). Corridor width presumably interacts with the presence or absence of breaks to affect the movement of species along a corridor (Figure 11.2). On the other hand, breaks facilitate the movement of some species across corridors that normally act as a barrier to them (as when native mammals or livestock cross highways through pipes or under bridges). Note that the *break area*—a small area within and immediately surrounding a break—plays an especially critical role in species movement both along and across a corridor (Figure 11.2). Studies of breaks, a conspicuous structural characteristic of landscapes, are particularly needed to help us better understand their effect on corridor functions.

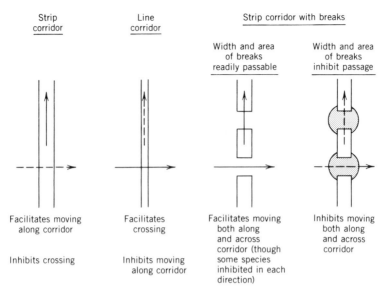

| Strip corridor | Line corridor | Strip corridor with breaks | |
| --- | --- | --- | --- |
| | | Width and area of breaks readily passable | Width and area of breaks inhibit passage |
| Facilitates moving along corridor | Facilitates crossing | Facilitates moving both along and across corridor (though some species inhibited in each direction) | Inhibits moving both along and across corridor |
| Inhibits crossing | Inhibits moving along corridor | | |

**Figure 11.2** *Effect of corridor width and breaks on movement across a landscape. The shaded areas indicate conditions inhibitory to movement and emphasize the critical importance of break areas (from Forman, 1983). (Courtesy of Ekologia CSSR.)*

## Hedgerow Function

**The Fence Effect.** Often the main purpose of constructing or maintaining hedgerows has been to fence in or block the movement of animals (many hedgerows are also called fencerows). Such structures may keep livestock in a pasture, or protect the crop in a field against livestock or the wild herbivores that roam in surrounding woods or open land.

The enclosure hedgerows in Europe were planted typically with hawthorn (*Crataegus*), willow (or sallow) (*Salix*), hazel (*Corylus*), and blackthorn (*Prunus*), any of which could be a barrier to herbivore movement. Some were "layered" by periodically cutting off the vegetation to keep height and width at one to two meters, and then weaving or binding the cut branches into the hedgerow to make a relatively impassable fence. Hedgerows are managed in many ways, including mechanical clipping (and pollarding), clearing of undergrowth, and leaving natural dense growth (Pollard et al., 1974; Yahner, 1982). Most European hedgerows tend to have one or few dominant species that may be either tree or shrub height. North American hedgerows in general are quite different. Since many grow up around a fence made of wire, wood, or stones, and management is lacking or minimal, the hedgerows are usually tree height and commonly are 4 to 15 m or more in width. Several species commonly predominate in a given hedgerow. Thorns, layering, wire, or stones in any hedgerow may produce the fence effect, inhibiting the passage of animals.

**Hedgerows as Conduits.**   It has been suggested that hedgerows are important corridors that facilitate the movement of plants and animals across an agricultural landscape (Sinclair et al., 1967; Pollard et al., 1974; Helliwell, 1975; Forman and Godron, 1981; Forman, 1981, 1983; Baudry, 1984; Burel, 1984; Merriam, 1984). Considerable indirect and some direct evidence is available to evaluate this hypothesis and determine its generality.

Some studies of small mammals, birds, and shrubs suggest that hedgerows are not efficient conduits for movement across a landscape (Sinclair et al., 1967; Pollard et al., 1974; Helliwell, 1975). The evidence in favor of uniform movement along hedgerows is less direct but diverse. McAtee's (1945) summary of pheasant management states that pheasants (*Phasianus*) use fencerows for travel in both Ohio and the northeastern United States. Presst (1971, cited in Pollard et al., 1974) studied a snake species that moved along ditch-and-bank hedgerows, between summer and winter quarters, to a distance of almost two kilometers. Two studies in England and two in Ontario report that small rodents move along hedgerows (Pollard and Relton, 1970; Eldridge, 1971; Wegner and Merriam, 1979; Merriam, 1984). MacClintock et al. (1977) found (in point samples) more bird species within woods that were connected by a wide wooded corridor to other woods than in isolated woodlots, and hypothesized that the corridor was important. Chapter 10 indicated that the fauna in hedgerows near an attached woods differs from that in more distant portions of a hedgerow, suggesting some movement along the hedgerow. In other linear strips of vegetation, McAtee (1945) indicated that pheasants move along ditches in Utah, and Nip-Van der Voort et al. (1979) reported that herbs moved sequentially down roadsides on dykes in Holland. Bull et al. (1976) and Wegner and Merriam (1979) both consider hedgerows to be important routes of movement between avian centers in a landscape. Finally, our casual observations of footprints in New Jersey and elsewhere suggest that deer (*Odocoileus*), raccoons (*Procyon*), and people use the hedgerow boundary for movement across an agricultural landscape more frequently than any other route except a road or stream corridor.

The evidence available leads us to conclude that hedgerows function as corridors for movement across a landscape by many species. For animals, both cover and food for foraging are involved. Wide tree and shrub hedgerows apparently are more effective corridors than are shrub hedgerows (Figure 11.3). Finally, in landscapes with few woodlots, hedgerows are probably, over the long term, critical "refuges" enabling the survival and dispersal of many woodland species.

**Figure 11.3** *A network of planted hedgerows near Dill City, Oklahoma (United States), varying from one to six trees in width. The shrubby narrows here, such as in the horizontal foreground windbreak, are on permeable soil that is only about 60 cm deep, whereas the nearby larger trees are on up to three times as much permeable soil. The scale of heterogeneity of soil conditions on this sandy plain in a warm grassland climate is finer than the heterogeneity of fields, windbreaks, roads, and farmyards. We expect that some species cross a landscape along such a network. (Courtesy of USDA Soil Conservation Service.)*

**Hedgerow Networks and Flows.**   The driving forces of wind, water, and locomotion are affected in major ways by hedgerow networks. Air moving across a network landscape has a turbulent lower surface pattern as it interfaces with both hedgerow vegetation and plants of the enclosed fields. From point to point, wind speed and desiccation at ground level are extremely variable. Average wind velocity is lower in a hedgerow landscape than in one without hedgerows. For example, Jensen (1954) found average wind speed to be 15% lower in a hedgerow landscape than in a comparable open field landscape in Denmark.

Hedgerow networks are important in the regulation of stream flows. One study compared two landscapes near each other in Brittany (France) with and without hedgerow networks (Merot and Ruellan, 1980). In winter (the rainy season) stream flow was lower in the hedgerow landscape than in the open landscape, whereas in summer the opposite was observed. The total annual stream flow of the two watersheds was essentially the same. Apparently, during the wet season the hedgerow network inhibits surface water runoff and stream flooding. During the drier season, higher average wind velocities in the open landscape may accelerate evapotranspiration. In the hedgerow landscape stream flow is less variable through the year, and presumably floods are less frequent.

The hedgerow network can also decrease soil loss by wind (The Shelterbelt Project, 1934). In addition, it is likely that more insects, other windblown organisms, and particulate matter carried from afar are deposited in hedgerow landscapes as a result of the turbulent wind flow patterns (Lewis, 1969a, 1969b; Brunel and Cancela da Fonseca, 1979; Reiners, 1983).

Although various birds and mammals appear to move effectively along hedgerows, the movement of a woodland species across a landscape using a hedgerow network (Figure 11.3) has apparently not yet been described. The movement of open field species across a hedgerow landscape would presumably be less efficient in a fine-mesh network, because of the fence effect of frequent hedgerow lines acting as barriers. In contrast, a coarser network, or one with breaks in the hedgerows, would enable greater movement of such open field species. Note that both types of movement, flow along hedgerows and flow across hedgerows, would be affected by the orientation of the network relative to the direction of movement.

## FLOWS AND THE MATRIX

As we examine how objects move through the matrix of a landscape, seven matrix characteristics and their effects will be explored.

### Matrix Connectivity

A matrix with high connectivity is subdivided by few or no barriers that would interrupt an object moving across it. Heat, dust, and seeds dispersed by wind may move in a relatively uniform laminar flow over the matrix. An animal, a pest, or a fire may spread through a nearly unbroken expanse of a particular type of landscape element (Elton, 1958; Foster, 1983). Thus, in fire-prone areas (see Figure 7.21) (Heinselman, 1973; Forman and Boerner, 1981; Grimm, 1984), people construct fire breaks to decrease matrix connectivity (and stop fires), where natural fire breaks are scarce. On the other hand, to protect certain interior species that will not cross narrow corridors (Wilson and Willis, 1975; Karr, 1982), we must increase the connectivity of a matrix or patch.

We expect, therefore, the highest average rates of movement where the matrix is highly connected. Where there is a paucity of barriers, we also expect relatively little genetic variability and population differentiation.

### Landscape Resistance

The structural characteristics of a landscape that affect the rate of flow of objects may collectively be termed the **resistance of the landscape** to movement. Landscape resistance results from two boundary characteristics, (a) boundary crossing frequency and (b) boundary discreteness, plus two landscape element characteristics, (c) hospitableness and (d) length of each element.

Because flows by water, wind, and locomotion are generally slower crossing boundaries, we expect boundary crossing frequency (Chapter 10) to be a general, easily measured indicator of landscape resistance. The **discreteness of a boundary**—that is, whether it is abrupt (discrete) or gradual—probably also significantly affects the rate of flow. On the one hand, physical flows such as water and heat energy readily cross discrete boundaries between landscape elements (Opdam et al., 1983). On the other hand, we expect that movements of animals and plants are inhibited more by a highly discrete boundary than by a gradual boundary; but this is considered as a hypothesis to be tested. The resistance of a landscape is strongly affected by the degree of suitability or *hospitableness* of each landscape element to the object moving (see Chapter 10). Hospitableness of a landscape element must be estimated or measured for each species or object considered. The total length of each landscape element crossed is also readily measured (as was done for the New York and French landscapes presented in Chapter 5).

### Narrows

In some places the matrix is narrow enough along the route of movement that the object moving is affected by the matrix width. Such narrows in the matrix may speed up or slow down the rate of movement. Objects carried by wind or water speed up in the vicinity of the narrows, because of the so-called Venturi effect. In Chapter 9, for example, we saw how wind accelerates when it passes through the gaps of a windbreak.

Locomoting objects probably slow down, as a rule, exercising caution in passing through a narrows. For example, pioneers crossing the North

American continent often took considerable time passing through narrow gorges, both because of the terrain and their concern about attacks from residents of the area. Such narrows function as **bottlenecks,** concentrating objects on the arriving side, as happens with a group of wasps entering a wasp nest, caribou funneled through a passage under the Alaska pipeline, and ships waiting to get through a lock. The presence of narrows is important in flows, but perhaps of greater importance is the nature of the area in and adjacent to the narrows, just as in the case of break areas (Figure 11.2). Large herbivores will have difficulty passing, if a leopard or a village appears in a narrows (see Figure 10.2). In planning or managing a landscape, narrows are of special significance and need to be pinpointed at the outset.

## Porosity and Interaction Among Patches

High matrix porosity—numerous patches pockmarking the matrix—may have a major or a minor effect on objects moving across the matrix, depending on the nature of flows between patches and matrix (Julander and Jeffery, 1964; Thomas et al., 1976; Thomas, 1979; Lyon and Jensen, 1980; Hanley, 1983). If patches are inhospitable or if predators or hunters concentrate in patches waiting for animals to pass by in the matrix, movement of the animals across the matrix will be slow and hazardous. For example, the foxes described in Chapter 10 had to detour around farmyards in the agricultural landscape (Storm et al., 1976). Conversely, a highly porous landscape where the patches are particularly hospitable can facilitate saltatory movement across the landscape. There are rest stops or stepping stones as the animal repeatedly crosses boundaries between matrix and patches.

The degree of interaction between similar patches would depend upon the distance between them. For some types of flows, the area of the patches might also be important (MacClintock et al., 1977) (see Appendix to Chapter 5). As yet, to describe the movement of objects across a matrix we have no formula that incorporates the factors of high or low connectivity, resistance, frequency of narrows, and porosity.

## Influence Fields

Geographers use the term **influence field** for the area under the influence of a particular node or patch (Bartholomew, 1973; Taaffe and Gauthier, 1973; Bailey, 1975; Haggett et al., 1977). The intensity of this influence may vary with distance from the patch. In population centers, influence fields might be the areas affected by a transportation network, the local news media, sulfur dioxide pollution, or the spread of a disease (Bailey, 1975).

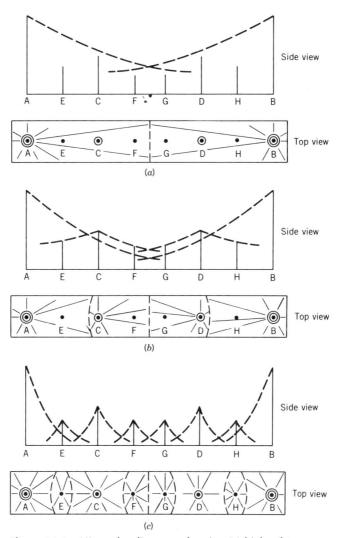

**Figure 11.4** *Hierarchy diagrams showing (a) high-, (b) middle-, and (c) low-order flows, and consequent influence fields. a. Points A and B are sources of strong high-order flows (indicated by the curved dashed lines) that dominate or overwhelm any flows from other points. The result is two-equal-sized influence fields to the right and left of the vertical dashed line. b. Middle-order flows from points C and D dominate only in areas distant from points A and B, resulting in four influence fields. c. Low-order flows from points E, F, G, and H dominate only in their immediate surroundings, resulting in eight influence fields (Edward J. Taaffe and Howard L. Gauthier,* Geography of Transportation, *© 1973, pp. 26,27. Adapted by permission of Prentice-Hall, Inc., Englewood Cliffs, N.J.)*

The influence fields from a given patch will be different for different flows. We must differentiate, therefore, between *high-order, middle-order,* and *low-order flows,* referring to the distance over which moving objects exert a significant effect (Taaffe and Gauthier, 1973). In high-order flows, small nodes near a large node have no significant influence compared to larger nodes (Figure 11.4). In contrast, with low-order flows, even small nodes may exert a significant influence. We can also identify "remote," or unaffected areas relative to a particular type of flow. For example, relative to high- and middle-order flows, no area is remote in the first two cases (Figure 11.4), whereas three remote areas are present in the third case (around point *E,* around *F* and *G,* and around *H*).

There are obvious applications of this kind of analysis to the influence fields of, for example, different animal species, seeds dispersing from trees, dust and heat radiating from bare areas, pollution from point sources, and the like. Antelope are high-order flows, while dairy cows are low-order. In a specific study of devastated vegetation extending for kilometers around a smelter (see Figure 9.15), the investigators found that different air pollutants extended different distances (Nash, 1975). Sulfur dioxide at a toxic level extended less than a kilometer, whereas the high-order zinc oxide extended out several kilometers and was primarily responsible for the extensive vegetation damage.

Influence fields for different objects representing high, medium, and low orders may be calculated and mapped (Figure 11.5). The classification of different flows into orders, reveals a **hierarchical spatial structure** that is striking in the mapped landscape. Only a few small areas are remote from the high-order activities, whereas most of the total area of the landscape is remote from the low-order activities (Figure 11.5). This classification is a more precise approach to understanding the effects of matrix porosity.

## Peninsular Interdigitation

The dendritic pattern, with "fingers" of vegetation projecting up stream valleys, is one of the most pervasive shapes in most landscapes. The landscape element type between the stream corridor fingers also presents another series of fingers, that is, the intervening ridges (Figure 11.6). This pattern of peninsular interdigitation or interfingering of two landscape element types is common (Chapter 3) and basically results from erosion.

This landscape configuration should show distinctive species diversity patterns. We hypothesize that total species diversity is highest in the central portion of interdigitating peninsulas (Figure 11.6), where species from both landscape elements are present. Yet most of the species in the narrow peninsulas are edge species. Therefore, the diversity of interior

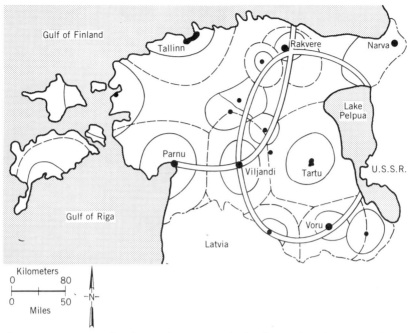

**Figure 11.5** *Hierarchical spatial structure of a landscape based on several different order flows considered simultaneously, in Estonia (USSR). Double lines enclose influence fields of high-order flows from Tartu and Tallinn. Dashed lines enclose influence fields of middle-order flows. Single solid lines enclose influence fields of low-order flows. Only four areas are remote from all flows—in the islands, above the word "Latvia," in the southeastern corner, and between Narva and Rakvere. Also note that a particular point may be the source of several types of flows, as is Tartu, which has high-, medium-, and low-order flows indicated by nearly concentric rings. (Based on Edgar Kant, 1951, and Taaffe and Gauthier, 1973).*

species and particularly of uncommon species, should be highest in the homogeneous areas on either side of the interdigitated area.

The rate of movement of objects across an area of peninsular inter-digitation should differ markedly according to the direction of flow. Movement parallel to the fingers on the average is rapid, since the peninsulas act as conduits with minimal boundary crossing frequency. Movement at right angles to the fingers on the average is slow, since boundary crossing frequency is exceptionally high.

One special case of peninsular interdigitation is seen, for example, when both flat valley bottoms and flat ridge tops are pastured (Figure 11.7), and the slopes between the pasture areas are forested. The moist pastures alternate with drier pastures, and a narrow, extremely sinuous forested corridor separates them.

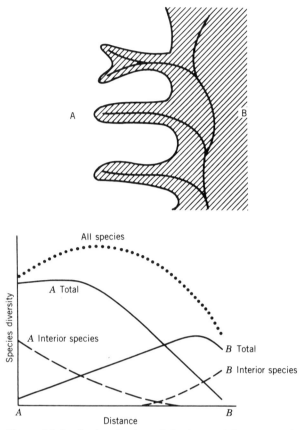

**Figure 11.6** *Peninsular interdigitation and the expected species diversity patterns. A and B are two ecosystem types, say upland and lowland, respectively. The graph indicates the expected average species diversity (number of species) based on the sampling of many horizontal lines across the area. In this example A arbitrarily has a higher diversity than B.*

## Spatial Orientation Relative to Flows

Patch shape is of major importance, affecting several ecological characteristics in a landscape, as well as the species present within the patch (Chapter 3). A key factor in this interaction is the spatial orientation of a landscape structure relative to the direction of flow of objects, that is, the *angle of interaction*. The long axis of a patch may be parallel or perpendicular (or diagonal) to the directions of flows, such as prevailing wind, slopes, or dispersal from a species source (Figure 11.8).

**Figure 11.7** *Peninsular interdigitation, where forested slopes separate open uplands from lowlands. Central Indiana (United States). Interdigitation ultimately resulting from the basic process of erosion is common in many landscapes. Note the several field peninsulas and the several forest peninsulas. (R. Forman).*

For example, an elongated patch parallel to the movement of species from a source is likely to intercept fewer moving individuals than if the patch is oriented at right angles to the direction of flow (Figure 11.8). Soil desiccation in a forest, caused by incoming heat energy in a savanna, is less when the long axis of the woods is parallel to the prevailing wind than when the two are at right angles. Coupling shape and relative orientation is of considerable ecological significance, but has been little studied. Nevertheless, the concept of angle of interaction can be directly applied in landscape planning and management.

## Distance

A straight line connecting two points represents the shortest distance (Euclidean distance) between them. In considering flows between two points we are usually more interested in the route that permits the most rapid movement, called the **time-distance.** Sometimes the straight line distance is the fastest route, but often some impediment to movement

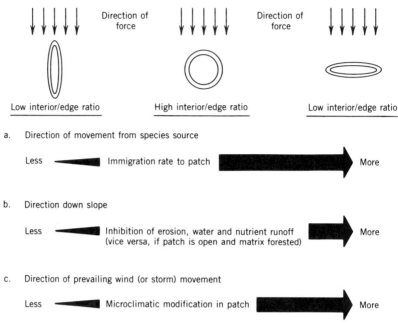

**Figure 11.8** *The importance of the angle of interaction in several landscape functions. Above, the patch orientation and the interior-to-edge ratio are given relative to the direction of movement of a major force. Below, the relative amount of landscape functioning is indicated.*

lies along the straight line and must be circumvented. For example, fish swimming upriver will make faster progress when they move from side to side through slowly moving water, than when they go directly up the channel against rapidly moving water. Straight-line distance is measured in distance units (e.g., meters and kilometers), whereas time-distance is measured in time units (e.g., minutes and days). We should also note that the shortest time-distance from one point to a second point may differ from the shortest route going in the opposite direction. One-way streets in towns, and the routes of birds flying upwind versus downwind in a windy landscape are good examples of this directionality feature.

A third type of distance is distance in **topological space.** The mathematical discipline known as topology is a qualitative geometry dealing with "the continuous connectedness between the points of a figure" (Lowe and Moryadas, 1975). Maps of most bus, train, and airplane routes are maps in topological space (Figure 11.9). Topological space is elastic, but in it the order of points, lines, and areas is maintained. Figure 11.9 shows Euclidian maps with a scale given in kilometers. On the right,

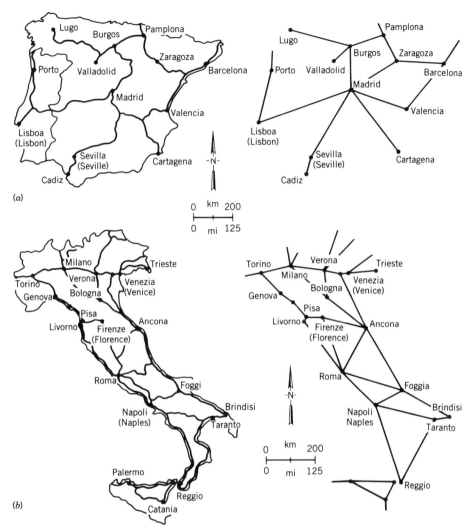

**Figure 11.9** *Actual and topological maps of major railroads in (a) Spain and Portugal and (b) Italy. Compare the routes among Madrid, Sevilla, Cartagena, and Valencia on the two maps of Spain. Then compare the round trip route from Napoli (Naples) to Reggio, Taranto, Brindisi, Foggia, and back to Napoli on the actual versus the topological maps of Italy.*

topological maps accurately represent the spatial ordering, but are only roughly proportional to the distance and the length of time necessary to cover a route. The passenger is primarily interested in *What order?*, *How far?*, and *How long?* Few passengers are interested in all the bends along the route or the precise locations of the various stops. Consequently, topological space is particularly used in transportation theory involving the movement of people.

Time-distance appears to be the most relevant concept in landscape ecology, though straight-line distance and topological space will be useful when dealing with certain principles. We also note that in many landscapes, curved features and winding roads are straightened and main-

**Figure 11.10** *Overlapping networks of different corridor types in Nevada County, California. Geometrization or linearization of landscapes, straightening or eliminating curved natural landscape features, plus the maintenance of geometrization increasingly result from fossil fuel energy use. How many types of corridors can be identified here? (Courtesy of USDA Soil Conservation Service.)*

**414** LANDSCAPE DYNAMICS

tained with machinery (Figure 11.10). In other words, humans increasingly depend on large amounts of fossil fuel energy to "linearize" landscapes in order to reduce time-distances.

## NETWORKS

Networks are widespread, overlapping, and of many types in most landscapes (Figure 11.10). Thus, it is not surprising that scholars in diverse fields, including geography, transportation, communications, and mathematics, have a sustained interest in networks (King, 1969; Taaffe and Gauthier, 1973; Isard, 1975; Bartlett, 1975; Lowe and Moryadas, 1975; Haggett et al., 1977; Odum, 1983; MacDonald, 1983). The flows of energy, materials, and species studied in landscape ecology appear to have the most direct analogies with the principles of the geography of transportation—that is, the movement of people. A number of these principles can be utilized or modified for landscape ecology.

### Nodes and Corridors

**Nodes** have two functions in flows: as intersection areas of corridors, and as sources or sinks (destinations) of flowing objects. Thus, cities are nodes for vehicle movement along highways, and water holes are nodes for animal paths in arid areas. A corridor or route usually connects nodes, and a network is a series of interconnected corridors (Figure 11.11). Nodes of course vary in type and size. They also vary in their "time-discreteness," that is, the times at which flows take place. For example, commuters enter a city in peak numbers once a day in the morning. Desert bighorn sheep (Figure 10.10) visit a water hole in peak numbers twice a day, at morning and at dusk (Leslie and Douglas, 1979).

Nodes often function as relayers of movement rather than as ultimate destinations, and certain controls on flows take place at **relay nodes.** The controls may (a) amplify or speed up flows, (b) reduce "noise" or "irrelevancies" in flows, and (c) provide temporary storage. Just as a telephone operator serves as a critical relay node for the flow of information, a landing area by a logging road provides temporary storage for sorting, preparing, and transporting logs (Peters, 1978; Bryer, 1983). An isolated lake on a wildlife refuge serves as a critical relay node for waterfowl migrating across a landscape. Such a relay node may provide food (amplification), eliminate weaker birds (reduce noise), and accumulate huge flocks waiting for a favorable weather front to arrive (temporary storage). This example of an isolated lake reminds us that the location of nodes relative to one another is critical to the flows or use of nodes.

**Figure 11.11** *Nodes, loops, and trunklines in a network. The nodes are oil well and gas drilling sites connected by road corridors. The oldest nodes are 50 years old—in an arid climate, such marks on a landscape heal slowly. (Courtesy of Dick Randall.)*

The configuration of transportation networks generally reflects efforts to minimize the time-distance along corridors between nodes. **Loops,** or alternative routes, increase the efficiency of movement by channeling flows around landscape sections, decreasing the use of those sections for movement (Figure 11.11). Without these conduits, the rate of movement would be slower, because locomoting organisms would have to undertake a search procedure to move between nodes. A major consequence of corridor networks is "nodal accessibility;" that is, isolated nodes and adjacent areas are more easily reached.

Just as in railroad networks, we may recognize major routes of flow—*trunk lines* or corridors—along which large numbers of objects move

(Figure 11.11). Examples are the migration routes of caribou or wilde-beest. *Feeder lines* or corridors link remote areas to the trunk lines. Often trunk lines go through a *gateway,* a main entry and exit point for a landscape or portion of a landscape. The gateway may function as an important control point in flows across a landscape. Hunters wait near a major deer trail and bag deer as they pass, while bears snag salmon below a waterfall.

## Network Connectivity

The degree to which all nodes in a system are linked by corridors is referred to as **network connectivity.** Connectivity therefore is one index of the simplicity or complexity of the network. Several methods are available for calculating the complexity of networks (Lowe and Moryadas, 1975; Taaffe and Gauthier, 1973; Haggett et al., 1977; Sugihara, 1983). Two common methods used in geography appear particularly useful in landscape ecology, the gamma index and the alpha index.

The **gamma index** of network connectivity is the ratio of the number of links in a network to the maximum possible number of links in that network. The number of links present is counted directly. The maximum possible number of links can be determined by counting the number of nodes present. With three nodes present, only three links are possible, but with four nodes present, three additional links are possible, making a total of six. Assuming no new intersections are formed, the maximum number of links rises by three each time a node is added. Thus, we have the gamma index for connectivity

$$\gamma = \frac{L}{L_{max}} = \frac{L}{3(V - 2)}$$

where $L$ is the number of links, $L_{max}$ is the maximum possible number of links, and $V$ is the number of nodes. The gamma index varies from zero, indicating that none of the nodes is linked, to 1.0, indicating that every node is linked to every other possible node.

In Figure 11.12 the network on the left has 15 links and 16 nodes, with a connectivity of

$$\gamma = \frac{L}{3(V - 2)} = \frac{15}{3(16 - 2)} = \frac{15}{42} = 0.36$$

whereas the network on the right with 20 links and 16 nodes has a connectivity of

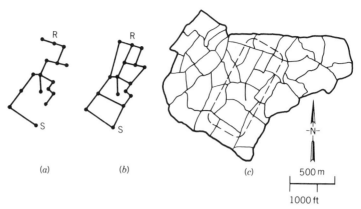

**Figure 11.12** *Two networks in topological space that differ in both connectivity and circuitry. Simple indices are given in the text for evaluating the amount of both variables that together are a measure of network complexity. Network b represents the dotted area of map c, indicating hedgerows of a medieval field pattern in Devon, England. This farm of late Saxon origin is shown in the* Domesday Book *of 1086, probably as pastureland. The characteristic small and irregular fields were created in the following century (adapted from Hoskins, 1955).*

$$\gamma = \frac{L}{3(V - 2)} = \frac{20}{3(16 - 2)} = \frac{20}{42} = 0.48$$

We therefore say that the first network is 36% connected, and the second network is 48% connected. Thus, for an animal using corridors to cross a landscape from point $R$ to point $S$, the route will be long in the first network. In the second network, the shortest route for the animal between two distant nodes $R$ and $S$ is closer to the straight-line distance between the nodes.

### Loops and Circuitry

The second network index, the **alpha index,** is a measure of **circuitry,** the degree to which "circuits" that connect nodes in a network are present. Circuits are defined as loops that provide alternative routes for flow. A minimally connected, or circuitless, network (with no isolated or unconnected nodes) has one less link than the number of nodes ($L = V - 1$) (Figure 11.12). If we add a link to this minimally connected network, a circuit or loop is formed. Therefore, when circuits are present, $L > V - 1$. The number of circuits present, i.e., the number of links present minus the number of links for a minimally connected network, may be expressed as $L - V + 1$. This expression represents the actual number of independent circuits in the network.

The alpha index for the degree of network circuitry is the ratio of the actual number of circuits in the network to the maximum number of possible circuits in that network. The maximum possible number of circuits is the maximum number of links—determined above as $3(V - 2)$—less the number of links in a minimally connected network $(V - 1)$, that is, $3(V - 2) - (V - 1)$, which equals $2V - 5$. Thus, the degree of network circuitry as indicated by the alpha index, is

$$\alpha = \frac{\text{actual number of circuits}}{\text{maximum number of circuits}} = \frac{L - V + 1}{2V - 5}$$

The index ranges from zero, for a network with no circuits, to 1.0 for a network with the maximum possible number of loops present.

In the networks of Figure 11.12 the alpha value for the network on the left is

$$\alpha = \frac{L - V + 1}{2V - 5} = \frac{15 - 16 + 1}{2 \times 16 - 5} = \frac{0}{27} = 0$$

and for the network on the right is

$$\alpha = \frac{L - V + 1}{2V - 5} = \frac{20 - 16 + 1}{2 \times 16 - 5} = \frac{5}{27} = 0.19$$

The first network has no circuitry, and in the second network, circuitry is 19%. An animal crossing a landscape along the first network has no choice of routes. An animal using the second network can take various routes to avoid disturbances or predators and minimize its time-distance.

The alpha index could be seen as an alternative way to calculate the connectivity of the network, because in a real sense circuitry is a way of being connected. However, we have chosen to use the alpha index in the narrower sense, as a measure of the degree of circuits present. Together, connectivity and circuitry, as measured by the gamma and alpha indices, indicate the degree of **network complexity.**

We must remember that these principles are based on topological space (using graph theory), which is a useful abstraction permitting us to focus on only nodes and links (Figure 11.9). However, it is a model or abstraction. The actual distance, the degree of linearity, the direction of links, and the precise location of nodes (all of which are largely ignored in topological space) are also of considerable import to certain flows in landscape ecology.

Several other simple indices are used in transportation and communication theory, to calculate, for example, the accessibility of a node from other nodes, the "central place" or most accessible node in the network, the number of routes one could take between two nodes, the linkage intensity or number of linkages per node, the degree of dispersion or compactness of a network, the delineation of regions based on the amounts of flow, the network configurations, the effects of hierarchies of node size, and the effects of hierarchies of route capacity (Lowe and Moryadas, 1975; Haggett et al., 1977). All such indices should be applied with caution in landscape ecology until we know more about the flows of animals, plants, energy, and mineral nutrients along corridors in networks.

## Gravity Model

In the above discussion on connectivity and circuitry, we made the useful but simplifying assumption that all nodes are equal, and thus that the complexity of the links is of primary interest. This assumption is often quite appropriate. However, where the nodes differ sharply, as when woodlots vary from tiny to huge, or when human population centers vary from cities to farmhouses, the nature of the node is an important factor, along with linkage complexity, that governs flows.

A widely used way to measure interaction between nodes is based on the **gravity model** (derived from the law of gravity in physics). It may be written (in a modified form)

$$I_{ij} = K \frac{P_i \times P_j}{d^2}$$

to describe the amount of interaction (I) between nodes $i$ and $j$, where $P_i$ is the population size or amount of objects at node $i$, $P_j$ is the population size or amount of objects at node $j$, and $d$ is the distance between the two nodes. $K$ is simply a constant to relate the equation to the particular objects being studied, such as heat energy, water molecules, or aardvarks.

The greater the size of the two nodes, the greater is the interaction between them. The greater the distance between two nodes, the less is interaction between them. In Figure 11.13, nodes $A$ and $C$ are closer and therefore have more interactions than $B$ and $C$. Furthermore, $A$ and $C$ are larger in combination and therefore have more interactions than $C$ and $D$. What pair has more interactions, $B$ and $C$ or $C$ and $D$? Use the gravity model formula above, and it will be found that nodes $C$ and $D$ have twice as many interactions as nodes $B$ and $C$. This fact emphasizes how important distance is in the interactions between nodes.

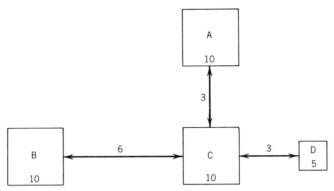

**Figure 11.13** *Gravity model diagram showing the combined effect of distance and node size on expected interactions between nodes. A, B, C, and D are nodes, with their sizes given in arbitrary units. Numbers on the arrows indicate the distance between the nodes. Which two connected nodes have the least interactions? See text for answer and formula that calculates the expected interaction between the nodes.*

Gravity models have been used to describe passenger flows by air and highway between California cities, and volumes of telephone calls between Canadian cities. Such models could be useful in describing the flow across a landscape of objects such as birds or wind-dispersed seeds moving between woodlots (McQuilkin, 1940; Buell et al., 1971; Carkin et al., 1978; Whitcomb, 1977; McDonnell, 1984). In addition to their predictive potential, gravity models emphasize that both the amount of objects in the origin node and the amount in the destination node affect flow rates in networks.

## Spatial Diffusion Processes

**Diffusion** is the process of spreading out. Biologists generally use it in a narrower sense to refer to the movement of particles from an area where they are more concentrated to an area of less concentration. The movement may be passive (or spontaneous) or due to heat energy. Here, we will use diffusion in the broader sense of spreading familiar to social scientists and the public. We use this sense when we speak of the diffusion of ideas across a country, of substances in the bloodstream to parts of the body, of air masses across a continent, and of defoliating insect pests and nonnative species across a landscape (Figure 11.14) (Gunn and Rainey, 1979; Rabb and Kennedy, 1979). Geographers, anthropologists, and other social scientists have identified a variety of diffusion patterns

(Sauer, 1952; Rogers, and Shamaker, 1971; Hagerstrand, 1965, 1967; King, 1969; Levin, 1974; Isard, 1975; Bartlett, 1975; Lowe and Moryadas, 1975; Haggett et al., 1977; Chesson, 1981), a few principles of which appear to be particularly useful in landscape ecology.

Previously we compared continuous versus saltatory movement. Whereas some objects diffuse uniformly through space, and others move in "jumps," a combination of the two is probably most common in ecology. Species (or "innovations" in geography) often jump from one node to several surrounding nodes and then spread locally around the new nodes. When a hierarchy of nodes is recognizable, as in the case of population centers that vary in size from city to farmhouse, the process is called *hierarchical diffusion* (Lowe and Moryadas, 1975). In landscape ecology, we might expect the spread of some newly introduced nonnative species (Figure 11.14) (Elton, 1958) to be a hierarchical diffusion process when, for example, the landscape is a mosaic of patches ranging in habitat quality from good to unsuitable. Note that directionality is an important characteristic of hierarchical diffusion.

The difference between expansionary diffusion and relocation diffusion also seems useful and important in landscape ecology. In *expansionary diffusion,* the objects expand their area of coverage while continuing to occupy the original position. For example, heat energy from a large black parking lot on a windless sunny day spreads into the surrounding area. A plant species undergoes expansionary diffusion when seeds germinate in the area surrounding the parent tree. In *relocation diffusion,* in contrast, the objects leave one area and move to another area. Water from a rainstorm in a high-elevation tropical rain forest flows down to the plain below (sometimes as a lethal wall of water crashing down stream beds). A pair of kangaroos leaves one grassy patch in a landscape and hops into another.

Diffusion processes have been investigated using a wide range of mathematical models. One of the most frequently-used approaches (called Monte Carlo simulation) investigates the effects of distance, time, barriers to dispersal, and other factors on diffusion flows, assuming that objects move in random directions (Hagerstrand, 1965; Cliff and Ord, 1973). A variety of other modelling approaches to diffusion is also available (Brown and Moore, 1969; Levin, 1974, 1978; Haggett et al., 1977; den Boer, 1981). Diffusion model approaches may be useful for identifying possible patterns or principles relating to movement across a landscape. However, because of their often oversimplified assumptions that do not take into account much of the richness of landscape flows—such as patchiness, the orientation of corridors, locomotion patterns, age and sex differences, and the like—the application of these models should be approached with caution and the results should be seen as hypotheses to be tested.

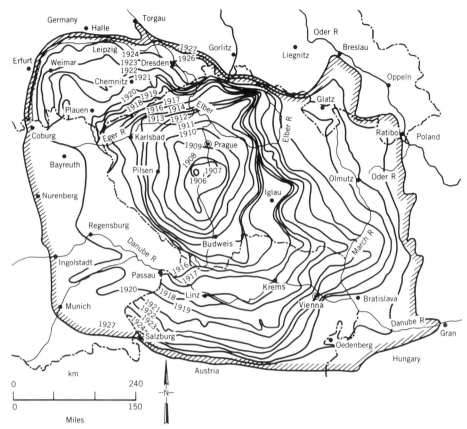

**Figure 11.14** *Spread of the nonnative muskrat in Czechoslovakia and surrounding countries in the 22 years (1905 to 1927) following its introduction from North America. The diffusion process of this semiaquatic mammal (*Ondatra zibethica*) that is trapped for its fur was relatively even in all directions. (From C. Elton, 1958,* The Ecology of Invasions by Animals and Plants, *Methuen & Co. Publishers. Based on Ulbrich, 1930.)*

## Optimization

The process of *optimization,* or the increasing of efficiency, is routine in many areas of human endeavor including landscape management. Usually one or a number of selected things in a system are maximized, and other components of the system are ignored and for the most part minimized (Cline, 1949). In studying optimal foraging strategies for animals we generally focus on the movements that maximize the detection and capture of food items. In network analysis, we may be looking for the shortest path between two points, the best place to add a link, or the links that, if broken, would cause the greatest change in the system (Fahrig et al., 1983).

Lowe and Moryadas (1975) introduce the question of minimum-distance paths as follows.

In order to obtain the flavor of optimization problems, let us first consider the Konigsberg Bridge problem which was introduced by the Swiss mathematician Euler in 1736. . . . [Figure 11.15] is a map of a portion of the city of Konigsberg (now Kaliningrad) in East Prussia, which, because of its location on the banks and on two islands of the river Pregel, has seven bridges.

It was the custom of the burghers to take a Sunday stroll through town and the question was asked, ''Is it possible to plan a promenade so that, starting from an origin one can return there after having crossed each of the seven bridges only once?'' Since we are not concerned with the width of the bridges or the distance between them, we may, as Euler did, convert the map to a graph [Figure 11.15]. . . . The four parts of the city are now the [nodes] . . . , and the . . . [links] represent the bridges.

Euler showed that this graph cannot be traversed in a simple circular path without backtracking because a single circular path would have to enter each [node] as many times as it departs from it; i.e., *each node must have an even number of [links]*. We see in [Figure 11.15] that this condition is not fulfilled. Subsequently, Euler was able to specify completely and prove the sufficient and necessary conditions for a graph that allows a cyclic path (called a Euler line) running through all links just once. The two conditions are: (1) the graph must be fully connected; (2) the path must enter and exit the same number of times at each node. . . . In this way, Euler established the foundations for a rigorous consideration of a variety of shortest-route problems. . . . (*The Geography of Movement*, by John C. Lowe and S. Moryadas, pp. 269–270. Copyright 1975 by Houghton Mifflin Company. Used by permission).

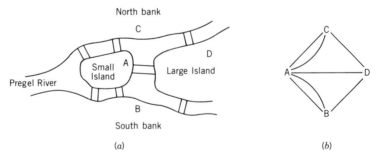

**Figure 11.15** *The four nodes and seven bridges of Konigsberg (now called Kaliningrad, East Prussia, USSR). Actual (a) and topological (b) maps have nodes labelled A, B, C, and D. What route would start and end at the same point, crossing each bridge only once? (See text.) Adapted from O. Ore,* Graphs and Their Uses, © *1963, Random House, Inc.*

This example leads us to consider the solution to the familiar "traveling salesman" problem.

Consider how a traveling salesman might complete a circuit starting from say, Charleston, West Virginia (USA), visiting one specified city in each of the remaining 47 conterminous states in the United States, and returning to the origin, so that the overall distance is minimized. From the origin, there are 47 choices; once this choice is made, there are 46 remaining choices; and so on. Altogether, the total number of alternative circuits, forced by the constraint that the journey must end at the starting point, is equal to 47! . . . Factorial numbers escalate very rapidly in value; thus, $47! = 2.5862^{59}$, which involves several million alternative routes. However, there is only *one* optimal (shortest) route. . . . (Lowe and Moryadas, 1975) (ibid).

Finally, we mention a landscape management plan for a mountainous area, containing villages, in southwestern New Hampshire. Optimization there related two major landscape functions, the flow of wildlife and the flow of people. A key to the plan emerged from seeing how early colonization patterns related to topography (C. Steinitz, personal communication). Parallel mountain ridges alternate with narrow river valleys, and villages are located at intervals along a river valley, only where tributaries could originally be dammed up for small mills. Today the top priority expressed by local residents is to maintain the identity of each village, and to prevent strip development along roads connecting villages.

The planners recommended a "multiple-use" plan that attempted to optimize several characteristics including future housing development, forestry, and wildlife. Proposed housing was concentrated around certain villages, and forestry and wildlife were concentrated on the mountain ridges. The mountain ridges were then connected by proposed forest corridors that crossed the river valley between the tributaries. These connecting corridors played a critical dual function. They would effectively separate villages by preventing strip development, and they would provide a network of different routes for the movement of wildlife between mountain ridges. Optimizing of a third major landscape function, namely, the flows associated with rivers and streams, can easily be incorporated into such a landscape management plan by adding along streams, corridors that are linked to or a part of the proposed forest corridors.

## SUMMARY

Corridors serve as conduits and as filters for much of the movement of animals, plants, materials, and water across the landscape. Network and matrix characteristics affect movements in contrasting ways, depending on whether the objects cross corridors or use corridors as conduits. Landscape functioning integrates flows both between adjacent ecosystems and across a landscape, for instance, as well as through a particular spatial configuration of ecosystems.

Movement through a matrix depends on its connectivity, its hospitableness, and the boundaries crossed between landscape elements. Species moving along a connected matrix may be inhibited by having to pass through narrows between nearby patches, whereas species moving from patch to patch are inhibited by large distances between patches in a matrix with low porosity. Influence fields, representing flows of high and low orders, overlap and form a hierarchical spatial structure of flows in a landscape. Peninsulas of two contrasting ecosystem types often interdigitate as a result of erosion. Flows across such an area are heavily dependent on the orientation of the structure relative to the direction of movement.

Networks are composed of corridors and nodes, and trunk lines handle high-volume flows. Network complexity combines the connectivity and the circuitry of the network, which can be measured by the gamma and alpha indices, respectively. Diffusion as a spreading-out process involves either relocation or expansion, depending on whether the objects cease or continue to occupy the original position. Optimization of flows through a network is done for the movement of people and is important for other ecological objects in landscape planning and management.

## QUESTIONS

1. What are the four major functions of corridors? Give an example of each from your own landscape.
2. Why is a "string of lights" configuration so important?
3. A comparison of two landscapes, one with and the other without a hedgerow network, concluded that total stream flow (of water) was essentially the same in each. How could this be so? What water and mineral nutrient differences would you expect?
4. Evaluate the concept of landscape resistance.
5. How could a highly porous matrix enhance movement across the landscape by one species, and inhibit a second species?
6. Diagram an example of peninsular interdigitation and discuss the question of movement across such an area.
7. Which is more important in landscape ecology, time-distance or topological space? Why?
8. Compare a network with low complexity to one with high complexity.
9. How is diffusion of objects different in the gravity model, in hierarchical diffusion, and in relocation diffusion? Give examples.
10. State the three major points you would make if you were giving a talk on how landscape structure affects landscape functioning.

# 12
# *Landscape Change*

*Change*
*Nature's mighty law*
**Robert Burns**

Screams and terrible cracking noises awakened the people of San Francisco. Streets were shaking, deep chasms were appearing, buildings were tilting and walls crumbling. Wood stoves were overturning and flames were escaping, people were being crushed or were racing for the streets. The earthquake struck in the early morning of 18 April 1906, and lasted forty seconds (Figure 12.1). The urban landscape was shaken, but several more days passed before it was really transformed. The earthquake had broken the water lines of the city. Countless small fires were fanned by a wind. Soon a fiery holocaust was in the making. Demolition teams appeared, blowing up rows of city blocks with explosives, trying to stop the gathering fire. The San Francisco landscape was blackened.

In October 1871, Mrs. O'Leary's cow is said to have upset a kerosene lamp in a small barn, causing a similar effect in the Chicago landscape. Warplanes caused major transformations of London in December 1940 and of Cologne in May 1942. Massive herbicide spraying transformed the Mekong River delta landscape in 1966. The completion of huge dikes in Holland in the twelfth, thirteenth, and twentieth centuries created whole new landscapes. In 1953, an ocean storm perforated the Dutch dikes, and an enormous 160,000-hectare area was flooded.

The above are dramatic "overnight" changes in landscapes, and the list could go on and on. Large landscape changes like these also take place over longer time frames. Suburbanization, deforestation, reforestation, desertification, and irrigation are pervasive processes that may convert an entire landscape into quite a different one on the same stretch of land (Figure 12.2). Furthermore, numerous small gradual changes in landscapes are taking place around us all the time. In this chapter, we are interested in how a landscape changes as a whole (Watt, 1947; Curtis, 1956; Darby, 1956; Sears, 1962; Raup, 1966; Gomez-Pompa et al., 1972; Heinselman, 1973; Brender, 1974; Peterken, 1976; Johnson and Sharpe, 1976; Johnson, 1977; Miller, 1978a; Fabos, 1979; Soule and Wilcox, 1980; Loucks, 1970; West et al., 1981; Shugart and West, 1981;

**427**

**Figure 12.1** *Transformation of the urban landscape of San Francisco. This photograph of City Hall was taken in the hours after the 1906 earthquake before fire spread across the city and reduced this and other structures to rubble. Photo from the files of California Department of Conservation, Division of Mines and Geology. Photographer unknown.*

Sharpe et al., 1981; Ruzicka et al., 1982; Romme and Knight, 1982; Romme, 1982; Minnich, 1983; Weinstein and Shugart, 1983).

## STABILITY

The forest fire that introduced Chapter 3 and the hunt using corridors at the opening of Chapter 4 were phenomena that took place within a landscape and in less than a day. Many factors affecting whole landscapes, however, operate at broader levels of both spatial and temporal scale. Thus, successional processes (Chapter 7) usually operate over decades or centuries, geomorphic processes (Chapter 6) take millennia or longer, and major groups of organisms have evolved over millions of years. It is possible, however, by understanding how the parameters that determine a landscape vary over time, to evaluate and compare all three of these time scales.

**Figure 12.2** *Coastal sand dune moving over a pine forest. The 25-meter-high maritime pine forest* (Pinus pinaster) *versus the 105-m-high Dune de Pilat, the highest dune in Europe, south of Bordeaux, France. (R. Forman).*

## Variation Curves

Regardless of which time scale is of interest, we begin by carefully examining the shapes of the curves that describe variation of the landscape as a function of time. These **variation curves** can be characterized by three independent parameters.

1. The **general tendency** of change (increasing, decreasing, or level).
2. The relative **amplitude of oscillation** around the general tendency (large or small).
3. The **rhythm of oscillation** (regular or irregular).

In the real world, these three simple parameters are combined and produce the temporal patterns illustrated by the curves in Figure 12.3. A wide range of important changing characteristics can be studied in a landscape, such as patch shapes, corridor widths, matrix porosity, network development, productivity, nitrogen levels, biotic diversity, rare bird species, successional rate, flows of water between landscape elements, insect movement across the landscape, total biomass, and so forth. Several examples of variation curves are instructive.

Changes in biomass over 1000 years in the Appalachian hardwood

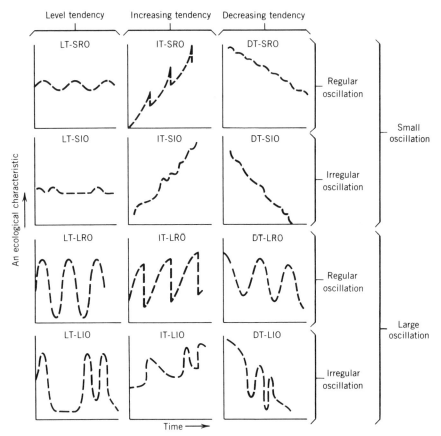

**Figure 12.3** *Examples of the twelve variation curves of ecological systems. Three basic attributes underlie these curves—general tendency, amplitude of oscillation, and rhythm of oscillation. Abbreviations used for the curves represent these three attributes—for example, LT-SRO is level tendency with small regular oscillation; DT-SIO is decreasing tendency with small irregular oscillation. These particular curves represent biomass changes in various landscapes over various time scales.*

forest of Tennessee (Figure 12.4*a*), estimated with a mathematical model (FORET), show a level general tendency with large irregular oscillations (variation curve LT-LIO in Figure 12.3). An area of woodland near Cambridge, England (Figure 12.4*b*), shows over the past four centuries a decreasing tendency with small irregular oscillations (curve DT-SIO in Figure 12.3). Carbon dioxide concentration in the air over more than two decades (Figure 12.4*c*), shows a marked increasing tendency with large regular oscillations (curve IT-LRO in Figure 12.3).

Of the dozen curves in Figure 12.3, we need to find out which are the most common trajectories for major landscape parameters, and why. Additional characteristics of variation could be added to these curves. For example, the shape of troughs may be symmetric or asymmetric, or the amplitude of oscillations may increase or decrease over time.

Often we can simply "eyeball" the trajectory of a landscape parameter, such as that in Figure 12.4c, and determine which of the dozen fundamental variation curves it is. We can also use simple statistical measures (such as time-series analysis—Box and Jenkins, 1970; Box, 1981). Generally, we find out if the observed values of the parameter can be significantly represented by a straight line (a linear regression) with level, positive, or negative slope. Then we determine how large the amplitude of oscillation is and whether the variability of the observed values above and below the line represents a significant regular oscillation. Such determinations are a good point of departure for characterizing the stability, or instability, of the landscape.

## Stability and Instability

All landscapes are subject to climatic fluctuations, and many parameters characterizing the landscape oscillate in the short term, that is, over the seasons (Figure 12.4c). In addition, most landscapes follow a long-term tendency, such as an increase in biomass over several successions (Figure 12.4a), or an increase in contrast between landscape elements as human influence increases. Therefore, it seems reasonable to say that a landscape is ("globally") **stable,** if (a) the long-term variability of its parameters is significantly represented by a horizontal line, and (b) the amplitude and degree of periodicity of oscillations around the line are (statistically) characterizable. Thus, only variation curves with a level tendency and small or large regular oscillations are stable (LT-SRO and LT-LRO in Figure 12.3).

This definition of stability is broad, but its necessity emerges when we recognize that the stability of a biological system is never "absolute," since no living system can be absolutely constant. Biological stability is, in true terms, a **metastability**; that is, the system is in **equilibrium**—it oscillates around a central position—and may also escape to a different equilibrium position. As long as the landscape system oscillates around a central position, it is in a metastable equilibrium.

**Instability** characterizes the landscape if a small environmental change is sufficient to divert the system out of its regime of oscillation around a central position. In this case a new trajectory appears that leads the system toward a different central position. Instability (or an unstable system) is the case in which the regime of fluctuation (i.e., the combination of general tendency, amplitude, and periodicity) is changing or unpredictable.

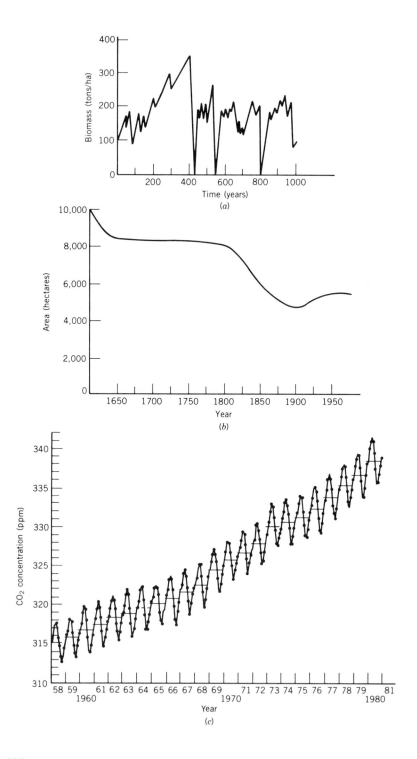

Two types of instability appear to exist. In one, the system changes and reaches a new regime of predictable oscillations—a new metastable equilibrium—after disturbance. In the other, no new (statistically) predictable regime of fluctuation appears. In other words, instability is either temporary or persistent. Temporary instability appears, for example, where mature hardwood forest is replaced by an equilibrium of regular cultivation. Persistent instability usually appears after the plowing of arid grasslands, as in southern Tunisia where wheat and barley crops cannot be dependably established because of frequent droughts (Floret and Pontanier, 1982).

Numerous terms have been proposed to refer to the stability of ecological systems (such as resistance, persistence, amplitude, deflection, elasticity, hysteresis, inertia, malleability, recovery, resilience, and vulnerability), making the current terminology chaotic (Woodwell and Smith, 1969; Westman, 1978). Nevertheless, some of these terms are particularly useful for dealing with major properties of landscape change. **Persistence,** as a measure of stability, refers to the time period during which a certain characteristic of a landscape continues to be present (or present at a given level). For example, the persistence of unbroken stream corridors, fine-mesh networks, certain species, or certain energy flow or mineral nutrient levels may be a distinct measurable characteristic of a landscape (Hairston et al., 1968; Odum, 1969; McNaughton, 1977; Van Voris et al., 1980; Ruzicka et al., 1978; Vitousek and Reiners, 1975; Dorney and Hoffman, 1979; Klotzli, 1980; Balser et al., 1981; Likens et al., 1977; LaMotte, 1983).

Another widely used approach is one that considers stability in terms of the response of a system to a disturbance or perturbation (e.g., Smith, 1972; May, 1973; Hurd and Wolf, 1974; Mellinger and McNaughton, 1975; Holling, 1973; Stolina, 1982; Grubb and Hopkins, 1985). In this case, stability is the product of two rather dissimilar characteristics of the system, resistance and recovery. **Resistance** is the ability of the system,

---

**Figure 12.4** *Three of the variation curves. (a) Predicted biomass of the Appalachian hardwood forest in Tennessee (United States) over a millennium (Reprinted by permission,* American Scientist, *journal of Sigma Xi, "Long-term Dynamics of Forest Ecosystems," by H. H. Shugart and D. C. West, 69:649 (1981). (b) Area of the Rockingham forest near Cambridge, England, over the past four centuries (from Peterken, 1976). (Courtesy of Blackwell Scientific Publications Ltd.) (c) Carbon dioxide concentration of the atmosphere on Mauna Loa, Hawaii, over 22 years. (Courtesy of D. Keeling). The upward trend is the result of fossil fuel combustion and forest destruction. The annual oscillation is due to respiration and photosynthesis of vegetation in the northern hemisphere (from Woodwell, 1983, based on MacCracken and Moses, 1982). (Courtesy of G. M. Woodwell and Springer-Verlag, New York, Inc.)*

when subjected to an environmental change or potential disturbance, to withstand or resist variation. **Recovery** or resilience is the ability of the system to bounce back or return after being changed. Resistance is measured as the inverse of the amount of deflection of a system from its initial trajectory. In essence, a large deflection means low resistance. Recovery is measured as the time required to return to the initial trajectory.

More generally, a characteristic of a system could be called stable if a disturbance causes a small total amount, or "integral," of variation in the system (Van Voris et al., 1980). The integral combines the resistance (amplitude of change) with the time-lag for recovery to the initial trajectory of the system. This approach is useful, especially for a mathematical model of the system. However, when combining these two characteristics (resistance and recovery) to produce a single number representing the degree of stability, we lose some of our ability to interpret causes. For example, we must clearly differentiate between two landscapes with the same total integral response, if the first one changes drastically but returns rapidly to its initial state, whereas the second one changes only slightly but recovers very slowly to its initial state. Therefore, in stability studies it is best to measure and express resistance and recovery as separate components of stability.

There is another reason why response to disturbance appears to be a valuable measure of landscape stability. San Francisco burned only about 50 years after it became a city. Because it did not persist unaltered for long (Figure 12.1)—only 50 years—we might incorrectly conclude that it had low stability (relative to fire). On the other hand, we could observe the same system for millennia during which no disturbance of this magnitude occurred. In this case, we would correctly conclude the system was highly persistent, but could not say it was highly stable. The reason for these different conclusions has nothing to do with the characteristics of that landscape system. Rather, in the second case simply by chance no strong disturbance occurred during the period of observation. Hence, the determination of stability must include observations during a period with strong environmental changes. We will now explore an example of this concept.

### An Example of Stability Followed by Degradation

The landscapes of the Sahel steppe or savanna belt south of the Sahara are thought to have scarcely changed from 1000 to 1900 A.D. Despite marked oscillations between dry and wet seasons, the landscape characteristics remained at a relatively constant average over several centuries. In other words, the landscapes exhibited a stability of type LT-LRO (Figure 12.3), a level tendency with large regular oscillations.

During rainy seasons in this area, annual plants germinate and develop a large biomass in a few weeks, while perennial plants put out leaves and build up reserves necessary for survival through the dry season. Biomass decreases during dry periods. This regular variability is an inherent characteristic of these landscapes. Plant and animal species are adapted to these climatic cycles, and the nomad shepherds wisely optimized the grazing process by moving their flocks over hundreds of kilometers (Brown, 1971b). The ecologist considers this landscape to be stable, as if it were the same sequence in a movie film repeated indefinitely. On the whole, during these centuries the ecological systems had relatively low production and supported a scattered human population.

Since about 1900, however, the traditional societies have been changing their way of life. Governments have tried to settle the nomads by digging wells, aiding in the construction of homes, and modifying the system of political control of citizens living far from administrative capitals. Consequently, the human population density has risen, and the mobility of flocks of sheep has diminished. For many years, this new system seemed to be metastable, with oscillations around a central position. But a decade of drought that began around 1970 (Zonneveld, 1980) revealed that this new equilibrium was unstable. In response to severe drought, the flocks totally destroyed the vegetation in the vicinity of the wells (see Figure 5.5), and finally, therefore, became decimated themselves. Since the 1970s, then, the landscape system has undergone variations characterized by a decreasing tendency with large irregular oscillations (DT-LIO of Figure 12.3).

## METASTABILITY

### Models

The relationship between stability and instability in ecological systems is essentially dialectic, since instability progressively gives way to stability, and stability is always ephemeral. It is as some physicians consider good health: "a temporary state between periods of ill health." To clarify this relationship, we return to the idea of metastability as a keystone. Metastability is the type of stability that permits us to live and in fact underlies all biological phenomena. To understand its nature, let us consider the movement of a marble on a "Russian hills" model (Figure 12.5) (Godron and Forman, 1983; Godron, 1984).

If the marble were placed on the summits at L, M, or N, it would be in an unstable equilibrium (Figure 12.5). The most stable equilibrium position for the marble is point A, because it can descend no further. But it can also remain at points B, C, or D, even if the system is shaken with environmental changes, as long as the changes are not too strong. Thus,

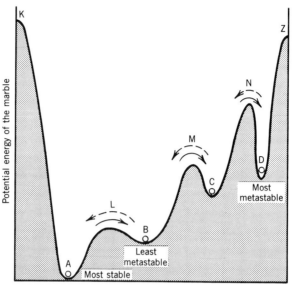

**Figure 12.5**  *The "Russian hills" model of the stability and metastability of a physical system. A marble moves from trough to trough depending upon the intensity (energy level) of an environmental change such as shaking (from Godron and Forman, 1983). (Courtesy of Springer-Verlag New York, Inc.)*

by definition, points *B, C*, and *D* are metastable equilibrium positions. The points are "highly" metastable if the troughs are deep. At no other point on the Russian hills can the marble be in an equilibrium state, since at any other point it would move between equilibrium points and therefore be unstable. Metastability, therefore, is not an intermediate condition between instability and stability. Rather, it is a combination of the two with new properties.

The Russian hills model helps to understand the nature of metastability and stability. As is always the case with a physical system, however, the model does not give sufficient understanding of an ecological system with its photosynthesizing plants, heterogeneous structure, and feedback mechanisms. A more elaborated "metastability model" (Figure 12.6) provides further insight and predictability into landscape change and should account for the following ecological patterns.

1. The landscape develops directly from points *A* to *B* to *C* to *D*, as biomass (potential energy) progressively accumulates in the absence

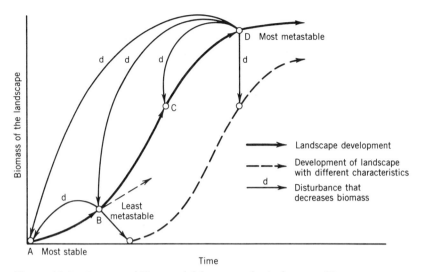

**Figure 12.6** *A metastability model for an ecological system. Biomass accumulates through succession, and most disturbances decrease biomass. Increasing metastability means that greater environmental changes are necessary to disturb the system. Some disturbances so change the system that it has quite different characteristics as biomass subsequently accumulates. Points A, B, and D represent the three basic types of stability.*

of disturbance (Figure 12.6). Biomass levels off in a sigmoid fashion as the landscape reaches its maximum biomass.

2. Disturbances such as pollution, overgrazing, or hurricanes may decrease biomass or—less commonly—increase it, e.g., by extended rain in a grassland, fertilizer, or the abrupt reduction of a major grazer population. Systems are less likely to return to their predisturbance level from biomass-increasing disturbances (subsidies) (Mellinger and McNaughton, 1975; Odum et al., 1979) than from biomass-decreasing ones.

3. "Most-stable" physical or mineral systems cannot lose biomass, but may change rapidly to a low metastable landscape—either by landscape development (biomass accumulation) or biomass-increasing disturbance—or remain unchanged. The difference depends on the ability of green plants to colonize.

4. "Low-metastable" systems have little resistance to disturbances of either sort but may recover rapidly from biomass-decreasing disturbance if seeds or sprouts are abundant.

5. "High-metastable" systems have high resistance to many disturbances of either sort but commonly recover very slowly (if at all), because their feedback loops are destroyed and considerable biomass is lost.

6. Disturbance may change characteristics of a landscape (e.g., landscape element types, human influences, or predominant species) without changing its potential energy level. Disturbance may also result in characteristics different from those of the previous S-shaped trajectory of biomass accumulation.
7. The level of metastability depends on the depth of a trough, not the amount of potential energy. Thus, a highly metastable system (e.g., long-term agriculture) may be maintained at a low biomass level by constant inputs of human energy or fossil fuel.

In Figure 12.5, potential energy and the depth of troughs are plotted. It should now be obvious that several additional ecological characteristics are critical in determining the stability characteristics of landscapes. Furthermore, we now have a framework for answering a nagging question (Horn, 1975) that might be posed as follows. Which is more stable, the often-disturbed field that returns immediately to field, or the seldom-disturbed old forest that takes so long to return to forest?

The landscape mosaic is composed of landscape elements in different states of instability and stability. Three basic types of stable landscape elements are usually present.

1. Rock outcrops and paved corridors, for example, are "most stable"— that is, they possess **physical-system stability** (point A in Figure 12.6), with a negligible amount of photosynthetic surface or energy stored in biomass.
2. "Low metastability" elements (point B in Figure 12.6) represent resilience or **recovery stability,** with relatively low biomass and many short-lived, rapidly reproducing species.
3. "High metastability" elements (point D in Figure 12.6) represent **resistance stability,** with large biomass and many long-lived species such as trees and large mammals.

The first type of landscape element is essentially a closed system, while the last two are open systems.

In this fashion, changes within a landscape, and change of a whole landscape, are directly related to (a) the types of stability present in specific landscape elements and (b) the spatial structure of the landscape.


## Species Coexistence Patterns

The biotic diversity principle introduced in Chapter 1 included the idea that species coexistence increases with increased landscape heterogeneity. The question of how a large number of species coexist in a particular ecosystem has sparked considerable interest and insight. Two opposite solutions are proposed to this problem. The first is a stable equilibrium that embraces three characteristics.

1. If two species occupy the same (ecological) niche in the same stable community, one will become extinct.
2. No two species observed in a stable community are direct competitors limited by the same resources; the species differ in niche in ways that reduce competition between them.
3. The community is a system of interacting, niche-differentiated populations that tend to complement one another, rather than directly competing, in their uses of the community's space, time resources, and possible kinds of interactions (Whittaker, 1975).

These three **competitive equilibrium** characteristics lead to the conclusion that species coexistence results directly from competition (e.g., Slatkin, 1974).

The second solution is radically different.

Alternatively, communities may be organized under conditions which prevent the attainment of competitive equilibrium. . . . Competitive assortment and the resultant succession toward equilibrium may be halted by events having three characteristics.

1. The effective disturbance event creates an environment that, at least temporarily, favors species with poorer competitive abilities than the competitive dominants in the closed community. Such environments will periodically appear as gaps or patches in the canopy of dominants and they may vary internally or grade into the dominant canopy.
2. The event must create patches at time intervals shorter than those required for exclusion of poor competitors throughout a region. A ''region'' includes a number of sites that are potential sources of propagules of all species in the succession (see also Pickett and Thompson, 1978).
3. Patches must be spatially disturbed such that they are accessible to the poorer competitors (Pickett, 1980).

As Pickett observes, these three requirements of nonequilibrium coexistence would seem to be provided by many of the agents that create patches in nature. In this view, the characteristics of the system largely oscillate around an average value or central position (Chapter 2) (see, e.g., Connell, 1978).

It would be astonishing if these two solutions were absolutely contradictory, and the laws of evolution and coadaptation of species left only the choice between two mutually exclusive solutions. It seems rather that we have a metastable equilibrium combining two types of structures.

1. In agreement with the competitive equilibrium solution, plant or animal communities may reach an equilibrium where heterogeneous vertical structure is combined with a rather uniform horizontal structure. For example, in an equatorial rain forest, herbivorous parrots, monkeys, and pigs would be found wherever you walked in the forest but would separate out at different vertical levels in the forest.
2. In agreement with the nonequilibrium solution, the animal or plant community may be composed of patches in different successional stages next to one another with specialized species in each type of patch.

In fact, over time ecological systems attain several metastable equilibria, because none is perfectly stable. Each is sufficiently stable to last until a disturbance arrives to send the system to another metastable state (Loucks, 1970; White, 1979).

## PATTERNS OF OVERALL LANDSCAPE CHANGE

Landscape change was a major theme in the early study of ecology. The works of Kerner (1863) in the Danube Basin and of Clements (1916, 1920) and Cowles (1901) in the midwestern United States emphasized the importance of succession, as it described the change of many ecological systems. These authors showed that the systems progressively tended to stabilize themselves and would follow a new succession after being disturbed.

Numerous careful studies have described the stages or types of community that succeed one another when a parcel of bare land is invaded, or reinvaded, by vegetation (e.g., Cowles, 1901; Cooper, 1913; Oosting, 1942; Bard, 1952; Gaussen, 1954; Botkin et al., 1972; Schmidt, 1975; Noble and Slatyer, 1978; Bazzaz, 1979; West et al., 1981). In landscape ecology we look at the sequence of each individual landscape element, and also at how the integrated whole changes (Shugart et al., 1973; Pickett, 1976; Whittaker and Levin, 1977; West et al., 1981; Shugart and West, 1981; Franklin and Hemstrom, 1981; Ruzicka et al., 1982). We must perceive landscape "cinematics," that is, the sequence of stages and changing proportions of landscape element types over the whole landscape. For example, if many of the patches of shifting cultivation scattered in a tropical rain forest matrix are abandoned, the structure of the whole may change, because matrix porosity (Chapter 5) diminishes, the forest animals that used the clearings become less numerous, and the paths or corridors linking the cultivated openings to the village disappear. In a small temperate nature reserve, the bird community changed over two decades as a result of both vegetation change on the reserve and an influx of new birds associated with surrounding suburbanization (Butcher et al., 1981; Aldrich and Coffin, 1980). In southern Ontario, the disappearance of several animal species such as the black bear (*Ursus americanus*) is reported to have coincided approximately with the threshold of 50% of the forest matrix being cleared (Dorney and Hoffman, 1979; Balser et al., 1981). It is possible to condense all such landscape changes into a precise format, presenting them in the form of a "transition matrix" (Waggoner and Stephens, 1970; Bledsoe and Van Dyne, 1971; Godron, 1973; Peden et al., 1973; Levin and Paine, 1974; Auclair, 1976; Zeimetz et al., 1976; Johnson and Sharpe, 1976; Enright and Ogden, 1979; Horn, 1976; Usher, 1979; West et al., 1981; Johnson, 1983).

## The Transition Matrix

Let us consider two maps of the same landscape drawn several years apart and look at how each landscape element is maintained or replaced by another type of element in the interval between mappings. We can place a grid of points over each map and note how many points landing on landscape element type *A* on the first map become type *B* points on the second map, or become type *C, D,* and so forth (Figure 12.7). The percentage change for each of these conversions, based on the total number of points observed, is called a transition or **replacement rate.** A simple way to organize these replacement rates is to list the replacements from *A* to *B, A* to *C, A* to *D,* and so forth on a line (Figure 12.7). Then on a second line, the replacement rates from *B* to others are listed, on a third line those from *C* to others, continuing until there is one line for each type of landscape element present. This collection of lines containing replacement rates makes up a table called a **transition matrix** (using the word "matrix" in its purely mathematical sense).

Transition matrices are used in several disciplines, such as medicine (to study probabilities of infection), genetics (chromosome crossovers), or physics (nuclear reactions). In these applications, the percentages are probabilities that remain constant over time, and the results of a transition matrix are therefore determined by a mathematical process called a Markov chain. In the case of landscapes, replacement rates appear rarely to remain constant over time. However, observed changes and simulations of desired changes have been described with transition matrices for landscape management (Godron, 1973; Godron and Lepart, 1973; Johnson and Sharpe, 1976; Auclair, 1976; Zeimetz et al., 1976; Debussche et al., 1977; Franklin, 1979; Kessell and Potter, 1980; Floret and Pontanier, 1982).

If transition rates remain constant within a landscape, the proportion of surface area covered by each landscape element type would tend

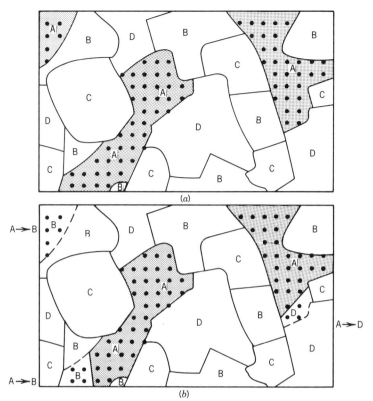

**Figure 12.7** *Landscape change for analysis with a transition matrix. Letters A, B, C, and D represent four types of landscape elements in an area mapped at two points in time. In the first map, (a), 80 grid points represent type A. In the follow-up map (b), 67 points (84%) remained as type A, 10 points (12%) were replaced by B, no points (0%) were replaced by type C, and 3 points (4%) were replaced by type D. The percentages are called transition or replacement rates.*

toward a stable equilibrium. To understand this idea, let us consider a plain in central Europe, where pastures or artificial grasslands last an average of eight years. They are followed by a period of grain cultivation lasting two years, and then by a reseeding of the pasture legumes and grasses. Each year, $\frac{1}{8}$ (or 12.5%) of the pastures are put in cultivation, and $\frac{7}{8}$ remain as pasture. Since the crop fields only last two years, half of their area each year is transformed into pasture, and the other half remains in cultivation.

The transition matrix that describes this double rhythm of change is as follows:

| | Pastures in the Following Year | Cultivated Fields in the Following Year |
|---|---|---|
| Pastures, in the first year | 87.5% | 12.5% |
| Cultivated fields, in the first year | 50% | 50% |

To show how this transition matrix works, we will start with an area that contains 1000 hectares in pasture and 1000 hectares in cultivation. After one year, the area in pasture will be

$$(87.5\% \times 1000\ ha) + (50\% \times 1000\ ha) = 875 + 500 = 1375\ ha$$

and the area of cultivated fields will be

$$(12.5\% \times 1000\ ha) + (50\% \times 1000\ ha) = 125 + 500 = 625\ ha$$

At the end of the second year, the areas are

$$(87.5\% \times 1375) + (50\% \times 625) = 1516\ ha\ in\ pasture, and$$
$$(12.5\% \times 1375) + (50\% \times 625) = 484\ ha\ in\ cultivation$$

After the third year, the areas are

$$(87.5\% \times 1516) + (50\% \times 484) = 1568\ ha\ in\ pasture, and$$
$$(12.5\% \times 1516) + (50\% \times 484) = 432\ ha\ in\ cultivation$$

Continuing these calculations for several years gives the following:

$1568 \to 1588 \to 1596 \to 1598 \to 1599 \to 1600 \to 1600$ ha in pasture
$432 \to 412 \to 404 \to 402 \to 401 \to 400 \to 400$ ha in cultivation

Figure 12.8 illustrates this landscape change along with two other sequential changes that begin with extremely different proportions of landscape element types. Interestingly, the final equilibrium appears not to be affected by the initial proportions of elements in a landscape but to depend only on the replacement rates. In the above example, the equilibrium level is 1600 ha and 400 ha, or a 4 : 1 ratio of pasture to cultivation in the landscape, no matter what the initial conditions were on the landscape (Figure 12.8). This ratio (and the areas of each land use) could be predicted from the average lengths of time a pasture and a cultivated field last, that is, 8 years versus 2 years, or a 4 : 1 ratio. Note that the predicted equilibrium, 1600 ha pasture and 400 ha cultivation, is based on the important assumption or observation that the replacement rate remains constant.

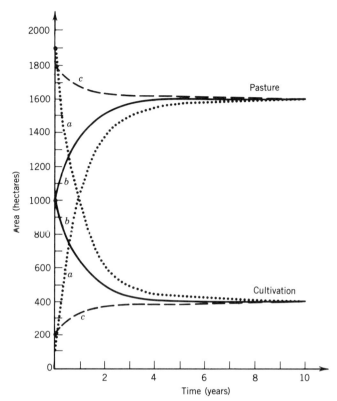

**Figure 12.8** *Change in three hypothetical landscapes using the same transition matrix, but beginning with different proportions of landscape elements. Landscape a begins with 19 times as much cultivation as pasture; b with equal proportions of the two; and c with 9 times as much pasture as cultivation.*

Transition matrices are constructed with a constant unit of time corresponding, for example, to the number of years separating two records in a regular sequence of aerial photographs. If we observe change at extremely short intervals (making processes appear almost continuous) or if the number of types of elements is numerous, other models may be used (Weinstein and Shugart, 1983). On the whole, since landscapes are complex systems, simplifying mathematical models are useful to gain understanding, but any model must be used (and the results interpreted) with caution considering the assumptions that have allowed the simplification.

In the pasture and cultivation example, the equilibrium is not static because part of the landscape changes each year. Therefore, it differs from the competitive equilibrium stability summarized by Whittaker (1975) but corresponds precisely with the nonequilibrium, regular replacement of patches described by Pickett (1980).

## The Shifting Mosaic

Mosaic changes have been studied within an ecosystem, where patches are different stages of a successional sequence.[1] Despite the presence of disturbances and progressive transformations in the patches, the ecosystem as a whole may be in steady state (Bormann and Likens, 1979, 1981), losing biomass (degrading), or accumulating biomass (aggrading).

In contrast, a landscape is composed of different types of landscape elements (such as rock outcrops, cultivated fields, woods, and paved roads), plus patches of different successional ages. Nevertheless, over a long term it may be stable, degrading, or aggrading. During long-term gradual change, short-term conversions of one landscape element to another take place, often at a rapid rate. A system exhibiting a pattern of long-term change along with short-term, internal spatial conversions is called a *shifting mosaic*.

In fact, this exact pattern occurred over a four-decade period in agricultural and urbanizing landscapes of southern Wisconsin (United States) (Sharpe et al., 1981). In the agricultural landscape studied from 1963 to 1975, the amount of "other natural vegetation" (excluding forest) remained constant at 187 hectares (Figure 12.9). Each year approximately seven hectares of this natural vegetation was lost, while seven hectares of other land-use areas were converted to it. In other words, the total for the landscape element type "other natural vegetation" remained absolutely stable, whereas patches of it appeared and disappeared at the average rate of about 4% per year (i.e., 84 hectares over the 12-year interval).

In the agricultural landscape of Wisconsin, crop and pastureland remained quite stable over the entire four-decade period, and the other types of landscape elements varied only slightly more (Figure 12.9). In the urbanizing landscape, on the other hand, forest and other natural vegetation also remained relatively stable, while a sharp drop in crop and pastureland was counterbalanced by a sharp increase in the landscape element type called "urban uses."

Ruzicka et al. (1982) recognized the concept of a shifting mosaic when they compared the stability of seven Czechoslovakian landscapes over either one or two centuries. For each landscape a stability index was

---

[1]See, for instance, Cooper, 1913; Watt, 1947; Whittaker, 1953; Barclay-Estrup, 1970; Heinselman, 1973; Shugart et al., 1973; Pickett, 1976; Grubb, 1977; Oliver and Stephens, 1977; Lorimer, 1977; King, 1977; Gimingham et al., 1979; Denslow, 1980; Shugart and West, 1981; Paine and Levin, 1981; Runkle, 1981; Forman and Boerner, 1981; Boerner and Forman, 1982; Minnich, 1983; Johnson, 1983.

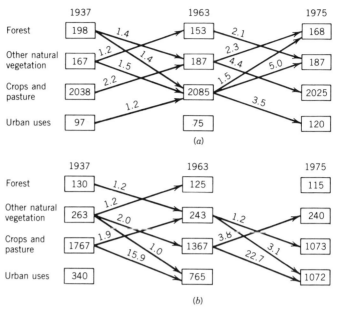

**Figure 12.9** *Changes in agricultural (a) and urbanizing (b) landscapes over 38 years. Boxes indicate total areas of each landscape element type in hectares. Arrows indicate average land use or cover changes in hectares per year. Each of these landscape areas, which are near Milwaukee, Wisconsin (United States) is 25 km² (from Sharpe et al., 1981). (Courtesy of D. M. Sharpe and Pudoc-Centre for Agricultural Publishing and Documentation.)*

calculated that was based on the stabilities and relative areas of the different landscape element types present in the mosaic. The stability of each landscape element type in turn was based on estimating the persistence or change in eight characteristics (energy fixation, biomass structure, species diversity, moisture, and so forth) over the time period. Six of the seven landscapes were decreasing in stability according to this analysis. Only a relatively eroded, hilly agricultural area with some forests showed a slight increase in stability over the past century. This study also showed that within a landscape certain landscape elements were much more stable than others.

## LANDSCAPE DYNAMICS

The ideas presented so far in this chapter provide only glimpses into a growing area of investigation. As stated in the *Newsletter* of the International Association of Ecology (1983), "The presence or absence of constant performance [and] . . . [t]he nature of stability, equilibrium, and change [are] still a central problem of ecology."

To resolve this problem, we might begin by delineating the level at which a landscape P is so modified that it is no longer landscape P and becomes landscape R. It could be agreed, for example, that this significant change is attained only when (a) a different landscape element type becomes the matrix, (b) several percentages of surfaces covered by element types have sufficiently changed, or (c) a new type of landscape element appears in the landscape and attains a certain threshold of coverage.

Each of these three proposed solutions is significant, because changes in the structure of a landscape are related to changes in its functioning. Present structure is the result of past functioning. But present structure also determines future functioning. Because of this tight linkage, it appears important to address *landscape organization,* a concept that unifies structure and functioning by integrating the spatial configuration with the patterns of flows in a landscape. This concept leads to a broader, more fundamental integration because it focuses on the active forces that drive landscape dynamics.

## Active Forces

When people cut down a forest or construct a superhighway, or buildings, the forces that produced the change are evident. When purely natural phenomena produce the change it is not so easy to understand all the forces that acted. The natural forces that act in a landscape include not only purely physical forces such as gravitation, mountain uplift, grinding glaciers, and the impact of raindrops, but also include the muscular activity of animals, from the insect or earthworm to the elephant or bison.

A striking example of the role animals play in a landscape is visible on an ancient plateau in western Kenya (Raunet, 1979). Hills with gentle slopes are covered with a red and yellow soil that is several meters deep, slightly moist (even through the dry season), composed of sand, silt, and clay (30% silt), and thoroughly mixed by termites. Wind and water sweep silt particles down from the grassy hills to the wide valleys below. The silt-rich soils of the valley support woody vegetation, thus giving the landscape a much-branched corridor appearance (Figure 12.10). All these flows are controlled by the muscle action of termites, which thoroughly breaks up and mixes all of the soil of the upland plateau. Only after this "soil muscle" process are the soil particles available for wind and water transport.

The most general biological force in the landscape is the vertical growth of plants that continually drives foliage upward (Chapter 7). Vegetation

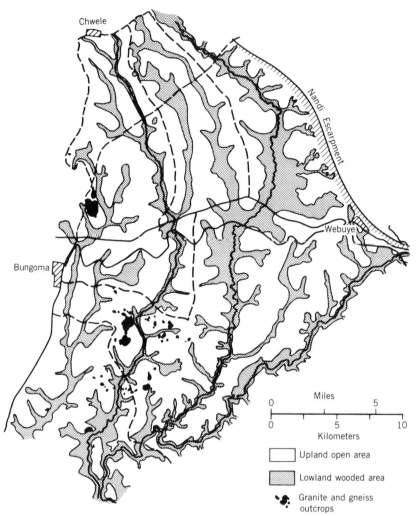

**Figure 12.10** *Ridge and valley landscape in western Kenya controlled by termite activity. Note the corridor structure and peninsular interdigitation (from Raunet, 1979). (Courtesy of the Institut des Recherches Agronomiques Tropicales.)*

colonizes bare areas over time, and the height of the green mantle tends to increase progressively, in the absence of disturbance. In the vertical dimension, however, the upward plant growth force causes a striking heterogeneity to appear. Vertical structure or layers become evident, with different animals and plants active at different levels within this structure (McClure, 1966; Harrison, 1962; Horn, 1971; Halle et al., 1978; Trabaud, 1984).

We should also mention the role of inertia. The processes of increasing biomass accumulation and increasing soil uniformity (see Chapter 6, the law of zonality) proceed more and more slowly, with oscillations increasingly dampened. In effect, inertia becomes an important stabilizing force.

The ways these forces act on a landscape suggest one of the emerging principles of landscape ecology (Chapter 1). Landscapes tend toward stability—slowly, and sometimes with detours due to disturbance—but nonetheless inexorably.

When we focus on the process, rather than the end product of the process, the point becomes obvious. If all rates diminish, the system varies less and less and remains persistently identical to itself. A landscape in an equilibrium is in a trough of metastability, at the center of dampened oscillations. The system escapes the trough only when a strong disturbance causes it to do so, in which case the system usually soon gets caught in another trough (Figure 12.5).

## Levels of Force

**Elasticity and Rupture in a Physical System.** Building on the conceptual bases of the preceding sections, we now add an idea that permits us to refine the distinction between metastability and instability. When we observe a simple system, such as a metal rod being stretched by the force of tension, we see two thresholds, the *rupture point* and the *elasticity limit*. Well known to engineers and mechanics, they will help us to sharpen up several observations.

1. If the force applied passes the rupture point $C$, the metal rod breaks, and the system is destroyed (Figure 12.11).
2. If the force is very much weaker than the rupture point, the rod returns exactly to its original form when it is no longer under tension. This elastic deformation has an upper boundary, the elasticity limit $E$ (Figure 12.11). (The elongation of the rod $D$ is proportional to the force applied $F$. In other words, $D = kF$, where $k$ is a coefficient of elasticity for the metal rod.)
3. If the force, however, is between the two points $E$ and $C$, we say the system is in the area of permanent or inelastic deformation. In this case, when the force is relaxed, the metal rod shortens a bit but does not return exactly to its original length. It remains permanently stretched or deformed. Similarly, hammering a metal bar with a force between $E$ and $C$ will flatten the bar, producing a deformation that remains. An interesting consequence of this resulting deformation is that the bar becomes tougher.

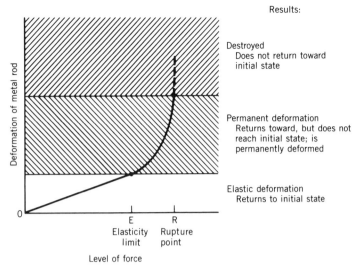

Results:

Destroyed
Does not return toward
initial state

Permanent deformation
Returns toward, but does not
reach initial state; is
permanently deformed

Elastic deformation
Returns to initial state

E                R
Elasticity    Rupture
limit          point

Level of force

**Figure 12.11**   *Effects of increasing force on a physical system such as a metal rod.*

**Ecological Responses to Varying Levels of Force.**   These physical system characteristics appear to be useful in understanding ecological systems. In fact, they can serve as a model for characterizing landscape change. Low-level forces result in the *landscape oscillation* illustrated by figure 12.12. That is, minor environmental changes cause landscape characteristics to change but only as fluctuations around a central position, and the landscape remains in its equilibrium. For example, a dry year may cause small stream corridors to dry out, but the following wet year results in fewer-than-average dried-out corridors, and the recovery of the scattered, previously-affected landscape elements is facilitated. When the level of force reaches *D*, it acts as a disturbance, causing a landscape characteristic to exceed its equilibrium range of oscillation. The landscape is no longer in equilibrium; it is unstable.

It is often difficult to distinguish between disturbance and minor environmental change. Information on changes in landscape characteristics over many years is generally required if we are to determine the type of variation curve present (Figure 12.3). Determining this is also of interest because a level of force that causes a stable pattern of variation to deviate significantly is a disturbance.

Moderate disturbance levels result in *landscape recovery* to the previous equilibrium (Figure 12.12). For example, three to five drought years in a row may cause a significant number of patches to burn and stream corridors to dry out, a significant deviation from the normal range and type of oscillation previously observed. The normal rains come again,

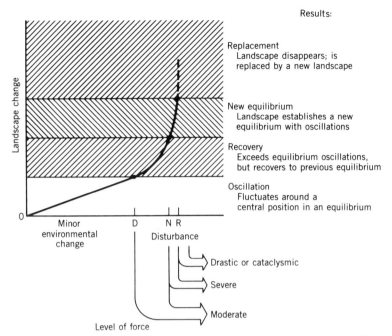

**Figure 12.12** *Effects of increasing force on an ecological system such as a landscape.*

though, and the landscape begins to recover. Whether the return to the original equilibrium is rapid or slow, it does take place.

Severe disturbance results in a *new landscape equilibrium* (Figure 12.12). In this case, the level of force exceeds *N*, and the landscape does not reequilibrate to the previous equilibrium level. A 24-year drought from 1276 to 1299 A.D. in parts of what is now the southwestern United States converted a landscape of shrubland and agriculture to a very open shrubland with few or no agricultural clearings (Watson, 1953). This new equilibrium with its altered proportion of landscape elements occurred because the Pueblo Indians departed from their nearby cliff dwellings (Figure 12.13) in response to 24 years with little water, little food, and the apparent wrath of the gods.

Drastic or cataclysmic disturbance causes *landscape replacement.* Above force level *R,* the original landscape disappears, and a new one takes its place on the same stretch of ground (Figure 12.12). As an example— what is powerful, noisy, and pushy, and exhibits the remarkable ability to both create or destroy whole landscapes? The bulldozer, of course. The force of the bulldozer exceeds *R,* and in a desert as well as a forest it may very effectively convert either landscape to suburbia—not only a new equilibrium, but a new landscape.

**Figure 12.13** *Cliff dwellings in Canyon de Chelley, Arizona (United States), abandoned 680 years ago as a result of a severe disturbance. Remains of the mud brick homes are present (center) by the stream corridor trees at the base of the sandstone cliff and on a ledge above them. A 24-year drought forced the Pueblo Indians to move from this site, which bordered both the stream valley below and the grass and shrub desert plain above. (R. Forman.)*

The new landscape has its own stability (that may be sustainable only with fossil fuel energy), and a new strong disturbance would be necessary to send it back nearly to its original equilibrium. The deforestation of some New York and New England landscapes resulted in an agricultural landscape equilibrium for a hundred years, but in the mid-ninteenth century many farmers moved to rich lands in the midwestern United States, and the terrain reverted toward the former forested equilibrium (Figure 12.14) (Raup and Carlson, 1941; Raup, 1966; Johnson and Sharpe, 1976; Marks, 1983). Areas near Angkor Wat in Cambodia and some former Mayan cities underwent landscape replacement to support these

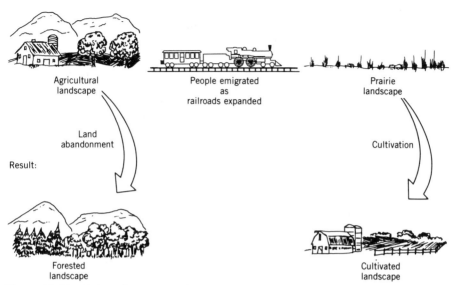

The Northeast

The Midwest

Agricultural
landscape

People emigrated
as
railroads expanded

Prairie
landscape

Land
abandonment

Cultivation

Result:

Forested
landscape

Cultivated
landscape

**Figure 12.14** *Linkage between mid-nineteenth-century landscape changes in the Northeast and Midwest of the United States.*

civilizations, and then subsequent reversion toward a natural landscape occurred.

**Comparison of Some Physical and Ecological Systems.** The models of change in Figures 12.11 and 12.12 offer a special glimpse into the difference between physical and ecological systems, a difference that is critical in the decisions made by society. For example, some scholars consider that the cell can be understood only with known physical and chemical laws. Others note that the cell obeys those laws but also exhibits biological characteristics such as adjustment to altered conditions and adaptation through reproduction.

At a more familiar level, the engineer, faced with the need to dispose of some toxic material, and with a nearby lake, calculates what the average concentration of the material will be if added to the lake, and finds it so low as to be quite safe for the many uses of the lake. The biologist modifies this physical system result by considering in addition the necessary ecological factors, such as lake stratification, the probability of material being especially absorbed by certain organisms, and the ecological accumulation up through the food chain, which result in quite high toxicity to the fish or the fisherman.

Comparing the cases of changes in the metal rod and in the landscape

(Figures 12.11 and 12.12) shows many similarities between the physical and ecological systems. However, when the intermediate force level is between E and R, the metal bar is permanently deformed, whereas the landscape either recovers directly or moves to a new equilibrium while retaining the capacity for eventual recovery. The toughening of the metal rod resulting from its deformation is an interesting analogy, because the landscape is probably often more resistant to a disturbance following recovery, largely because of shifts in some of the species present (Cocking and Forman, 1983).

The terms irreversible and permanent are sometimes used in relation to change in a physical system (Ayyad and Le Floc'h, 1983). But ecologists rarely employ these terms because of the remarkable adjustment, adaptation, and recovery abilities in ecological systems. Above the R force level, we may say that a landscape is destroyed, or disappears, or is replaced by another landscape (Figure 12.15). We may set a certain arbitrary level, say of some landscape structural characteristic, above which we say the landscape is gone. However, the stretch of land is still there, and the characteristic observed is usually still there in a much larger or smaller amount. Hence, we can destroy a desert landscape by irrigating it for agriculture, or we can destroy that agricultural landscape by turning off the water. In neither case is the change irreversible or permanent.

## Stabilizing Properties

We have presented several major forces that operate together to create landscape organization. Some of these forces underlie destabilizing and others stabilizing processes in the landscape. Now we will recognize three general processes that drive a landscape to become more stable.

First, as discussed previously, light energy is fixed into plant biomass. The amount of biomass accumulation varies through space according to the landscape structure of patches, corridors, and matrix. This internal heterogeneity—with its related flows of animals, plants, water, mineral nutrients, and energy among landscape elements—provides an inherent

**Figure 12.15** *Transformation of a citrus grove landscape (a) to a suburban one (b) in 28 years (1950 to 1978), Santa Clara County, California. The road network has remained largely intact as the primary organizing structure. Streams, in contrast, have largely been channeled, straightened, or eliminated. Many former farmhouse areas have remained as distinct patches present in the matrix of homes. Wetlands and citrus groves have essentially been eliminated. In some ways the citrus grove landscape represented an even greater transformation from the earlier native grass and shrub landscape. (Courtesy of USDA Soil Conservation Service.)*

(a)

(b)

flexibility to the system that allows it to absorb environmental changes, and if disturbed, to recover.

Second, the landscape system is open to immigration and emigration of species, to mineral nutrient inputs and outputs, and to water flows. In fact, the amount flowing through an ecological system often exceeds the amount present in the system. Precipitation can quickly end a drought, and river flow can end a flood. Colonization from windblown seeds and spores can cover bare land overnight. Withdrawal of a locust plague or a military force can result in rapid landscape recovery. Wind-borne mineral nutrients refertilize overexploited land, and rivers can carry off extensive sediment deposits from floods. These flows through open landscapes, enhancing the resistance and recovery processes, in turn depend on the birth, growth, and mortality of plants and animals.

The third and most unique process is evolution. A pair of animals may produce a large group of furry babies that differ from one another. The young grow and disperse across the landscape, and certain of them survive and reproduce. If a disturbance hits the landscape, a different set of the animals will survive and reproduce. This set is generally more resistant to the disturbance and in turn will produce resistant babies. Natural selection has taken place, and the species remains in the landscape with a slight genetic change. Since many plant and animal species in the landscape contain this capacity for genetic change in response to environmental change, evolution helps provide the resistance that keeps the landscape in equilibrium and helps it recover from disturbance.

## LINKAGES AMONG LANDSCAPES

Usually the boundaries separating landscapes are relatively distinct and easily determined, especially at the scale of aerial photographs. The bases for this fact lie in the three processes that form landscapes—geomorphic change, natural disturbance, and human influence. Most geomorphic processes leave relatively distinct boundaries. The effects of most natural disturbances are similar across a single geomorphic area. Human influences, in contrast, may be superimposed on a landscape or may cross a natural boundary and be superimposed in similar form on parts of two or more landscapes. At this level of scale, human influences generally tend to make fuzzy boundaries that appear as gradations or a strip of mosaic.

The same forces that drive flows between landscape elements drive the flows between landscapes—namely, mass flow and locomotion (Chapter 9). The five vectors (wind, water, flying animals, ground animals, and people) are also the same, but their relative importance is quite different in flows between landscapes. Flying and ground animals are normally the least important, while wind and people are most important. Water flowing overland from one landscape to another is channeled in rivers. Water in evapotranspiration from a well-vegetated landscape is also blown downwind and drops as precipitation in mountainous landscapes or as humidity or precipitation in low, less vegetated landscapes.

Wind is a major transport vector carrying moisture, particles, insects, algae, spores, seeds, aerosols, pollutants, and heat energy between landscapes. Pests such as the gypsy moth (*Lymantria dispar*) and white pine blister rust (*Cronartium ribicola*) cross landscape boundaries by wind. So do sandstorms and dust storms—as has happened in Australia, Africa, and the "dust bowl" of the 1920s and 1930s in the midwestern United States (see Figure 5.1). So do light seeds and spores that colonize bare surfaces. And so does heat energy, passing from a dry, sparsely-vegetated landscape to desiccate the vegetation of one downwind.

People are of greatest importance in inter-landscape flows. They transport animals, plants, mineral nutrients, and water, and they do it in cars, buses, trains, boats, and planes. They also do it in irrigation ditches, in heat liberation from nuclear power plants, in long distance drives of sheep and cattle, and in many other ways. The cumulative effects of these human-caused transports mold the form of most landscapes on earth. For most of these landscapes, the molding process is directly dependent on nonrenewable resources, specifically fossil fuel and mineral concentrations.

A different dimension of the human impact dwarfs even the above. It is the "decision catalyst" (or trigger or stimulus) transmitted by communication. In other words, decisions made in one landscape (often urban) are sent to and change other landscapes. History is rich with examples of such decisions and far-off effects. Decisions made in Rome affected hundreds of landscapes in the Roman Empire, from Turkey to Britain. Decisions made in Spain affected landscapes in the Spanish colonies from the southern tip of South America to the Phillipines. A decision in Rio de Janeiro to build a new capital, Brasilia, created new landscapes a thousand kilometers away in the Amazon basin.

The spreading of one landscape at the expense of an adjacent landscape is a competition and results in human and natural conflicts. Desertification is commonly a spreading of an arid landscape into an adjacent grassland or savanna that is being overgrazed. Sand and dust increasingly pour over the adjacent landscape. Irrigation, expanding like giant bubbles in an arid grassland or desert, will turn portions of it into temporarily productive agriculture. Suburban landscapes all around the world are expanding at the expense of almost every other landscape type (Figure 12.15). Only the urban landscape frequently outcompetes suburbia, as cities gobble up once-suburban neighborhoods.

## SUMMARY

To characterize landscape change, one must take the following steps.

1. See whether there is a general tendency or direction of landscape change over time.
2. See how the oscillations (large or small relative to the changing average) are superimposed on the general tendency.
3. Determine whether the oscillations are regular or irregular.
4. Locate the deflections or breaks in rhythm and see whether a new regime is established or not.
5. Determine the forces that have broken the regime—that are, therefore, the disturbances.

Stability in a variation curve is rarely definitive but rather emerges in the form of a sequence of levels that are separated by phases of instability. The passage from one metastability trough to another can be described with a transition matrix. A landscape progresses away from the "most stable" state to deeper troughs of metastability. Therefore, a mature landscape is very metastable (i.e., in a deep trough), yet once disturbance causes it to leave its trough, there is little chance that the system will rapidly return to this state.

Heterogeneity has emerged as a keystone of this chapter. A landscape is a mosaic of landscape elements that exhibit three different kinds of stability: (a) physical system stability, (b) recovery stability, and (c) resistance stability.

Wind and people are the predominant vectors in the interactions between whole landscapes, and human decisions often act as the catalysts that transform landscapes. Since landscapes are rarely in steady state, understanding how the spatial configuration of ecosystems affects a shifting mosaic is a key to understanding landscape change.

## QUESTIONS

1. When you see a graph showing changes in a landscape characteristic through time, how do you determine which variation curve it represents? What variation curves are most common in landscapes?
2. Is it possible to define stability and metastability without having defined what a disturbance is? Explain.
3. Give three landscape element examples for each of the three major types of stability.
4. Why is it useful, in order to understand landscape change, to consider the mechanisms of species coexistence (e.g., competitive equilibrium or nonequilibrium coexistence)?

5. Does a transition matrix always lead to an equilibrium? Could a particular equilibrium be predicted directly by measuring the areas of landscape element types at a point in time? Or from simply knowing the replacement rates? Explain.
6. Under what circumstances would you expect a shifting mosaic to be in steady state? How is this important to a forester or a range manager?
7. What are the major stabilizing forces in a landscape? The major destabilizing forces?
8. How do the metal rod under tension and the landscape subjected to environmental change differ in response?
9. In what primary ways do linkages among landscapes differ from linkages among landscape elements?
10. Does it seem normal that a biological system would commonly show a regime of oscillation? Justify your response with at least two different arguments.
11. Are there predictable patterns in the way mosaics change over time? Explain. Indicate how this fact is important to one of the following: geography, forestry, crop science, range management, wildlife management, or nature conservation.

# Part IV
# Heterogeneity and Management

# 13
# *Heterogeneity and Typology*

*Landscape . . . the widely rolling plateau*
*with countless broad ridges and domes*
*which crowd upon one another*
*in endless number of wearying monotony*
*like storm-driven waves of a sea.*
**Anton Kerner, 1863**
*The Plant Life of the Danube Basin*

In the final two chapters of this book, we will attempt to build further on the structural, functional, and dynamic concepts and foundations already set up. Heterogeneity has emerged as a keystone in several chapters, and so now we will focus specifically on the relations between heterogeneity and functioning (Figure 13.1). We begin with the basic laws of thermodynamics and consider the response of animals to heterogeneity. The result of heterogeneity is a multitude of landscapes on earth that have yet to be classified. Guidelines or options for an eventual classification will be identified. We consider descending, ascending, and phylogenetic typologies, recognizing both an inherent hierarchy in nature, and the need for a fundamental theoretical underpinning for a typology.

## LANDSCAPE HETEROGENEITY

In view of the diverse equilibrium processes presented in the previous chapter, is it even possible to find a general trend in landscape heterogeneity? Perhaps it is, because ecological processes and the problems of landscape planning, conservation, and management emanate from the same roots. Their ultimate foundations are evolutionary, the flow of matter, and thermodynamic. The evolutionary process, based on reproduction and genetic change in animal and plant species, was discussed in Chapter 7, and the flow of matter in Chapter 9. Now we consider the fundamental process of thermodynamics in landscape ecology.

**463**

**Figure 13.1** *Landscape functioning determined by a mosaic of pine forest and rock surfaces. Flows of water, wildlife, heat, and fire across the landscape are strongly controlled by its pattern of heterogeneity. The rock surfaces with little biomass present have very high stability (Chapter 12). Yosemite National Park, central California. (R. Forman)*

## Thermodynamic Laws

When energy is converted from one form to another, say in the process of making electricity from coal, making leaf tissue using sunlight, or converting beetles to woodpecker tissue (Figure 13.2), the total amount of energy present before and after the process remains constant. This fact is the **first law of thermodynamics,** and it means that energy can neither be created nor destroyed.

We also know that nothing can be 100% efficient. The amount of electrical energy generated is less than the energy contained in the coal. The explanation for this apparent paradox is that some of the coal energy, indeed the majority, is given off as heat during the conversion process. The coal energy precisely equals the electrical energy plus the heat en-

**Figure 13.2**  *Wire, post, and pasture systems. The wire exchanges long-wave or heat energy with its surroundings, and negligible amounts of materials. The post exchanges heat energy and energy in biomass (woodpeckers make large holes and consume the beetles that make small holes) with its surroundings, plus the materials in biomass and wood decay. The pasture exchanges short-wave or visible energy (through photosynthesis), long-wave energy, and materials with its surroundings. Brown County, Wisconsin (United States). (Courtesy of USDA Soil Conservation Service.)*

ergy. More generally, in each energy conversion in an ecological system, the amount of "usable" energy decreases, because of the fact that some energy is given off as heat. When we eat chocolate-covered ants, we add only a portion of the available energy to our tissue, and give off the rest as body heat. When a flea bites us, the energy extracted is split between flea fat and flea heat.

This explanation follows from the **second law of thermodynamics** (or Carnot principle)—an isolated system increases in entropy. An **isolated system** is one that has no exchange of energy or matter with its surrounding environment.[1] **Entropy** is a measure of the disorder (or unavailable energy) in a system. The "second law" signifies that an isolated system progressively loses its structure and tends toward a homogeneous mixture of all the molecules composing it. In other words, no new structure can appear within an isolated system.

When a system is not isolated, its entropy may decrease and its structure may increase. For example, a red-hot molten wire plunged into cold water loses heat (entropy) and hardens (i.e., builds structure). Biological phenomena that produce new structures (sociological, ecological, morphological, genetic, and biochemical) are not exceptions to the second law, because they produce their structure in ecosystems. An ecosystem is not an isolated system, because it receives energy and matter from its surroundings (Bertalanffy, 1950; Prigogine and Nicolis, 1971). The critical solar energy arrives in the visible "high-quality" wavelengths that are used in photosynthesis as a base of almost all life (see Figure 2.2). Mineral nutrients enter from parent rock material and from other ecosystems. Human modification of natural ecosystems typically increases the inputs and outputs of matter, and makes the system more open.

Within the biosphere, as biological systems develop, they accumulate "information" (Margalef, 1957; Pielou, 1966; Medvedkov, 1967; Godron, 1968; Webber, 1972; Phipps, 1981a, 1981b), which is commonly considered equivalent to a decrease in entropy (Boltzmann, 1896; Brillouin, 1962; Odum, 1983; Godron, 1984; Phipps, 1984). This process takes place for two reasons.

1. The biosphere builds structure and information from the high quality energy of short-wave-length solar radiation (as indicated by the "paradox of Schrodinger").

[1]Coupled with this concept of an isolated system from physics, an "open system" exchanges both energy and matter with its surroundings, and a "closed system" exchanges energy but not matter with its surroundings (e.g., Bruhat, 1962; Bertin et al., 1979). Alternatively, some authors use the term "open system" when referring to a system that exchanges energy, matter, or both with its surroundings, and "closed system" when referring to a system that exchanges no energy or matter with its surroundings.

2. All biological systems possess feedback mechanisms that depend on flows of matter, energy, and information. These exchanges are necessary in biological systems in order to reach metastable equilibria beyond the "most stable," purely mineral state (Figure 13.1).

## Mechanisms Causing Heterogeneity

All equilibria are established at a molecular level of scale. Each molecule has its own characteristics, such as number and type of atoms or rate and direction of movement. However, a gas as a whole, for example, has additional broader characteristics such as pressure, volume, and temperature. The laws of thermodynamics link these two levels of integration. The sum of innumerable interactions of myriads of molecules of gas are expressed by simple "macroscopic" principles, such as the relationship linking temperature, volume, and pressure of a gas in a system (Boltzmann, 1896). In any nonisolated system, usable energy flows from state to state and may build structure and heterogeneity. However, where heat energy accumulates, entropy increases resulting in less structure and more homogeneity.

The sequence of mechanisms that cause the heterogeneity of landscapes on earth operates at an even more macroscopic scale, but a general pattern may now be recognized. The starting point is a mass of randomly moving atoms or molecules, characterized by a maximum level of entropy (Figure 13.3). According to many scholars, the earth originated from the sun as a hot rotating mass of atoms some 4.5 billion years ago. As the earth continues to spin away from the sun, it cools and thus shrinks. The earth's interior is squeezed, so that it is kept hot and provides soil and water bodies with a small amount of heat that is important during cold periods. The energy contained in the earth (i.e., ancient solar energy) in this ongoing formative process has produced plate tectonics and many consequent landforms (Figure 13.3). These are the primary mechanisms that produce heterogeneity from an original more homogeneous state.

The remaining mechanisms typically augment the amount of heterogeneity present and depend more or less directly on solar radiation today (Figure 13.3). For example, climatic patterns are determined by light, temperature, and wind, all of which are under solar control and modified by landforms. Erosion and deposition, plant and animal colonization, biomass accumulation, food web development, natural disturbances, and human influences all depend mainly on solar energy (Figure 13.4). Under certain conditions, these processes may increase homogeneity, but generally they produce more heterogeneous conditions.

Of course, these mechanisms do not work independently but are interconnected by various feedback loops (see Figure 7.12). Widespread

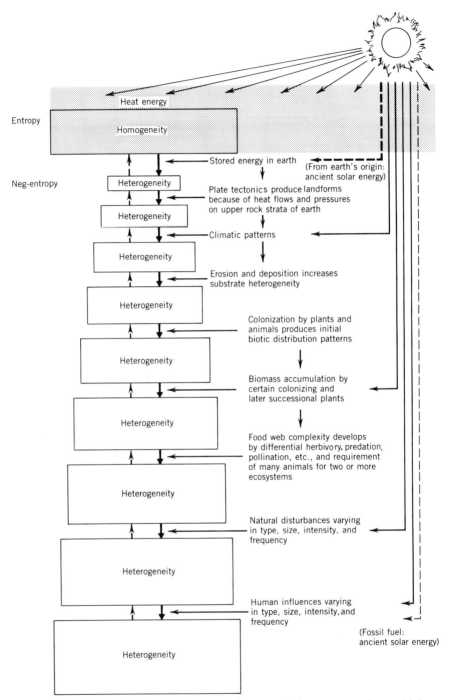

**Figure 13.3** *Heterogeneity-producing mechanisms. Solar energy at three widely separated time periods drives processes that progressively increase the heterogeneity of the planet and its landscapes. Many feedbacks among the processes exist.*

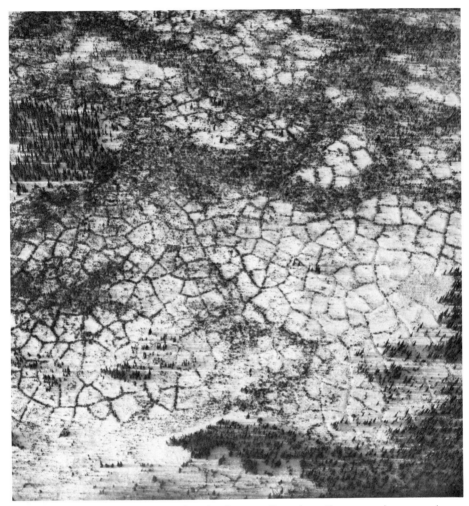

**Figure 13.4** *Heterogeneous tundra of polygon soils and coniferous patches caused mainly by solar radiation. The polygons, produced by freezing and thawing processes, are about 30 to 40 m across, and the snow is about 0.5 m deep. Spruce (Picea) and shrubby areas contain Sphagnum moss. This is a glaciated landscape above the Artic Circle near Ft. Yukon, Alaska (Tedrow, 1977; Bliss et al., 1981). (Courtesy of USDA Soil Conservation Service.)*

human influences are superimposed on the many other processes. In many landscapes these human influences are primarily based on fossil fuel energy that was extracted from former solar energy by plants tens or hundreds of millions of years ago. In these cases the structure and type of landscape depends directly on both fossil fuel and today's solar energy.

## ANIMAL RESPONSE TO HETEROGENEITY

Let us consider how the results of this chain of heterogeneity-producing processes directly affects landscape functioning—in this case, the use of the landscape by animals. A considerable literature on animal populations in patchy ecosystems provides insight into habitat selection, population dynamics, competition, predation, foraging, home ranges, behavior, and genetic variability (e.g., Gause, 1934; Huffaker, 1958; Pimentel, 1961; Pianka, 1966; Den Boer, 1970, 1981; Levin and Paine, 1974; Cody, 1975; Levin, 1976; Wiens, 1976; Price, 1975; Connell, 1978; Wiens, 1985). Here we will focus on the movement of animals relative to the landscape and its heterogeneity.

Potentially useful energy accumulates in portions or patches within a landscape. Heterogeneity is therefore a result of thermodynamics, and it is also a source of flows between areas. These two fundamental characteristics of heterogeneity link thermodynamics and landscape dynamics.

Heterogeneity in landscapes is specifically required by many animals that live in two or more landscape elements. The case of the Japanese beetle (*Coleoptera: Popillia japonica*) is typical. This beetle can be noxious to crop cultivation and finds optimal living conditions in humid environments (Regniere et al., 1983). Such sites in a landscape, therefore, are areas of aggregation and breeding and also centers where their predators are concentrated. During favorable years, the Japanese beetles multiply prodigiously in humid places. They also colonize, more or less regularly, drier patches where predators do not find sufficient concentrations of them to form persistent predator colonies. During dry years, predation remains intense in humid places and can lead to drastic beetle mortality. The rate of beetle survival therefore may be higher in the dry patches dispersed in the matrix. The investigators conclude

. . . [T]he density and stability of populations of the Japanese beetle are probably determined to a large extent by the proportion of total area in each habitat type.. . . [T]he Japanese beetle exhibits several characteristics which enhance the species performance in heterogeneous environments (Regniere et al., 1983).

This example is not unusual; most animals play hide-and-go-seek with their predators. This dodging game suggests a resolution to a problem that has been boiling among ecologists in recent decades. Initially, ecologists supposed that assemblages of species become increasingly diversified and increasingly stable up to the point of ecosystem maturity (Odum, 1969). When computers permitted the construction of models that predicted the equilibrium conditions of assemblages of species, it was found that the models often became increasingly unstable when species complexity increased (May, 1973; DeAngelis, 1975; Lawlor, 1978; Pimm and Lawton, 1978). Experimental studies suggested that stability and species diversity were not closely related, and also that predators play a key role in controlling both characteristics (Tansley and Adamson, 1925; Hairston et al., 1968; Paine, 1966; Dodson, 1974; Harper, 1977; Lubchenco, 1978; Pimm, 1982). Scientific interest in how species coexist was rekindled. Why don't dominant species simply eliminate less dominant ones?

An important answer emerges when we observe the movements of animals in a landscape. Animals often use different landscape elements in the cluster of ecosystems present for different functions (Figure 13.5). The most protected type of landscape element is for sleeping and raising young, the most productive is for feeding, and so on. The moose (*Alces americana*) in North America feeds in marshes or along streams and hides in the thickest woods when it sleeps (Goddard, 1970; Van Ballenberghe and Peek, 1971; Le Resche et al., 1974). In contrast, the royal eagle (*Aquila chrysaetos*) in Europe builds its nest in the mountains on steep,

**Figure 13.5** *Chamois in an alpine meadow in the Alps. These animals move among and require several landscape elements, including meadows for grazing, south-facing slopes for heat on cold days, and rocky areas to hide and rest in, as the two young chamois are doing here. (Irene Vandermolen.)*

TABLE 13.1 *Wildlife using more than one type of landscape element.*

| Species | Landscape elements | Reference |
|---|---|---|
| 1. Elk and deer | Forest, shrubland, and grassland—90% of use occurs within 200 m on both sides of forested edge | Thomas et al., 1979 |
| 2. Ruffed grouse | Forest—equal proportions of four stand size classes, all intersecting at a common point to provide feeding (mature stand), breeding (pole stand), and roosting (regeneration stand) habitat | Gullion, 1977 |
| 3. Pheasant | Agricultural land—10 to 25% of land in hay crops that provide nesting and roosting cover | Joselyn et al., 1968; Warner, 1981 |
| 4. Canvasback, Redhead duck, Mallard duck, Canada goose | Agricultural land, grassland, and open water—agricultural residue and forage for feeding geese and mallards; fingernail clams and aquatic vegetation for feeding canvasbacks and redheads. All species require terrestrial and aquatic habitats | Bellrose et al., 1979 |
| 5. Black bear | Uplands and lowlands—acorns from upland oaks in summer and fall; acorns from lowland oaks in winter and spring | Landers et al., 1979 |

*Source:* Risser et al. (1984) and others.

exposed rocky cliffs (that give protection from small mammals that like its eggs), but it finds its prey in cultivated fields or wooded edges (Lheritier, 1975). In wildlife management and in pest management it is common to find animals that use, and probably require, two or more nearby ecosystem types (Table 13.1) (e.g., Huot, 1974; Wetzel et al., 1975; Liberg, 1980; Arnold, 1983; Morris and Lemon, 1983; Gilmer and Stewart, 1983; Armstrong et al., 1983; Collins and Urness, 1983).

Animal use of the cluster of ecosystems in a landscape appears to be a general principle of landscape ecology (Chapter 1). It implies considerable movement across edges and through convergency points (Chapter 6) (Harris, 1981) and emphasizes the importance of understanding boundary function.

The use of different ecosystems by animals further suggests that the concept of the "ecological niche,"—as the sum of all the roles and factors that involve a species—must be expanded or at least viewed from a broader angle. The niche of an animal is not well represented by a box within a network of interconnected boxes depicting a food web, or by a series of tolerance curves plotted along a series of environmental gradients (Chapter 2). Both of these have to be augmented by the combination of uses found in a heterogeneous assemblage of ecosystems in a landscape (Figure 13.5). A detailed example will be seen in the following chapter.

The movements of some animals near boundaries reveal yet another landscape pattern. The exclusion or *repulsion zone* is the area adjacent to a landscape element where a species is inhibited by an effect of that landscape element. Roads inhibit red foxes (*Canis vulpes*) for at least 90 m, elk (*Cervis canadensis*) for about 200 to 400 m, and some birds for a few hundred meters to over a kilometer in the case of a busy highway (Storm et al., 1976; Rost and Bailey, 1979; Irwin and Peek, 1983; Lyon, 1983; Veen, 1973; Van der Zande et al., 1980). The spreading of heat, road salt, lead, other chemicals, herbivores, and predators from landscape elements also effectively creates a repulsion zone for certain organisms (Figure 13.6) (e.g., Muller and del Moral, 1966; Lagerwerff and Specht, 1970; Hofstra and Hall, 1971; Smith, 1971; Muller, 1970; Bartholomew, 1970; Mierau and Favara, 1975; Jaksic and Fuentes, 1980).

So far we have explored the nature of heterogeneity from the molecular level to the use by animals of a cluster of ecosystems within a landscape. Now let us broaden our perspective further to consider how to categorize a landscape and compare or even relate the landscapes present on earth.

## GUIDELINES FOR LANDSCAPE TYPOLOGY

The physician begins by sequentially observing the external symptoms of an illness and makes a diagnosis by comparing the case with other

**Figure 13.6** *A repulsion zone surrounding a shrub patch in the California chaparral. The shrub patch keeps the adjacent grassy area bare in one or more ways, by (a) secreting organic chemicals that inhibit the annual grasses; (b) harboring herbivores that feed intensively near the shrub cover; or (c) absorbing water in extended roots. The shape of the shrub (Salvia leucophylla) patch suggests that it is a spreading element (see Figure 5.10). (Courtesy of C. H. Muller.)*

known cases. Diagnosis is reached by systematically arranging the symptoms and comparing them with established criteria. The physician thus performs the process of **classification.** Similarly, the alchemists and chemists of the eighteenth century spent their time classifying the substances they encountered, distinguishing acids, bases, salts, and so forth. Early zoologists and botanists recorded the characteristics of objects to construct classifications that remained fluid and finally stabilized a century later.

Landscapes as we have considered them have become an object of scientific study only in recent decades, and our description of the structure and functioning of landscapes represents only the infancy of landscape ecology. Do we now know enough about landscapes to propose a classification? The honest answer is no, and we wish especially to avoid the emergence of a sterile dogmatism. However, we can learn a lot by exploring the foundations or bases of a **typology,** that is, a study of types or a preclassification (Robert, 1972).

The principal reason to remain cautious is seen in the following two examples. Mendeleiev, the discoverer of the periodic table of chemical elements, was trying to compare types of chemical elements. One day he had the idea of taking a sequential list, in order of the increasing atomic weight of the elements, and winding the list around a cylinder. The "true" classification then appeared to him (Figure 13.7). Fluorine, chlorine, bromine, and iodine were lined up together and appeared to have similar characteristics. Oxygen, sulfur, selenium, and tellurium were also lined up and related, and so it went. The most admirable aspect of this discovery was that it anticipated, by more than a century, the knowledge of the number of electrons in the outer rings of atoms (Figure 13.7). These numbers are the basis of the chemical similarities among elements and the fundamental basis of their classification.

A similar phenomenon occurred in the development of the classification of plants and animals. The naturalist Carl Linnaeus (known for his nomenclatural system for plants and animals) developed an early classification of plants based on the number of stamens (male reproductive organs) in the flower. This classification was severely constrained by the selection of a single **attribute,** that is, an inherent characteristic of an object.

In a constrained closed nomenclature, the arrival of an intruder disrupts the entire framework, and requires revision of the whole dictionary. The price paid for something rigid or too tightly constructed is splitting or shattering. (Dagognet, 1970)

Some years later an alternative approach was taken by Adanson, who accorded value to every attribute of the organism.

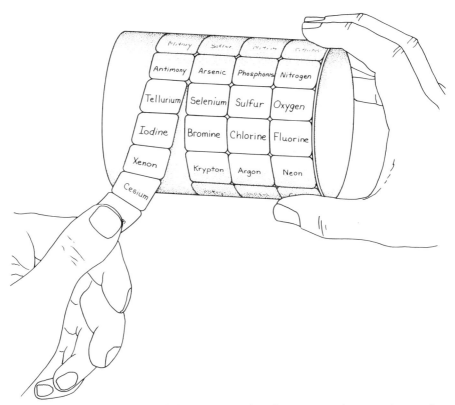

**Figure 13.7** *A list of chemical elements (in order of atomic weight) wound around a cylinder. This process was a key step in Mendeleiev's discovery. Over a century later, oxygen, sulfur, selenium, and tellurium were found to have six electrons, and fluorine, chlorine, bromine, and iodine were found to have seven electrons in their outer shell. These were major steps in the establishment of the periodic table of chemical elements.*

> . . . [T]he inverse error of Linnaeus. Adanson gathered everything without distinction. He hoped to extract . . . the method of true similarity and relationships.. . . [This was] an exceptionally rational undertaking but it fell apart under its own weight because he refused to shorten the operations and to subordinate certain attributes to others. (Dagognet, 1970)

Finally, in the nineteenth century a solution that avoided both the snag of a unique characteristic and the undifferentiated morass of measurements was proposed by de Jussieu. He formed a hierarchy of attributes. Reproductive characteristics of plants received priority among the possible attributes for classification because they are less variable, and perhaps because they enclose in the seed or embryo the "organizational plans" or genetic blueprint that will give rise to the future adult organism.

Thus, this diagnosis chose as priorities for the hierarchical classification the most fundamental attributes and also those that predict the future.

When de Jussieu selected his position, he had as much luck, or genius, as Mendeleiev, because the morphological classification thus constructed anticipated the "phylogenetic" classifications later devised based on evolution and underpinned by the fossil record. Implicit were the real origins, the relationships or connections among species, genera, families, and orders of organisms, and even the fact that the morphological units are based on genetic similarities. We can see, at least schematically, the junction between the morphological and the genetic aspects of a good classification, and now realize that we must try to link, in just as elegant a fashion, the spatial and the temporal components of landscapes as we prepare their typology.

If history repeats itself without stumbling, the science of landscapes should begin by being descriptive, until the day when someone discovers the key to the fundamental organization of landscapes. We believe this key is largely thermodynamic, as discussed earlier, but its shape remains the puzzle. An **ascending typology** or approach to landscape classification, one that begins with the individual landscapes on earth and builds up to the broadest groupings of them, will be presented shortly. For convenience, we first discuss the opposite approach, a **descending typology** that begins by distinguishing the most general units and then proceeds to the specific landscapes.

## THE INHERENT HIERARCHY IN NATURE

Before descending the stairs of the typological pyramid, let us look at its plan. No natural typology gives all attributes equal priority, because a latent or inherent hierarchy always exists. Any plan describing nature today gives different weights or priorities to different attributes, and generally the attributes are then arranged in a hierarchy. We should ask, though, whether the human mind is thus constructing an artificial hierarchy for nature or whether an inherent hierarchy exists in nature.

Duck feet are webbed and eagle feet are covered with feathers. Is one of these attributes hierarchically superior to the other? *A priori*, nothing permits us to say. Similarly, the spiny fins of the perch are not inherently superior to the flexible fins of a carp. Even the presence of feet is not inherently superior to the presence of fins, and Adanson was right, when beginning a classification, to place all characteristics on the same level without forming a hierarchy. But now let us consider the whole group of ducks, eagles, perch, and carp, using the same attributes just considered. A hierarchy now appears obvious—ducks and eagles have feet, whereas perch and carp have fins. Feet versus fins is the higher category, and ducks versus eagles and perch versus carp is the lower category in the hierarchy.

In other words, even if all the attributes in a typology of natural objects are placed on the same level, without any *a priori* hierarchy, the comparison of the organisms (with different attributes) will make the inherent hierarchy evident. The perceptive or cantankerous soul will point out that reality is not as simple as this example, because there are birds with spiny feet and fish with webbed fins. But a close examination of the spines of bird feet reveals that they are not at all comparable anatomically to fish spines.

Our first step in typology is the search for attributes, and the second is to establish their hierarchy (Godron, 1975; Allen and Starr, 1982). In observing landscapes we will see, for example, that those with interconnected corridors and those with unconnected corridors, are related. Furthermore, the characteristic "presence of corridors" is higher in the hierarchy than characteristics such as "line corridors" or "strip corridors." More generally, an implicit hierarchy in landscapes results from their spatial character (Neef, 1963; Haase, 1976). Areas with valley glaciers are included in mountainous landscapes, and oases are included in desert landscapes. An intriguing question then comes to mind. "Could the summit of the pyramid, for this landscape hierarchy, be a spatial characteristic useful in mapping?"

## Five Levels in a Descending Hierarchy

**Finding the Summit Level—Zonal Climates.**  In searching for primary attributes, for a landscape hierarchy, we first examine a range of broad-scale mapping approaches and forest site classification systems.[2] These studies suggest that ecological classifications and maps usually have quite small basic units because the integrating of several ecological characteristics mainly results in small homogeneous areas. Geographical and planning classifications usually have large basic homogeneous units associated with fewer, broader-scale criteria, and thus more abstraction (Troll, 1968; Neef, 1968; Herz, 1973; Schreiber, 1977). Some approaches are hierarchical. They may be based, for example, on plant formations and species associations, climate, or on "ecosystem regions"

[2]See, for example, Troll, 1950; Tuxen, 1955; Ellenberg, 1956; Schmithusen, 1963; Godron et al., 1964; Schlenker, 1964; Kuchler, 1964, 1967; Haase, 1964, 1968; Christian and Stewart, 1968; Neef, 1968; Lacate, 1969; Diershke, 1969; Jurdant et al., 1972; Rowe, 1972; Isachenko, 1973; Bruneau, 1973; Wertz and Arnold, 1975; Long et al., 1975; Soil Survey Staff, 1975; Leser, 1976; Hills, 1976; Whyte, 1976; Walter, 1977; Schreiber, 1977; Wiken and Ironside, 1977; Jurdant et al., 1977; Stumpel and Kalkhoven, 1978; Bailey et al., 1978; Cowardin et al., 1979; Brossard and Wieber, 1980; Pfister and Arno, 1980; Davis, 1980; Spurr and Barnes, 1980; Ruzicka and Miklos, 1981; Rowe and Sheard, 1981; Marchal, 1981; Barnes et al., 1982; Klopatek et al., 1983; Naveh and Lieberman, 1984.

(clusters of landscapes) (Koppen, 1931; Braun-Blanquet, 1932; Braun, 1950; Bailey, 1976, 1978) and may show how finer-scale units aggregate to form broader-scale units (Pattee, 1973; Gardner et al., 1982; Allen and Starr, 1982). Although the mapping and classification approaches are exceedingly diverse, the possible attributes tend to sort into two categories. Those attributes used mainly by ecologists (including flora, fauna, life form, appearance, and species associations) are usually lower in a classification. Those used widely by both geographers and ecologists (such as climate, topography, bedrock, and human influence) are commonly the highest attributes in a classification. We conclude that we must find the summit of the landscape typology pyramid among this latter set of variables.

At the global scale, bedrock type can only be used as a first and very broad discriminating variable that pinpoints the large continental plates or shields. In effect, major mountain chains such as the Rocky Mountains and the Himalayas offer mosaics of highly varied rock types, topographic relief, and contrasting climates (Figure 13.8). Consequently, such major mountain chains are not usefully defined as constituting a single landscape. The surface of flat sedimentary basins is generally covered with relatively fine soil particles. However, it is quite heterogeneous with sands and clays providing radically different ecological conditions for animals and plants, commonly only a few hundred meters apart. Human influence also cannot be mapped precisely at this broad scale, since human influences commonly cause sharp environmental differences, often only a few meters apart (Figure 13.8).

Therefore, because bedrock, topographic relief, and human influence vary at a relatively fine scale, the summit level of a descending hierarchy within continents must be related to climate (Pecsi and Samogyi, 1969). At this highest level, the spatial units are the major climatic zones or **zonal climates,** principally correlated with latitude (Chapter 7), that are conspicuous over the globe (Koppen, 1918).

If we map climates at a broad scale, we draw upon characteristics linked to large air masses circulating over the surface of the globe (Chapters 2 and 7). This approach is well illustrated in the Mediterranean climatic zone, where summer drought is the most ecologically important climatic factor. All slopes on mountains in the Mediterranean region experience the summer drought and thus are a part of the Mediterranean climatic zone (Emberger, 1930, 1955; Di Castri and Mooney, 1973). In other words, Mediterranean landscapes are not just those of the sunny Riviera, with mild winters, where romantics revel or attempt to overcome their melancholies, but also include the Atlas Mountains of North Africa where more than a meter of snow falls. These landscapes also encompass all the territory in Europe, Africa, Chile, California, and Australia where air masses produce a summer drought. In short, the climate of a major

**Figure 13.8** *Large variability in a mountainous region and an abrupt human-caused boundary. Mountainous regions typically include a number of landscapes at different altitudes, such as the grassland of an extensive valley, the coniferous forest area, and the alpine areas shown here. The rangeland on the left, planted with wheatgrass and alfalfa (Agropyron, Medicago), produces four times as much forage as the native range plants on the right. The fence is much used by many birds and other animals, and concentrations of animal tramplings, droppings, and associated organisms are typically found along its length. Sange de Cristo Mountains, near Westcliffe, Colorado (United States). (Courtesy of USDA Soil Conservation Service.)*

climatic zone permeates all the landscapes and slopes within it (Bailey, 1983).

**Climatic Regions.** Within each of the major climatic zones (presented in Chapter 7) it is useful to distinguish smaller units, with the help of observations collected by meteorological stations. We can then view climatic variations relative to such physical characteristics of a region as its distance from the sea, the direction of its important winds, its altitude, and the like. These meteorological observations describe the effects of the movements of air masses. The broad zonal climates can be subdivided into smaller areas, each with distinctive climatic conditions—generally called **climatic regions**—that can normally be objectively distinguished using statistical methods.

Of course, these regions are affected by political, economic, or cultural modifications. Even so, the landscapes within a climatic region almost always share a direct or indirect affinity. The similarities in animal and plant forms present among landscapes in a region attest to the common climatic characteristics.

Most of New York and New England, or most of the southeastern United States, constitutes a climatic region. Within such a region many landscapes are present (e.g., agricultural, urban, and montane), but they have similar ranges of solar radiation, rainfall, and the like that are characteristic of a regional climate. Furthermore, the ranges of most native animal and plant species extend over most of a climatic region.

This role of climate was recognized by de Candolle, a nineteenth-century natural scientist, when he observed that the visible limits of natural vegetation are often linked with climatic moisture, whereas the limits attained by cultivation are linked with temperature. The explanation is that for over five thousand years, people have learned how to control the water on the land they cultivate, by irrigation or drainage, but it is much harder to control temperature. In other words, it is easier to create grasslands in the Pakistan desert than to make tomatoes ripen in the fields of Canada.

**Vegetation Belts.** In considering landscapes within a climatic region, what is the third level of the descending typology? Soulavie (1780–1784) seems to have scientifically examined this question when he drew a map of Ardeche in central France well before the similar classic works of Humboldt (1807), Kerner (1863), and Schimper (1903). In effect, a map must rest on a typology (which indeed, is often summarized in the legend of the map). It appeared logical to Soulavie, as he explored on foot and horseback, that landscapes were linked to levels of altitude, termed by him vegetation belts or levels.

These altitudinal levels are now often appropriately called **bioclimatic units,** because they roughly correspond to the distribution of climates as well as animals and plants. A **vegetation belt** is the distinctive plant community of a bioclimatic unit. Vegetation belts are clearly visible evidence of the bioclimatic units in most mountainous areas, such as the slopes of Mt. Fuji or the Southern Alps of New Zealand. For instance, in parts of the Rocky Mountains (Figure 13.8) the vegetation belts are dominated in sequence by alpine vegetation, spruce-fir (*Picea engelmannii, Abies lasiocarpa*), Douglas-fir (*Pseudotsuga menziesii*), pine (*Pinus ponderosa*), and grassland. In the Swiss Alps, the vegetation belts may be alpine vegetation, larch (*Larix decidua*), spruce (*Picea abies*), and pine (*Pinus sylvestris*) or deciduous forest.

Within each vegetation belt several soil types, vegetation types, and land uses coexist. The concept of the bioclimatic unit, with its usually conspicuous vegetation belt, unifies the landscape elements present, one next to the other, at the same altitudinal level. Each belt contains and is covered throughout by a unique combination of landscape elements caused primarily by soil variations, exposure, and human influence.

A vegetation belt is a single landscape if it fulfills the essential characteristic of a landscape—that is, that a particular cluster of ecosystems is repeated in similar form throughout its kilometers-wide extent. Hence, if conifer forest, roads, and weekend cabins predominate throughout the vegetation belt, it is a single landscape. But if in a wide portion of this belt the cluster of ecosystems is rocky pasture, shrubland, and conifer forest, this is a separate landscape within the vegetation belt (Figure 13.9). Similarly, if suburbia has spread over a wide portion of the belt, this also is a separate landscape.

On flat plains, climatic differences through space of course are much less, and meteorological observations are easily interpolated to show whether more than one bioclimatic unit is present (Emberger, 1930; Rey, 1960).

**Geomorphic Units.** Within each bioclimatic unit, soil conditions are commonly distinctive, and they merit closer examination (Hubrich, 1967;

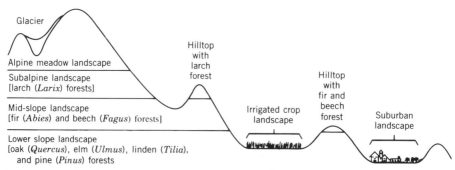

**Figure 13.9** *Landscapes in a mountainous region (the Swiss Alps). Altitudinal limits are determined by climate, whereas different landscapes within an altitudinal belt are determined by soil conditions or human influence. Hilltop with fir and beech woods is an "unusual feature" within the lower slope landscape, as is a single small city within a large surrounding suburban landscape.*

Kugler, 1976; Pecsi and Samogyi, 1969; Jurdant et al., 1972; Maarleveld and De Lange, 1972). Over large zones, general soil development is regulated by the law of zonality (Chapter 7), but local site conditions may strongly modify that development. For example, areas where rocks are close to the ground surface do not support the same type of soil, vegetation, or fauna as areas where rocks are deep underground. Wet areas will support marshes, bogs, or swamps. Where these distinctive geomorphic units, or nonzonal soils, extend for kilometers within a vegetation belt, they support a separate landscape. The rocky pasture-shrubland-conifer forest landscape just mentioned is an example (Figure 13.9). Consequently, in the hierarchy, such geomorphic characteristics normally appear just below the vegetation belt (or bioclimatic unit) characteristics.

**Human Influences.**   Finally, human activities, which generally differ among climatic types and geomorphic types, are the fifth hierarchical level in the descending landscape typology. The presence of an urban or suburban landscape within a geomorphic unit is a striking example common around the world (Figure 13.9). An irrigated agricultural landscape or a forest plantation landscape within a geomorphic unit of a vegetation belt are further examples.

## A Parallel Hierarchy

The hierarchy just outlined is quite parallel to a hierarchy of vegetation units, such as formations, associations, and community types (Braun-Blanquet, 1932; Du Rietz, 1921). Vegetation hierarchies are often highly structured, especially when developed primarily for the purposes of mapping.

For example, the precise vegetation hierarchy of Vinogradov (1976) contains 14 levels of typological organization, from "phytosere" to "population." The mapping scale ranges from extremely broad (1:300,000,000) to extremely fine (1:100), and the size of the smallest unit from $10^6$ to $10^{-7}$ km. This hierarchy is based on the assumption that the sizes of ecological units in nature are mathematically, indeed logarithmically, distributed. In view of the extreme variability in the size of landscape elements within a landscape, and of sizes of landscapes within a region, the mathematical assumption may or may not be warranted. Nevertheless, an inherent hierarchy in the groupings of organisms in nature does exist that parallels the hierarchy of landscapes described above.

## Map Overlay Approach

In regions where maps of topography, climate, soils, forests, economic factors, and the like have been made, the maps can be superimposed on each other to obtain a preliminary typology. This approach has been useful in understanding the geography of diverse regions in landscape architecture, and in regional planning (e.g., Joly, 1959; Godron, 1963; McHarg, 1969; Le Floc'h et al., 1973; Bied-Charreton et al., 1973; Bailey, 1983).

The map overlay method has the advantage of being "open," that is, it is always possible to insert a new attribute at the time of mapping. This approach also permits the inclusion in the typology of social or economic attributes that are not directly visible in the field, such as population density, commercial flows, and type of administration. Results are produced that can rapidly be understood and communicated by scientists, other investigators, local officials, and decision makers.

The only major limitation of the map overlay method, always assuming that maps have been carefully checked for accuracy, is that for most regions the desirable or necessary maps are unavailable or nonexistent. In these cases use of the available maps must be combined with the methods of ascending typology.

## ASCENDING TYPOLOGY

The ascending approach begins with extensive measurement, as in the Adanson approach, but handles the measurements to produce a hierarchy in the most judicious way possible. Often mathematical techniques are used. Since computers permit the handling of masses of data, calculation methods have sprung up like blooms in a desert after rain.

The advantage of the ascending method is that it begins with a basis of concrete objects and does not a *priori* reject those objects that might be considered atypical or nonconforming. The lower portion of the pyramid of classification is solidly based on distinct and well-defined objects. At the outset, of course, it is uncertain whether the summit will ever emerge clearly. Nevertheless, the first step always consists of making observations according to a precise protocol for each of the attributes included.

### The Landscape Attributes

Numerous attributes in a landscape can be observed in preparing for an ascending typology. A preliminary collection of attributes can be obtained by directly extracting them sequentially from the preceding chapters. Each time we delineated a characteristic of a landscape, we implicitly recognized this potential application.

In Chapter 3, for example, patches were first distinguished according to the four most frequent origins (disturbance patches, remnant patches, environmental resource patches, and planted patches). To construct the base of an ascending typology, we can now simply make an inventory or repertoire of the characteristics of landscapes in the order they have been examined in the book (Table 13.2). Note that this is a repertoire for the total organization of a landscape, including structural, functional, and dynamic characteristics.

## Multivariate and Direct Methods for Typology Construction

Two principal sets of methods can be employed to elaborate ascending typologies. The simplest is a series of multivariate methods that deal with many variables concurrently.

**Multivariate Methods.** The scientists who first assembled a large number of attributes to build a typology appear to have been psychologists. Their challenge was to combine the results of countless psychological tests (used in schools as well as industry) in order to characterize personalities, in determining "intelligence," for example. Intelligence here is a set of attributes that can, at least in part, replace one another. Memory is another set of attributes, more or less independent of intelligence, and so on. This problem is relatively close to ours, since we must relate all the basic landscape attributes cited in Table 13.2 to build our typology.

The methods psychologists have developed focus on relationships among attributes that are the answers to questions on psychological tests. Attributes are compared two by two. When a linear relationship between two attributes makes sense, it may be expressed as a "correlation coefficient," a measure of how closely or tightly the two attributes are related (Figure 13.10). The general idea is to group the relationships (generally correlation coefficients in a mathematical matrix) to make sets of attributes automatically appear. We then identify a set of attributes with a predominant trait of an individual, such as intelligence, memory, attention span, intuition, creativity, and so on.

For this purpose, each attribute (the range of answers by the people tested to a question) becomes an axis on a graph, and the result of the whole test is a graph with many axes or dimensions, instead of the usual two dimensions of most graphs. When two attributes are linearly related, their relationship is represented by a ("regression") line, around which the values for all the individuals tested fall (Figure 13.10). When several attributes, two by two, show strong relationships, the corresponding regression lines are grouped in a bundle, like the ribs of an umbrella that may be open or closed. If the umbrella is nearly closed, the ribs corresponding to the regression lines are grouped in a tight bundle, and the main shaft of the umbrella seems to quite satisfactorily represent all the

TABLE 13.2 *Characteristics that give rise to landscape organization*

*Patches*

| | |
|---|---|
| Disturbance patches | Small and large patches |
| Chronic disturbance patches | Patch edge or edge effect |
| Remnant patches | Isodiametric and elongated patches |
| Regenerated patches | Rings |
| Planted patches | Peninsulas |
| Homes or habitations | Interdigitated peninsulas |

*Corridors*

| | |
|---|---|
| Disturbance, remnant, environmental resource, planted, regenerated corridors | Line, strip, and stream corridors |
| | Shelterbelts |
| Curvilinear and straight corridors | Width effect |
| Breaks | Stream orders |
| Narrows | Corridors higher or lower than surroundings |
| Nodes and mini-nodes | |
| String-of-lights pattern | |

*Matrix and network*

| | |
|---|---|
| Relative area of matrix | Spreading and relict elements |
| Matrix connectivity | Network intersections |
| Control over dynamics | Mesh size |
| Porosity | Homogeneity |
| Concave and convex boundaries | |

*Overall Structure*

| | |
|---|---|
| Levels of scale | Spatial linkage |
| Micro- and macroheterogeneity | Low and high contrast |
| Distinctive configurations | Grain size |
| Regular, aggregated, linear, and parallel configurations | Unusual landscape features |

*Natural Processes in Development*

| | |
|---|---|
| Geomorphology | Plant and animal establishment |
| Landforms | Speciation |
| Openness | Increase in vegetation stature |
| Depth effect | Soil development, law of zonality |
| River systems, equilibrium profiles | Role of decomposers |
| Bedrock | Net ecosystem production |
| Climate | Aggrading and degrading ecosystems |
| Rhexistasy, biostasy | Natural disturbance |

*Human Role in Development*

| | |
|---|---|
| Natural rhythm modifications | Managed landscapes, hamlets |
| Farmyards, greenhouses | Cultivated landscapes—Open-field and enclosure methods, villages, traditional agriculture, modern agriculture, geometrization |
| Cultivation, livestock, irrigation | |
| Fire control | |
| Forest management, $CO_2$ buildup | |
| Modification methods and tools | Suburban landscapes, cities, sacred monuments, politics |
| Hunting, domestication, fire use, mineral extraction | Urban landscapes, specialization, writing, districts, structural models |
| Fallowing, input of animal labor and fossil fuel, fertilizers and pesticides | Megalopolis |

TABLE 13.2   *(Continued)*

*Flows Between Adjacent Elements*

Vectors—wind, water, flying animals, ground animals, people
Forces—diffusion, mass flow, locomotion
Boundary function
Sources, sinks
Laminar and turbulent airflows
Streamlined and bluff objects
Cool air drainage
Sound movement
Impaction

Soil porosity
Flows of particulates and dissolved substances
Surface and subsurface flows
Binding factors
Land-to-stream flows
Gravitational transport
Hedgerow effects on fields
Matrix effects on hedgerows

*Animal and Plant Movement*

Continuous and saltatory movements
Boundary crossing frequency
Rest stops, stepping stones
Animal dispersal
Latitudinal and vertical migration

Remoteness
Long and short distance plant dispersal
Nonnative species invasions
Intersection effect in networks

*Landscape Functioning*

Corridor as habitat, conduit, barrier, and source of effects on matrix
Functions of breaks
Break area
Fence effect
Matrix connectivity
Resistance to movement
Boundary discreteness
Hospitableness
Narrows function, bottlenecks
Interaction among patches
Influence fields
High and low order flows

Hierarchical spatial structure
Peninsular interdigitation effects
Angle of interaction
Time-distance and topological space
Relay nodes
Loops
Trunk and feeder lines, gateways
Network connectivity, circuitry, and complexity
Spatial diffusion
Expansionary and relocation diffusion
Optimization

*Landscape Change*

Variation curves
General tendency, amplitude of oscillation, rhythm of oscillation
Stability, instability, equilibrium, metastability
Persistence, resistance, recovery
Physical system stability, recovery stability, resistance stability
Species coexistence

Competitive equilibrium, nonequilibrium coexistence
Transition replacement rate
Dynamics, active forces
Rupture point, elasticity limit
Stabilizing properties
Linkages among landscapes

*Heterogeneity*

Isolated and nonisolated systems
Heterogeneity-producing mechanisms

Animal use of cluster of ecosystems

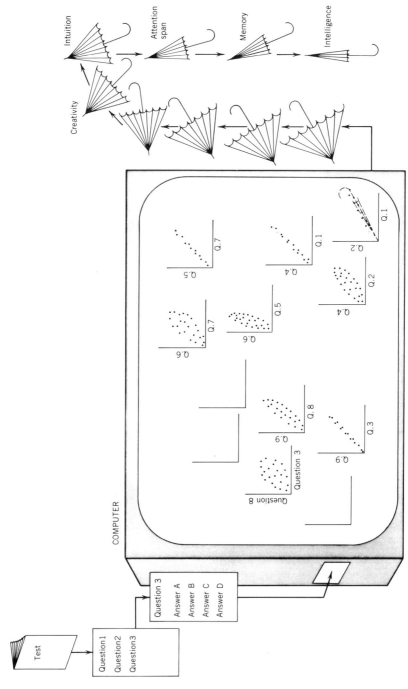

**Figure 13.10**  Schematic stages in a multivariate method for identifying significant characteristics. Attributes—that is, answers to test questions—are compared two-by-two by the computer in order to find clusters of attributes that are highly correlated with one another. Each attribute is represented here by the rib of an umbrella. Thus, the first umbrella (representing the characteristic "intelligence") identified by the computer, has the most tightly bound ribs, i.e., the most highly correlated attributes. Each subsequent characteristic has progressively less correlated attributes (more open umbrella), and hence is less clearly identified.

regression lines. This shaft then represents one of the sets of attributes we are looking for.

If the umbrella is more open, the regression lines are more separated from one another, and the shaft represents a set of attributes with less precision (Figure 13.10). The mathematical techniques used provide a nice overview of the mass of data collected, because sets of attributes appear in sequential order with the most tightly bound sets first. Thus an individual's traits most clearly characterized by the psychological test appear first. These techniques are chosen in such a manner that the sets of attributes are statistically independent (orthogonal) of each other.

This type of method has been used in ecology for more than two decades (Dagnelie, 1973) and is widely adopted now. The simplistic image just given only portrays a tiny part of the gamut of methods developed (factor analysis *sensu lato*, principal components analysis, classification methods, factorial analysis of correlations, canonical analysis, multivariate analysis of variance, and so forth). To lighten the vocabulary, we simply group these methods, which concurrently analyze many variables often with the interactions among them, as *multivariate analysis*.

In spite of the use of powerful statistical techniques and large computers, these methods are not always as objective as their appearance would lead one to believe (Beals, 1973; Speight, 1976). They normally require assumptions that are rarely fulfilled in reality, and they also require arbitrary choices of levels, units, and mathematical rules of procedure (algorithms) by the observer. Their advantage is that they enable treatment of the totality of observations collected, and often also identification of distinct breaks in the sequential ordering of sets of attributes (Figure 13.10) (Speight, 1976). But their shortcoming is that they provide evidence only on the broad outlines of the problem at hand. They provide an image whose imperfections are embedded in the mass, to the point where it is almost impossible to reveal either the bias in sampling or the small errors committed in field observations and their transcription.

**Direct Methods.** On the other hand, we may use all portions of the available information sequentially, searching for relationships between pairs of attributes before grouping them in sets. The goal of direct methods, in other words, is immediately to visualize each of the threads of the tapestry before providing a total view of the motif represented.

The shortcoming of direct methods is that they initially provide partial views, and we must restrain ourselves from interpreting too much from them too fast. On the other hand, these methods use simple mathematics instead of letting complex mathematical rules of procedure do the syntheses. The advantages of direct methods are threefold.

1. They stick to reality.
2. They allow errors to appear directly for immediate correction.
3. They provide immediate information or guidance for continued sampling (Godron, 1968; Mavrommatis, 1971; Daget and Godron, 1982).

At present, direct methods linking attributes two by two are regularly combined with, and nicely complemented by, multivariate methods (Darracq et al., 1984). Methods permitting the direct calculation of relationships between presences and absences of attributes taken three by three are only sketchy and rarely used, but appear to be potentially useful.

## TOWARD A PHYLOGENETIC TYPOLOGY

The ascending and the descending routes are not perfect. They provide only descriptive (empirical) typologies, and with them we are not likely to find the true key to landscape classification. To consider a more general route to this key, perhaps we should return to the example of Mendeleiev and de Jussieu.

In both cases, the key was an anticipation of a general rule that was based on the atomic or molecular structure of the phenomena observed. The columns that appeared on Mendeleiev's cylinder each listed elements that had the same number of electrons in the outer ring of the atom. Mendeleiev did not guess that his classification, which rested on a conventional macroscopic attribute (atomic weight) would be, many years later, related to the properties of subatomic particles that are the true fundamental base of the typology. Similarly, the rules of plant relationships proposed by de Jussieu foreshadowed the combinations of mutations and chromosomal alterations, resting on molecular phenomena, which were discovered long afterward.

Can we hope that landscape classification will one day rest on such a solid foundation? It would be presumptuous to say so, but we already have two indications that point in this direction. The first, which is at the heart of this book, consists of the recognition that a landscape is essentially a spatially heterogeneous entity developed in an environment that is even more heterogeneous (Figure 13.11). Consequently, the forces that determine the nature of the whole landscape are those that cause heterogeneity both in the characteristics of a landscape and in the overall environment. The laws of thermodynamics show that any macroscopic heterogeneity is ultimately controlled by the underlying agitation of molecules, and we suspect that this general rule may be a basis of the future key to landscape typology.

The second guideline to follow is much more concrete. It rests on a commonplace fact observed by Aristotle (384-322 B.C., *On Generation*

**Figure 13.11** *A landscape mosiac molded by biological and human influences in an underlying heterogeneous physical environment. Coffee shrubs under scattered shade trees cover the valley by the city of Antigua. View is from the side of 4250-m Volcan d'Agua, Guatemala. (R. Forman.)*

*and Corruption,* II, 10), and known to ecologists for a long time. That is, all landscapes tend toward a "globally" stable state, following an S-shaped (or logistic) curve. Such a process begins with positive feedbacks, reaches a point of inflexion, and ends up leveling off because of negative feedbacks. Humans generally oppose this tendency, displacing the equilibrium of the landscape toward a different state characterized by a particular management regime (Chapters 8 and 12). This antagonism of two forces, simple in principle and complex in detail (Godron, 1984), is likely to be one of the fundamental rules of a true classification. Such a classification will be *phylogenetic;* that is, the present degree of relationship can be linked with past functioning (see Figure 7.19).

## SUMMARY

The ultimate basis for the heterogeneity of landscapes is thermodynamic, that is, it results from the energy flow that originates in solar radiation.

The solar energy that produces our present spatial heterogeneity comes from three different time periods: (a) the original formation period of the earth with its hot core and subsequently cooled surface; (b) the flourishing period of the ancient plants that became fossilized and have subsequently been extracted in the form of coal, oil, and gas; and (c) the present. All energy flows according to the first and second laws of thermodynamics.

Many animal species use, and appear to require, two or more landscape elements. For example, an animal may sleep or raise young in one and feed in another. This fact is of considerable importance both in understanding species coexistence, and the ecological niche, and in wildlife and pest management.

A classification of landscapes would be premature, but the basic characteristics of a landscape typology can be recognized. Nature contains an inherent hierarchy. Therefore, we develop descending and ascending typologies that go from the broadest category down to individual landscapes, or vice versa. A descending typology proceeds from zonal climate to regional climate to vegetation belts (or bioclimatic units) to geomorphic units to human influences. In constructing an ascending typology, multivariate methods permit us to progressively aggregate landscapes into sets according to their total similarity. Direct methods, on the other hand, typically identify relationships between pairs of particular attributes before grouping landscapes into sets. The fundamental rules of a true phylogenetic classification—where the present degree of relationship can be linked with past functioning—probably would relate the molecular to the "macroscopic" landscape level, and also take into account thermodynamics, stability, and disturbance.

## QUESTIONS

1. How are the laws of thermodynamics useful in understanding a landscape?
2. Landscape heterogeneity results from solar radiation during three widely separated time periods. Discuss this statement.
3. For each of three different types of landscapes, give an example of an animal species that uses two ecosystems. Give an example of one that uses three or more ecosystems in any landscape.
4. Why were the Mendeleiev and de Jussieu classifications so much more successful than the others?
5. Give an example in which geomorphic characteristics are more important than climatic characteristics in a typological hierarchy. Under what circumstance could human influence be above climate in a hierarchy?
6. Order the following three characteristics hierarchically in terms of their effect on the formation of landscapes: human influences, geomorphic units, and bioclimatic units. Explain the rationale.
7. What is an ascending method for typology construction?

8. In what ways is a multivariate approach superior to a direct approach in comparing attributes? What are its shortcomings?
9. What are the basic prerequisites for a phylogenetic classification of landscapes?
10. Understanding heterogeneity is the key to understanding the ecology of a landscape. Evaluate this statement.
11. Choose two photographs from Chapter 13, and indicate where the limits between different landscapes are. Give the rationale for choosing these limits.

# 14
# Landscape Management

*We cannot command nature except by obeying her.*
**Francis Bacon, circa 1610**

One of the oldest texts known tells the unhappy story of Shukallituda, perhaps the first landscape architect, who invented windbreaks more than 5000 years ago on the scorching plains of Mesopotamia.

Shukallituda . . . , when he poured water on the furrows,
when he dug channels around squares of land . . . ,
The furious winds, with all they carry,
With the dust of mountains, struck him in the face. . . .
In the garden, at five or six inaccessible places,
on each place, he planted a tree as protective shade.
The protective shade of this tree—the sarbatus with full foliage—
The shadow it gives, at dawn,
At noon and at dusk, never disappeared. (Kramer, 1957)

The goddess Inanna, tired from travels across Mesopotamia, approached the garden and found the shade of the trees planted as windbreaks so refreshing that she rested there. Shukallituda spotted her, a sleeping beauty clad in simple attire, and made love to her while she slept. Upon awakening, the goddess took vengeance. She caused a calamity to devastate the land and forced the gardener into exile. As in so many myths, the brazen gardener ended up returning happily to his garden after serving his exile. Nevertheless, the punishment inflicted by Inanna foreshadowed the first plague of far-off Egypt. The waters of that country were "turned into blood" because the presumptuous gardener had made an attempt on the integrity of the goddess.

Could this Mesopotamian myth have been a sign that early farmers were conscious of hurting the nourishing Mother Earth when they labored to plant their crops? Was this the seed that much later gave rise to today's conservation movement and land ethic? Did the farmers not know that Mother Nature can respond to abuse by washing away the soil, choking the rivers and fish with sediments, taking away animals, and introducing plagues of pests?

**495**

## WHERE HUMANS GATHER

The human species, from the beginning, was an animal of the edge (Figure 14.1). Except perhaps in the tropical rain forest, most terrestrial animals today also live in several environments sequentially: to feed, to get cover or shelter, and to reproduce.

The arboreal and fruit-eating primates that gave rise to the first hominoids (humans and human-like animals) lived in the dense forest. When the climate became drier near the end of the Tertiary period (see Appendix

**Figure 14.1** *Human changing the sex ratio of deer. Both species reside near the borders of wooded and open areas. The productivity of wildlife populations is altered by the harvesting of only males, only old animals, or any animal. The female deer on the left is a decoy (from a fourteenth-century manuscript,* Livre de la Chasse, *by Gaston Phoebus, Comte de Foix). (Courtesy of H. Roger Viollet, Photo Harlingue-Viollet.)*

to Chapter 7), they probably began to use more open forests and savannas, to become omnivorous, and to profit from the great diversity of environments available. This development was a prelude to the conquest by this least specialized mammal of the infinite variety of environments available today around the world. Humans are slower than ungulates (Figure 14.1), less water-wise than marine mammals, less endowed for struggle than carnivores, less agile for climbing trees than related primates, but more versatile than any of them. Although humans are not "number one" in every region, they compete rather well almost anywhere. Analogously, students know that their chances of entering a certain university are better if they do well in all subjects rather than having a single very strong talent and several weak points.

Near the end of the Ice Age (15,000 to 13,000 B.C.), evidence at one of the oldest known hamlets shows that humans knew how to combine diverse landscape elements to choose an optimal living site. At Pincevent in northern France, people settled where two corridors crossed—at a ford, where a terrestrial mammal track crossed a river full of fish.

Later, on European plains, villages and their fields were often dispersed in the forest matrix in such a way as to form large concentric circular patches. A central village was adjacent to cultivation that was surrounded by pasture and then by woods that provided fuel and construction materials. This spatial arrangement is still used in certain forested savanna regions of tropical Africa (de Miranda, 1979). In more hilly or mountainous regions, villages are often aligned along a fault line or at the base of a slope. These places are basically edges that separate, for example, an alluvial basin for cultivation from a more rocky plateau for pasturing and hunting. Cliff dwellings, often several dozen meters above a plain, are aligned along the boundary between lowland and upland landscape elements (see Figure 12.13). Similarly, in Mediterranean regions villages are often strung out along the rim of a plateau, close to a number of landscape elements.

Among the ten largest cities of the world, eight [Tokyo, New York, Shanghai, Paris, Buenos Aires, Beijing (Peking), London, and Los Angeles] are near the sea, on a major ecological border where the globe is divided between continent and ocean. There the cities profit from the complementarity of resources that come from two contrasting environments. Cities such as Venice and New Orleans have even used sites where the land and sea are intimately intertwined, providing fresh, brackish, and salt water resources.

These examples suggest that human communities capitalize on the inherent heterogeneity of landscapes and then increase it, as the story of Shukallituda testifies. This combined heterogeneity provides the flexibility essential to long-term community equilibrium.

# PRODUCTION IN LANDSCAPES

A landscape is a thermodynamic machine that receives short-wave visible energy from the sun, reflects part of it (about 30%), temporarily absorbs about 70% of the energy and then reemits it in long-wave heat radiation (see Figure 2.2). Such a system tends over time toward an equilibrium, tracing the well-known S-shaped curve or trajectory. The accumulation of plant biomass in a landscape tends toward a maximum that often is determined primarily by climatic conditions (temperature and precipitation).

This outline is usefully applied to human utilization of the landscape. When we attempt to harvest the production of a natural landscape covered with mature vegetation, we tend to destabilize it. If only a small amount is harvested, the system remains in equilibrium or returns to equilibrium at a natural rate (see Figures 12.5 and 12.6). A larger harvest for short-term gain, on the other hand, acts as a disturbance to the landscape, and a similar harvest is then impossible until a period of fallow or waiting has passed. Where vegetation is thin—for example, when invading bare soil—little production can be extracted from a landscape. Production is maximum in intermediate states where the forester or farmer profits from previous ecosystem products, such as humus, sprouting, biotic diversity, water level stabilization, and nitrogen accumulation.

Let us explore this overview in more detail. Animals harvest some primary production but they then return nearly all of their harvest to the atmosphere in the form of $CO_2$. When *Homo sapiens* extracts a small portion of biomass from mature vegetation, the basic process of vertical growth tends to immediately reestablish the equilibrium of the vertical biomass distribution. In effect, the vegetation provides a positive net production equal to the biomass harvested. Thus, the system does not leave its trough of metastability (Figures 12.5 and 12.6).

Similarly, when people harvest some of the animals living in a natural landscape (Figure 14.1), the proportion removed determines whether the landscape equilibrium is altered or not. Harvesting of animals also modifies the age distribution of a species—for example, the balance among prereproductive, reproductive, and postreproductive animals. In some cases, the harvesting of reproductive animals may lead to a population crash, as in the case of the American bison. On the other hand, harvesting of old animals may lead to a new equilibrium more productive than the original (Ellison, 1975).

Since the agricultural revolution of the early Holocene, people have known that they can "rejuvenate" ecological systems to stretch production and live on resources more predictable than those from hunting and gathering. Agricultural intensification still seems possible in some productive regions, and yields continue to increase with inputs of both photosynthetic and fossil fuel energy in a number of areas, for example the Parisian basin and Manitoba, Canada.

Maintaining highly productive equilibria, however, has a cost—an economic, social, ecological, and energy cost. Everything in a productive system, such as an agricultural system, can be reduced to a common unit, calories, including even the long-term quality of the soil and the fatigue and intellectual work of the farmer (Odum, 1971; Pimentel et al., 1975, 1978; Zucchetto and Jansson, 1979a, 1979b; Odum and Odum, 1981; Hansen et al., 1982; Costanza et al., 1983). With this view we gain major insights into the relative costs of each input to the producing of yields. However, we must further refine even these caloric estimates and consider the quality of the inputs and outputs. For example, the cost of producing a calorie of petroleum differs from that of a calorie of firewood or of mutton. Here ecology cannot dissociate itself from economics.

Our problems involving production of renewable resources can be reduced to the following question. How can we shift the equilibria of natural landscapes to other metastable equilibria that will provide the regular annual extraction of energy we need in the form of plant or animal biomass? New equilibria can range from natural reserves to agriculture to cities. In addressing this problem clearly it is inadequate to think simply in terms of managing such and such an ecosystem. We need to focus on the assemblage of ecosystems that comprise a landscape.

To see the future clearly, we must absorb and build on history as it is mirrored in the present. Perhaps the most informative mirrors of the present are our degraded landscapes. They are depauperate in animals and plants and usually suffer from mineral nutrient imbalances. Most striking, however, is the loss of much of their internal structure of corridors and patches. The surface area of degraded landscapes extends year by year almost inexorably, especially in some tropical countries and arid zones. But the study of the dynamics of a particular degraded landscape is often not too informative because the rate of change is so slight. In fact, the single greatest difficulty in managing most landscapes is our lack of knowledge of the forces that underlie landscape change.

## PLANNING AND MANAGEMENT OF MAJOR LANDSCAPE TYPES

In Chapter 8, we saw how landscape characteristics such as patches, corridors, and flows of objects changed along a gradient of landscape modification by human influence. Now we will examine management operations along a similar gradient—from the natural landscape to the landscape with forestry, the agricultural landscape, and finally the landscape with buildings. In each case we are particularly interested in how some of the previous landscape ecology principles are being or could be used in management. There are overlaps among these categories, of course, as when an agricultural landscape includes nature reserves, woodlots for forestry, and homes. Management of all these landscapes (Klotzli, 1980; Vos et al., 1982; Harms et al., 1984) must begin with a survey of (a) the landscape elements present, (b) the flows among them, and (c) the changes in them over time.

## The Natural Landscape

Extensive areas of the globe have natural landscapes that are inhospitable or little used for agriculture, forestry, or homes. These include tundra, boreal forest, desert, and tropical rain forest regions. Elsewhere—in many temperate deciduous forest, grassland, and Mediterranean-type regions— natural landscapes are nearly absent, but remnant landscape elements of them usually remain. The problems of management in these two types of situations are fundamentally different (Gomez-Pompa et al., 1972; Westhoff, 1970; Duffey, 1974; Van der Maarel and Stumpel, 1974; Peterken, 1977; Ratcliffe, 1977; Bakker, 1979; Council on Environmental Quality, 1980; Van der Maarel, 1980; Soule and Wilcox, 1980; Game and Peterken, 1984).

**Managing Natural Landscapes.** If the management objective is to maintain or restore the natural landscape, the survey of landscape elements must focus on their sensitivity to human influence. The key management protection effort is related to the degree of sensitivity. That is, human activities must be dispersed, low in intensity, and inversely proportional to the sensitivity of each landscape element. Certain forms of recreation and scientific endeavor are often particularly appropriate. In areas with very fragile soils or rare plant species or animals requiring remoteness, even these human activities may be incompatible with the maintenance of a landscape in its natural condition (i.e., without significant human impact).

The survey of flows of animals, plants, energy, water, and mineral nutrients among landscape elements pinpoints key areas of movement within a landscape. Many of these will be found to take place in corridors, and so special management to avoid breaks and narrows and to maintain adequate width, nodes, and connectivity may be required. The annual movement of animals up and down mountains, or across a landscape, for example, requires that the integrity of valley migration routes be protected (Figure 14.2). The movement of water, particulate matter, and dissolved nutrients calls for our particular attention to slopes and stream corridors. If not, big floods appear and fish disappear.

Finally, the survey of changes in landscape elements over time pin-

**Figure 14.2**  *Oil pipeline corridor (south of Delta Junction, Alaska) that caribou (Rangifer) will cross on their migration route. Shown here is an above-ground portion of the 100-km-long north-south pipeline across Alaska. Roads and vehicular tracks in the tundra are extremely persistent because of the short growing season. (Courtesy of USDA Soil Conservation Service.)*

points the roles and locations of natural disturbances of different types, sizes, and intensity. Fire, floods, blowdowns, and insect outbreaks may be common and essential phenomena in a landscape in its natural condition without significant human influence. Thus, rather than considering natural disturbances—even huge ones—detrimental, we may have to manage in a way that ensures they occur and have a natural spread. Fire control with equipment, water control with dams, and insect control with pesticides may have to be minimized or eliminated. Landscape heterogeneity and the relative abundance or rarity of all species in a landscape depend on the natural disturbance regimes.

**Managing Natural Remnants.**   Surrounded by rangeland, forests for logging, cultivation, suburbia, or a city, remnants of the natural landscape which are to be managed as nature reserves involve additional considerations. Two major problems are isolation and human impacts from the matrix (Figure 14.3). Isolation primarily affects the interior species. Therefore patch size, shape, number, and configuration are critical (Chapters 3, 5, and 11), as are, also, corridor width and connectivity (Chapters 4

**Figure 14.3** *Isolation and human influences from the matrix—two special issues of remnant nature reserves. The two patches in the foreground have corridors to a species source, whereas other patches are isolated. These small patches are heavily influenced by the human activities in the surrounding landscape elements (northern New York state). (R. Forman.)*

and 11). Patches must have characteristics adequate to support the interior species. Both corridors and patches have a configuration that permits rapid recolonization when an interior species becomes locally extinct in a patch (Figure 14.3).

Management of the flows of objects from the matrix to the nature reserve is the other major focus. Since the matrix is often strongly human-influenced, generally the management process is to minimize or eliminate these flows (Figure 14.3). Some can be affected by modifying the edge characteristics, but the primary effort is on control of the adjacent landscape elements surrounding the nature reserve, especially those located uphill, upwind, and in the direction of buildings.

Wildlife managers have often focused on maximizing the amount of edge to encourage wildlife in a landscape. Nature conservation managers and foresters are more concerned with the critical role of large patches for interior species and for logging operations (Leopold, 1933; Giles,

1978; Terborgh, 1976; Soule and Wilcox, 1980; Cubbage, 1983; Noss, 1983). These concepts can be quite compatible in landscape management as a whole. Maintaining and creating large patches as a top priority, and then surrounding these with a high density of corridors and small patches—containing edges—accomplishes all these objectives and more.

Natural remnants are very much an integral part, of course, of their human-influenced landscape. Thus, the cluster of ecosystems present (Chapter 1) may be a better basic unit for management to consider than the isolated landscape element.

### Landscapes with Forestry

When forest areas are large and the human population low, the management of forests basically consists of three operations: cut the trees, haul them away, and wait decades before repeating the process (Figure 14.4). This process must be analyzed in terms of the size, shape, and location of cuts, and the location of hauling roads and landings, because each of these variables affects mineral nutrient flows, stream quality, microclimate, and natural tree regeneration.

In the wooded landscapes of densely inhabited regions, foresters face different problems. They begin with forest regeneration following cutting. After regeneration, the stand passes through a series of stages from a seedling bed to an old forest. When regeneration takes place on an entire tract of managed land, the forest tract may be called **even-aged** or regular. Alternatively, we may manage the tract as a mosaic that is composed of patches or landscape elements of different ages. The result is a **mosaic tract** of even-aged patches.

In a mosaic tract, foresters must use a different operation or strategy for each patch of the mosaic. Mature trees are cut and replaced by seeds. Seedlings of the best trees are selected and favored during their early years. *Thinning,* the cutting-out of certain less desirable individuals, is done when the young trees are dense. Even at a broad scale the overall tract or forest mosaic is uneven, because foresters tend to aggregate similar age patches in different portions of the mosaic, to facilitate harvesting.

Whether even-aged or mosaic management is applied depends to a large extent on the pattern of natural disturbance in a forest. If extensive fires, pest outbreaks, and the like are present, then whole natural tracts are typically even-aged stands. If small fires, floods, or blowdowns are present, a finer scale mosaic of even-aged stands is naturally produced. If the natural disturbance is at an even finer scale—such as single tree blowdowns and defoliations—a *multi-aged* stand develops naturally. It is primarily in the third case that the forester has a choice whether to manage for even-aged or mosaic tracts.

**Figure 14.4** *A multi-aged and multi-layered forest patch many centuries old. A canopy of coastal redwoods (Sequoia gigantea) covers subcanopy, understory, shrub, and herb layers. Many individuals in a layer, although varying by two or more times in diameter, may be similar in age, indicating they started together following a disturbance. This old forest contains considerable standing and fallen dead wood, important to many animals and plants. Nearby forest patches of different ages constitute a mosaic tract managed for a sustained yield of wood products. Wheeler Creek Natural Area, Oregon, United States. (U. S. Forest Service; courtesy of J. F. Franklin.)*

For several thousand years wood was the prime fuel for domestic heating, as well as for baking bricks, tiles, and pottery, making glass, smelting iron, and the metallurgy and potash industries. When the population-to-forest ratio is low, tree trunks are generally cut for firewood. When the ratio is high, local firewood largely comes from branches (or young stems). It may be taken from the crowns of cut trees or from the lower branches of standing trees. Management in these areas is particularly important, since the lack of firewood is emerging as a global problem.

In some areas, **coppice wood**—young stems of species able to sprout from stumps of cut trees—is a particularly valuable source of even-sized firewood and other wood products. When we cut all the shoots in a parcel, we call it a *simple coppice*. If only certain shoots are selected for cutting it is a *selective coppice*. When we systematically leave some old trees (standards) standing (such as trunks of seed origin with clear space or "elbow room" around them), we obtain a distinctive forest structure, namely a *coppice with standards* (or simply coppice woods), with dense sprouts under an open forest canopy. In this manner, we combine the production of firewood from coppice and timber from canopy trees on the same parcel (Rackham, 1975, 1976, 1980). This management technique was well adapted to the needs of rural European communities, where farmers regularly cut coppice wood for heating and for woodworking—carpentry, furniture making, and wagon construction. When the standard trees were occasionally cut for major beams in construction, the careful farmer replanted them, even transplanting particularly promising individuals of the same species to replace the old giants that had been harvested.

Many other types of forest management exist (Marien, 1983), but they all have a general problem in common. Timber products only become available in the long term. Therefore, a major concern of management is to obtain a **sustained yield**—a soil quality and a gradation of ages or sizes of stems capable of assuring the regular replacement of the old tree by the young (Figure 14.4). An idealized J-shaped (or hyperbolic) curve, relating the number of stems in each of several size classes, characterizes a tract managed for sustained yield. In this situation, there are many small stems, progressively fewer intermediate sized stems, and few large stems. Both a mosaic tract and an uneven-aged forest, as well as (of course) an multi-aged stand, can be managed in this way.

Forest management requires a document that summarizes the ecological conditions present and the management objectives. A key step is to divide the land into categories, grouping together parcels that become units of management and treatment. Within each unit, a balanced heterogeneity is recognized and maintained. It acts as the spatial counterpoint to the temporal rotation of harvests that is necessary to assure sustained yield. For example, if you annually cut coppice when it is 15 years old, you must divide your forest into fifteen equal parts and cut one part each year. The landscape for forestry is the result of past management and its present heterogeneity gives rise to the staggering of human actions over time.

## The Agricultural Landscape

Globally, the great majority of managed landscapes are agricultural. We will begin as landscape detectives, reading the landscape for clues to the type of management used by the farmers there.

The farmer's life is directly affected by the percentages of cultivated fields, forests, and pastures in the landscape (Figure 14.5). Ancient terms for these—*ager, sylva* and *saltus*—are still used in parts of Europe (Kuhn-holtz-Lordat, 1958; Barry, 1960). The **agro-sylvo-pastoral equilibrium** is a keystone of Mediterranean agriculture. A break in this balance causes the risk of erosion, one of the most fundamental causes of major landscape change in that climate (Naveh, 1982b; Naveh and Dan, 1973). An equilibrium among these three landscape element types is thus our first clue.

A second more direct clue is readily deciphered from the first glimpse of a landscape with regular rotation cropping and a fallow period. The length of the fallow period can be deduced from the percentage of cultivated surfaces present (de Miranda, 1979). The plains of western Europe commonly have a biennial alternation of wheat and sugar beet (or corn) that results in almost exactly equal areas of the two crops (see Chapter 12). Checkerboard squares regularly alternate color each season and each year.

In an open landscape the major clue is sparsely dispersed clumps of small shrubs or grasses in a cold dry climate, a common result of extensive grazing, seen in a range of landscapes from Kashmir in the Himalayas to Patagonia at the tip of South America. In certain warmer pastured landscapes, however, trees are tolerant, and tell us more. For example, the gnarled trunk of the argan-tree (*Argania*) in southern Morocco serves as a ladder enabling goats to browse the leaves of an "aerial pasture." In southern Spain and Portugal, acorn-producing oaks are scattered in a park-like arrangement indicative of animal farming such as of pigs.

Another major clue to agricultural management processes comes from the types of buildings that a farming operation must possess. In fact, the buildings depend directly on the proportion of types of landscape elements present. Sheds and hay barns are consistently present in pasture farms in temperate regions. Grinding windmills once commonly graced grain country, and windmills that pump water for livestock are common in some dry landscapes of Mexico and Texas. In Bordeaux and Riesling country, the storehouses for wine are lined up as outbuildings around the chateaus. The typical white fences of farms in Ireland and (in the United States) New England and Kentucky are directly linked to the breeding and pasturing of horses.

In each case presented, the structure in the agricultural landscape is the clue; it both mirrors and tells the management regime. Myriad opportunities exist to use landscape ecology concepts in this management.

**Figure 14.5** *Cultivation, pasture, and forest on a 65-degree slope. A cornfield (Zea mays) with horizontal lines (right) and a pasture for livestock with criss-cross lines (left) have been cut in this montane rain forest near Merida, Venezuela, at an elevation of about 2000 m. Erosion and sedimentation are severe in the area. (R. Forman.)*

To illustrate, think of the effects of field size on agricultural production and on natural processes. Of the shapes of fields and the peninsulas present. Of the mesh size of windbreak networks. Of the width and connectivity of stream corridors. Of the density of remnant patches or landscape porosity. Of the frequency and spatial distribution of natural disturbances. Of the spread of species from roads and farmyard areas.

Of unusual landscape features. Of the pattern of spread of pests and pesticides. Of objects producing turbulent airflow. Of rest stops, stepping stones, relay nodes, bottlenecks, and boundary crossing frequency. Of hierarchical spatial structure and the angle of interaction. Of network intersections and circuitry. Of stabilizing processes. Of remoteness. Of linkages with other landscapes. Each of these is of particular importance in the agricultural landscape; and in fact, most are critical to both agricultural production and natural processes.

## The Built Landscape

According to classical canons, a landscape becomes artificial when it includes objects built by artisans or artists. The examples in Chapter 8 showed that isolated homes, villages, cities, and communication routes are early human-created types of landscape elements. A perception that combines buildings with the physical environment may be described in the following manner.

The builders of traditional buildings in the rural environment have always known, through an intuitive perception of natural phenomena, how to produce an ingenious response to climate in each location. . . . The traditional habitat presents architectural characteristics which permit inhabitants to be naturally protected from climate. (Groleau, 1981)

We find this perception mirrored in landscapes when we observe the distribution of different types of homes. In western Europe, for example, the Latin home is covered with curved Roman tiles. A Gallic or northern home, once covered with thatched straw, today has slate or flat tiles. A line separating the areas using these two types of buildings coincides almost exactly with the line bordering the area that receives an average 2000 hours of sunlight in a year and has an average annual temperature of 11.5°C (53°F) (Groleau, 1981) (Figure 14.6). These two styles of homes are both a cultural heritage and a direct "adaptation" to climatic differences. The author observed a similar pattern linking climate with types of homes in northeastern Brazil and in Central America.

When buildings are aggregated in groups—villages, towns and cities—the management challenges relate largely to problems of circulation (Chapter 8). The inputs, outputs, and flows within the system just as in a cell or a vertebrate body, require controls and management.

As just described for the agricultural landscape, a large proportion of the landscape ecology concepts apply to, and are critical in, the built landscape. This is because high spatial heterogeneity, numerous flows among landscape elements, and rapid landscape change are all prominent and conspicuous in the built landscape.

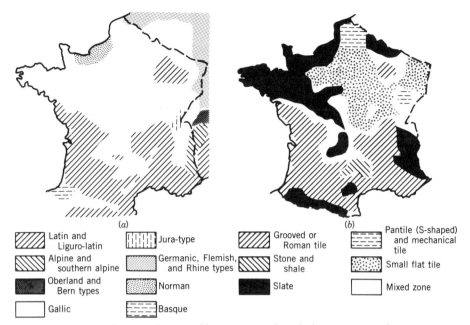

| | Latin and Liguro-latin | | Jura-type | | Grooved or Roman tile | | Pantile (S-shaped) and mechanical tile |
|---|---|---|---|---|---|---|---|
| | Alpine and southern alpine | | Germanic, Flemish, and Rhine types | | Stone and shale | | Small flat tile |
| | Oberland and Bern types | | Norman | | Slate | | Mixed zone |
| | Gallic | | Basque | | | | |

**Figure 14.6** *Distribution of types of homes (a) and roofs (b) in France. The major boundaries correlate closely with annual solar radiation and temperature (from D. Groleau, 1981). (Courtesy of* Amenagement et Nature.*)*

## LANDSCAPE QUALITY

There is an old dictum that one does not question tastes and colors. Landscape quality can be appreciated from several more or less subjective points of view (Williamson, 1979; Coltman, 1984). The artist, the scientist, the economist, and the sociologist will not consider the same things equally in making judgments, and no one can say that one point of view is better than another.

### A Direct Method of Estimating Landscape Quality

Several methods permit some objectivity in the estimation of landscape quality. Perhaps the most direct method involves the use of a large photographic collection, say of pictures of two landscapes, a plain and an area of low mountains. In a study by Brun-Chaize (1976), the photographs were paired, one from each landscape. Sixty-five pairs were selected and presented to a sample population of 324 persons who came from both urban and rural areas. Each person was asked which of the two photographs in each pair he or she preferred.

The results were analyzed statistically (e.g., with factor analysis) and relationships between the opinions of different observers emerged. The result of this analysis is an image in which a cloud of points corresponding to the relationships is projected onto a grid with coordinates. The two photographs in a pair were represented by nearby points on the grid, if many of the observers either liked or rejected both of them. Two photographs in a pair are represented by two widely separated points if the opinions of the 324 people were divergent on which was preferable.

Several interesting results emerge from this image of the relationships among the observers' opinions.

1. When the photographs included considerable geometrization of objects, the cloud of points spread out widely. This result means that the population had widely differing perceptions of what a lot of straight lines meant as an indication of landscape quality. Moderate or intermediate levels of geometrization produced more agreement among people and represented good landscape quality.
2. Exactly the same result was found for curvilinearity.
3. The cloud of points is also spread out when more "artificialization" was present, as indicated by homes, cultivated fields, roads, forestry activities, or domestic animals.

The persons questioned constituted a heterogeneous sample. The older the people, the more they preferred geometric and artificialized landscapes. Those with higher education or in a more intellectual profession, along with those in cities, appreciated the wild landscapes more. The luxuriance of vegetation seemed to play only a minor role in the impressions of the observers.

## Survey Questionnaires

Polls and survey questionnaires are widely used to gather public opinions, on subjects from politics to ping-pong. When such questionnaires include many criteria for evaluating landscape quality, and the responses for each criterion are interrelated, we can combine the responses to obtain an overall score. Many classical data analysis techniques may be used—as well as some newer ones like those based on "fuzzy sets" (MacDougall, 1981)—to interpret responses.

Unfortunately, all the methods of evaluation of landscape quality by inquiry suffer a severe handicap. The landscape itself affects the perception of people (Stilgoe, 1981). A townsperson does not appreciate a landscape in the same way as a forester. A townsperson may romantically admire the twisted trees that are the despair of the forester looking to a forest for wood production. The inhabitant of a natural landscape who understands the "balance of nature" may view predator control measures as misguided, whereas the suburbanite views wild predators as nothing but a nuisance or danger.

Sociologists have tried to analyze this type of self-suggestion, the dependence of sociological behavior on the physical characteristics of the landscape. R. Mucchielli (personal communication) has observed that tropical forest landscapes (Figure 14.7) exhibit three characteristics that influence human behavior.

1. In these regions, nature is so powerful that humans cannot resist it. They remain in a passive rather than building mood, leaving protection mainly in the hands of rites or magic.
2. Environmental stability over the seasons and years provides a permanent nourishment. Societies have no need to establish collective structures for production and they remain composed of small tribal families.
3. The restricted horizon and the closed world (Figure 14.7) favor the blossoming of myths where humans are surrounded by oppressive and vengeful powers.

## Perception of Landscape Quality by Animals

The methods described above are concerned with the perception of landscape quality by the human intellect. Would it be possible to more directly evaluate the well-being or satisfaction that the primate *Homo sapiens* feels in a landscape? Because nature and culture are so intermingled for us, it is easier to study the behavior of large wild animals whose movements can be related with variations in environmental conditions (Wiens, 1976, 1985).

Over the past two decades, many studies, particularly on hoofed herbivores in cool regions, have elucidated the population dynamics and feeding habits of the animals. We might mention the wild boar in Europe (Mauget, 1979), the desert bighorn sheep in arid areas of western United States (Woolf et al., 1970; Oldemeyer et al., 1971; Shannon et al., 1975; Bailey, 1980), the wild sheep in Czechoslovakia (Sabados and Manica, 1977), the chamois in the Alps (Kramer, 1969), the white-tailed deer in Minnesota and Wisconsin (USA) (Wetzel et al., 1975; Larson et al., 1978), the red deer in Scotland (Staines, 1976), the roe deer in Denmark (Andersen, 1953), the mule deer in New Mexico (USA) (Boeker et al., 1972), and the ibex in Mongolia (Dzieciolowski et al., 1980). Despite this richness of information, studies that relate animal movements to the heterogeneity of the environment are scarce.

Let us briefly go up a magnificent Mediterranean mountain to share in the work, pleasure, and significance of one study that explicitly focused

**Figure 14.7** *Perception of landscape quality according to where an observer lives. Living in this rain forest landscape strongly determines your evaluation of its quality and its potential. The long curving shoots are chusque bamboo (Chusquea) in the understory of this montane rain forest near Merida, Venezuela, at an elevation of about 3000 m. (R. Forman.)*

on a landscape, that is, a heterogeneous system. Wild sheep or mouflon (*Ovis ammon musimon*) near Caroux, France, live on the flank of a massive mountain and move from summits swept by cool Atlantic winds to valleys bathed in the mild Mediterranean climate (Auvray, 1982). The vegetation, long influenced by people, includes forests in four bioclimatic units or belts plus open or closed shrubland (heaths), a few crops, and rocky outcrops. The mouflon move through exceptionally diverse landscapes, in search of both food where it is available, and a comfortable microclimate, or a secure resting place. In this study we are particularly interested in which landscape elements or landscapes are perceived by the animal as being of high quality, and how this perception changes through time.

Our first step (which required being in shape) was a backpack reconnaissance of all the environments present. The objective was to tentatively determine the primary characteristics important to the animal. The broad result was a sensation of awe, beauty, fear, and endurance in the complex of landscapes. Closer to the scientific objective, it appeared that the major variables affecting the mouflon were altitude, vegetation type, dominant plant species, topographic location, exposure, and slope angle.

A rough preliminary synthesis was diagrammed to characterize the types of landscape elements and show the overall structure of the region. Four bioclimatic belts were drawn on a fine scale map (1/10,000). The landscapes corresponded to the bioclimatic levels thus mapped. The investigator then established four routes through the area that were walked at least twice monthly. At each one of a series of panoramic observation points at least 15 minutes of observations were made on each visit. Each time, a data sheet was filled in that indicated meteorological conditions, the number of animals observed, their behavior, the landscape element used by the mouflon and so on. In total, 2667 data sheets were completed; 580 corresponded to observation points where no mouflon was observed and 2087 censused 10,767 individual animals.

The completion of data sheets when no animals are observed is important in this type of study. In studying population dynamics, the calculations are generally done only with data where animals are observed. But when we wanted to know how the landscape was used by the mouflon, absences of animals are just as important as presences. Absences indicated sites where the mouflon did not like to live. In other words, "empty" points modify the significance of the final overall interpretation and thus are critical in a landscape study.

The main problem in this type of study is how to link animal observations and ecological characteristics. The animals are sensitive to a combination of characteristics, not just a single one in isolation. To overcome this problem, a direct method of analysis was used that focuses on the combinations of characteristics (e.g., contingency tables transformed into "corrected frequencies"; Godron, 1968; Daget and Godron, 1982). Such an analysis showed, for example, that the mouflon frequent the western and northern exposed slopes primarily when there is little wind, but generally move to eastern slopes in strong (usually northwest) winds. The animals rest and spend much of their time on the more rocky landscape elements. Finally, the analysis showed that they move from grasslands in spring, to open forests occasionally throughout the year, to shrubby heathlands in summer and fall, and to dense forests in winter.

Overall, the study showed what landscape elements were preferred by the mouflon—as a combined function of microclimate and feeding—and how these changed over time. It also showed the primary routes or corridors used. This kind of analysis of the structure of landscapes, and their functioning over time, is precisely the foundation necessary for good management of an area.

In addition, the results permitted detection of other areas around the Mediterranean region, where the appropriate combination of landscape elements is also present, and an analogous management regime would be appropriate for mouflon. (Furthermore, the investigator was in exceptional physical shape at the end and could compete with mouflon in covering terrain.) Finally, concerning the animal's perception of landscape quality, it was apparent that the mouflon was an "amateur" in finding food in these diversified mountainous landscapes. The animal is far from its native lowland prairie, which has disappeared altogether and would have to be reconstructed.

## Protection of Landscape Quality

When a landscape is excessively modified or artificialized, the natural mechanisms of regulation are no longer efficient enough to restore quality. Informed citizens then must sound what might be called the *Alarm Cry of Plato* (c. 360 B.C.).

. . . [I]n those days the country . . . yielded far more abundant produce . . . [I]n comparison of what then was, there are remaining only the bones of the wasted body, as they may be called . . . all the richer and softer parts of the soil having fallen away, and the mere skeleton of the land being left. But in the primitive state of the country, its mountains were high hills covered with soil, and the plains, as they are termed by us, of Phellus were full of rich earth, and there was abundance of wood in the mountains which now only afford sustenance to bees, not so very long ago there were still to be seen roof of timber cut from trees growing there, which were of a size sufficient to cover the largest houses; and there were many other high trees, cultivated by man and bearing abundance of food for cattle. Moreover, the land reaped the benefit of the annual rainfall, not as now losing the water which flows off the bare earth into the sea, but, having an abundant supply in all places, and receiving it into herself and treasuring it up in the close clay soil, it let off into the hollows the streams which it absorbed from the heights, providing everywhere abundant fountains and rivers, of which there may still be observed sacred memorials in places where fountains once existed. . . .

Such was the natural state of the country, which was cultivated . . . (*Critias*, 111.b,c,d)

In Plato's Mediterranean basin, forests were the best protection of the landscape, and Roman consuls were later charged with their protection ("silvae sunt consules dignae"). In medieval Europe, the preservation of the forests, which were the most sensitive element of the landscapes, was recognized in one of the chapters of the early Charlemagne edict (about 810 A.D.): "Where there are forests, no one is permitted to take too much from them and damage them, and everyone guards the animals well."

Today, on the one hand we see the accelerating degradation of nature, and on the other hand efforts to limit that degradation are increasingly being pursued by international organizations, nations, local bodies, and individuals. Behind the first process are the increase in the human population and the increasing use of fossil and nuclear energy. Behind the second process are partly economic self interest, in greater part governmental legislation—often reflecting the will of the people—but perhaps most of all a **land ethic** (Leopold, 1949; Hills, 1974; Wilson, 1984), that is, a self-imposed limitation on the degree to which one will modify or destroy the landscape. When two forces are both accelerating in opposite directions the quite predictable outcome is rupture or breakdown of the system. The outcome can be modified, though, and landscape quality may be the keystone. What steps can be taken?

## MODELLING AND LANDSCAPE MANAGEMENT

Since the beginning of this century, scientists have realized that the early analytic methods developed by René Descartes and John Stuart Mill no longer suffice for frontiers with highly complex objects. When a large number of forces combines to make a system develop, it is no longer efficient to search for how only one of the forces acts, "other things being equal." In ecology since the 1960s, teams of investigators engaged in large ecological projects have shown that **systems analysis** (the study of the behavior of, and interactions among, components in a model of a complex system) is useful to begin to understand ecosystem functioning. This systematic approach is quite natural when we view the landscape as a product of its past functioning. Clearly, management of the group of ecosystems that makes up a landscape requires at least the outline of a **model**—a simplified verbal (at first), graphic, or mathematical description used to help visualize a complex object.

Apparently the first useful models for landscape ecology were suggested by von Thunen (Hall, 1966) and formalized by Christaller (1933, 1938). They express simultaneously the spatial distribution of human activities and a logic of functioning. Individuals and human groups are distributed regularly in space so as to optimize the use of resources. This produces hexagonal structures organized around **central places** that in turn are surrounded or boxed in (Figure 14.8) (Losch, 1940, 1954; Woldenberg, 1972). Certain long-term activities take place only in these central places or principal centers that in turn govern the activities of secondary centers. For example, the rural habitat dispersed in hexagonal structures (Einzelhof) across the landscape results in homogeneity in the distribution of water resources and in the control of agricultural production.

The central place model stimulated considerable interest and controversy. Some geographers saw hexagons everywhere; others saw none. More important, though, was the research that could link the hexagonal or other spatial structures to flows in the landscape. Thus, if a barrier is present that blocks and channels flows within a landscape, any geometric spatial structure will accordingly be distorted (Losch, 1954). If one direction in space is unique or "privileged," say, because of a drainage or communication corridor, the basic landscape distribution will become linear (Figure 14.8), as have the characteristic "rangs" in the settlements of eastern Canada, and as in the Marshufendorf and Waldhufendorf areas of Germany. If one point on the landscape governs activity, a radiating pattern of flows and structure will be evident. We see this on limestone plateaus where a deep well is used for an entire community, and in the rotation of land around a village in the early open-field type of European agriculture (Chapter 8).

All these spatial structures are linked to functioning. Conversely, it is possible to deduce functioning from the observation of spatial structure. For this purpose we use maps at an intermediate level of scale in beginning a landscape ecology study.

## Models from Maps

Many types of maps may be used to manage landscapes (Chapter 13), and it is also possible to build models from these maps. For example, landscape planning and management for the North and South River watersheds near Boston was done with an extensive mapping and modeling process (Steinitz, 1979; and C. Steinitz, personal communication), that is both fascinating and instructive for us. The data base was composed of a grid of 78,400 squares, each 100 m on a side. Fifty-three maps were constructed, including the following.

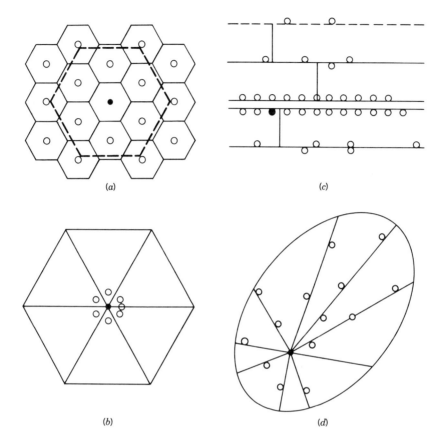

● Primary center
○ Secondary center

**Figure 14.8** *Patterns of resource use and division of space. (a) Hexagonal structure on a homogeneous distribution of resources, where primary centers are equidistant and secondary centers under the loose influence of a primary center are equidistant. (b) Control is centralized, so secondary centers are near the primary center. (c) Resources are homogeneously distributed, but primary centers are aligned on a social rather than on a resource axis. (d) Resources are heterogeneously distributed, leading to an elliptic or asymmetric polygon structure. [After von Thunen (Hall, 1966); Christaller, 1933; Hagget et al., 1977]*

1. Geology.
2. Topography (altitude, slope, exposure).
3. Soils (soil depth, water table depth, types according to two classifications, permeability, pH, resistance to slumping).
4. Hydrology (type of surface water, direction and order of water courses, watershed characteristics).

5. Climate (average precipitation, average temperature, maximum hourly precipitation).
6. Vegetation (vegetation type, tree height, tree density, type of usage) and animals.
7. Land occupation (type of habitation, green space, type of commerce, type of industry, roads, communication lines, airports, public services, historic monuments).
8. Land value.
9. Recreation potential.
10. Visibility of historic sites.
11. Zoning.
12. Administration.
13. Census results.

A first series of models was constructed from these maps. They included, in particular, the following.

1. A model of soil evaluation that characterized the risks of water erosion (from the universal soil loss equation developed by Wischmeier and Smith, 1965, 1978—Chapter 9) and showed that erosion may reach 20 tons of soil per hectare per year (about five dump truck loads for a football field-sized area) in 33,820 squares of the grid, and may exceed in 1,447 squares 200 tons. The costs of combatting erosion were also included for each hectare-square.
2. Three submodels relative to water resources. The first calculated the needs of people, industry, commerce, and so forth. The second treated the water balance (precipitation, interception, evapotranspiration, effects of urbanization, local accumulation, outputs). The third estimated variations in water quality. A model integrating these was applied to both watersheds and included the effects of the salt marshes near their mouths.
3. A model related to land use and the disturbance effect of urban management, including the "diversity" of adjacent squares, and natural succession.
4. An evaluation model of land value (from an empirical linear regression), where parameters were density of homes, distance from a superhighway interchange, a slope limiting the installation of a septic system, date of sale, and proximity to a road.
5. A model that put together the inventory of historic sites, the land having views of them, and visual preferences in order to propose options for creating protected zones and foreseeing necessary financial resources. A difficult choice remained—whether to manage for the present situation, in which buildings surround the historic sites (as preferred by many local residents)—or manage historic places by

attempting to recreate their original environment, which in some cases was forested (as preferred by many conservationists).

6. A model of site selection desirable for recreation.
7. A model analyzing the factors involved in locating industries (availability of labor, transportation, mineral and water resources, waste treatment, fiscal inducements).
8. A transportation model with different alternatives for the daily commuting schedules of workers.

Each of these models results from a specific objective or question posed by the investigators, a modeling step necessary for dealing with the huge mass of raw mapping data. (The complexity here was too great to synthesize all the models into a single huge model.) With the models, the investigators were able to develop management recommendations and options that were spatially focused. That is, the information could be related to an individual square in the grid, to an aggregation of squares, or to the entire grid, which covered parts of more than one landscape. Management guidelines and priorities differed at different levels of scale.

## Model Construction

To build a model, we must generally take five successive steps.

1. Describe the objective.
2. Detect the principal cogs or linkages.
3. Assemble them in a temporary fashion.
4. Try to make the assemblage work or function.
5. Observe the discrepancies between reality and the model and return to steps one, two, or three.

In the case of landscape management, the objective of the model is easy to conceptualize. We want to describe simplified images of the landscape as it changes, contrasting the results of each of the alternative management policies envisioned.

To figure out the principal cogs of the system, it is useful to begin by drawing a rough diagram of the processes that affect landscape change. Several conditions must be met by the model. Most importantly, it must include the spatial diversity of the land to be managed. This purpose can be served by the maps available, especially land use or occupation maps that integrate vegetation types, "artificialization" (including building density), and dominant species. These maps also permit the rapid establishment of a dialogue between the landscape planners and the ecologists, geographers, foresters, range managers, and other people involved.

Finally, it is helpful to diagram schematically the land use methods that have been used over the preceding years as well as those that can be anticipated for the future. These diagrams are needed to prepare so-called "tensor models" for management.

### Tensor Models in Management

The use of each individual landscape element can be represented by a (mathematical) matrix (see Chapter 12). In this case each horizontal row represents a characteristic parameter of land use such as wheat production, protection of rare species, value of the soil, or aesthetic value. The columns are sequential time intervals, essentially describing the change of each parameter over time. The combination of several such matrices produces an array of several dimensions that is called a **tensor** in mathematics (Robert, 1972; Pillet, 1981). A tensor for a landscape is composed of a pile of as many matrices as there are landscape elements present. It may be compared to a booklet of which each matrix is a page. The tensor is a model that shows the change in all those elements, that is, the change in the landscape as a whole. The usefulness of the tensor is that it can be developed for each landscape management strategy proposed (Figure 14.9), and thus the expected changes through time can be compared.

One such tensor functions directly with the four arithmetical operations $(+, -, \times, \div)$ to provide a general idea of how the parameters vary over time relative to the area of each landscape element. This model is, therefore, the simplest usable one for landscape management. It is easily enriched with more powerful mathematical tools, such as a transition matrix (Chapter 12), a process that is convenient for integrating the changes in land use through time (Godron, 1973).

Tensors will be used here in their basic form, for two objectives, (a) to delineate land potential and (b) to estimate the direct consequences of the alternative management options.

**The Land Potential Tensor.**  Discussions between ecologists and economists often lead to considerations of *land potential,* that is, the possible uses and values of an area.

1. One major type of land potential is the production that can be harvested or extracted using available technology and directly given an economic value.
2. Another major type of land potential, extremely difficult to calculate in its totality in economic terms, is the basic role of a landscape in the ecological regulation that is necessary to maintain it in equilibrium. Familiar examples are natural vegetation that prevents flooding (Figure 14.9), erosion, and pest outbreaks, salt marshes that control estuarine

**Figure 14.9** *Officers stranded by rapid surface runoff upriver. The flood level results from past decisions of a specific landscape management approach. Alternative options are readily compared with tensor and other models. For each option we must evaluate a landscape element on the basis of its role in ecological regulation, its aesthetic and inspirational value, and its economic value. Wichita County, Texas (United States). (Courtesy of the* Iowa Park Leader *and USDA Soil Conservation Service.)*

fish and shellfish populations, and predators that prevent herbivore populations from overusing the land.

3. A third major land potential type transcends simple economic terms and should not be reduced to them—the aesthetic, therapeutic, and inspirational value of the land to humans, illustrated so vividly by art, literature, religious sites, and personal experience.

For example, the economic production of eucalyptus or pine plantations involves change over time in several parameters such as tree height, diameter, and density; accumulated primary production; and thinnings. We may add the cost in money and energy of each silvicultural operation along with the change in recreational and other values. All these data are assembled in a two-dimensional matrix for each landscape element, and the matrices are brought together like a booklet to form the tensor model for the landscape.

To better understand how the land potential tensor is built, we will take two simple examples from a study done in the province of Bouchir, Iran (Godron and Koohafkhan, 1982). In this province it is possible to improve pastures on warm limestone slopes dominated by a shrub, common jujube (*Zizyphus spina-Christi*), by means of a ban on cattle grazing during the winter months. Since the year this management approach was initiated several important parameters have changed. The first is above-ground biomass, because a large number of annual species, including grasses (*Stipa capensis*) and legumes (*Astragalus siliquosus*), has increased. The second is plant production consumed by the herd of cattle. The third is the growth of the herd. The fourth is the portion of cattle production consumed by the local inhabitants, and the fifth is commercial revenue from sales on the local meat market. The sixth is the cost of tending the herd. Finally, the seventh is the quantity of feed (generally barley) that must be given to the herd during the temporary grazing ban.

The change in these parameters over time can be represented on a matrix in which each row refers to one of the parameters and the columns represent time. One such matrix shows the potential of these slopes if a grazing ban is used. In this case, the time interval selected is one year, and each column corresponds to one year. The matrix therefore simply shows how each of the landscape parameters changes over time. The observations indicated that, in the pastures on these warm slopes plant cover resulting from the grazing ban increased for three years and leveled off thereafter.

A second matrix can be developed for pastures on cooler limestone soils. Here the wormwood shrub (*Artemisia herba-alba*) is predominant, but it is common to plant a different shrub, sea orach (*Atriplex halimus*), to create extra forage for grazing. In this case, the increase in forage value is slower and does not stabilize until the fifth year.

For these warmer and cooler pastures, we have a total of thirteen parameters related to possible management. The values for each parameter as it changes over time are written across a row. Each matrix therefore, with thirteen rows and ten columns that represent ten consecutive years, effectively describes how the pastureland changes over a ten-year period. These two matrices (one for warmer pastures and one for cooler pastures) can then be placed one below the other like the pages of a booklet to form a two-page tensor model. In this case, it is a land potential tensor. We could build tensor models in similar fashion for a reconstruction of the recent past in a landscape, or for future landscape changes if left to natural processes.

Note that the results of a tensor model depend on the parameters included in the rows. In this example we only included direct economic parameters. A complete landscape management plan would of course also include key parameters related both to ecological regulation and aesthetics.

**Improvement Tensors.** In this example we will consider only range improvements in the same extensive area of Bouchir. For complete management we would have to add the actions that pertain to meat production, the economic system, the inhabited areas, biotic diversity, stream quality, and numerous other parameters, following exactly the same process described below.

The actions envisioned here are pastoral improvements of direct interest to the farmers and have to do with the characteristics of each landscape element on the slopes of the area. Four management options are considered.

1. A two-month grazing ban (during the period of vegetation regeneration—November and December) followed by carefully limited grazing during the remainder of the year.
2. A two-month grazing ban, coupled with the planting of annual forage species [like milk vetch (*Astragalus siliquosus*)].
3. A three-month grazing ban, coupled with the planting (or replanting) of perennial herbaceous forage species [such as Siberian wheatgrass (*Agropyron desertorum*) or bromegrass (*Bromus tomentellus*)].
4. A three-month grazing ban, coupled with the planting of woody forage species [such as sea orach (*Atriplex halimus*), four-wing saltbush (*A. canescens*), and acacia (*Acacia arabica*)].

These actions, of course, must be combined with the purchase of feed for the animals during the grazing ban.

The effects of the envisioned range improvements were calculated for these four scenarios using tensors, and the results compared. It appeared that the actions would have to be implemented over several years, because the costs of the actions would not be compensated by the predicted improvements until after a delay of several years. Thus, use of the model averted premature selection and implementation of one of the proposed range modifications. The next step would be to build a "sequence model"; that is, one that compares the results of different management actions applied in a sequence of time periods.

## Model Sensitivity, Risks, and Timing

The sensitivity of a model can be estimated by means of a simulation that simply varies inputs artificially or mathematically. The simulation determines the ratios of outputs to inputs. That is, when inputs vary, how much effect does this variation have on outputs? For our purpose, the inputs are the management parameters listed on the rows of each page of the land potential tensor. By artificially varying the intensity of a parameter and calculating the effect on, say, range improvement or cattle production, we can estimate the sensitivity of each management parameter.

For example, if management increases plant production of a pasture by 10%, the average plant production of the landscape will be increased much less if the pasture is poor than if it is rich. In Bouchir, for example, the sensitivities for the first 11 parameters show that the most efficient action to improve animal production is presently the winter ban on grazing of the common jujube shrub (*Zizyphus*).

This example is quite schematic, its basic goal being to illustrate the progressive steps of the method. It is not, however, in multiplying the details that tensors may provide the most interesting applications. It is rather in considering the probability of risk, in optimizing the more important results, and in coupling them with a management sequence, that tensors can be used to greatest benefit.

Risk assessment is one of the most useful applications of modeling, but not the easiest to perform. For example, in the arid climate of Iran the principal hazard is the risk of drought. It directly affects plant production, which is easy enough to measure or estimate. Woody plant production is relatively constant, but production of annual plants varies greatly and must be observed in detail. It would be possible to construct a submodel to delineate this point (e.g., as Floret and Pontanier, 1982; Rambal, 1984; and Naveh, 1982b did elsewhere in the Middle East), but precipitation variation over time is not sufficiently well documented in the region for such a submodel to be useful. We would do better to simply recognize that the contrast between dry years and moist years is marked and to construct two tensors to distinguish those two types of years.

The other primary risks there, are eruptions of new species, cattle diseases, and the movements of human populations. In addition, even the most rigorous predictions are always modified by the decisions of interested persons that in turn are generally unpredictable. It is possible, though, to introduce this unpredictability in assessing risk into the model and to evaluate the consequences to the system of disturbances at different times.

At times in history our predecessors have managed their natural heritage with a remarkable wisdom that respected nature and implicitly recognized its finely tuned sequence of events. The seasonal migration of wild herbivores (Figure 14.10), and flocks of sheep with shepherds, between summer and winter pastures is a natural response to fluctuating environmental conditions. Human population pressures and today's living conditions have changed, and such former ecological or management solutions are too often interrupted today and will be lost tomorrow without wise management.

It is inherently interesting to rediscover the spirit, if not the letter, of the finely tuned management of our predecessors. When we do so we can then optimize the chronological order of management operations and resource use, as was formerly done through observation and expe-

**Figure 14.10**  *Elk (*Cervus canadensis*) on winter range before altitudinal migration in spring. Maintenance of such a species requires the protection of both summer and winter habitat, as well as the migratory corridors. Northern Yellowstone National Park, Wyoming (United States). (Courtesy of Dick Randall.)*

rience. Nevertheless, in a heterogeneous landscape we must be sure to marry this timing of management operations to a spatial model.

Each of the landscape elements in a landscape—not just the "rich" elements from which an immediate profit can clearly be made—may require a different kind of management. A model that sets priorities on management actions in each landscape element will usually identify "production-poor" environments as urgently requiring management that may range from the constructing of buildings to the protection of the natural state. For example, in the Mississippi delta the upland forest—often of mature, sometimes stunted or dying live oak trees (*Quercus virginiana*)—

is among the least productive areas of the delta (Costanza et al., 1983). However, these forests are elements essential to the movement of animals and people on the plain. They cover and protect the levee ridges that rise above the extensive marshlands, and harbor rare species of the landscape.

## SOME BROADER PERSPECTIVES

As we close this chapter on management and this book on landscape ecology, it is time to again broaden our horizons. We observed in an earlier chapter that human decisions are the most widespread catalysts of change in landscapes. What general ecological concepts can guide us in making such planning and management decisions?

Let us suppose that we are planning to transform a patch (or corridor or matrix) in a landscape to, say, a group of homes, a forest plantation, a road, or a nature reserve. First, we must evaluate the "patch-matrix interactions," that is, how the heterogeneous surroundings will affect the proposed new patch, and conversely how it will affect them (see Chapter 9). Are there major sources of airborne particles or aerosols upwind, or large herbivore populations nearby, or frequent wildfires in adjacent vegetation, or excessive surface runoff upstream, that would render the location inappropriate for the new element? Is the location part of an important corridor for wildlife, a protection against floods downstream, or a stabilization against the deposit of soil downwind?

Next we evaluate the characteristics of the present patch at the proposed location. We must begin by evaluating the present landscape element by two criteria, relative uniqueness and replacement or recovery time. The value of the present element is directly proportional to the sum of these two criteria. **Relative uniqueness** is a measure of how many comparable examples of this landscape element exist at different levels of scale, from the local area to the nation, even the globe. **Recovery time** is a measure of how long it would take to replace the existing landscape element in comparable form if it were disturbed or destroyed. A high relative uniqueness or a high recovery time often renders the location inappropriate for a proposed new landscape element. If the present element has a low relative uniqueness and recovery time we can then proceed to evaluate how the proposed new ecosystem would affect the surroundings.

Finally, we need to plan the intensity of human influence appropriate to the natural conditions of the site. At a minimum we must develop a simple **input-output model.** We view the site as a box (a "black box," no less) and simply list its characteristics quantitatively—say, the amount of standing wood, the native species diversity, the annual production of fruits, the human population density, the amount of water retention, and so on. These are measured in terms of number or weight per unit area.

Then we describe the inputs to the system. In simplest form, we recognize three classes—atmospheric inputs, soil inputs, and direct human inputs. Atmospheric and soil inputs include those due to both natural and human actions, such as precipitation, sulfur dioxide, blowing seeds, mice, humic acids, and toxic substances in ground water. Direct human inputs include objects brought in by vehicles, seeds planted, pesticides applied, house cats, and people themselves. These are measured in terms of number or weight per unit area per unit time. Similarly, we describe the outputs from the system, again recognizing three classes of outputs—atmospheric, soil, and direct human outputs. The human outputs include harvests of wood, crops, and livestock, and the atmospheric and soil outputs include any pollutants generated at the site.

Using this simple input-output model we can estimate both the optimum and the maximum levels of human influence appropriate to the site. We look at three primary results of the model.

1. The ratio of direct human input to human output, often described in financial terms, also describable in caloric terms. This ratio, however, is only one portion of the economic, social, and ecological cost that must be evaluated.
2. The difference between the pollutant levels of the incoming and outgoing atmospheric and soil flows. Any increase is a cost to the surroundings.
3. The change in the level of storage (or standing crop) of characteristics within the box representing the site. This measure is basically of whether the proposed new landscape element would cause the system to aggrade, remain in steady state, or degrade.

All three characteristics of the model must be given major weight when arriving at a planning or management decision on the optimum and maximum levels of human influence on the site. In integrating the three characteristics, we realize different ecological characteristics can be ordered according to their sensitivity to disturbance including human influence.

In evaluating potential degradation, the following changes, in progressive order, can easily be observed or assayed (beginning with the most sensitive first).

1. The relative abundance of species begins to change.
2. Sensitive species begin to disappear and native species diversity begins to decrease.
3. Nonnative species begin to colonize.

4. Biomass and cover begin to decrease.
5. Production begins to decrease.
6. Erosion begins to increase.

Exceptions exist, and additional ecological characteristics can and should be integrated with these. Still, these general patterns provide readily usable guidelines to the landscape planner, manager, and ecologist.

The final decision on whether, where, and at what level of human influence to change a landscape element is of course a human judgment. It must weigh the ecological, economic, and social benefits against their costs (Figure 14.11). This decision will be significantly enhanced by evaluations of the three factors described:

1. *Site-matrix interactions.*
2. *Relative uniqueness and recovery time.*
3. *The three basic results of the input-output model.*

In conclusion, the wise management of ecosystems approaches them as elements that interact with other ecosystems in a heterogeneous landscape, and not as isolated elements. Wise management also builds on the recognition that change is the norm in both landscape elements and landscapes. We should not be detoured by the human penchant for homogeneity or the status quo, but rather try to manage using both heterogeneity and change. Wise management further leads to ecologically sound economic production, in spatial compatibility with the natural areas of a landscape. The ecological integrity of our entire planet depends on our understanding of and respect for structure, function, and change in its landscapes.

## SUMMARY

Humans have tended to settle near boundaries between two distinct areas of resources, and have then increased the heterogeneity present in order to provide the flexibility involved in long-term stability. Ecological systems can be stretched, in the intermediate phase represented in the S-shaped biomass accumulation curve, to provide larger and more predictable production for harvest. The harvest increase must be balanced against its economic, social, ecological, and energy cost.

The three key elements of natural landscape management are the tailoring of human usage to the sensitivity of each landscape element, the maintenance of the integrity of the major corridors, and the allowance of the natural disturbance regime. Natural remnants in a different matrix are managed with two additional objectives—to minimize the isolation

**Figure 14.11** *A corridor resulting from landscape planning and management. This form is the current and temporary product of trial and error, plus the experience of professionals in every generation over time (in this case, millennia). Economic, social, and ecological factors—such as transportation for agricultural harvests, connecting villages to a city, avoiding most floods of a nearby river, and providing shade and a windbreak—were all important in planning this corridor. Current management here involves road maintenance, periodic pollarding of trees, and eliminating most natural vegetation and wildlife. The text describes three major landscape ecology criteria for evaluating change, the basic ingredient in planning and managing the landscapes of the future. Languedoc, France. (R. Forman.)*

of interior species and to control the detrimental flows that enter from surrounding areas. Landscapes that are managed for sustained forest yield may be even-aged, a mosaic of even-aged patches, or multi-aged. Firewood is increasingly in short supply; various kinds of coppice are useful for producing even-sized wood. Management of the agricultural landscape often involves the balancing of cultivation, pastures, and natural vegetation.

Landscape quality may be estimated by using paired photographs, survey questionnaires, and even by studying animal movements. The protection of landscape quality may involve government legislation but depends in a major way on acceptance of a land ethic combined with the watchfulness exemplified by the "Alarm Cry of Plato."

Models have been developed that simplify complex phenomena. These models may be verbal, graphic, or mathematical, and are often usefully developed from maps. For example, a tensor model may effectively reveal the change possible in each landscape element and in a whole landscape under different management options.

In planning the management of a landscape element, we must evaluate patch-matrix interactions and the relative uniqueness and replacement time of the present site. We then develop a simple input-output model to estimate (a) the ratio of direct human input to harvest; (b) the difference in pollutant levels between incoming and outgoing atmospheric and soil flows; and (c) the change in the characteristics of the site. Wise management also recognizes the natural rhythms of change.

## QUESTIONS

1. In choosing the placement of a new city, what landscape ecological principles would you consider to be the most important?
2. Why is it that net production of crops and livestock is greatest near the midpoint of the modification gradient from natural to urban landscapes?
3. What are the primary differences between managing a natural landscape and managing natural remnants in a different landscape?
4. How do sustained yield, natural disturbance, and a mosaic forest relate to one another in a landscape managed for forestry?
5. Compare the primary methods of estimating landscape quality.
6. How are aesthetics and the ecological structure of a landscape related?
7. How do the land ethic and the "Alarm Cry of Plato" complement one another in practice?
8. What is a model? How does one develop a model from a few maps of a landscape?
9. What are the advantages and disadvantages of a tensor model?
10. We often develop a simple input-output model in planning or managing a

landscape. What are the major results of this model that can guide our decision making?

11. If a herd of antelopes in an ecosystem is regulated according to the logistic equation

$$\frac{dN}{dt} = rN \frac{K - N}{K}$$

what population size $N$ would give the highest growth rate? You may calculate this mathematically or simply show it on a graph. How could this result be modified by the adjacent ecosystem?

12. If the mortality rate of pines in a plantation is 20% over 10 years, how many seedlings must be planted to yield 600 trees/ha after 80 years? Draw the corresponding curve on a graph. How could this result be modified by the adjacent landscape element?

13. Consider a landscape of pastures, cultivation, hedgerows, and scattered woods. Assuming there is no change in the relative numbers of these landscape element types, what primary guidelines would a wildlife manager use to increase wildlife? A forester, to increase wood products? A range manager, to increase livestock production? A biological conservationist, to increase biotic diversity?

# References

Aber, J. D., D. B. Botkin, and J. M. Melillo. 1978. Predicting the effects of differing harvesting regimes on forest floor dynamics in northern hardwoods. *Can. J. Forest Res.* 8:306–315.

Agger, P., and J. Brandt. 1984. Registration methods for studying the development of small-scale biotope structures in rural Denmark. In Brandt, J., and P. Agger, eds., *Proceedings of the First International Seminar on Methodology in Landscape Ecological Research and Planning (Vol. 2)*. Roskilde, Denmark: Roskilde Universitetsforlag GeoRuc. Pp. 61–72.

Aldrich, J. W., and R. W. Coffin. 1980. Breeding bird populations from forest to suburbia after thirty-seven years. *Amer. Birds* 34:3–7.

Alexander, W. B. 1932. The bird population of an Oxfordshire farm. *J. Animal Ecol.* 1:58–64.

Allen, T. F. H., and T. Starr. 1982. *Hierarchy Perspectives for Ecological Complexity*. Chicago: University of Chicago Press.

Allison, L. E. 1964. Salinity in relation to irrigation. *Adv. in Agron.* 16:139–180.

Ambuel, B., and S. A. Temple. 1983. Area dependent changes in the bird communities and vegetation of southern Wisconsin forests. *Ecology* 64:1057–1068.

Andersen, J. 1953. Analysis of Danish roe deer population. *Danish Rev. Game Biol.* 2:127–155.

Anderson, S. H. 1979. Changes in forest bird species composition caused by transmission-line corridor cuts. *Amer. Birds* 33:33–36.

————, K. Mann, and H. H. Shugart, Jr. 1977. The effect of transmission-line corridors on bird populations. *Amer. Midl. Natur.* 97:216–221.

Antonovics, J., and A. D. Bradshaw. 1970. Evolution in closely adjacent plant populations. VIII. Clinal patterns at a mine boundary. *Heredity* 25:349–362.

Antrop, M. 1984. Structural analysis of landscapes using remote sensing documents and visual image interpretation. In Brandt, J., and P. Agger, eds., *Proceedings of the First International Seminar on Methodology in Landscape Ecological Research and Planning* (Vol. 2). Roskilde, Denmark: Roskilde Universitetsforlag GeoRuc. Pp. 29–37.

Armstrong, E., D. Euler, and G. Racey. 1983. White-tailed deer habitat and cottage development in central Ontario. *J. Wildl. Manage.* 47:605–612.

Arnold, G. W. 1983. The influence of ditch and hedgerow structure, length of hedgerows and area of woodland and garden on bird numbers on farmland. *J. Appl. Ecol.* 20:791–850.

Arrenhius, O. 1921. Species and area. *J. Ecol.* 9:95–99.

Art, H. W., F. H. Bormann, G. K. Voight, and G. M. Woodwell. 1974. Barrier island forest ecosystems: role of meteorologic nutrient inputs. *Science* 184:60–62.

Ashton, P. S. 1976. Mixed dipterocarp forest and its variation with habitat in the Malayan lowlands: a re-evaluation at Pasoh. *Malayan Forester* 39:56–65.

Asmussen, L. E., J. M. Sheridan, and C. V. Booram, Jr. 1979. Nutrient movement in streamflow from agricultural watersheds in the Georgia Coastal Plain. *Trans. Amer. Soc. Agric. Engin.* 22:809–815, 821.

Auclair, A. N. 1976. Ecological factors in the development of intensive-management ecosystems in the midwestern United States. *Ecology* 57:431–444.

———, and G. Cottam. 1971. Dynamics of black cherry (*Prunus serotina*) in southern Wisconsin oak forests. *Ecol. Monogr.* 41:153–177.

Austin, R. F. 1981. The shape of West Malaysia's districts. *Area* 13:145–150.

Auvray, F. 1982. Le massif du Caroux-Espinouse. *Bull. Mens. Off. Nat. Chasse* 59:10–14.

Axelrod, D. I. 1960. The evolution of flowering plants. In Tax, S., ed., *Evolution After Darwin*. Volume 1. *The Evolution of Life. Its Origin, History and Future*. Chicago: University of Chicago Press. Pp. 227–305.

Ayyad, M., and E. Le Floc'h. 1983. An ecological assessment of renewable resources for rural agricultural development in the western Mediterranean coastal region, Remdene. Alexandria, Egypt: University of Alexandria. 104 pp.

Bailey, J. A. 1980. Desert bighorn forage competition and zoogeography. *Wildl. Soc. Bull.* 8:208–216.

Bailey, N. T. J. 1975. *The Mathematical Theory of Infectious Diseases and its Applications*. London: Charles Griffin.

Bailey, R. G. 1976. *Ecoregions of the United States*. Ogden, Utah: U. S. Dept. Agric., Forest Service Report.

———. 1978. *Description of the Ecoregions of the United States*. Ogden, Utah: U. S. Dept. Agric., Forest Service Report. 77 pp.

———. 1983. Delineation of ecosystem regions. *Environ. Manage.* 7:365–373.

———, R. D. Pfister, and J. A. Henderson. 1978. Nature of land and resource classification—a review. *J. Forestry* 76:650–655.

Baker, R. H. 1971. Nutritional strategies of myomorph rodents in North American grasslands. *J. Mammal.* 52:800–805.

Baker, R. R. 1978. *The Evolutionary Ecology of Animal Migration*. London: Hodder and Stoughton.

Bakker, P. A. 1979. Vegetation science and nature conservation. In Werger, M. J. A., ed., *The Study of Vegetation*. The Hague: Junk. Pp. 249–288.

Ballard, J. T. 1979. Fluxes of water and energy through the Pine Barrens ecosystems. In Forman, R. T. T., ed., *Pine Barrens: Ecosystem and Landscape*. New York: Academic Press. Pp. 133–146.

Balser, D., A. Bielak, G. De Boer, T. Tobias, G. Adindu, and R. S. Dorney. 1981. Nature reserve designation in a cultural landscape, incorporating island biogeographic theory. *Landscape Planning* 8:329–347.

Banfield, A. W. F. 1954. Preliminary investigation of the barren ground caribou. Part I. Former and present distribution, migration and status. Part II. Life history, ecology and utilization. *Wildl. Manage. Bull. (Ottawa), Series 1, No. 10A and B*. 79 and 112 pp.

Barclay-Estrup, P. 1970. The description and interpretation of cyclical processes in a heath community. II. Changes in biomass and shoot production during the *Calluna* cycle. *J. Ecol.* 58:243–249.

Bard, G. E. 1952. Secondary succession on the Piedmont of New Jersey. *Ecol. Monogr.* 22:195–215.

Barila, T. Y., R. D. Williams, and J. R. Stauffer. 1981. The influence of stream order and selected stream bed parameters on fish diversity in Raystown Branch, Susquehanna River Drainage, Pennsylvania. *J. Applied Ecol.* 18:125–131.

Barloy, J. 1980. Conséquences sur la production végétale agricole de l'aménagement du bocage dans l'Ouest de la France. *Bull. Tech. Inf.* 353–355: 783–828.

———, A. Cherouvrier, R. Delecolle, J. C. Simon. 1976. Influence des talus boisés sur la culture adjacente, en pays de bocage. In *Les Bocages: Histoire, Ecologie, Economie,* published jointly by Institut National de la Recherche Agronomique, Centre National de la Recherche Scientifique, and Université de Rennes, Rennes, France. p. 275–282.

Barnes, B. V., K. S. Pregitzer, T. A. Spies, and V. H. Spooner. 1982. Ecological forest site classification. *J. Forestry* 80:493–498.

Barrett, S. W., and S. F. Arno. 1982. Indian fires as an ecological influence in the northern Rockies. *J. Forestry* 80:647–651.

Barry, J. P. 1960. Contribution a l'étude de la végétation de la region de Nîmes. *Ann. Biol.* 36:311–567.

Bartholomew, B. 1970. Bare zone between California shrub and grassland communities: the role of animals. *Science* 170:1210–1212.

Bartholomew, D. J. 1973. *Stochastic Models for Social Processes.* New York: Wiley.

Bartlett, M. S. 1975. *Statistical Analysis of Spatial Patterns.* London: Chapman and Hall.

Bates, C. G. 1937. The vegetation of wayside and hedgerow. *J. Ecol.* 25:469–481.

Baudry, J. 1984. Effects of landscape structure on biological communities: The case of hedgerow network landscapes. In Brandt, J., and P. Agger, eds., *Proceedings of the First International Seminar on Methodology in Landscape Ecological Research and Planning* (Vol. 1). Roskilde, Denmark: Universitetsforlag GeoRuc. Pp. 55–65.

Baudry, J., and F. Baudry-Burel. 1982. La mesure de la diversité spatiale. Relations avec la diversité specifique. Utilisation dans les évaluations d'impact. *Oecol. Applic.* 3:177–190.

———, and F. Burel. Landscape project: "Remembrement:" Landscape consolidation in France. *Landscape Plann.* 11. In press.

Baumgartner, A., and E. Reichel. 1975. *The World Water Balance.* Munich: R. Oldenbourg.

Bazzaz, F. A. 1979. The physiological ecology of plant succession. *Ann. Rev. Ecol. Systematics* 10:351–372.

Beals, E. 1973. Ordination: mathematical elegance and ecological naivete. *J. Ecol.* 61:23–36.

Beard, J. S. 1953. The savanna vegetation of North Tropical America. *Ecol. Monogr.* 33:149–215.

————. 1955. The classification of tropical American vegetation types. *Ecology* 36:89–100.

Beasom, S. L., E. P. Wiggers, and J. R. Giardino. 1983. A technique for assessing land surface ruggedness. *J. Wildl. Manage.* 47:1163–1166.

Beaujeu-Garnier, J. 1977. *Images Economiques du Monde.* Paris: Soc. Education Enseign. Sup.

Beckwith, S. L. 1954. Ecological succession on abandoned farmlands and its relation to wildlife management. *Ecol. Monogr.* 20:349–375.

Bell, H. 1973. *Rangeland Management for Livestock Production.* Norman, Oklahoma: University of Oklahoma Press.

Bellis, E. D., and H. B. Graves. 1971. Deer mortality on a Pennsylvania interstate highway. *J. Wildl. Manage.* 35:232–237.

Bellrose, F. C., F. L. Paveglio, Jr., and D. W. Steffeck. 1979. Waterfowl populations and the changing environment of the Illinois River Valley. *Illinois Natur. Hist. Surv. Bull.* 32:1–54.

Beranek, L. L., ed. 1971. *Noise and Vibration Control.* New York: McGraw-Hill.

Bergen, J. D. 1969. Cold air drainage on a forested mountain slope. *J. Appl. Meteorol.* 8:884–895.

Bertalanffy, L. Von. 1950. The theory of open systems in physics and biology. *Science* 111:23–29.

Bertin, M., J. P. Faroux, and J. Renault. 1979. *Cours de Thermodynamique.* Paris: Dunod.

Bider, J. R. 1968. Animal activity in uncontrolled terrestrial communities as determined by a sand transect technique. *Ecol. Monogr.* 38:269–308.

Bied-Charreton, M., J. Bonvallot, G. Dandois, J. P. Raison, M. Portais, and B. Hugot. 1973. *Madagascar, Conditions Geographiques de la Mise en Valeur Agricole.* Tananarive, Madagascar: Madagascar Sect. Geogr. 129 pp.

Billings, W. D., and K. M. Peterson. 1980. Vegetational change and ice-wedge polygons through the thaw-lake cycle, arctic Alaska. *Arctic Alpine Res.* 12:413–432.

Bingham, S. C., P. W. Westerman, and M. R. Overcash. 1980. Effect of grass buffer zone length in reducing the pollution from land application areas. *Trans. Amer. Soc. Agric. Engin.* 23:330–335.

Blair, D. J., and T. H. Biss. 1967. *The Measurement of Shape in Geography: An Appraisal of Methods and Techniques.* Nottingham, England: University of Nottingham, Department of Geography, Bulletin of Quantitative Data for Geographers, No. 11.

Blavoux, B., M. Dray, and P. Merot. 1976. Comparison des écoulements sur deux bassins versants élémentaires, bocager et "ouvert," à l'aide du tracage par $O^{18}$. In *Les Bocages: Histoire, Ecologie, Economie.* Institut National de la Recherche Agronomique, Centre National de la Recherche Scientifique, Université de Rennes, Rennes, France. Pp. 153–158.

Bledsoe, L. J., and G. M. Van Dyne. 1971. A compartment model simulation of secondary succession. In Patten, B. C., ed., *Systems Analysis and Simulation in Ecology* (Vol. 1). New York: Academic Press. Pp. 479–511.

Bliss, L. C., D. W. Heal, and J. J. Moore, eds. 1981. *Tundra Ecosystems: A Comparative Analysis.* International Biological Program Report 25.

Blondel, J. 1979. *Biogeographie et Ecologie.* Paris: Masson.

Bobek, H., and J. Schmithusen. 1967. *Die Landschaft im Logischen System der Geographie.* Zum Gegenstand und zur Methode der Geographie, Darmstadt. Pp. 254–276.

Boeker, E. L., V. E. Scott, H. G. Reynolds, and B. A. Donaldson. 1972. Seasonal food habits of mule deer in southwestern New Mexico. *J. Wildl. Manage.* 36:56–63.

Boerner, R. E. J., and R. T. T. Forman. 1982. Hydrologic and mineral budgets of New Jersey Pine Barrens upland forests following two intensities of fire. *Can. J. Forest Res.* 12:503–510.

Boltzmann, L. 1896. *Vorlesungen uber Gastheorie.* 2 vols. Leipzig.

Bongiorno, S. F. 1982. Land use and summer bird populations in northwestern Galicia, Spain. *Ibis* 124:1–20.

Bormann, F. H. 1953. The statistical efficiency of sample plot size and shape in forest ecology. *Ecology* 34:474–487.

———, and G. E. Likens. 1967. Nutrient cycling. *Science* 155:424–429.

———, and G. E. Likens. 1979. Catastrophic disturbance and the steady state in the northern hardwood forest. *Amer. Scientist* 67:660–669.

———, and G. E. Likens. 1981. *Pattern and Process in a Forested Ecosystem.* New York: Springer-Verlag.

Bornkamm, R., J. A. Lee, and M. R. D. Seaward, eds. 1982. *Urban Ecology.* Oxford: Blackwell Scientific Publishers.

Botkin, D. B., and M. J. Sobel. 1975. Stability in time-varying ecosystems. *Amer. Natur.* 109:625–646.

———, J. F. Janak, and J. R. Wallis. 1972. Some ecological consequences of a computer model of forest growth. *J. Ecol.* 60:849–873.

Bowen, G. W., and R. L. Burgess. 1981. *A Quantitative Analysis of Forest Island Pattern in Selected Ohio Landscapes.* Oak Ridge, Tennessee: Oak Ridge National Laboratory, Environmental Sciences Division, Publication ORNL-TM-7759. 111 pp.

Box, E. O. 1981. *Macroclimate and Plant Forms: An Introduction to Predictive Modeling in Phytogeography.* The Hague: Junk.

Box, G., and G. Jenkins. 1970. *Time Series Analysis Forecasting and Control.* San Francisco: Holdenday.

Braakhekke, W. G., and E. I. Braakhekke-Ilsink. 1976. Nitrophile Saumgesellschaften im Sudosten der Niederlande. *Vegetatio* 32:55–60.

Brabec, E., P. Kovar, and A. Drabkova. 1981. Particle deposition in three vegetation stands: a seasonal change. *Atmospheric Environment* 15:583–587.

Bradshaw, A. D. 1972. Some evolutionary consequences of being a plant. *Evol. Biol.* 5:25–47.

Brandt, J., and P. Agger, eds. 1984. *Proceedings of the First International Seminar on Methodology in Landscape Ecological Research and Planning.* 5 vols. Roskilde, Denmark: Roskilde Universitetsforlag GeoRuc. Pp. 118, 150, 153, 171, 235.

Braun, E. L. 1950. *Deciduous Forests of Eastern North America.* Philadelphia: Blakiston.

Braun-Blanquet, J. 1932. *Plant Sociology.* New York: McGraw-Hill.

———. 1964. *Pflanzensoziologie Grundzuge der Vegetationskunde,* 3rd ed. Vienna: Springer-Verlag.

Brender, E. V. 1974. Impact of past land use on the lower Piedmont forest. *J. Forestry* 72:34–36.

Brillouin, L. 1962. *Science and Information,* 2nd ed. New York: Academic Press.

Brinson, M. H., H. S. Bradshaw, R. N. Holmes, and J. B. Elkins, Jr. 1980. Litterfall, stemflow, and throughfall nutrient fluxes in an alluvial swamp forest. *Ecology* 61:827–835.

Brockmann-Jerosch, H. 1912. Baumgrenze und Klimacharakter. *Beitr. Geobot. Landesaufn Schweiz* 6:1–256.

Bromley, S. W. 1935. The original forest types of southern New England. *Ecol. Monogr.* 5:61–89.

Brooks, K. N., and D. B. Thorud. 1971. Antitranspirant effects on the transpiration and physiology of tamarisk. *Water Resources Res.* 7:499–510.

Brossard, T., and J. C. Wieber. 1980. Essai de formulation systémique d'un mode d'approche du paysage. *Bull. Assoc. Geogr. France (Paris)* 468:103–111.

Brown, J. H. 1971a. Mammals on mountaintops: non-equilibrium insular biogeography. *Amer. Natur.* 105:467–478.

——, and G. A. Lieberman. 1973. Resource utilization and coexistence of seed-eating desert rodents in sand dune habitats. *Ecology* 54:788–797.

Brown, L. A., and E. G. Moore. 1969. Diffusion research in geography: a perspective. *Progr. in Geogr.* 1:119–157.

Brown, L. H. 1971b. The biology of pastoral man as a factor in conservation. *Biol. Conserv.* 3:93–100.

Brown, R. B., G. F. Kling, and N. H. Cutshall. 1981. Agricultural erosion indicated by $^{137}$Cs redistribution: II. Estimates of erosion rates. *Soil Sci. Soc. Amer. J.* 45:1191–1197.

Bruhat, G. 1962. *Thermodynamique.* Paris: Masson.

Brun-Chaize, M. 1976. *Le Paysage Forestier. Analyse des Préférences du Public.* Orléans: Institut National de la Recherche Agronomique, Publ. No. 76-14. 83 pp.

Bruneau, M. 1973. Dynamique des paysages et organisation de l'espace dans la plaine de Sukhotai (Thailande). *L'Espace Géogr.* 2:207–223.

Brunel, E., and J. P. Cancela da Fonseca. 1979. Concept de la diversité dans les écosystems complexes. *Bull. Ecol.* 10:147–163.

Brush, G. S., C. Lenk, and C. Smith. 1980. The natural forests of Maryland: an explanation of the vegetation map of Maryland. *Ecol. Monogr.* 50:77–92.

Bryer, J. B. 1983. The effects of a geometric redefinition of the classical road and landing spacing model through shifting. *Forest Sci.* 29:670–674.

Bucht, S., and B. Elfving. 1977. Thinning response and increment in a strip-thinned stand. *Sver. Skogsvordsforb. Tidskr.* 75:323–345.

Buckley, R. 1982. The habitat model of island biogeography. *J. Biogeogr.* 9:339–344.

Buckner, C. H. 1957. Population studies on small mammals of southeastern Manitoba. *J. Mammal.* 38:87–97.

Budowski, G. 1956. Tropical savannas, a sequence of forest felling and repeated burning. *Turrialba* 6:1–2, 23–33.

Budyko, M. I. 1974. *Climate and Life,* ed. D. H. Miller. New York: Academic Press.

Budyko, M. I. 1980. *Ecologie Globale.* Moscou: Editeur Progrés.

Buell, H. F., and R. T. T. Forman. 1983. Three decades of research at Hutcheson Memorial Forest, New Jersey (USA). *William L. Hutcheson Mem. For. Bull.* 6(2):24–32.

Buell, M. F., H. F. Buell, J. A. Small, and T. G. Siccama. 1971. Invasion of trees in secondary succession on the New Jersey Piedmont. *Bull. Torrey Bot. Club.* 98:67–74.

Bull, A. L., C. J. Mead, and K. Williamson. 1976. Bird-life on a Norfolk farm in relation to agricultural changes. *Bird Study* 23:163–182.

Bunge, W. 1966. *Theoretical Geography.* Lund, Sweden: Lund Studies in Geography, Series C, General and Mathematical Geography No. 1.

Bunnell, S. D., and D. R. Johnson. 1974. Physical factors affecting pika density and dispersal. *J. Mammal.* 55:866–869.

Burdon, J. J., and G. A. Chilvers. 1977. Preliminary studies on a native Australian eucalypt forest invaded by exotic pines. *Oecologia* 31:1–12.

Burel, F. 1984. Use of landscape ecology for the management of rural hedgerow network areas in western France. In Brandt, J., and P. Agger, eds., *Proceedings of the First International Seminar on Methodology in Landscape Ecological Research and Planning* (Vol. 2). Roskilde, Denmark: Roskilde Universitetsforlag GeoRuc. Pp. 73–81.

Burgess, R. L., and D. M. Sharpe, eds. 1981. *Forest Island Dynamics in Man-dominated Landscapes.* New York: Springer-Verlag.

Burgess, T. M., R. Webster, and A. B. McBratney. 1981. Optimal interpolation and isarithmic mapping of soil properties. IV. Sampling strategy. *J. Soil Sci.* 32:643–659.

Burrough, P. 1981. Fractal dimensions of landscapes and other environmental data. *Nature* 294:240–242.

Busack, S. D., and S. B. Hedges. 1984. Is the peninsular effect a red herring? *Amer. Natur.* 123:266–275.

Buson, C. 1979. *Une Approche Pédologique de Problème de l'Epandage: Caracterisation Hydrique des Sols Bruno sur Schistes Briovériens de la Région de Vire (Calvados). Effet des Epandages de Laiterie sur les Sols et les Eaux.* Thèse Doc. Ing., Ecole Nationale Superieure Agronomie Rennes, Rennes, France. 118 pp.

Butcher, G. S., W. A. Niering, W. J. Barry, and R. H. Goodwin. 1981. Equilibrium biogeography and the size of nature preserves: an avian case study. *Oecologia* 49:29–37.

Caborn, J. M. 1957. *Shelterbelts and Microclimate.* Forestry Commission, Bull. 29. London: H.M.S.O.

Caborn, J. M. 1976. Changements du paysage et protection contre le vent. In *Les Bocages: Histoire, Ecologie, Economie.* Institut National de la Recherche Agronomique, Centre National de la Recherche Scientifique, Université de Rennes, Rennes, France. Pp. 109–114.

Cailleux, A., and G. Taylor. 1954. *Cryopédologie: Etude des Sols Gelés.* Paris: Hermann.

Cain, S. A., and G. M. de O. Castro. 1959. *Manual of Vegetation Analysis.* New York: Harper and Row.

Cameron, R. A. D., K. Down, and D. J. Pannett. 1980. Historical and environmental influences on hedgerow snail faunas. *Biol. J. Linn. Soc.* 13:75–87.

Campbell, C. J. 1970. Ecological implications of riparian vegetation management. *J. Soil Water Conserv.* 25:49–52.

Cancela da Fonseca, J. P. 1980. Introduction à la théorie des catastrophes et à ses applications en écologie. Paris: Cahiers Centre Economie, Espace, Environment, No. 2. Pp. 120–137.

Cannell, M. G. R., compiler. 1982. *World Forest Biomass and Primary Production Data.* London: Academic Press.

Cantor, G. 1969. Fondements d'une théorie générale des ensembles. *Trad. Cahiers pour l'Analyse* 10:35–52.

Carkin, R. E., J. F. Franklin, J. Booth, and C. E. Smith. 1978. Seeding habits of upper-slope tree species. IV. Seed flight of noble fir and pacific silver fir. Portland, Oregon: U. S. Forest Service Research Note PNW–312.

Carlquist, S. J. 1974. *Island Biology.* New York: Columbia University Press.

Carol, H. 1956. Zur Diskussion um Landschaft und Geographie. *Geographica Helvetica* 11:111–133.

Carpenter, J. R. 1935. Forest edge birds and exposures of their habitats. *Wilson Bull.* 47:106–108.

Carrero, O. 1983. *Distribution Horizontale des Principales Essences Commerciales d'une Forêt Tropophile Tropicale et Variations du Milieu (Réserve Forestière de Ticoporo, Etat de Barinas, Venezuela).* Montpellier, France: Université de Sciences et Techniques de Languedoc. 50 pp.

Chaney, R. W. 1940. Tertiary forests and continental history. *Bull. Geol. Soc. Amer.* 51:469–488.

Chapman, J. A., and G. A. Feldhamer, eds. 1982. *Wild Mammals of North America: Biology, Management, and Economics.* Baltimore, Maryland: Johns Hopkins Press.

Chapman, W. M. M. 1939. The bird population of an Oxfordshire farm. *J. Animal Ecol.* 8:286–299.

Charley, J. L., and S. W. Cowling. 1968. Changes in soil nutrient status resulting from overgrazing and their consequences in plant communities of semi-arid areas. *Proc. Ecol. Soc. Austral.* 3:28–38.

Charnov, E. L. 1976. Optimal foraging theory: attack strategy of a mantid. *Amer. Natur.* 110:141–151.

Chasko, G. G., and J. E. Gates. 1982. Avian habitat suitability along a transmission-line corridor in an oak-hickory forest region. *Wildl. Monogr.* 82:1–41.

Chessel, D. 1978. Description non paramétrique de la dispersion spatiale des individus d'une espèce. *Biométrie et Ecol.* 1:45–135.

Chesson, P. L. 1981. Models for spatially distributed populations: the effect of within-patch variability. *Theor. Pop. Biol.* 19:288–325.

Chettleburgh, M. R. 1952. Observations on the collection and burial of acorns by jays in Hainault Forest. *Brit. Birds* 45:359–364.

Chevallier, D. 1980. *Valorisation Energétique des Petits Bois à Mardiex (Manche).* Diplome Agronomie Approfondie. Paris-Grignon: Institut National Agronomie. 67 pp.

Chisholm, M. D. I. 1962. *Rural Settlement and Land Use: An Essay in Location.* Chicago: Aldine.

Chorley, G. A., and R. J. Haggett. 1970. *Social and Economic Models in Geography*. London: Methuen.

Chorley, R. J., D. E. G. Malm, and H. A. Pogozelski. 1957. A new standard for estimating basin shape. *Amer. J. Sci.* 255:138–141.

Christaller, W. 1933. *Die Zentralen Orte in Suddeutschland*. Jena: Fischer.

———. 1938. Rapports fonctionnels entre les agglomérations urbaines et les campagnes. *Comptes Rendus Congr. Int. Geogr.* 2:123–138.

Christian, C. S., and G. A. Stewart. 1968. Methodology of integrated surveys. *UNESCO Recherche Resourc. Natur.* 6:233–280.

Clapham, A. R. 1932. The form of the observational unit in quantitative ecology. *J. Ecol.* 20:192–197.

Clark, P. J., and F. C. Evans. 1954. Distance to nearest neighbor as a measure of spatial relationships in populations. *Ecology* 35:445–453.

———, and F. C. Evans. 1979. Generalization of a neighbor measure of dispersion for use in *K* dimensions. *Ecology* 60:316–317.

Clarke, C. H. D. 1940. *A Biological Investigation of the Thelon Game Sanctuary*. Ottawa: National Museum of Canada Bull. 96, Biol. Ser. 25. 135 pp.

Clayton, J. L. 1976. Nutrient gains to adjacent ecosystems during a forest fire: an evaluation. *Forest Sci.* 22:162–166.

Clements, F. E. 1916. *Plant Succession: An Analysis of the Development of Vegetation*. Washington, D.C.: Carnegie Institute Publication 242. 512 pp.

———. 1920. *Plant Indicators*. Washington, D.C.: Carnegie Institute.

Cliff, A. D., P. Haggett, J. K. Ord, K. Bassett, and R. B. Davies. 1975. *Elements of Spatial Structure: A Quantitative Approach*. Cambridge: Cambridge University Press.

Cliff, A. D., and J. K. Ord. 1973. *Spatial Autocorrelation*. London: Pion.

Cline, M. G. 1949. Basic principles of soil classification. *Soil Sci.* 67:81–91.

Cocking, W. D., and R. T. T. Forman. 1983. Vegetation responses of an old-field ecosystem to single and repeated sulfur dioxide disturbance. *William L. Hutcheson Mem. For. Bull.* 6:4–19.

Cody, M. L. 1975. Towards a theory of continental species diversities: Bird distributions over Mediterranean habitat gradients. In Cody, M. L., and J. M. Diamond, eds., *Ecology and Evolution of Communities*. Cambridge, Massachusetts: Belknap Press. Pp. 214–257.

Cole, G. A. 1983. *Textbook of Limnology*, 3rd ed. St. Louis: Mosby.

Cole, B. J. 1981. Colonizing abilities, island size, and the number of species on archipelagoes. *Amer. Natur.* 117:629–638.

Collins, S. L., and G. E. Uno. 1983. The effect of early spring burning on vegetation in buffalo wallows. *Bull. Torrey Bot. Club* 110:474–481.

Collins, W. B., and P. J. Urness. 1983. Feeding behavior and habitat selection of mule deer and elk on northern Utah summer range. *J. Wildl. Manage.* 47:646–663.

———, P. J. Urness, and D. D. Austin. 1978. Elk diets and activities on different lodgepole pine habitat segments. *J. Wildl. Manage.* 42:799–810.

Coltman, R. 1984. Environmental chart and checklist. *Architectural Technology* 2:44–48.

Comins, H. N., W. D. Hamilton, and R. M. May. 1980. Evolutionarily stable dispersal strategies. *J. Theor. Biol.* 82:205–230.

Connell, J. H. 1978. Diversity in tropical rain forests and coral reefs. *Science* 199:1302–1310.

Connor, E. F., and E. D. McCoy. 1979. The statistics and biology of the species-area relationship. *Amer. Natur.* 113:791–833.

Constant, P. M., C. Eybert, and R. Mahed. 1976. Avifaune reproductrice du bocage de l'Ouest. In *Les Bocages: Histoire, Ecologie, Economie.* Institut National de la Recherche Agronomique, Centre National de la Recherche Scientifique, Université de Rennes, Rennes, France. Pp. 327–332.

Cooper, W. S. 1913. The climax forest of Isle Royale, Lake Superior, and its development. I. *Bot. Gaz.* 55:1–44.

Coppock, D. L., J. E. Ellis, J. K. Detling, and M. I. Dyer. 1983. Plant-herbivore interactions in a North American mixed-grass prairie. II. Responses of bison to modification of vegetation by prairie dogs. *Oecologia* 56:10–15.

Costanza, R., C. Neill, S. C. Leibowitz, J. R. Fruci, L. M. Bahr, Jr., and J. W. Day, Jr. 1983. *Ecological Models of the Mississippi Deltaic Plain Region: Data Collection and Presentation.* Washington, D.C.: U. S. Fish and Wildlife Service Publication FWS–OBS–82–68. 342 pp.

Cottam, G., and J. T. Curtis. 1956. The use of distance measures in phyto-sociological sampling. *Ecology* 37:451–460.

Council on Environmental Quality. 1980. *Biological Diversity.* (Prepared by E. A. Norse.) Eleventh Annual Report of the Council on Environmental Quality. Washington, D.C.: U. S. Government Printing Office. 50 pp.

Covich, A. P. 1976. Analyzing shapes of foraging areas: some ecological and economic theories. *Ann. Rev. Ecol. Systematics* 7:235–257.

Cowardin, L. M., V. Carter, F. C. Golet, and E. T. LaRoe. 1979. *Classification of Wetlands and Deepwater Habitats of the United States.* Washington, D.C.: U. S. Fish and Wildlife Service Report FWS/OBS–79/31. 103 pp.

Cowles, H. C. 1901. The physiographic ecology of Chicago and vicinity: a study of the origin, development, and classification of plant societies. *Bot. Gaz.* 31:73–108, 145–182.

Craighead, J. J., G. Atwell, and B. W. O'Gara. 1972. Elk migration in and near Yellowstone National Park. *Wildl. Monogr.* 29:1–48.

Cubbage, F. W. 1983. Tract size and harvesting costs in southern pine. *J. Forestry* 81:430–433.

Curtis, J. T. 1956. The modification of mid-latitude grasslands and forests by man. In Thomas, W. L., Jr., ed., *Man's Role in Changing the Face of the Earth.* Chicago: University of Chicago Press. Pp. 721–736.

———. 1959. *The Vegetation of Wisconsin. An Ordination of Plant Communities.* Madison: University of Wisconsin Press.

———, and R. P. McIntosh. 1951. An upland forest continuum in the prairie-forest border region of Wisconsin. *Ecology* 32:476–496.

Daget, P. 1979. La nombre d'espèces par unité d'échantillonnage de taille crois-sante. *La Terre et la Vie* 32:461–470.

———, and M. Godron. 1982. *Analyse de l'Ecologie des Espèces dans les Com-munautés.* Paris: Masson.

Dagnelie, P. 1973. L'analyse factorielle. In *Ordination and Classification of Communities*. ed. R. H. Whittaker. The Hague: Junk. Pp. 223–248.

Dagognet, F. 1970. *Le Catalogue de la Vie: Etude Méthodologique sur la Taxinomie*. Paris: Presses Universitaires Françaises.

Damagnez, J. 1976. Bioclimatologie: rapport de synthèse. In *Les Bocages: Histoire, Ecologie, Economie*. Institut National de la Recherche Agronomique, Centre National de la Recherche Scientifique, Université de Rennes, Rennes, France. Pp. 105–108.

Dansereau, P. 1957. *Biogeography. An Ecological Perspective*. Ronald Press, New York.

Darby, H. C. 1956. The clearing of the woodland in Europe. In Thomas, W. L., ed., *Man's Role in Changing the Face of the Earth*. Chicago: University of Chicago Press. Pp. 183–216.

Darley-Hill, S., and W. C. Johnson. 1981. Acorn dispersal by the blue jay (*Cyanocitta cristata*). *Oecologia* 50:231–232.

Darlington, P. J. 1957. *Zoogeography: The Geographic Distribution of Animals*. New York: Wiley.

Darracq, S., M. Godron, and F. Romane. 1984. *Typologie Forestière de la Region des Garrigues du Gard*. Nancy, France: Ecole Nationale Génie Rural Eaux et Forêts. 181 pp.

Darwin, C. 1842. *The Structure and Distribution of Coral Reefs. Being the First Part of the Geology of the Voyage of the Beagle, Under the Command of Capt. Fitzroy, R. N., During the Years 1832–36*. London: Smith, Elder.

Darwin, F., ed. 1958. *The Autobiography of Charles Darwin and Selected Letters*. New York: Dover.

Daubenmire, R. F. 1968. *Plant Communities: A Textbook of Plant Synecology*. New York: Harper and Row.

———. 1978. *Plant Geography: With Special Reference to North America*. New York: Academic Press.

Davenport, D. C., P. E. Martin, E. B. Roberts, and R. M. Hagan. 1976. Conserving water by antitranspirant treatment of phreatophytes. *Water Resources Res.* 12:985–990.

Davis, L. S. 1980. Strategy for building a location-specific, multipurpose information system for wildland management. *J. Forestry* 78:402–406.

Davis, M. B. 1976. Pleistocene biogeography of temperate deciduous forests. *Geoscience and Man* 13:13–26.

Davis, W. 1899. The geographical cycle. *Geogr. Jour.* 14:481–504.

Davison, S. E., and R. T. T. Forman. 1982. Herb and shrub dynamics in a mature oak forest: A thirty year study. *Bull. Torrey Bot. Club* 109:64–73.

Davison, V. E. 1941. Wildlife borders—an innovation in farm management. *J. Wildl. Manage.* 5:390–394.

Day, G. M. 1953. The Indian as an ecological factor in the northeastern forest. *Ecology* 34:329–346.

De Angelis, D. L. 1975. Stability and connectance in food web models. *Ecology* 56:238–243.

———, C. C. Travis, and W. M. Post. 1980. Persistence and stability of seed-dispersed species in a patchy environment. *Theor. Pop. Biol.* 16:107–125.

De Blij, H. J. 1977. *Human Geography.* New York: Wiley.

Debussche, M., J. Escarre, and J. Lepart. 1982. Ornithochory and plant succession in Mediterranean abandoned orchards. *Vegetatio* 48:255–266.

———, M. Godron, J. Lepart, and F. Romane. 1977. An account of the use of a transition matrix. *Agro-ecosystems* 3:81–92.

Decamps, H. 1984. Towards a landscape ecology of river valleys. In Cooley, J. H., and F. B. Golley, eds. *Trends in Ecological Research for the 1980's.* New York: Plenum. Pp. 163–178.

De Jong, C. B., M. Begg, and R. G. Kachanoski. 1983. Estimates of soil erosion and deposition for some Saskatchewan soils. *Can. J. Soil Sci.* 63:607–617.

Delcourt, H. R., P. A. Delcourt, and T. Webb, III. 1983. Dynamic plant ecology: the spectrum of vegetational change in space and time. *Quat. Sci. Rev.* 1:153–175.

Delelis-Dusollier, A. 1973. *Contribution a l'étude des haies, des fourrés préforestiers, des manteaux sylvatiques de France.* Thèse Doctorat d'Etat, Université de Lille, Lille, France. 146 pp.

Den Boer, P. J. 1970. On the significance of dispersal power for populations of carabid beetles (Coleoptera, Carabidae). *Oecologia* 4:1–28.

———. 1981. On the survival of populations in a heterogeneous and variable environment. *Oecologia* 50:39–53.

Denslow, J. S. 1980. Patterns of plant species diversity during succession under different disturbance regimes. *Oecologia* 46:18–21.

Desabie, J. 1966. *Théorie et Pratique des Sondages.* Paris: Dunod.

Detwyler, T., ed. 1971. *Man's Impact on the Environment.* New York: McGraw-Hill.

Deveaux, D. 1976. Repartition et diversité des peuplements en carabiques en zone bocagère et arasée. In *Les Bocages: Histoire, Ecologie, Economie.* Institut Nationale de la Recherche Agronomique, Centre National de la Recherche Scientifique, Université de Rennes, Rennes, France. Pp. 377–384.

De Walle, D. R. 1983. Wind damage around clearcuts in the ridge and valley province of Pennsylvania. *J. Forestry* 81:158–159.

Diamond, J. M. 1972. Biogeographic kinetics: estimation of relaxation times for avifaunas of southwest Pacific islands. *Proc. Nat. Acad. Sci. USA* 69:3199–3203.

———. 1975. The island dilemma: lessons of modern biogeographic studies for the design of natural reserves. *Biol. Conserv.* 7:129–146.

———, and R. M. May. 1976. Island biogeography and the design of natural reserves. In May, R. M., ed., *Theoretical Ecology.* Philadelphia: Saunders. Pp. 163–186.

Di Castri, F., and H. A. Mooney, eds. 1973. *Mediterranean Type Ecosystems. Origin and Structure.* Berlin: Springer-Verlag.

Dickerman, C. W. 1869. *How to Make the Farm Pay; Or the Farmer's Book.* Philadelphia: Zeigler, McCurdy.

Dickinson, R. E. 1970. *Regional Ecology: The Study of Man's Environment.* New York: Wiley.

Dierschke, H. 1969. Die naturraumliche Gliederung der Verdener Geest. *Forsch. Deutsch. Landeskunde.* 177:1–113.

————. 1974. *Saumgesellschaften im Vegetations- und Standortsgefalle an Wald-randern.* Gottingen: Verlag Erich Goltze KG.

Dietrich, W. E., and T. Dunne. 1978. Sediment budget for a small catchment in mountainous terrain. *Z. Geomorphol. Suppl.* 29:191–206.

Diggle, P. J. 1981. Binary mosaics and the spatial pattern of heather. *Biometrics* 37:531–539.

Dodson, S. I. 1974. Zooplankton composition and predation: an experimental test of the size efficiency hypothesis. *Ecology* 55:605–613.

Dokuchaev, V. V. 1898. *Writings,* (in Russian). Reprinted 1951. Vol. 6. Akad Nauk, Moscow. 381 pp.

Dorney, R. S., and D. W. Hoffman. 1979. Development of landscape planning concepts and management strategies for an urbanizing agricultural region. *Landscape Planning* 6:151–177.

————, and P. W. McLellan. 1984. The urban ecosystem: its spatial structure, its scale relationships, and its subsystem attributes. *Environments* 16:9–20.

Doxiadis, C.A. 1968. *Ekistics; An Introduction to the Science of Human Settlements.* London: Hutchinson.

Dregne, H. E. 1977. Desertification of arid lands. *Econ. Geogr.* 53:322–331.

Dudzinski, M. L., W. J. Muller, W. A. Low, and H. J. Schuh. 1982. Relationship between dispersion behavior of free-ranging cattle and forage conditions. *Appl. Animal Ecol.* 8:225–241.

Duffey, E. 1974. *Nature Reserves and Wildlife.* London: Heinemann.

Dunbar, C. O., and K. M. Waage. 1969. *Historical Geology,* 3rd ed. New York: Wiley.

Duncan, P. 1983. Determinants of the use of habitat by horses in a Mediterranean wetland. *J. Animal Ecol.* 52:93–109.

Dunford, E. G., and P. W. Fletcher. 1947. Effect of removal of streambank vegetation upon water yield. *Trans. Amer. Geophys. Union* 28:105–110.

Durango, S. 1951. Om tornskatans (*Lanius collurio* L.) spetsning av bytesdjur. *Fagelvarld* 10:49–65.

Du Rietz, G. E. 1921. *Zur Methodologischen Grundlage der Modernen Pflanzensoziologie.* Wien: Adolf Holzhausen.

Duval, J. 1980. *Les Jardins Suspendus de Babylone.* Geneva: Farnot.

Dyksterhuis, E. J. 1949. Condition and management of rangeland based on quantitative ecology. *J. Range Manage.* 2:104–115.

————, 1957. The savannah concept and its use. *Ecology* 38:435–442.

Dzieciolowski, R., J. Krupka, Bajandelger, and R. Dziedzic. 1980. Argali and Siberian ibex populations in the Khuhsyrh Reserve in Mongolian Altai. *Acta Theriologica* 25(16):213–219.

Eckbo, G. 1975. *The Landscape We See.* New York: McGraw-Hill.

Ehanno, B. 1976. Faune entomologique de bocage breton: punaises *Miridae* des vegetaux des talus. In *Les Bocages: Histoire, Ecologie, Economie.* Institut National de la Recherche Agronomique, Centre National de la Recherche Scientifique, Université de Rennes, Rennes, France. Pp. 385–389.

Ehrlich, P., R. Holm, and D. Parnell. 1974. *The Process of Evolution.* New York: McGraw-Hill.

Eldridge, J. 1971. Some observations on the dispersion of small mammals in hedgerows. *J. Zool.* 165:530–534.

Elfstrom, B. A. 1974. *Tree Species Diversity and Forest Island Size on the Piedmont of New Jersey.* Master's thesis. Rutgers University, New Brunswick, New Jersey. 73 pp.

Ellenberg, H. 1939. Uber Zusammensetzung, Standort und Stoffproduktion bodenfeuchter Eichen- und Buchen-Mischwaldgesellschaften Nordwestdeutschlands. *Mitt. Flor.-soz. Arbeit. Niedersachsen* 5:3–155.

———. 1956. *Aufgaben und Methoden der Vegetationskunde.* Stuttgart: Ulmer.

———. 1962. Wald in der Pampa Argentiniens. *Geobot. Inst. Eidg. Techn. Hochschule, Stiftung Rubel (Zurich)* 37:39–56.

———. 1978. *Vegetation Mitteleuropas mit den Alpen in Okologischer Sicht.* 2nd ed. Stuttgart: Ulmer.

Ellison, L. 1975. *Théorie de la Récolte Maximale Soutenue.* Montpellier, France: Institute Botanique Publication. 2 pp.

Elton, C. S. 1958. *The Ecology of Invasions by Animals and Plants.* London: Methuen.

———, and M. Nicholson. 1942. The ten-year cycle in numbers of the lynx in Canada. *J. Animal Ecol.* 11:215–244.

Emberger, L. 1930. La végétation de la région mediterranéenne: essai d'une classification des groupements végétaux. *Rev. Gen. Bot.* 42:641–662.

———. 1954. Observations sur la fréquence en forêt dense équatoriale. *Vegetatio* 7:169–176.

———. 1955. Une classification biogéographique des climats. *Récents Travaux des Laboratoires Botaniques, Geologiques et Zoologiques, Université des Sciences et Techniques, (Languedoc, Montpellier)* 7:3–45.

Emlen, J. T. 1978. Density anomalies and regulatory mechanisms in land bird populations on the Florida peninsula. *Amer. Natur.* 112:265–286.

———. 1981. Divergence in the foraging responses of birds on two Bahama islands. *Ecology* 62:289–295.

Enright, N., and J. Ogden. 1979. Applications of transition matrix models in forest dynamics. *Araucaria* in Papua, New Guinea and *Nothofagus* in New Zealand. *Austral. J. Ecol.* 4:3–24.

Erhart, H. 1967. *La Genèse des Sols en tant que Phénomène Géologique.* Paris: Masson.

Erickson, R. O. 1945. The *Clematis Fremontii* var. *Riehlii* population in the Ozarks. *Ann. Missouri Bot. Gard.* 32:413–460.

Eschener, A. R., and J. H. Patric. 1982. Debris avalanches in eastern upland forests. *J. Forestry* 80:343–347.

Evans, F. C. 1956. Ecosystem as the basic unit in ecology. *Science* 123:1227–1228.

———, and E. Dahl. 1955. The vegetation structure of an abandoned field in southeastern Michigan and its relation to environmental factors. *Ecology* 36:685–706.

Eyre, S. R. 1977. *Vegetation and Soils: A World Picture.* 2nd ed. London: Arnold.

Fabos, J. G. 1979. *Planning the Total Landscape: A Guide to Intelligent Land Use.* Boulder, Colorado: Westview Press.

Fahrig, L., L. Lefkovitch, and G. Merriam. 1983. Population stability in a patchy environment. In Lauenroth, W. K., G. V. Skogerboe, and M. Flug, eds., *Analysis of Ecological Systems: State-of-the-Art in Ecological Modelling.* New York: Elsevier. Pp. 61–67.

Fairchild, W. W., and C. I. Tulcea. 1970. *Sets*. Philadelphia: Saunders.

———. 1971. *Topology*. Philadelphia: Saunders.

Ferguson, J. A. 1916. *Farm Forestry*. New York: Wiley.

Ferris, C. R. 1979. Effects of Interstate 95 on breeding birds in northern Maine. *J. Wildl. Manage.* 43:421–427.

FitzPatrick, E. A. 1983. *Soils. Their Formation, Classification and Distribution*. London: Longman.

Flaccus, E. 1959. Revegetation of landslides in the White Mountains of New Hampshire. *Ecology* 40:692–703.

Fletcher, J. L., and R. G. Busnel, eds. 1978. *Effects of Noise on Wildlife*. New York: Academic Press.

Floret, C. 1981. Dynamique de systèmes écologiques de la zone aride. *Acta Oecol.* 2(3):195–214.

———, and R. Pontanier. 1982. *L'Aridité en Tunisie Présaharienne. Climat, Sol, Végétation, et Aménagement*. Paris: Office de la Recherche Scientifique et Technique d'Outre Mer. 544 pp.

Forman, R.T.T. 1964. Growth under controlled conditions to explain the hierarchical distributions of a moss, *Tetraphis pellucida*. *Ecol. Monogr.* 34:1–25.

———. 1975. Canopy lichens with blue-green algae: A nitrogen source in a Colombian rain forest. *Ecology* 56:1176–1184.

———, ed. 1979a. *Pine Barrens: Ecosystem and Landscape*. New York: Academic Press.

———. 1979b. The New Jersey Pine Barrens, an ecological mosaic. In Forman, R. T. T., ed., *Pine Barrens: Ecosystem and Landscape*. New York: Academic Press. Pp. 569–585.

———. 1981. Interactions among landscape elements: a core of landscape ecology. In Tjallingii, S. P., and A. A. de Veer, eds., *Perspectives in Landscape Ecology*. Wageningen: Centre for Agricultural Publication and Documentation. Pp. 35–48.

———. 1983. Corridors in a landscape: their ecological structure and function. *Ekologia (CSSR)* 2:375–387.

———, and J. Baudry. 1984. Hedgerows and hedgerow networks in landscape ecology. *Environ. Manage.* 8:495–510.

———, and R. E. J. Boerner. 1981. Fire frequency and the Pine Barrens of New Jersey. *Bull. Torrey Bot. Club.* 108:34–50.

———, and M. Godron. 1981. Patches and structural components for a landscape ecology. *BioScience* 31:733–740.

———, and M. Godron. 1984. Landscape ecology principles and landscape function. In Brandt, J., and P. Agger, eds., *Proceedings of the First International Seminar on Methodology in Landscape Ecological Research and Planning*. (Vol. 5). Roskilde, Denmark: Roskilde Universitetsforlag GeoRuc. Pp. 4–15.

———, and D. C. Hahn. 1981. Spatial patterns of trees in a Caribbean semievergreen forest. *Ecology* 61:1267–1274.

———, A. E. Galli, and C. F. Leck. 1976. Forest size and avian diversity in New Jersey woodlots with some land use implications. *Oecologia* 26:1–8.

Foster, D. R. 1983. The history and pattern of fire in the boreal forest of southeastern Labrador. *Can. J. Bot.* 61:2459–2471.

————, and G. A. King. 1984. Landscape features, vegetation and developmental history of a patterned fen in south-eastern Labrador, Canada. *J. Ecol.* 72:115–143.

Franklin, J. F. 1979. Ecosystem studies in the Hoh River drainage, Olympic National Park. In Starkey, E. E., J. F. Franklin, and J. W. Mathews, eds., *Ecological Research in National Parks of the Pacific Northwest.* Corvallis, Oregon: Oregon State University Forest Research Laboratory Publication, pp. 1–8.

————, and M. A. Hemstrom. 1981. Aspects of succession in the coniferous forests of the Pacific Northwest. In West, D. C., H. H. Shugart, Jr., and D. B. Botkin, eds., *Forest Succession: Concepts and Application.* New York: Springer-Verlag. Pp. 212–229.

Fritts, S. H., and L. D. Mech. 1981. Dynamics, movements, and feeding ecology of a newly protected wolf population in Minnesota. *Wildl. Monogr.* 80:5–82.

Galli, A. E., C. F. Leck, and R. T. T. Forman. 1976. Avian distribution patterns within different sized forest islands in central New Jersey. *Auk* 93:356–364.

Gallusser, W. A. 1978. Der Wiederaufbau der Nordamerikanischen Zivilisationslandschaft durch Staatliche Massnahmen, am Beispiel von Wisconsin. *Erdkunde* 32:142–157.

Game, M. 1980. Best shape for nature reserves. *Nature* 287:630–632.

————, and G. F. Peterken. 1984. Nature reserve selection strategies in the woodlands of central Lincolnshire, England. *Biol. Conserv.* 29:157–181.

Gardner, R. H., W. G. Cale, and R. V. O'Neill. 1982. Robust analysis of aggregation error. *Ecology* 63:1771–1779.

Garwood, N. C., D. P. Janos, and N. Brokaw. 1979. Earthquake-caused landslides: a major disturbance to tropical forests. *Science* 205:997–999.

Gates, J. E., and L. W. Gysel. 1978. Avian nest dispersion and fledgling success in field-forest ecotones. *Ecology* 59:871–883.

————, and J. A. Mosher. 1981. A functional approach to estimating habitat edge width for birds. *Amer. Midl. Natur.* 105:189–192.

Gause, E. F. 1934. *The Struggle for Existence.* Baltimore: Williams and Wilkins. (Reprinted, New York: Hafner, 1964.)

Gaussen, H. 1954. *Géographie des Plantes,* 2nd ed. Paris: Colin.

Gauthier, B. 1979. Presentation du phytobenthos limnétique. *Mem. Soc. Linn. Québec* 1:1–79.

Gautier, E. 1952. *Le Passé de l'Afrique du Nord.* Paris: Payot.

Geier, A. R., and L. B. Best. 1980. Habitat selection by small mammals of riparian communities: evaluating effects of habitat alterations. *J. Wildl. Manage.* 44:16–24.

Geiger, R. 1965. *The Climate Near the Ground.* Cambridge, Massachusetts: Harvard University Press.

Geophysics Research Forum. 1984. *Studies in Geophysics: Groundwater Contamination.* Washington, D. C.: National Academy Press.

Gerasimov, I. P., V. S. Preobrazhensky, R. P. Zimina, and T. V. Zvonkova. 1979. Soviet physical and biological geography. *Geoforum (Moscow)* 10:261–265.

Getz, L. L., F. R. Cole, and D. L. Gates. 1978. Interstate roadsides as dispersal routes for *Microtus pennsylvanicus. J. Mammal.* 59:208–212.

Ghiselin, J. 1977. Analyzing ecotones to predict biotic productivity. *Environ. Manage.* 1:235–238.

Gibbs, J. P. 1961. A method for comparing the spatial shapes of urban units. In Gibbs, J. P., ed., *Urban Research Methods.* New York: Van Nostrand. Pp. 99–106.

Gilbert, L. E. 1980. The equilibrium theory of island biogeography: fact or fiction? *J. Biogeogr.* 7:209–235.

Giles, R. H., Jr. 1978. *Wildlife Management.* San Francisco: W. H. Freeman.

Gilg, A. W. 1973. A study in agricultural disease diffusion. *Inst. Brit. Geogr. Publ.* 59:77–97.

Gilmer, D. S., and R. E. Stewart. 1983. Ferruginous hawk populations and habitat use in North Dakota. *J. Wildl. Manage.* 47:146–157.

Gilpin, M. E. 1981. Peninsula diversity patterns. *Amer. Natur.* 118:291–296.

Gimingham, C. H., S. B. Chapman, and N. R. Webb. 1979. European heathlands. In Specht, R. L., ed., *Heathlands and Related Shrublands of the World. A. Descriptive Studies.* Amsterdam: Elsevier. Pp. 365–413.

Givnish, T. J. 1981. Serotiny, geography, and fire in the Pine Barrens of New Jersey. *Evolution* 35:101–123.

Gleason, H. A. 1926. The individualistic concept of the plant association. *Bull. Torrey Bot. Club* 53:7–26.

———, and A. Cronquist. 1964. *The Natural Geography of Plants.* New York: Columbia University Press.

Goddard, J. 1970. Movements of moose in a heavily hunted area of Ontario. *J. Wildl. Manage.* 34:439–445.

Godron, M. 1963. *Carte des Régions Naturelles du Maroc.* Rabat, Morocco: Institut National de la Recherche Agronomique.

———. 1966. Application de la théorie de l'information à l'étude de l'homogénéité et de la structure de la végétation. *Oecol. Plantarum* 1:187–197.

———. 1968. Quelques applications de la notion de fréquence en écologie végétale (recouvrement, information mutuelle entre espèces et facteurs écologiques, échantillonnage). *Oecol. Plantarum* 3:185–212.

———. 1971. Comparaison d'une courbe aire-espèce et de son modèle. *Oecol. Plantarum* 6:207–213.

———. 1972. Echantillonnage linéaire et cartographie. *Investigacion Pesquera* 36:171–174.

———. 1973. Analyse d'un échantillonnage en ligne dans la savane de Lamto (Côte d'Ivoire). *Ann. Univ. Abidjan, Serie E* 6(2):25–31.

———. 1975. Préservation, classification et évolution des phytocénoses et des milieux. *Biologia Contemporanea* 1:6–14.

———. 1982. L'étude du "grain" de la structure de la végétation. Application à quelques exemples mediterranéens. *Ecologia Mediterranea* 8:191–195.

———. 1984. *Ecologie de la Végétation Terrestre.* Paris: Masson.

———, and A. M. Bacou. 1975. Sur les limites "optimales" séparant deux parties d'une biocénose hétérogène. *Ann. Univ. Abidjan, Série E* 8(1):317–324.

———, and R. T. T. Forman. 1983. Landscape modification and changing ecological characteristics. In Mooney, H. A., and M. Godron, eds., *Disturbance and Ecosystems: Components of Response.* New York: Springer-Verlag. Pp. 12–28.

————, and A. Koohafkhan. 1982. Un exemple de modélisation de l'aménagement d'un territoire grace à des tenseurs. *Jour. Recherche Develop. Milieu Rural* 18:1–14.

————, and J. Lepart. 1973. Sur la représentation de la dynamique de la végétation au moyen de matrices de succession. In *Sukzessionforschung Rinteln*. Vaduz: Cramer. Pp. 269–287.

————, P. Daget, L. Emberger, E. Le Floc'h, G. Long, J. Poissonet, C. Sauvage, and J. P. Wacquant. 1968. *Code pour le Relevé Méthodique de la Végétation et du Milieu*. Paris: Centre National de la Recherche Scientifique. 292 pp.

————, G. Grandjouan, A. Heaulme, E. Le Floc'h, J. Poissonet, and J. P. Wacquant. 1964. *Notice Détaillée, Carte Phyto-écologique et Carte de l'Occupation des Terres de Sologne*. Paris: Centre National de la Recherche Scientifique. 192 pp.

Golley, F. B., J. T. McGinnis, R. G. Clements, G. I. Child, and M. J. Duever. 1975. *Mineral Cycling in a Tropical Moist Forest Ecosystem*. Athens, Georgia: University of Georgia Press.

Gomez-Pompa, A., C. Vazquez-Yanes, and S. Guevara. 1972. The tropical rain forest, a non-renewable resource. *Science* 177:762–765.

Gonzalez-Bernaldez, F. 1981. *Ecología y Paisage*. Madrid: Blume.

Good, R. E., N. F. Good, and J. W. Andresen. 1979. The Pine Barren plains. In Forman, R. T. T., ed., *Pine Barrens: Ecosystem and Landscape*. New York: Academic Press. Pp. 283–295.

Gordon, A. G., and E. Gorham. 1963. Ecological aspects of air pollution from an iron-sintering plant at Wawa, Ontario. *Can. J. Bot.* 41:1063–1078.

Gorham, E., P. M. Vitousek, and W. A. Reiners. 1979. The regulation of chemical budgets over the course of terrestrial ecosystem succession. *Ann. Rev. Ecol. Systematics* 10:53–84.

Gosz, J. R., D. G. Brookins, and D. I. Moore. 1983. Using strontium isotope ratios to estimate inputs to ecosystems. *BioScience* 33:23–30.

Gottfried, B. M. 1979. Small mammal populations in woodlot islands. *Amer. Midl. Natur.* 102:105–112.

Grace, J. 1977. *Plant Response to Wind*. New York: Academic Press.

Graustein, W. C., and R. L. Armstrong. 1983. The use of strontium-87/strontium-86 ratios to measure atmospheric transport into forested watersheds. *Science* 219:289–292.

Gregory, K. J., and D. E. Walling. 1973. *Drainage Basin Form and Process*. New York: Wiley.

Greig-Smith, P. 1952. The use of random and contiguous quadrats in the study of the structure of plant communities. *Ann. Bot. London* 16:293–316.

————. 1964. *Quantitative Plant Ecology*. 2nd ed. London: Butterworth.

Grier, C. C. 1975. Wildfire effects on nutrient distribution and leaching in a coniferous ecosystem. *Can. J. Forest Res.* 5:599–607.

Griffin, D. R. 1973. Oriented bird migration in or between opaque cloud layers. *Proc. Amer. Philos. Soc.* 117:117–141.

Grimm, E. C. 1984. Fire and other factors controlling the Big Woods of Minnesota in the mid-nineteenth century. *Ecol. Monogr.* 54:291–311.

Groleau, D. 1981. Intégration climatique et habitat traditionnel rural. *Aménagement et Nature* 63:6–10.

Grose, D. 1957. *The Flora of Wiltshire.* Devizes, England: Wiltshire Archaeology and Natural History Society.

Grossman, L. 1977. Man-environment relationships in anthropology and geography. *Assoc. Amer. Geogr. Ann.* 67:126–144.

Grubb, P. J. 1977. The maintenance of species richness in plant communities: the importance of the regeneration niche. *Biol. Rev.* 52:107–145.

Grubb, P. J., and A. J. M. Hopkins. Resilience at the level of the plant community. In Dell, B., A. Hopkins, and B. Lamont, eds., *Resilience in Mediterranean Type Ecosystems.* The Hague: Junk. In press.

Grue, C. E., R. R. Reid, and N. J. Silvy. 1983. Correlation of habitat variables with mourning dove call counts in Texas. *J. Wildl. Manage.* 47:186–195.

G'sell, S. 1913. *Histoire Ancienne de l'Afrique du Nord.* Paris: Hachette.

Gullion, G. W. 1977. Forest manipulation for ruffed grouse. *North Amer. Wildl. and Natur. Resourc. Conf. Trans.* 42:449–458.

Gunn, D. L., and R. C. Rainey, eds. 1979. Strategy and tactics of control of migrant pests. *Trans. Roy. Philos. Soc.* (London) *B* 287:249–488.

Guyot, G., and B. Seguin. 1976. Influence du bocage sur le climat d'une petite region. In *Les Bocages: Histoire, Ecologie, Economie.* Institut National de la Recherche Agronomique, Centre National de la Recherche Scientifique, Université de Rennes, Rennes, France. Pp. 121–130.

———, and M. Verbrugghe. 1976. Etude de la variabilité spatiale du microclimat à l'échelle parcellaire en zone bocagère. In *Les Bocages: Histoire, Ecologie, Economie.* Institut National de la Recherche Agronomique, Centre National de la Recherche Scientifique, Université de Rennes, Rennes, France. Pp. 131–136.

Gysel, L. W. 1951. Borders and openings of beech-maple woodlands in southern Michigan. *J. Forestry* 49:13–19.

Haase, G. 1964. Landschaftsokologische Detailuntersuchung und naturraumliche Gliederung. *Petermanns Geogr. Mitt.* 109:8–30.

———. 1968. Inhalt und Methodik einer umfassenden landwirtschaftlichen Standortkartierung auf der Grundlage landschaftsokologischer Erkundung. *Wiss. Veroff. Deutsch. Inst. Landerkund. N. F. (Leipzig)* 25–26:309–349.

———. 1975. Zur Methodik grossmassstabiger landschaftsokologischer und naturraumlicher Erkundung. *Wiss. Abh. Geogr. Ges. D. D. R.* 5:35–128.

———. 1976. The chorical structure of the natural landscape. *XXIII Congr. Int. Geogr. (Moscow)* 6:14–18.

———. 1984. The development of a common methodology of inventory and survey in landscape ecology. In Brandt, J., and P. Agger, eds., *Proceedings of the First International Seminar on Methodology in Landscape Ecological Research and Planning* (Vol. 5). Roskilde, Denmark: Roskilde Universitetsforlag GeoRuc. Pp. 68–106.

Haber, W. 1980. Raumordungskonzepte aus der Sicht der Okosystemforschung. *Forschungs. -und Sitzungberichte der Akad. fur Raumforschung und Landesplanung (Hannover)* 131:12–24.

Hack, J. T. 1960. Interpretation of erosional topography in humid temperate regions. *Amer. Sci.* 258:80–97.

Haffer, J. 1969. Speciation in Amazonian forest birds. *Science* 165:131–137.

Hagar, C. C. 1960. The interrelationship of timber, birds, and timber regeneration in the Douglas fir region of northwestern California. *Ecol.* 41:116–125.

Hagerstrand, T. 1965. A Monte Carlo approach to diffusion. *Archiv. Europ. Sociol.* 6:43–67.

Hagerstrand, T. 1967. *Innovation Diffusion as a Spatial Process.* Chicago: University of Chicago Press.

Haggett, P., A. D. Cliff, and A. Frey. 1977. *Locational Analysis in Human Geography.* New York: Wiley.

Hairston, N. G., J. D. Allen, R. K. Colwell, D. J. Futuyma, J. Howell, M. D. Lubin, J. Mathias, and J. H. Vandermeer. 1968. The relationship between species diversity and stability: an experimental approach with protozoa and bacteria. *Ecology* 49:1091–1101.

Hall, E. R., and K. R. Kelson. 1959. *The Mammals of North America.* New York: Ronald Press.

Hall, P. G., ed. 1966. *Von Thunen's Isolated State.* Translated by C.M. Wartenberg. London: Pergamon.

Halle, F., R. A. Oldeman, and P. B. Tomlinson. 1978. *Tropical Trees and Forests: An Architectural Analysis.* Berlin: Springer-Verlag.

Hamilton, T. H., R. H. Barth, Jr., and I. Rubinoff. 1964. The environmental control of insular variation in bird species abundance. *Proc. Nat. Acad. Sci. USA* 52:132–140.

Hanes, T. L. 1971. Succession after fire in the chaparral of southern California. *Ecol. Monogr.* 41:28–52.

Hanley, T. A. 1983. Black-tailed deer, elk, and forest edge in a western Cascades watershed. *J. Wildl. Manage.* 47:237–242.

Hansen, K. L., H. T. Odum, and M. T. Brown. 1982. Energy models for Volusia County, Florida. *Florida Scientist* 45:209–228.

Hansson, L. 1977. Landscape ecology and stability of populations. *Landscape Plann.* 4:85–93.

Harmon, W. H. 1948. Hedgerows. *Amer. For.* 54:448–450.

Harms, W. B., A. H. F. Stortelder, and W. Vos. 1984. Effects of intensification of agriculture on nature and landscape in The Netherlands. *Ekologia (CSSR)* 3:281–304.

Harper, J. L. 1977. *Population Biology of Plants.* London: Academic Press.

Harris, L. D. 1981. Forest and wildlife dynamics in the Southeast. *Trans. North Amer. Wildl. Natur. Resources Conf.* 45:307–322.

———, and P. Kangas. 1979. Designing future landscapes from principles of form and function. In *Our National Landscape, Techniques for Analyzing and Management of Visual Resources.* Washington, D. C.: U. S. Dept. Agric., Forest Service, General Technical Report PSW–35. Pp. 725–729.

Harrison, J. L. 1962. The distribution of feeding habits among animals in a tropical rain forest. *J. Animal Ecol.* 31:53–64.

Hasel, A. A. 1938. Sampling error in timber surveys. *J. Agric. Res.* 57:713–736.

Hasler, A. D., ed. 1975. *Coupling of Land and Water Systems.* New York: Springer-Verlag.

Hastings, H., R. Pekelney, R. Monticciolo, D. Von Kannon, and D. Del Monte. 1982. Time scale, persistence and patchiness. *Biosystems* 15:281–289.

Havlick, S. 1974. *The Urban Organism*. New York: Macmillan.

Hedberg, O. 1955. Vegetation belts of the East African mountains. *Sven. Bot. Tidskr.* 45:140–202.

Heezen, K. L., and J. R. Tester. 1967. Evaluation of radio-tracking by triangulation with special reference to deer movements. *J. Wildl. Manage.* 31:124–141.

Heinselman, M. L. 1973. Fire in the virgin forests of the Boundary Waters Canoe Area, Minnesota. *J. Quaternary Res.* 3:329–382.

Heller, H. 1969. Lebensbedingungen und Abfolge der Flussauenvegetation in der Schweiz. *Mitt. Schweiz. Anst. Forstl. Versuchswesen* 45:3–124.

Helliwell, D. R. 1975. The distribution of woodland plant species in some Shropshire hedgerows. *Biol. Conserv.* 7:61–72.

———. 1976. The effects of size and isolation on the conservation value of wooded sites in Britain. *J. Biogeogr.* 3:409–416.

Herz, K. 1973. Beitrag zur Theorie der landschaftsanalytischen Massstabsbereiche. *Petermanns Geogr. Mitt.* 117:91–96.

Hessing, M. B., C. D. Johnson, and R. P. Balda. 1981. Secondary succession of desert grassland in north-central Arizona powerline corridors. *J. Environ. Manage.* 13:55–69.

Heusser, C. J. 1974. Vegetation and climate of the southern Chile lake district during and since the last interglaciation. *J. Quaternary Res.* 4:290–315.

Hewes, L., and C. Jung. 1981. Early fencing on the middle western prairie. *Ann. Assoc. Amer. Geogr.* 71:177–201.

Higgs, A. J. 1981. Island biogeography theory and nature reserve design. *J. Biogeogr.* 8:117–124.

———, and M. B. Usher. 1980. Should nature reserves be large or small? *Nature* 285:568–569.

Hill, M. O. 1973. The intensity of spatial pattern in plant communities. *J. Ecol.* 61:225–235.

Hills, G. A. 1960. Regional site research. *For. Chron.* 36:401–423.

———. 1974. A philosophical approach to landscape planning. *Landscape Plann.* 1:339–371.

———. 1976. An integrated iterative holistic approach to ecosystem classification. In *Proceedings of the First Meeting of the Canadian Commission on Ecological (Bio-physical) Land Classification*, Petawawa, Ontario. Pp. 73–97.

Hocking, J. G., and G. S. Young. 1961. *Typology*. Reading, Massachusetts: Addison-Wesley.

Hodson, N. L. 1966. A survey of road mortality in mammals (and including data for the grass snake and common frog). *J. Zool. London* 148:576–579.

Hofstra, G., and R. Hall. 1971. Injury on roadside trees: leaf injury on pine and white cedar in relation to foliar levels of sodium chloride. *Can. J. Bot.* 49:613–622.

Holdridge, L. R. 1947. Determination of world plant formations from sample climatic data. *Science* 105:367–368.

———. 1967. *Life Zone Ecology*. San José, Costa Rica: Tropical Science Center.

Holling, C. S. 1973. Resilience and stability of ecological systems. *Annu. Rev. Ecol. Systematics* 4:1–24.

Hooper, M. D. 1976. Historical and biological studies on English hedges. In *Les*

*Bocages: Histoire, Ecologie, Economie.* Institut National de la Recherche Agronomique, Centre National de la Recherche Scientifique, Université de Rennes, Rennes, France. Pp. 225–227.

Hooper, M. D. 1970. Hedges and birds. *Birds* 3:114–117.

Hoover, H. 1965. *The Long-shadowed Forest.* London: Souvenir Press.

Hopkins, M. N., and E. P. Odum. 1953. Some aspects of the population ecology of breeding mourning doves in Georgia. *J. Wildl. Manage.* 17:132–143.

Horn, H. S. 1968. The adaptive significance of colonial nesting in the Brewer's Blackbird (*Euphagus cyanocephalus*). *Ecology* 49:682–694.

———. 1971. *The Adaptive Geometry of Trees.* Princeton: Princeton University Press.

———. 1975. Forest succession. *Sci. Amer.* 232:90–98.

———. 1976. Markovian properties of forest succession. In Cody, M. L., and J. M. Diamond, eds., *Ecology and Evolution of Communities.* Cambridge, Massachusetts: Belknap Press. Pp. 196–211.

Horton, R. E. 1945. Erosional development of streams and their drainage basins; hydrophysical approach to quantitative morphology. *Bull. Geol. Soc. Amer.* 56:275–370.

Hoskins, W. G. 1955. *The Making of the English Landscape.* New York: Penguin.

Houghton, R. A., J. E. Hobbie, J. M. Melillo, B. Moore, B. J. Peterson, G. R. Shaver, and G. M. Woodwell. 1983. Changes in the carbon content of terrestrial biota and soils between 1860 and 1900: A net release of $CO_2$ to the atmosphere. *Ecol. Monogr.* 53:235–262.

Houte de Lange, S. M. ten. 1978. Zur futterwahl des Alpensteinbockes (*Capra ibex* L.). Eine Untersuchung an der Steinbockkolonie am Piz Albris bei Pontresina. *Zeit. Jagdwiss.* 24:113–138.

———. 1984. Effects of landscape structure on animal population and distribution dynamics. In Brandt, J., and P. Agger, eds., *Proceedings of the First International Seminar on Methodology in Landscape Ecological Research and Planning* (Vol. 1). Roskilde, Denmark: Roskilde Universitetsforlag GeoRuc. Pp. 19–31.

Howe, R. W. 1979. Distribution and behavior of birds on small islands of northern Minnesota. *J. Biogeog.* 6:379–390.

Hubbell, S. P. 1979. Tree dispersion, abundance, and diversity in a tropical dry forest. *Science* 203:1299–1309.

Hubrich, H. 1967. Die landschaftsokologische Catena in reliefarmen Gebieten dargestellt an Beispielen aus dem nordwestsachsischen Flachland. *Petermanns Geogr. Mitt.* 111:13–18.

Huffaker, C. B. 1958. Experimental studies on predation: dispersion factors and predator-prey oscillations. *Hilgardia* 27:343–383.

Humboldt, A. von. 1807. *Essai sur la Géographie des Plantes.* Paris: Schoell.

Huntley, B., and H. J. B. Birks. 1983. *An Atlas of Past and Present Pollen Maps for Europe: 0–13000 Years Ago.* Cambridge: Cambridge University Press.

Huot, J. 1974. Winter habitat of white-tailed deer at Thirty-one Mile Lake, Quebec. *Can. Field-Natur.* 88:293–301.

Hurd, L. E., and L. Wolf. 1974. Stability in relation to nutrient enrichment in arthropod consumers of old field successional ecosystems. *Ecol. Monogr.* 44:465–482.

Hutchinson, G. E. 1957. *A Treatise on Limnology* (Vol. 1). New York: Wiley.

Hynes, H. B. N. 1975. The stream and its valley. *Verh. Int. Ver. Limnol.* 19:1–15.

Iacopi, R. 1973. *Earthquake Country.* Menlo Park, California: Sunset Books.

Ilvessalo, Y. 1920. Entragstafeln fr Kiefern-, Fichten- und Birkebestande in der Sdhalfe von Finland. *Acta. For. Fenn.* 15:1–96.

Irwin, L. L., and J. M. Peek. 1983. Elk habitat use relative to forest succession in Idaho. *J. Wildl. Manage.* 47:664–672.

Isachenko, A. G. 1973. *Principles of Landscape Science and Physical-Geographic Regionalization.* Melbourne: Melbourne University Press.

Isard, W. 1975. *Introduction to Regional Science.* Englewood Cliffs, New Jersey: Prentice Hall.

Isenmann, P. 1976, 1977. L'error demographique et spatial de la Mouelt-sieuse en Europe. *L'Oiseau* 46:337–366, and 47:26–40.

Jacobsen, R., and R. Adams. 1958. Salt and silt in ancient Mesopotamian agriculture. *Science* 128:1251–1258.

Jacquot, A. 1931. *Manuel Pratique de Sylviculture.* Paris: Bailliere.

Jaksic, F. M., and E. R. Fuentes. 1980. Why are native herbs in the Chilean matorral more abundant beneath bushes: microclimate or grazing? *J. Ecol.* 68:665–669.

Jakucs, P. 1972. *Dynamische Verbindung der Walder und Rasen.* Budapest: Akademiai Kiado, Verlag Ungarischen Akad.

Janzen, D. N. 1970. Herbivores and the number of tree species in tropical forests. *Amer. Natur.* 102:501–528.

Jennrich, R. I., and F. B. Turner. 1969. Measurement of non-circular home range. *J. Theoret. Biol.* 22:227–237.

Jenny, H. 1980. *The Soil Resource: Origin and Behavior.* New York: Springer-Verlag.

Jensen, M. 1954. *Shelter Effect: Investigations into the Aerodynamics of Shelter and its Effect on Climate and Crops.* Copenhagen: Danish Technical Press.

Johnson, E. A. 1983. The role of history in determining vegetation composition—an example in the western subarctic. *Nordicana* 47:133–140.

Johnson, R. R. 1970. Tree removal along southwestern rivers and effects on associated organisms. *Amer. Philos. Soc. Trbk.* 1970:321–322.

Johnson, W. C. 1977. A mathematical model of forest succession and land use for the North Carolina Piedmont. *Bull. Torrey Bot. Club* 104:334–346.

———, and N. R. French. 1981. Soviet Union. In Kormondy, E. J., and J. F. McCormick, eds., *Handbook of Contemporary Developments in World Ecology.* Westport, Connecticut: Greenwood Press. Pp. 343–383.

———, and D. M. Sharpe. 1976. An analysis of forest dynamics in the northern Georgia Piedmont. *Forest Sci.* 22:307–322.

———, R. K. Schreiber, and R. L. Burgess. 1979. Diversity of small mammals in a powerline right-of-way and adjacent forest in East Tennessee. *Amer. Midl. Natur.* 101:231–235.

Johnston, D., and E. P. Odum. 1956. Breeding bird populations in relation to plant succession on the piedmont of Georgia. *Ecology* 37:50–62.

Johnston, V. 1947. Breeding birds of the forest edge in Illinois. *Condor* 49:45–53.

Joly, F. 1959. *Une Carte au 1/1,000,000 de l'Utilisation du Sol au Maroc.* Rabat, Morocco: Com. Nat. Geogr. 114 pp.

Jones, D. D. 1975. The application of catastrophe theory to ecological systems. In Innis, G. S., ed., *New Directions in the Analysis of Ecological Systems* (Vol. 5). La Jolla, California: Simulation Council Proceedings of the Series on Society and Computer Simulation. Pp. 133–148.

Jordan, C. F., and J. F. Kline. 1972. Mineral cycling: some basic concepts and their application in a tropical rain forest. *Annu. Rev. Ecol. Systematics* 3:33–50.

Joselyn, G. B., J. E. Warnock, and S. L. Etter. 1968. Manipulation of roadside cover for nesting pheasants—a preliminary report. *J. Wildl. Manage.* 32:217–233.

Julander, O., and D. E. Jeffery. 1964. Deer, elk, and cattle range relations on summer range in Utah. *Trans. North Amer. Wildl. Natur. Resource Conf.* 29:404–414.

Jurdant, M., J. L. Belair, V. Gérardin, and J. P. Ducruc. 1977. *L'Inventaire du Capital-Nature.* Québec: Serv. Etudes Ecol. Region., Dir. Region. Terres, Pêches, Environ. Canada. 202 pp.

———, J. C. Dionne, J. Beaubien, J. L. Belair, and V. Gérardin. 1972. An ecological survey of the Saguenay-Lac Saint Jean region. Québec, Canada. *Int. Geogr.* 1:259–261.

Kalamkar, R. J. 1932. Experimental error and the field plot technique with potatoes. *J. Agric. Sci.* 22:373–383.

Kant, E. 1951. Umland studies and sector analysis. In Gleerup, C. W. K., ed. *Studies in Rural-Urban Interaction.* Lund: University of Lund, Lund Studies in Geography, Series B, Human Geography, No. 3. Pp. 3–14.

Kareiva, P. 1982. Experimental and mathematical analyses of herbivore movement: quantifying the influence of plant spacing and quality on foraging discrimination. *Ecol. Monogr.* 52:261–282.

Karr, J. R. 1982. Population variability and extinction in the avifauna of a tropical land bridge island. *Ecology* 63:1975–1978.

———, and K. E. Freemark. 1983. Habitat selection of environmental gradients: dynamics in the "stable" tropics. *Ecology* 64:1481–1494.

———, and K. E. Freemark. Disturbance, perturbation, and vertebrates: an integrative perspective. In Pickett, S. T. A., and P. S. White, eds., *Natural Disturbance: A Patch Dynamic Perspective.* New York: Academic Press. In press.

———, and I. J. Schlosser. 1978. Water resources and the land-water interface. *Science* 201:229–234.

Kasriel, R. H. 1971. *Undergraduate Topology.* Philadelphia: Saunders.

Keller, E. A. 1972. Development of alluvial stream channels: a five stage model. *Geol. Soc. Amer. Bull.* 83:1531–1536.

Kendall, M., and A. Stuart. 1967. *The Advanced Theory of Statistics.* 2nd ed. 2 vols. London: Griffin.

Kendeigh, S. C. 1944. Measurement of bird populations. *Ecol. Monogr.* 14:67–106.

———. 1974. *Ecology with Special Reference to Animals and Man.* Englewood Cliffs, New Jersey: Prentice Hall.

Kerner, A. 1863. *Das Pflanzenleben der Donaulaender.* Innsbruck: University of Innsbruck. (*1978. The Background of Plant Ecology.* Translated by H. S. Conard. Salem, New Hampshire: Ayer Co.)

Kershaw, K. A. 1957. The use of cover and frequency in the detection of pattern in plant communities. *Ecology* 38:291–299.

———. 1958. An investigation of the structure of a grassland community. *J. Ecol.* 46:571–592; 47:31–33.

———. 1960. The detection of pattern and association. *J. Ecol.* 48:233–242.

———. 1975. *Quantitative and Dynamic Plant Ecology.* New York: Elsevier.

Kessell, S. R., and M. W. Potter. 1980. A quantitative succession model for nine Montana forest communities. *Environ. Manage.* 4:227–240.

Kiemstedt, H., ed. 1975. *Landschaftsbewertung fur die Erhohlung im Sauerland.* Dortmund, West Germany: Institut fur Landes- und Stadtentwicklungs Forschung des Landes Nordrhein- Westfalen.

Kimura, M., and G. H. Weiss. 1964. The stepping stone model of population structure and the decrease of genetic correlation with distance. *Genetics* 49:561–576.

Kincaid, W. B., and E. H. Bryant. 1983. A geometric method for evaluating the null hypothesis of random habitat utilization. *Ecology* 64:1463–1470.

King, L. J. 1969. *Statistical Analysis in Geography.* Englewood Cliffs, New Jersey: Prentice-Hall.

King, T. J. 1977. The plant ecology of ant-hills in calcareous grasslands. II. Succession on the mounds. *J. Ecol.* 65:257–278.

Kira, T. 1978. Community architecture and organic matter dynamics in tropical lowland rain forests of Southeast Asia with special reference to Pasoh Forest, West Malaysia. In Tomlinson, P. B., and M. H. Zimmerman, eds. *Tropical Trees as Living Systems.* Cambridge: Cambridge University Press. Pp. 561–590.

Klopatek, J. M., J. R. Krummel, J. B. Mankin, and R. V. O'Neill. 1983. A theoretical approach to regional environmental conflicts. *J. Environ. Manage.* 16:1–15.

Klotzli F., 1980. Okologie in der Orts-und Regionalplanung. In *Okologie in der Raumplanung.* Dokumentation und Information fur Schwerzisher Orts- Regional- unt Landesplanung Nr. 59/60. Zurich: Geobotanischen Institut. pp. 53–61.

Knight, D. H. 1975. A phytosociological analysis of species-rich tropical forest on Barro Colorado Island, Panama. *Ecol. Monogr.* 45:259–284.

Knowlton, F. F. 1960. Food habits, movement and populations of moose in Gravelly Mountains, Montana. *J. Wildl. Manage.* 24:162–170.

Koeppl, J. W., N. A. Slade, and R. S. Hoffmann. 1975. A bivariate home range model with possible application to ethological data analysis. *J. Mammal.* 56:81–90.

Kopecky, K. 1969. Zur Syntaxonomie der naturlichen nitrophilen Saumgesellschaften in der Tschechoslowakei und zur Gliederung der Klassa Galio-Urticetea. *Folia Geobot. Phytotax. (Praha).* 4:235–259.

Koppen, W. 1918. Klassification der Klimate nach Temperatur. *Niederschlag und Jahreslauf:* 193–203, 243–248.

———. 1931. *Grundriss der Klimakunde.* Berlin: de Gryter.

Kovar, P., E. Brabec, and J. Holubova. 1982. Particle deposition in Prague grasslands. *Ekologia (CSSR)* 2:251–256.

Kozlowski, T. T., and C. E. Ahlgren, eds. 1974. *Fire and Ecosystems.* New York: Academic Press.

Kozova, M. 1982. Spatial arrangement of landscape elements and possibilities of its expression. *Proceedings of the VIth International Symposium on Problems in Landscape Ecological Research*. Bratislava, Czechoslovakia: Institute for Experimental Biology and Ecology.

Kramer, A. 1969. Sozial Organisation und Sozialverhalten einer Gemspopulation (*Rupicapra rupicapra* L.) der Alpen. *Zeitschrift fur Tierpsychologie* 26:889–964.

———. 1972. *A Review of the Ecological Relationships Between Mule and White-tailed Deer*. Calgary: Alberta Department of Lands and Forests, Occasional Paper No. 3. 54 pp.

Kramer, S. 1957. *L'Histoire Commence à Sumer*. Grenoble: Arthaud.

Krebs, C. J. 1972. *Ecology. The Experimental Analysis of Distribution and Abundance*. New York: Harper and Row.

Krebs, J. R. 1971. Territory and breeding density in the great tit, *Parus major* L. *Ecology* 52:2–22.

———, J. C. Ryan, and E. L. Charnov. 1974. Hunting by expectation or optimal foraging? A study of patch use by chickadees. *Animal Behav.* 22:953–964.

Kroodsma, R. L. 1982. Bird community ecology on power-line corridors in East Tennessee. *Biol. Conserv.* 23:79–94.

Krystofovich, A. N. 1957. *Paleobotanica*, 4th ed. Nauch.-Tech. Izd. Neft. i. Gorono-Topliv. Lit. Leningrad: Gosudar.

Kuchler, A. W. 1964. *Potential Natural Vegetation of the Conterminous United States*. New York: American Geographical Society Special Publication 36. 150 pp.

———. 1967. *Vegetation Mapping*. New York: Ronald Press.

———. 1969. Natural and cultural vegetation. *Prof. Geogr.* 21:383–385.

———. 1973. Problems in classifying and mapping vegetation for ecological regionalization. *Ecology* 54:512–523.

Kugler, H. 1976. Zur Aufgabe der geomorphologischen Forschung und Kartierung in der D. D. R. *Petermanns Geogr. Mitt.* 120:154–160.

Kuhnholtz-Lordat, G. 1958. *La Terre Incendiée*. Nîmes: Maison Carrée.

Kuratowski, K. 1972. *Introduction to Set Theory and Topology*. Oxford: International Series of Monographs in Pure and Applied Mathematics No. 101 (1966. *Introduction à la Théorie des Ensembles et à la Topologie*. Geneva: Monographies de L'Enseignement Mathematique No. 15).

Lacate, D. S. 1969. *Guidelines for Bio-physical Land Classification*. Ottawa: Canadian Forest Service Publication 1204. 61 pp.

Lachenbruch, A. H. 1962. Mechanics of thermal contraction cracks and ice-wedge polygons in permafrost. *Geological Society of America, Special Paper* 70:1–69.

Lafforgue, G. 1969. *La Protohistoire*. Paris: Cultures, Arts, Lois.

Lagerwerff, J. V., and A. N. Specht. 1970. Contamination of roadside soil and vegetation with cadmium, nickel, lead, and zinc. *Environ. Sci. Technol.* 4:583–586.

La Motte, M. 1983. Research on the characteristics of energy flows within natural and man-altered ecosystems. In Mooney, H. A., and M. Godron, eds., *Disturbance and Ecosystems: Components of Response*. New York: Springer-Verlag. Pp. 48–70.

Landers, J. L., R. J. Hamilton, A. S. Johnson, and R. L. Marchington. 1979. Foods and habitat of black bears in southeastern North Carolina. *J. Wildl. Manage.* 43:143–153.

Langlois, G. 1973. *Traitement des Résidus Solides.* Paris: Bergerat-Monnoyeur.

Larson, T. J., O. J. Rongstad, and F. W. Terbilcox. 1978. Movement and habitat of white-tailed deer in southcentral Wisconsin. *J. Wildl. Manage.* 42:113–117.

Lawlor, L. R. 1978. A comment on randomly constructed model ecosystems. *Amer. Natur.* 112:445–447.

Lay, D. 1938. How valuable are woodland clearings to birdlife. *Wilson Bull.* 50:254–256.

Lebeau, R. 1969. *Les Grands Types de Structures Agraires dans le Monde.* Paris: Masson.

Le Clezio, P. 1976. Les ambiguités de la notion de maille optimale. In *Les Bocages: Histoire, Ecologie, Economie.* Institut National de la Recherche Agronomique, Centre National de la Recherche Scientifique, Université de Rennes. Rennes, France. Pp. 551–554.

Lecompte, M. 1973. Analyse des rapports climats-végétation par une méthod d'échantillonnage continu. *Bull. Soc. Sci. Nat. Phys. Maroc.* 53:37–61.

Leduc, J. P. 1979. Le rôle du bocage. *Recherche et Nature* 20:4–9.

Lee, J. J., and D. L. Inman. 1975. The ecological role of consumers—an aggregated systems view. *Ecology* 56:1455–1458.

Lee, R. 1980. *Forest Hydrology.* New York: Columbia University Press.

Lefeuvre, J. L., J. Missonnier, and Y. Robert. 1976. Caractérisation zoologique: écologie animale. In *Les Bocages: Histoire, Ecologie, Economie.* Institut National de la Recherche Agronomique, Centre National de la Recherche Scientifique, Université de Rennes. Rennes, France. Pp. 315–326.

Le Floc'h, E., G. Long, J. Poissonet, and M. Godron. 1973. Végétation. In *Atlas Régional du Languedoc-Roussillon.* Paris: Berger-Levrault. Pp. 1–35.

Lelong-Ferrand, J., and J. M. Arnaudies. 1980. *Cours de Mathématique - Analyse.* Paris: Dunod.

Leopold, A. 1933. *Game Management.* New York: Scribners.

———. 1941. Cheat takes over. *The Land* 1:310–313.

———. 1949. *A Sand County Almanac.* New York: Oxford University Press.

Leopold, L. B., M. G. Wolman, and J. P. Miller. 1964. *Fluvial Processes in Geomorphology.* San Francisco: W. H. Freeman.

Le Resche, R. E., R. H. Bishop, and J. W. Coady. 1974. Distribution and habitats of moose in Alaska. *Natur. Can. (Que.)* 101:143–178.

*Les Bocages: Histoire, Ecologie, Economie.* 1976. Institut National de la Recherche Agronomique, Centre National de la Recherche Scientifique, Université de Rennes, Rennes, France. 586 pp.

Leser, H. 1976. *Landschaftsokologie.* Stuttgart: Ulmer.

Leslie, D. M., Jr., and C. L. Douglas. 1979. Desert bighorn sheep of the River Mountains, Nevada. *Wildl. Monogr.* 66:5–56.

Levin, S. A. 1974. Dispersion and population interactions. *Amer. Natur.* 108:207–228.

———. 1976. Population dynamic models in heterogeneous environments. *Ann. Rev. Ecol. Systematics* 7:287–310.

———. 1978. Pattern formation in ecological communities. In Steele, J. H., ed., *Spatial Pattern in Plankton Communities*. New York: Plenum. Pp. 433–465.

———, and R. T. Paine. 1974. Disturbance, patch formation, and community structure. *Proc. Nat. Acad. Sci. USA* 71:2744–2747.

Levins, R. 1968. *Evolution in Changing Environments*. Princeton: Princeton University Press.

Lewis, T. 1969a. The distribution of insects near a low hedgerow. *J. Appl. Ecol.* 6:443–452.

———. 1969b. The diversity of the insect fauna in a hedgerow and neighboring fields. *J. Appl. Ecol.* 6:453–458.

Lhéritier, J. N. 1975. Les rapaces diurnes du parc national des Cévennes. *Mem. Trav. EPHE, Montpellier* 2:1–143.

Lhote, M. 1973. *A la Découverte des Fresques du Tassili*. Paris: Arthaud.

———. 1978. *Vers d'Autres Tassili*. Paris: Arthaud.

Liberg, O. 1980. Spacing patterns in a population of rural free roaming domestic cats. *Oikos* 35:336–349.

Lienenbecker, H., and U. Raabe. 1981. Veg auf Bahnhofen des Ost-Munsterlandes. *Ber. Naturw. Ver. Bielefeld* 25:129–141.

Lieth, H. 1975. Historical survey of primary production research. In Lieth, H., and R. H. Whittaker, eds., *Primary Productivity of the Biosphere*. New York: Springer-Verlag. Pp. 7–16.

Likens, G. E., and F. H. Bormann. 1974. Linkages between terrestrial and aquatic ecosystems. *BioScience* 24:447–456.

———, F. H. Bormann, and N. M. Johnson. 1969. Nitrification: importance to nutrient losses from a cut-over forested ecosystem. *Science* 163:1205–1206.

———, F. H. Bormann, N. M. Johnson, D. W. Fisher, and R. S. Pierce. 1970. Effects of forest cutting and herbicide treatment on nutrient budgets in the Hubbard Brook watershed-ecosystem. *Ecol. Monogr.* 40:23–47.

———, F. H. Bormann, N. M. Johnson, and R. S. Pierce. 1967. The calcium, magnesium, potassium, and sodium budgets in a small forested ecosystem. *Ecology* 48:772–785.

———, F. H. Bormann, R. S. Pierce, J. S. Eaton, and N. M. Johnson. 1977. *Biogeochemistry of a Forested Ecosystem*. New York: Springer-Verlag.

———, F. H. Bormann, R. S. Pierce, and W. A. Reiners. 1978. Recovery of a deforested ecosystem. *Science* 199:492–496.

Lind, O. T. 1979. *Handbook of Common Methods in Limnology*. 2nd ed. St. Louis: Mosby.

Lindberg, S. E., R. C. Harriss, and R. R. Turner. 1982. Atmospheric deposition of metals to forest vegetation. *Science* 215:1609–1611.

Little, S. 1979. Fire and plant succession in the New Jersey Pine Barrens. In Forman, R. T. T., ed., *Pine Barrens: Ecosystem and Landscape*. New York: Academic Press. Pp. 297–314.

Long, G. 1974. *Diagnostic Phyto-écologique et Aménagement du Territoire*. Paris: Masson.

———, P. Daget, M. Godron, J. L. Guillerm, M. Marlange, and J. Poissonet. 1975. *Diagnostic Phyto-écologique et Aménagement du Territoire. Application et Examen des Cas Concrets*. Paris: Masson.

Lorimer, C. G. 1977. The presettlement forest and natural disturbance cycle of northeastern Maine. *Ecology* 58:139–148.

Losch, A. 1940. *Die Raumliche Ordnung der Wirtschaft.* Jena: Gustav Fischer.

———. 1954. *The Economics of Location.* New Haven: Yale University Press.

Loucks, O. L. 1970. Evolution of diversity, efficiency and community stability. *Amer. Zool.* 10:17–25.

Lovejoy, S. 1982. Area-perimeter relation for rain and cloud areas. *Science* 216:185–187.

Lovejoy, T. E., R. O. Bierregaard, J. M. Rankin, and H. O. R. Schubart. 1983. Ecological dynamics of forest fragments. In Sutton, S. L., T. C. Whitmore, and A. C. Chadwick, eds., *Tropical Rain Forests: Ecology and Management.* Oxford: Blackwell Sci. Publ. Pp. 377–384.

———, J. M. Rankin, R. O. Bierregaard, Jr., K. S. Brown, Jr., L. H. Emmons, and M. E. Van der Voort. 1984. Ecosystem decay of Amazon forest remnants. In Nitecki, M. H., ed., *Extinctions.* Chicago: University of Chicago Press. Pp. 295–325.

Lovett, G. M., W. A. Reiners, and R. K. Olson. 1982. Cloud droplet deposition in subalpine balsam fir forests: hydrological and chemical inputs. *Science* 218:1303–1304.

Low, W. A., M. L. Dudzinski, and W. J. Muller. 1981. The influence of forage and climatic conditions on range community preference of shorthorn cattle in central Australia. *J. Appl. Ecol.* 18:11–26.

Lowe, J. C., and S. Moryadas. 1975. *The Geography of Movement.* Boston: Houghton Mifflin.

Lowenthal, D. 1976. Past time, present place: landscape and memory. *Geogr. Rev.* 65:1–36.

Lowrance, R., R. Todd, J. Fail, Jr., O. Hendrickson, Jr., R. Leonard, and L. Asmussen. 1984. Riparian forests as nutrient filters in agricultural watersheds. *BioScience* 34:374–377.

Lubchenco, J. 1978. Plant species diversity in a marine intertidal community: importance of herbivore food preference and algal competitive abilities. *Amer. Natur.* 112:23–39.

Luder, P. 1981. The diversity of landscape ecology. Definition and attempt at empirical identification. *Angewandte Botanik* 55:321–329.

Luey, J. E., and I. R. Adelman. 1980. Downstream areas as refuges for fish in drainage development watersheds. *Trans. Amer. Fish Soc.* 109:332–335.

Lundholm, B., and M. Stackerud, eds. 1980. *Environmental Protection and Biological Forms of Control of Pest Organisms.* Stockholm: Ecological Bulletin 31, Swedish Natural Science Research Council. 171 pp.

Lynch, J. F., and D. F. Whigham. 1984. Effects of forest fragmentation on breeding bird communities in Maryland, USA. *Biol. Conserv.* 28:287–324.

Lynch, K. 1960. *The Image of the City.* Cambridge, Massachusetts: M. I. T. Press.

Lyon, L. J. 1979. Habitat effectiveness for elk as influenced by roads and cover. *J. Forestry* 77:658–660.

———. 1983. Road density models describing habitat effectiveness for elk. *J. Forestry* 81:592–595.

———, and C. E. Jensen. 1980. Management implications of elk and deer use of clear-cuts in Montana. *J. Wildl. Manage.* 44:352–362.

Maarleveld, G. C., and G. W. De Lange. 1972. Een globale geomorfologische en landschappelijke kaetering en waardering van de uitwaarden van de nederlandes Grote Rivieren. *Landbouwkundig Tijdscher* 84:273–288.

Mabbutt, J. A. 1976. Physiographic setting as an indication of inherent resistance to desertification. In *Problems in the Development and Conservation of Desert and Semi-desert Lands.* New South Wales, Australia: Proceedings of the Symposium of the 23rd International Geographical Congress, University of New South Wales. Pp. 189–197.

MacArthur, R. H., and J. W. MacArthur. 1961. On bird species diversity. *Ecology* 42:597–598.

———, and E. O. Wilson. 1967. *The Theory of Island Biogeography.* Princeton: Princeton University Press.

MacClintock, L., R. F. Whitcomb, and B. L. Whitcomb. 1977. Evidence for the value of corridors and minimization of isolation in preservation of biotic diversity. *Amer. Birds* 31:6–16.

MacCracken, M., and H. Moses. 1982. The first detection of carbon dioxide effects. *Dept. Energy Conf. 8106 (Washington)* 214:3–44.

MacDonald, N. 1983. *Trees and Networks in Biological Models.* Chichester: Wiley.

MacDougall, E. 1981. Fuzzy set evaluation in landscape assessment. In *Regional Landscape Planning.* Amherst: University of Massachusetts Press. Pp. 165–169.

Mack, R. N. 1981. Invasion of *Bromus tectorum* L. into western North America: an ecological chronicle. *Agro-Ecosystems* 7:145–165.

Maley, J. 1980. Les changements climatiques de la fin du Tertiaire en Afrique: leur conséquence sur l'apparition du Sahara et de sa vegetation. In Martin, A. J., and H. Faure, eds., *The Sahara and the Nile. Quaternary Environments and Prehistoric Occupation in Northern Africa.* Rotterdam: Balkema. Pp. 63–86.

Mandelbrot, B. B. 1977. *Form, Chance, and Dimension.* San Francisco: W. H. Freeman.

———. 1981. *The Fractal Geometry of Nature.* New York: Freeman.

Marchal, M. 1981. Les paysages agraires en Haute-Volta. *Photo-interpretation* 1(6): pages unnumbered.

Marcot, B. G., and V. J. Meretsky. 1983. Shaping stands to enhance habitat diversity. *J. Forestry* 81:527–528.

Margalef, R. 1957. La teoría de la informacion en ecología. *Mem. R. Acad. Cienc. Art. Barcelona* 32:373–449.

———. 1958. Information theory in ecology. *Gen. Systems* 3:36–71.

———. 1963. On certain unifying principles in ecology. *Amer. Natur.* 97:357–374.

Marien, J. 1983. Forêt cultivée et forêt écologique. *Informations-Forêt* 2:123–134.

Marks, P. L. 1983. On the origin of the field plants of the northeastern United States. *Amer. Natur.* 122:210–228.

Marr, J. W. 1977. The development and movement of tree islands near the upper limit of tree growth in the southern Rocky Mountains. *Ecology* 58:1159–1164.

Marschner, F. J. 1959. *Land Use and its Pattern in the United States.* Washington, D. C.: U. S. Dept. Agric. Handbook 153.

Marsh, P. C., and J. E. Luey. 1982. Oases for aquatic life within agricultural watersheds. *Fisheries* 7:16–19, 24.

Marshall, J. K. 1967. The effect of shelter on the productivity of grasslands and field crops. *Field Crop Abstracts* 20:1–14.

Marshall, W. H., and J. J. Kupa. 1963. Development of radio-telemetry techniques for individually marking ruffed grouse. *Trans. No. Amer. Wildl. and Natur. Resourc. Conf.* 28:443–456.

Martin, P. 1971. Prehistoric overkill. In Detwyler, T., ed., *Man's Impact on the Environment.* New York: McGraw-Hill. Pp. 613–624.

Martin, T. E. 1980. Diversity and abundance of spring migratory birds using habitat islands in the Great Plains. *Condor* 82:430–439.

Matheron, G. 1965. *Les Variables Régionalisées et leur Estimation.* Paris: Masson.

Matthies, H. 1925. Die Bedeutung der Eisenbahnen und der Schiffahrt fur die Pflanzenverbreitung in Mecklenburg. *Arch. Ver. Freunde Naturg. Mecklenb. N. S.* 1:27–97.

Mattson, W. J., and N. D. Addy. 1975. Phytophagus insects as regulators of forest primary production. *Science* 190:515–522.

Mauget, R. 1979. Quelques problèmes de biologie et d'éco-éthologie chez le Sanglier. *Bull. Mens. Off. Nat. Chasse* 23:20–29.

Mavrommatis, G. 1971. *Recherches Phytosociologiques et Ecologiques dans le Massif de l'Ossa (Crête).* Montpellier, France: Institut Botanique. 73 pp.

May, R. M. 1973. *Stability and Complexity in Model Ecosystems.* Princeton: Princeton University Press.

Mayer, R., and B. Ulrich. 1978. Input of atmospheric sulfur by dry and wet deposition to two central European forest ecosystems. *Atmos. Environ.* 12:375–377.

Mayr, E. 1974. *Populations, Espèces et Evolution.* Paris: Hermann.

McAtee, W. L. 1945. *The Ring-necked Pheasant and its Management in North America.* Washington, D. C.: American Wildlife Institute.

McCashion, J. D., and R. M. Rice. 1983. Erosion on logging roads in northwestern California: How much is avoidable? *J. Forestry* 81:23–26.

McClure, H. E. 1966. Flowering, fruiting and animals in the canopy of a tropical rain forest. *Malayan Forester* 29:182–203.

McColl, J. G. 1978. Ionic composition of forest soil solutions and effects of clearcutting. *Soil Sci. Soc. Amer. J.* 42:358–363.

———, and D. F. Grigal. 1975. Forest fire: effects on phosphorus movement to lakes. *Science* 188:1109–1111.

McCreary, D. D., and D. A. Perry. 1983. Strip thinning and selective thinning in Douglas-fir. *J. Forestry* 81:375–377.

McDonnell, M. J. 1984. Interactions between landscape elements: dispersal of bird-disseminated plants in post-agricultural landscapes. In Brandt, J., and P. Agger, eds., *Proceedings of the First International Seminar on Methodology in Landscape Ecological Research and Planning* (Vol. 2). Roskilde, Denmark: Roskilde Universitetsforlag GeoRuc. Pp. 47–58.

———, and E. W. Stiles. 1983. The structural complexity of old field vegetation and the recruitment of bird-dispersed plant species. *Oecologia* 56:109–116.

McHarg, I. L. 1969. *Design with Nature.* Garden City, New York: Natural History Press.

McIntosh, R. P. 1967. The continuum concept of vegetation. *Bot. Rev.* 33:131–187.

McNaughton, S. J. 1977. Diversity and stability of ecological communities: a comment on the role of empiricism in ecology. *Amer. Natur.* 111:515–525.

———. 1979. Grassland-herbivore dynamics. In Sinclair, A. R. E., and M. Norton-Griffiths, eds., *Serengeti. Dynamics of an Ecosystem.* Chicago: University of Chicago Press.

McQuilkin, W. E. 1940. The natural establishment of pine in abandoned fields in the Piedmont Plateau region. *Ecology* 21:135–149.

Meckelein, W. 1980. *Desertification in Extremely Arid Environments.* Stuttgart: Geography Institute, University of Stuttgart.

Medvedkov, Y. V. 1967. The concept of entropy in settlement pattern analysis. *Regional Sci. Assoc. Papers* 18:165–168.

Meinig, D. W., ed. 1979a. *The Interpretation of Ordinary Landscapes.* Geographical Essays, Oxford: Oxford University Press.

———. 1979b. Reading the landscape. An appreciation of W. G. Hoskins and J. B. Jackson. In Meinig, D. W., ed., *The Interpretation of Ordinary Landscapes.* Geographical Essays, Oxford: Oxford University Press. Pp. 195–244.

Mellinger, M. V., and S. J. McNaughton. 1975. Structure and function of successional vascular plant communities in central New York. *Ecol. Monogr.* 45:161–182.

Melquist, W. E., and M. G. Hornocker. 1983. Ecology of river otters in west central Idaho. *Wildl. Monogr.* 83:5–60.

Mengel, R. M. 1964. The probable history of species formation in some northern wood warblers (Parulidae). *The Living Bird (Ornithol. Lab., Cornell Univ.)* 3:9–43.

———. 1970. The North American central plains as an isolating agent in bird speciation. In Kort, W., Jr., and J. K. Jones, Jr., eds., *Pleistocene and Recent Environments of the Central Great Plains.* Lawrence, Kansas: University of Kansas Press. Pp. 279–340.

Merot, A., and A. Ruellan. 1980. Pédologie, hydrologie des bocages: caractéristiques et incidences de l'arasement des talus boisés. *Bull. Tech. Inf.* 353–355:631–656.

Merriam, G. 1984. Connectivity: a fundamental characteristic of landscape pattern. In Brandt, J., and P. Agger, eds., *Proceedings of the First International Seminar on Methodology in Landscape Ecological Research and Planning* (Vol. 1). Roskilde, Denmark: Roskilde Universitetsforlag GeoRuc. Pp. 5–15.

Messenger, K. G. 1968. A railway flora of Rutland. *Proc. Bot. Soc. Brit. Isl.* 7:325–344.

Metzgar, L. H. 1972. The measurement of home range shape. *J. Wildl. Manage.* 36:643–645.

Meynier, A. 1970. *Les Paysages Agraires.* Paris: Armand Colin.

Middleton, J. D., and G. Merriam. 1983. Distribution of woodland species in farmland. *J. Appl. Ecol.* 20:625–644.

Mierau, G. W., and B. E. Favara. 1975. Lead poisoning in roadside populations of deermice. *Environ. Pollution* 8:55–64.

Mikesell, M. W. 1968. Landscape. *Int. Encyclo. Soc. Sci.* 8:575–580.

Miller, D. H. 1956. The influence of pine forest on daytime temperature in the Sierra Nevada. *Geogr. Rev.* 46:209–218.

————. 1977. *Water at the Surface of the Earth: An Introduction to Ecosystem Hydrodynamics*. New York: Academic Press.

————. 1978a. The factor of scale: ecosystem, landscape mosaic, and region. In Hammond, A., G. Macinio, and W. B. Fairchild, eds., *Sourcebook on the Environment, A Guide to the Literature*. Chicago: University of Chicago Press. Pp. 63–88.

Miller, D. R., J. D. Bergen, and G. Newroth. 1983. Cold air drainage in a narrow forested valley. *Forest Sci.* 29:357–370.

Miller, G. T., Jr. 1981. *Living in the Environment*. 3rd ed. Belmont, California: Wadsworth.

Miller, R. I. 1978b. Applying island biogeographic theory to an east African reserve. *Environ. Conserv.* 5:191–195.

————, and L. D. Harris. 1977. Isolation and extirpations in wildlife reserves. *Biol. Conserv.* 12:311–315.

Minnich, R. A. 1983. Fire mosaics in southern California and northern Baja California. *Science* 219:1287–1294.

de Miranda, E. 1979. *Etude des Déséquilibres Ecologiques et Agricoles d'une Region Tropicale Semi-aride au Niger*. Bordeaux: Publ. Institut de la Recherche et d'Application des Méthodes de Developpment, et Université de Bordeaux.

Mitchell, J. L. 1961. Mink movements and populations on a Montana river. *J. Wildl. Manage.* 25:48–54.

Moebius, K. 1877. *Die Auster und die Austernwirtschaft*. Berlin: Wiegand. (1880. *An Oyster-bank is a Biocoenose or a Social Community*. Translated and published in Report of the U.S. Fish Commission, Washington, D.C. Pages 683–751).

Moen, A. N. 1973. *Wildlife Ecology: An Analytical Approach*. San Francisco: W. H. Freeman.

————. 1974. Turbulence and the visualization of wind flow. *Ecology* 55:1420–1424.

Molinier, R., and P. Muller. 1938. La dissémination des espèces végétales. *Comm. SIGMA* 64:1–169.

Moore, N. W., and M. D. Hooper. 1975. On the number of bird species in British woods. *Biol. Conserv.* 8:239–250.

Moran, P. 1953. The statistical analysis of the Canadian lynx cycle. I. Structure and prediction. *Austral. J. Zool.* 1:163–173.

Moravec, J. 1975. Die Unterheinheiten der Assoziation. *Beitr. Natur. Forsch. Sudw. Dtl.* 34:225–232.

Moreau, R. E. 1972. *The Palaearctic-African Bird Migration Systems*. London: Academic Press.

Morgan, K. A., and J. E. Gates. 1982. Bird population patterns in forest edge and strip vegetation at Remington Farms, Maryland. *J. Wildl. Manage.* 46:933–944.

Morowitz, H. J. 1970. *Entropy for Biologists*. New York: Academic Press.

Morris, M. M. J., and R. E. Lemon. 1983. Characteristics of vegetation and topography near red-shouldered hawk nests in southwestern Quebec. *J. Wildl. Manage.* 47:138–145.

Muehlenbach, V. 1979. Contributions to the synanthropic (adventive) flora of the railroads in St. Louis, Missouri, USA. *Ann. Missouri Bot. Garden* 66:1–108.

Mueller-Dombois, D., and H. Ellenberg. 1974. *Aims and Methods of Vegetation Ecology.* New York: Wiley.

Muller, C. H. 1970. Phytotoxins as plant habitat variables. *Rec. Advan. Phytochem.* 3:105–121.

———, and R. del Moral. 1966. Soil toxicity induced by terpenes from *Salvia leucophylla. Bull. Torrey Bot. Club* 93:130–137.

Muller, T. 1962. Die Saumgesellschaften der Klasse Trifolio-Geranietea sanguinei. *Mitt. flor. -soz. ArbGemein. N. F.* 9:65–140.

Murie, O. J. 1951. *The Elk of North America.* Wildlife Management Institute. Harrisburg, Pennsylvania: Stackpole.

Murphey, R. 1951. The decline of North Africa since the Roman occupation: climatic or human. *Ann. Assoc. Amer. Geogr.* 41:116–132.

Nash, T. H., III. 1975. Influence of effluents from a zinc factory on lichens. *Ecol. Monogr.* 45:183–198.

Naveh, Z. 1982a. Landscape ecology as an emerging branch of human ecosystem science. *Adv. Ecol. Res.* 12:189–237.

———. 1982b. Mediterranean landscape evolution and degradation as multivariate-biofunctions: theoretical and practical implications. *Landscape Plann.* 9:125–146.

———, and J. Dan. 1973. The human degradation of Mediterranean landscapes in Israel. In DiCastri, F., and H. A. Mooney, eds., *Mediterranean-type Ecosystems: Origin and Structure.* Berlin: Springer-Verlag. Pp. 373–390.

———, and A. S. Lieberman. 1984. *Landscape Ecology. Theory and Application.* New York: Springer-Verlag.

Needham, J. 1954. *Science and Civilization in China.* Cambridge, England: Cambridge University Press.

Neef, E. 1963. Topologische und chorologische Arbeitsweisen in der Landschaftsforschung. *Petermanns Geogr. Mitt.* 107:249–259.

———. 1967. *Die Theoretischen Grundlagen der Landschaftslehre.* Geographisch-Kartographische Anstalt Gotha. Leipzig: Hermann Haack.

———. 1968. Der Physiotop als Zentralbegriff der Komplexen Physischen Geographie. *Petermanns Geogr. Mitt.* 112:15–23.

Nicholson, M. 1970. *The Environmental Revolution.* New York: McGraw-Hill.

Niemi, A. 1969. On the railway vegetation and flora between Esbo and Inga, southern Finland. *Acta Bot. Fenn.* 83:1–28.

Niering, W. A., and R. H. Goodwin. 1974. Creation of relatively stable shrublands with herbicides: arresting succession on rights-of-way and pastureland. *Ecology* 55:784–795.

Nip-Van der Voort, J., R. Hengeveld, and J. Haeck. 1979. Immigration rates of plant species in three Dutch polders. *J. Biogeogr.* 6:310–318.

Noble, I. R., and R. O. Slatyer. 1978. The effect of disturbances on plant succession. *Proc. Ecol. Soc. Austral.* 10:135–145.

Noss, R. F. 1983. A regional landscape approach to maintain diversity. *BioScience* 33:700–706.

Noy-Meir, I. 1973. Desert ecosystems: environments and producers. *Ann. Rev. Ecol. Systematics* 4:25–51.

Nye, P. H., and D. J. Greenland. 1960. *The Soil Under Shifting Cultivation.*

Harpenden, England: Commonwealth Agricultural Bureau of Soils. Technical Communication 51.

Odum, E. P. 1959. *Fundamentals of Ecology*. Philadelphia: Saunders.

———. 1969. The strategy of ecosystem development. *Science* 164:262–270.

———. 1971. *Fundamentals of Ecology,* 3rd ed. Philadelphia: Saunders.

———, J. T. Finn, and E. H. Franz. 1979. Perturbation theory and the subsidy-stress gradient. *BioScience* 29:349–352.

Odum, H. T. 1957. Trophic structure and productivity of Silver Springs, Florida. *Ecol. Monogr.* 27:55–112.

———. 1983. *Systems Ecology: An Introduction*. New York: Wiley.

———, and E. C. Odum. 1981. *Energy Basis for Man and Nature*. New York: McGraw-Hill.

Oetting, R. B., and J. F. Cassel. 1971. Waterfowl nesting on interstate highway right-of-way in North Dakota. *J. Wildl. Manage.* 35:774–781.

Oldemeyer, J. L., W. J. Barmore, and D. L. Gilbert. 1971. Winter ecology of bighorn sheep in Yellowstone National Park. *J. Wildl. Manage.* 35:252–269.

Oliver, C. D., and E. P. Stephens. 1977. Reconstruction of a mixed-species forest in central New England. *Ecology* 58:562–572.

O'Loughlin, C. L., and A. J. Pearce. 1976. Influence of Cenozoic geology on mass movements and sediment yield response to forest removal, North Westland, New Zealand. *Bull. Int. Assoc. Engineering Geol.* 14:41–46.

Omernik, J. M., A. R. Abernathy, and L. M. Male. 1981. Stream nutrient levels and proximity of agricultural and forest land to streams: some relationships. *J. Soil Water Conserv.* 36:227–231.

Oosting, H. J. 1942. An ecological analysis of the plant communities of the Piedmont, North Carolina. *Amer. Midl. Natur.* 28:1–126.

Opdam, P. 1984. Methodological problems in interdisciplinary landscape studies. In Brandt, J., and P. Agger, eds., *Proceedings of the First International Seminar on Methodology in Landscape Ecological Research and Planning* (Vol. 2). Roskilde, Denmark: Roskilde Universitetsforlag GeoRuc. Pp. 5–14.

———, H. van Dam, S. M. ten Houte de Lange, J. T. R. Kalkhoven, F. Kragt, and A. H. P. Stumpel. 1983. A comparative study of spatial patterns in a landscape. Leersum, The Netherlands: *Annual Report, Research Institute for Nature Management.* Pp. 66–82.

Orians, G. H., and N. E. Pearson. 1978. On the theory of central place foraging. In Horn, D. J., G. R. Stairs, and R. D. Mitchell, eds., *Analysis of Ecological Systems.* Columbus: Ohio State University Press. Pp. 155–177.

Orndorff, K. A., and G. E. Lang. 1981. Leaf litter redistribution in a West Virginia hardwood forest. *J. Ecol.* 69:225–236.

Orwin, C. S., and C. S. Orwin. 1967. *The Open Fields.* Oxford: Clarendon Press.

Owen, O. 1971. *Natural Resource Conservation*. New York: Macmillan.

*The Oxford English Dictionary* (12 vols. plus supplements). Oxford: Clarendon, 1933.

Oxley, D. J., M. B. Fenton, and G. R. Carmody. 1974. The effects of roads on populations of small mammals. *J. Appl. Ecol.* 11:51–59.

Ozenda, P. 1964. *Biogéographie Végétale*. Paris: Doin.

Paine, R. T. 1966. Food web complexity and species diversity. *Amer. Natur.* 100:65–75.

————, and S. A. Levin. 1981. Intertidal landscapes: disturbance and the dynamics of pattern. *Ecol. Monogr.* 51:145–178.

Park, R. E. 1968. *Human Communities. The City and Human Ecology.* New York: The Free Press.

Parton, W. J., W. D. Gould, F. J. Adamsen, S. Torbit, and R. G. Woodmansee. 1980. $NH_3$ volitilization model. In Van Veen, , and Frissel, eds., *Simulation of Nitrogen Behavior in Soil-plant Systems.* Wageningen: Centre for Agricultural Publication and Documentation. Pp. 233–244.

Pattee, H. H. 1973. *Hierarchy Theory: The Challenge of Complex Systems.* New York: Braziller.

Patterson, R. D., and K. D. Haze. 1979. Micrometeorological study of an urban valley. *Boundary Layer Meteorol.* 17:175–186.

Patton, D. R. 1975. A diversity index for quantifying habitat edge. *Wildl. Soc. Bull.* 394:171–173.

Pechanec, J. F., and G. Stewart. 1940. Sagebrush-grass range sampling studies: size and structure of sampling unit. *Amer. Soc. Agron. Jour.* 32:669–682.

Pecsi, M., and S. Samogyi. 1969. Subdivision and classification of the physiographic landscapes and geomorphological regions of Hungary. In *Research Problems in Applied Geography.* Budapest: Akad. Kiado. Pp. 7–24.

Peden, L. M., J. S. Williams, and W. E. Frayer. 1973. A Markov model for stand projection. *Forest Sci.* 19:303–314.

Peet, R. K. 1974. The measurement of species diversity. *Ann. Rev. Ecol. Systematics* 5:285–307.

————, and O. L. Loucks. 1977. A gradient analysis of southern Wisconsin forests. *Ecology* 58:485–499.

Pellek, R. 1983. Depletion of the Mauritanian forest. *J. Forestry* 81:320–321.

Penck, A. 1910. Versuch einer Klimaklassification auf Physiographischer Grundlage. *Sitzler Pr. Ak. Wiss.* 12:236–246.

Penman, H. 1948. Natural evaporation from open water, bare soil and grass. *Proc. Roy. Soc. London A* 193:120–145.

Perrier, A. 1975. Etude physique de l'évapotranspiration dans les conditions naturelles. *Ann. Agron.* 26:1–18, 105–123, 229–243.

Perrier de la Bathie, B. 1921. *La Végétation Malgache.* Paris: Challamel.

Peterken, G. F. 1974. A method of assessing woodland flora for conservation using indicator species. *Biol. Conserv.* 6:239–245.

————. 1976. Long-term changes in the woodlands of Rockingham Forest and other areas. *J. Ecol.* 64:123–146.

————. 1977. Habitat conservation priorities in British and European woodlands. *Biol. Conserv.* 11:223–236.

Peters, P. A. 1978. Spacing of roads and landings to minimize timber harvest cost. *Forest Sci.* 24:209–217.

Peterson, R. L. 1955. *North American Moose.* Toronto: University of Toronto Press.

Petrides, G. A. 1942. Relation of hedgerows in winter to wildlife in central New York. *J. Wildl. Manage.* 6:261–280.

Pfister, R. D., and S. F. Arno. 1980. Classifying forest habitat types based on potential climax vegetation. *Forest Sci.* 26:52–70.

Phillipson, J., R. J. Putnam, J. Steel, and S. R. J. Woodell. 1975. Litter input, litter decomposition and the evolution of carbon dioxide in a beech woodland—Wytham Wood, Oxford. *Oecologia* 20:203–217.

Phipps, M. 1981a. Entropy and community pattern analysis. *J. Theor. Biol.* 93:253–273.

———. 1981b. Information theory and landscape analysis. In Tjallingii, S. P., and A. A. de Veer, eds., *Perspectives in Landscape Ecology.* Wageningen: Centre for Agricultural Publication and Documentation. Pp. 57–64.

———. 1984. Rural landscape dynamics: the illustration of some key concepts. In Brandt, J., and P. Agger, eds., *Proceedings of the First International Seminar on Methodology in Landscape Ecological Research and Planning* (Vol. 1). Roskilde, Denmark: Roskilde Universitetsforlag GeoRuc. Pp. 47–54.

Pianka, E. R. 1966. Latitudinal gradients in species diversity: a review of concepts. *Amer. Natur.* 100:33–46.

Pickett, S. T. A. 1976. Succession: an evolutionary interpretation. *Amer. Natur.* 110:107–119.

———. 1980. Non-equilibrium coexistence of plants. *Bull. Torrey Bot. Club* 107:238–248.

———. 1982. Population patterns through twenty years of old-field succession. *Vegetatio* 49:45–59.

———, and J. N. Thompson. 1978. Patch dynamics and the design of nature reserves. *Biol. Conserv.* 13:27–37.

Pielou, E. C. 1965. The spatial pattern of two-phase patchworks of vegetation. *Biometrics* 20:156–167.

———. 1966. Species-diversity and pattern-diversity in the study of ecological succession. *J. Theoret. Biol.* 10:370–383.

———. 1967. A test for random mingling of the phases of a mosaic. *Biometrics* 23:657–670.

———. 1969. *An Introduction to Mathematical Ecology.* New York: Wiley.

———. 1974. *Population and Community Ecology.* New York: Gordon and Breach.

———. 1977. *Mathematical Ecology.* New York: Wiley.

———. 1979. *Biogeography.* New York: Wiley.

Pigott, C. D., and K. Taylor. 1964. The distribution of some woodland herbs in relation to the supply of nitrogen and phosphorus in the soil. *J. Ecol.* 52 (Suppl.):175–185.

Pihan, J. 1976. Bocage et érosion hydrique des sols en Bretagne. In *Les Bocages: Histoire, Ecologie, Economie.* Institut National de la Recherche Agronomique, Centre National de la Recherche Scientifique, Université de Rennes. Rennes, France. Pp. 185–192.

Pillet, P. 1981. Organisation et évolution des unités écologiques du parc national des Cévennes. *Bull. Ecol.* 12:187–224.

Pimentel, D. 1961. An ecological approach to the insecticide problem. *J. Econ. Entomol.* 54:108–114.

———, and C. A. Edwards. 1982. Pesticides and ecosystems. *BioScience* 32:595–600.

———, W. Dritschilo, J. Krummel, and J. Kutzman. 1975. Energy and land constraints in food protein production. *Science* 190:254–261.

———, J. Drummel, D. Gallahan, J. Hough, A. Merrill, I. Schreiner, P. Vittum,

F. Koziol, E. Back, D. Yen, and S. Fiance. 1978. Benefits and costs of pesticide use in United States food production. *BioScience* 28:772, 778–784.

Pimm, S. L. 1982. *Food Webs.* New York: Chapman and Hall.

———, and J. H. Lawton. 1978. On feeding on more than one trophic level. *Nature* 275:542–544.

Pires, J. M., T. Dobzhansky, and G. A. Black. 1953. An estimate of the number of species of trees in an Amazonian forest community. *Bot. Gaz.* 114:467–477.

Platt, W. J. 1975. The colonization and formation of equilibrium plant species associations on badger disturbances in a tall-grass prairie. *Ecol. Monogr.* 45:285–305.

Poissonet, J., M. Godron, P. Poissonet, and G. Long. 1973. A comparison of sampling methods in dense herbaceous vegetation. *J. Range Manage.* 26:65–67.

Pollard, E. 1968. Hedges. III. A comparison between the Carabidae of a hedge and field site and those of woodland glades. *J. Appl. Ecol.* 5:649–656.

———. 1971. Hedges. VI. Habitat diversity and crop pests: a study of *Brevicoryne brassicae* and its syrphid predators. *J. Appl. Ecol.* 8:751–780.

———, M. D. Hooper, and N. W. Moore. 1974. *Hedges.* London: Collins.

———, and J. Relton. 1970. Hedges. V. A study of small mammals in hedges and cultivated fields. *J. Appl. Ecol.* 7:549–557.

Porteous, I. R. 1981. *Topological Geometry,* 2nd ed. Cambridge: Cambridge University Press.

Portmann, A. 1969. *Animal Forms and Patterns.* New York: Schocken Books.

Powell, E. P. 1900. *Hedges, Windbreaks, Shelters and Live Fences.* New York: Orange Judd.

Preobrazhensky, V. S. 1984. International symposium on landscape ecology. *Soviet Geogr.* 6:453–463.

Presst, I. 1971. An ecological study of the viper *Vipera berus* in southern Britain. *J. Zool.* 164:373–418.

Preston, F. W. 1962. The canonical distribution of commonness and rarity. *Ecology* 3:185–215.

Price, P. W., ed. 1975. *Evolutionary Strategies of Parasitic Insects and Mites.* New York: Plenum.

Prigogine, I., and G. Nicolis. 1971. Biological order, structure and instabilities. *Quart. Rev. Biophys.* 4:107–148.

Puglisi, M. J., J. S. Lindzey, and E. D. Bellis. 1974. Factors associated with highway mortality of white-tailed deer. *J. Wildl. Manage.* 38:799–807.

Pye, V. I., R. Patrick, and J. Quarles. 1983. *Groundwater Contamination in the United States.* Philadelphia: University of Pennsylvania Press.

Rabb, R. L., and G. G. Kennedy, eds. 1979. Movement of highly mobile insects: concepts and methodology in research. In *Proceedings of a Conference on Movement of Selected Species of Lepidoptera in the Southeastern United States.* Raleigh: North Carolina State University.

———, R. E. Stinner, and R. Van den Bosch. 1976. Conservation and augmentation of natural enemies. In Huffaker, D. B., and P. S. Messenger, eds., *Theory and Practice of Biological Control.* New York: Academic Press. Pp. 233–254.

Rackham, O. 1975. *Hayley Wood: Its History and Ecology.* Cambridge: Cambridgeshire and Isle of Ely Naturalists' Trust.

————. 1976. *Trees and Woodlands in the British Landscape*. London: Dent.

————. 1980. *Ancient Woodland*. London: Edward Arnold.

Rambal, S. 1984. Un modèle de simulation du pâturage en Tunisie pré-sahari-enne. *Oecol. Gen.* 5:351–364.

Ramensky, L. G. 1924. Die Grundgesetzmassigkeiten im Aufbau der Vegeta-tionsdecke. *Bot. Centbl., N. F.* 7:453–455.

Ranney, J. W., M. C. Bruner, and J. B. Levenson. 1981. The importance of edge in the structure and dynamics of forest islands. In Burgess, R. L., and D. M. Sharpe, eds., *Forest Island Dynamics in Man-dominated Landscapes*. New York: Springer-Verlag. Pp. 67–96.

————, and W. C. Johnson. 1977. Propagule dispersal among forest islands in southeastern South Dakota. *The Prairie Naturalist* 9:217–244.

Rapoport, A. 1969. *House Form and Culture*. Englewood Cliffs, New Jersey: Prentice Hall.

————. 1982a. *The Meaning of the Built Environment: A Nonverbal Commu-nication Approach*. Beverly Hills: Sage.

Rapoport, E. H. 1982b. *Areography. Geographical Strategies of Species*. Fun-dacion Bariloche Series No. 1. New York: Pergamon Press.

Rapp, A. 1960. Recent developments of mountain slopes in Karkevagge and surroundings, northern Scandinavia. *Geogr. Ann.* 42:71–200.

Ratcliffe, D. A., ed. 1977. *A Nature Conservation Review* (2 Vols.). Cambridge: Cambridge University Press.

Raunet, M. 1979. Importance et interactions des processus géochimiques, hy-drologiques et biologiques (termites) sur les surfaces d'aplanissement tropi-cales granito-gneissiques. *Agron. Tropic.* 34:40–53.

Raunkiaer, C. 1918. Recherches statistiques sur les formations végétales. *Det. Kgl. Danske Vidensk. Selskab. Biologiske Meddeleiser* 13:11–78.

————. 1934. *The Life Forms of Plants and Statistical Plant Geography*. (Being the collected papers of C. Raunkiaer). Oxford: Oxford University Press.

Raup, H. M. 1966. The view from John Sanderson's farm: a perspective for the use of the land. *Forest Hist.* 10:2–11.

————, and R. E. Carlson. 1941. *The History of Land Use in the Harvard Forest*. Petersham, Massachusetts: Harvard Forest Bulletin 20.

Raveling, D. G. 1969a. Roost sites and flight patterns of Canada geese. *J. Wildl. Manage.* 33:319–330.

————. 1969b. Social classes of Canada geese in winter. *J. Wildl. Manage.* 33:304–318.

Ravera, O. 1969. Seasonal variation of the biomass and biocoenotic structure of plankton of the Bay of Ispra (Lago Maggiore). *Verh. int. Ver. Limnol.* 17:237–254.

Regniere, J., R. Rabb, and R. Stinner. 1983. *Papillia japonica* (Coleoptera: Scar-abaeidae): distribution and movement of adults in heterogeneous environ-ments. *Canad. Entomol.* 115:287–294.

Reiners, W. A. 1983. Disturbance and basic properties of ecosystem energetics. In Mooney, H. A., and M. Godron, eds., *Disturbance and Ecosystems*. New York: Springer-Verlag. Pp. 83–96.

————, and G. E. Lang. 1979. Vegetational patterns and processes in the balsam fir zone, White Mountains, New Hampshire. *Ecology* 60:403–417.

Resler, R. A. 1972. Clearcutting: beneficial aspects for wildlife resources. *J. Soil Water Conserv.* 27:250–259.

Rey, P. 1960. *Essai de Cinétique Biogéographique.* Paris: Centre National de la Recherche Scientifique.

Richard, P. 1977. *Histoire Post-Wisconsinienne de la Végétation du Quebec Méridional.* Quebec: Direction Generale des Forêts. 312 pp.

Richards, P. W. M. 1928. Ecological notes on the bryophytes of Middlesex. *J. Ecol.* 16:267–300.

———. 1964. *The Tropical Rain Forest.* Cambridge: Cambridge University Press.

Richardson, L. F. 1926. Atmospheric diffusion shown on a distance-neighbour graph. *Proc. Roy. Soc. London Ser. A* 110:709–737.

Ricou, G., and V. Lecomte. 1976. Influence de la structure bocagère sur l'entomofaune. In *Les Bocages: Histoire, Ecologie, Economie.* Institut National de la Recherche Agronomique, Centre National de la Recherche Scientifique, Université de Rennes. Rennes, France. Pp. 411–417.

Ridley, H. N. 1930. *The Dispersal of Plants Throughout the World.* Kent: L. Reeve.

Ripley, B. D. 1981. *Spatial Statistics.* New York: Wiley.

Risser, P. G., E. C. Birney, H. D. Blocker, S. W. May, W. J. Parton, and J. A. Wiens. 1981. *The True Prairie Ecosystem.* Stroudsburg, Pennsylvania: Hutchinson and Ross.

———, J. R. Karr, and R. T. T. Forman. 1984. *Landscape Ecology: Directions and Approaches.* Champaign: Illinois Natural History Survey, Special Publication 2.

———, and W. J. Parton. 1982. Ecosystem analysis of the tall-grass prairie: nitrogen cycle. *Ecology* 63:1342–1351.

Ritchie, J. C., C. M. Cooper, J. R. McHenry, and F. R. Schiebe. 1983. Sediment accumulation in Lake Chicot, Arkansas. *Environ. Geol.* 5:79–82.

———, and J. R. McHenry. 1977. The distribution of $^{137}$Cs in some watersheds in the eastern United States. *Health Physics* 32:101–105.

Roach, S. A. 1968. *The Theory of Random Clumping.* London: Methuen.

Robbins, C. S. 1980. Effect of forest fragmentation on bird populations. In DeGraaf, R. M., and K. E. Evans, compilers, *Management of North Central and Northeastern Forests for Nongame Birds.* U. S. Dept. Agric., Forest Service General Technical Report NC-51. Pp. 198–212.

Robert, P. 1972. *Dictionnaire de la Langue Francaise.* Paris: Soc. Nouv. Littré.

Robinette, G. O. 1972. *Plants, People and Environmental Quality.* Washington, D.C.: U.S. Dept. Interior, Nat. Park Serv., and Amer. Soc. Landscape Architects Foundation. U.S. Gov. Printing Office.

Rodoman, B. 1970. *The Organized Anthroposphere.* Ekistics 29. No. 175.

Rogers, E. M., and F. F. Shamaker. 1971. *Communication of Innovations.* New York: Free Press.

Romme, W. H. 1982. Fire and landscape diversity in subalpine forest of Yellowstone National Park. *Ecol. Monogr.* 52:199–221.

———, and D. H. Knight. 1982. Landscape diversity: the concept applied to Yellowstone Park. *BioScience* 32:664–670.

Rongstad, O. J., and J. R. Tester. 1969. Movements and habitat use of white-tailed deer in Minnesota. *J. Wildl. Manage.* 33:366–379.

Rood, J. P. 1970. Ecology and social behavior of the desert cavy (*Microcavia australis*). *Amer. Midl. Natur.* 83:415–454.

Root, R. B. 1973. Organization of a plant-arthropod association in simple and diverse habitats: the fauna of collards (*Brassica oleracea*). *Ecol. Monogr.* 43:95–124.

Rosenberg, N. J., B. L. Blad, and S. B. Verma. 1983. *Microclimate: The Biological Environment.* New York: Wiley.

Rossetti, C. 1962. Un dispositif de prises de vues aériennes à basse altitude et ses applications pour l'étude de la physionomie des végétations ouvertes. *Bull. Serv. Carte Phytogeogr. B* 7:211–238.

Rost, G. R., and J. A. Bailey. 1979. Distribution of mule deer and elk in relation to roads. *J. Wildl. Manage.* 43:634–641.

Roughgarden, J. D. 1978. Influence of competition on patchiness in a random environment. *Theoret. Pop. Biol.* 14:185–203.

Rouse, W. R. 1984a. Microclimate at arctic tree line. 1. Radiation balance of tundra and forest. *Water Resour. Res.* 20:57–66.

———. 1984b. Microclimate at arctic tree line. 2. Soil microclimate of tundra and forest. *Water Resour. Res.* 20:67–73.

Row, C. 1978. Economies of tract size in timber growing. *J. Forestry* 76:576–582.

Rowe, P. B. 1963. Streamflow increases after removing woodland-riparian vegetation from a southern California watershed. *J. Forestry* 61:365–370.

Rowe, S. J. 1972. *Forest Regions of Canada.* Canadian Forest Service Publication 1300. 172 pp.

———, and J. W. Sheard. 1981. Ecological land classification: a survey approach. *Environ. Manage.* 5:451–464.

Royama, T. 1984. Population dynamics of the spruce budworm *Choristoneura fumiferana. Ecol. Monogr.* 54:429–462.

Roze, F. 1981. Caractérisation et évaluation de l'importance des haies lors des pré-études écologiques aux operations de remembrement. In Gehu, J. M., and A. Delelis-Dusollier, eds., *Phytosociologie et Remembrement des Terres.*

Ruhe, R. V., and P. H. Walker. 1968. Hillslope models and soil formation. I. Open systems. *Int. Congr. Soil Sci. Trans.* 4:551–560.

———. 1975. *Geomorphology, Geomorphic Processes and Surficial Geology.* Boston: Houghton Mifflin.

Rumney, G. R. 1968. *Climatology and the World's Climates.* New York: Macmillan.

Runkle, J. R. 1981. Gap regeneration in some old-growth forests of the eastern United States. *Ecology* 62:1041–1051.

Russell, E. W. B. 1983. Indian set fires in the forests of the northeastern United States. *Ecology* 64:78–88.

Ruthsatz, B. 1983. Kleinstrukturen im Raum Ingolstadt: Schutz- und Ziegerwert Teil I: Hochstaudenfluren an Entwasserungsgraben. *Tuexenia* 3:365–388.

———, and W. Haber. 1981. The significance of small-scale landscape elements in rural areas as refuges for endangered plant species. In Tjallingii, S. P., and A. A. de Veer, eds., *Perspectives in Landscape Ecology.* Wageningen: Centre for Agricultural Publication and Documentation. Pp. 117–124.

Ruzicka, M., A. Jurko, M. Kozova, F. Zigrai, and V. Svetlosanov. 1982. Evaluation methods of landscape stability on agricultural territories in Slovakia. In *Proceedings of the VIth International Symposium on Problems in Landscape Ecological Research*. Bratislava, Czechoslovakia: Institute for Experimental Biology and Ecology. Pp. 1–31.

————, and L. Miklos. 1981. Methodology of ecological landscape evaluation for optimal development of territory. In Tjallingii, S. P., and A. A. de Veer, eds., *Perspectives in Landscape Ecology*. Wageningen: Centre for Agricultural Publication and Documentation. Pp. 99–107.

————, and L. Miklos. 1984. Methodology of syntheses in landscape ecological planning—LANDEP. In Brandt, J., and P. Agger, eds., *Proceedings of the First International Seminar on Methodology in Landscape Ecological Research and Planning*. Roskilde, Denmark: Roskilde Universitetsforlag GeoRuc. Pp. 163–174.

————, H. Ruzickova, and F. Zigrai. 1978. Krajinne zlozky, prvky a struktura V biologickon planovani krajinpy. *Quaestiones Geobiologicae* 23:7–63.

Rydberg, P. A. 1954. *Flora of the Rocky Mountains and Adjacent Plains*. 2nd ed. New York: Hafner.

Saarinen, E. 1965. *The City*. Cambridge, Massachusetts: M. I. T. Press.

Sabados, K., and M. Manica. 1977. Alimentation du mouflon en Slovaquie en dehors de la période de croissance. *Folia Venatoria* 7:81–94.

Saint-Girons, H. 1976. Les petits mammifères dans l'écosystème du bocage. In *Les Bocages: Histoire, Ecologie, Economie*. Institut National de la Recherche Agronomique, Centre National de la Recherche Scientifique, Université de Rennes. Rennes, France. Pp. 343–346.

————, and R. Duguy. 1976. Les reptiles du bocage. In *Les Bocages: Histoire, Ecologie, Economie*. Institut National de la Recherche Agronomique, Centre National de la Recherche Scientifique, Université de Rennes. Rennes, France. Pp. 347–349.

Sands, A. 1980. *Riparian Forests in California: Their Ecology and Conservation*. Davis, California: Institute of Ecology, University of California.

Satoo, T., and H. A. I. Madgwick. 1982. *Forest Biomass*. The Hague: Martinus Nijhoff/Junk.

Sauer, C. O. 1925. The morphology of landscapes. *Univ. Calif. Publ. Geogr.* 2:19–53.

————. 1952. *Agricultural Origins and Dispersals*. New York: American Geographical Society.

————. 1963. The morphology of landscapes. In Leighly, J., ed., *Land and Life: A Selection from the Writings of Carl Ortura Sauer*. Berkeley: University of California Press. Pp. 315–350.

Savage, J. M. 1960. Evolution of a peninsula herpetofauna. *Systematic Zool.* 9:184–212.

Schemnitz, S. D., ed. 1980. *Wildlife Management Techniques Manual*. 4th ed. Washington, D. C.: The Wildlife Society.

Schimper, A. F. W. 1903. *Plant-Geography*. Revised ed. 2 vols. Oxford: Oxford University Press.

————. 1935. *Pflanzen-geographie auf Physiologischer Grundlage*. 2 vols. Jena: Gustav Fischer.

Schlenker, G. 1964. Entwicklung des in Sudwestdeutschland angewandten Verfahrens der forstlichen Standortskunde. In *Standort, Wald und Waldwirtschaft in Oberschwaben, "Oberschwabische Fichtenreviere."* Stuttgart: Pp. 5–26.

Schlesinger, W. H., and W. A. Reiners. 1974. Deposition of water and cations on artificial foliar collectors in fir krummholz of New England mountains. *Ecology* 55:378–386.

Schlosser, I. J., and J. R. Karr. 1981a. Water quality in agricultural watersheds: impact of riparian vegetation during base flow. *Water Resources Bull.* 17:233–240.

———. 1981b. Riparian vegetation and channel morphology impact on spatial patterns of water quality in agricultural watersheds. *Environ. Manage.* 5:233–243.

Schmid, J. A. 1975. *Urban Vegetation: A Review and Chicago Case Study.* Chicago: University of Chicago, Department of Geography Research Paper 161. 266 pp.

Schmithusen, J. 1963. Der wissenschaftliche Landschaftsbegriff. *Mitt. flor. soz. Arbgem. N. F. (Stolzenau/Weser.)* 10:9–19.

———. 1964. *Was ist eine Landschaft?* Erkundliches Wissen, Part 9. Wiesbaden: Franz Steiner.

———. 1967. *Fliesengefuge der Landschaft und Oekotop.* Zum Gegenstand und zur Methode der Geographie, Darmstadt, West Germany. Pp. 444–464.

Schoener, T. W. 1971. Theory of feeding strategies. *Ann. Rev. Ecol. Systematics* 2:369–404.

Schreiber, K. F. 1968. Les conditions thermiques du canton de Vaud. *Beitr. Geobot. Landesaufn. Schweiz.* 49:1–31.

———. 1977. Landscape planning and protection of the environment. *Appl. Sci. and Develop.* 9:128–139.

Schreiber, R. K., and J. H. Graves. 1977. Powerline corridors as possible barriers to the movement of small mammals. *Amer. Midl. Natur.* 97:504–508.

Schuerholz, G. 1974. Quantitative evaluation of edge from aerial photographs. *J. Wildl. Manage.* 38:913–920.

Schumm, S. A. 1956. Evolution of drainage basins and slopes in badlands at Perth Amboy, New Jersey. *Bull. Geol. Soc. Amer.* 67:595–646.

Schuster, L. 1950. Uber den sammeltrieb des Eichelhahers (*Garrulus glandarius*). *Vogelwelt* 62:239–240.

Sears, P. B. 1962. *The Biology of the Living Landscape; An Introduction to Ecology.* London: Allen and Unwin.

Section d'Agriculture de l'Institut de France. 1822. *Nouveau Cours Complet d'Agriculture* (Vol. 8). Paris.

Seib, R. L. 1980. Baja California. A peninsula for rodents but not for reptiles. *Amer. Natur.* 115:613–620.

Seignobos, C. 1978. Les systèmes de defense végétaux pré-coloniaux. *Annals de l'Université de Tchad, Serie Lettres, Langues Vivantes et Sciences Humaines.* Numero Special. Tchad (Chad).

Shaffer, M. L. 1981. Minimum population sizes for species conservation. *BioScience* 31:131–134.

Shannon, C. E., and W. Weaver. 1949. *The Mathematical Theory of Communications.* Urbana: University of Illinois Press.

Shannon, N. M., R. J. Hudson, V. C. Brink, and W. D. Kitts. 1975. Determinants of spatial distribution of Rocky Mountain bighorn sheep. *J. Wildl. Manage.* 39:387–401.

Sharpe, C. F. S. 1938. *Landslides and Related Phenomena.* New York: Columbia University Press.

Sharpe, D. M., F. W. Stearns, R. L. Burgess, and W. C. Johnson. 1981. Spatio-temporal patterns of forest ecosystems in man-dominated landscapes of the eastern United States. In Tjallingii, S. P., and A. A. de Veer, eds., *Perspectives in Landscape Ecology.* Wageningen: Centre for Agricultural Publication and Documentation. Pp. 109–116.

*The Shelterbelt Project.* 1934. (Published statements by numerous separate authors.) *J. Forestry* 32:952–991.

Shirer, H. W., and J. F. Downhower. 1969. Radiotracking of dispersing yellow bellied marmots. *Trans. Kansas Acad. Sci.* 71:463–479.

Shugart, H. H., Jr., T. R. Crow, and J. M. Hett. 1973. Forest succession models: a rationale and methodology for modeling forest succession over large regions. *Forest Sci.* 19:203–212.

———, and D. C. West. 1981. Long-term dynamics of forest ecosystems. *Amer. Scientist* 69:647–652.

Siccama, T. G., G. Weir, and K. Wallace. 1976. Ice damage in a mixed hardwood forest in Connecticut in relation to *Vitis* infestation. *Bull. Torrey Bot. Club* 103:180–183.

Simberloff, D. S. 1976. Experimental zoogeography of islands: effects of island size. *Ecology* 57:629–648.

———, and L. G. Abele. 1976. Island biogeography theory and conservation practice. *Science* 191:285–286.

———, and E. O. Wilson. 1970. Experimental zoogeography of islands: a two-year record of colonization. *Ecology* 51:934–937.

Simonds, J. O. 1983. *Landscape Architecture: A Manual of Site Planning and Design.* New York: McGraw-Hill.

Simpson, G. G. 1964. Species density of North American recent mammals. *Syst. Zool.* 13:57–73.

Sinclair, A. R. E., and M. Norton-Griffiths, eds. 1979. *Serengeti. Dynamics of an Ecosystem.* Chicago: University of Chicago Press.

Sinclair, N. R., L. L. Getz, and F. S. Bock. 1967. Influence of stone walls on the local distribution of small mammals. *Univ. Conn. Occas. Papers Biol. Sci. Series* 1:43–62.

Sivery, G. 1977. *Structures Agraires et Vie Rurale dans le Hainaut à la Fin du Moyen Age.* Lille, France: Publications de l'Université de Lille III.

Slatkin, M. 1974. Competition and regional coexistence. *Ecology* 55:128–134.

Smith, A. J. 1975. Invasion and ecesis of bird-disseminated woody plants in a temperate forest sere. *Ecology* 56:19–34.

Smith, D. M. 1962. *The Practice of Silviculture.* New York: Wiley.

Smith, F. E. 1972. Spatial heterogeneity, stability, and diversity in ecosystems. In Deevey, E. S., ed., *Growth by Intussusception. Ecological Essays in Honor of G. Evelyn Hutchinson. Trans. Conn. Acad. Sci.* 44:309–335.

Smith, R. L. 1979. *Ecology and Field Biology.* New York: Harper and Row.

Smith, W. H. 1971. Lead contamination of roadside white pine. *Forest Sci.* 17:195–198.

Smith, W. P. 1983. A bivariate normal test for elliptical home-range models: biological implications and recommendations. *J. Wildl. Manage.* 47:613–619.

Snow, D. W. 1965. The relationship between census results and the breeding population of birds on farmland. *Bird Study* 12:287–304.

Snyder, D. P. 1950. Bird communities of the coniferous forest biome. *Condor* 52:17–27.

Soil Survey Staff. 1975. *Soil Taxonomy: A Basic System of Soil Classification for Making and Interpreting Soil Surveys.* Washington, D. C.: U. S. Dept. Agric., Soil Conservation Service, Agriculture Handbook 436.

Sochava, V. B. 1967. *Problèmes Théoriques de la Régionalisation Naturelle et l'Expérience des Recherches dans cette Direction en Sibérie.* Prague: Geographie Congrés.

Soulavie, J. L. 1780–1784. *Histoire Naturelle de la France Méridionale.* Paris, Nîmes: Quillan.

Soule, M. E., and B. A. Wilcox. 1980. *Conservation Biology.* Sunderland, Massachusetts: Sinauer Associates.

Soule, M. E., B. A. Wilcox, and C. Holtby. 1979. Benign neglect: a model of faunal collapse in the game reserves of east Africa. *Biol. Conserv.* 15:259–272.

Sousa, W. P. 1980. The responses of a community to disturbance: the importance of successional age and species' life histories. *Oecologia* 45:72–81.

Southwood, T. R. E., and M. J. Way. 1970. Ecological background to pest management. In Rabb, R. L., and F. E. Guthrie, eds., *Concepts in Pest Management.* Raleigh: North Carolina State University. Pp. 6–29.

Speight, J. G. 1976. Towards explicit procedures for mapping natural landscapes. *XXIII Congr. Int. Geogr. (Moscow)* 5:126–130.

Spirn, A. W. 1984. *The Granite Garden. Urban Nature and Human Design.* New York: Basic Books.

Spooner, B., and H. S. Mann, eds. 1982. *Desertification and Development: Dryland Ecology in a Social Perspective.* London: Academic Press.

Sprugel, D. G. 1976. Dynamic structure of wave-regenerated *Abies balsamea* forest in the northeastern United States. *J. Ecol.* 64:889–911.

Spurr, S. H., and B. V. Barnes. 1980. *Forest Ecology,* 3rd ed. New York: Wiley.

Staines, B. W. 1976. The use of natural shelter by red deer (*Cervus elaphus*) in relation to weather in Northeast Scotland. *J. Zool. London* 180:1–8.

Stapleton, J., and E. Kiviat. 1979. Rights of birds and rights of way. *Amer. Birds* 33:7–10.

Stearns, F. W., and R. Montag, eds. 1974. *The Urban Ecosystem: A Holistic Approach.* Stroudsburg, Pennsylvania: Dowden, Hutchinson and Ross.

Steavenson, H. A., H. E. Gearhart, and R. L. Curtis. 1943. Living fences and supplies of fence posts. *J. Wildl. Manage.* 7:256–261.

Steinitz, C. 1979. Simulating alternative policies for implementing the Massachusetts Scenic and Recreational Rivers Act: The North River Demonstration Project. *Landscape Plann.* 6:51–89.

Stenseth, N. C. 1977. The importance of spatio-temporal heterogeneity for the population dynamics of rodents: towards a theoretical foundation of rodent control. *Oikos* 29:545–552.

————. 1981. How to control pest species: application of models from the theory of island biogeography in formulating pest control strategies. *J. Appl. Ecol.* 18:773–794.

Stewart, G., W. P. Cottam, and S. S. Hutchings. 1940. Influence of unrestricted grazing on northern salt desert plant associations in western Utah. *J. Agric. Res.* 60:289–316.

Stiles, E. W. 1979. Animal communities of the New Jersey Pine Barrens. In Forman, R. T. T., ed., *Pine Barrens: Ecosystem and Landscape*. New York: Academic Press. Pp. 541–553.

————. 1980. Patterns of fruit presentation and seed dispersal in bird-disseminated woody plants in the Eastern Deciduous Forest. *Amer. Natur.* 116:670–688.

Stilgoe, J. R. 1981. Fair fields and blasted rock. American land classification systems and landscape aesthetics. *Amer. Studies* 22:21–33.

Stinner, R. R., R. L. Rabb, and J. R. Bradley, Jr. 1977. Natural factors operating in the population dynamics of *Heliothis zea* in North Carolina. In *Proc. XV Int. Congr. Entomol.* Washington, D. C. Pp. 622–642.

Stoddart, D. 1965. The shape of coral atolls. *Marine Geol.* 3:369–383.

Stolina, M. 1982. Stabilita smredovych ekosystemov prirodzenych a kulturnych lesov. *Ekologia (CSSR)* 1:237–250.

Storm, G. L., R. D. Andrews, R. L. Phillips, R. A. Bishop, D. B. Sniff, and J. R. Tester. 1976. Morphology, reproduction, dispersal and mortality of midwestern red fox populations. *Wildl. Monogr.* 49:5–82.

Strahler, A. N. 1952. Hypsometric (area-altitude) analysis of erosional topography. *Bull. Geol. Soc. Amer.* 63:1117–1142.

Strahler, A. N. 1957. Quantitative analysis of watershed geomorphology. *Trans. Amer. Geophys. Union* 38:913–920.

Strojan, C. L. 1978. Forest leaf litter decomposition in the vicinity of a zinc smelter. *Oecologia* 32:203–212.

Stumpel, A. H. P., and J. R. T. Kalkhoven. 1978. A vegetation map of the Netherlands based on the relationship between ecotopes and types of potential natural vegetation. *Vegetatio* 37:163–173.

Stumpf, W. A., and C. O. Mohr. 1962. Linearity of home range of California mice and other animals. *J. Wildl. Manage.* 26:149–154.

Sugihara, G. 1983. Peeling apart nature. *Nature* 304:94.

Sukachev, V., and N. Dylis. 1964. *Fundamentals of Forest Biocoenology*. Edinburgh and London: Oliver and Boyd.

Suominen, J. 1969. The plant cover of Finnish railway embankments and the ecology of their species. *Ann. Bot. Fenn.* 6:183–235.

Swank, W. T., and J. E. Douglass. 1974. Streamflow greatly reduced by converting deciduous hardwood stands to pine. *Science* 185:857–859.

Swanson, F. J., R. L. Fredriksen, and F. M. McCorison. 1982. Material transfer in a western Oregon forested watershed. In Edmonds, R. L., ed., *Analysis of Coniferous Forest Ecosystems in the Western United States*. Stroudsburg, Pennsylvania: Hutchinson Ross. Pp. 233–266.

Swingland, I. R., and P. J. Greenwood, eds. 1983. *The Ecology of Animal Movement*. Oxford: Clarendon Press.

Taaffe, E. J., and H. L. Gauthier, Jr. 1973. *Geography of Transportation*. Englewood Cliffs, New Jersey: Prentice Hall.

Talbot, L. M., and M. H. Talbot. 1963. *The Wildebeest in Western Masailand*. Washington, D. C.: The Wildlife Society, Wildlife Monograph 12.

Tamm, C. O., and T. Troedsson. 1955. An example of the amounts of plant nutrients supplied to the ground in road dust. *Oikos* 6:61–70.

Tansley, A. G. 1935. The use and abuse of vegetational concepts and terms. *Ecology* 16:284–307.

———, and R. S. Adamson. 1925. Studies on the vegetation of the English chalk. III. The chalk grasslands of the Hampshire-Sussex border. *J. Ecol.* 13:177–223.

Taylor, M. E. 1971. Bone disease and fractures in east African viverrids. *Can. J. Zool.* 49:1035–1042.

Taylor, M. W. 1977. A comparison of three edge indexes. *Wildl. Soc. Bull.* 5:192–193.

Taylor, R. J., and P. J. Regal. 1978. The peninsular effect on species diversity and the biogeography of Baja California. *Amer. Natur.* 112:583–593.

Tedrow, J. C. F. 1977. *Soils of the Polar Landscapes*. New Brunswick, New Jersey: Rutgers University Press.

Telfer, E. S. 1974. Logging as a factor in wildlife ecology in the boreal forest. *For. Chron.* 50:186–190.

Terborgh, J. 1974. Preservation of natural diversity: the problem of extinction prone species. *BioScience* 24:715–722.

———. 1976. Island biogeography and conservation: strategy and limitations. *Science* 193:1029–1030.

———, and B. Winter. 1983. A method for siting parks and reserves with special reference to Colombia and Ecuador. *Biol. Conserv.* 27:45–58.

Termier, H., and G. Termier. 1968. *Biologie et Ecologie des Premiers Fossiles*. Paris: Masson.

Tester, J. R., and K. L. Heezen. 1965. Deer response to a drive census determined by radio tracking. *BioScience* 15:100–104.

Thellung, A. 1905. Einteilung der Ruderal- und Adventivflora in genetische Gruppen. *Vjschr. Naturf. Ges. Zurich* 50:232–305.

Thom, R. 1969. Topological models in biology. *Topology* 8:313–335.

———. 1977. *Stabilité Structurelle et Morphogenèse*. 2nd ed. Paris: Inter-Editions.

Thomas, J. W., ed. 1979. *Wildlife Habitats in Managed Forests: The Blue Mountains of Oregon and Washington*. U. S. Dept. Agric., Forest Service, Agriculture Handbook 553.

———, H. Black, Jr., R. J. Scherzinger, and R. J. Peterson. 1979. Deer and elk. In Thomas, J. W., ed, *Wildlife Habitats in Managed Forests of the Blue Mountains of Oregon and Washington*. U. S. Dept. Agric., Forest Service, Agriculture Handbook 553. Pp. 104–127.

———, R. J. Miller, H. Black, J. E. Rodiek, and C. Maser. 1976. Guidelines for maintaining and enhancing wildlife habitat in forest management in the Blue Mountains of Oregon and Washington. *Trans. North Amer. Wildl. and Natur. Resour. Conf.* 41:452–476.

Thomas, W., Jr., ed. 1955. *Man's Role in Changing the Face of the Earth*. Chicago: University of Chicago Press.

Thompson, D. 1961. *On Growth and Form* (abridged ed.). Bonner, J. T., ed. Cambridge: Cambridge University Press.

Thompson, H. R. 1958. The statistical study of plant distribution patterns using a grid of quadrats. *Austral. J. Bot.* 6:322–343.

Thompson, J. N., and M. F. Willson. 1978. Disturbance and the dispersal of fleshy fruits. *Science* 200:1161–1163.

Thompson, W. A., I. B. Vertinsky, and W. G. Wellington. 1979. The dynamics of outbreaks: further simulation experiments with western tent caterpillar. *Res. Pop. Ecol.* 20:188–200.

Tjallingii, S. P., and A. A. de Veer, eds. 1981. *Perspectives in Landscape Ecology.* Wageningen: Centre for Agricultural Publication and Documentation.

Tomek, W. 1973. Birds of the western part of the Ciezkowice uplands (translated from Polish). *Acta Zoologica Cracoviensia* 18:437–497.

Trabaud, L. 1984. Changements structuraux apparaissant dans une garrigue de chêne kermés soumise à différents régimes de feux contrôlés. *Oecol. Applic.* 5:127–143.

Tribus, M., and E. McIrvine. 1971. Energy and information. *Sci. Amer.* 225:179–184.

Tricart, J. 1965. *Principes et Methodes de la Geomorphologie.* Paris: Masson.

Trimble, G. R., and E. H. Tryon. 1966. Crown encroachment into openings cut in Appalachian hardwood stands. *J. Forestry* 64:104–108.

Troll, C. 1950. Die geographische Landschaft und ihre Erforschung. *Studium Generale (Heidelberg)* 3:163–181.

———. 1966. *Okologische Landschaftsforschung und Vergleichende Hochge-birgsforschung.* Erdkundliches Wissen. Schriflenfolge fur Forschung und Praxis. Heft II. Wiesbaden: Franz Steiner.

———. 1968. Landschaftsokologie. In Tuxen, R., ed., *Pflanzensoziologie und Landschaftsokologie.* The Hague: Junk. Pp. 1–21.

———. 1971. Landscape ecology (geo-ecology) and bio-ceonology—a terminology study. *Geoforum* 8:43–46.

Tuan, Y. 1974. Space and place: humanistic perspective. *Progr. in Geogr.* 6:211–252.

Tuxen, R. 1955. Das System der nordwestdeutschen Pflanzengesellschaften. *Mitt. Forist.-soziol. Arbeitsgem.* 5:155–176.

———. 1967. Ausdauernde nitrophile Saumgesellschaften Mitteleuropas. *Contributions Botaniques de Cluj,* 431–453.

Udvardy, M. D. F. 1970. *Dynamic Zoogeography, with Special Reference to Land Mammals.* New York: Van Nostrand Reinhold.

Ulbrich, J. 1930. Die Bisamratte: Lebensweise, Gang ihrer Ausbreitung in Europa, wirschaftliche Bedeutung und Bekampfung. Dresden.

Ulrich, R. S. 1984. View through a window may influence recovery from surgery. *Science* 224:420–421.

United Nations, 1977. *Desertification: Its Causes and Consequences.* Oxford: Pergamon.

Urquhart, F. A. 1960. *The Monarch Butterfly.* Toronto: University of Toronto Press.

U. S. Environmental Protection Agency. 1972. *Noise Pollution.* Washington, D.C.: U. S. Government Printing Office. 13 pp.

Usher, M. B. 1979. Markovian approaches to ecological succession. *J. Animal Ecol.* 48:413–426.

Van Ballenberghe, V., and J. M. Peek. 1971. Radiotelemetry studies of moose in northeastern Minnesota. *J. Wildl. Manage.* 35:63–71.

Van den Bosch, R., and A. D. Telford. 1964. Environmental modification and biological control. In DeBach, P., ed., *Biological Control of Insect Pests and Weeds.* New York: Reinhold. Pp. 459–488.

Van der Hammen, T., and G. Correal Urrego. 1978. Prehistoric man on the Sabana de Bogotá: Data for an ecological prehistory. *Paleogeogr., Paleoclimatol., Paleoecol.* 25:179–190. (Reprinted in Van der Hammen, T., ed. 1978. *The Quaternary of Colombia.* Vol. 6. Amsterdam: Elsevier. Pp. 179–190).

Van der Maarel, E. 1980. Towards an ecological theory of nature management. *Verh. Gesellschaft fur Okologie* 9:13–24.

———, and A. H. P. Stumpel. 1974. Landschaftsokologische Kartierung und Bewertung in den Niederlanden. *Verh. Gesellsch. fur Okologie* 3:231–240.

Van der Pijl, L. 1969. *Principles of Dispersal in Higher Plants.* Berlin: Springer-Verlag.

Van der Plank, J. E. 1960. Analysis of epidemics. In Hansfall, J. G., and A. E. Dimeno, eds., *Plant Pathology, Vol. III. Diseased Population Epidemics and Control.* New York: Academic Press. Pp. 229–289.

Van der Zande, A. N., W. J. der Keurs, and W. J. van der Weijden. 1980. The impact of roads on the densities of four bird species in an open field habitat—evidence of a long-distance effect. *Biol. Conserv.* 18:299–321.

Van Eimern, J., R. Karschon, L. A. Razumova, and G. W. Robertson. 1964. *Windbreaks and Shelterbelts.* World Meteorological Organization Technical Note 59. 188 pp.

Van Hylckama, T. E. A. 1970. Water use by saltcedar. *Water Resources Res.* 6:728–735.

Van Leeuwen, C. G. 1965. Het verband tussen natuurlijke en anthropogene landschapsvormen, bezien vanuit de betrekkingen in grensmilieu's. *Gorteria* 2:93–105.

———. 1966. A relation theoretical approach to pattern and process in vegetation. *Wentia* 15:25–46.

———. 1973. Oecologie en natuurtechniek. *Natuur en Landschap.* 27:57–67.

———. 1982. From ecosystem to ecodevice. In Tjallingii, S., and A. de Veer, eds., *Perspectives in Landscape Ecology.* Wageningen: Centre for Agricultural Publication and Documentation. Pp. 29–34.

Van Voris, P., R. V. O'Neill, W. R. Emanuel, and H. H. Shugart, Jr. 1980. Functional complexity and ecosystem stability. *Ecology* 61:1352–1360.

Vance, D. R. 1976. Changes in land use and wildlife populations in southeastern Illinois. *Wildl. Soc. Bull.* 4:11–15.

Vannote, R. L., G. W. Minshall, K. W. Cummins, J. R. Sedel, and C. E. Cushing. 1980. The river continuum concept. *Can. J. Fish. Aquat. Sci.* 37:130–137.

Veen, J. 1973. De verstoring van weidevogelpopulaties stedeb. *Volkshuisv.* 53:16–26.

Verry, E. S., and D. R. Timmons. 1982. Waterborne nutrient flow through an upland-peatland watershed in Minnesota. *Ecology* 63:1456–1457.

Verts, B. J. 1967. *The Biology of the Striped Skunk*. Urbana: University of Illinois Press.

Vestal, A. G. 1949. Minimum areas for different vegetations: their determination from species-area curves. *Univ. Illinois Biol. Monogr.* 20:1–70.

Villa R., B., and E. L. Cockrum. 1962. Migration in the guano bat *Tadarida brasiliensis mexicana* (Saussure). *J. Mammal.* 43:43–64.

Vink, A. 1980. *Landschapsecologie en Landgebruik*. Utrecht: Bohn, Scheltema and Holkema.

Vinogradov, B. V. 1966. Les nouvelles méthodes d'interprétation des photographies aériennes pour la cartographie de la couverture végétale. *Technip (Paris)* 2:93–96.

———. 1976. Hierarchy of topological units of vegetation cover. *Biogeog. and Soil Geog. (Moscow)* 4:133–137.

———. 1980. Dynamic structure of anthropized ecosystems (translated from Russian). *Doklady Akademii Nauk SSSR* 249:753–756.

Vitousek, P. M. 1983. Mechanisms of ion leaching in natural and managed ecosystems. In Mooney, H. A., and M. Godron, eds., *Disturbance and Ecosystems. Components of Response*. New York: Springer-Verlag. Pp. 129–144.

———, J. R. Gosz, C. C. Grier, J. M. Melillo, W. A. Reiners, and R. L. Todd. 1979. Nitrate losses from disturbed ecosystems. *Science* 204:469–474.

———, and W. A. Reiners. 1975. Ecosystem succession and nutrient retention: a hypothesis. *BioScience* 25:376–381.

Vos, W., W. B. Harms, A. H. F. Stortelder. 1982. *Vooronderzoek Naar Landschapsecologische Relaties Tussen Ecosystemen*. Rapport 246. Wageningen: De Dorschkamp.

Waddington, C. H. 1975. *A Catastrophe Theory of Evolution. The Evolution of an Evolutionist*. Ithaca, New York: Cornell University Press.

Waggoner, P. E., and G. R. Stephens. 1970. Transition probabilities for a forest. *Nature* 225:1160–1161.

Wales, B. A. 1967. Climate, microclimate and vegetation relationships on northern and southern forest boundaries in New Jersey. *William L. Hutcheson Mem. For. Bull.* 2:1–60.

———. 1972. Vegetation analysis of northern and southern edges in a mature oak-hickory forest. *Ecol. Monogr.* 42:451–471.

Walker, B. H. 1981. Is succession a viable concept in African savanna ecosystems? In West, D. C., H. H. Shugart, Jr., and D. B. Botkin, eds., *Forest Succession: Concepts and Application*. New York: Springer-Verlag. Pp. 431–448.

Wallace, A. 1880. *Island Life or the Phenomena and Causes of Insular Faunas and Floras Including a Revision and Attempted Solution to the Problem of Geological Climates*. London: Macmillan.

Walter, H. 1964. *Die Vegetation der Erde in Öko-physiologischer Bertrachtung, Band 1: Die Tropischen und Subtropischer Zonen*. Jena: Gustav Fischer.

———. 1968. *Die Vegetation der Erde, Band 2: Die Gemassigten und Arktischen Zonen*. Jena: Gustav Fischer.

———. 1977. *Vegetationszonen und Klima*, 3rd ed. Stuttgart: Ulmer.

Warner, R. E. 1981. Illinois pheasants: population, ecology, distribution, and abundance, 1900–1978. Champaign: *Illinois Natur. Hist. Surv., Biol. Notes* 115.

Watson, D. 1953. *Indians and the Mesa Verde.* Washington, D. C.: U. S. Dept. Interior, National Park Service.

Watt, A. S. 1947. Pattern and process in the plant community. *J. Ecol.* 35:1–22.

Watts, M. T. 1975. *Reading the Landscape: An Adventure in Ecology.* New York: Macmillan.

Way, D. 1978. *Terrain Analysis. A Guide to Site Selection Using Aerial Photographic Interpretation.* New York: Van Nostrand Reinhold.

Weaver, J. E., and F. W. Albertson. 1956. *Grasslands of the Great Plains: Their Nature and Use.* Lincoln, Nebraska: Johnsen.

Weaver, M., and M. Kellman. 1981. The effects of forest fragmentation on woodlot tree biotas in southern Ontario. *J. Biogeogr.* 8:199–210.

Webb, L. J. 1958. Cyclones as an ecological factor in tropical lowland rain forest, North Queensland. *Austral. J. Bot.* 6:220–228.

Webb, T., III. 1981. The past 11,000 years of vegetational change in eastern North America. *BioScience* 31:501–506.

Webber, M. J. 1972. *Impact of Uncertainty on Location.* Cambridge, Massachusetts: M. I. T. Press.

*Webster's Third New International Dictionary of the English Language (Unabridged).* 1963. Springfield, Massachusetts: Merriam.

Wegner, J. F., and G. Merriam. 1979. Movements by birds and small mammals between a wood and adjoining farmland habitats. *J. Appl. Ecol.* 16:349–358.

Weinstein, D. A., and H. H. Shugart, Jr. 1983. Ecological modeling of landscape dynamics. In Mooney, H. A., and M. Godron, eds., *Disturbance and Ecosystems. Components of Response.* New York: Springer-Verlag. Pp. 29–45.

Weller, F., and K. F. Schreiber. 1965. Le noyer comme moyen auxiliaire pour déceler les risques de gelée tardive sur un terrain. *Phytoma (Paris)* 17:26–30.

Wellington, W. G., P. J. Cameron, W. A. Thompson, J. B. Vertinsky, and A. S. Landsberg. 1975. A stochastic model for assessing the effects of external and internal heterogeneity on an insect population. *Res. Pop. Ecol.* 17:1–28.

Wertz, W. A., and J. F. Arnold. 1975. Land stratification for land-use planning. In Bernier, B., and C. H. Winget, eds., *Forest Soils and Forest Land Management.* Quebec: Laval University Press. Pp. 617–629.

West, D. C., H. H. Shugart, Jr., and D. B. Botkin, eds. 1981. *Forest Succession: Concepts and Application.* New York: Springer-Verlag.

Westhoff, V. 1970. New criteria for nature reserves. *New Scientist* 16:108–113.

Westman, W. E. 1978. Measuring the inertia and resilience of ecosystems. *BioScience* 28:705–710.

Wetzel, J. F., J. R. Wambaugh, and J. M. Peek. 1975. Appraisal of white-tailed deer winter habitat in northeastern Minnesota. *J. Wildl. Manage.* 39:59–66.

Whitcomb, R. F. 1977. Island biogeography and "habitat islands" of eastern forest. *Amer. Birds* 31:3–5.

———, C. S. Robbins, J. F. Lynch, B. L. Whitcomb, M. K. Klimkievitcz, and D. Bystrak. 1981. Effects of forest fragmentation on avifauna of the eastern deciduous forest. In Burgess, R. L., and D. M. Sharpe, eds., *Forest Island*

*Dynamics in Man-Dominated Landscapes.* New York: Springer-Verlag. Pp. 125–206.

White, E. J., and F. Turner. 1970. A method of estimating income of nutrients in catch of air borne particles by a woodland canopy. *J. Appl. Ecol.* 7:441–461.

White, J. 1979. The plant as a metapopulation. *Ann. Rev. Ecol. Systematics* 10:109–145.

White, P. S. 1979. Pattern, process and natural disturbance in vegetation. *Bot. Rev.* 45:229–299.

Whiteside, R. W., and F. S. Guthery. 1983. Ring-necked pheasant movements, home ranges, and habitat use in west Texas. *J. Wildl. Manage.* 47:1097–1104.

Whitmore, T. C. 1975. *Tropical Rain Forests of the Far East.* Oxford: Oxford University Press.

Whittaker, R. H. 1953. A consideration of climax theory: the climax as a population and pattern. *Ecol. Monogr.* 23:41–78.

———. 1967. Gradient analysis of vegetation. *Biol. Rev.* 42:207–264.

———., ed. 1973. *Ordination and Classification of Communities.* The Hague: Junk.

———. 1975. *Communities and Ecosystems,* 2nd ed. New York: Macmillan.

———, and S. A. Levin. 1977. The role of mosaic phenomena in natural communities. *Theoret. Pop. Biol.* 12:117–139.

———, S. A. Levin, and R. B. Root. 1973. Niche, habitat, and ecotope. *Amer. Natur.* 107:321–338.

———, and G. M. Woodwell. 1969. Structure, production and diversity of the oak-pine forest at Brookhaven, New York. *J. Ecol.* 57:157–174.

———. 1973. Retrogression and coenocline distance. *Handbook Veg. Sci. (Rinteln)* 5:53–73.

Whyte, R. O. 1976. *Land and Land Appraisal.* The Hague: Junk.

Whyte, W. H. 1968. *The Last Landscape.* Garden City, New York: Doubleday.

Wiens, J. A. 1973. Pattern and process in grassland bird communities. *Ecol. Monogr.* 43:237–270.

———. 1976. Population responses to patchy environments. *Annu. Rev. Ecol. Systematics* 7:81–120.

———. Vertebrate responses to environmental patchiness in arid and semi-arid ecosystems. In Pickett, S. T. A., and P. S. White, eds., *Natural Disturbance: A Patch Dynamic Perspective.* New York: Academic Press. In press.

———, and M. I. Dyer. 1975. Rangeland avifaunas: their composition, energetics, and role in the ecosystem. In Smith, D. R., ed., *Proceedings of a Symposium on Management of Forest and Range Habitats for Nongame Birds.* Washington, D. C.: U. S. Dept. Agric., Forest Service Technical Report WO-1. Pp. 146–182.

Wiken, E. B., and G. Ironside. 1977. The development of ecology (biophysical) land classification in Canada. *Landscape Plann.* 4:273–375.

Wilcox, B. A. 1980. Insular ecology and conservation. In Soule, M. E., and B. A. Wilcox, eds., *Conservation Biology: An Evolutionary-Ecological Perspective.* Sunderland, Massachusetts: Sinauer Associates. Pp. 95–118.

Wilder, R. L. 1965. *Introduction to the Foundations of Mathematics,* 2nd ed. New York: Wiley.

Williams, R. C., and J. M. Williams. 1970. Radiotracking of homing and feeding flights of a neotropical bat, *Phyllostomus hastatus. Animal Behav.* 18:302–309.

Williamson, D. 1979. Scenery as a natural resource. *Landscape Australia* 4:94–100.

Williamson, K. 1969. Habitat preferences of the wren on English farmland. *Bird Study* 17:30–96.

Willis, E. O. 1974. Populations and local extinctions of birds on Barro Colorado Island, Panama. *Ecol. Monogr.* 44:153–169.

Willmot, H. 1980. Special reference to age of hedges in Church Broughton Parish, Derbyshire. *J. Ecol.* 68:269–285.

Wilmanns, O., and J. Brun-hool. 1982. Irish mantel and saum vegetation. *J. Life Sci., Roy. Dublin Soc.* 3:165–174.

Wilson, A. G. 1967. A statistical theory of spatial distribution models. *Transpn. Res.* 1:253–269.

Wilson, E. O. 1984. *Biophilia.* Cambridge: Harvard University Press.

———, T. Eisner, R. Briggs, R. Dickerson, R. Metzenberg, R. O'Brien, M. Susman, and W. Boggs. 1973. *Life on Earth.* Stamford, Connecticut: Sinauer Associates.

———, and E. O. Willis. 1975. Applied biogeography. In Cody, M. L., and J. M. Diamond, eds., *Ecology and Evolution of Communities.* Cambridge, Massachusetts: Belknap Press. Pp. 522–534.

Wiman, B. 1981. Aerosol collection by Scots pine seedlings: design and application of a wind tunnel method. *Oikos* 36:82–92.

Wischmeier, W. H., and D. D. Smith. 1965. Predicting rainfall-erosion losses from cropland east of the Rocky Mountains. Washington, D. C.: U. S. Dept. Agric., Handbook 282.

———. 1978. *Predicting Rainfall Erosion Losses—A Guide to Conservation Planning.* Washington, D. C.: U. S. Dept. Agric., Handbook 537.

Wistendahl, W. A. 1958. The flood plain of the Raritan River, New Jersey. *Ecol. Monogr.* 28:129–153.

Woldenberg, M. 1972. The average hexagon in spatial hierarchies. In Chorley, R. J., ed., *Spatial Analysis in Geomorphology.* London: Methuen. Pp. 323–354.

Wolman, M. G., and R. Gerson. 1978. Relative scales of time and effectiveness of climate in watershed geomorphology. *Earth Surf. Processes* 3:189–208.

Woodcock, A., and M. Davis. 1978. *Catastrophe Theory.* New York: Penguin Books.

Woodmansee, R. G. 1978. Additions and losses of nitrogen in grassland ecosystems. *BioScience* 28:448–453.

———. 1979. Factors influencing input and output of nitrogen in grasslands. In French, N. R., ed., *Perspectives in Grassland Ecology.* New York: Springer-Verlag. Pp. 117–134.

Woodwell, G. M. 1967. Radiation and the patterns of nature. *Science* 156:461–470.

———. 1983. The blue planet: of wholes and parts and man. In Mooney, H. A., and M. Godron, eds., *Disturbance and Ecosystems: Components of Response.* New York: Springer-Verlag. Pp. 2–10.

———, and H. H. Smith, eds. 1969. Diversity and stability in ecological systems. *Brookhaven Symp. Biol.* 22:1–264.

————, and R. H. Whittaker. 1968. Primary production in terrestrial ecosystems. *Amer. Zool.* 8:19–30.

Woolf, A., T. O'Shea, and D. L. Gilbert. 1970. Movements and behavior of bighorn sheep on summer ranges in Yellowstone National Park. *J. Wildl. Manage.* 34:446–450.

Wright, H. E., Jr. 1974. Landscape development, forest fires, and wilderness management. *Science* 186:487–495.

Yahner, R. H. 1982. Avian use of vertical structures and plantings in farmstead shelterbelts. *J. Wildl. Manage.* 46:50–60.

————. 1983a. Seasonal dynamics, habitat relationships, and management of avifauna in farmstead shelterbelts. *J. Wildl. Manage.* 47:85–104.

————. 1983b. Small mammals in farmstead shelterbelts: habitat correlates of seasonal abundance and community structure. *J. Wildl. Manage.* 47:74–84.

Yapp, W. B. 1973. Ecological evaluation of a linear landscape. *Biol. Conserv.* 5:45–47.

Yarranton, G. A., and R. G. Morrison. 1974. Spatial dynamics of a primary succession: nucleation. *J. Ecol.* 62:417–428.

Yates, P., and J. A. Sheridan. 1983. Estimating the effectiveness of vegetated flood-plains and wetlands as nitrate-nitrite and orthophosphorus filters. *Agric. Ecosystems Environ.* 9:303–314.

Yi, B. G. 1976. *Croissance du Cèdre de l'Atlas* (Cedrus atlantica *Manetti*) *en Relation avec Quelques Variables du Milieu en Languedoc-Roussillon (France)*. Thèse Doctorat Ingenieur, Université des Sciences et Techniques du Languedoc, Montpellier, France. 193 pp.

Yoakum, J., W. P. Dasman, H. R. Sanderson, C. M. Nixon, and H. S. Crawford. 1980. Habitat improvement techniques. In *Wildlife Management Techniques Manual*. Washington, D. C.: Wildlife Society. Pp. 344–345.

Yoshino, M. M. 1975. *Climate in a Small Area: An Introduction to Local Meteorology*. Tokyo: University of Tokyo Press.

Young, A. 1978. A twelve-year record of soil movement on a slope. *Z. Geomorphol. Suppl.* 29:191–206.

Zarnovican, R. 1972. *Etude de la Structure Horizontale d'une Tourbière*. Québec: Université Laval. 109 pp.

Zeeman, E. C. 1976. Catastrophe theory. *Sci. Amer.* 334:65–83.

Zeimetz, K. A., I. E. Pillon, E. E. Hardy, and R. C. Otte. 1976. *Dynamics of Land Use in Fast Growth Areas*. Agric. Econ. Rept. 325. Washington, D. C.: U. S. Dept. Agric., Economic Research Service. 48 pp.

Zonneveld, I. S. 1979. *Land Evaluation and Land(scape) Science*. Enschede, The Netherlands: International Training Center. 134 pp.

————. 1980. Some consequences of the mutual relationship between climate and vegetation in the Sahel and Sudan. *Int. Training Cen. Jour. (Enschede)* 2:255–296.

Zube, E. H. 1970. *Landscapes: Selected Writings of J. B. Jackson*. Amherst: University of Massachusetts Press.

————, R. O. Brush, and J. G. Fabos, eds. 1975. *Landscape Assessment: Values,*

*Perception and Resources*. Stroudsburg, Pennsylvania: Dowden, Hutchinson, and Ross.

Zucchetto, J., and A. M. Jansson. 1979a. Integrated regional energy analysis for the island of Gotland, Sweden. *Environ. and Plann. A* 11:919–942.

———, and A. M. Jansson. 1979b. Total energy analysis of Gotland's agriculture: a northern temperate zone case study. *Agro-Ecosystems* 5:329–344.

# Glossary

**Adaptation**  a process of gradual change resulting from environmental constraints and variation among individuals in a population.

**Adjustment period**  a time following disturbance during which the rate of species dynamics (colonization, extinction, population size changes) is elevated.

**Age of Copper and Age of Bronze**  the first human cultural and technological phases with a widespread use of metal.

**Aggrading**  gradually increasing in biomass or structure.

**Agro-sylvo-pastoral equilibrium**  a persistent balance in areas devoted to cultivation, forest, and pasture.

**"Alarm Cry of Plato"**  a citizens' alert to landscape degradation.

**Allelochemics**  organic substances secreted by one organism that affect another organism.

**Alluvial deposit**  eroded soil deposited by flowing water.

**Alpha index**  the ratio of the actual number of circuits in a network to the maximum possible number of circuits, i.e., a measure of circuitry.

**Amplitude of oscillation**  the amont of fluctuation around the general tendency of a variation curve.

**Anemochore**  a wind-blown propagule.

**Angle of interaction**  the spatial orientation of a landscape structure relative to the direction of flow of objects.

**Animal dispersal**  a one-way movement of an individual from one home range to a new home range.

**Aquifer**  a layer of sand or porous rock filled with water.

**Arcto-Tertiary flora**  deciduous and coniferous trees dominating the high latitudes north of the equator during the Tertiary.

**Ascending typology**  a study beginning with the individual attributes and building up to the broadest groupings of them.

**Attribute**  an inherent characteristic of an object.

**Barochore**  a heavy propagule dispersed by gravity, although animals may also play a role.

**Basin**  *see* Watershed.

**Binding factors**  the amounts of organic matter, acidity, and roots present that affect the aggregation of soil particles.

**Binon**  a unit of information (in information theory).

**Biocenosis**  *see* Ecosystem.

**Bioclimatic unit**  terrain (e.g., an altitudinal band) with a distinctive climate, vegetation, and animal community.

**Biogeocenosis**  *see* Ecosystem.

**Biomass** the total weight or mass of living organisms in an area.

**Biostasy** a geologic interval when the predominant process was a biological and chemical dissolving and depositing of minerals.

**Bit** *see* Binon.

**Bluff object** one with a broad flattened end which causes the boundary layer of flowing air to separate from the surface.

**Bottleneck** a narrows that concentrates moving objects on the arriving side.

**Boundary crossing frequency** a measure of the number of borders per unit of length that an object crosses in moving between two points.

**Boundary discreteness** the degree of abruptness between landscape elements.

**Boundary function** the effect of the edge on flows, analogous to a semipermeable membrane.

**Boundary layer air** a layer of flowing air closest to the surface of an object.

**Break** a discontinuity or gap.

**Break area** a small area within and immediately surrounding a gap in a corridor.

**Broad scale** in spatial proportion, referring to a large area where the ratio of map length to true length is small. Opposite of fine scale.

**Carrying capacity** the maximum number of individuals or maximum biomass that a particular environment can support.

**Catastrophe point** a threshold at which the continuity in structure and function of a system is easily and significantly altered or broken.

**Cation exchange capacity** the ability of many positively charged nutrients (or cations) to attach chemically to clay particles (primarily) and later be released from them.

**Central place** a principal center with long-term activities and control over surrounding secondary centers.

**City** an area with a large aggregation of people who have specialized and diversified roles.

**Circuit** a loop that provides alternative routes for flow.

**Circuitry** *see* Network circuitry.

**Classification** a systematic arrangement of characteristics of objects.

**Climatic region** a subdivision with a distinctive climate within a zonal climate.

**Climax community** an assemblage of species that can successfully reproduce and remain where they are.

**Cluster of ecosystem types** the kinds of landscape elements found near a point, typically within several hundred meters of it.

**Coarse scale** *see* Broad scale.

**Cold air drainage** a downslope movement of air replacing warm air at night.

**Collective** a communally run aggregation of people, buildings, and land, generally larger than a farm and smaller than a village.

**Community or ecological community** an assemblage of species at a particular time and place.

**Competitive equilibrium** a persistent coexistence of species resulting directly from competition.

**Configuration** the location and juxtaposition of landscape elements.

**Congruity** spatial coincidence of boundaries when different components are mapped.

**Connectivity** a measure of how connected or spatially continuous a corridor or matrix is. *See also* Network connectivity.

**Continuous movement** moving between points without stopping.

**Continuum** a gradual change in species composition along an environmental gradient.

**Contrast** the degree of difference and the abruptness of transition between adjacent areas.

**Control burn** an intentional fire set at certain times of the year for management purposes.

**Convergency line** a line corridor separating two types of landscape elements, thus providing three types in close proximity.

**Convergency point** a location where three or more types of landscape elements intersect.

**Coppice with standards** a wood with scattered old trees over a dense layer of sprouts from stumps.

**Coppice wood** an area where young stems of species are sprouting from stumps of cut trees.

**Corridor** a narrow strip of land that differs from the matrix on either side.

**Corridor filtration** selective absorption or blocking that prevents objects from crossing a corridor.

**Covert** *see* Convergency line; Convergency point.

**Cultivated landscape** a landscape dominated by plowed land for crops, but usually with patches of natural and managed land present.

**Curvilinearity** a measure of the convolutions or amount of winding of a linear feature.


**Degrading** gradually decreasing in biomass or structure.

**Dendritic** treelike branching pattern, such as a stream with tributaries.

**Depth effect** the number of surfaces visible at different horizontal distances.

**Descending typology** a study that begins by distinguishing the most general groupings and then proceeds to the specific types.

**Desertification** a process of severe reduction of biological productivity and soil quality, leading to desertlike conditions.

**Detritus** dead organic matter.

**Diffusion** a movement of materials from a region of high concentration to one of lower concentration. Also, a process of spreading out.

**Dispersal** *see* Animal dispersal; Plant dispersal.

**Dispersion** the pattern of spatial arrangement of individuals, such as regular, random, or clustered.

**Dissolved substances** materials that chemically break apart in water and pass into solution.

**Distinctive configuration** a significantly nonrandom spatial pattern.

**Disturbance** an event that causes a significant change from the normal pattern in an ecological system.

**Disturbance patch** an area that has been disturbed within a matrix.

**Dominance** the degree to which one or a few species predominate in a community in terms of numbers, biomass, or dynamics.

**Dynamic balance**   a state of equilibrium reached within a system subject to two opposing forces.

**Ecological community**   *see* Community.
**Ecological niche**   the functional role of a species in a community, together with the environmental variables affecting the species.
**Ecology**   the scientific study of the relationships between organisms and their environment.
**Ecosystem**   all of the organisms in a given place in interaction with their nonliving environment.
**Ecotone**   a relatively narrow overlap zone between two communities.
**Edge**   an outer band of a patch that has an environment significantly different from the interior of the patch.
**Edge effect**   a distinctive species composition or relative abundance in the outer band of a patch (i.e., different from the species composition or relative abundance of the patch interior).
**Edge species**   a species found only or primarily near the perimeter of a landscape element.
**Elasticity limit**   a threshold of force below which a system returns to its original state and above which it is somewhat deformed.
**Enclosure**   a pasture or cultivated field surrounded by a hedgerow network.
**Entropy**   a measure of the disorder, or unavailable energy, in a system.
**Environmental resource patch**   an area where environmental resources, such as soil moisture or rock type, differ from the surrounding matrix.
**Ephemeral patch**   an area caused by animal social behavior or by low-intensity, short-lived fluctuations in environmental factors within a matrix.
**Equilibrium**   oscillation around a central position.
**Equilibrium profile**   a curve on a graph representing river elevation versus percent of the total distance from source to sea.
**Erosion**   a process by which particles are removed from the soil surface and carried away by water, wind, etc.
**Euphotic zone**   the upper portion of a water body penetrated by sunlight.
**Evapotranspiration**   the evaporation of water molecules from the surfaces of plants, soil, and other objects.
**Even-aged**   composed of canopy trees of the same age.
**Evolutionary change**   an alteration in the frequencies of genes in a population from generation to generation.
**Expansionary diffusion**   a process by which objects extend their area of coverage while continuing to occupy the original position.
**Extinction-recolonization hypothesis**   the idea that the pattern of decreasing species diversity from base to tip of a peninsula is caused by species colonization from the mainland and extinction at different points along the peninsula.

**Fallowing**   a temporary setting aside of land for natural regrowth and improvement of soil conditions.
**Feedback**   a loop in which one component affects a second component that in turn affects the first component.

**Fine scale** in spatial proportion, referring to a small area, where the ratio of map length to true length is large. Opposite of broad or coarse scale.

**First law of thermodynamics** energy can neither be created nor destroyed.

**First-order stream** *see* Stream order.

**Flood frequency** the probability, expressed as a percentage, that a particular maximum flood level will be attained during any single year (based on past 100-year periods).

**Flood level or stage** a water level attained by a particular flood frequency.

**Force** a power acting to move an object by expending energy.

**Form and function principle** the interaction between two objects is proportional to their common boundary surface.

**Function** the flow of mineral nutrients, water, energy, or species.

**Funnel effect** a concentration of species movements through an area such as a peninsula.

**Gamma index** the ratio of the number of links in a network to the maximum possible number of links, i.e., a measure of network connectivity.

**Gateway** a main entry or exit point for movement.

**Gene flow** the mixing of genes through interbreeding.

**General tendency** an overall increasing, decreasing, or level pattern for a variation curve.

**Geometrization** the formation of predominantly linear or polygonal features.

**Geomorphology** study of the forms of the land surface and the processes producing them. Also, study of the underlying rocks or parent materials and the landforms present, which were formed in geological time.

**Gradient** a gradual change with distance.

**Grain size of a species** the distance or area to which a species is sensitive in carrying out its functions, such as foraging or absorbing mineral nutrients.

**Grain size of a landscape** the average, and the variability in, diameter or area of the landscape elements present.

**Gravitational transport** the movement of materials on steep slopes by gravity.

**Gravity model** an equation relating the amount of interaction or flow to the distance between and the size of each of two nodes.

**Gross production** the amount of organic matter produced by the process of photosynthesis.

**Ground water** a continuous body of water in soil where spaces between soil particles are saturated.

**Hamlet** a little cluster of homes.

**Heterotroph** an organism that consumes or absorbs chemical energy stored in large organic molecules.

**Hierarchical diffusion** a spreading of objects among nodes of different size.

**Hierarchical spatial structure** a group of influence fields for objects representing different order flows.

**Hierarchy** a sequence of sets composed of smaller subsets.

**High-order flow** the movement of objects that exert an influence or effect over a long distance.

**Holocene** the period since the last major glaciation, about 10,000 years ago.

**Home range**   the area around an animal's home that is used for feeding and other daily activities.

**Homogeneous**   having all parts identical to each other.

**Hospitableness**   the suitability or avoidance of an area by a species.

**Humus**   well-decomposed layer of organic matter beneath the litter and above the mineral soil.

**Hydrochore**   a propagule dispersed by water.

**Impaction**   the adherence of materials carried by wind on plants and other surfaces.

**Influence field**   an area under the control of, or affected by, a particular node or patch.

**Information (in information theory)**   the knowledge, expressed in binons or bits, that is gained from observing an event. Also, the logarithm (base 2) of the inverse of the probability of an event. Also, considered equivalent to neg-entropy, the opposite of entropy.

**Innovation**   a new technique or idea that causes a significant effect.

**Input-output model**   a simple (black-box) model that describes the number of objects within, and the number of objects entering and leaving a system.

**Instability**   a state in which a small environmental change is sufficient to divert a system out of equilibrium, its regime of oscillation around a central position.

**Interior species**   a species located only or primarily away from the perimeter of a landscape element.

**Intersection effect**   ecological conditions being modified significantly by the presence of an interconnection of corridors.

**Iron Age**   the human cultural and technological phase characterized by the widespread use of iron.

**Island biogeographic theory**   theory explaining the number of species on islands as related to an island's area, isolation, and age, as caused by the balance between colonization and extinction.

**Isolated system**   one that has no exchange of energy or matter with its surrounding environment.

**Isolation or isolating mechanism**   a factor or process which prevents random reproduction among individuals of a population and generally leads to genetically different subpopulations.

**Laminar airflow**   layers or streams of air moving in parallel fashion, one on top of another.

**Land ethic**   a self-imposed limitation on the degree to which one will modify or destroy the landscape.

**Landform**   a geomorphic feature of the earth's surface.

**Land potential**   the possible uses and values of a land area.

**Landscape**   a heterogeneous land area composed of a cluster of interacting ecosystems that are repeated in similar form throughout. Landscapes vary in size, down to a few kilometers in diameter.

**Landscape change**   the alteration in the structure and function of the ecological mosaic over time.

**Landscape development**   formation resulting from three mechanisms operating within a landscape's boundary: specific geomorphological processes taking place over a long time, colonization patterns of organisms (including humans), and local disturbances of individual ecosystems over a shorter time.

**Landscape ecology** a study of the structure, function, and change in a heterogeneous land area composed of interacting ecosystems.

**Landscape element** the basic, relatively homogeneous, ecological unit, whether of natural or human origin, on land at the scale of a landscape.

**Landscape function** the flows of energy, materials, and species among the component ecosystems.

**Landscape organization** the integration of structure and function, i.e., the spatial configuration and the patterns of flows in a landscape.

**Landscape oscillation** a regime, subject to minor environmental changes, that fluctuates but remains in equilibrium.

**Landscape recovery** the return of a system, subjected to a moderate disturbance level, to its original equilibrium.

**Landscape replacement** the destruction of a system by drastic or cataclysmic disturbance, and its replacement by a new one.

**Landscape resistance** the effect of structural characteristics of a landscape on the rate of flow of objects.

**Landscape structure** the distribution of energy, materials, and species in relation to the sizes, shapes, numbers, kinds, and configurations of landscape elements or ecosystems.

**Large scale** *see* Broad scale; Fine scale.

**Latitudinal migration** a north-south seasonal movement of animals across landscapes.

**Law of zonality** within a climatic zone, the process by which soils developed from different underlying rocks, together with their assemblages of plants and animals, tend to converge toward an increasingly uniform ecological system.

**Lentic** relating to slow-moving water, such as in lakes and bogs.

**Line corridor** a narrow band essentially dominated throughout by edge species.

**Litter** relatively undecomposed organic matter in the top layer of soil.

**Littoral zone** the shallow area near the shore of water bodies.

**Locomotion** movement of an animal from one place to another by its expenditure of energy.

**Long-distance dispersal** movement to a different landscape.

**Loop** a circuit or alternative route in a network.

**Lotic** relating to fast-moving water, such as in most streams and rivers.

**Low-order flow** the movement of objects that exert an influence or effect over a short distance.

**Macroheterogeneity** a pattern whereby the assemblage of landscape element types differs markedly in the extreme portions of the area examined.

**Mainland** a wide area from which a peninsula extends. Also in island biogeographic theory, a large land area serving as a species source for an archipelago.

**Managed landscape** a landscape, such as rangeland or forest, where native species are harvested.

**Mass flow**   movement of matter along an energy gradient.

**Matrix**   the most extensive and most connected landscape element type present, which plays the dominant role in landscape functioning. Also, a landscape element surrounding a patch.

**Megalopolization**   a process of forming a number of cities surrounded by suburbia.

**Mesh size**   in a network, the average distance between lines or the average area of elements enclosed by the lines.

**Metastability**   a state of being in equilibrium (oscillating around a central position), but susceptible to being diverted to another equilibrium.

**Microclimate**   the climate of a small area, such as within vegetation.

**Microheterogeneity**   a pattern where the assemblage of landscape element types around a point is similar wherever the point is located in the landscape.

**Migration**   a cyclic movement of animals between separated areas that are used during different seasons.

**Mini-node**   a widening in a corridor that is too narrow to be called a separate landscape element.

**Model**   a simplified verbal, graphic, or mathematical description used to help understand a complex object.

**Moraine**   a deposit of rocks and debris carried and dropped by a glacier.

**Mosaic tract**   a tract of patches of different aged trees.

**Multi-aged stand**   a naturally developed stand (usually) with trees of many ages.

**Multivariate analysis**   methods that concurrently analyze many factors, plus the relationships among the factors.

**Narrows**   an area in the form of an isthmus.

**Natural landscape**   an area where human effects, if present, are not ecologically significant to the landscape as a whole.

**Natural selection**   a sorting process involving overproduction of offspring, variability, competition, and survival of the fittest offspring.

**Negative feedback**   a loop where one component stimulates a second component, but the second inhibits the first.

**Net ecosystem production**   the gain or loss of organic matter in an ecosystem during a certain time period. Also, net plant production less the respiration of herbivores, carnivores, and decomposers.

**Net plant or primary production**   the organic matter produced by photosynthesis less that lost in plant respiration.

**Network circuitry**   the degree to which circuits or loops in a network are present.

**Network complexity**   the combination of network connectivity and circuitry.

**Network connectivity**   the degree to which all nodes in a system are linked by corridors.

**New landscape equilibrium**   the condition in which a landscape subjected to severe disturbance does not return fully to its previous equilibrium level.

**Node**   a patch attached to a corridor, both of the same landscape element type. Also, an intersection of corridors, and a source or sink of flows of objects.

**Noise**   unwanted sound.

**Nonequilibrium coexistence**   survival of species with irregular fluctuations because of disturbance or unpredictable (stochastic) events.

**Oasis effect** desiccation of an area due to advection.

**Open field** a post-forest landscape in a European area with a social system that directly controls land-use practices.

**Openness** a measure of the horizontal distance visible from a point.

**Optimal foraging** a process of searching for food on a cost-benefit basis.

**Optimization** a process of increasing efficiency or planning for increased efficiency, usually of one among several characteristics.

**Paleolithic** the human cultural and technological phase characterized by the use of stone tools, before the widespread use of metal. In some regions this was followed by the Neolithic phase with abundant polished stone tools.

**Particulates or particulate matter** fine material that is not dissolved in water.

**Patch** a nonlinear surface area differing in appearance from its surroundings.

**Patchiness** the density of patches, or the fineness of a mosaic.

**Patch turnover** the rate of appearance and disappearance of patches.

**Peninsula** a narrow extension or lobe of a landscape element.

**Peninsular interdigitation** a case where peninsulas of one landscape element interfinger with peninsulas of a second landscape element.

**Percolate** to move water down in a near-vertical direction through soil.

**Persistence** a measure of stability, referring to the time period during which a certain characteristic continues to be present at a given level.

**Phylogenetic** a pattern of ancestry which relates current similarities to past relationships.

**Physical-system stability** the most stable state of a system, with a negligible amount of photosynthetic surface or energy stored in biomass.

**Phytoplankton** floating aquatic plants, particularly algae.

**Plant-dispersal** a process of plant propagule movement that results in establishment of the species at a new site.

**Plate tectonics** the study of the movement of huge, sometimes continent-size, rock shields that underlie the earth's surface.

**Population** a group of individuals of the same species located in a particular time and place. Some definitions add that the individuals regularly exchange genes through reproduction.

**Population differentiation** the process of dividing a population into genetically different subpopulations.

**Porosity (of a landscape matrix)** the measure of the density of patches in a landscape.

**Positive feedback** a loop where one component stimulates a second component and the second stimulates the first.

**Production** the accumulation of organic matter by organisms.

**Propagule** a reproductive structure, or diaspore, produced by a plant for dispersal.

**Proximate factor** an event or characteristic that has a direct or relatively direct effect on an organism.

**Rain shadow** a dry area downwind of a ridge caused by moist air being forced up the ridge where it cools and loses moisture by precipitation.

**Recovery** ability of a system to return to an earlier state after being changed.

**Recovery stability**   a state of low metastability, with relatively low biomass and many short-lived, rapidly reproducing species.

**Recovery time**   a measure of how long it would take to replace a characteristic with a comparable one if it were disturbed or destroyed.

**Regenerated patch**   an area that becomes free of disturbance within a chronically disturbed matrix.

**Region**   an area, usually containing a number of landscapes, that is determined by a complex of climatic, physiographic, biological, economic, social, and cultural characteristics.

**Relative uniqueness**   a measure of how many comparable examples of a characteristic exist at different levels of scale, from the local area to the globe.

**Relaxation period**   a time following disturbance during which the species extinction rate is elevated.

**Relay node**   a transmittal point that may speed up flows, reduce "noise" in flows, and provide temporary storage.

**Relict element**   a landscape element in the process of diminishing, usually with concave boundaries.

**Relocation diffusion**   a process by which objects leave one area and spread to another area.

**Remnant patch**   an area remaining from a former large landscape element and now surrounded by a disturbed area.

**Remoteness**   a state of being distant from edges or other landscape elements.

**Replacement rate**   a percentage change of conversions over time from one type to another in a transition matrix.

**Repulsion zone**   an area adjacent to a landscape element where a species is inhibited by an effect of that element.

**Resilience**   *see* Recovery.

**Resistance**   the ability of a system, when subjected to an environmental change or potential disturbance, to withstand or resist variation.

**Resistance stability**   a state of high metastability, with large biomass and many long-lived species present.

**Resolution**   the degree to which small objects are distinguishable.

**Rest stop**   a spot where an object stops for a brief period before moving on.

**Reticulate pattern**   a structure composed of linear features that interconnect and form circuits or loops.

**Rhexistasy**   a geologic interval when the predominant process was mechanical erosion, which flattens mountains and accumulates heavier deposits at their feet.

**Rhythm of oscillation**   a regular or irregular fluctuation around the general tendency of a variation curve.

**Ridge and valley topography**   a series of more or less parallel ridges composed of hard resistant rock alternating with valleys of softer rock.

**Ruggedness**   the sum of the slopes, valleys, peaks, exposures, and elevations present.

**Rupture point**   a threshold above which a force destroys a system.

**Saltatory movement**   stopping a number of times while moving between two points.

**Scale**   the level of spatial resolution perceived or considered. Also, spatial proportion, or the ratio of length on a map to true length.

**Second law of thermodynamics**   in transforming energy from one level or form to another, some useful energy is always given off or lost as heat.

**Selection**   *see* Natural selection.

**Selective coppice**   the cutting of only selected sprouts in a stand.

**Sequent occupance**   landscape changes produced when a sequence of different cultures occupies the same area.

**Set of disturbance regimes**   the intensities, frequencies, and types of perturbations (disturbances) characterizing each ecosystem type in a cluster of ecosystem types.

**Shelterbelt**   a corridor with woody species planted in a number of rows.

**Shifting mosaic**   a system exhibiting a pattern of long-term change along with short-term internal spatial conversions.

**Short-distance dispersal**   movement, usually meters to hundreds of meters, of a species to a new area within a landscape.

**Simple coppice**   the cutting of all the sprouts in a stand.

**Sink**   an area or ''reservoir'' that absorbs objects.

**Small scale**   *see* Broad scale; Fine scale.

**Soil**   the top layer of the earth's surface where rocks have been broken down into relatively small particles through biological, chemical, and physical processes.

**Soil fertility**   a measure of the richness of a soil based on cation exchange capacity and the amount of positively charged nutrients.

**Soil loss equation (universal)**   an expression of the five major factors affecting erosion of soil.

**Soil porosity**   the proportion of air space in a soil, which affects the ability of air or water to move through it.

**Soil texture**   the distribution of sizes of mineral particles, especially sand, silt, and clay.

**Soluble substances**   *see* Dissolved substances.

**Sound**   a form of energy, measured by frequency and intensity, that moves through space in a linear trajectory with undulations or waves around the trajectory.

**Source**   an area or ''reservoir'' that gives off objects.

**Speciation**   the process of forming new species.

**Species-area curve**   the relationship plotted between increasing area and the number of species.

**Species composition**   the particular species present, for example in a community.

**Species diversity**   the number of species present. Also called ''species richness.'' Sometimes an index (Shannon-Wiener) of species diversity is calculated, which includes not only the number but the relative abundance (evenness) of species.

**Species dynamics**   changes in a community due to colonization, extinction, and population size fluctuation.

**Species source**   an area (usually large) from which species come in colonization.

**Spreading element**   a landscape element in the process of expanding, usually with convex boundaries.

**Stability** the condition of a system characterized by a variation curve with a level general tendency and a large or small regular oscillation.

**Stepping stone** a spot that is colonized by a species, that is, when the species arrives and successfully reproduces and grows.

**Stream corridor** a band of vegetation bordering a stream or river.

**Streamlined** characteristic of an object for which the boundary layer of flowing air closely follows the surface of the object.

**Stream order** a pattern of connecting tributaries in which a length of stream is numbered according to how many upstream tributaries have joined it (e.g., a first-order stream is a small feeder stream with no upstream tributaries; a fifth-order stream has four upstream tributaries).

**String-of-lights** a pattern consisting of a series of nodes attached to a corridor.

**Strip between home ranges** a band, sometimes used for animal dispersal, that separates areas used by individuals on each side.

**Strip corridor** a wide band with a central interior environment that contains an abundance of interior species.

**Subsurface flow** the more or less horizontal movement of water and dissolved substances beneath the soil surface.

**Suburban landscape** a town and country area with a heterogeneous patchy mixture of residential areas, commercial centers, cropland, managed vegetation, and natural areas.

**Succession** a directional species replacement process, often leading through a series of recognizable stages to a climax community.

**Surface runoff** the movement of water over a soil surface.

**Sustained yield (in forestry)** the regular replacement of old trees by young trees as a result of soil quality and a gradation of ages or sizes of stems.

**Systems analysis** the study of the behavior of, and interactions among components in, a model of a complex system.


**Tensor** a combination of a number of mathematical matrices producing an array of several dimensions.

**Territorial behavior** the establishment, and usually defense, of a certain small area ("territory") against intrusions by other individuals of the same species.

**Tessera** the smallest homogeneous unit visible at the spatial scale of a landscape.

**Thermodynamics** see First law of thermodynamics; Second law of thermodynamics.

**Thinning** selectively cutting out of certain less desirable individuals.

**Time-distance** a route that permits the most rapid movement between two points.

**Topological space** a map that accurately represents the spatial ordering, but is not proportional to the distance and the length of time necessary to cover a route. Also, a geometry dealing with the continuous connectedness between the points of a figure.

**Traditional agriculture** a heterogeneous fine-grained matrix with scattered, irregularly shaped cultivated fields next to grazed fallow patches.

**Transition matrix** a table of replacement rates over a time period for all landscape elements present.

**Trophic level** a step in a food chain, such as producer or herbivore.

**True synthesis**   an operation in which parts or elements of an object are transformed into new forms when combined.

**Turbulent airflow**   irregular air motion, usually with up and down currents.

**Typology**   a study of types, or a preclassification.

**Ultimate factor**   an event or characteristic, e.g., in evolution or geologic history, that causes or controls a proximate factor.

**Unusual landscape feature**   a rare type of landscape element, or an area in a landscape that differs significantly in geomorphology, disturbance regime, or cluster of ecosystem types from virtually any other area of the landscape.

**Urban landscape**   a landscape with a densely built-up matrix.

**Variation curve**   a line describing the fluctuation of a system through time, characterized primarily by its general tendency, and its amplitude and rhythm of oscillation.

**Vascular plant**   a plant with conducting tissue or tubes for internal vertical movement of liquids.

**Vector**   a transport mechanism. Also a symbol of a spatial trend.

**Vegetation belt**   a distinctive plant community of a bioclimatic unit.

**Vertical migration**   a seasonal movement of animals between higher and lower elevations in mountains.

**Village**   a cluster of homes in a rural area, somewhat larger than a hamlet, which includes at least one common building or market place.

**Watershed**   the area drained by a river or stream and its tributaries.

**Weathering**   a process of forming soil from the breakdown of rock or other parent material.

**Width effect**   a pattern where species distributions are related to the width of a landscape element.

**Wind**   air movement caused by differences in air pressure.

**Yield**   the edible harvest. More precisely, the organic matter remaining from gross production after subtracting losses due to plant respiration, herbivory, decomposition, and nonedible portions.

**Zonal climate**   a major extensive area, principally correlated with latitude, that has similar climatic conditions throughout.

**Zonality, law of**   *see* Law of zonality.

**Zoochore**   a propagule dispersed by animals.

# Index

Accessibility, of patch, 188
Acidity, 44, 341
Active forces in landscape dynamics,
    447–454
Adaptation:
    concept of, 57–58
    to human disturbance, 275–276
    to natural disturbance, 44, 266–267,
        275–276
Adaptive radiation, 60
Adjustment period, 90–91
Advection, 27, 161
Aerosol, 332
Agde, France, 159–162, 185, 196–200,
    203–204, 217
Age:
    even- and multi- in forestry, 503–505
    pyramid, 50–51
    see also Bronze; Copper; Iron age
Aggrading system, 264
Aggregated or aggregation, of objects,
    317–320. See also Cluster;
    Configuration
Agricultural landscape:
    change in, 90–92, 158, 183–184,
        291–297, 442–446, 452–453
    structure of, 8–9, 19–23, 116, 125,
        217, 290, 344, 506–508
    types of buildings in, 276–277, 506
    see also Agriculture
Agriculture:
    harvests, 284–285, 498–499
    and hedgerows, 132–134, 183–184,
        351
    introduction of methods, 259, 282–285,
        393–394
    modern, 276–277, 296, 392–394
    production in, 71, 351, 498–499,
        520–526
    shifting or swidden, 280, 284
    traditional, 296

see also Agricultural landscape; Fallow
    or fallowing
Agro-sylvo-pastoral equilibrium, 506–507
Airflow:
    characteristics of, 320–333
    direction altered or reversed, 326–328
    filtration by vegetation, 332–333
    over hill, 320–322
    laminar, 320
    turbulent, 320–328
    past two structures, 325–328
    past windbreak, 321–326
    see also Wind
Air pollution, 339, 408
Alarm cry of Plato, 514–515
Albedo, 36, 130
Allelochemic, 331–332, 474
Alluvium or alluvial deposit, 41, 150–152
Alpha index, 418–419
Alpine, 37–39, 240, 254, 471. See also
    Tundra
Amplitude of oscillation, 429–432
Anemochore, 381
Angiosperm, 243, 248
Angle of interaction, 410–412
Animal:
    abundance over geologic time, 248
    establishment in landscapes, 246–250
    flying, as vector, 315, 333
    foraging, 55, 111, 175
    ground, as vector, 315, 333–335
    movement, 24, 357–381
    relationship to other factors, 249–250
    in soil, 40–44, 447–448
    use of cluster of ecosystems, 471–473,
        511–514
    see also Dispersal; Migration;
        Movement
Aquatic environment, 44–49
Aquifer, 45, 342
Arctic, see Tundra

Arcto-tertiary flora, 243–245, 270–271
Area, see Matrix; Patch size; Species
Arid, see Desert
Artificialization, 286, 508–510. See also
    Landscape modification
Ascending hierarchy, 477, 484–490
Assimilation, 73
Association, see Configuration; Link or
    linkage, spatial
Atlas cedar, 202–203
Atlas Mountains, 200–204, 217
Attribute:
    concept of, 475, 478
    of landscape, 484–488
Aufwuchs, 46

Badlands, 214–215
Barochore, 381
Barrier:
    corridor as, 162, 334, 342–346,
        398–402
    farmyard, lake, river, and town as,
        369–372
    for fox, 369–372
    within patch, 111, 115
    perceived by animal, 364–381
    see also Corridor; Filter or filtration;
        Hedgerow
Basin, 13
Beaver, 152–154
Bedrock, 41, 233–235, 261, 339, 479
Beginning position, 207–210, 223
Belt, vegetation, 229, 481–482
Bighorn sheep, desert, 372–374
Binding factors in soil, 341
Binon, 202–203, 222–224
Biocenosis, 14–15
Bioclimatic unit, 481–482
Biogeocenosis, 14–15, 29
Biogeography:
    in geologic time, 68
    island, 29, 66–67, 102–105
    plant and animal, 29
Biological:
    desert in ocean, 48
    dilution and magnification, 75
Biomass:
    change, 27–28, 264, 432, 436–437
    concept of, 50
    in production, 71, 285, 346
    pyramid, 69–70
    vertical distribution, 256–259
Biophilia, 306
Biosphere, 35
Biostasy, 233–235, 241

Biotic diversity, see Diversity
Biotic potential, 51–53
Biotope, 12
Bit, 202–203, 222–224
Bloom, phytoplankton, 47
Bluff object, 320–322
Boreal, see Coniferous forest
Bottleneck, 406
Boundary:
    closed, 168–169
    concave, 175–176
    congruity, 98
    convex, 175–177
    crossing frequency, 359, 405
    discreteness, 405
    fluctuation, 382
    function, 314–315
    humans gather near, 497
    of landscape, 11, 456
    layer air, 320–322
    open, 168–169
    of patch, 17
    shape, 174–177
    see also Ecotone; Edge
Break:
    airflow through, 324–326
    area, 400
    in corridor, 125–127, 178–179, 206,
        324–326
    effect on species movement, 178–179
        400–401
Broader perspectives, 526–528
Bronze, age of, 247, 278
Brownian movement, 256
Buffalo wallow, 15
Buildings or built landscape:
    in agricultural landscape, 276–277, 5
    in city, 298–307
    in hamlet, 289, 497
    related to climate, 508–509
    in village, 10, 267, 293–294

Calorie, see Heat
Capillary water, 44
Carbon:
    cycle, 75
    dioxide, 264, 281, 430–432
Carboniferous, 243, 270–271
Carnivore, 68–70, 73–76
Carrying capacity, 52–53
Catastrophe or catastrophic:
    ecology, 338
    point, 268
    theory, 267–268
Cation exchange capacity (CEC), 34

Central places, 516–517
Cheatgrass, 382–386
Chernozem, 259
Cinematics, 440
Circuitry, 418–419. *See also* Loop in
    network
City:
    historical overview, 298–302
    location near boundary, 497
    modern, ecology of, 306–309
    specialization in, 304
    structure and function, 303–310
    *see also* Megalopolis or
        megalopolization; Urban
Classification:
    of chemical elements, 475–476
    concept of, 475
    geographical, ecological, and planning,
        478–479
    hierarchical, 476–484
    phylogenetic, 262–263, 477, 490–491
    of plants and animals, 475–478
    of soil, 262–263
    of vegetation, 256, 483
Clay, 43, 260–261. *See also* Soil
Climate or climatic:
    characteristics of, 35–40, 249–250, 260
    of cold regions, 239–241
    continental, 37, 259
    of desert, 238
    equatorial, 235–236
    Mediterranean, 238–239, 479–480
    post-glacial, 246–247
    regions, 480–481
    and stasic processes, 233–235
    temperate, 239
    tropical, 236–237
    zones or zonal, 36–38, 259, 478–480
Climax community, 64–65
Cline, 60
Closed system, 466
Cluster:
    along sample line, 223–224
    of ecosystems used by animals,
        471–473, 511–514
    of ecosystem types, 8–11, 105, 380
    of rain forest trees, 213–214
Coexistence, species, 26, 438–440,
    471–473
Cold air drainage, 328. *See also* Climate;
    Polar or climatic
Collective, 295–296
Colonization:
    -extinction, 66–67, 113–115
    human, 289

of island, 66–67
of peninsula, 113
*see also* Immigration to patch
Community, ecological:
    of animals, 98
    characteristics of, 60–68
    climax, 64–65
    horizontal pattern of, 60–62
    spatial structure, 60–63
    unit theory, 61
    vertical stratification in, 60
    *see also* Diversity
Competition:
    characteristics of, 52–53
    between landscapes, 457
Competitive:
    equilibrium, 439–440
    exclusion principle, 53
Complexity, network, 24, 418–419
Concentric zone model, 306–307
Concept areas, *see* Landscape ecology
Conduit, 334
    corridor as, 398–400, 402
    perceived by animal, 364–381
Configuration:
    aggregated, 206, 209–210
    determining distinctive, 207–211
    distinctive, 198, 204–211
    linear, 206
    parallel, 206, 218, 239
    of patches, 118–119, 194
    regular, 205, 218
    spatial linkage, 206–210, 224
Congruity of boundaries, 98
Coniferous forest:
    animals, 54–55, 251–253
    biomass, 256–257
    climate and soil, 36–39, 42, 259
    landscape, 10, 19–23, 205
    succession in, 64, 84
Connectivity:
    corridor, 127
    gamma index of, 417–418
    matrix, 162–165, 168–169, 288,
        404–405
    network, 412, 417–418
Conservation:
    biological, 105, 117
    of matter, law, 74
Continental:
    climate, 37, 259
    shelf zone, 48
    *see also* Plate tectonics
Continous, *see* Movement
Continuum, 61

Contrast, 200
  characteristics of, 211–216, 224,
    358–359
  high, 215–216, 284
  low, 211–215
Control burn, 65–66, 279
Convergency point and line, 207
Copper, age of, 247, 278
Coppice:
  selective and simple, 505
  with standards, 122, 505
  wood, 505
Coral reef, 49
Corridor:
  concept of, 23, 123, 151–155, 397
  as conduit, 111, 163, 398–402
  convergency line, 207
  disturbance, 124
  environmental resource, 124
  filtration, 162, 334, 342–346, 398–402
  and flows, 397–404
  and fox movement, 369–372
  higher than surroundings, 144–146
  hiker's view of, 125–127
  human use of, 121–122
  intersection efect, 178–181, 388–390
  line, 131–142, 288, 401, 501
  lower than surroundings, 142–144
  management, 124–125, 500
  microenvironment within, 130–131
  origin of, 124
  planted, 124
  regenerated, 124
  remnant, 124
  strip, 131–133, 142–146, 184, 206,
    288, 401
  vulture's view of, 125–127, 448
  see also Connectivity; Hedgerow;
    Network; Stream corridor; Width
    effect; Windbreak
Cover, 50, 171
Covert, see Convergency point and line
Criteria for distinguishing matrix, 159–168
Cultivation, see Agriculture
Culture, 7, 273
Curvilinearity, 125–126
Cycle:
  atmosphere-organism aand soil-
    organism, 75
  carbon and phosphorus, 75
  hydrologic, 45

Deciduous forest:
  temperate:
    climate and soil, 37–39, 252, 259,
      289–291
    landscape, 101, 143, 158, 171
  tropical, 39
Decision catalyst, 285–286, 457
Decomposers and decomposition, 43, 71,
  263–264
Deformation, permanent or inelastic,
  449–450
Degrading system:
  characteristics of, 264–265, 499,
    527–528
  example of, 434–435, 514–515
Delta, landscape within desert, 238
Dendritic, 127, 148–149, 177
Density:
  as characteristic, 50, 171
  dependent factor and independent
    factor, 55
  road, 183
Deposition:
  by glacier, 239–241
  by water, 40, 150–152, 230–231, 234
  by wind, 41, 158
  see also Sedimentation
Depth effect, 231
Descending hierarchy, 477–483
Desert:
  animal in, 372–374
  cold, 36–39
  geomorphology of, 238
  interior, delta landscape of, 238
  origin of, 68, 166–168
  people in, 14, 452
  soil, 42, 234
  warm and cold, 6, 14, 36–39, 234,
    334
  see also Desertification
Desertification, 157, 166–168, 283
Detritus, 46–48, 69
Development:
  housing, 303
  of landscapes, 229–268, 273–310
  of vegetation, 256–262
Devonian, 242–243, 270–271
Diffusion:
  characteristics of, 316–318, 421–423
  expansionary and relocation, 422
  hierarchical, 422
Dike, 142
Directionality, of airflow, 320, 326–328
Direct methods for typology, 489–490
Discreteness, see Boundary; Time
Dispersal:
  animal, 361–362
  of fox, 368–372

jump, 359
long-distance and short-distance,
    381–382
plant, 381
of river otter, 375–376
seed, 212–214
Dispersion, 50, 189
Dissolved nutrient or substance, 45, 337
Distance:
Euclidean, 411
in management, 500–501
minimum path, 424
time-, 411–415
in topological space, 412–414
see also Isolation
Distinctive configuration, see
    Configuration
District, 306
Disturbance:
chronic or repeated, 87–91, 99, 339
concept of, 9–10
intensity, 27, 274
line, 109
in management, 500–503
in metastability model, 435–438
natural, 265–268, 274–276
patch, 85–89, 99, 287, 386
and patches, 118–119
result of, 26–27, 289–291
and rhythms, 274–276
set of, regimes, 9–10
spread of, 400
Ditch, 142
Diversity:
biotic, 25–26, 47, 60, 63, 236,
    470–471
habitat, 104–105, 111, 140
insect, 140–141, 324
measurement of, 63
species:
    in hedgerow, 140–141, 179–181
    in interdigitating peninsulas, 408–410
    in island biogeography, 66–67,
        102–104
    in landscape modification gradient,
        289–291, 297, 302–303, 306, 309
    in landscape patches, 104–105
Dominance, 60
Drainage density and pattern, 149
Drumlin, 241
Dynamic or dynamics:
balance, 274
control over, in matrix. 164–166
landscape, 227, 446–456
species, 84, 124

Ecological:
dilution and magnification, 75
regulation, 520–521
Ecology, science of, 29, 33, 229. See also
    Landscape ecology
Ecosystem:
characteristics of, 9, 13–15, 29
model, 76–77
net production of, 264
stability, 77, 264
Ecotone, 60–61, 94
Ecotope, 11–12
Edge:
effect, 108–109
of patch or corridor, 108, 132, 147,
    332
production and nutrients in, 99–102
species, 26, 109, 136, 144–146,
    178–180
structure, 101
width of, 108
see also Boundary
Efficiency of energy transfer, 73, 464–466
Elasticity limit, 449–450
Element types, 12–13. See also Landscape
Enclosure, 163, 293, 401–402
Endemic species, 255
End position, 207–210, 223
Energy flow:
in ecosystem, 68–76
heat, 26–27, 36, 466–468
long- and short-wave, 35–36, 465–466
pyramid, 70
Entropy, 222, 466–468
Environmental:
gradient, 61–62, 114
heterogeneity, 114
resistance, 52–53
resource patch, 88, 93–94, 99, 287
see also Diversity, habitat
Equatorial, see Climate or climatic;
    Tropical rain forest
Equilibrium:
agro-sylvo-pastoral, 506–507
colonization-extinction, 113–115
competitive, 439–440, 445
new, for landscape, 451
non-, 53–56, 439–440, 445
profile, 232–233
in stability, 24, 33, 431, 435–436
in transition matrix, 442–444
Erosion:
characteristics of, 214–215, 230,
    318–319
soil loss equation, 340, 518

Erosion (*Continued*)
  and stream corridor, 344
  in time of Plato, 514–515
  by water, 45, 146–148, 151, 166, 237,
    242, 338–341, 518
  by wind, 158, 166–168, 237–238,
    383
Establishment of life, *see* Animal; Plant
Estuary, 45–48
Ethic:
  biophilia, 306
  land, 515
  linkage, 313–314, 315–320, 456–457
Eucalypt, Australian, 386–388
Euphotic zone, 45–48
Evaporation, 45, 347–349
Evapotranspiration, 38–40, 45, 344–345
Evolutionary:
  change, 57–58
  ecology, 57–60
Exclusion, *see* Repulsion zone
Exponential increase, 34, 51–53, 256,
    337–338, 386, 505
Extinction:
  of birds, 275
  characteristics of, 52–53, 382
  colonization, 66–67, 113–115
  on islands, 66–67
  of large mammals, 250
  of major groups, 248, 270–271
  in patches, 87–91

Fallow or fallowing, 280, 283, 293, 506
Farmyard, 276–277, 506
Feedback loop or system:
  characteristics of, 3, 33, 467
  example of, 3, 26, 33–34, 40, 44, 47,
    249–250
  negative, 33, 53–54, 119, 260
  positive, 34, 137, 260
Feeder line, 417
Fence:
  effect, 401–402
  in pastureland, 465–466, 480
  *see also* Hedgerow
Fertilizer, 285
Filter or filtration:
  corridor as, 162, 334, 342–346,
    398–402
  effect of soil, 336–337, 342
  effect of stream corridor, 146–147,
    342–346
  vegetation as, in airflow, 332–333
  *see also* Barrier
Financial monument, 300–302

Fire:
  adaptation to, 44, 266
  control burn, 65–66, 279
  effect of wildfire control, 65–66
  frequency, 266, 279
  use by indigenous populations,
    280–282
Firewood, 121–122, 504–505
Flood:
  frequency, 150–153, 240, 266–267
  level, 150–152, 234, 521
  plain, 147, 151–153, 266–267
  and stream corridor, 146–148,
    344–345
  *see also* Stream; Stream corridor
Flow:
  across landscape, animal and plant,
    357–394
  and angle of interaction, 410–412
  and corridors, 111, 162–163, 334,
    342–346, 397, 404
  high-order, middle-order, and low-
    order, 407–409
  impedance, 344
  mass, 316–318
  in matrix, 404–415
  rate, 46
  relative to spatial orientation, 357,
    409–419
  in soil, 335–346
  *see also* Energy flow; Function or
    functioning; Interaction
Flowering plant, 243, 248, 270–271
Food chain:
  in aquatic system, 46–48
  characteristics of, 73–74
  detritus, 69, 73–74
  grazing, 69, 73–74
Food web, 73–74
Footpath, 128–130
Foraging, 55, 111, 175
Force:
  active, in landscape stability, 447–449
  levels of:
    in ecological system, 450–453
    in physical system, 449
  stabilizing properties, 274, 454–456
  underlying vectors and flow, 24,
    315–320
  *see also* Vector
Forestry:
  characteristics of, 71, 183, 229
  coppicing, 122, 505
  even-aged, multi-aged, and mosaic
    tract, 503–504

firewood, 121–122, 504–505
with high population-to-forest ratio, 281, 502–503
sustained yield, 505
thinning, 503
Form and function principle, 177
Fossil fuel use, 243, 264, 270–271, 310, 468–469
Fox, red, 367–372
Frequency:
absolute, 161, 222–223
boundary crossing, 359
fire, 266, 279
flood, 150–153, 240, 266–267
relative, 161–162
in sound, 329
Function or functioning:
concept, 399
of corridor, 397–404
of landscape, 11, 24–25, 357–394, 397–426, 464
of matrix, 404–415
of network, 415–425
see also Flow; Interaction
Functional displacement, 386
Funnel effect, 113, 207, 219

Gain, initial species, 67
Gamma index, 417–418
Gap:
within community, 61
in windbreak, 324–326
Garden, 298
Gas, 331–332, 467
Gatekeeper, 399
Gateway, 417
Gause's principle, 53
Gelifract, 240
Gene flow, 17, 59, 163, 254
Generalist species, 63
General tendency, 429–432
Genetic:
drift, 58
memory, 275
variability, 249, 254
Geological time, 247–248, 270–271
Geometrization, 279, 290, 296, 414, 510
Geomorphic unit, 482–483
Geomorphology:
characteristics of, 9–10, 223–241
cold region, 239–241
desert, 238
equatorial, 235–236
landform in, 230–232
Mediterranean, 238–239

temperate, 239
tropical, 236–237
Glaciation:
characteristics of, 231, 240–241, 245–246, 270–271
and speciation, 251–254
see also Pleistocene
Global:
ecology, 35
harvests, 284–285
see also Biosphere
Government monument, 300–302. See also Politics
Gradient:
community, 131, 195
environmental, 61–62, 114, 195, 219
Grain size:
of landscape, 216–218
of species, 182, 217, 381
Grassland:
cool or steppe, 39, 290, 382–386, 521–524
modification of, by people, 278–279, 290, 521–524
origin of, 68
rangeland and animals, 15, 258–259, 392, 480, 521–524
soil, 42, 259, 392
Gravitation, 256
Gravitational transport, 345
Gravity model, 420–421
Grid approach, 210–211
Ground water, 342
Growth form, 60
Guild, 60, 63
Gymnosperm, 243, 248, 270–271

Habitation, 95–96, 288
Hamlet, 289, 497
Harvests, 284–285, 498–499. See also Agriculture; Production; Yield
Heat, 26–27, 35, 38–40, 464–468
Hedge, see Hedgerow
Hedgerow:
affected by field, 352–353
affected by home, 353
affected by woods, 352–353
animal community of, 137–141
attached to woods, 181–182, 352
as conduit, 380, 390, 402
fence effect, 401–402
forest species in, 388–392
function, 401–404
intersection, 179–180, 388–392
as line corridor, 132–141

Hedgerow (*Continued*)
  literature, 29, 132–134
  microenvironment within, 130–131
  network, 392, 403–404
  origin, 134–136
  as refuge, 402
  second hedgerow downwind, 347–349
  as source of predators on pests, 351
  structure, 126, 134–137
  used by skunk, 365–367
  vegetation of, 135–139, 179–181
  width, 388–390
  *see also* Corridor; Hedgerow effect;
    Shelterbelt; Windbreak
Hedgerow effect:
  on crop production, 351
  on evaporation, 347–349
  on field, 347–353
  on field organisms, 350–351
  on microclimate, 347–349
  on water, erosion, and mineral
    nutrients, 348–350
  on wind speed, 347–349
  *see also* Hedgerow; Interaction
Herbivore or herbivory, 68–71, 73–76
Heterogeneity:
  animal response to, 380, 470–473
  concept of, 26, 184–186, 463–473
  of landscape, 25–27, 267, 463–469,
    490
  of matrix, 184–186, 215
  measurement of, 202–204, 218–225
  mechanisms causing, 467–470
  micro- and macro-, 194–204, 215–216
  in rain forest, 211–214, 219, 254, 258
  related to scale, 198–200, 403
  and thermodynamics, 464–467, 470
  *see also* Diversity; Homogeneity
Heterotroph or heterotrophic:
  animal as, 246
  city as, 304–306
  succession, 65
Hexagonal structure, 516–517
Hierarchy or hierarchical:
  ascending, 477, 484–490
  descending, 477–483
  in nature, 476–484
  parallel, 483
  spatial structure, 407–409
  vegetation, 483
Higher carnivore, 68–70, 74–76
Hill, airflow over, 320–322
Holocene, 68, 246–247
Home range, 361, 380
  range, 361, 380

*see also* Habitation
Homogeneity:
  causal mechanism, 27, 211–215, 254,
    467–468
  characteristics of, 13, 185, 254, 290
  and hospitableness of habitat, 358, 367,
    379, 387–388
  related to scale, 185, 198–200
  *see also* Heterogeneity
Hospitableness, 358, 380, 405
Human:
  gathering, 496–497
  influence in ascending typology, 483
  as vector, 315
  *see also* Landscape modification
Humus, 41, 76, 260
Hunting, 121–123, 292, 496
Hydrochore, 381
Hydrologic cycle, 45

Ice age, *see* Glaciation; Pleistocene
Immigration to patch, 87–91, 104–105.
  *See also* Colonization
Impaction, 332–333
Improvement tensor, 522–523
Individualistic theory, 61
Inertia, 449
Influence field, 406–408
Information:
  in biomass or biological systems, 28,
    466–467
  characteristics of, 202
  index, 63
  measurement of, 202–203, 209–210,
    222–225
Infrared photography, 36
Inhospitable patch, 367, 379–380. *See*
  *also* Hospitableness
Innovation, 283
Input-output model in management,
  526–528
Insect:
  diversity, 140–141, 324
  movement, 324, 332–333, 363,
    392–394
  termite action, 447–448
Instability, 341–432
Intensity of sound, 329
Interaction:
  between adjacent landscape elements,
    111, 263–264, 313–353, 502
  angle of, 410–412
  between landscapes, 456–457
  between land and stream, 342–346
  between nodes in a network, 420–421

between woods and field, 112
in cluster of ecosystems, 471–473
patch-matrix or site-matrix, 526–528
see also Flow; Function or functioning
Interdigitation of peninsulas, 116,
   408–410, 448
Interior:
   -to-edge ratio, 110–115, 177, 412
   of landscape element, 132, 147
   species, 109, 136–137, 144–146,
      178–180, 410
Intersection:
   effect, 178–181, 388–390
   of tributaries, 399
Intrinsic rate of increase, 51–53
Invasion of nonnative species, 29,
   382–388, 423
Iron age, 247, 278
Irradiation, 265
Irrigation, 279
Island biogeography, see Biogeography
Isolation, isolated, or isolating
   mechanism:
   in island biogeography, 103–105
   of patches, 171–173, 188–189,
      420–421, 501–502
   problem in management, 501–502
   in selection or speciation, 58–59, 255,
      372
   system, 466

J-shaped curve, 34, 51–53, 256,
   337–338, 386, 505

Kin selection, 58

Land:
   ethic, 515
   evaluation, 30
   potential, 520
Landform, 7, 230–232, 237
Landscape:
   architecture, 4, 30, 298, 495
   in art, 4–6
   attributes, 484–487
   change, 11, 27, 285–286, 427–457
   closed, 231–232
   component, 12
   concept, scientific, 11, 193, 482
   concept in dictionary, 4
   concept in social science, 5–8
   development:
      human role in, 11, 23–24, 273–310
      natural processes in, 11, 23, 229–271
   differentiating between, 224–225

dynamics, 227, 446–456
as ecosystem, 15
element, 11–13, 164
element type, 12–13
feature, unusual, 10, 218–219, 381,
   482
function or functioning, 11, 24–25,
   357–394, 397–426, 464
grain size, 216–218
heterogeneity, 25–27, 267, 463–469,
   490
hierarchical spatial structure, 407–409
managed, 286–291
megalopolis, 309–310
natural, 61, 215–216, 265, 287–289,
   500–503
as new equilibrium, 451
open, 231–232
open-field, 292–293
organization, 447, 486–487
oscillation, 450–451
overall patterns of change, 440–446
planning, 4, 30, 314, 478–479
principles, 17–28
quality indicated by animals, 250
recovery, 450–451
replacement, 451–455
resistance, 405
significance of, 3
structure, 11, 23–29, 81, 191–225,
   274–276, 286–310, 360
suburban, 286–288, 298–303
typology, 473–491
urban, 286–288, 303–309
see also Landscape ecology; Landscape
   modification; Stability
Landscape ecology:
   concept, 6–13
   concept areas of, 17–24
   on different continents, 30
   origin of, 28
Landscape modification:
   characteristics of, 30, 184, 216
   corridor characteristics in, 288
   in cultivated landscapes, 286–288,
      291–297
   gradient, 286–310
   in managed landscapes, 286–291
   matrix characteristics in, 288
   methods of, 281–286
   patch characteristics in, 287–288
   in suburban landscapes, 286–288,
      298–303
   in urban landscapes, 286–288,
      303–309

Landslide or landslip, 64
Land-stream interaction, 342–346
Lentic system, 45–46
Life:
  form, 60
  origin of, 241, 270–271
Light, wavelength, 35–36, 465–466
Linearity, 125–126, 296, 414–415
Line or linear, sampling with segments,
    159–162, 185–186, 196–204,
    207–210, 222–225. *See also*
    Configuration; Corridor
Link or linkage, spatial:
  between landscape elements,
    315–320
  among landscapes, 456–457
  in network, 417–419
  *see also* Configuration
Literature, major, 28–31
Litter, 41, 76
Littoral zone, 45–49
Livestock:
  overgrazing, 166–168, 279, 282–285,
    383–385
  production and soil, 282–285, 289,
    343, 392, 521–524
Locomotion, 316–320, 333–335
Loess, 41
Loop in network, 180, 381, 416–419
Lotic system, 45–46

Macroheterogeneity, 195, 200–204
Madro-Tertiary flora, 245
Mainland, 113
Management:
  of agricultural landscape, 506–508
  of built landscape, 508
  decision catalyst, 285–286, 457
  landscape, 495–529
  of landscape with forestry, 71, 183,
    229, 281, 503–505, 515
  modelling and, 515–526
  of natural landscape, 500–501
  of natural remnants, 501–503
  sensitivity, risk, and timing, 523–526
  wildlife, 132–134, 142, 472, 502–503,
    515
  *see also* Landscape
Mantel, 101, 108–109
Map:
  models from, 516–519
  overlay approach, 483–484
Mapping, 62–63, 193, 223, 478–479
Marine environment, 47–49
Mass flow, 316–318

Matrix:
  as binding material, 159, 162–166
  characteristics of, 23, 83, 157–177,
    184–186
  combining three criteria for
    determining, 165–166
  concept, 157–159
  control over dynamics, 164–166
  criteria for distinguishing, 159–168
  criteria influence change, 166–168
  flows in, 404–415
  heterogeneity, 184–186, 215
  as homogeneous mass, 159–162,
    165–166
  in mathematics, 520
  as mold, 159, 164–166
  relative area of, 160–162, 165, 288
  transition, 441–445
  *see also* Connectivity
Mediterranean type landscape:
  characteristics of, 20–23, 474, 479–480
  climate and geomorphology of,
    238–239, 479–480
  mouflon on mountain in, 511–514
  origin of, 68
Megalopolis or megalopolization,
    309–310
Mesh size, 182–183, 404
Mesozoic era, 243, 247–248, 270–271
Metal rod or wire, 449–450, 453–454,
    465–466
Metastability:
  characteristics of, 431, 435–440
  high-metastable, low-metastable, most-
    stable systems, 437–438
  models, 435–438
  *see also* Equilibrium; Stability
Methods of landscape modification,
    281–286
Microclimate, 40, 130, 347–349
Microheterogeneity, 194–200, 203–204,
    215–216
Migration:
  of animal, 249, 362
  of flora, 245–246, 381
  latitudinal, 362–363
  vertical, 362–364, 525
Mineral nutrient, *see* Nutrient
Minimum patch point, 67
Mini-node, 126–127, 178
Model and modelling:
  central places and hexagons, 516–517
  concentric, multiple-nuclei, and sector
    zones, 306–307
  concept of, 515

construction, 519–520
improvement tensor, 522–523
input-output, in management, 526–528
land potential tensor, 520–522
from maps, 516–519
metastability, 435–438
Russian hills, 435–436
sensitivity, risks, and timing in,
    523–526
systems analysis, 515
tensor, 520–523
Monument
    financial, 300–302
    government, 300–302
    sacred, 299–302
Moose, 251–253
Moraine, 239–240
Morocco, 200–204, 217
Mortality, 50
Mosaic:
    checkerboard, 278, 281
    community, 65
    shifting, 445–446
    tract in forestry, 503–504
Mouflon in mountain landscape,
    511–514
Mountain:
    landscapes, 25, 191–194, 479–482
    openness and depth, 231–232
    ruggedness, 232
    soil, 42
    see also Tundra
Movement:
    across landscape, 357–394
    in agriculture, 392
    animal, 24, 357–381
    continuous, 357–359, 388–391
    insect, 324, 332–333, 363, 392–394
    locomotion, 316–320, 333–335
    patterns of, 357–361
    in pest control, 392–394
    plant, 24, 381–394
    rate of, 371
    saltatory, 357–361, 371, 381, 388–391
    saltatory with local spread, 389–391
    see also Corridor; Dispersal; Migration
Multiple nuclei model, 306–307
Multivariate analysis or methods for
    typology, 485–489
Mutation, 57

Nant, France, 208–210, 218, 223–225
Narrows, 126, 206, 405–406
Natural:
    disturbance, 265–268, 274–276

landscape, 61, 215–216, 265,
    287–289, 500–503
selection, 58, 249, 254, 456
Nature reserve, 105, 117
Neg-entropy, 222, 468
Neolithic, 278
Neritic zone, 48
Network:
    canal, fern-like or hand-like, 279
    characteristics of, 23, 178–184,
        415–425
    circuitry, 418–419
    complexity, 24, 418–419
    connectivity, 412, 417–418
    effect on stream flow, 404
    effect on wind, 403–404
    factor determining structure, 183–184
    hedgerow, 392, 403–404
    intersection, 178–180
    and landscape modification, 288
    mesh size of, 182–183
    reticulate pattern of, 180–182
    urban, 305
    see also Corridor; Hedgerow
Niche, ecological:
    concepts of, 63, 473
    fundamental and realized, 63
    width, 63
Nitrogen, 289–291, 343–345, 392
Node:
    interaction between, 420–421
    as landscape element, 125–127
    in network, 415–421
    relay, 415
Noise, 329–330
Nonequilibrium coexistence, 53–56,
    439–440, 445
Nonnative, see Species
Nutrient:
    in aquatic system, 47–49
    cycling, 74–76
    in landscape modification gradient,
        289–291, 297, 302
    movement by animals, 392
    redistribution, 26, 392
    runoff, 146–147

Oasis effect, 27, 161
Ocean, 48–49
Ohio landscapes, 170–174
Open:
    -field, 292–293
    system, 466
Openness, 231–232
Optimization, 423–425

Orientation relative to flow, 357, 409–412
Oscillation:
   amplitude of, 429–432
   landscape, 450–451
   of population, 52–55
   rhythm of, 429–432
Otter, river, 374–376
Overgrazing, 166–168, 279, 283,
      383–385

Paleolithic, 247, 277–278
Paleozoic, 241–243, 247–248, 270–271
Pangaea, 243
Parallel configuration, 206, 218, 239
Parent material, see Bedrock
Particulates or particulate matter, 337
Patch:
   accessibility, 188
   causative mechanism for, 84
   characteristics of, 83, 171, 205
   chronic or repeated disturbance, 87–91,
      99
   configuration, 118–119, 412
   density, 117–118, 171–173, 287
   dispersion, 189
   disturbance, 85–89, 99, 287, 386
   elongated, 110–111
   environmental resource, 88, 93–94, 99,
      287
   ephemeral, 97–98
   habitation or home, 95–96, 288
   interaction among, 189, 406
   introduced, 94–96, 99, 287
   isodiametric, 110–111
   isolation, 171–173, 188–189,
      420–421, 501–502
   and landscape modification,
      286–309
   patch- interaction in management,
      526–528
   in network, 163
   orientation, 412
   origin, 83–99
   persistence, 98–99
   planted, 94–95
   post-disturbance species dynamics, 85
   regenerated, 91–92
   remnant, 84, 88–93, 99–102, 287
   shape, 106–117, 171–173, 188, 287,
      410–412
   species dynamics of, 84–85, 95
   stability, 98–99
   turnover, 85
   see also Patch size
Patchiness, 61, 207, 218

Patch size:
   characteristics of, 25–26, 67, 98–105,
      110
   in different landscapes, 171–173, 287
   effect on energy and nutrients, 99–102
   species and, of islands, 102–104
Path:
   in landscape element, 128–130
   minimum-distance, 424
Pelagic zone, 45, 48–49
Peninsula:
   characteristics of, 113–117
   funnel effect, 113, 207
   interdigitation, 116, 408–410, 448
   mainland of, 113
   population differentiation on, 117
   tip of, 115–117, 207
People as a vector, 315. See also Human;
      Landscape modification
Percolate, 341
Perennial herb border, 101, 108–109
Periglacial, 240
Persistence:
   of patch, 98–99
   in stability, 433
Pesticide, 285
Pest and pest control, 96, 351, 392–394
Phosphorus cycle, 75–76
Phylogenetic, 262–263, 477, 490–491
Physical system:
   comparison with ecological system,
      436–437, 449–454
   stability, 28, 438
   and thermodynamics, 465–466
Phytoplankton, 46–47, 70
Pine:
   Barrens, 259, 265
   California, 386–388
Pipeline, 501
Planning, see Landscape; Management
Plant:
   abundance over geological time, 248
   dispersal, 212–214, 381–382
   establishment in landscapes, 241–246
   see also Movement
Plate tectonics, 230, 243, 467–468
Pleistocene, 68, 251–254. See also
      Glaciation
Podzol, 259
Polar, 36–37, 239–240
Politics, 302
Pollarding, 122
Pollination, 243–244, 254
Pollution, air, 339, 408
Polygon soil, 469

Population:
  characteristics of, 49–60
  differentiation, 117, 372
  growth, 51–53
  regulation, 55–57
Porosity:
  landscape:
    characteristics of, 168–174, 207
    in different landscapes, 170–174
    and flows, 406
    importance of, 169–170
  soil, 43–44, 336, 341
Power-line, 142–144
Preadapted, 386
Precipitation:
  amount and effect on vegetation,
    37–40, 235–236
  effect on soil and stream, 335–337
Predation and predator-prey cycle, 33,
  53–55
Prey, see Predation and predator-prey
  cycle
Primary era, 241–243, 247–248, 270–271
Principles, emerging in landscape
  ecology, 24–28
Production:
  in agriculture, 71, 284–285, 351,
    498–499, 520–526
  of aquatic system, 47
  consumer, 73
  in forestry, 121–122, 281, 502–505
  gross, 70–71
  in landscape modification gradient,
    289, 293, 296–297, 302, 308–309
  net:
    for animals, 73, 498, 520–523
    for ecosystem, 264
    for plants, 70–72, 264
  for people, 498–499, 520–523
  plant and animal, 70–73
  primary, 71–72
  secondary, 73
  of vegetation, 71–72, 346, 455–456,
    498
  and yield, 71
  see also Biomass, Harvests
Propagule, 381
Proximate factor, 34–35
Psychological test, 485–489
Pyramid, see Age; Biomass; Energy flow
Pyrophytic, 266

Quality of landscape:
  a direct method of estimating, 509–510
  perception by animals for, 511–514

protection of, 514–515
survey questionnaires for, 510–511
Quaternary, 245–246, 270–271

Radiotracking or radiotelemetry, 365,
  369–370
Railroad, 142
Rainfall, see Precipitation
Rain forest, temperate, 39. See also
  Tropical rain forest
Rain shadow, 37, 68
Random, 316–317
Rangeland, see Grassland; Livestock
Recombination, 57–58
Recovery:
  related to disturbance and stability, 28,
    434, 450–451
  time in management, 526–528
Regenerated, see Corridor; Patch
Region:
  characteristics of, 13, 29, 35
  climatic, 480–481
Regular, see Configuration
Relative:
  area in determining a matrix, 160–162,
    165, 288
  uniqueness in management, 526–528
Relaxation period, 89–91
Relict element, 175–176
Remnant, managing natural, 501–503.
  See also Corridor; Patch
Remoteness or remote area, 368, 380,
  407–409
Replacement:
  of landscape, 451, 454–455
  rate, 441–443
Repulsion zone, 473–474
Resistance:
  to disturbance, 28, 433–434
  to movement across landscape, 405
Resolution, 193
Resource extraction and alteration,
  281–282
Respiration, 71–73
Rest stop, 360–361
Reticulate pattern, 180–182
Retrogression, 264. See also Degrading
  system
Rhexistasy, 233–235, 241
Rhythm:
  daily 275–277
  disturbance and, 274–276
  modification of, 274–281
  of oscillation, 429–432
  seasonal, 275–279

Rhythm (*Continued*)
    of several years or centuries, 279–281
Richness, *see* Diversity
Ridge and valley topography, 206, 239
Ring, 111–113
Riparian, *see* Stream corridor
River:
    as conduit and filter, 380
    system, 232–233
    *see also* Flood; Stream
Road and roadside:
    as barrier, 380, 398–399
    as conduit, 380, 398–399
    corridor, 129, 141–142, 454–455
    density, 183
    and repulsion zone, 473–474
Ruggedness, 232
Runoff, *see* Nutrient; Surface runoff;
    Water
Rupture point, 449–450
Russian hills model, 435–436

Sacred, monument, 299–302
Saltatory, 357–361, 371, 381, 388–391
Sand, 43, 260–261. *See also* Soil
Saum, 101, 108–109
Savanna:
    animal effects on, 283, 361, 434–435,
        448, 506
    climate and fire, 37–39, 215–216, 279
    structure and vegetation, 195, 215–217,
        434–435, 448, 506
Scale:
    broad or coarse, 191–193
    characteristics of, 6, 15, 191, 218
    fine, 191–193
    and heterogeneity, 198–200, 403
    levels of, 16–18, 198–200, 366
    spatial and temporal, 16–17
Seascape, 6–7
Seasonality, 38–39, 46–47, 275–279
Secondary era, 243, 247–248, 270–271
Second law, 70, 464–467
Sector model, 306–307
Sedimentation, 146–147, 340. *See also*
    Deposition
Selection, 58, 249, 254, 456
Sequent occupance, 301
Set of disturbance regimes, 9–10. *See also*
    Disturbance
Seven wonders of ancient world, 299
Shannon-Wiener index, 63
Shape:
    boundary, 174–177
    and foraging, 107

lake, 106
    of patch, 106–117, 171–173, 188, 287,
        410–412
    of sample plot, 106–107
Shelterbelt, 179. *See also* Corridor;
    Hedgerow; Windbreak
Shifting:
    agriculture, 280, 284
    mosaic, 445–446
Shrubland, 37, 382–386, 521–524
Shuttle analysis, 202–204, 224
Sigmoid curve, 52, 257, 491
Silt, 43. *See also* Sedimentation; Soil
Siltation, 146–147, 340
Silurian, 241–242, 270–271
Sink, 75, 315
Site-matrix interaction in management,
    526–528
Skunk, 365–367
Social dominance hierarchy, 56
Soil:
    animals in, 40–44, 447–448
    binding factors, 341
    brown, 259
    cation exchange capacity (CEC), 341
    characteristics of, 40–44
    chemistry, 44
    classification, 262–263
    clay, 43, 260–261
    decomposer, 43, 71, 263–264
    development, 259–264
    erosion, *see* Erosion
    fertility, 341
    filtration, 336–337, 342
    flows in, 335–346
    formation of, 40–41
    horizon, 41, 261
    loam, 43
    loss equation, universal, 340, 518
    moisture, 44, 348
    organic, 326
    pollution, 339
    porosity, 43–44, 336, 341
    profile, 42
    relationship to other factors,
        249–250
    sandy, 43, 260–261
    texture, 43, 341
    type, 43, 259
Solar energy, 35–40, 464–469
Soluble substance, 45, 337
Sound:
    characteristics of, 328–331
    frequency and intensity, 329
    noise, 329–330

Source:
  and sink, 315
  species, 113, 412
Spatial diffusion, see Diffusion
Spatial orientation, 359, 409–412
Specialist species, 63
Speciation:
  characteristics of, 57–60, 251–256
  gradual and punctuated, 59
  of moose, 251–253
  of plants, 254–256
  of warblers, 251–253
Species:
  -area curve, 67, 103
  coexistence, 26, 438–440, 471–473
  composition, 60
  dynamics, 84, 124
  edge, 26, 109, 136, 144–146, 178–180
  endemic, 255
  flow, 26
  generalist, 63
  grain size of, 182, 217, 381
  interior, 109, 136–137, 144–146,
      178–180, 410
  nonnative, 96, 294–295, 302–303,
      382–388
  nonnative invading, 382–388, 423
  pool, 26, 67
  rare, 60, 339
  source, 113, 412
  specialist, 63
  village, 294–295
  see also Diversity
Spreading element, 175–176, 474
S-shaped curve, 52, 257, 491
Stability:
  concept of, 27, 431, 428–435,
      445–446, 449
  of ecosystem, 77, 264
  equilibrium and, 431, 435–436
  followed by degradation, 434–435
  high-metastable, low-metastable, and
      most-stable systems, 437–438
  metastability and, 431, 435–440
  of patch, 98–99
  persistence, 433
  physical system, 28, 438
  recovery, 28, 434, 438
  resistance, 28, 433–434, 438
  variation curve in, 429–432
  see also Stabilizing properties
Stabilizing properties, 454–455. See also
    Stability
Standing crop, 70–71, 76–77
Stasic processes, 233–235

Steppe, 39, 290, 382–386, 521–52. See
    also Grassland
Stepping stone, 360–361
Stone age, old and new, 247, 277–278
Stratification:
  of aquatic system, 46–47
  in community, 60
Stream:
  as barrier and conduit, 380
  clear cool, 336
  drainage density and pattern, 149
  effect of land on, 342–346
  first-, second-, and third-order,
      148–150
  network effect on, 404
  order, 148
  output in, 337–338
  see also River; Stream corridor
Stream corridor:
  beaver in, 152–154
  characteristics of, 23, 131–133,
      146–153
  effect on erosion, 344
  effect on species movement, 146–148,
      334
  effect on stream, 146–148, 342–346
  filtration effect on animals, 342–343
  filtration effect on nutrients and water,
      146–147, 345–346
  intersection of tributaries, 399
  and landscape modification, 288,
      296–297
  open strip within, 147, 152, 334
  structure, 146–147
  width of, 148, 346
  see also Corridor; Stream
Streamlined object, 320–322, 328
String of lights, 127, 399
Strip:
  corridor, 131–133, 142–146, 184, 206,
      288, 401
  cropping, 290
  cut, 133, 144
  between home ranges, 381
  mining, 276
  open within stream corridor, 152
  see also Corridor
Subsurface flow, 45, 318, 341–342
Suburban, 298–303, 286–288
Succession:
  characteristics of, 64–66, 440
  cyclic, 64–65
  heterotrophic, 65
  point, 65
Surface runoff, 45, 318, 521

Survivorship curve, 50–51
Sustained yield, 504–505
Synthesis, true, 194
Systems analysis, 515

Taiga, see Coniferous forest
Temperate:
    rain forest, 39
    zone geomorphology, 239
    see also Deciduous forest
Temperature, 37–40, 46–47, 235, 348
Tendency, general, 429–432
Tensor model:
    concept of, 520
    improvement, 522–523
    land potential, 520–522
Territory or territorial behavior, 56–57,
    361
Tertiary, 68, 243–249, 270–271
Tessera, 11–13, 164–215
Thermocline, 47
Thermodynamic or thermodynamics:
    first law of, 464
    and heterogeneity, 464–467, 470
    second law of, 70, 464–467
    system, 222
Thinning, 503
Time:
    -discreteness, 415
    -distance, 411–415
Tools for landscape modification,
    278–286, 384
Topography, 173–174, 206, 239, 479
Topology or topological space, 412–414,
    424
Tornado, 267
Transition matrix, 441–445
Transmission line, 142–144
Transportation, 30, 414
Traveling salesman problem, 425
Trophic level, 69
Tropical:
    climate, 235–237
    dry region, 236–237
    Tertiary flora, 243–245
    see also Tropical rain forest
Tropical rain forest:
    characteristics of, 19–23
    contrast in, 211–214, 235
    effect on human perception, 511–512
    grain size of, 218
    heterogeneity in, 211–214, 219, 254,
        258
    human effect in, 212, 219, 235–237,
        280, 284

lowland, 19–23, 35–39, 235–236,
    254–255
montane, 21, 37–39, 212, 507, 512
soil, 41–42
Through effect, 129–130
Trout, 46, 336
Trunk line, 416
Tundra:
    alpine, 37–39, 240, 254, 471
    animal in, 97, 358
    arctic, 37–39, 259, 469
    soil, 41–42, 469
Turbidity, 46
Turnover, patch, 85
Typology:
    ascending, 477, 484–490
    concept of, 475
    descending, 477–483
    direct methods for, 489–490
    landscape, guidelines for, 473–477
    multivariate methods for, 485–489
    phylogenetic, 490–491

Ultimate factor, 34–35
Unusual landscape feature, 10, 218–219,
    381, 482
Upwelling, 49. See also Aquatic
    environment
Urban, 96, 286–288, 303–310, 427–428,
    434. See also City
Urbanization, 30

Variation:
    curve, 429–432
    in populations, 57–58
Vascular plant, 241
Vector, 315, 456–457. See also Force;
    Locomotion; Mass flow
Vegetation:
    belt, 229, 481–482
    classification, 256, 483
    development, 256–262
    over geological time, 241–247
    post-glacial, 247
    relationship to other factors, 249–250
    stature, increase in, 256–259, 447–448
    type, 38–39, 98, 259
Verge, see Road and roadside
Vertebrate, see Animal
Village:
    characteristics of, 10, 267, 293–296
    species, 294–295
Volcanic activity, 266–267

Warblers, 251–253

Wastes, 306–309, 343
Water:
    amount of flow, 337–338
    flow, characteristics of, 45, 146–147, 240
    as mass flow or vector, 315
    quality, 146–147
    see also Flood; Stream
Watershed, 13
Weather, see Climate
Weathering, 40
Width effect, 142–146, 388–390, 400–401
Wildlife management, 132–134, 142, 472, 502–503
Wind:
    erosion, 41
    as mass flow or vector, 315, 318
    network effect on, 403–404
    polar front, prevailing westerly, and trade, 36–37
Windbreak:

characteristics of, 297, 321–326
dense, 323–325
porous, 323–325
snow accumulation by, 321, 324–325, 383
see also Hedgerow
Woodstock, New York, 159–162, 185
Woody mantle, 101, 108–109
Writing, 304

Yield, 71. See also Harvests; Production

Zonality, law of, 259–262
Zone, zonal, or zonation:
    altitudinal and latitudinal, 37–38
    climate, 478–480
    euphotic, littoral, continental shelf, and pelagic, 45–49
    repulsion, 473–474
    temperate, 239
Zoochore, 381
Zooplankton, 47

# About the Authors

Richard Forman is PAES Professor of Landscape Ecology in the Graduate School of Design at Harvard University, where he teaches ecology and landscape ecology. He has served as a Rutgers University professor, Fulbright scholar, Centre National de la Recherche Scientifique (CNRS) researcher, editorial board member of *Ecology* and *BioScience*, President of the Torrey Botanical Club, and Vice President of the Ecological Society of America and the International Association of Landscape Ecology. The landscapes that have molded his thinking are in the Southeast, Southwest, northern Midwest, Middle Atlantic States, New England, and Ontario in North America, and in the Caribbean, Central America, Colombia, France, and England. His current interests are the development of landscape ecology concepts and research relating patch and corridor configuration to the diversity and movement of plants and animals.

Michel Godron teaches ecology at the Université Montpellier II and is a research scientist and former director of the Centre Louis Emberger, CNRS in Montpellier, France. He coordinates an ecological program with UNESCO and serves on the scientific councils of two national parks and the Institut des Amenagements Régionaux et de l'Environment. He was a visiting professor at the Université Laval (Quebec) and has authored or edited five books, including *Analyse de l'Ecologie des Espèces* (Masson, 1982), *Disturbance and Ecosystems* (Springer, 1983), and *Ecologie de la Végétation Terrestre* (Masson, 1984). His perspectives have been molded by the landscapes of central, northeastern, and southern France, and by his principal projects in Brazil, Mexico, the United States, Canada, Ivory Coast, Morocco, Algeria, Tunisia, Iran, and China. His current interests include landscape ecology, the methods and basis of spatial heterogeneity, and resource management in developing countries.